EGYPT to CANAAN

A COMPREHENSIVE STUDY

EGYPT to CANAAN

A COMPREHENSIVE STUDY

ROBERT SURGENOR

EGYPT TO CANAAN
By Robert Surgenor
Copyright © 2010
GOSPEL FOLIO PRESS
All Rights Reserved

Published by
GOSPEL FOLIO PRESS
304 Killaly St. W.
Port Colborne, ON L3K 6A6
CANADA

ISBN: 9781926765068

Cover Design by Philip Rockey

All Scripture quotations from the
King James Version unless otherwise noted.

Printed in Canada

Table of Contents

Acknowledgements 7
Preface 9
1. Egypt to Canaan 11
2. MOSES IN MIDIAN 33
3. MOSES BEFORE PHARAOH 77
4. THE PASSOVER 99
5. THE MIXED MULTITUDE 125
6. THE PILLAR OF A CLOUD 147
7. CROSSING THE RED SEA 175
8. MARAH AND ELIM 199
9. THE MANNA 211
10. REPHIDIM THE SMITTEN ROCK 235
11. MOSES AND JETHRO 251
12. MOSES AND THE LAW 273
13. PROVIDING FOR THE TABERNACLE 315
14. ISRAEL LEAVES SINAI 333
15. THE CONSECRATION OF THE PRIESTS 345
16. VARIOUS ORDINANCES AND HAPPENINGS 371
17. THE LAW OF JEALOUSY 377
18. THE LAW OF THE NAZARITE 385
19. THE OFFERING OF THE PRINCES 397
20. THE CONSECRATION OF THE LEVITES 411
21. THE PASSOVER & THE CLOUD 429
22. THE TWO TRUMPETS OF SILVER 449

23. THE MIXT MULTITUDE 471
24. AARON and MIRIAM'S SLANDER 493
25. FAILURE TO ENTER IN 503
26. THE SABBATH BREAKER
    THE RIBBAND OF BLUE 537
27. THE REBELLION OF KORAH 543
28. AARON'S ROD THAT BUDDED 567
29. THE RED HEIFER 573
30. MIRIAM AND AARON'S DEATH 585
31. THE SERPENT OF BRASS 593
32. WATER AND WAR 607
33. BALAK AND BALAAM 613
34. THE DAUGHTERS OF MOAB 635
35. THE NEW CENSUSTHE DAUGHTERS
    OF ZELOPHEHAD 647
36. JOSHUA'S INAUGURATIONWAR ON
    THE MIDIANITES 655
37. REUBEN AND GAD – COMING SHORT 673
38. JOSHUA AND RAHAB 691
39. CROSSING JORDAN 711
40. GILGAL 725

Acknowledgements

In some parts of our country farmers have a yearly problem and it is this. When they plow their fields to prepare them for sowing, small rocks always come to the surface. They work their way up from underneath the soil. The diligent farmer clears his fields of these unwanted "visitors." However, the next year the same thing occurs again! More rocks emerge from underneath. There seems to be no end to clearing the rocks from the fields.

In writing a book, there is a similar problem. One may read a manuscript over a number of times, removing misspelled words and grammatical errors. In spite of such diligence, more "rocks" always seem to come to the surface. That is why any sensible author employs others to enter his manuscripts to "pick rocks." At times, it almost seems like an endless task.

To avoid a host of errors two great helpers have come to my rescue to eliminate the surfacing "rocks." As the author, I pay them tribute from extreme appreciation and respect; namely my wife Wilda, and Philip Rockey, of the Newington Assembly in Connecticut. They have labored much over the writings of this book for 14 months and seeing that I am not an intellectual, they have filled a number of trucks with rocks and hauled them away, so that this book can show some degree of respect grammatically. Even with such diligence, you may find a "rock" or two, but be easy on us, for we are only frail mortal men at our best.

Preface

In writing this book we have kept four basic things in mind.

(1) To cover the subject more thoroughly than other books dealing with the same subject.

(2) To present the subject at a reading level that will allow the simplest saint to fully understand.

(3) To avoid "intellectual coldness," and present truths with a warm, personal, and faithful approach.

(4) To avoid what is termed, "political correctness," and in love, apply the plain truths of the Word of God to the believer's personal life.

To make the reading easier for older saints, we have employed 12 point Times Roman type, which is larger than what is used in most books. Subtitles have been inserted in the text for quick reference, and all Scripture references have been spelled out, and not abbreviated.

We trust that this book will prove to be a blessing to all that read it. That the meditation of its contents will produce a greater love to Christ, and a greater resolve to live not unto one's self, but rather unto Him Who died for them and rose again.

1

Egypt to Canaan

Before us lies one of the most intriguing stories ever recorded for mankind – the deliverance of Israel from Egypt, and their journey to the land of Canaan. As we commence this sacred history of Israel, the question naturally arises, why so much attention in the divine writings of this historical event? The answer is simple – it all originated as a result of a covenant that God made with a man called Abraham. Consequently, in commencing our journey with Israel as a new and redeemed nation, we go back in history four hundred and thirty years to the call of Abraham from Ur of the Chaldees. When God made His promise to Abraham, it was exactly 430 years later, *"even the selfsame day,"* that the nation of Israel marched out of Egypt to commence their unique journey to the land of Canaan (Ex. 12:41). Some have thought that Israel was bound in Egypt for 430 years, but this is not so, as a careful consideration of the Holy Scriptures will show. In reality, their time in Egypt was only half of the supposed time of 430 years. To prove this let us consider what the Spirit records.

> *"And He said unto Abram, know of a surety that thy seed shall be a stranger in a land that is not theirs, and shall serve them; and they shall afflict them four hundred years; And also that nation, whom they shall serve, will I judge: and afterward shall they come out with great substance. And thou shalt go to thy fathers in peace; thou shalt be buried in a good old age. But in the fourth generation they shall come hither again: for the iniquity of the Amorites is not yet full"* (Gen. 15:13-16).

EGYPT TO CANAAN

"And God spake on this wise, that his seed should sojourn in a strange land; and that they should bring them into bondage, and entreat them evil four hundred years" (Acts 7:6).

"And this I say, that the covenant, that was confirmed before of God in Christ, the law, which was four hundred and thirty years after, cannot disannul, that it should make the promise of none effect" (Gal. 3:17).

"Now the sojourning of the children of Israel, who dwelt in Egypt, was four hundred and thirty years. And it came to pass at the end of the four hundred and thirty years, even the selfsame day it came to pass, that all the hosts of the LORD went out from the land of Egypt" (Ex. 12:40-41).

God's promise to Abraham was given in Genesis 12:2-3, that He would make of him a great nation, and bless him, and make his name great, and that he would be a blessing to others in the fact that through him all the nations of the earth would be blessed. This promise was confirmed when he entered into the land. You will remember that he said to the Lord God, *"Whereby shall I know that I shall inherit it?"* (Gen. 15:8). God instructed him, and a sacrifice was made consisting of a three year old heifer, a she goat of three years, a ram of three years, a turtledove, and a young pigeon. Thus, Abraham was taught that the foundation of every blessing, and the security of every promise, rested on a blood sacrifice. Thus we read, *"In the same day the LORD made a covenant with Abram, saying, Unto thy seed have I given this land, from the river of Egypt unto the great river, the river Euphrates"* (Gen. 15:18). When God sets the time on this occasion, He is dating it from the birth of Isaac, which took place 30 years after Abraham left Ur of the Chaldees. He left Ur at the age of 70, but delayed in Haran, not departing from there until he was *"seventy and five years old"* (Gen. 12:4). Twenty-five years later, Isaac was born, Abraham now being one hundred years of age. Thus, when the Spirit, through Stephen, records the departure date for Israel from Egypt, He relates it from the birth of Isaac, a space of 400 years. Yet the Spirit, through Paul, tells us in Galatians 3:17 that the space of time was 430 years. There is no conflict, for He is simply setting Israel's departure date back to the time when Abraham came into the land, thirty years before the birth of Isaac. You will also notice the wording of Galatians 3:17. *"The law, which was four hundred and thirty years after"* … That is a vital point, proving without any shadow of a doubt that from the time of the promise to Abraham until the coming out of Israel from Egypt was exactly 430 years, for the law was not given until after Israel left Egypt.

Also consider the fact that it was designed that four generations were to exist in Egypt before Israel's coming out (Gen. 15:16). These generations are recorded in Exodus 6:16-20. Levi, Kohath, Amran, Moses and Aaron. Moses and Aaron were the fourth generation. The iniquity of the Amorites in the land of Canaan was full, the time of their judgment had come, and their punishment would be inflicted by the invading army of Israel – it was now time for God to act, and to bring His people out from bondage!

GOD'S TIMETABLE

Embracing this correct view leads us to another unique truth regarding God's timetable. According to historians, from the creation of Adam to the time of Noah's flood involved 1,656 years. From Noah's flood to God's covenant with Abraham was 430 years, making a total of 2086 years from the creation of Adam to God's covenant with Abraham. Now notice! From God's covenant to Abraham to the giving of the law was 430 years, and from that date to the crucifixion of our Lord was 1,656 years, making a total of 2,086 years from God's covenant to Abraham and the crucifixion! In other words, the covenant of God to Abraham stands directly in the middle of God's timetable, not only from the flood to the giving of the law, but also from the creation of the first Adam to the crucifixion of the last Adam, our blessed Lord!

Three hundred and fifty years had passed since Abraham had entered into a covenant with God regarding the land of Canaan. Now He begins to move, making preparation for the tremendous event of Israel's exodus out of Egypt. Eighty years were employed by God to train a man to fulfill His divine purpose regarding Israel. Moses was born. He would be a mediator, deliverer and saviour of the nation. First of all, enrollment in the school of God would be needed. This would involve forty years of training in Egypt, followed by forty years of training in the backside of the desert. Then, and not before then, would God's servant be sufficiently prepared for the tremendous task that would employ him for the last forty years of his life, namely marching them out of Egypt and leading them through a waste-howling wilderness.

CONVICTION OF SIN

Before God raised up a deliverer for the nation, He brought that nation to the place of desperation for deliverance. Relating this to our day we can scripturally say that until a sinner is convicted of his sins by the divine operation of the Holy Spirit, he never will seek salvation. One way of producing false professors is to simply tell a non-convicted soul to *"believe on the Lord Jesus Christ, and thou shalt be saved"* (Acts 16:31). If there is a response, it will involve simply a mental assent to a Bible verse, and a mental recording that they are consequently saved. However, such people, having never been awakened to the enormity of their sins, never convicted before God of their true condition, and never seeing themselves as vile in God's sight and on the way to hell, are not truly saved, they are simply professors of a saying and not the possessors of salvation. Thus we see the importance in the declaration of the gospel, to preach much about sin, and the need of repentance, before exposing God's way of deliverance. As one godly preacher advised me. "When preaching the gospel, give them a big rope of law and a wee thread of grace at the end." David exclaimed, *"For mine iniquities are gone over mine head: as an heavy burden they are too heavy for me. I am troubled; I am bowed down greatly; I go mourning all the day long"*

(Ps. 38:4,6). There is no mere mortal that can produce this conviction in the heart of a sinner. It is solely the work of the Holy Spirit of God. Thus, the wise preacher declares the message and leaves the results with God. Human interference, and pressuring sinners into a profession can produce one of two things; a prematurely born child, weak from the start, or a false professor, still dead.

"And the children of Israel were fruitful, and increased abundantly, and multiplied, and waxed exceeding mighty; and the land was filled with them. Now there arose up a new king over Egypt, which knew not Joseph" (Ex. 1:7-8). The word "knew not" can be taken two ways. Either he had never met Joseph, or, knowing of Joseph, he did not regard or appreciate him. The Chaldean translates it as, "Who confirmed not the decree of Joseph." This pharaoh broke all covenants between Joseph and the previous pharaoh. His policy was to eventually exterminate the nation of Israel which dwelt in his land. The same phraseology is employed in Judges 2:10. *"And also all that generation were gathered unto their fathers: and there arose another generation after them, which knew not the LORD, nor yet the works which he had done for Israel."* That is, they regarded not the LORD, nor His former works.

THREE POSITIONS

Before going further it would be well to explain the three positions in which Israel was found, namely, the land of Egypt, the Wilderness, and the land of Canaan. Israel in Egypt affords us a picture of Christians in the world, a world under the dominion of sin and Satan, its prince and god. Israel in the wilderness displays to us a picture of Christians as pilgrims and strangers journeying on to their eternal rest in heaven. Israel in the land pictures the Christians seated with Christ in the heavenlies, enjoying their spiritual blessings. These three positions are referred to first in the First Corinthian epistle, where we find an assembly in the world and its influence permeating that assembly. Second, the saints being pilgrims and strangers are viewed as such in Peter's first epistle. The third position, speaking of Christians enjoying their spiritual blessings, as Israel would in the land, are brought before us in Paul's epistle to the Ephesians.

PHARAOH AND THE DEVIL'S PLAN

In Exodus 1, Israel gives us a graphic picture of a sinner being dealt with by God. Pharaoh, being a picture of Satan, he was a cruel master over his slaves. *"Come on, let us deal wisely with them,"* was his agenda. The word means, "Let us deal cunningly, or, craftily with them." In the Greek language, the thought is, "Let us outwit them." Sinners today are totally outwitted by the master of deception and craft. Little does the world realize the cruel master they are under. He leads them on in various avenues to suit their personality, until at the end, he gleefully watches them plunge into the eternal abode where their worm dieth not, and the fire is not quenched.

Pharaoh's plan of Israel's annihilation was to cast all the male children into the Nile River. Basically, it was a subtle plan by Satan to destroy the seed whereby Messiah would come. There is a practical application to this event. The world in which God's people live would like to destroy our children. Christians are exhorted to bring their children up in the nurture and admonition of the Lord, instilling into them God's Word. Through the parent's programming, the child is to learn the fear of the Lord, obedience to its parents, and its need of a Saviour. The world despises and hates such programming, as can easily be seen by the attitude and teachings of our public school system. Thomas Jefferson devised a public school system for the purpose of instilling into the children the Holy Scriptures. What a change has taken place! One cannot find a public school where the Scriptures are read daily and prayer is offered in the classrooms. Muhammadism, and a host of other isms and cults are taught in our schools, but the Holy Word of God is not allowed! Today, we have a public school system permeated with liberals that not only condone, but also blatantly teach humanism (self-esteem), atheism (no moral code), materialism (self-satisfaction), evolution (no Creator), no spanking, homosexualism, sex education (abortion), no respect for Judeo-Christian morals, and liberties that violate Holy Scripture. What has been the result? The results are horrific, for we have five-year old children stabbing teachers, school shootings, and pregnant children with no husbands, no fear of parents, policemen, or anyone. Dope addiction runs rampant. There is an epidemic of shoplifting, road-rage, and a total disregard for law and order. Over 52% of marriages end in divorce. The structure and fabric of family life has been torn apart to the point of near extermination. The world says to the Christian, "Give me your children and I will teach them." The fearful question is, "What will they teach them?"

TRAINING CHILDREN

It is imperative for parents to train up their children in the way that they should go. Solomon, with God-given wisdom, wrote, *"Train up a child in the way he should go: and when he is old, he will not depart from it"* (Prov. 22:6). You will notice that Scripture does not say, "in the way he **would** go," but rather, "in the way he **should** go." Parents are not encouraged to raise their children by *rationalism*, that is, by their own opinion. They are not to raise their children by *traditionalism*, which is simply conforming to the way that it has been done. Nor are they to follow *pragmatism*, meaning, that which seemingly works is good. No, these worldly methods will never do! What the Christian parent is enjoined to do is to raise their children according to *scripturalism* – what saith the Lord. Generally speaking, psychologists are antagonistic to the Word of God. The word "Christian psychologist" is a misnomer.

Children are the fruit of a couple's oneness. Parents are privileged to cooperate with God, in bringing souls into this world. This privilege is denied to angels. A newborn infant comes into this world as raw material that is flexible and moldable. He has no mental patterns, habits of life, attitudes, or emotional reactions. The infant is plastic, yet born with a bias toward evil. This starts in the womb as David confessed, *"Behold, I was shapen in iniquity; and in sin did my mother conceive me"* (Ps. 51:5). Isaiah speaks of being a transgressor from the womb (Isa. 48:8). Charles Bridges remarked, "All choose from the first dawn of reason, the broad road of destruction."

In the light of all this, what are parents called upon by God to do? The Holy Scriptures provide the answer! Remember, parents are God-appointed mediators within the framework of the home. They are commanded to hold the reins of government and the rod of authority. Their offices are three-fold, (1) Prophet, (2) Priest, (3) and King. Let me explain. As a PROPHET they are to declare the will of God to their children. *"And these words, which I command thee this day, shall be in thine heart: And thou shalt teach them diligently unto thy children, and shalt talk of them when thou sittest in thine house, and when thou walkest by the way, and when thou liest down, and when thou risest up"* (Deut. 6:6-7).

As a PRIEST they are to pray on their behalf. Consider God's servant Job in this respect. He offered burnt offerings daily on behalf of his sons, lest they had sinned (Job 1:5). Abraham was like a KING to his household. God testifies with these words. *"For I know him, that he will command his children and his household after him, and they shall keep the way of the LORD, to do justice and judgment"* (Gen. 18:19). Abraham would not stand for questioning, reasoning, disputing, delaying, or answering back from his household. When a parent tells a child to do something, that child has no right to question its parent by asking why. Neither does it have the right to delay in performing the parent's command. Let us consider the mental capacity of a little child with the use of medical terms. There are three categories, an Idiot, an Imbecile, and a Moron. The idiot has the mental capacity of a child up to three years of age. He needs complete custodial care. The imbecile's thinking ability ranges from three years to seven years of age. He needs supervision regarding his personal care. Finally, the moron has the brain capacity of a child from eight to twelve. He is capable of a routine work schedule, but he cannot think in terms of duty, responsibility, or moral choice. He needs others.

It is amazing to me to observe how many Christians there are who think that a child psychologist, or a family counselor knows more than God, and follows his advice. Yes, some Christian parents think that they too know more than God when it comes to raising their children. I have been invited to homes where the children act like wild animals, showing no respect to God or man. Their parents tell them to be nice, to quiet down, but their words fall on deaf ears as they continue to tear about in a most unmannerly fashion. What is the problem? It is that the parents think that they know more than God. Then, I have been in homes where the little ones are very subdued. They are polite and quiet to the point of being bashful. It is lovely to see and wonderful and refreshing to behold. Why do they act thus? They behave properly because the parents are raising them in the fear of God and following the guidelines of Holy Scripture. Authors are to say little about themselves, but I must relate this. When I was a little boy I had a no-nonsense Irish father that shaved with a straight razor. That razor required frequent sharpening, which was accomplished with a leather strap. That dreaded strap hung in the bathroom adjacent to the kitchen. Many times I felt the intense sting of that strap when discipline was needed. In all of my life, never once did I talk back to my father. I didn't dare to! If I even looked at him the wrong way, I experienced a strapping. Consequently, even though I loved my father, I feared him. He was good to me and provided me with many things that would bring joy to a lad's heart, but he would not stand for any act of disobedience to his word. My dear mother backed him up 100%, and if punishment was needed when he was at work, she never said, "Wait until you father comes home." She would immediately administer the needed punishment with a stick. Thus, from my earliest recollections, I learned reverence, respect and healthy fear. I feared my parents; consequently, I feared my school teachers and the law enforcement agencies. We see this lacking in most youth of today. Consequently, a society has emerged that is uncontrollable in the classroom, in the workforce, and in society in general. Ask any policeman what he thinks of our society today. His answer will invariably be negative. The pattern God has given for raising children has been set aside.

Parents acting under divine authority see four important things in Proverbs 22:15. Let us consider them carefully. *"Foolishness is bound in the heart of a child; but the rod of correction shall drive it far from him."* First of all, the problem is perceived. *"Foolishness is bound in the heart of a child."* Not just found in the heart, but *bound* in the heart! It is part of the child – foolishness. Now this word doesn't mean just being silly. That is the way it is used today, but when the scriptures were translated into English, "foolishness" meant, "folly of an ungodly nature; wickedness; irreverence; stubbornness; selfishness; anger; lying; rebellion." This is not childishness, but rather wickedness. No matter how little the child may be, all of these unsavory things are part of his fallen nature and will bring him into serious trouble later in life if correction is withheld. The second thing to observe is its intensity. It is bound in the heart. It is part of his "warp and woof." It is not an additive, or a paste on. Ah no, it is an integral part of his fallen nature. It is his nature. The third thing the godly parent sees is the divine instrument to be administered, namely, the rod of correction. I have heard of all kinds of excuses for the word "rod." God informs us in no uncertain terms that it is a "beating rod" (Prov. 23:13). The fourth thing is that consistent punishment of this character will drive his perverse behavior far from him.

Having established this divine principle, let us consider the ways in which the disciplining rod is used. It is to be administered **early** and with determination. *"Chasten thy son while there is hope, and let not thy soul spare for his crying"* (Prov. 19:18). I know a godly couple that raised a very large family. In every assembly meeting, those children sat quietly for over one hour with only a Bible and a hymnbook on their lap. At the age of five months, their correction began by their mother. She certainly didn't beat a five-month old child when it became restless, but she did inflict a little pain with a pinch, so that they soon associated her "shhh" with pain. It didn't take long for them to associate the warning with pain if not obedient. Those children are now adults that manifest deepest respect for their parents, and are a credit to the community in which they live. All but two profess to be saved. They were chastened early in life.

Consistency is another vital additive in administering punishment. *"He that spareth his rod hateth his son: but he that loveth him chasteneth him betimes* (diligently)*"* (Prov. 13:24). It is useless to punish a child one day for misbehaving, and then not punish him for misbehaving at a later time. Furthermore, sparing the rod manifests a lack of true love in the parent's heart for their child. A child is soon to perceive a weakness in its parent if consistency is not practiced.

Every human has a will and a spirit. Parents should never seek to break the spirit of a child, but they must **break their child's will**, or else the child will soon rule them. If a parent does not break the will of their child, the day will come when that child will break their heart. Parents either rule their children, or their children rule them. I have seen mothers totally embarrassed over the behavior of their child in public. I have also witnessed parents wondering why they and their family were never invited back to another's home for dinner. Of course the reason in many cases was that their children were unruly in the home to which they were invited. Who wants visitors whose children will damage valued items in their home? Notice what God says. *"The rod and reproof give wisdom: but a child left to himself bringeth his mother to shame"* (Prov. 29:15). You will notice that it is the mother, not the father that is publicly shamed. The reason being, that it is basically the mother's responsibility to train that child, for she is with her child (being in the home), while the father is away from the home during the day, earning a living for his family.

"Correct thy son, and he shall give thee rest; yea, he shall give delight unto thy soul" (Prov. 29:17). Thus, we see that diligent correction by the parent produces a **peaceful home**. Some homes are like madhouses, with the children tearing about, yelling, jumping on furniture, throwing objects, and manifesting no regard for parents or visitors. How pleasant and refreshing to visit a home where the children are subdued. There used to be a saying when I was a child, and it went like this: "Children should be seen and not heard."

Another thing we wish to consider is **firmness**. *"Withhold not correction from the child: for if thou beatest him with the rod, he shall not die. Thou shalt beat him with the rod, and shalt deliver his soul from hell"* (Prov. 23:13-14). The force of the word "beat" is, "to be attacked and captured." Some punishment requires more severity than others, depending on the offense. Psychologists try to convince the naive public that spanking produces a violent child. However, crime statistics reveal that parents who have been brutally beaten by their children, over 98% of those children were never spanked in their childhood. It is the undisciplined child that is likely to manifest violence in later years than the corporally punished child. Make no mistake about that!

Having considered these vital points, let me remind you that God disciplines His children, sometimes severely. *"If his children forsake My law, and walk not in My judgments; If they break My statutes, and keep not My commandments; Then will I visit their transgression with the rod, and their iniquity with stripes"* (Ps. 89:30-32). Notice that God afflicted the writer of Psalm 119. *"Before I was afflicted I went astray: but now have I kept Thy word ... It is good for me that I have been afflicted; that I might learn Thy statutes ... I know, O LORD, that Thy judgments are right, and that Thou in faithfulness hast afflicted me"* (vv. 67, 71, 75). God afflicted the psalmist for going astray. The force of that word *"afflicted"* is, "chasten," or, "deal hardly with." To the church at Laodecia, Christ writes, *"As many as I love, I rebuke* (show one his fault) *and chasten* (chastise with blows, to scourge): *be zealous* (get busy) *therefore, and repent."* Thus, we see that parents are under divine orders to punish their children, even as Christ punishes His children. Yet there are "Christians" that question God Himself, considering the psychiatrist of more authority and wiser than God!

Christian fathers are exhorted: *"Provoke not your children to wrath: but bring them up in the nurture and admonition of the Lord"* (Eph. 6:4). One can provoke their child to wrath by imposing impossible commands upon them. In other words, expecting too much. Such behavior on the parent's part will possibly frustrate the child and produce anger, or even tears. *"Nurture"* is discipline that regulates character *"Admonition"* is putting the child in mind of the Lord's claims. The final expression, *"of the Lord,"* simply means that the discipline and admonition are prescribed by the Lord, and administered in His name. Before closing this train of thought, let me turn you to Hebrews 12:5-11.

> *"And ye have forgotten the exhortation which speaketh unto you as unto children, My son, despise not thou the chastening of the Lord, nor faint when thou art rebuked of Him: For whom the Lord loveth He chasteneth, and scourgeth every son whom He receiveth. If ye endure chastening, God dealeth with you as with sons; for what son is he whom the father chasteneth not? But if ye be without chastisement, whereof all are partakers, then are ye bastards, and not sons. Furthermore we have had fathers of our flesh which corrected us, and we gave them reverence: shall we not much rather be in subjection unto the Father of spirits, and live? For they verily for a few days chastened us after their own pleasure; but He for our profit, that we might be partakers of His holiness. Now no chastening for the present seemeth to be joyous, but grievous: nevertheless afterward it yieldeth the peaceable fruit of righteousness unto them which are exercised thereby."*

Elders are required to rule well their own house, having their children in subjection with all gravity (1 Tim. 3:4). For if a man cannot rule a little child in his own home, how can he possibly rule mature saints in God's assembly?

God's word to Israel was, *"These words, which I command thee this day, shall be in thine heart: And thou shalt teach them diligently unto thy children, and shalt talk of them when thou sittest in thine house, and when thou walkest by the way, and when thou liest down, and when thou risest up"* (Deut. 6:6-7). God required an intensive teaching of the Holy Scriptures on the part of the parents to their children. Parents, please do not leave the total teaching of the word of God to the Sunday school teacher. It is your responsibility to bring into your child's mind and heart the divine writings. Paul relates to Timothy how his mother and grandmother made known to him the scriptures. *"And that from a child thou hast known the holy scriptures, which are able to make thee wise unto salvation through faith which is in Christ Jesus"* (2 Tim. 3:15). Robert Raikes is credited with pioneering Sunday schools in the 1780's, of which the Holy Scriptures makes no mention.

MOSES' PARENTS

There was a godly couple who *"were not afraid of the king's commandment"* (Heb. 11:23), Amram and Jochebed by name (Ex. 6:20). Both were of the tribe of Levi. They married within their own camp. This activity provides a spiritual lesson for saints today. Christians have no permission from the Lord to marry an unsaved person. Such a union is termed an unequal yoke. *"What part hath he that believeth with an infidel?"* (2 Cor. 6:15). The word *"part"* means sharing in a common object such as marriage.

Not only this, Paul informs the Christian widow *"she is at liberty to be married to whom she will; only in the Lord"* (1 Cor. 7:39). I take this to mean one acknowledging the Lordship of Christ. Generally speaking, denominationalism does not totally acknowledge the Lordship of Christ. The Lord's Supper is not practiced every Lord's day, women gather without a head covering, one-man ministry is condoned; unbelievers and believers sit together at the so-called Lord's supper. Individual wafers are employed instead of one loaf of bread, and individual cups are used rather than one cup. Ministers are salaried for their "services," and a host of other unscriptural practices are condoned and practiced. The believer, bowing to the Lordship of Christ, is separated from all of these inconsistencies and certainly would not consider marrying a person so engaged. Moses' parents were careful to marry within their own tribe.

Their first child was Miriam, followed about eleven years later with Aaron. Three years after the birth of Aaron, Moses was born *"exceeding fair,"* or, "exceeding fair to God" (margin—Acts 7:20).

In the eyes of his parents there was something different. *"He was a proper child"* (Heb. 11:23). It may have been at the time of Moses' birth that the parents received a divine revelation in which to place their faith. The fact that he was *"exceeding fair"* would be to them a token from God that the child was sent by God to do a great work, his beauty assuring their faith. They endangered their own lives by hiding their newborn son, but they were unable to conceal him more than three months. Amram means, "exalted people," and Jochebed means, "Jehovah is glory." To give such names to their children would seem to indicate the godliness of Moses' grandparents, their reverence to Jehovah, and their concern for the nation to which they belonged.

Faith is not blind neither does it deliberately court danger. Seeking means to overcome the danger, they acted in faith. The very river that spoke of death to every Israelite newborn would be the hiding place of refuge for a person that was going to make the deepest imprint in history up to the day of Christ's coming into the world. It certainly is not a lack of faith to avoid danger with necessary precautions. Fanaticism acts foolishly - faith acts wisely. Don't leave the keys to your automobile in the ignition and expect God to protect your vehicle from theft. If God has given the means to protect your property, be diligent to employ those means. Fanaticism tempts God, while faith trusts God.

There is another principle involved in this episode, and that is, when the powers that be go beyond their God-given boundary and command God's people to disobey the word of God, then the Christian has no recourse but to disobey the command and obey his God. You will remember when the Jewish council commanded that Peter and the other apostles not teach in this Name (Jesus), Peter was not slow to tell them in no uncertain terms, *"We ought to obey God rather than man"* (Acts 5:29). When a government acts within the boundaries that God has given it, we of all people, should be very conscious to obey the powers that be, for if we resist, we are basically resisting God. With this thought, Romans 13:1-2 comes into view. *"Let every soul be subject unto the higher powers. For there is no power but of God: the powers that be are ordained of God. Whosoever therefore resisteth the power, resisteth the ordinance of God: and they that resist shall receive to themselves damnation"* (Rom. 13:1-2).

MOSES' SISTER

"She laid it in the flags by the river's brink" (Ex. 2:3), thus securing it from being swept downstream by the current. *"And his sister stood afar off, to wit what would be done to him"* (v. 4). The life of this little girl, Miriam, is interesting, and affords us warnings as to our behavior. At this point she is perhaps fourteen or fifteen years of age, and seemingly quite intelligent. We see her sisterhood. More than likely she was positioned afar off by her godly mother, for the object of reporting any happenings of her infant brother to her mother. All of a sudden, out of all the daughters of Pharaoh, came a particular one whom Jewish tradition has named Bathya. God directed her eye and touched her heart, all on behalf of the babe. Notice the shrewdness of Jochebed's fifteen-year-old daughter. Innocently, she proposes a sensible plan to Pharaoh's daughter. *"Shall I go and call to thee a nurse of the Hebrew women, that she may nurse the child for thee?"* What swiftness! What strategy! What sagacity! The little girl is calm and collected, and her suggestion was well suited to the great monarch's daughter's mind. She in no way endangered the family by revealing the mother of the babe. She simply suggested, "Shall I go and call to thee a nurse of the Hebrew women, that she may nurse the child for thee?" She automatically places herself at a much lower level by asking a question.

Her attitude reminds me of the Samaritan woman at Jacob's well. Let me expose you to another version. *"Come see a Man, which told me all things that ever I did: can this be the Christ?"* (John 4:29). She was a woman addressing men, consequently, she was not telling them, she was asking them, thus taking a low place and throwing out her inquiry for their examination. In other words, "Can you help me?" That's it. That's the avenue in approaching sinners to influence them. A "know-it-all" attitude will turn a person away, but a lowly attitude will more than likely attract persons to you. *"Learn of Me,"* says the Lord, *"for I am meek and lowly in heart."*

The heart of Pharaoh's daughter was moved with compassion. *"The babe wept."* How touching, and how wonderful, just to think that those tears moved the heart of a very important lady. Ah yes, but it was not only Moses' tears that moved her heart, it was Moses' God. Let us ever remember, that *"the king's heart is in the hand of the LORD, as the rivers of water: He turneth it whithersoever He will"* (Prov. 21:1). *"He doeth according to His will in the army of heaven, and among the inhabitants of the earth: and none can stay His hand, or say unto Him, What doest Thou?"* (Dan. 4:35). Nothing can stay the divine purposes of God. A man was to be raised up with a full knowledge of worldly wisdom, and divine wisdom, for a specific work. That man was Moses!

Miriam is next seen on the shores of the Red Sea where we observe her *song* of twenty-one words (Ex. 15:20). Then we sadly read of her *slander* in Numbers 12:1, followed by her being *shut out* of the camp in verse 15. Finally, she is laid to *sleep* in the desert of Zin (Num. 20:1). There is a tone of sadness to the history of Miriam who started the journey singing, but who ended it sour. A merry woman turned to a murmuring woman. Her name, meaning "rebellion," fits her history. How sad it is to see saints start well, but not finish well. Once happy and vibrant, they have turned into sour and complaining discontents. In some, envy has made their bones rotten. In others, pride has brought them low, while others, holding grudges, have become like sour grapes fallen from the vine. May the good Lord keep us happy, and may we keep ourselves humble, so that the joy of the Lord will become our strength.

MOSES' MOTHER

Taken to its mother, the child grew. Not only physically, but mentally too. We are not considering an ordinary person when we observe Moses. I can picture his delighted mother daily teaching him his responsibilities to God and God's people. The whole story is absolutely amazing to say the least! Not only did the government protect the child, but it also supported the family financially to raise their own child! It is stranger than fiction! How unsearchable are God's judgments and His ways past finding out. Some Hebrew women nursed their children to the age of five. How long Moses was nursed of his mother I am not prepared to say, but one thing I do know, and it is this, that every single moment was vitally important to her to instill into that infant's growing mind all that she knew about Jehovah, the God of the Hebrews. To Jochebed, God had allotted a certain amount of time to accomplish her purpose. There would be seriousness coupled with intensity in training this child. Her opportunity had come, but it would not be for long.

Mothers, let me implore you regarding your little ones. How intense are you in instilling into your children's mind the divine truths? How many moments a day do you spend with them? The day will come when they will reach maturity and if you have not taught them the ways of God by then, you will have lost the game. God *says "thou shalt teach (the holy scriptures) them diligently unto thy children"* (Deut. 6:7). The word *"diligently"* is used mostly for the sharpening of arrows, and swords. Sharpening makes them more effective. In other words, we are to teach our children effectively. Sunday schools can be effective, even though a man-made invention. However, in many cases, Sunday schools have degenerated into religious entertainment classes, play-acting for grown up people, and craft classes for the mechanical mind. What a perversion! It is to be detested. Many Sunday school songs are a disgrace, and the antics manifested while singing or shouting them is even a greater disgrace. Try to picture the Lord acting the way some do in Sunday school activities. You can't! Let us examine ourselves. Are the songs scriptural? Are they related to the unsaved? Do they reveal the sinner's need and the simple way of salvation? Teaching the word of God to little ones should never be for entertainment, but rather for enlightenment.

As a child, when our Lord went to the School of the Book, it was for the purpose of teaching the little ones the five Books of Moses, and to memorize the Book of Leviticus. Yes, memorize the whole Book of Leviticus. They were serious about it, they were intent with it, and they were dogmatic about it! I have seen little ones memorize whole chapters from the Bible. It can be done, and it should be done. When little Moses was taken to Pharaoh's daughter to be incorporated into that wealthy and influential godless family he was equipped with divine truths that would govern him the rest of his days on earth. His mother was a wise woman. Are you mothers wise?

MOSES' EDUCATION

History relates that Pharaoh's daughter dearly loved Moses. He was given the very best education of the day. He was one of 10,000 students drawn from the whole known world, being sent to Heliopolis, by the River Nile. His education would be moral and mental, the subjects being Orthography, Grammar, Arithmetic, Geometry, then special studies such as History, Theology, Medicine, Astronomy, and Engineering. I have heard it said that God had to send him to the backside of the desert for 40 years to unlearn the 40 years of learning in Egypt. This way of thinking is a lot of nonsense. What he learned in Egypt would be of value to him in his labors for God. There is an interesting verse in 1 Kings 4:30, and it reads like this. *"And Solomon's wisdom excelled the wisdom of all the children of the east country, and all the wisdom of Egypt."* One can see by this that the educational system that Egypt afforded was second only to the wisdom of Solomon. Moses received the most advanced education of his day.

MOSES' LIFE – THREE SEGMENTS

The life of Moses can be divided into three equal segments of time. First—he was *a prince in Egypt* and saw his *importance*. Second—he was *a shepherd in Midian,* and realized his *impotence*. Third—he was *a deliverer for Israel* and saw God's *omnipotence.* It is interesting to note that not until two thirds of his lifetime were spent did he begin to publicly function for God. Eighty years of training for forty years of work. That seems to be God's way for His servants. Elijah spent time in solitude before meeting Ahab. He seems to step out of nowhere to stand before the king. Later, he is summoned to spend time alone from public gaze at the brook Cherith, then on to Zarephath to dwell with a widow woman and her son before standing before the prophets of Baal and the nation to challenge them concerning the true God. Paul went to Arabia (Gal. 1:17) to be alone with God before engaging in missionary travels.

The life of Moses was packed with 120 years of action for God. He was noted as a *statesman,* an illustrious *soldier* who led the Egyptian army against the Ethiopian city of Meroe, totally defeating it, and bringing back the spoils. He was a *scholar*, and became a *shepherd,* a *songwriter,* a *scribe,* and finally a *shadow* of Christ in at least ninety-nine ways. Six times the Scriptures speak of him as a *"man of God."* His name is inscribed on holy writ 848 times in 187 chapters. In 13 chapters of the Bible, we see him engaged in prayer. The words *"and the Lord spake unto Moses"* are found no less than 99 times, and *"the Lord said unto Moses"* 51 times. He knew a unique intimacy with God, thus he had power with men.

MOSES' CHOICE

Moses had grown in forty years to become great, powerful, and important. He *"was learned in all the wisdom of the Egyptians."* After forty years in the desert, he would manifest himself before Pharaoh to be *"mighty in words and in deeds"* (Acts 7:22). At forty years of age, he was a mature man. He had passed the impulsiveness of youth and was able to estimate the important implications of his decision. Habits are hard to change at forty, but the whole thing had been weighed in the sanctuary of God. Thus we read, *"it came into his heart to visit his brethren the children of Israel"* (Acts 7:23). Seeing one of his brethren wronged by an Egyptian, he defended and avenged him, smiting the Egyptian, and hiding his body in the sand. He supposed that his brethren would have understood his calling of God to deliver them, but they understood not. God was not going to deliver His people using a soldier with a sword. Ah no, He was going to redeem His people out of Egypt by using a shepherd with a rod. This reminds us of that One Who was to enter the realm of time from eternity, to deliver us from this present evil world, even the Great Shepherd of the sheep, our Lord Jesus Christ.

In faith's hall of fame we read these monumental words in Hebrews eleven: *"By faith Moses, when he was come to years, refused to be called the son of Pharaoh's daughter; Choosing rather to suffer affliction with the people of God, than to enjoy the pleasures of sin for a season; Esteeming the reproach of Christ greater riches than the treasures in Egypt: for he had respect unto the recompence of the reward. By faith he forsook Egypt, not fearing the wrath of the king: for he endured, as seeing Him who is invisible."* Faith has an eagle's eye and a lion's heart. Moses was probably destined to be the coming ruler in the greatest nation of his day, but he refused. Promised a future of luxury and pleasurable living, he declined. He was willing to exchange a palace for a tent, and a wealthy city for a waste-howling wilderness. One may say that he possessed tremendous insight. Let me change that term to "tremendous faith-sight."

Exchanging treasures for reproach is certainly not the human way of thinking. The natural man would call it madness. Festus reckoned the apostle Paul a madman for relinquishing his position in the nation of Israel to become a Christian. He couldn't understand it. It was beyond his mental capacity, for he was a natural man, and Paul's choice was spiritual (Acts 26:24). *"But the natural man receiveth not the things of the Spirit of God: for they are foolishness unto him: neither can he know them, because they are spiritually discerned"* (1 Cor. 2:14).

Not only is the natural man blind to spiritual truths, he is also blind as to the spiritual man himself, as the next verse relates. *"But he that is spiritual judgeth* (discerneth) *all things, yet he himself is judged* (discerned) *of no man"* (1 Cor. 2:15). The natural man cannot understand the godly Christian's way of thinking. They cannot understand a man being reviled, persecuted, and evil spoken of, yet rejoicing and being exceedingly glad because of such treatment. It is not normal, it is not expected, and it is simply not a worldly reaction. But why are such attitudes shown? They are shown simply because the Lord has told them to react that way. Read it for yourself in Matthew 5:11-12.

Saintly Christians let their light shine before men, that they might see their good works, thus glorifying their Father which is in heaven (v. 16). Moses made his choice. He had respect unto the recompense of the reward. The word "respect" simply means "to turn one's eyes away from other things and fix them on something, with a steadfast mental gaze." He apprehended not by his senses, but through his soul. Having made that choice, God was going to further prepare his man to play a role in accomplishing His divine purposes. The backside of the desert would prove a valuable experience for Moses in the school of God.

2

MOSES IN MIDIAN

God is careful to reveal to us that this mighty man was a compassionate, considerate, and righteous individual. This revelation is contained in two verses. *"Now the priest of Midian had seven daughters: and they came and drew water, and filled the troughs to water their father's flock. And the shepherds came and drove them away: but Moses stood up and helped them, and watered their flock"* (Ex. 2:16-17). Greedy and inconsiderate fellows were these shepherds. It had been their habit to take advantage of these seven women. After these women labored in drawing the water, these men would habitually appear on the scene and take for themselves the water the women had labored to draw. The reason I perceive that this had been going on for quite some time is because of the fact that when Moses helped them, they returned home earlier than at other times. You will remember that Reuel said to them, *"How is it that you are come so soon today?"* That is the only time you read that particular expression, *"Moses stood up."* He was to stand before Pharaoh (Ex. 9:10), but the expression we are considering involves more that a physical position. It would seem to me that it means that he stood up to their perverse actions. He acted against them. We use that expression in our day. A fellow has something against another so he goes and stands up to him. I believe that is what we have here.

Then the question arises, how could one eighty-year-old man stand up against a group of shepherds? Could it be that the presence of God was so manifested in Moses that they were afraid of him? Evidently, he spoke to them with authority and was able to drive them away. Not only this, he was not too lofty to physically help the shepherdesses, for he drew the water for them. One can readily see how God prepares men for great tasks. First He employs them with small tasks. Here was a man that would be standing before Pharaoh, the greatest monarch of the day, but first he stands up before nomad shepherds in the wilderness. He was going to be used of God in bringing relief and help to a nation of perhaps two million people, but first he is called upon to bring help to seven women. He would be calling forth tons of water from the flinty rock to satisfy a whole nation, but first he is used to draw water from a well to satisfy a small flock of sheep. Can you not see how God works? His school is unique. The training is slow and very deliberate, and the eye of God carefully observes it.

NO "SKIPPING GRADES"

To accomplish great exploits for God, one must start accomplishing little things for God. That is His way of training. There are no "skipping grades" in the school of God. There are no rush courses in His agenda. The man who is a profitable and profound teacher was not always so. Ah no, his beginning was very small. He was an insignificant disciple, alone in the study, pouring over the Holy Writings, seeking, in humility, to glean some "gold, silver, and precious stones" from above. He considered his time very valuable and consequently he redeemed it. The attractions of the world had no magnetic affect upon his soul, the legitimate pleasures of life did not draw away his precious time for studying the Scriptures. In assembly gatherings, he was a good listener, learning and applying precious truths as they fell from the lips of the more knowledgeable. He meditated upon holy things, giving himself wholly to them.

Then the day came when recognition became his neighbor. He acquired a good report of the brethren. Older brethren, one by one, passed off the scene, until, all of a sudden, he was an older saint being looked upon for help from those younger and untaught. God began to use him, and saints began to look to him with respect and for spiritual help. Yes, it took most of a lifetime to graduate, if I may so use that term. These are the kind of men that are desperately needed in God's assemblies today. We are becoming like Israel and Judah in Hosea's day, *"destroyed for lack of knowledge"* (4:6). Moses had graduated from the highest worldly university of his day, and now he has been placed in the "kindergarten" of God's school, forty years away from graduation.

MOSES' MARK

When questioned by Reuel (or Jethro) regarding Moses, his daughters described him as *"an Egyptian."* Egypt had left its mark on the comparatively young Hebrew. How often, in our association with this world, it leaves its mark on some Christians. One is known by the company he keeps. At least 35 years of Moses' 40 years on earth had been spent in the company of the Egyptians. Consequently, it had left its mark. Let us remember, as the sanctified people of God, we may be in this world, but we are not of this world. We are not incorporated into its system. Our status is that of strangers away from our heavenly home, and pilgrims on our way to that home. Like Abraham, we look for a city whose Builder and Maker is God. Our Lord has made this very clear in His teaching. *"If ye were of the world, the world would love his own: but because ye are not of the world, but I have chosen you out of the world, therefore the world hateth you"* (John 15:19*). "They* (Christ's own) *are not of the world, even as* I (Christ) *am not of the world"* (John 17:16).

It is one thing to be isolated, and another thing to be separated. Unlike monks and other cultic orders, Christians do not shut themselves up in a walled monastery, totally isolating themselves from society. If that were the case, how could we ever let our light shine among men? No, no, we move in and out among the ungodly. We "rub shoulders" with them on the street and in the business world. We live beside them, we walk before them, and we witness to them - all in hopes of winning them to Christ. Thus, we are *in the world*, however, we are not *of this world*.

DIFFERENT PURSUITS

Their pursuits in life are not our pursuits. Their goals are far different than ours. They live for themselves; we live not unto ourselves, but unto Him Who died for us and rose again. They practice the lusts of the flesh; we seek to crucify the flesh with the affections and lusts thereof. Their pleasure is found in sports. Our pleasure is in reading the Scriptures. The pleasures of sin attract them, while the right hand of God attracts us, for at His right hand there are pleasures for evermore. They live for today, we live in view of eternity. They look for fleeting security, we look for the Saviour Who shall change our bodies as He escorts us into the realms of heavenly bliss. What a vast difference in the earth dweller, and the child of God, the citizen of heaven! There is no comparison whatsoever! God help us from the mark of the world being stamped on our image. Well may we pray like David: *"Unto thee will I cry, O LORD my Rock; be not silent to me: lest, if Thou be silent to me, I become like them that go down into the pit"* (Ps. 28:1).

In Gideon's day there were two men, Zebah, and Zalmunna who slew some men at Tabor. When asked who the slain men were, they answered Gideon, *"As thou art, so were they; each one resembled the children of a king"* (Judg. 8:18). *"Now when they* (the rulers of the people) *saw the boldness of Peter and John, and perceived that they were unlearned and ignorant men, they marvelled; and they took knowledge of them, that they had been with Jesus"* (Acts 4:13). Do you get the point? Associations leave their mark on us. Let us all then, with open face beholding as in a glass the glory of the Lord, experience that continual changing into the same image from glory to glory, even as by the Spirit of the Lord (2 Cor. 3:18). Let us spend much time with Christ that we may be like Christ. That in essence is godliness.

MOSES' SONS

Moses was a stranger in the desert of Midian, and it was there that he secured a Gentile bride. From that union, God

MOSES IN MIDIAN

gave him two sons. Often in biblical times, children received their name relative to the conditions that prevailed in their parent's life at that particular time. I have no doubt that this was the case with Moses when his first son was born. The child's name, Gershom, meaning "a stranger here," gives us an insight into the feeling of Moses while away from his people, being confined to Midian. Perhaps he was depressed. One thing he did know, and it was this, that he was a stranger in his present location.

I wonder how much we realize our strangership in this world of activity and prosperity? Is it true that we are all taken up with temporal things, so much so, that the golden celestial city has become very dim in our spiritual vision, and the glorious heavenly land seems very far off? Or, on the other hand, are we living in such a way that the things of this world are very dim to our eye, for we have our hope, our sight, and our expectation set on things above? Is not this one of the exhortations of Paul to the Colossian saints? *"If (since) ye then be risen with Christ, seek those things which are above, where Christ sitteth on the right hand of God. Set your affection (mind) on things above, not on things on the earth"* (Col. 3:1-2).

In other words, now that you are saved from a godless society and brought nigh unto God, be careful to act in reference to heavenly things as you formerly did regarding the things of this earth. Let your earnestness in heavenly things even surpass your former earnestness regarding those things of earth that are transient and perishing. He reminded them that they were dead to all hopes of happiness from the present world, consequently, they should not even have one hunger pang for the former things that they enjoyed while in their unconverted state. They now possessed a treasure, and that treasure was in heaven, consequently, that is where their heart should also be.

Allow me to approach this in different words so that a double impression will be imbedded in your mind, for this is a supremely vital truth that has been set aside by many of God's people today.

As Christ presently lives in heaven, so we too should live for heaven, and firmly set our mind, our affections there. Those blessed things which are above, we are to seek as objects of pursuit and deep affection, ever striving to secure them. Are we prepared to dwell with Him? He is in the heavenlies. Are our affections there? What about our mind, our thoughts? Are we occupied about the things where our Lord now dwells? Do we think often where our final home will be? Is our interest there? Or, like many professing Christians, is our mind occupied with worldly wealth, honor, and its fading pleasure? Are our affections fixed on our houses, our automobiles, our property, our fashionable clothing, or our worldly pleasures, so prevalently found in the theater, the sports arena, and worldly tours? How can we that are dead to sin and to the world set our affections on such trivial things? What a colossal waste of energy and precious time! Are we not to seek FIRST the kingdom of God? Certainly we are, and the Lord, while here, has provided for us in His life, the divine pattern. Certainly, the great object of our contemplation should be the heavenly world. Nothing short of this will bring pleasure to the heart of our God.

Moses' second son, Eliezer, meaning, "my God is a help," is not mentioned until Israel had experienced deliverance (Ex. 18:4). It will not be until Israel has been fully restored to God, that the nation will see how greatly Jehovah has helped them. Samuel experienced this in a partial way during his conflict with the Philistines, setting up a stone to commemorate the event. *"Then Samuel took a stone, and set it between Mizpeh and Shen, and called the name of it Ebenezer, saying, Hitherto hath the LORD helped us"* (1 Sam. 7:12). What a tremendous day for Israel when their Messiah and Redeemer will come in mighty power. God will make His enemies the footstool of Christ's feet, as the Son of Man totally defeats the enemies of Israel, sets up His earthly kingdom, and establishes Israel as the head of the nations. Israel will confess in that day, *"All nations compassed me about ... thou hast thrust sore at me that I might fall: but the LORD helped me. The LORD is my strength and song, and is become my salvation"* (Ps. 118:10, 13-14).

ISRAEL CRYING

While Moses was content in the backside of the desert, Israel was in Egypt crying. The divine record says, they sighed (from weariness); they cried (from desperation); and God heard their groaning (from burdens). *"And God looked upon the children of Israel, and God had respect unto them"* (Ex. 2:25). He observed and comprehended their case. He heard and He looked. Let us ever remember that *"the eyes of the LORD are upon the righteous, and His ears are open unto their cry"* (Ps. 34:15). Satan would seek to convince us in times of severe trial that the Lord has forgotten about us, that He is not interested in our plight. Nothing could be farther from the truth. *"For the eyes of the LORD run to and fro throughout the whole earth, to shew Himself strong in the behalf of them whose heart is perfect toward Him"* (2 Chron. 16:9).

Paul relates his trial before the Roman Government. *"At my first answer no man stood with me, but all men forsook me: I pray God that it may not be laid to their charge. Notwithstanding the Lord stood with me, and strengthened me; that by me the preaching might be fully known, and that all the Gentiles might hear: and I was delivered out of the mouth of the lion"* (2 Tim. 4:16-17). What a tremendous statement! How often saints have held tenaciously to that wonderful, and assuring promise in the Epistle to the Hebrews, namely, *"Let your* conversation (manner of living) *be without covetousness; and be content with such things as ye have: for He hath said, I will never leave thee, nor forsake thee. So that we may boldly say, The Lord is my helper, and I will not fear what man shall do unto me"* (13:5-6). Unknown to Israel, God was watching, and listening, and God was about to move on their behalf.

MOSES THE SHEPHERD

Moses kept the flock of Jethro his father-in-law, who was a priest in Midian. Jethro probably officiated a sacerdotal priest for the family, interceding on their behalf to God. The value of the word *"kept"* is to be noticed and appreciated. It is used to describe a person that becomes acquainted with something, to associate with, to rule, to tend a flock, and to lead it to good grazing pastures. A good shepherd would be careful not to lead his flock to poisonous plants, but would seek to afford them the best possible food in the area. He would be quick to observe an injury, or strange behavior in any of his sheep. His eye would be keen. In other words, Moses was a good shepherd. He understood the sheep that were committed to his care. He knew what they needed, but not only that, he loved them and had an affectionate care for them. He was down to their level in associating himself with them. He would be keen to observe any disorder in any sheep and seek immediately to cure that malady. He valued the flock, and considered himself a servant to them.

JEHOVAH THE SHEPHERD

Jehovah pictures Himself as a Shepherd in four aspects to Israel in Isaiah 40:10. (1) *"He shall feed His flock like a shepherd."* Thus bringing satisfaction to His people. (2) *"He shall gather the lambs with His arm."* Such action would secure the otherwise defenseless little ones. (3) *"And shall carry them in His bosom."* This would indicate His support for them, and manifest a heartwarming affection for them. (4) *"And shall gently lead those that are with young."* This indicates His sympathy, consideration, and gentleness to those experiencing weakness. A good shepherd never drives sheep; he leads them, and that gently.

Not only in the prophecy of Isaiah does the Lord reveal His qualities as a Shepherd, but also in the writings of Ezekiel. In chapter 34 and verses 15 and 16, we discover six exposures of the Shepherd character of our blessed Lord. (1) *"I will feed My flock."* Thus the Lord exposes Himself as a Minister of food. How precious are the quiet moments when we turn aside to the quietness of His sanctuary and allow Him to feed us with the finest of the wheat. How wonderful to be able to say, *"I sat down under His shadow with great delight, and His fruit was sweet to my taste"* (Song 2:3). Jeremiah discovered this and exclaimed, *"Thy words were found, and I did eat them; and Thy word was unto me the joy and rejoicing of mine heart: for I am called by Thy name, O LORD God of hosts"* (Jer. 15:16). The world can never afford experiences of this nature.

(2) *"I will cause them to lie down."* The Lord is a Man of peace to His people. The peace of God is that which passeth all understanding. The human mind cannot begin to fully comprehend it. It is in a quiet and settled state that sheep can more effectively digest their food. The world is full of turmoil. It has its inhabitants rushing here and rushing there. People are constantly on the go. Their eyes are never satisfied with seeing, nor their ears with hearing. They are constantly in an unsettled state. However, the godly Christian has learned a vital truth, and it is exposed in Paul's exhortations to Timothy. We are told to *pray "for kings, and for all that are in authority; that we may lead a quiet and peaceable life in all godliness and honesty"* (1 Tim. 2:2). In other words, it is in the atmosphere of quietness and peace that godliness grows.

Some Christians are always on the go, rushing here and there, hardly ever taking time out to be alone with God in the quietness of the sanctuary, and never seem to grow up into godliness. Their diverse interests in temporal things occupy most of their precious time. What a tremendous loss for eternity! Just saved so as by fire. When their life is finally over, when they have lived their allotted time, they enter the courts above, but there is no abundant entrance.

Peter exhorts God's people to give all diligence to add to their faith, so that they may abound, not being barren or unfruitful, thus making their calling and election sure. Then he implies, that if these things are evident in the life, they shall never fall. Then when the time comes to enter heaven, Peter exclaims, *"For so an entrance shall be ministered unto you abundantly into the everlasting kingdom of our Lord and Saviour Jesus Christ"* (2 Pet. 1:11).

THE HOMECOMING HERO

In other words, it can be compared to soldiers returning home after a war. The ordinary soldier returns quietly. There are no bands playing a heart-warming welcome. There is no fanfare. No, he is just another soldier that did as little as he could, and made it back home safe and sound. However, in that same location, there is a man who returns a hero. His fame has been spread from shore to shore. Ah, the scene is far different for this individual. The town officials are ready, the band is ready, and the parade is about to begin down Main Street. The crowds are gathered on both sides of the street. The train pulls into the little town's station and out steps the hero. The crowd cheers, the band strikes up a tune, the mayor holds out his hand to the hero, and the homecoming parade begins. What a day! What an abundant entrance! The hero and the ordinary soldier were both safely home, but what a vast difference in the reception! What a glorious entrance into heaven that must be for the martyr! What an abundant reception for the saint who has sacrificed his whole life for Christ. Many have borne reproach. Multitudes have forfeited worldly fame and fortune for the cause of Christ. Think what an abundant entrance they experienced.

Let me ask you, what kind of an entrance are you going to experience? We may never experience an entrance like the Apostle Paul's, but let us seek, in our fleeting lifetime, to live with that coming entrance in view, that it may be abundant.

(3) *"I will seek that which was lost"* (Ezek. 34:16). A lost sheep is one that has wandered away from the flock. Unless found and brought back, it may die from surrounding circumstances. The true shepherd is a person who goes into the wilderness to seek that lost sheep with the purpose of bringing it back into the fold. To spiritualize this expression, the lost sheep represents a backslider, a saint who has lost heart, and no longer is seen in happy fellowship with other believers as was seen in days past. A diligent shepherd keeps an attendance record, and when it is perceived that the lack of attendance is not due to physical sickness, but rather spiritual sickness, he moves quickly, and

deliberately. Such visits require much wisdom, compassion, and understanding. One is reminded of Paul's exhortation to shepherds in Galatians 6:1. The person considered did not slowly drift away from the flock, which is characteristic of a backslider, but rather was quite suddenly overpowered by a sinful action. Sin had successfully made its surprise attack upon this person. He *was "overtaken."* Thus, the exhortation; *"Brethren, if a man be overtaken in a fault, ye which are spiritual, restore such an one in the spirit of meekness; considering thyself, lest thou also be tempted"* (Gal. 6:1). It would seem in this case that at least two spiritual persons visit the fallen one. The object would be to "reset the broken bone," for that is what the word *"restore"* implies. The healing process was to be done in the spirit of meekness.

Meekness is a powerful tool! The world knows nothing about it. They consider meekness to be weakness. However, the spiritual man perceives that meekness is simply strength and power under divine control. Our Lord was all-powerful, yet *"meek and lowly in heart."* It is always wise to look at yourself and consider the fact that you too, under certain circumstance, could suddenly be overtaken in a fault. Such awareness of self definitely helps in dealing with erring ones.

(4) I will *"bring again that which was driven away."* They call them, "sheep stealers." Who are they? Well, they are individuals who lead certain weak saints astray. Paul warns the Ephesians of the danger of being carried away with every wind of doctrine. With craftiness, the thief lies in wait to deceive (Eph. 4:14). *"They creep into houses (through the TV or the radio), and lead captive silly women"* (2 Tim. 3:6). There is an eminent danger exposing one's self to certain media preachers. Men that shepherds would not allow on their platform to preach, have ways of influencing naive saints by way of the radio and television. Through this media, they "creep into houses" influencing the minds of simple Christians to their own destruction.

I can relate to a scriptural assembly of 42 people, where some began listening to radio preachers, who convinced them that the wearing of a head covering in the Corinthian assembly was purely cultural, and not doctrinal. These people were convinced through the smooth words that the previous teaching they had received was faulty. Not only this, some were convinced that women were allowed to speak in the church. One thing led to another, until finally the day came when 21 left that assembly after 21 years of fruitful fellowship. The devil had done his work well, and the testimony was hurt. Efforts were made to reconcile them to the truth and to God's assembly, but it was to no avail.

CHRISTIAN PSYCHOLOGY?

There is another danger that should alarm shepherds to awareness, and that is the intrusion of Christian psychology, which is the study of mental processes and behavior. The description "Christian psychology" is certainly a misnomer. According to Dave Hunt of Bend Oregon,

> "C.T. (Christianity Today, founded by Billy Graham in 1956) upholds Christian psychology. Christian psychology claims that the Word of God and the power of the Holy Spirit, sufficient in the past, are insufficient today. The C.T. author insists that churches and pastors relying solely upon God and His Word, lack the expertise to deal with emotional problems; the help of professionals trained in psychology is required … Every psychologist or psychiatrist, whether Christian or atheist, must take the same courses, give the same answers to pass the same tests and be licensed by the same government bureaus."

Shepherds should speak to Christian parents who flatly reject God's way of disciplining their children, by not using the rod, and instead adhere to the psychologist's theory. Imagine, setting the Book of Proverbs on the shelf as insufficient and outdated, and picking up some psychologist's writings on raising children as the criteria of the day! Such attitudes and actions can lead to nothing short of disaster in the home and for the child. The faithful shepherd will seek that which was driven away.

(5) I *"will bind up that which was broken."* Thus the shepherd is a skillful surgeon. This has already been discussed, but perhaps we could add a little more. The erring one has been overtaken in a fault. It is a fault, not something serious enough to call for excommunication. It is an unintentional error. The restoration process may be painful, but in the end, it will be very helpful, because it will restore the erring one to more effective usefulness again. This takes time, patience, expertise, and love, on the part of the shepherd. The object of the shepherd's work should be for the glory of God, the honor of Christ, the betterment of the assembly, and the restored effectiveness of the faulty one. Just as a skillful surgeon has valuable tools to aid him in his work, so also the shepherd has an indispensable tool to accomplish his work – the Holy Word of God.

(6) I *"will strengthen that which was sick."* It takes a keen eye to discern spiritual sickness. The sickness of vanity sometimes creeps in. The clothing gradually changes. Colors become more "eye-catching," and flagrant. The garment has become tighter around the body, displaying more shape, and jewelry begins to adorn the body. Modesty is no longer seen, and attraction to self seems to be the ultimate goal. Does a shepherd notice? He should! Does a shepherd act? He should! But does he? Ah, who wants to confront a vain woman and her stand-by husband? However, the solemn responsibility is there, right at his doorstep.

PRIDE

Then we have the disease of pride. A brother has climbed to the top of the workforce ladder. He has become very important to the company that employs him. He begins to feel himself to be somebody. Rather than looking up to the saints, he now begins to look down on them. He feels that he is indispensable in the assembly. His humble walk has turned into a prominent strut. He seemingly can't hide his pride, and as an old-timer would candidly say, "it's sticking out all over." He loves the praise of men, and expects it. None can preach as good as he. Not many have a better home than he. His automobile is the best, at least according to him, and, unknown to him, he has become actually useless for God. How does a shepherd approach a proud man? How can he bring him back? These are questions that a fruitful shepherd can answer, for he has had experience in that field. Near every medical institution of any worth there is a library consisting of records of the success rate of all nearby physicians. Needless to say, it is not open to the public, but the record is indelibly written in black and white. You shepherds, you spiritual physicians, how does your record book stand? Is it positive, or is it negative?

FIVE SHEPHERDS

Now that we have spent 2,322 words explaining that little word *"kept,"* I think that we had better move on to the unique bush that met the gaze of Moses at Horeb. However, let me say one more thing. Speaking of shepherds, there are five who definitely point to Christ. (1) Abel, the righteous shepherd that was slain by his brother. He is a picture of Christ, crucified and slain by His own. (2) Jacob, the resourceful shepherd, who manifested care for his sheep, reminds us of all the resources God's people experience in their great Shepherd. (3) Joseph, the rejected shepherd, sold by his brethren to slavery, even as Judas sold our Lord for the price of a gored slave, being thirty pieces of silver. (4) Moses, the returning shepherd, who at the first was rejected, but returned forty years later to lead God's people out of Egyptian bondage. He is a figure of Him Who is yet to come in power to redeem the nation of Israel from world tyranny, making them the head of the nations and not the tail. (5) David, the royal shepherd, who risked his life for the sheep, confronting a lion and a bear, thus pointing to that blessed One Who entered the battle against the powers of darkness, and defeated him who had the power of death, that is the devil.

THE UNCONSUMED BUSH

Speaking of the bush, let us be clear about one thing. The bush was not in the fire! It was rather the opposite; the fire was in the bush. There is an analogy to this unique sight. If the bush would have been in the fire, then we could say that it represented Israel in the midst of the fires of persecution, yet not consumed. But that was already known, so what is the picture here? It is simply this. Out of the midst of a bush, appears a flame of fire, which was the appearance of the angel of the LORD. The word "angel," according to Strong, is: "mal'ak mal-awk' from an unused root meaning to dispatch as a deputy; a messenger; specifically, of God, i.e. an angel ... ambassador."

I believe the presence of the representative angel to be a sign to Moses, that Jehovah, the covenant-keeping God, was revealing Himself to be in the midst of His persecuted people, typified by the fact that the bush burned. In the midst of all Israel's persecution, dwelt the Lord Himself! What a revelation! What a comfort and assurance to the man Moses, who God was going to use to deliver His people! The bush was not consumed. Egypt, with its hopes of annihilating God's people, could never succeed. God, in the midst, was not there to destroy His people. Quite the opposite, He was in their midst to help them, and deliver them. What a wonderful God they had, and they had to be made aware of this magnificent fact.

Do we appreciate God in our midst? Our God is a consuming fire, yet He dwells in the midst of His gathered- out people and wonder of wonders, they are not consumed. God was going to dwell in the midst of His earthly people, thus the Tabernacle was set up, and God was pleased to dwell in the holiest of holies. Only once a year was Aaron allowed to enter into that sacred place to make atonement for the nation. There would be much fear connected with that entry through the veil, lest through a slight error on his part, he would die.

Today, we as the sons of God, as holy priests, have continual access into the immediate presence of God. How can this be?

Ah, it is a precious thought – the blood of Christ has afforded us the way! Do we appreciate the privilege; do we take advantage of it? Elizabeth Darks words are appropriate here.

> "Lamb of God, through Thee we enter
> Inside the veil;
> Cleansed by Thee, we boldly venture
> Inside the veil:
> Not a stain; a new creation;
> Ours is such a full salvation;
> Low we bow in adoration
> Inside the veil."

Israel is described as a bush. Unfortunately, our English translation gives no indication of what type of bush it was, but the Hebrew text reveals that it was a bramble, or thorn bush. That in itself is interesting, for it gives us a graphic picture of what Israel was at that time. What fruit can a thorn bush bear? What use is it, except to intensify a fire? Israel at its present state could bear no fruit for God; it was like a lowly bush.

The development of a thorn is equally interesting. A thorn is produced from an abortive leaf or branch. It has proven incapable of fulfilling its original purpose. Was not this a perfect description of Israel in the burning of Egyptian persecution and bondage? What could the nation do for God while in Egypt? Absolutely nothing! Egypt speaks of the materialistic world, and the question arises, what can a materialistic worldling accomplish for God? Nothing! Man may invent wonderful devices to accomplish his various purposes, but what does it all amount to for God? Nothing! Man has developed civilization, but what has civilization produced for God? Nothing. The space program with all its outstanding accomplishments, what has the space program offered to the heart of God? Nothing! What can a dead man produce? Nothing! The human race is dead in trespasses and sins, consequently, unregenerate mankind are the children of wrath, totally incapable of producing any fruit for God (Eph. 2:2-3). Israel was likened to a thorn bush.

THREE DESCRIPTIONS

It is equally interesting to consider the various horticultural descriptions of Israel in the Scriptures. She is likened to a **vine**, relating to her historic past. *"Thou hast brought a vine out of Egypt: thou hast cast out the heathen, and planted it"* (Ps. 80:8). Paul speaks of Israel in its present condition as **an olive tree.** *"For if thou wert cut out of the olive tree which is wild by nature, and wert graffed contrary to nature into a good olive tree: how much more shall these, which be the natural branches, be graffed into their own olive tree?"* (Rom. 11:24). Regarding the kingdom of God, the nation is likened to **a fig tree.** *"Then said he unto the dresser of his vineyard, Behold, these three years I come seeking fruit on this fig tree, and find none: cut it down; why cumbereth it the ground?"* (Luke 13:7). The Lord had sought fruit from Israel during His three years of ministry, only to find none. *"Now learn a parable of the fig tree; When his branch is yet tender, and putteth forth leaves, ye know that summer is nigh"* (Matt. 24:32).

DOUBLE CALLS

While God is observing Moses, the shepherd turns aside to see this great sight. Never before had Jehovah approached a person in this fashion. Upon looking on the bush, Moses receives a double call, *"Moses, Moses."* There seems to be urgency when one receives a double call from the Lord. There are seven of them in Scripture. (1) *"And the angel of the LORD called unto him out of heaven, and said, **Abraham, Abraham**: and he said, Here am I"* (Gen. 22:11). The sacrificial knife was prepared for Isaac's bosom, but God suddenly intervened, and Isaac was spared, a substitute being provided. Thus: the Provision of God – **Preservation**

(2) *"And God spake unto Israel in the visions of the night, and said, **Jacob, Jacob**. And he said, Here am I. And He said, I am God, the God of thy father: fear not to go down into Egypt; for I will there make of thee a great nation"* (Gen. 46:2-3). Thus: the guidance of God – **Pathway**.

(3) *"And when the LORD saw that he turned aside to see, God called unto him out of the midst of the bush, and said,* **Moses, Moses.** *And he said, Here am I"* (Ex. 3:4). Thus: the holiness of God – **Promise**.

(4) *"And the LORD came, and stood, and called as at other times,* **Samuel, Samuel.** *Then Samuel answered, Speak; for thy servant heareth"* (1 Sam. 3:10). Thus: the calling of God – **Prophecy**.

(5*) "And the Lord said,* **Simon, Simon***, behold, Satan hath desired to have you, that he may sift you as wheat: but I have prayed for thee, that thy faith fail not"* (Luke 22:31). Thus: the consolation of God – **Prayer**.

(6) *"And he fell to the earth, and heard a voice saying unto him, Saul, Saul, why persecutest thou Me?"* (Acts 9:4). Thus: the convicting power of God – **Persecution**.

(7) *"And Jesus answered and said unto her, Martha, Martha, thou art careful and troubled about many things"* (Luke 10:41). Thus: the rebuke of God – **Provision**.

So you can readily see a degree of urgency in all of these double calls from God to men. God sees that Moses is now ready for the tremendous task that He was about to lay on his shoulders. What a miracle, a mere man standing before a mighty monarch. A meek shepherd influencing about two million slaves and bringing them out of Egypt with might and power! This was only accomplished because Jehovah was working to fulfill His covenant promise to Abraham, Isaac, and Jacob.

"HOLY" AND "SAINT"

Having answered the double call, Moses was now commanded to put off his shoes, for the place where he was now standing was holy ground. It was the presence of God that made it holy. What makes a gathered-out company of God's people holy? Is it pleasant surroundings? Not at all! Is it a steeple with a cross on the top? Hardly! Artistic glass stained windows and pictures of ancient saints? Never! Nothing of a temporal nature makes a place holy. No amount of ritual, religious pageantry, musical concert, or robes and religious garb constitutes a place holy. There is only one requirement to position a place as being holy, and that is the unhindered presence of God. Exodus 3:5 affords us the first occasion of the word "holy" in the Bible. It is elsewhere translated, "saint," and carries the thought of something set apart, or separated. There are 544 references to the word "holy" in the Scriptures and 98 references to the word "saint." The Spirit of God, the brethren, certain women, the Scriptures, the temple of God (the local assembly), the heavenly city, God's effective calling, God Himself, and His Son, are all termed "holy." Let us always remember, God's assembly is holy, for He is in the midst. This should affect our conduct, dress, speech, and attitude.

CHILDREN IN THE ASSEMBLY GATHERING

Teachers are warned not to defile the temple of God with frivolous teaching, lest God destroy them. Children are to be taught that the gathering is holy and to act accordingly. What a disgrace to see unruly children in an assembly gathering, and to hear babies screaming to have their own way and parents giving in to them. Also, to see children bribed with goodies in an effort to make then behave, this being the result of heeding the utter nonsense of psychologists. Gullible parents, allowing the theories of psychologists to permeate their minds regarding child rearing, usually results in producing unruly little ones. That will never do.

Our children are to be firmly taught that the gathering is holy and that they are to fearfully manifest due reverence in the presence of a holy Lord God. Parents teach your children the divine precepts diligently, and unless they are in physical pain, or mentally retarded, they will sit quietly for one hour, with reverence. I have seen that goal accomplished time and time again by godly parents. While composing this chapter, I am ministering the Word of God for a few weeks to an assembly of mostly young couples. To my delight, all of the little ones have been sitting night after night without toys, cereal, candy, or silly books. They sit at attention because their parents demand it of them. The question arises, how do these parents accomplish what the world considers impossible? The solution is very easy. Hanging on the kitchen wall is an effective persuader to obedience. It is called a paddle, and these parents are convinced that God is right when He says:

> "He that spareth his rod hateth his son: but he that loveth him chasteneth him betimes. Chasten thy son while there is hope, and let not thy soul spare for his crying. Foolishness is bound in the heart of a child; but the rod of correction shall drive it far from him. Withhold not correction from the child: for if thou beatest him with the rod, he shall not die. Thou shalt beat him with the rod, and shalt deliver his soul from hell. The rod and reproof give wisdom: but a child left to himself bringeth his mother to shame. Correct thy son, and he shall give thee rest; yea, he shall give delight unto thy soul" (Prov. 13:24; 19:18; 22:15; 23:13-14; 29:15,17).

If I went into the paddle-making business and was able to sell one for 25 cents to every parent that had unruly children, I would become a millionaire in less than one year. And if they were all put to wise and diligent use, the law enforcement agencies would have a season of great relief in just a few years. But of course, all of this is just wishful thinking.

Godly, Robert Chapman, who lived to be 100, carefully wrote these beautiful words.

> "Thy name is holy, O our God!
> Before Thy throne we bow;
> Thy bosom is Thy saints abode,
> We call Thee Father now."

THE HOLINESS OF OUR LORD

The holiness of God is to be appreciated. In our Lord's pre-incarnate state, holy seraphim cried one to another and said, *"Holy, holy, holy, is the LORD of hosts: the whole earth is full of His glory"* (Isa. 6:3). At the time of our Saviour's birth, the angelic announcement came to Mary; *"The Holy Ghost shall come upon thee, and the power of the Highest shall overshadow thee: therefore also that holy thing which shall be born of thee shall be called the Son of God"* (Luke 1:35).

After living for thirty years in total obscurity in the despised city of Nazareth, our Lord stepped forth to commence His unique ministry. As He went about doing good, the demons confessed His holiness before His face, saying, *"Let us alone; what have we to do with Thee, Thou Jesus of Nazareth? art Thou come to destroy us? I know Thee who Thou art; the Holy One of God"* (Luke 4:34).

Coming to the sin offering which typified Christ, we read, *"Speak unto Aaron and to his sons, saying, This is the law of the sin offering: In the place where the burnt offering is killed shall the sin offering be killed before the LORD: it is most holy"* (Lev. 6:25).

Regarding His burial and resurrection, Christ prophetically spoke, *"For thou wilt not leave My soul in hell; neither wilt Thou suffer Thine Holy One to see corruption"* (Ps. 16:10).

After His ascension to heaven, while walking in the midst of the seven churches of Asia, He is still holy. *"And to the angel of the church in Philadelphia write; These things saith He that is holy, He that is true, He that hath the key of David, He that openeth, and no man shutteth; and shutteth, and no man openeth"* (Rev. 3:7).

During the great tribulation, slain saints will cry with a loud voice saying, *"How long, O Lord, holy and true, dost Thou not judge and avenge our blood on them that dwell on the earth?"* Later, as the judgments of God are poured out upon this earth and the kingdom of the beast, souls will be heard to sing the song of Moses, containing these words: *"Who shall not fear Thee, O Lord, and glorify Thy name? for Thou only art holy: for all nations shall come and worship before Thee; for Thy judgments are made manifest"* (Rev. 15:4).

What sublime scriptures these are that uphold the holiness of our blessed Lord. He was holy prior to becoming human. He was holy at His birth, during His life, burial and resurrection, and He is presently holy while abiding in heaven. He will always be acknowledged as *"holy, holy, holy."* Jesus Christ, the same yesterday (holy), today (holy), and forever (holy). His character is eternal, and it never changes.

PUTTING OFF ONE'S SHOES

Allow me to make an application regarding the command to Moses to put off his shoes (Ex. 3:5). There was to be no approach through a man-made convenience. Christendom adores its cathedrals, ostentatious buildings, altars, beautifully glass-stained windows, pipe organs, images, relics, and a host of other man-devised ornaments to supposedly assist and inspire worship by its adherents. The intelligent Christian, who is a true worshipper, realizes that *"God is a Spirit: and they that worship Him must worship Him in spirit and in truth"* (John 4:24). That is, his worship corresponds to the nature of God. He worships in spirit, meaning that his eyes are not occupied with material objects or sacrifices. Not only this, he worships in truth. If this were to be taken *subjectively*, it would mean that he worships in sincerity, and integrity of character. If the expression were taken *objectively*, then it would mean that the worshipper would worship according to divinely revealed truth. In reality, both cases are true.

In our everyday walk of life we wear shoes, but drawing nigh to God on this particular occasion was different. No shoes were to be worn in Moses' approach. The application is simply this; I certainly hope that there is more reverence in your heart entering an assembly gathering than entering a grocery store. There is a vast difference between a business gathering, or social gathering, than a gathering of God's people with the Lord in the midst. Do we realize this? Our demeanor should be one of sobriety. Our dress should measure up to the set standards of the society of the country in which we live. In the Aaronic order of the priesthood, the death penalty hung over the head of every officiating priest. It was either dress according to God's pattern, or die (Ex. 28:42-43). Casualness should find no resting place in God's assembly. For high-level presidential gatherings, a suit and tie are required. Undertakers are required to wear suits because of the occasion. Airline pilots must measure up to their company's dress code, usually a white shirt and tie. Some grocery stores require their young male employees to wear a white shirt and tie to convey respect to their customers. Are assembly gatherings on a higher platform than those just mentioned? I think so, but do you? I hope so! An old, godly preacher, advised me, "When you are doing something for God, act your best, speak your best, and dress your best - for He is worthy of nothing but your best."

KNOWING GOD

Having drawn near to God, the LORD is now going to reveal Himself to Moses. It is only on holy ground, and acting in obedience, that God reveals Himself to His people. Many saints know about God, but not all actually know God. The apostle Paul had known God for over twenty years, yet he writes, *"That I may know Him, and the power of His resurrection, and the fellowship of His sufferings, being made conformable unto His death"* (Phil. 3:10). Paul coveted an even more intimate relationship with his God. Intensive study of the Bible and religious books can perhaps give one a good knowledge of God. We can thus learn His attributes, His ways, His history with the human race, and a host of other intellectual truths. This is all well and good, however, it takes more than intensive study to actually know God in a personal and experiential way. There is a man living in back of our home on the next street. I know of him, I say hello to him, and recognize him as a neighbor when meeting him elsewhere. However, I really do not know him in a personal way. Many

Christians know about God, like I know about my neighbor, but they do not know God in an intimate way. The problem is that they have never lived with Him. Their times of deep communion with Him are nonexistent. Ah yes, they can preach, they can teach, giving the Greek of this and the Hebrew of that, but something is lacking, and it is simply this, they do not intimately know God. Moses was now entering into an intimate relationship with the One he was about to serve.

THE FEAR OF GOD

God now speaks. *"I am the God of thy father, the God of Abraham, the God of Isaac, and the God of Jacob. And Moses hid his face; for he was afraid to look upon God"* (Ex. 3:6). The psalmist manifested the same attitude, and exclaimed. *"For who in the heaven can be compared unto the LORD? who among the sons of the mighty can be likened unto the LORD? God is greatly to be feared in the assembly of the saints, and to be had in reverence of all them that are about Him"* (Ps. 89:6-7). Not just feared, but *"greatly to be feared."* Because we are under grace and not law, it is no excuse for laxness in the presence of a Holy God! What is your behavior in a holy gathering with the Lord in the midst? Ignorance of God begets unhallowed familiarity. Jacob, in the presence of God *"was afraid, and said, How dreadful is this place! this is none other but the house of God, and this is the gate of heaven"* (Gen. 28:17).

Regarding Samson's parents, when the flame went up toward heaven from off the altar, and the angel of the LORD ascended in the flame of the altar, Manoah and his wife looked on it, and fell on their faces to the ground (Judg. 13:20).

How lovely to see the bowed heads of God's people gathered together on a Lord's Day morning to remember their Lord. There is no chattering or lightness, but a recognition of the solemnity of the occasion. The fear of God is over the place and the saints are very subdued, lest they grieve the Holy Spirit, Who, with the Lord Jesus, is in their midst. Such scenes are most lovely to behold.

MOSES IN MIDIAN

Notice how God first revealed Himself. *"He said, I am the God of thy father, the God of Abraham, the God of Isaac, and the God of Jacob"* (Ex. 3:6). Never before had God linked Himself in such a statement with these three men together. The expression is also found in Exodus 3:15, 3:16, and 4:5. When confronting the Sadducees regarding the resurrection, the Lord Jesus refers to this expression in three gospels; Matthew 22:32, Mark 12:26, and Luke 20:37. Peter, in his address to the nation, quotes it in reference to God glorifying His Son Jesus (Acts 3:13), and Stephen relating this event before the council quotes it (Acts 7:32). Other than those occasions, it is not found elsewhere in the Scriptures. What does it imply? To find the answer one must turn back to Exodus 2:24-25. *"And God heard their groaning, and God remembered **His covenant** with Abraham, with Isaac, and with Jacob. And God looked upon the children of Israel, and God had respect unto them."* He perceived, He ascertained by seeing. The time had arrived when He was to fulfill His word given to Abraham, Isaac, and Jacob. Those men had received the promise, but they had never witnessed the fulfillment of it. Israel was about to actually see and experience the fulfillment of that ancient promise given about 215 years prior to the fire in the bush. That is why, all of a sudden, Jehovah identifies Himself with Abraham, Isaac, and Jacob. He is a covenant-keeping God.

JEHOVAH

God further makes known to Moses that He was the LORD (Jehovah). Notice carefully the expression.

> *"And I appeared unto Abraham, unto Isaac, and unto Jacob, by the name of God Almighty, but by My name JEHOVAH was I not known to them. And I have also established **My covenant** with them, to give them the land of Canaan, the land of their pilgrimage, wherein they were strangers. And I have also heard the groaning of the children of Israel, whom the Egyptians keep in bondage; and I have remembered My covenant"* (Ex. 6:3-5).

Now it seems to some that there is a discrepancy in that statement, *"by My name JEHOVAH was I not known unto them,"* for time and time again we read of JEHOVAH in the Book of Genesis, and many times in connection with Abraham. What then does God mean when He says, *"by My name JEHOVAH was I not known"*? The answer is simple. He had appeared unto Abraham, Isaac, and Jacob by the name of God Almighty (El-Shaddai). The name means "God all-sufficient, the dispenser, the pourer-out of gifts." God had proven Himself to them in this way many times, thus they knew Him as such. However, the word JEHOVAH means, "the self-existent, eternal One." It indicates "the accomplishment of promises already made. To bring into existence."

However, *"these all died in faith, not having received the promises, but having seen them afar off, and were persuaded of them, and embraced them, and confessed that they were strangers and pilgrims on the earth"* (Heb. 11:13). Thus, they did not know what the name JEHOVAH implied. God had never acted in this fashion, in this role, on their behalf, but now He was going to act as the One accomplishing the promises. Thus, Moses and Israel would know Him as JEHOVAH, a privilege that Abraham, Isaac, and Jacob, never experienced. The title, *"The God of Abraham, the God of Isaac, and the God of Jacob,"* and the title JEHOVAH all hinge around the promised covenant. The first expression, *"The God of Abraham, the God of Isaac, and the God of Jacob,"* links God with the announcement of the covenant, but that expression "JEHOVAH" associates God with the actual fulfilling of that covenant.

MOSES' PLEAS

Following his meeting with God at the burning bush, we discover four problems in Moses' mind. One could almost term them "his excuses" or, "his pleas," and the consideration of them proves very interesting to the careful reader.

Moses' First Plea

(I) *"And Moses said unto God, Who am I, that I should go unto Pharaoh, and that I should bring forth the children of Israel out of Egypt?"* (Ex. 3:11). I suppose that one could consider a note of humility associated with this plea. We see the same expression with David regarding his being associated in an intimate way with the king. *"And David said unto Saul, Who am I? And what is my life, or my father's family in Israel, that I should be son in law to the king?"* (1 Sam. 18:18). Later in David's life, the same attitude is shown regarding his house and the kingdom. *"Then went king David in, and sat before the LORD, and he said, Who am I, O Lord GOD? and what is my house, that Thou hast brought me hitherto?"* (2 Sam. 7:18). David was thankful for being able to serve God. *"But who am I, and what is my people, that we should be able to offer so willingly after this sort? for all things come of Thee, and of Thine own have we given Thee"* (1 Chron. 29:14). Solomon also manifests the same spirit as his father David, saying, *"But who is able to build Him an house, seeing the heaven and heaven of heavens cannot contain Him? who am I then, that I should build Him an house, save only to burn sacrifice before Him?"* (2 Chron. 2:6).

Do you feel important? Do you consider yourself superior to others? Are you indispensable? Think again my friend, for really, in yourself you are "a nothing!" Just be thankful that God has designed it in His eternal counsels and plans to employ redeemed beings to labor with Him in the accomplishment of His divine purposes. At the tomb of Lazarus, our Lord could have commanded the stone to roll away of itself, but that was not His design. Ah no. Instead, He spoke to those standing there, *"Take ye away the stone"* (John 11:39). In other words, He was going to allow them to have a part in this tremendous miracle of raising the dead. God doesn't need you to save a sinner, but it has pleased Him to design it in such a way that Scripture must exclaim, *"How then shall they call on Him in whom they have not believed? and how shall they believe in Him of Whom they have not heard? and how shall they hear without a preacher?"* (Rom. 10:14).

The plea of Moses was answered with these assuring words from God. *"Certainly I will be with thee; and this shall be a token unto thee, that I have sent thee: When thou hast brought forth the people out of Egypt, ye shall serve God upon this mountain"* (Ex. 3:12). The miracle of the bush and the fire was a token to Moses that God would be sending him, and not only that, but also that He would be with Moses. This assurance is similar to what we find the Lord giving to His own upon Him leaving them after His resurrection. He assures them of the fact that all power has been given unto Him in heaven and in earth, and because of this, they are to teach all nations, baptizing them in the name of the Father, and of the Son, and of the Holy Ghost; teaching them all things that He had commanded them, and then the promise is given, *"and, lo, I am with you alway, even unto the end of the world. Amen"* (Matt. 28:18-20). Is it not the same with God's servants today as they seek, by His grace, to take the gospel to the regions beyond, with the divine promise ringing in their ears, *"I will never leave thee nor forsake thee"*? What a privilege to be able to prove the presence and the power of God out of sight from the brethren, looking totally to a Father in heaven Whose resources never run dry.

Moses' Second Plea

(II) The next thing we discover with Moses is, that his plea is of not having a message. *"And Moses said unto God, Behold, when I come unto the children of Israel, and shall say unto them, The God of your fathers hath sent me unto you; and they shall say to me, What is His name? what shall I say unto them?"* (Ex. 3:13). It is possible to run and not to be sent. How vexing it is to hear men spewing out bushels of words, without even spoonfuls of thought. They are what are termed, "word-merchants." Their vocabulary is voluminous. They sway people by their emotions. They have more stories than a skyscraper, and they speak highly of themselves, and what they have accomplished. The limelight attracts them like a moth is attracted to a light in the darkness. Their memory is keen and they can "rattle off" verse after verse, impressing their audience with their tremendous ability to fluently quote scripture, and also the book, chapter, and verse. They impress people that don't know any better. Such men are dangerous, for in their natural ability, they seemingly can produce converts in automobile assembly-line fashion, which in few years infiltrate the assemblies, only to bring those assemblies to ruin. Strange children in the assemblies of God! I am afraid that the percentage is rising higher and higher as the coming of the Lord draws nigh.

What is needed today are plain men, with plain messages from God. Not "pretty sermons," but rather "plain searching." Messages that will dig deep into the heart, producing a reflection in the soul of the hearer regarding their ways, thus causing a deep searching of one's heart, and a producing of repentance to restoration. Well might we cry like Habakkuk, *"O LORD, I have heard Thy speech, and was afraid: O LORD, revive Thy work in the midst of the years, in the midst of the years make known; in wrath remember mercy"* (Hab. 3:2). The day is coming when the fire will try every teacher's work of what sort it is. It is to be feared that much will go up in smoke, being just wood hay, and stubble, instead of gold, silver, and precious stones (1 Cor. 3:12). Moses pleaded that he had no message.

"I AM THAT I AM"

Upon asking what he should say to the children of Israel, immediately God provides the answer. *"And God said unto Moses, I AM THAT I AM: and He said, Thus shalt thou say unto the children of Israel, I AM hath sent me unto you"* (Ex. 3:14). The expression literally means, "I will be that I will be." In the Greek language it is thus expressed; "I am He that exists, the existing One." In Arabic it would be translated, "The eternal One Who passeth not away." Consequently, in this title, we perceive God's underived, eternal, unchangeable, existence, contrary to the gods of Egypt. It conveys the thought of our absolute God acting with unfettered ability and self-dependence. C.H. Macintosh referred to the title as Jehovah furnishing a blank check to be filled up to any amount. *"I AM."* What a profound statement! What an awe-inspiring revelation!

In connection with this portion, F. W. Grant contributes an interesting thought. *"***The Almighty** is the name God took with Abraham; **I Am** or **Jehovah** is that which He took with Israel; **The Highest** is that which He will show Himself to be in millennial times. None of these in themselves declare His nature, or the character of His ways toward us. But in the mouth of the Lord Jesus, **Father** has become indeed a revealing name, and we know God as He was never revealed before."

It is also interesting to note God's continual association with these three men, Abraham, Isaac, and Jacob. This conveys a very interesting thought to us. In Abraham and Isaac we see in Genesis 22 a father and a son. Who could read that portion and not see the beautiful picture of the Father and the Son going to Calvary? As the God of Abraham, we see the Father aspect of God. As the God of Isaac, we notice the Son aspect of God, for is not Isaac a beautiful type of our Lord Jesus Christ? Also, God is not ashamed to be called the God of Jacob. It was in Jacob that God displayed His power, grace, patience, and guidance. It is through the Holy Spirit that the power and grace of God is seen in the lives of His redeemed people. It is He Who dwells within every believer, guiding him, empowering him, and providing for him the truths of Holy Scripture. Thus in the God of Abraham, Isaac, and Jacob, we see the Father, the Son, and the Holy Spirit.

"I AM THAT I AM," is a name that tells what He is in Himself. This explains His name Jehovah, and signifies that He is self-existent; He has His being of Himself, and has no dependence upon any other. Thus, being self-existent, He cannot but be self-sufficient, and therefore all sufficient, and the inexhaustible fountain of being and bliss. The name also implies that He is eternal and unchangeable, always the same, yesterday, today, and forever: He will be what He will be, and what He is. Furthermore, He is faithful and true to all His promises,

unchangeable in His word as well as in His nature, and not a man that He should lie. *"God said unto Moses, I AM THAT I AM: and He said, Thus shalt thou say unto the children of Israel, I AM hath sent me unto you"* (Ex. 3:14). A name that speaks what He is to His people."

You will remember that our Lord employs this during His sojourn here. None but God Himself could ever do this. Coming upon His own, walking on a stormy sea, He quieted their fear with these sublime words; *"Be of good cheer, I AM"* (John 6:20, Newberry margin). Speaking to a sinful woman that expression is used again. *"I AM that speak unto you"* (John 4:26). Again, notice the expression to questioning Jews. *"Before Abraham was, I AM"* (John 8:58). Finally, at His betrayal, He reveals Himself as the great I AM. He asks of them Whom they were seeking. *"They answered Him, Jesus of Nazareth. Jesus saith unto them, I AM (the word "he" not being in the original text). And Judas also, which betrayed Him, stood with them. As soon then as He had said unto them, I AM, they went backward, and fell to the ground"* (John 18:6). In other words, stepping back in awe and amazement, they fell forward on their faces before Him. Thus, for an instantaneous flash, we get a glimpse of that coming day, when nations shall fall down before Him, the King of Kings, LORD of Lords, and the great I AM!

It is also interesting to note that it is the Gospel of John that so graphically portrays our Lord's deity, and the fact that He is the great I AM in a prepared human body. Just consider with me for a few moments that expression I AM, in various exposures of Him.

(1) *"And Jesus said unto them,* **I am** *the bread of life: he that cometh to Me shall never hunger; and he that believeth on Me shall never thirst"* (John 6:35). Christ, the source of SATISFACTION. The world has much to offer, but the end thereof are the ways of death. The earth dweller's eye is never satisfied with seeing, nor his ear with hearing. Those who come to Christ, accepting Him as Lord and Saviour, immediately find an inward satisfaction that the world

cannot offer. When men accumulate wealth, something happens within. They develop a love for more wealth. One cannot love something that they do not possess. A beggar cannot have the love of money, but with the wealthy, that is another situation, for most of them fall in love with their riches and are never content, but always craving more.

A WONDERFUL FAMILY

There is a personal friend of mine that I admire. I first became acquainted with him and his wife in 1970 when they had only two little children. God came in and saved them, and through the years, gave them a total of six sons and six daughters. They lived in an extremely humble dwelling on a farm consisting of hundreds of acres. The land was mountainous, so there certainly was no large income from growing crops. The children were raised with two great instruments, one a Bible, and the other a rod of correction. The Bible was read in their home daily, and the children were committed into God's hand by prayer daily, before leaving their home for school. Today, all but two daughters profess to be saved, and some are married and live nearby. They have a few vehicles adorned with rust and old age. There is no insurance on anything that they own. A large garden and some cattle supply them with food. They have never had the desire to "go on a vacation," nor do they have a television in their home. The grandchildren surround them and provide wholesome entertainment as they romp and play about the house and yard.

Many times I have sat at their breakfast table at 6:55 A.M. to feast with some of their sons and daughters. The meal always consists of fresh eggs right out of the nest, a huge pile of pancakes, with butter, maple syrup, or gravy if you like. Oh yes, this is also accompanied with home grown and home canned sausage, bacon, orange juice, coffee, tea and milk. Oh my, don't let me forget those delicious home-fried potatoes either!

ONE MILLION DOLLARS REFUSED

One day, the father of this wonderful family received visitors to his humble dwelling. They were developers, big business men with a lot of money. Their desire was to acquire a small portion of my friend's farm for a housing development. It was a fair distance down the lane and up the highway, and wouldn't interfere with their lifestyle in any way. The proposition was made and they said to my friend, "We will pay you one-million dollars in cash for the property." What an opportunity to be immediately rich!

Well now, let me give you my friend's immediate answer. Looking at them he quietly said, "Now what would I ever do with a million dollars? You fellows may as well leave now, I'm not the least bit interested." I am sure an amazed look covered their faces. Not interested? Not interested in one million dollars? No, my friend was not the least bit interested. Why? Well, what did the Lord say? Have you forgotten that already? *"I am the bread of life: he that cometh to Me shall never hunger; and he that believeth on Me shall never thirst."* My friend was proving that truth. He was proving that *"godliness with contentment is great gain"* (1 Tim. 6:6). Is it true that some saints lie when singing certain spiritual songs?

THE WORLDLY MIND

Let me illustrate. "Mr. Worldy-minded" heartily sings in the gospel meeting, "I tried the broken cisterns Lord, but ah the waters failed. E'en as I stooped to drink they fled and mocked me as I wailed. Now none but Christ can satisfy, none other name for me. There's life, and peace, and lasting joy, Lord Jesus found in Thee." However, the next day, Mr. Worldly-minded is found cheering his lungs out at a football, or a soccer game? And before Friday rolls around, he has been to a theater, a musical concert, and a bowling alley. Yet he sings, "now none but Christ can satisfy." What is he singing? Why the answer is simple. He is singing a lie! Ah no my friend, the godly soul confesses like the psalmist, *"All my springs are in Thee"* (Ps. 87:7). *"Thou wilt shew me the path of life: in Thy presence is fulness of joy; at Thy right hand there are pleasures for evermore"* (Ps. 16:11).

> "I thirst, but not as once I did,
> The vain delights of earth to share;
> Thy wounds, Emmanuel, all forbid
> That I should seek my pleasure there.
> It was the sight of Thy dear Cross
> First weaned my soul from earthly things,
> And taught me to esteem as dross
> The mirth of fools and pomp of kings."
> William Cowper

(2) *"Then spake Jesus again unto them, saying, **I am** the light of the world: he that followeth Me shall not walk in darkness, but shall have the light of life"* (John 8:12). Christ is the source of GUIDANCE. John the Baptist was sent to bear witness of that true (genuine) Light that came into this world. As the Light, He *"lighteth every man"* (John 1:9). Divine illumination has its source in Christ. Notice divine guidance in the experiences of Paul at Corinth. *"Then spake the Lord to Paul in the night by a vision, Be not afraid, but speak, and hold not thy peace: For I am with thee, and no man shall set on thee to hurt thee: for I have much people in this city. And he continued there a year and six months, teaching the word of God among them"* (Acts 18:9-11) As the Light, the Lord saves us from ignorance, from grave mistakes, and from sin. He is the true Light!

(3) *"**I am** the Door: by Me if any man enter in, he shall be saved, and shall go in and out, and find pasture"* (John 10:9). Christ is the source of SALVATION. Thus, we see a number of truths contained in this statement. First of all, the singleness of salvation. He is not simply "a door," but rather *"the Door."* There is no other way. He is the divine channel to salvation – *"by Me."* Salvation is inclusive – it is universal. There is no limited atonement connected with it whatsoever, as some would claim. It is unto

all and upon all them that believe: for there is no difference" (Rom. 3:22). *"Enter in,"* gives us the thought of simplicity. Not a number of steps to attain to. No years of vain efforts to better one's self. No amount of penance, prayers, or payments, can secure salvation. It is a "one step" experience, if I may put it that way. It is a one-time act of faith, taking place at a definite time and place, a divine transaction between the soul and God. How wonderfully pure and simple! There is a divine absoluteness to salvation. Christ said, *"he shall be saved."* Not "he may be, or might be." No, no, that would never do. That would never bring eternal rest and peace to a soul. Our Lord is very definite about the whole thing; *"he **shall** be saved."*

(4) ***I am*** *the good Shepherd: the good Shepherd giveth His life for the sheep"* (John 10:11). Christ is the source of COMFORT. The true Shepherd would be one that entered in the fold of the sheep (Israel) by the door (the door of prophecy). Christ answered all that was written of Messiah, and took that path of God's will in presenting Himself to the nation. He fulfilled all the prophetic utterances regarding Messiah's first coming. To Him the porter openeth (John the Baptist), introducing Him to the people as the Lamb of God that taketh away the sin of the world. How blessed to have a Shepherd that knows and loves and cares! We can say like the psalmist, *"The Lord is my Shepherd, I shall not want."* As **the Good Shepherd,** He gave His life for us. As **the Great Shepherd,** He lives in heaven on our behalf (Heb. 13:20). Finally, as **the Chief Shepherd,** He will award crowns of glory to the under-shepherds, who being ensamples to the flock, have labored faithfully for Himself (1 Pet. 5:4).

(5) *"Jesus said unto her, **I am** the resurrection, and the life: he that believeth in Me, though he were dead, yet shall he live"* (John 11:25). Christ is the source of our RESURRECTION. He is "the resurrection" to those sleeping, and "the life" to those that are alive. *"Though he were dead"* is not a verb, but an adjective. Thus, it should read, "Though he has died physically, yet shall he live." The nature of our resurrection is explained in 1 Corinthians 15.

How vital the resurrection of Christ is, for if Christ be not risen, we are yet in our sins, we have no blessed hope, and we of all men would be most miserable. What a tremendous miracle was His resurrection, where words exposing the most comprehensive power of God are employed in Ephesians chapter one. His resurrection is the absolute guarantee of ours, blessed be His name!

(6) *"Jesus saith unto him,* **I am** *the way, the truth, and the life: no man cometh unto the Father, but by Me"* (John 14:6). Christ is the source of our APPROACH. He provides us the life necessary to approach, and he provides the truth as to how to approach. Through the blood of Jesus, we enter the holiest. How vital to have a Great High Priest at God's right hand, affording us the liberty to enter into the immediate presence of God. Only one man in Israel had this privilege and that only once a year – the high priest on the Day of Atonement. What a change! What a privilege! We, the redeemed of the Lord are bidden to come at anytime and as often as we may. What unfathomable value and worth is found in Him Who is the way! Do we take advantage, as we should, of our privilege?

(7) *"***I am*** the Vine, ye are the branches: He that abideth in Me, and I in him, the same bringeth forth much fruit: for without Me ye can do nothing"* (John 15:5). Christ is the source of UNION, and FRUIT-BEARING. Union with Christ makes a man fruitful for God. His desire is not only "fruit," but also "more fruit," accompanied with "much fruit," as His words in John 15 convey. He is the Vine and we are the branches. Not welded on, glued on, tied on, or bolted on. Oh no, we are an integral part of the Vine, obtaining all our substance necessary for fruit bearing in Him. Paul reminds the Colossian assembly with these words. *"That ye might walk worthy of the Lord unto all pleasing, being fruitful in every good work, and increasing in the knowledge of God"* (Col. 1:10). Only union in Christ can produce this in the life of a soul.

Moses' Third Plea

(III) Having addressed the title of God, we now come to the third plea, or excuse of Moses. His claim was that he had no authority. *"And Moses answered and said, But, behold, they will not believe me, nor hearken unto my voice: for they will say, The LORD hath not appeared unto thee"* (Ex. 4:1).

A SNAKE

The miracles that took place on that occasion have manifold applications, but we will mention only a few. Moses is told to cast the rod in his hand to the ground, and upon doing so, the rod immediately turned into a snake. It probably was a dangerous snake, for Moses fled from before it. Then *"the LORD said unto Moses, put forth thine hand, and take it by the tail. And he put forth his hand, and caught it, and it became a rod in his hand"* (Ex. 4:4). Anyone familiar with snakes knows that you certainly don't pick up a snake by the tail. Doing so, more or less, guarantees that you will be bitten. The safest way is to grab the snake by the back of the head, that way it cannot twirl around and strike you. The lesson one sees in this is, no matter what God says, even though it may appear to be wrong, yet it has to be right. Is this not what Frederick Faber's thoughts were when he wrote the following words?

"Ill that God blesses is our good,
And unblest good is ill;
And all is right that seems most wrong,
If it be His sweet will."

Moses does not question God. That is the point I want to make. Do we question God? When we are called upon to do something for God that does not appeal to us, do we do it? Would we stand for a godly principle at the expense of our income? If the Lord called upon us to make a tremendous sacrifice, would we exercise the faith in God's ability to help us make that sacrifice successfully? It is easy to trust God when it costs us nothing, but it is quite another thing to trust God in something, that to the natural man, seems wrong. There was no hesitation on Moses' part. He put forth his hand and caught the snake by the tail. I don't read that God told him prior to his act, that the snake would be turned back to a rod in his hand. It appeared to be a very dangerous move to make, yet if God said it, it must be right. Thus, in faith, Moses acted with unquestioning obedience. Moses put his life in danger, with the assurance that God would preserve him, simply because he was doing what God had told him to do.

To an Egyptian, the snake was an emblem of royal and divine power. It was seen on the diadem of every pharaoh. However, consider the snake as a picture of Satan, that old serpent, the devil. The rod is an emblem of government and power. Let us go back to Eden where we find Adam crowned with glory and honor. The psalmist exclaimed; *"Thou madest him to have dominion over the works of Thy hands; Thou hast put all things under his feet"* (Ps. 8:6). Adam held the rod of government and power. However, through his sin, he forfeited that position, and Satan grasped it for his own. Consequently, when Satan showed the Lord all the kingdoms of the world in a moment of time, he said to Jesus, *"All this power will I give Thee, and the glory of them: for that is delivered unto me; and to whomsoever I will I give it. If Thou therefore wilt worship me, all shall be Thine"* (Luke 4:6-7). That was no vain boast, for the Lord never rebuked him.

Today, Satan holds the power and glory of the kingdoms of this world. However, the day is coming when Christ will *"take the serpent by the tail,"* and will regain the power and glory of the kingdoms of this world for Himself. Prior to the setting up of His kingdom, the thundering announcement is made by the seventh angel, accompanied by *"great voices in heaven, saying, The kingdoms of this world are become the kingdoms of our Lord, and of His Christ; and He shall reign for ever and ever"* (Rev. 11:15). Christ will take Satan's power away and will hold the rod. *"And out of His mouth goeth a sharp sword, that with it He should smite the nations: and He shall rule them with a rod of iron: and He treadeth the winepress of the fierceness and wrath of Almighty God"* (Rev. 19:15).

A LEPROUS HAND

God then gave Moses another sign.

"And the LORD said furthermore unto him, Put now thine hand into thy bosom. And he put his hand into his bosom: and when he took it out, behold, his hand was leprous as snow. And He said, Put thine hand into thy bosom again. And he put his hand into his bosom again; and plucked it out of his bosom, and, behold, it was turned again as his other flesh. And it shall come to pass, if they will not believe thee, neither hearken to the voice of the first sign, that they will believe the voice of the latter sign" (Ex. 4:6-8).

Moses was about to receive authority to inflict and then remove the plagues that were about to fall upon Egypt. Also seen is the fact that the seat of man's loathsome disease of sin and uncleanness lies in his bosom (his heart). Even as the Lord Himself exposed this saying, *"For from within, out of the heart of men, proceed evil thoughts, adulteries, fornications, murders, thefts, covetousness, wickedness, deceit, lasciviousness, an evil eye, blasphemy, pride, foolishness: All these evil things come from within, and defile the man"* (Mark 7:21-23). It is not the hand that affects the heart. Quite the contrary, it is rather the heart that affects the hand. Thus, the works of man produce nothing of value to God. The natural man can never better his inward condition by good works, for *"his heart is deceitful above all things, and desperately wicked"* (Jer. 17:9). Society endeavors to "rehabilitate" criminals by incarcerating them for long periods of time, pouring into their minds philosophical ideas for their betterment. They try to cure the leprous hand, not understanding that it is the heart that is unclean. Their thought is that there is some good in everyone; no matter how wicked they may act. I term this "sophisticated nonsense!" Nothing short of the power of God, visiting a soul with salvation, can change the corruptness of man. A God-cured heart can change the hand of man. Moses is bidden to thrust his hand back into his bosom, and doing so, upon drawing it out again, the leprosy was gone, his hand was completely healed.

Do we not see in this miracle that true cleansing must begin with the heart? The leprous heart represents sin that is hidden, and the leprous hand shows us sin exposed.

WATER INTO BLOOD

The third sign given to Moses to perform in case the first two signs were not received, was taking water from the river and pouring it upon the dry land In doing so, God would turn the poured out water into blood. Thus, Moses was given a threefold power from God, to convince the elders of Israel that the Lord had appeared unto him, and would be using him as His instrument in delivering Israel from Egyptian bondage.

There is a similarity in the New Testament regarding Paul proving to the questioning Corinthians that he truly was an apostle sent from God. Three things were necessary regarding an apostle's verification. (1) He must have seen the Lord Jesus Christ, and been commissioned personally by Him. (2) He must work signs, wonders, and mighty deeds. (3) His ministry must prove to be successful. Paul writes to the Corinthians to remind them of these proofs seen in him. *"Am I not an apostle? am I not free? have I not seen Jesus Christ our Lord? are not ye my work in the Lord? If I be not an apostle unto others, yet doubtless I am to you: for the seal of mine apostleship are ye in the Lord"* (1 Cor. 9:1-2). *"Truly the signs of an apostle were wrought among you in all patience, in signs, and wonders, and mighty deeds"* (2 Cor. 12:12).

There are no apostles today, but there are laborers, working in the harvest field for God. What is needed for the unsaved to be convinced that such workers are truly sent from God? The sign gifts are past, the era of the apostles is gone, but one thing the laborer has today that those in apostolic times did not possess is the complete, divine revelation of God in the Holy Scriptures. This is all the worker needs today to work successfully for God in the winning of souls to Christ. The complete Word, accompanied by a godly life, gives the child of God all the authority and power needed. *"For God hath not given us the spirit of fear* (timidity); *but of power* (dunamis, dynamite), *and of love* (affection or benevolence), *and of a sound mind* (discipline, self control)" (2 Tim. 1:7). Moses needed three signs to convince his brethren. We need two things to win souls; a consistent godly life, and the Holy Scriptures.

MOSES AT THE INN

Moses is now equipped for the task of meeting and convincing his brethren, but one thing remains. His house must yet be set in order. On his way to Egypt with his wife and his sons, while stopping at an inn, the Lord met him, and sought to kill him. One might think that such an action on the part of God was strange and extreme. However, consider the character of God and the mission of Moses. God was about to fulfill His covenant to Abraham, of which circumcision was the sign, yet that sign had not been carried out in Moses' own house. The holiness of God demanded that His ambassador have his own house in order, acknowledging that covenant. This was to be done by Moses having his own sons circumcised. In other words, a man is not fit for public work if he is lax in his own house. Moses submitted to the claims of God in spite of the distress of his wife, thus God spared him.

Having circumcised her two sons, Zipporah and her sons are sent back home, while Moses continues his journey to Egypt alone. In relating this, one cannot but help think of God's similar requirements for an overseer today. He must be *"one that ruleth well his own house, having his children in subjection with all gravity; (for if a man know not how to rule his own house, how shall he take care of the church of God?)"* (1 Tim. 3:4-5). It just stands to reason that if a man cannot control a five-year-old child, how can he possibly control a fifty-year-old man? A man may know the scriptures, contribute to the Bible-readings, and even visit the sick, but if he can't control his children, God disqualifies him from the position of being an overseer.

The wife of Moses was not in sympathy with God's requirements concerning her husband; nevertheless Moses maintained the position of ruling his own house, regardless of the feelings and attitude of his wife. We have seen men that are controlled by their wives. Behind the scenes, they are manipulating their husbands to do things their way. This can be increasingly troublesome when such women thus control elders in an assembly. As Moses journeyed on alone toward Egypt, already on the way to meet him was his older brother, Aaron. Consequently, in the time of disappointment and perhaps loneliness, God provided encouragement and comfort to his faithful servant. Aaron *"met him in the mount of God, and kissed him"* (Ex. 4:27). What a tender meeting! Having not seen each other for forty years, they now meet and embrace. Thus we see two men, alone in the desert at the mount of God, who are going to make everlasting history and change the course of two nations. Moses had much to say on that memorable occasion. *"And Moses told Aaron all the words of the LORD Who had sent him, and all the signs which He had commanded him"* (Ex. 4:28). There is something sweet observing these two men walking together. One was a man who had endured the burden of Egyptian tyranny; the other was a man who had enjoyed the luxuries of a palace, and then the solitude of the desert. Their circumstances in life were at the opposite ends of the spectrum, but their purpose of heart was exactly the same.

WORKING TOGETHER

How often such patterns can be seen today, such as two men of an entirely different disposition, and an entirely different upbringing, yet by the grace of God working together for the furtherance of the gospel. Consider a man who was a college professor, preaching with a man who was a common laborer, or a man who was raised in wealth, preaching with a man who was raised in poverty. A man raised in religion, preaching with a man who had been a drunkard. It is simply amazing! More than that, it is beautiful to behold! Oh, the transforming power of God, seen in the lives of men from all walks of life. Can we not all say, "By the grace of God, I am what I am?" "Behold how good, and how pleasant it is for brethren to dwell together in unity." Look at the disciples as they join together from all walks of life. We observe a fisherman, a doctor, a tax collector, a profound scholar in Judaism, and all of them with oneness of mind. Time and time again, Luke records how that they all were with one accord. It is beautiful to the sight! The world must stand back and exclaim, "We cannot accomplish this!" No, but our great God can! What transforming power, what wondrous grace, seen in the transformation of these men. What glory brought to the name of our God! What dignity clothing the message of the gospel!

Not only in the gospel arena do we see such a miracle, but in the local assembly as well. Often noticed are people of all ages, from all walks of life, and with varying personalities, sitting together in a circle with their Lord in the midst. Their mind is one, their purpose is one, and they are there to remember their Lord in the breaking of the bread and the drinking of the cup. There is no "minister" to officiate. There are no printed programs to follow. There is no confusion. What is happening? Well, they are sitting in reverent silence waiting for the Great Director to lead them into song and worship. One may say, "Who is the Great Director?" We answer, "The Holy Spirit." Nothing can compare to this on earth. No human engineering, no physical director, nothing but the divine leading and prompting of the Holy Spirit, as He graciously moves the Lord's people, just at the appropriate time, to rise and function.

A BIBLE CONFERENCE EXPERIENCE

I remember on one occasion being at a "Bible conference" (convention) and there were a number of preachers present. They were all different in their personalities. There was no program, no human guidance, no master of ceremonies, but we all sat in silence waiting for the Holy Spirit to place a man on the platform with a message from God. Remember, the Spirit in all His profound wisdom not only provides His servants with an appropriate message, but He also knows the order, relative to other speakers, when that man is to rise with his particular message. After much prayer, a man arose, then another man, and then another man. Each one seemed to follow the previous speaker in thought. Then the fourth man arose, and his message also tied in with what had previously been said. Five men spoke, and then the correspondent of that assembly rose to his feet to give out the announcements. In doing so, he remarked, "We have seen the Lord working today, and we have all been spoken to. It would be well for all of us, upon returning to our homes, to get down on our knees and confess our sins to God and seek His favor." That was an experience, not to be forgotten. The presence and guidance of God had been remarkably felt in that gathering. How precious such gatherings are.

3

MOSES BEFORE PHARAOH

The divine record then brings us to the meeting of Moses and Aaron with the elders of the children of Israel (Ex. 4:29-31). When having received the testimony of God accompanied with the miracles, they believed and bowed their heads and worshipped. The hope of better days ahead caused their hearts to ascend in holy worship to the God of Abraham, the God of Isaac, and the God of Jacob.

Is it not so today with many of God's dear people that are in the furnace of affliction? Instead of looking at apparent dark and dismal days lying ahead on earth, their spirits rise above the cloudy atmosphere of earth and they look heavenward upon the things that are not seen. They behold a glorious city foursquare of pure gold awaiting them. They see the risen Lamb of God, in all His glorious dignity, power, glory, and love waiting to receive them, and what does this spiritual gaze produce? It causes God's persecuted saints to worship in spite of all their trials. The psychologist cannot explain it! The worldly genius stands dumbfounded! The humanist cries, "This can't be!" The atheist withdraws in silence! The doctors of philosophy mutter in confusion! How can a human being in the most dire and distressing circumstance leap for joy, laugh in hope, and raise his heart in holy worship and praise to One Whom he has never actually seen by his natural eye? Ah my friend, if you are a true child of

God you most certainly have the answer, don't you? The answer is simple. *"In Whom ye also trusted, after that ye heard the word of truth, the gospel of your salvation: in Whom also after that ye believed, ye were sealed with that Holy Spirit of promise"* (Eph. 1:13). And what is the Holy Spirit of promise called? Notice the Saviour's description. *"But the Comforter, which is the Holy Ghost, whom the Father will send in My name, He shall teach you all things, and bring all things to your remembrance, whatsoever I have said unto you"* (John 14:26). Isn't that beautiful? Isn't that most comforting? We are indwelt with a Comforter. That particular word simply means: "a Consoler, an Advocate. One Who draws alongside to comfort and help."

The Scripture, and this world's history are full of the testimonies of men and women rejoicing in the midst of their trials. What power is resident in the child of God! The world with all its "wisdom" knows nothing about it, but we do, those of us who are His own. The groaning elders of Israel worshipped!

PHARAOH'S FIRST RESPONSE

The first audience with Pharaoh brings this ungodly response: *"Who is the LORD, that I should obey His voice to let Israel go? I know not the LORD, neither will I let Israel go"* (Ex. 5:2). Instead of complying with the request, Pharaoh increases the burdens of Israel, withdrawing the materials necessary for work, and at the same time demanding more work. Satan is now stirred and concerned. Whenever a work for God is about to begin, you can be sure that the devil will be very aware of it, and he too will begin to act to hinder that work.

The LORD God of Israel had said, *"Let My people go, that they may hold a feast unto Me in the wilderness."* Consequently Satan silently sows the seed of discord among the elders of Israel to discredit Moses in their eyes, and to hinder his work for God. What a master of deception he is.

PAUL AND SATAN

Consider God's faithful servant Paul as he seeks to serve the Lord. Look at Satan in the shadows. *"The Jews stirred up the devout and honourable women, and the chief men of the city, and raised persecution against Paul and Barnabas, and expelled them out of their coasts"* (Acts 13:50). *"The unbelieving Jews stirred up the Gentiles, and made their minds evil affected against the brethren"* (Acts 14:2). *"And when the seven days were almost ended, the Jews which were of Asia, when they saw him in the temple, stirred up all the people, and laid hands on him"* (Acts 21:27). Relating to his labors Paul himself testified: *"By honour and dishonour, by evil report and good report: as deceivers, and yet true"* (2 Cor. 6:8). Satan was employing unconverted Jews to stir up people against Paul.

SMYRNA, PHILADELPHIA, AND SATAN

Notice what the Lord terms their synagogue when addressing the church at Smyrna. *"I know thy works, and tribulation, and poverty, (but thou art rich) and I know the blasphemy of them which say they are Jews, and are not, but are the synagogue of Satan"* (Rev. 2:9). Also, our Lord says to the church at Philadelphia. *"Them of the synagogue of Satan, which say they are Jews ..."* (Rev. 3:9). Paul exclaimed, *"For we wrestle not against flesh and blood, but against principalities, against powers, against the rulers of the darkness of this world, against spiritual wickedness in high places"* (Eph. 6:12).

EVANGELISTS AND SATAN

Many evangelists can testify that on occasions, there is no opposition, no interest on the part of the people, and no evidence of God working. Consequently, there is no attack from the enemy. All is quiet, and comfort reigns. However, any laborer with experience can testify, that when God is going to work, Satan is right there to oppose. His devices are many.

Sometimes he stirs up so-called church leaders against the invading soldiers of the Cross, and they influence their congregations against the preachers. Gospel tents have been burned to the ground. Automobile tires have been slashed. Lives have been threatened. False reports have been circulated. Satan has many workers to further his kingdom of darkness.

A DEMON WORSHIPPER

On one occasion, in a little village in the mountains, a woman from California visiting her folks, raised the report that the man preaching in the tent was a demon worshipper. However, instead of the religious community acting against the evangelist, through curiosity, they flocked into the tent to see what a demon worshipper looked like. God began to work, and a number of souls were saved! Thus, through the false report, the devil was defeated through his own devices!

Standing before the elders of Israel, Moses stands accused. There is no rebuttal on his part. Godly men do not strike back at negative remarks leveled at them. What does Moses do? Notice; *"And Moses returned unto the LORD, and said ..."* (Ex. 5:22). He took the matter to the LORD. Is not this the Christian's recourse when things seemingly are going wrong, when things are happening that we least expect? We often sing the words of Joseph Scriven:

> "What a Friend we have in Jesus,
> All our sins and griefs to bear!
> What a privilege to carry
> Everything to God in prayer!
> O what peace we often forfeit,
> O what needless pain we bear!
> All because we do not carry
> Everything to God in prayer."
> "Have we trials and temptations?
> Is there trouble anywhere?
> We should never be discouraged:

Take it to the Lord in prayer!
Can we find a friend so faithful,
Who will all our sorrows share?
Jesus knows our every weakness:
Take it to the Lord in prayer."

When turning to God, Moses was exhorted to take comfort from His name: *"I am the LORD: And I appeared unto Abraham, unto Isaac, and unto Jacob, by the name of God Almighty, but by My name JEHOVAH was I not known to them"* (Ex. 6:3). He was also to take comfort from His covenant: *"And I have also established My covenant with them, to give them the land of Canaan, the land of their pilgrimage, wherein they were strangers"* (Ex. 6:4). Another source of comfort to Moses would be from God's compassions: *"And I have also heard the groaning of the children of Israel, whom the Egyptians keep in bondage; and I have remembered My covenant"* (Ex. 6:5).

With these words ringing in Moses' heart, the LORD then unfolds His seven precious promises, employing the words, *"I will."* Notice:

(1) *"Wherefore say unto the children of Israel, I am the LORD, and **I will** bring you out from under the burdens of the Egyptians"* (RELIEF).

(2) *"And **I will** rid you out of their bondage"* (RIDDANCE).

(3) *"And **I will** redeem you with a stretched out arm, and with great judgments"* (REDEMPTION).

(4) *"And **I will** take you to Me for a people"* (RELATIONSHIP).

(5) *"And **I will** be to you a God: and ye shall know that I am the LORD your God, which bringeth you out from under the burdens of the Egyptians"* (REFUGE).

(6) *"And **I will** bring you in unto the land, concerning the which I did swear to give it to Abraham, to Isaac, and to Jacob"* (ROUTING).

(7) *"And **I will** give it you for an heritage: I am the LORD"* (RICHES) (Ex. 6:6-8).

The promises correspond as well to New Testament truths.

(1) We were all under sin, but then freed from sin (Rom. 3:9; 6:8).

(2) We are as redeemed ones, dead to sin (Rom. 6:2).

(3) "In whom we have redemption through His blood, the forgiveness of sins, according to the riches of His grace" (Eph. 1:7).

(4) "And because ye are sons, God hath sent forth the Spirit of His Son into your hearts, crying, Abba, Father" (Gal. 4:6).

(5) "That by two immutable things, in which it was impossible for God to lie, we might have a strong consolation, who have fled for refuge to lay hold upon the hope set before us" (Heb. 6:18). *"Let your conversation be without covetousness; and be content with such things as ye have: for He hath said, I will never leave thee, nor forsake thee"* (Heb. 13:5).

(6) "Blessed be the God and Father of our Lord Jesus Christ, which according to His abundant mercy hath begotten us again unto a lively hope by the resurrection of Jesus Christ from the dead, to an inheritance incorruptible, and undefiled, and that fadeth not away, reserved in heaven for you" (1 Pet. 1:3-4).

Even with these promises presented to the children of Israel by Moses, they hearkened not for anguish of spirit, and for cruel bondage. The word *"anguish of spirit"* can be translated, "shortness of breath," thus indicating that their bondage was so cruel, that they scarcely had time to breathe. However, unknown by them, God was about to move on their behalf through Moses and Aaron.

GOD'S PURPOSED DELAY

It is profitable to understand that God does not always act immediately in accomplishing His purposes. There was going to be a period of time from the announcement of deliverance to the elders, to that actual deliverance itself. True, there are times when God moves suddenly, but on most occasions, the wheels of God's government move slow but sure. God never moves on impulse as we humans are prone to do. However, God does move very deliberately, and nothing can hinder His purposes from being fulfilled. Moses is about to become the greatest miracle worker in the Old Testament; Egypt is about to be laid in ruins, and God is about to deliver His people out of bondage. The process of the development of these things will prove to be most interesting, as we shall see.

Two reasons for the apparent delay in Israel's deliverance can be found in Romans chapter nine. *"For the scripture saith unto Pharaoh, even for this same purpose have I raised thee up, that I might shew My power in thee, and that My name might be declared throughout all the earth"* (v. 17). The word *"power"* is "dunamis," meaning "force, and especially miraculous power." It is that word from which we derive our word "dynamite." Consequently, Egypt, and the then-known world for that matter, would learn of the power of God and that His name would be magnified among them. What a revelation to the world would the miracles produce.

Not only this, the seeming delay would also serve in punishing Egypt for their cruelty to God's earthly people. It would also make the Egyptians glad to see Israel leave their country, so much so, that they would be willing to enrich them with their substance, which included gold and silver.

When the time finally would arrive for Israel to leave, they would by that time be fully assured of God's hand being with them. It would also give them an intense feeling of their dependence upon their God, and a deeper appreciation of their exodus. They would be leaving Egypt with a great story to tell to their children in years to come, convincing them of the greatness of their God.

LESSONS FROM JONAH AND ISAIAH

Moses is not left to his own wisdom and intellect when confronting Pharaoh, neither is he left to determine the time of his various approaches to this mighty monarch. Ah no! All is in the controlling hand of the Almighty. Let me inject this thought relevant to our day. When men approach the victims of darkness to proclaim deliverance, in reality, they are attacking the devil and all his host. They come with a message that is termed *"the power of God."* That message is the gospel. Now then, what do they declare, and for how long do they declare it? Well, consider the most successful preacher of Old Testament times and what do you find? What does God instruct Jonah? Simply this: *"Arise, go unto Nineveh, that great city, and preach unto it the preaching that I bid thee"* (Jon. 3:2). Isaiah was concerned about how long he should preach. He certainly had no bookings did he? Notice his concern. *"Then said I, Lord, how long? And He answered, until the cities be wasted without inhabitant, and the houses without man, and the land be utterly desolate"* (Isa. 6:11). Thus, we see the complete control of God over these men regarding the message to be delivered and the time element involved. How is it with us today? I am afraid that in many circles we have deteriorated into a position of self-will, thus giving the Spirit of God, as it were, a back seat. How wonderful to behold godly men that totally rely on God for an appropriate message, and keep preaching those God-given messages in a given locality until the Spirit of God gives them the signal to cease.

SIGNS, WONDERS, PLAGUES

Thus, God commands Moses: *"Thou shalt speak all that I command thee: and Aaron thy brother shall speak unto Pharaoh, that he send the children of Israel out of his land"* (Ex. 7:2). God then goes on to explain to Moses that He will harden Pharaoh's heart, and multiply His *signs* and *wonders* in the land of Egypt. In relation to Egypt, these signs and wonders were called *plagues*, for that is exactly what they were to the Egyptians (9:14). However, to Israel they would be signs and wonders. You may ask, "What is a sign?" Well it is simply this, these miracles performed would carry a moral significance, manifesting the different features which would mark this world as under judgment. The word *"wonders"* comes from the root word *"persuade,"* thus they were events to produce conviction and lead to obedience.

The plagues (signs and wonders) were ten. God was about to inflict judgment upon the gods (demons) of Egypt (Num. 33:4), and demonstrate Himself above all gods (Ex.18:11). Psalm 78 mentions six of the plagues; Psalm 105 eight of them; and Psalms 135 and 136 one of them. Similarities of these plagues are to be seen in Revelation chapters 8, 9, 15, and 16.

INTROVERSION

It is most interesting to notice the order in which the plagues were inflicted, and their divine design. There was nothing haphazard about them, for God is a God of order. The careful reader will notice that there is what is called "an introversion" connected with the plagues. Starting with the first plague and linking it with the last plague, we notice a similarity. In the first plague, the river is turned into blood – a symbol of death. In the last plague we find actual death, the death of all of Egypt's firstborn. The lack of the sprinkling of a lamb's blood, invoked the shedding of the firstborn's blood.

Moving inward from the first and the last plague, we come to plagues number two and nine. Here we discover that in the second plague, we have frogs, creatures of the night, while in the ninth plague we have a thick darkness which could be felt (Ex. 10:21-22). Moving inwardly again we come to plagues number three and eight, thus finding in number three the confession of the magicians, *"This is the finger of God,"* and in number eight, the confession of Pharaoh, *"I have sinned against the LORD your God, and against you."*

Coming next to plagues number four and seven, in both incidences Goshen is mentioned as being exempted. Finally, in the two center plagues, numbers five and six there is a mention in both of the cattle being attacked, the first with a very grievous murrain, and the second a boil breaking forth with blains (Ex. 9:3, 9).

Not only do we have an introversion connected with these plagues, but we also discover that the first nine plagues are linked together into groups of three. In the first group we notice:

BLOOD (Ex. 7:14-25); FROGS (Ex. 8:1-7); LICE Exodus 8:16-19). The first took place in the morning by the river, and affected all.

FLIES (Ex. 8:20-34); MURRIAN (Ex. 9:1-7); BOILS AND BLAINS (Ex. 9:8-12) The first took place in the morning by the river, and only affected Egypt, Israel was exempt.

HAIL AND LIGHTNING (Ex. 9:13-35); LOCUSTS (Ex. 10:3-19); DARKNESS (Ex. 10:21-23). The first took place in the morning, and only affected Egypt. Israel was exempt.

In each of these three triads, there is a divine pattern as to the warnings. The pattern is the same in all three, namely this. The first plague in each group brings a long time interval between the warning and its accomplishment. The second plague in each triad brings a shorter warning, and in the last plague of each triad, there is no warning. In other words, the plagues of BLOOD, FLIES, and HAIL AND LIGHTNING bring a long warning with them. The plagues of FROGS, MURRAIN, and LOCUSTS, bring a shorter warning. However, in the plagues of LICE, BOILS, and BLAINS, and DARKNESS, there is no warning given whatsoever!

This pattern brings before us a most sobering truth regarding God's dealings with mankind, and it is this. Our God is a longsuffering God. He is not willing that any should perish, but that all should come to repentance (2 Pet. 3:9). However, as Solomon stated, *"Because sentence against an evil work is not executed speedily, therefore the heart of the sons of men is fully set in them to do evil"* (Eccl. 8:11). Man takes advantage of the longsuffering of God, and heeds not the warnings. *"For God speaketh once, yea twice, yet man perceiveth it not"* (Job 33:14). Then the time comes in the life of many that is described in the following verse. *"For man also knoweth not his time: as the fishes that are taken in an evil net, and as the birds that are caught in the snare; so are the sons of men snared in an evil time, when it falleth suddenly upon them"* (Eccl. 9:12).

We may also state, that the first triad of plagues interfered with their *comfort*, while the second triad of plagues affected their *possessions*, and the third triad of plagues brought *desolation and death*. Finally, the worst of all plagues came upon the Egyptians – *"And Moses said, thus saith the LORD, about midnight will I go out into the midst of Egypt: And all the firstborn in the land of Egypt shall die, from the firstborn of Pharaoh that sitteth upon his throne, even unto the firstborn of the maidservant that is behind the mill; and all the firstborn of beasts"* (Ex. 11:4, 5). *"And it came to pass, that at midnight the LORD smote all the firstborn in the land of Egypt, from the firstborn of Pharaoh that sat on his throne unto the firstborn of the captive that was in the dungeon; and all the firstborn of cattle"* (Ex. 12:29). God says, *"Be not deceived; God is not mocked: for whatsoever a man soweth, that shall he also reap"* (Gal. 6:7). Eighty years before, Pharaoh had decreed that all the male children born to the children of Israel be slain by casting them into the river. Pharaoh was now going to reap what he had sowed, in the death of all Egypt's firstborn. The wheels of God's government sometimes grind very slow, but they move very sure, for there is not a thing purposed in the government of God that will ever be aborted or lack fulfillment. Evil and wickedness abound on every hand, yet sinners seem to prosper in this life with seemingly no serious consequences. However, God has decreed that *"the wicked shall be turned into hell, and all the nations that forget God"* (Ps. 9:17). The psalmist was awakened to this fact. Consider his words. *"For I was envious at the foolish, when I saw the prosperity of the wicked ... They are not in trouble as other men; neither are they plagued like other men ... Behold, these are the ungodly, who prosper in the world; they increase in riches ... When I thought to know this, it was too painful for me; Until I went into the sanctuary of God; then understood I their end. Surely Thou didst set them in slippery places: Thou castedst them down into destruction. How are they brought into desolation, as in a moment! they are utterly consumed with terrors"* (Ps. 73:3, 5, 12, 16-19).

THE RICH MAN IN HELL

Consider the rich man mentioned by our Lord in Luke chapter sixteen. Ah yes, he was clothed in the garment of royalty, and fared sumptuously every day, indicating that he enjoyed great wealth and good health. Suddenly, he dropped dead, lifting up his languid eyes in hell – forever lost. Had he been previously warned? Most certainly! He had saved parents and was raised in a home where the Word of God was reverenced, yet in spite of these privileges, he refused to repent. He could only serve one master, either God or mammon. He chose to serve the latter to his own ruin and destruction. He chose to be devoted to riches and despised God (Luke 16:13). His warnings were perhaps many. Yet in spite of it all, the day came, that without any apparent warning, he lost his silver, his station in life, but worst of all, he lost his precious soul.

A CARELESS YOUTH

I remember a youth of Christian parents being repeatedly warned of God about his soul. The various warnings went unheeded until the day came, while rounding a severe curve in the highway, he lost control and plunged into the ditch, immediately breaking his neck. His flight from earth was made into hell, in a moment of time. Later, someone lamented to me that he never had a chance. I replied, "He had over twenty years of chances."

How solemn to "play loose" with God. To spurn His grace,

to break His laws, until His longsuffering ceases, only resulting in the immediate retribution of the sinner, which ushers them into hell - the place of their longsuffering for eternity.

Not only were these plagues a public manifestation of the power of God, they were a divine visitation of God's wrath upon Egypt for their cruel treatment of the Hebrews. It certainly was a divine manifestation of the superiority of Jehovah above all the false gods of Egypt, these plagues in themselves being a judgment upon Egypt's gods, as stated in Numbers 33:4. *"Upon their gods also the LORD executed judgments."* The Egyptians were affected physically, mentally, and spiritually, until finally, after the seventh plague, *"Pharaoh's servants said unto him ... knowest thou not yet that Egypt is destroyed?* (Ex. 10:7). The word *"destroyed"* indicates, "we are perishing and there is no escape." These "servants" were the principle men that were about Pharaoh. They were men that were nobles, and counselors to this obstinate monarch.

"SHOCK WAVES" TO OTHER NATIONS

What a situation to be brought into! The whole land, once prosperous above all nations was now lying totally desolate, in absolute ruin! I am sure that the nations of the world in that day were "sitting up and taking serious notice." The "shock waves" from the dynamite activities of Jehovah in Egypt would be shaking all neighboring nations. I often wonder what it will be like in that coming day when the LORD of hosts *"will shake the heavens, and the earth, and the sea, and the dry land,"* and when He will shake all nations, and the desire of all nations shall come: and He will fill His house with glory (Hag. 2:6-7). Three days later, after this divine utterance, the word of the LORD came again to Haggai, and he was told to tell Zerubbabel the governor of Judah: *"I will shake the heavens and the earth; And I will overthrow the throne of kingdoms, and I will destroy the strength of the kingdoms of the heathen; and I will overthrow the chariots, and those that ride in them; and the horses and their riders shall come down, every one by the sword of his brother"* (Hag. 2:21-22).

As we are all aware, this promise was given to the nation of Israel after they had returned to the Land from their captivity in Babylon. They were small, they were weak, and they were discouraged. Thus; the LORD provides them with a promise that projected the nation on to a future state of divine glory, when the Messiah would come as the King of kings and the Lord of lords, to set up His glorious kingdom in which Israel would be the head and not the tail of all nations. The Persian Empire, at that time, occupied two million square miles of subdued territory and reigned supreme. However, God made His people to realize His all-sufficiency, stating, *"The silver is Mine, and the gold is Mine, saith the LORD of hosts."* Now tell me, would that not be a word of encouragement to a downtrodden people – pointing them on to the day of millennial bliss and glory? Brethren, looking ahead has a purifying effect upon the people of God no matter what dispensation may be their portion.

Consider ourselves. Look at 1 John 3:2-3, and what does it say? Simply this: *"Beloved, now are we the sons of God, and it doth not yet appear what we shall be: but we know that, when He shall appear, we shall be like Him; for we shall see Him as He is. And every man that hath this hope in Him* (set on Christ) *purifieth himself, even as He* (Christ) *is pure."* Living a life filled with the expectation of His coming has a purifying effect upon us. It strengthens us, it stabilizes us, it soothes us, and it supplies us with perception and power to live a consistent Christian life in a world that has no hope.

The children of Israel in Egypt were downtrodden, they were just mere slaves. However, the fact that the LORD of hosts had so manifested Himself on their behalf as to bring the powerful nation of Egypt down to desolation, must have had a stimulating effect on God's elect at that time. Even though Pharoah's servants realized their plight, yet three more plagues were to follow. One is reminded of the words of Romans 11:22: *"Behold therefore the goodness and severity of God: on them which fell, severity."*

THE LOCUSTS

The eighth plague brought locusts. Any residue which remained in Egypt would be eaten. When they came, *"they covered the face of the whole earth, so that the land was darkened; and they did eat every herb of the land, and all the fruit of the trees which the hail had left, and there remained not any green thing in the trees, or in the herbs of the field, through all the land of Egypt"* (Ex. 10:15). The coming of these creatures is remarkable indeed. In the first place, even though locusts were common in Arabia, yet they were comparatively rare in Egypt; the Red Sea forming a sort of barrier against them. Locusts are not known to cross seas, or engage in long flights. However, God Who controls the winds of Earth, caused a strong east wind to transport this menace across the Sea into the land of Egypt. The Scripture states: *"The Lord brought an east wind upon the land all that day, and all that night; and when it was morning, the east wind brought the locusts"* (Ex. 10:13).

Consider the word *"brought."* It is remarkable, as it has the import of *guiding, leading, directing one's course*. It is interesting to note, that the prevailing winds which blow in Egypt are six months from the south, and six months from the north. However a strong wind from either the north or the south would not assist the locusts across the Red Sea from Arabia into Egypt – there was a necessity for an east wind, which, of course, was no problem to Him Who holds the wind in His hand

It must have been a horrible experience. Clouds of them so thick that daylight became dark. *"And the locusts went up over all the land of Egypt, and rested in all the coasts of Egypt: very grievous were they ; before them there were no such locusts as they, neither after them shall be such"* (Ex. 10:14). The houses would have been full of them. It would be impossible to eat a bite of food without them crawling into one's mouth. Whatever vegetation of the country was left, soon disappeared, as they gnawed on every form of vegetable life. Trees and plants would have been stripped of their leaves and reduced to naked boughs and stems. The sound of their devouring vegetation would have been heard from a great distance. Resting at night, there would have been at least a depth of four inches of them on the ground. In Canada locusts have been known to invade the wheat fields, stripping them bare in a matter of hours. Their bodies covering the roads made driving almost impossible as automobiles running over them would produce slippery slime from their crushed carcasses, causing the vehicles to careen off the roads. The whole scene would only remind us of the spiritual barrenness of this world. It is a desolate waste. There is nothing in it for God, neither is there anything in it for the spiritual man who is feasting on Christ. John Nelson Darby wrote; "This world is a wilderness wide, I have nothing to seek or to choose."

What a contrast we see in God employing a strong east wind in Exodus 14, for there the wind was not bringing dismay and destruction, but rather delight and deliverance, as God employed it to part the Red Sea and dry its exposed bed, providing a passage for His people from Egypt. It was also used by God to destroy Israel's enemies, making them a free and redeemed people.

DARKNESS

The next plague, being the ninth, brought darkness for three days that could be felt. The Egyptians *"saw not one another, neither rose any from his place."* Not only this, but Psalm 78 reveals that *"He cast upon them the fierceness of His anger, wrath, and indignation, and trouble, by sending evil angels among them"* (Ps. 78:49). Rabbis say that the devil and angels were let loose, producing fearful apparitions, which resulted in fearful shrieks and groans. It was a darkness they could feel. The same Hebrew word in the original is used to express the darkness which covered the deep at the time just prior to the six days of God reconstructing this Earth as a suitable habitation for man. The darkness of Genesis 1:2 was the result of God's judgment, just as we find it here in Exodus 10:21. The sun was one of the deities of Egypt, and in that country, any darkening of his light in the day time was as extremely rare occurrence. What consternation must have seized the inhabitants at such a phenomenon. Afraid to venture out of their homes, they sat, horror stricken, shrouded in thick darkness, never before experienced. What profit was their sun god to them now?

This whole episode portrays to us the spiritual condition of this world as a result of sin. The situation is most distressing. There is the darkness of ignorance. In Ephesians chapter four, we read of the ungodly walking in the vanity of their mind, *"having the understanding darkened, being alienated from the life of God through the ignorance that is in them, because of the blindness of their heart"* (v. 18). What makes it even more sobering, is the fact that men love darkness rather than light, because their deeds are evil (John 3:19). One of the objects in preaching the gospel is *"to open their eyes, and to turn them from darkness to light, and from the power of Satan unto God, that they may receive forgiveness of sins"* (Acts 26:18). Things will worsen after the rapture of the Church. Revelation 16:10 reveals: *"And the fifth angel poured out his vial upon the seat of the beast; and his kingdom was full of darkness; and they gnawed their tongues for pain."*

Not only is this world enshrouded in spiritual darkness, but most of its inhabitants are heading for a place called *"the blackness of darkness"* (Jude 1:13), a darkness that is everlasting, and a darkness in which the smoke of their torment shall ascend up for ever and ever, where they will have no rest day nor night (Rev. 14:11).

CALVARY'S DARKNESS

In speaking of darkness, one is reminded of another occasion when there was supernatural darkness, not for three days as in Egypt, but for three hours in Jerusalem, which is spiritually called Egypt (Rev. 11:8). What a scene that must have been, when our blessed Lord bare our sins in His own body on the tree. He became a sin offering for us, and as He sank beneath the judgment waters of God's divine wrath, we read, *"And it was about the sixth hour, and there was a darkness over all the earth until the ninth hour"* (Luke 23:44).

EGYPT TO CANAAN

Thank God, as a result of Calvary's darkness and the bearing of our sins in His own body on the tree, we have been called out of darkness, into His marvelous light! (1 Pet. 2:9). Involved in that effectual calling, we have been delivered from the power of darkness, and God has translated us into the kingdom of His dear Son (Col. 1:13). Egypt's ninth plague was darkness – a darkness which could be felt. What lessons are involved in this plague for us!

It will perhaps be profitable to mention one more thing regarding the plagues. In sending these plagues, God was inflicting judgments upon Egypt's false gods. This was previously mentioned and Numbers 33:4 was quoted. *"Upon their gods also the LORD executed judgments."* The Nile was extremely important to Egypt, for overflowing its banks yearly, it covered the land with fertilizing silt, vital to the maturity of Egypt's crops. From its banks, irrigation systems were devised so that water was drawn from this mighty river to water their crops. Unlike the land of Canaan, rain from heaven was a foreign thing in Egypt. Consequently, the Nile god, **"Hap,"** was worshipped as a beneficial deity. Upon this god, judgment fell. The river was turned into blood. Egypt's source of life and refreshment was gone! Is this not a picture of this world? It is morally dead, a place with a stench that can bring no life and refreshment to those dwelling in it. Spiritual death reigns.

The next plague brought frogs in abundance upon the land. Egyptians worshipped a frog-headed deity named **"Hekt,"** to them a symbol of fruitfulness and affluence. These loathsome creatures invaded their homes entering their bedchambers, their ovens, and their kneadingtroughs (or, dough). John writes: *"And I saw three unclean spirits like frogs come out of the mouth of the dragon, and out of the mouth of the beast, and out of the mouth of the false prophet. For they are the spirits of devils, working miracles, which go forth unto the kings of the earth and of the whole world, to gather them to the battle of that great day of God Almighty"* (Rev. 16:13-14). Frogs inflate themselves and symbolize pride, and self-sufficiency. They speak of evil influences. Where was their god Hekt to protect them from this unclean invasion?

The next plague involved Aaron smiting *"the dust of the earth, and it became lice in man, and in beast; all the dust of the land became lice throughout all the land of Egypt"* (Ex. 8:17). Where was Egypt's earth god, *"Seb,"* to deliver them? These tiny creatures would invade the bodies of all, making their priests ceremonially unclean. Their worship would come to an abrupt halt. *"Sep"* amounted to nothing!

The fourth plague brought forth flies (the Scarabaeus beetle). This *"Scarabaeus"* was a symbol of the sun, and of the abiding life of a soul. Consequently, a carving of this beetle was seen on every mummy-chest. This was the god of the sun and of creative power. But where was he in their time of need? Nowhere!

The worshipping of *"Apis, the sacred bull,"* involved brute worship, but lo and behold, where was he, as God Almighty inflicted a grievous murrain (pestilence) upon the horses, asses, camels, oxen, and upon the sheep? (Ex. 9:3). The horses belonged to the wealthy. The asses were the property of the poor. The camels belonged to merchants, to bear their merchandise to market. The farmers used the oxen to plow the ground, and the sheep provided wool for clothing. All was lost, and every phase of Egyptian society suffered severely. *Apis* was of no help to them.

The next divine judgment came upon *"Typhon,"* the evil genius. Human sacrifices were offered to this god to ward off plagues, but now, the terrible plague of boils fell upon the inhabitants of Egypt, and where was their god, who was supposedly their protector? (Ex. 9:8-12).

As the seventh plague was about to descend, God had a message for Pharaoh. *"And the LORD said unto Moses, Rise up early in the morning, and stand before Pharaoh, and say unto him, Thus saith the LORD God of the Hebrews, let My people go, that they may serve Me. For I will at this time send all My plagues upon thine heart, and upon thy servants, and upon thy people; that thou mayest know that there is none like Me in all the earth. For now I will stretch out My hand, that I may smite thee and thy people with pestilence; and thou shalt be cut off from the earth"* (Ex. 9:13-15). **"Shu,"** the god of the atmosphere was about to be found ineffective as far as protecting the possessions of the Egyptians. God sent a very grievous hail, the worst in intensity that Egypt had ever experienced in its history. It smote all that were in the field, man and beast. Every herb and tree were smitten, and so severe was the judgment that Pharaoh cried out; *"I have sinned this time: the Lord is righteous, and I and my people are wicked"* (Ex. 9:27).

Egypt's protector against the locusts was **"Serapia."** What folly to trust in false gods! The God of Israel brought a myriad of locusts to invade the land, and He removed them. The protection that the Egyptians thought that *"Serapia"* would provide, entirely evaporated in their time of great need and distress. God's judgment mightily fell upon their false god.

THE FIRSTBORN SLAIN

The intensity of God's plagues constantly increased, until finally, "the mother of all plagues" fell upon that darkened and devastated land – God slew all of their firstborn. What a solemn and terrifying announcement – *"all the firstborn in the land of Egypt shall die, from the firstborn of Pharaoh that sitteth upon his throne, even unto the firstborn of the maidservant that is behind the mill; and all the firstborn of beasts"* (Ex. 11:5). It was a blow which wounded where the heart is most susceptible. The firstborn was the pride, hope, and joy of every Egyptian family, but God took that from them in one stroke at midnight.

What bitterness there must have been in the hearts of fathers and mothers as they viewed their healthy firstborn lying cold and still in death. The breathless clay, never again to lie in its mother's bosom. He that is sick may be restored, but he that is dead has bid a "forever farewell" to those he loved. Aroused from the blackness of night, perhaps from the dying groans of their loved ones, they were suddenly hurled into the chamber of deep grief and sorrow, so much so, that the Scripture relates,

"And there shall be a great cry throughout all the land of Egypt, such as there was none like it, nor shall be like it any more" (Ex. 11:6).

As previously stated, they had killed the children of Israel's newborn sons, and now eighty years later, God slew their firstborn sons. They had finally reaped what they had sown. *"Be not deceived; God is not mocked: for whatsoever a man soweth, that shall he also reap"* (Gal. 6:7).

Consider with me for a moment a worse death, called the second death. Incarcerated in the Lake of Fire, the damned shall weep and wail, as they are eternally tossed upon the waves and billows of God's fierce wrath. They will experience eternal separation from all loved ones, and the frivolous pleasures that they vainly pursued in their vapor of lifetime on Earth. I thoroughly believe that if we Christians had a deeper knowledge of the state of the eternally lost, that it would produce in us a deeper love for souls, and a more energetic spirit in seeking to reach them with the saving message of the gospel. Lord, help us to be more fully aware of the sinner's plight!

Thus, we see the working of the Almighty, as He, one by one, inflicted judgment on the gods that the blinded Egyptians considered so powerful. Truly, *"all the inhabitants of the earth are reputed as nothing: and He doeth according to His will in the army of heaven, and among the inhabitants of the earth: and none can stay His hand, or say unto Him, What doest Thou?"* (Dan. 4:35). Our God is great!

With Egypt lying in total desolation and ruin, the time was then ripe for Israel's exodus. One thing more was needed – the redemption of Israel's firstborn through the blood of a lamb.

4

THE PASSOVER

What lessons the Passover afford us as the people of God! The apostle Paul saw the importance of it when, by the Spirit, he wrote; *"Even Christ our Passover is sacrificed for us"* (1 Cor. 5:7). Thus we see, that in this ancient rite that was given to the children of Israel, a shadow, a type, and a prophetic view of Christ Himself! Ask any Orthodox Jew today what the Passover means to him, and he will tell you that the Passover is one of the most important events of the year – a reminder to him of the great deliverance his ancient fathers experienced by the hand of the LORD, in bringing them out of Egypt. Even until this day, it is a very sacred day in Jewish reckoning.

In the Passover, the Christian observes a lamb chosen; a lamb without blemish; a lamb slain; a lamb roast with fire; a lamb eaten; and a lamb's blood applied to the lintel and doorpost. Are there lessons in all of this? Most certainly! It is very evident that Peter had this ancient rite in mind when he penned; *"Forasmuch as ye know that ye were not redeemed with corruptible things, as silver and gold, from your vain conversation received by tradition from your fathers; But with the precious blood of Christ, as of a lamb without blemish and without spot: Who verily was foreordained before the foundation of the world, but was manifest in these last times for you, who by Him do believe in God, that raised Him up from the dead, and gave Him glory; that your faith and hope might be in God"* (1 Pet. 1:18-21). There are a number of things that Peter is appreciating; First, that Christ was the Lamb, a sacrificial Lamb, for He had no character defect and was unstained by sin. Truly, He is *"a lamb without blemish and without spot."* Second, that Christ the Lamb was foreordained before the foundation of the world. This proclaims the eternity of Christ. Third, that Christ was manifested, thus drawing attention to His humanity, the Word incarnate, God manifest in the flesh! Finally, Peter exclaims that God *"raised Him up from the dead, and gave Him glory,"* displaying the fact of His power over death and His unique exaltation and preeminence, in that God gave Him glory.

Israel was looking for the Messiah, the Christ, the Anointed One, Who would come in power and glory and subdue their enemies, trampling them underneath His feet and establishing His kingdom on Earth, with Israel positioned as the head of all nations. They certainly were not looking for a meek and lowly One, a Lamb to be crucified and forsaken by God. They were not looking for a Messiah coming out of Galilee, a mere carpenter of poor and lowly parents. Ah no, they were not looking for a Lamb, they were looking for a man, who in their eyes, would fulfill the role of a King of kings, and a Lord of lords. But Who came, or should I say, in what manner did He come? Go to the River Jordan and behold Him at the age of about thirty, and what do you see? You see a a lowly Man, clothed in the garments of the poor. Ah yes, but what did John see? Listen to his divinely given words. *"Behold the Lamb of God, which taketh away the sin of the world"* (John 1:29). What a tremendous and inspired statement! It has been indelibly inscribed on the holy pages of Scripture, making it eternal. What depth, what height, what breadth and length it reaches to. It is worthy to be proclaimed to the four corners of the Earth. What hope it breathes for poor mortal man, ruined and hell-bound as a result of sin! What a cure, what a blessed truth – *"the Lamb of God, which taketh away the sin of the world."*

Coming back to Exodus 12, we discover God's instructions to the nation regarding this newly appointed feast, to be called "the Passover." The word in itself has great meaning, and is found seventy one times in the Scriptures, the first three occasions being in Exodus 12. The last mention is in Hebrews 11:28, which is referring to the Passover of Exodus 12. The word Passover simply means a pretermission, or exemption. The word comes from *"pacach"* a primitive root; to hop, i.e. (figuratively) skip over (or spare); by implication, to hesitate. In the New Testament, apart from the Gospels, it is only mentioned in 1 Corinthians 5:7, and Hebrews 11:28. Connected with the word "Passover" we see various qualities of our blessed Lord, such as, **His prophecy** to His disciples (Matt. 26:2); **His perception** in the midst of the doctors (Luke 2:41-47; **His purging** of the Temple (John 2:13-16); **His power and perfuming** at Bethany (John 12:1-3). **His pouring** of water on the disciples feet (John 13:1-5); and finally, **His Passion** at the crucifixion (John 19:13-18). When Paul refers to the Passover in 1 Corinthians 11:28, it is in connection with the assembly **purging** itself from the old leaven.

Israel's first feast is spoken of in at least five different ways. It was to be a *memorial*, for their memory (Ex. 12: 14). It was also to be a *feast*, thus promoting fellowship (v. 14). It was also an *ordinance*, for it was an appointed law (v. 24). The children of the next generation would be speaking of it as a *service* (v. 26), indicating ministry on the people's part. Finally, it was a *sacrifice* (v. 27), something that would produce worship in the hearts of His people.

SEVEN PASSOVERS

Scripture records seven Passovers, the first one being here in the land of Egypt. The second Passover was carried out *"in the wilderness of Sinai, in the first month of the second year after they were come out of the land of Egypt"* (Num. 9:1). Not until we come to Gilgal, thirty nine years later, do we read of Israel keeping the Passover (Josh. 5:10). The fourth mention is found in Joshua's day. The wilderness journey was over, and they were finally in the land eating the old corn of the land. It was at Gilgal, where the reproach of Egypt was rolled away, that Israel sat down as inheritors of the promise, and with great joy did eat the Passover. What a memorable occasion that was! Years later, coming to 2 Chronicles 30, we read of the fifth recording of Israel's Passover. It was kept as a result of

Hezekiah's letters to all Israel and Judah, also to Ephraim and Manasseh, requesting their presence at Jerusalem for the occasion. Those that humbled themselves came, but there were others that simply laughed the king's messengers to scorn, and mocked them.

When messengers of the Cross bid sinners to come to Christ the Passover Lamb, they too, like Hezekiah, experience the same reactions. When the gospel is preached, there are those that humble themselves, and come to Christ, while others laugh the preacher to scorn and mock him. Consider all the occasions in which this befell the beloved apostle Paul in his endeavors to wins souls to Christ.

Not until the remnant had been back from their Babylonian captivity and dwelling in the land for twenty years, do we read of Israel keeping the Passover. It was upon the completion of the house of God that the sixth Passover in recorded history took place. Seven is the number of completeness and divine perfection, and it was at the seventh recorded Passover that we find the Lord Himself with great desire, keeping it with His disciples. His very presence there, made the occasion perfect and divinely complete to those with Him on that sacred occasion. It was there that He instituted the Lord's Supper, that we might be held in constant remembrance of Him, the true Pascal Lamb.

Whether Israel realized the full import of the Passover, is to be seriously questioned. There are numerous types and shadows of Christ in the Old Testament, that were never fully perceived by most of God's people. However, it is easy to look back after perceiving the truths revealed in the New Testament and see Christ foreshadowed throughout the Old Testament writings.

> The New is in the Old concealed,
> But the Old is in the New revealed.

CHRIST OUR PASSOVER

Considering the fact that our Lord is described as a Lamb, and also as our Passover, with delight we trace Him in Exodus 12. The first thing we notice is His all-sufficiency. *"In the tenth day of this month they shall take to them every man a lamb, according to the house of their fathers, a lamb for an house: And if the household be too little for the lamb, let him and his neighbour next unto his house take it according to the number of the souls; every man according to his eating shall make your count for the lamb* (v. 3-4). Never is the lamb spoken of as being too little for the house. Oh no, that would never do. Christ is sufficient for, not just a select few, but rather for all. Thus, God can proclaim that He desires *"ALL men to be saved"* (1 Tim. 2:4); *"that **WHOSOEVER** shall call upon the name of the Lord shall be saved"* (Acts 2:21); *"That through His name **WHOSOVER** believeth in Him shall receive remission of sins"* (Acts 10:43); *"That **WHOSOVER** believeth in Him should not perish, but have everlasting life"* (John 3:16).

God instructed Israel regarding the quality of the Lamb to be chosen. *"Your lamb shall be without blemish"* (v. 5). The word *"without blemish"* is also translated: "undefiled, perfect, complete, integrity, truth." Thus, we see the purity of the Lamb of God. Peter describes Christ as *"a Lamb without blemish and without spot"* (1 Pet. 1:19). Being without blemish reveals that there was no *character defect* in the Son of God. A person could purchase a spotless garment from a manufacturer, but if stamped "imperfect," that would indicate that there was a fault in its manufacture. We often call such garments, "seconds."

Due to Adam's fall, the whole human race was born defective. Through Adam, we all inherited a character defect from the day of conception. We all came into this world with a depraved and ruined nature. We were all born sinners. We entered this scene blemished. But wait! How did Christ come into this world? Ah, His coming was far different than ours! Just read that tremendous angelic statement in Luke 1:35, and you will see this – He was born holy! He came into this world without blemish, faultless, and unblamable. There was a holiness connected with the first Adam, but he had a nature that was capable of sinning. The last Adam came into this world holy, and with a nature incapable of sinning. The divine record plainly states: *"In Him is no sin"* (1 Jn. 3:5).

Notice, Christ is not only without blemish, but He is also defined as *"without spot."* Not only was there no character defect in His birth, but there was no spot in His life. There was no personal sin. He was never stained by the evil that surrounded Him – He was *"without spot!"* There were never any sins laid to His account as a result of His walk here. He ate with sinners, yet was never stained as a result. He was holy, harmless, undefiled, and separate from sinners in all their perverted ways. What a wonderful Lamb, a Lamb without blemish and without spot! This unique quality qualified Him to be the accepted sacrifice for our redemption.

It is interesting to notice the pronouns used in connection with the word *"lamb." "A lamb"* (v. 3); *"the lamb"* (v. 4); and *"your lamb"* (v. 5). Thus, the gospel preacher would apply those statements this way. Christ is *"a Lamb."* In other words, there are other prophets, that He is only one of many. The Mohammedan would admit that Jesus was a Prophet, but that Mohammad was a greater prophet. Next comes that expression, *"the lamb."* Thus, nominal Christianity would cry out and say, "No, no! Jesus Christ is the only Lamb, there is no other way." However, that last expression is most precious, and it is this; *"your lamb"* (v. 5). In other words, the Lamb of God is mine in a personal way. He is my own personal Saviour, He is my Lamb.

A SPIRITUAL BIRTHDAY

What an occasion the Passover was! *"This month shall be unto you the beginning of months: it shall be the first month of the year to you"* (v. 2). In other words, this event was the nation's spiritual birthday. Their civil new year, Rosh Hashanah, fell in October, but now they were going to experience another new year's day, a sacred new year, in the month of Abib, which is April (Ex. 13:4).

THE PASSOVER

The Passover initiated a new beginning, and so it is with us. The moment we trusted Christ, the Passover Lamb, we commenced a new beginning. We obtained a new relationship with God. God became our Father, Christ became our Lamb, our Saviour, and Shepherd, and the Holy Spirit became our Comforter. These most blessed relationships are totally unknown and unexperienced by the ungodly. We were taken off the broad way and placed on the narrow. We became a new creation in Christ. We obtained a power never experienced before, the power of the indwelling of the Holy Spirit. No longer dwelling in darkness, we became the children of light. Our desires changed. Our manner of life changed. Our outlook changed. What a tremendous transformation took place upon receiving Christ! It was just as Charles Wesley wrote:

> "Soon as my all I ventured,
> On the atoning blood.
> The Holy Spirit entered,
> And I was born of God."

Have you noticed that even though there must have been literally thousands of lambs slain, yet the Spirit of God, when recording this memorable event, is careful to use the singular when speaking of the Passover. The word "lambs" is never employed, but rather the word "lamb." Why is this? Why didn't God say, "Your lambs shall be without blemish? Simply because the Spirit of God had Christ in view, the true Lamb of God! All of these lambs pointed to one Lamb, the Lamb of God which taketh away the sin of the world. How accurate are the Holy Scriptures. Every jot and tittle, every little mark employed with the Hebrew letters, divinely, and carefully placed by the Holy Spirit to project the exact meaning of every syllable and word.

It is wise to observe, not only the instructions relative to the Passover, but also the divine order in which they were given. For simplicity we will number them.

(1) It was to be *"a male of the first year"* (v. 5). A male was accounted more excellent than a female. Being in its first year,

105

a lamb retains, during that period, its lamb-like harmlessness, with also its flesh being more tender at that period. Thus we have portrayed the excellence of Christ, mirrored in His harmless and tender spirit.

(2) *"Ye shall take it out from the sheep, or from the goats"* (v. 5). We title this plain statement, **APPROPRIATION**. Even though allowance is made for the choosing of a goat, yet we never read that any of the congregation selected a goat. "Theodoret says the provision was made for the relief of the poorer class of persons; but practically it seems not to have taken effect. When people were poor, their richer neighbors supplied them with lambs (Kalisch)."[1]

In God's celestial abode, there are myriads of holy angels, yet not one of them was appropriated to be the ultimate sacrifice for sin. The government of God required blood, precious blood from a sinless human being, to accomplish eternal redemption for Adam's fallen race. Thus, our blessed Lord was "taken out" from all the host of heaven to be the Lamb for our redemption. Peter, in musing on the precious blood of Christ and His unblemished character as the Lamb, bursts forth with these sublime words: *"Who verily was foreordained before the foundation of the world, but was manifest in these last times for you"* (1 Pet. 1:20).

> Long before created worlds,
> Burst forth to fill God's space.
> God's Son was chosen as the Lamb
> Our vile sins to erase.
>
> Emergency, is not the thought,
> In God's eternal plan.
> Long, long, before man came to be,
> Was the plan too vast to scan![2]

---

1 George Rawlinson. Exodus. The Pulpit Commentary (Hendrickson Publishers, Peabody, MA). P.259.
2 Robert E. Surgenor, May 10, 2008

(3) The next thing to consider is **APPRECIATION**. *"And ye shall keep it up until the fourteenth day of the same month: and the whole assembly of the congregation of Israel shall kill it in the evening"* (Ex. 12:6). There were four days of testing and observation. I am sure that the children would become attached to the little lamb. This attachment would cause a greater impact upon them when the little creature was slain. Come with me to the apostles, especially John, and what do we find? Listen to his words concerning the Lamb of God. *"That which was from the beginning, which we have heard, which we have seen with our eyes, which we have looked upon, and our hands have handled, of the Word of life"* (1 Jn. 1:1).

Can you not see a growing intelligence and appreciation in the heart of John regarding the Lamb? As Jesus came to them, it was on the banks of Jordan that John heard the greatest prophet of Old Testament times declare, *"Behold the Lamb of God!"* (John 1:36). That same day he had the privilege of abiding in the Lord's dwelling, to hear His words. John said, *"we have seen with our eyes,"* meaning "to stare at."

However, John proceeds, and says, *"which we have looked upon."* Ah, now he has drawn closer to the Lamb and is viewing Him more intently, for that is what the word "looked upon" conveys. I see this displayed three years later in John 13, where we find John in the bosom of His Lord. The intimacy has increased with days.

How is it with us? Do we just view the Lamb with a casual glance, or do we view Him intently? Do we meet with Him, and visit with Him? Remember, that is what the word "looked upon," conveys. We live in a very busy world. It madly rushes on, and would drag us with it, thus leaving us very little time to quiet ourselves in the presence of God to feast upon the Lamb of God. May God exercise us and help us to give Him the priority in our lives, that we might have many precious moments of simply looking upon Him. What a blessed occupation. What blessed benefits accrue from such "looking."

If your attachment to Christ is not greater now than when you first professed, something is drastically wrong my friend. There are some people that the more you get to know them, the less you think of them. Not so with our Lamb! The more you know Him, the more you will love Him. It is a spiritually "automatic" reaction! It cannot be avoided!

I can picture the children as the lamb's throat was cut and the blood poured out into the bason. I am sure there would be tears. Come with me to Calvary, and what disciple do we find? We see John, the disciple whom Jesus loved. What a sight for his eyes to behold. He gazes upon his blessed Lord with a scourged body, cruelly nailed to an accursed tree. Do you think that he was looking all over the place, engaging in conversation with all that were nearby? Do you believe that he was laughing? Why the very thought of it all is repulsive. No, no! I see a sober, broken-hearted, and intently-looking disciple, with his eyes fixed on Him, the Lamb of God!

Come with me now to the Lord's Supper. What do you find? On some occasions you will find "saints" engaged in conversation prior to the commencement of the meeting. Their mind is not on Christ at all. On one occasion I observed two young ladies in the circle, passing photographs between themselves, and giggling while the emblems were being passed. The Spirit within was quenched, my heart was grieved, and I was angry. What was the problem? Either such folks are not saved, or if they are saved, they are out of touch with God. In contrast to this, how wonderful to walk into a gathering, and observe the saints sitting quietly, and subdued in His most holy presence. The Lord is there, and they realize it fully, and act accordingly. Such moments are precious to behold.

(4) *"The whole assembly of the congregation of Israel shall kill **it** in the evening."* Thus we have, **ATONEMENT**. The marginal rendering reads, *"shall kill **it** between the two evenings."* The collective singular for the plural is employed to emphasize the fact that even though there were thousands of lambs slain by thousands of

THE PASSOVER

people, it was considered a single act. The Holy Spirit designed the language this way, simply because this whole episode was to speak of Christ. *"The whole assembly of the congregation of Israel"* was credited with the killing of the lamb. Opening the pages of the New Testament, we find these startling words. *"Ye men of Israel, hear these words; Jesus of Nazareth ... Him ... ye have taken, and by wicked hands have crucified and slain"* (Acts 2:22-23). *"Ye denied the Holy One and the Just ... and killed the Prince of life"* (Acts 3:14-15). *"Ye slew and hanged on a tree"* (Acts 5:30).

The lamb actually was to be slain *"between the two evenings."* That is the marginal rendering in a good reference Bible.

"The Jews divided the day into *morning* and *evening*: till the sun passed the *meridian,* all was *morning* or *fore-noon;* after that, all was *afternoon* or *evening.* Their *first evening* began just after *twelve o'clock,* and continued until *sunset;* their *second evening* began at *sunset* and continued until *night,* i.e., during the whole time of *twilight;* between twelve o'clock, therefore, and the termination of *twilight,* the Passover was to be offered.

The day among the Jews had *twelve* hours (John 11:9). Their *first* hour was about six o'clock in the morning with us. Their *sixth* hour was our noon. Their *ninth* hour answered to our three o'clock in the afternoon. By this we may understand that the time in which Christ was crucified began at the *third* hour, that is, at nine o'clock in the morning, the ordinary time for the *daily morning sacrifice,* and ended at the *ninth hour,* that is, three o'clock in the afternoon, the time of the evening sacrifice (Mark 15:25, 33, 34, 37). Wherefore their *ninth* hour was their *hour of prayer,* when they used to go into the temple at the daily evening sacrifice (Acts 3:1); and this was the ordinary time for the Passover.

It is worthy of remark that God sets no particular *hour* for the killing of the Passover: any time between the two evenings, i.e., between twelve o'clock in the day and the termination of twilight, was lawful. The daily sacrifice (see Exodus 29:38-39) was killed at *half past the eighth hour*, that is, *half an hour* BEFORE *three* in the *afternoon*; and it was offered up at *half past the ninth hour*, that is, *half an hour* AFTER *three*. In the evening of the Passover it was killed at *half past the seventh hour*, and offered at *half past the eighth*, that is, *half an hour* BEFORE *three*: and if the evening of the Passover fell on the evening of the Sabbath, it was killed at *half past the* SIXTH *hour*, and offered at *half past the* SEVENTH, that is, *half an hour* BEFORE *two* in the afternoon.

The reason for this was, they were first obliged to kill the daily sacrifice, and then to kill and roast the paschal lamb, and also to rest the evening before the Passover. Agreeably to this *Maimonides* says 'the killing of the Passover is after mid-day, and if they kill it before it is not lawful; and they do not kill it till after the daily evening sacrifice, and burning of incense: and after they have trimmed the lamps, they begin to kill the paschal lambs until the end of the day.' By this time of the day God foreshowed the sufferings of Christ in the evening of times or in the last days (Heb. 1:2; 1 Peter 1:19-20): and about the same time of the day, when the paschal lamb ordinarily died, He died also, viz., at the *ninth* hour (Matt. 27: 46-50)."[3]

(5) *"And they shall take of the blood, and strike it on the two side posts and on the upper door post of the houses, wherein they shall eat it"* (Ex. 12:7). Thus, the fifth thing we notice is, **APPLICATION**. The lamb's blood was shed to redeem the firstborn, but that

---

3   Clark. Exodus (MacSword, Bible study software for Mac OS 10)

THE PASSOVER

alone was not sufficient. The blood from the lamb must be applied to the two side posts and on the upper door post of their houses. None was to be sprinkled on the door step. The blood was not to be stepped on.

In like manner, Christ the Passover Lamb was slain at Calvary. His blood was shed for the remission of sins. However, it avails nothing for the sinner until that sinner appropriates that blood to himself. Paul seems to be very concerned over those who have *"trodden under foot the Son of God,"* and have counted the blood of the covenant an unholy thing (Heb. 10:29). No Israelite, upon entering or leaving their dwelling, would be stepping on the blood of the lamb!

Regarding the application of the blood, it would seem that Peter had this in mind, when by the Spirit he penned these words: *"Elect according to the foreknowledge of God the Father, through sanctification of the Spirit, unto obedience and sprinkling of the blood of Jesus Christ: Grace unto you, and peace, be multiplied"* (1 Pet. 1:2). The sinner was known in Eternity past, and chosen. He then was set apart by the Spirit to be dealt with, and convicted of his sin. The message of the gospel came home to his heart and he believed. He applied the value of the Sacrifice, and thus was saved. In other words, he sprinkled the blood of the slain Lamb. This is an act of faith. It is not faith that shelters me from the coming judgment, it is rather the blood of the Lamb. Faith is only the element that links me with the shed blood.

ENGINE AND BOX CARS

Let me explain it this way. Come to a railroad siding and you will see some boxcars sitting there. They are at point A, but we want them to be moved to point B. However, they have no power in themselves to move one inch. The next thing we observe is an engine backing up to the cars. Still, they can't move, until one thing happens, and it is this, the brakeman couples the cars to the engine. The engineer applies the throttle, and the cars are now in motion, being moved from point A to point B. What is moving them, the coupler? Why no, the engine is moving them. All the ability and power is contained, not in the coupler, but in the engine. However, without the coupler, they would never come into the good of the engine's power to move them.

FAITH THE COUPLER

In like manner, faith is the coupler that links me to the Lamb. Let us be careful in our expressions, especially when preaching the gospel. I am sure that we are all aware that good works, prayers, penance, and reformation cannot save the soul, and those who preach such nonsense need to be saved themselves. No, no, it is none of those things. But let me go further, and this may startle you. It is not faith that saves the sinner, nor is it the finished work of Christ that saves the soul. Through faith I have been saved, but it wasn't my faith that saved me, it only linked me to the Lamb. You may argue and reply, "If trusting the finished work of Christ doesn't save me, what does save me?" Friend, the answer is very pure and simple, and it is found fourteen times in our Lord's own words in the Gospel of John. *"That whosoever believeth in Him should not perish, but have eternal life ... He that believeth on Him is not condemned ... He that believeth on the Son hath everlasting life"* (John 3:15,18,36). He never says, "That whosoever believeth on His finished work should not perish, but have eternal life ... He that believeth on His finished work is not condemned ... He that believeth on His finished work hath everlasting life." Ah no, it is Christ in Whom I trust, and in Him alone. The Christ of God, that finished the work! The Lamb of God Who was slain for me! Yes, He finished that tremendous work, but it is He, and He alone, that saves the soul!

(6) The next thing we want to consider is **ASSIMILATION**. *"They shall eat it"* (Ex. 12:7). It was to be eaten at night, and they were to have their loins girded, their shoes on their feet, their staff in their hand, and they were to eat it in haste. Not only this, they were not to break a bone of the lamb. Can you picture the scene? The destroyer is going through the land smiting all the Egyptian's firstborn. Great cries are going up. It is a dreadful

night for the Egyptians. How different is the scene with God's people. Sheltered by the blood of the lamb, they are having a feast inside their humble dwellings, a feast never to be forgotten – they are feasting on roast lamb!

The eating of the lamb would satisfy, sustain, strengthen, and sober them. By feasting on our Passover Lamb, we too experience true satisfaction. There are Christians who never seem to be satisfied. What is the problem? Simply this, they have ceased to feast on Christ. Their intimate communion with Him no longer exists. They seek satisfaction from indulgence in worldly things, but alas, such pleasures and aspirations can never satisfy. Paul told Timothy that, *"godliness with contentment is great gain"* (1 Tim. 6:6).

A journey lay before them. Their diet prior to their exodus was roast lamb. This would strengthen and sustain them for their journey. God was giving them a high protein, low cholesterol diet. Let me say this. Do you want to be strengthened for trials along the way, and sustained for the weary, tiresome days ahead? Then by all means, feast on Christ, and you will discover this, that God will strengthen and sustain you in most unexpected ways. One is reminded of the words of our blessed Lord. *"He that eateth My flesh, and drinketh My blood, dwelleth in Me, and I in him"* (John 6:56). This is a series of acts, the habit of spiritually feeding on Christ. And what does it indicate? Simply this, that one is truly and intimately connected with Him. Christ is manifesting Himself through them, and others observe it.

Many disciples, upon hearing the Lord speak these words said; *"This is an hard saying; who can hear it?"* Perhaps you wonder about it too, but let me explain. To eat a person simply means, to take that person, and make that person part of yourself, by meditating and enjoying that person. You have a similar expression from Jeremiah when he exclaimed; *"Thy words were found, and I did eat them; and Thy word was unto me the joy and rejoicing of mine heart: for I am called by Thy name, O LORD God of hosts"* (Jer. 15:16). That certainly doesn't mean that he actually chewed and swallowed the parchment on which the word was written. No, no! Nothing like that at all! He is simply telling us that he devoured the truth of the divine writings and bowed to their authority and lived them out in his life. Doing this caused a great joy and rejoicing in his heart.

In view of all this, let me ask you, what is your spiritual diet, what is your "main dish" if I may put it that way? Is it the daily newspaper, a worldly magazine, a story book, a novel (which is unscriptural), or perhaps even the radio, the television, or the internet? Or, are you a serious student of the Holy Scriptures, feeding and feasting on Christ as your daily portion?

Very often, one can detect the diet of another by listening to them talk. There is an old expression that I'm going to use and I will put it in italics. Did you ever try to talk about the Scriptures to a Christian, and find that getting them to engage in such conversation was like *trying to pull hen's teeth*? They can readily talk about the mechanics of tractors, cars, and other mechanical devices, but ask them about the truths of Scripture, and you draw a blank. Take them to Jabin king of Canaan, and his captain Sisera, which dwelt in Harosheth. Or, march them into the New Testament and ask them their thoughts on the Lion of the tribe of Judah, the Root of David, standing before the throne of God and taking the book out of the right hand of God. Ask them, and see what they say.

Then we have the "bookworms." Please don't misunderstand me, for good books are valuable friends. Commentaries, devotional writings, expository books, they are very valuable tools for the serious Christian. However, there are folks that spend the most of their reading time over books instead of THE BOOK. They ingest what this author has to say, and what that author has to say, but they never go with an open mind to the Bible itself to see what God has to say to them personally through the Holy Spirit. They may even sit for an hour with earphones listening to a preacher on a particular subject. This is all well and good, but if the personal reading and meditation of the Scriptures themselves are neglected, then it is not good. We need to get fresh thoughts for ourselves, straight from the throne of God, if we ever expect to develop godliness in our lives. Years ago, folks, at times, had to prime the well's pump to get the water to flow. Books should be used the same way. Through reading good books we obtain thoughts that prime the well, directing us to the Scriptures where the Spirit personally speaks to us with fresh thoughts from Himself. Israel was to eat roast lamb. We are to feast on Christ.

"Gazing on Thee, Lord in glory,
While our hearts in worship bow,
There we read the wondrous story
Of the cross, its shame and woe.

Gazing on it we adore Thee,
Blessed, precious, holy Lord;
Thou, the Lamb, art ever worthy;
This be earth's and heaven's accord."[4]

ACCOMPANIMENTS

Accompanying the lamb, they were to eat unleavened bread with bitter herbs. Unleavened bread reminds us of the impeccable humanity of our blessed Lord, that living Bread that came down from heaven. Bitter herbs speaks to us of the bitterness of His death, as He, by the grace of God tasted death for every man (Heb. 2:9). We muse on His holy life, we meditate on the sorrows, agony, and accursedness of His death, and bow in holy adoration and wonder.

ROAST WITH FIRE

The lamb was not to be eaten raw, nor sodden at all with water, but roast with fire. Nothing was to come between the fires of God's wrath and the Lamb of God. Nothing was to help

---

4   Centra Thompson. The Believer's Hymn Book. (John Ritchie Ltd. Kilmarnock, Scotland). P. 327

alleviate the severe pain of God's wrath and judgment. As He poured out His soul unto death, the waves and billows of God's unmitigated wrath poured over Him, sinking Him into deep mire, where there was no standing. We, frail mortals, cannot fathom it, we cannot comprehend it, we cannot perceive it in the least, but one thing we do fully know, and it is this: He gave Himself for our sins to redeem us back to God! Glory to His name! Hallelujah! What a Saviour!

The lamb was to be roasted with fire; his head with his legs, and with the purtenance thereof (Ex. 12:9). When I consider the *"head"* of Christ, I think of His holy **mind**. Looking at the *"legs,"* I am reminded of His holy **movements**, and when I view the inwards, the *"purtenance thereof,"* my mind is drawn to His holy **motives**. All were in perfect accord with His Father in heaven. Thus, He could rightfully exclaim, *"He that sent Me is with Me: the Father hath not left Me alone; for I do always those things that please Him"* (John 8:29).

LOINS, FEET, AND HAND

Moving down to verse eleven in Exodus chapter twelve, we come across a very unusual stipulation associated with the eating of the Passover lamb. *"Thus shall ye eat it; with your loins girded, your shoes on your feet, and your staff in your hand; and ye shall eat it in haste: it is the LORD'S Passover."* Those living in the East usually wear long, flowing garments, which, although convenient in postures of repose would pose a problem in working or walking. Thus, in girding up the loins, the person was more prepared for work or journeying. Wearing shoes in the house was not an accepted thing. Ceremonial politeness would require the removal of one's shoes. Also, there would be concern about bringing dirt into the dwelling, thus soiling the carpets. However, they were to have their shoes on their feet. Their staff, or walking stick, was to be in their hand. Now the picture is simply this. They were called upon to be ready to leave for the journey immediately upon notice from the Lord. They were to be alert and ready. In other words, don't be gathering up your garments and collecting them under your girdle when it is time to leave. When the call comes to go, don't be taking the time to put your shoes on. Don't be looking for your staff. Have it in your hand, and be ready to go at a moments notice! Even the lamb was to be eaten in haste.

THE WHOLE ARMOUR OF GOD

How would one apply this to our day? I think that if we turned to Romans 13:11-12, we would find a parallel. *"Now is our salvation (the Lord's coming) nearer than when we believed. The night is far spent, the day is at hand: let us therefore cast off the works of darkness, and let us put on the armour of light."* Just as Israel feasted on the lamb at night, so we are morally in a night season, feasting on Christ. Are we living in such a way that when the shout is given, that we will be ready? Are we wearing the whole armor of God? Have we girded up the loins of our mind? Do we possess a disciplined thought life? Are we sober, and hoping perfectly for the grace that is to be brought unto us at the revelation of Jesus Christ? (1 (Peter 1:13). Are our loins girded about with truth? In other words, is there sincerity, truthfulness, integrity, and reality seen in our lives? (Eph. 6:14). What about our feet? Are they shod with the preparation of the gospel of peace? (Eph. 6:15). Do we have a sure footing in the gospel? Is the spiritual staff in our hand, displaying the fact that we are pilgrims and strangers, journeying on to our heavenly home?

Our financial affairs, are they in order? If the Lord were to come today, would your creditors be at a great loss over your debt? Have you purchased items on time and they are no longer worth what you owe? It is wrong. God's command still remains, *"Owe no man anything"* (Rom. 13:8). Consider Proverbs 22:26-27. *"Be not thou one of them that strike hands, or of them that are sureties for debts. If thou hast nothing to pay, why should he take away thy bed from under thee?"* The striking of hands was when two persons made an agreement. That agreement was sealed when they struck each others hands.

THE CREDIT CARD CATCH

Let us draw a picture. Consider a young couple starting out in life. His wages should determine what their standard of living will be. However, they are not satisfied with that, and the ungodly merchants make it very easy for them to obtain whatever the lust of their eye dictates. So what happens? They purchase items that they presently cannot afford. The credit card enables them to fill their home with fine furniture. In the driveway sits a new automobile, with monthly payments attached. Whatever they see and want, they buy – on time. They are burdened with credit card interest, and monthly car payments. Their debt rises, and the point comes that the merchandise on which they owe money is no longer worth what they owe. With some, the time comes when their merchandise is repossessed. That is what is meant in those words, *"If thou hast nothing to pay, why should he take away thy bed from under thee?"* Now then, what if the Lord should come, and this couple is transported from earth to glory? They leave it all behind, but oh the disgrace, for their creditors have lost money over their unpaid debt. If the Lord should come today, would this be the kind of testimony that you would leave behind? God forbid! Thus, we have in verses 1-14 of Exodus 12, the directions for the first Passover.

NOTHING LEFT

It is interesting isn't it, that no roast lamb was to be left in their dwelling after their departure. *"Ye shall let nothing of it remain until the morning; and that which remaineth of it until the morning ye shall burn with fire"* (Ex. 12:10). Why is that? A few reasons have been given by various commentators, but William Warke, whom I labored with, made this remark: "God would not allow any Egyptian to feast on Israel's roast lamb." Israel left behind their dwellings and belongings in Egypt. The next day many Egyptians would be snooping about their houses to see what they could obtain. One thing for certain, there would be no roast lamb for them to feast upon! The spiritual application is simply this, that no unsaved person can enjoy Christ, the

Passover Lamb. He does not have the capability to ingest and enjoy spiritual truths. He cannot make Christ part of himself. As an intellect, he may study about Christ. He may accumulate volumes of data about Christ, but he cannot enjoy Christ in an intimate and personal way. It is absolutely impossible. No unsaved man can feast on the Passover Lamb. Only those possessed of divine life through the new birth can find peace, joy, and strength through feasting on Christ.

THOSE FORBIDDEN

God mentions others who were forbidden to partake of the Passover, namely, strangers, foreigners, hired servants, and uncircumcised persons. These can be likened spiritually to certain classes of people today. Paul speaks of the Ephesian believers prior to their salvation as, *"strangers from the covenants of promise."* One could hardly admit a person into assembly fellowship who was yet a stranger to grace and to God! Uncircumcised persons were those not under the covenant. They manifested insubjection to divine authority. The foreigner was a sojourner passing through, not intending to be a permanent resident.

Assemblies have experienced people on the road, passing by, stopping long enough to enter the hall on Lord's Day morning, prior to the Lord's Supper. They have no letter of commendation, but profess to be Christians. They attend a denominational "church" in their locality. They are foreigners. What is to be done with them? They are to be greeted with kindness, given a seat outside of the circle of fellowship, and told that they are more than welcome to observe the assembly carry out the Lord's supper. After the meeting, they should be invited to a home for a meal, and after the meal, sent on their way with prayer for their safety. Christians are to show goodness to all men, especially to those of the household of faith (Gal. 6:10).

The hired servant would represent the person that is working for divine favor and eternal life. He is confused, or deceived as to the way of salvation. He thus occupies, not a seat in the circle, but rather the seat of the unbeliever, as an observer. The partaking of the Passover was not for everyone, but just for those who were ceremonially, and morally clean, having been brought under God's covenant. The same principle applies to God's assemblies. There are limitations as to who is able to break bread with other believers. Let us be clear on the matter, that there are divinely appointed restrictions to the assembly and the Lord's Supper. Christendom knows nothing of these divine principles and they display their ignorance publicly when their billboard says, "Worship with us."

THE FEAST OF UNLEAVENED BREAD

Going back to verses 15-20, we have instructions for future celebrations. *"Seven days shall ye eat unleavened bread; even the first day ye shall put away leaven out of your houses: for whosoever eateth leavened bread from the first day until the seventh day, that soul shall be cut off from Israel"* (v. 15). Leaven is yeast, and it speaks of uncleanness. This is the first mention of it in the Bible, the last mention being in Galatians 5:9. The word is found 23 times.

The Feast of Unleavened Bread was the first of the seven feasts of Jehovah (Lev. 23), and is always linked with the Passover. The Passover was a one-day feast, the Feast of Unleavened Bread was a seven-day feast. It is profitable to notice that the one-day feasts portray what God has done FOR you, while the period-feasts declare what God is doing IN you. *"Christ our Passover is sacrificed for us"* (1 Cor. 5:7). That is what God has done for us. He has fully provided redemption for us through the offering of His Son. Now then, having experienced *"redemption through His blood, even the forgiveness of sins"* (Col. 1:14), I have the responsibility to purge out the old leaven. I have the duty to eliminate every single thing in my life that is unclean. Anything that would displease the Lord is to be put away.

The feast was for seven days, indicating a complete period of time. In other words, our whole lifetime should be free of leaven! Christ gave many warnings against the leaven of the

Pharisees, the Sadducees, and of Herod (Matt. 16:11; Mark 8:15). The leaven of the Pharisees was hypocrisy and ritualism. The leaven of the Sadducees was wrong doctrine. The leaven of Herod was politics. The leaven of the Galatians was legalism (Gal. 5:9), and the leaven at Corinth was vain glory, worldliness, and a toleration of evil (1 Cor. 5:7-8). Paul exhorts the saints at Rome. *"I speak after the manner of men because of the infirmity of your flesh: for as ye have yielded your members servants to uncleanness and to iniquity unto iniquity; even so now yield your members servants to righteousness unto holiness"* (Rom. 6:19). He also warns the Ephesian assembly. *"But fornication, and all uncleanness, or covetousness, let it not be once named among you, as becometh saints"* (Eph. 5:3). In like manner he addresses the Colossians. *"Mortify therefore your members which are upon the earth; fornication, uncleanness, inordinate affection, evil concupiscence, and covetousness, which is idolatry"* (Col. 3:5). Uncleanness, uncleanness, uncleanness! It is everywhere! It surrounds us, it crowds in upon us, it would seek to overpower us. God hates it, and we should hate it. May the Lord give us grace to say "NO" to all forms of uncleanness!

> "Break every barrier down,
> Thou Lamb of Calvary;
> Show me the awfulness of sin,
> The thing which grieveth Thee:
>
> Purge Thou my soul from dross,
> Cleanse me from every sin,
> Wash me in Thine atoning blood,
> And make me pure within."[5]

"Then Moses called for all the elders of Israel, and said unto them, Draw out and take you a lamb according to your families, and kill the Passover. And ye shall take a bunch of hyssop, and dip it in the blood that

---

[5] Bertha Mullen. The Believer's Hymn Book. (John Ritchie Ltd. Kilmarnock, Scotland) P.314.

is in the bason, and strike the lintel and the two side posts with the blood that is in the bason; and none of you shall go out at the door of his house until the morning. For the LORD will pass through to smite the Egyptians; and when He seeth the blood upon the lintel, and on the two side posts, the LORD will pass over the door, and will not suffer the destroyer to come in unto your houses to smite you. And ye shall observe this thing for an ordinance to thee and to thy sons for ever. And it shall come to pass, when ye be come to the land which the LORD will give you, according as He hath promised, that ye shall keep this service. And it shall come to pass, when your children shall say unto you, What mean ye by this service? That ye shall say, It is the sacrifice of the LORD's Passover, who passed over the houses of the children of Israel in Egypt, when He smote the Egyptians, and delivered our houses. And the people bowed the head and worshipped" (Ex. 12:21-27).

The first occasion of worship connected with the nation is found in Exodus 4:30. On that occasion, Moses and Aaron had gathered together all the elders of the children of Israel. *"And Aaron spake all the words which the LORD had spoken unto Moses, and did the signs in the sight of the people."* We then read that the people believed, and *"bowed their heads and worshipped."* A careful reader will notice the difference, and it is this. In Exodus 4:31, the people bowed their **HEADS** and worshipped, but in Exodus 12:27 they bowed the **HEAD** and worshipped. *"Bowed the head,"* brings before us a corporate unity. The whole nation was now linked together by the death of the lamb, they were all reckoned as one, thus the word **HEAD** in the singular is employed.

WAGES PAID

"And the children of Israel ... borrowed (requested) *of the Egyptians jewels of silver, and jewels of gold, and raiment."* Having found favor in the sight of the Egyptians, they gave them such things as

they required (Ex. 12:35-36). This was the fulfillment of the promise made to Abraham. *"And also that nation, whom they shall serve, will I judge: and afterward shall they come out with great substance"* (Gen. 15:14). In reality, they were only being paid their wages for all the years of their slavery. God sent them out full. *"The children of Israel went out with an high hand"* (Ex. 14:8). That is, they went out in power and dignity. They went out with all the materials needed to erect a sanctuary for God in the wilderness.

FULLY FURNISHED

In like manner, when God delivers a soul from bondage, and brings that soul into the kingdom of God, that soul is not poverty stricken. Ah no, he is fully furnished to function for God. He is immediately indwelt with the Holy Spirit, Who furnishes him. He is now able to pray, worship, witness, and live a godly life for his Redeemer. *"For God hath not given us the spirit of fear; but of power, and of love, and of a sound mind"* (2 Tim. 1:7).

When God saves a soul, what does that person immediately seek to accomplish? He wants to tell others. He certainly doesn't have to attend a college to accomplish that! He doesn't have to write his message out to do that. Why no! He is indwelt by the Holy Spirit, Who can give him holy boldness and utterance.

Look at the poor creature in Mark 5, indwelt and plagued by thousands of demons. What a terrible case was his! But just look at this wreck of humanity after the Lord saved him. What is he doing? Crawling off to some monastery to try to be holy? Nonsense! He is publishing in his hometown how great things Jesus had done for him. He couldn't keep quiet. What power! What ability! What a change! My friend, God has given you the ability to witness. Do you do it? Not only this, but he fully furnishes us with the ability to worship in a corporate way. There are small assemblies where every brother rises at the breaking of bread to audibly worship. How fragrant to behold! It is heartwarming to see. Men furnished and functioning. That is the way God would have it. There is no excuse for laziness in the house of God. *"He brought them forth also with silver and gold: and there was not one feeble person among their tribes"* (Ps. 105:37).

> "Heed we the steward's call,
> Work, brethren, work!
> There's room enough for all;
> Work, brethren, work!
> This vineyard of the Lord
> Constant labour doth afford;
> Yours is a sure reward;
> Work, brethren, work!
>
> Hear we the Shepherd's voice,
> Pray, brethren, pray!
> Would ye His heart rejoice?
> Pray, brethren, pray!
> Sin calls for constant fear,
> Weakness needs the strong One near,
> Long as ye struggle here;
> Pray, brethren, pray!
>
> Now sound the final chord,
> Praise, brethren, praise!
> Thrice holy is our Lord;
> Praise, brethren, praise!
> What more befits the tongues
> Soon to lead the eternal songs,
> While heaven the note prolongs?
> Praise, brethren, praise!"[6]

God, the Holy Spirit, has fully furnished us to accomplish what the hymn writer has exhorted us to do. Israel went out with sufficient material possessions to enable them to fully function for their God. We too, have been saved with the ability to acceptably serve our Redeemer.

---

6   Unknown. The Believer's Hymn Book. (John Ritchie Ltd. Kilmarnock, Scotland). P. 55.

5

THE MIXED MULTITUDE

> *"And the children of Israel journeyed from Rameses to Succoth, about six hundred thousand on foot that were men, beside children. And a mixed multitude went up also with them; and flocks, and herds, even very much cattle"* (Ex. 12:37-38).

The word *Rameses* means, *"under the sun,"* representing this present evil world. *Succoth* means, *"booths or tents,"* which portrays the thought of pilgrim character.

These people were leaving an Egyptian world in exchange for a pilgrim journey. Imagine, about two and one half million people leaving a way of life, and all their Egyptian-acquired possessions, and following one man, out of their environment, into a wilderness! What an amazing movement, what an astounding change! Can we not relate to this in our own salvation experience? Immediately, this mass exodus draws our attention to the words of our Lord, and the words of the Spirit through Peter. *"If ye were of the world, the world would love his own: but because ye are not of the world, but I have chosen you out of the world, therefore the world hateth you"* (John 15:19). *"Dearly beloved, I beseech you as strangers and pilgrims, abstain from fleshly lusts, which war against the soul"* (1 Pet. 2:11).

A *stranger* is a person away from home. A *pilgrim* is a person journeying to their home. We are in a wicked world, but strangers to it as we make our way down life's narrow way, on to our celestial home. You will notice in connection with this, that we are to be abstainers. There is to be no leavened bread in our dwellings. We are to abstain from fleshly lusts. I would say that this is a "full-time" effort, but the Holy Spirit within us will fully enable us to purge out all leaven if we allow Him to so work within.

THE MIXED MULTITUDE

There were people who had never experienced any association with the Passover, or the lamb, who joined the children of Israel in their departure from Egypt. They seemed to see an advantage for themselves being linked with the people of God. It would seem that self interest motivated them. Thus, we have *"a mixed multitude."* Who were they? We can only speculate, but some may have been linked to the Israelites through mixed marriages. Others may have been Egyptians of the poorer class, anxiously hoping to better their living standard. Perhaps some were slaves, seeing an opportunity for freedom, while others may have been vagabonds, adventurers, or debtors. We believe enthusiasm motivated them to join the exodus. However, it was not long before we discover that these are the people that *"fell a lusting."* They remembered Egypt's food, the fish, the cucumbers, the melons, the leeks, the onions, and the garlick (Num. 11:5).

Is there the possibility of having similar circumstances in the Dispensational Church today? Absolutely! There are multitudes professing to be Christians, that have never experienced redemption by the blood of the Lamb. They have joined the people of God in all denominations. They have also infiltrated God's assemblies of gathered out saints. David cried, *"Rid me, and deliver me from the hand of strange children"* (Ps. 144:11).

Paul manifested the same concern when he met with the elders of the Ephesian assembly. *"Take heed therefore unto yourselves, and to all the flock, over the which the Holy Ghost hath made you overseers, to feed the church of God, which He hath purchased* with His own blood. *For I know this, that after my departing shall grievous wolves enter in among you, not sparing the flock. Also of your own selves shall men arise, speaking perverse things, to draw away disciples after them"* (Acts 20:28-30).

Jude also expresses deep concern. *"For there are certain men crept in unawares, who were before of old ordained to this condemnation, ungodly men, turning the grace of our God into lasciviousness, and denying the only Lord God, and our Lord Jesus Christ"* (Jude 1:4). Even more interesting is the fact that, in the next verse, he exhorts his readers to remember *"that the Lord, having saved the people out of the land of Egypt, afterward destroyed them that believed not."*

THE SEVEN CHURCHES

Consider the seven Churches of Asia in Revelation 2 and 3. In spite of the newness of Christianity, we find an infiltration of strange children, we see a mixed multitude. Notice how the Church at Ephesus was very much aware of the danger of people creeping into the assembly who had never been born again. Christ said to them, *"I know thy works, and thy labour, and thy patience, and how thou canst not bear them which are evil: and thou hast tried them which say they are apostles, and are not, and hast found them liars"* (Rev. 2:2). The word *"tried"* is, *"to scrutinize, examine."*

This assembly was very aware of the fact that there were professing Christians that would seek to join themselves to them for personal gain. All applicants for fellowship into that local assembly were scrutinized. They were examined. There was no such thing as just walking in and being accepted.

Let me relate this to positions in certain agencies of our government. Do you think that you could apply for a job with the FBI, and with no questions asked, be heartily accepted? Think again! Before being accepted into that agency, your family history would be examined, and your relatives questioned. You also would be interrogated, and the answers would have to be right or you would be denied the privilege of being a member of that agency.

The church at Pergamos was plagued with worldliness, and Thyatira was no better, for in that assembly was Jezebel, who led people into a profession. There they were, defiling God's assembly with false doctrine. Sardis had a name to live, but they were dead, and Laodicea thought themselves to be rich and self-sufficient, but the divine appraisal was, *"thou art wretched, and miserable, and poor, and blind, and naked."* Why all the problems? The answer is simple – a mixed multitude!

THE TEN VIRGINS

In the parable of the ten virgins (Matt. 25), the Lord speaks of certain virgins that had lamps but no oil. Who do they represent? They speak to us of professors (lamps), but having no oil (the Holy Spirit). God plainly says, *"Now if any man have not the Spirit of Christ, he is none of His"* (Rom. 8:9). Outwardly, they seemed genuine, but when the Bridegroom came, the solemn reality was manifested, that they were not ready. They were left behind. I have heard of more than one preacher telling a congregation of "believers" that when the Lord came, there would be enough people in that assembly left behind to be able to continue to break bread. This is a very unpolitically correct statement, but some of those older preachers were not worried about being politically correct. I would say that being scripturally correct should be the model for all faithful preachers. It is, "What saith the Lord," that really counts!

THE LAYING ON OF HANDS

I have talked to more than one elder who expressed concern that some in their assembly were possibly not saved. What makes godly men come to such conclusions? Through observation of some individuals they do not see the marks of divine life. Oh yes, at first, when seeking reception into an assembly they seemed qualified. They convinced the church that they were saved. But perhaps their reception was too soon. They had not been observed for a long enough period of time.

You will remember the case of leprosy. If a man was suspected of having this dreadful disease, the priest would examine him. Not being able to evaluate the person accurately, the priest would shut that person up for seven days. If the spot on the skin spread, he would be pronounced unclean. However, if the spot spread not, the priest would pronounce him clean. Do you understand the principle here? It is simply this, you cannot come to a conclusion about a person without a time of careful observation. Paul warned Timothy, *"Lay hands suddenly on no man, neither be partaker of other men's sins: keep thyself pure"* (1 Tim. 5:22).

> "Some have understood that the laying on of hands was to heal the sick (Koppe); others of the laying on of hands to absolve penitents; but the obvious meaning is to refer it to ordination. It was usual to lay the hands on the heads of those who were ordained to a sacred office, or appointed to perform an important duty (1 Tim. 4:14) Compare Acts 6:6; 8:17. The idea here is, that Timothy should not be hasty in an act so important as that of introducing men to the ministry, he should take time to give them a fair trial of their piety; he should have satisfactory evidence of their qualifications, he should not at once introduce a man to the ministry because he gave evidence of piety, or because he burned with an ardent zeal, or because he thought himself qualified for the work. It is clear from this that the apostle regarded Timothy as having the right to *ordain* to the ministry; but not that he was to ordain alone, or *as a prelate*. The injunction would be entirely proper on the supposition that others were to be associated with him in the act of ordaining.

Neither be partakers of other men's sins. This is evidently to be interpreted in connection with the injunction *"to lay hands suddenly on no man."* The meaning in this connection, is, that Timothy was not to become a participant in the sins of another by introducing him to the sacred office. He was not to invest one with a holy office who was a wicked man or a heretic, for this would be to sanction his wickedness and error. If we ordain a man to the office of the ministry who is known to be living in sin, or to cherish dangerous error, we become the patrons of the sin and of the heresy. We lend to it the sanction of our approbation; and give to it whatever currency it may acquire from the reputation which we may have, or which it may acquire from the influence of the sacred office of the ministry. Hence the importance of caution in investing any one with the ministerial office. But while Paul meant, doubtless, that this should be applied particularly to ordination to the ministry, he has given it a general character. *In no way* are we to participate in the sins of other men."[7]

THE UNLEARNED

Let us go a step further with what Alfred Barnes says. The laying on of hands is the acknowledging of the approval of that particular person. In receiving into the local assembly, the elders must be satisfied that the applicant for fellowship is saved, and doctrinally and morally sound. A person may be saved but not sound in doctrine. He may be totally ignorant of the truth of separation, or he may not be sound on the truth of the security of the believer, or he may not understand why there should be only one loaf and one cup at the supper. Also, he may not be morally

---

7   Alfred Barnes. Notes on 1 Tim.5. (MacSword, Bible study software for Mac OS-10).

sound. He may see nothing wrong in ruining his health with tobacco and alcohol. His, or her dress, may show traces of immodesty. Perhaps, they are still adorning their bodies with silver and gold. These people may be truly saved, but they do not see some doctrinal truths and moral principles clearly. They are unlearned. What attitude is to be shown to such? Those in a responsible position in the assembly are to show them kindness and seek to teach them the right way. These untaught folks are to be given the *"seat of the unlearned"* during this period of ignorance, until they see things as they ought to be (1 Cor. 16:14). Receiving them with their errors, makes one a partaker of their sins.

THE FALSE PROFESSOR

What about the false professor? Let us suggest a supposed case. A young man, upon hearing the gospel, professes to be saved. He has been raised in a home whose parents are in God's assembly. Of course, his parents are very anxious for him to be in the assembly. He is encouraged by them to ask for baptism. He meets with the elders over the matter. They ask him how he was saved. His story is scriptural and very convincing. After all, he has learned the "language of Canaan," he knows the answers. However, there is a "fly in the ointment." This fellow's life has not drastically changed. He tells the elders, "I saw that I was a sinner, and that Jesus died for me, and I believed on the Lord Jesus Christ." However, there were no signs of deep remorse seen in this professor prior to his confession. There was no true conviction of sin. He could never exclaim like David, *"For mine iniquities are gone over mine head: as an heavy burden they are too heavy for me. I am troubled; I am bowed down greatly; I go mourning all the day long"* (Ps. 38:4, 6). Ah no, it was just the fact that he "believed."

A NEW CREATURE

Let us be aware of certain truths. First of all, *"if any man be in Christ, he is a new creature: old things are passed away; behold, all things are become new"* (2 Cor. 5:17). That means, when souls are saved, their way changes! They are taken off the broad way, and his feet are divinely placed on the narrow way that leads to life (Matt. 7). On that narrow way, their desires change. In some cases they change dramatically. I would say that the greater one's wickedness prior to conversion, the more dramatically will be the change. A timid, and obedient child of twelve, upon professing salvation, is certainly not going to manifest as drastic a change as a thirty year old libertine. No, no, such expectations would be unrealistic to say the least. We must be sensible about the whole thing. That is the reason that when little children profess, it may take a long time to see if they really have divine life. When they enter youth, then the evidence will make itself apparent. We wait and watch, and when they become teenagers they will manifest more readily if they truly have divine life or not.

THE WORLD

Another truth is this: *"Love not the world, neither the things that are in the world. If any man love the world, the love of the Father is not in him"* (1 Jn. 2:15). The term *world* seems to be used in the Scriptures in three senses:

(1) As denoting the physical universe; the world as it appears to the eye; the world considered as the work of God, as a material creation.

(2) The world as applied to the people that reside in it—"the world of mankind."

(3) As the dwellers on the earth are by nature acting under a set of maxims, aims, and principles that have reference only to this life.[8] It is in this last sense that John writes.

LOVING THE WORLD

John was a very tender man, but let me say, that he was a very blunt man! There were no gray areas with him. Of course,

---

8 Alfred Barnes. Notes on 1 John 2. (MacSword, Bible study software for Mac OS-10).

we recognize that he was moved by the Spirit in what he wrote. So what does he say? Simply this, that if you are saved, you are not to be in love with the world, that is, to covet what society likes. Matthew Henry, in his commentary, wrote: "This world is our passage, not our portion." How true! The world, with all its fanfare and fun, is not to be the portion of the pilgrim and stranger. However, the young man applying for baptism, and eventually reception into God's assembly, still loves the world. He frequents the sports events. He may even go bowling, or regularly attend the pool rooms, or attend the theaters, or the races. He loves that style of life. What is the problem? The difficulty is, that he has never been born again! There has been no indwelling of the Spirit to strengthen him against such lawless, and God-dishonoring activity. He has never been made a new creature. He has a new story, but his lifestyle is the same old thing. He loves the world.

You may accuse me of being too judgmental, but I beg your pardon – what does God say? It is as plain as plain can be. *"If any man love the world, the love of the Father is not in him."* That word ***"not"*** is a "little-big" word! All true saints have the love of the Father in them. It is an inborn trait, imbedded in the individual by the operation of the Holy Spirit. The man may say what he likes, his language may be convincing and scripturally correct, but something vital is sadly missing – the love of the Father is *NOT* in him! I say that such a position is desperately dangerous. They have made a profession, but their own hearts have deceived them, and they are still in their sins. Many Christians cease to pray for their salvation for they think them to be saved, so they lose the prayers of the saints for their salvation.

ASSEMBLY INVASION

However, there is something equally sad. The parents feel that he is saved, and they don't want to think otherwise. His relatives make excuses for him, and the pressure is put on the assembly to receive him. Some sensible and spiritual Christians may object, but they are put aside, and with great "joy" the false professor is baptized and received into the fellowship of that particular assembly. What has taken place? In reality, they have become partaker of his sins. The assembly has become defiled. Brethren, these are sobering realities. These are somber facts, not to be avoided or shoved aside. Denominational "churches" are full of false professors. God's assemblies are being invaded by virgins with no oil in their lamps. Their scent has not changed. The world is in their heart and the love of the Father was never implanted in their soul.

Shall we go further? Shall we draw an even darker picture? Why not? We need to be aware of things developing rapidly among us. Let us consider this same assembly. From time to time, they have a series of gospel meetings and souls are saved. Thank God for that! However, there are some, due to all the excitement that such meetings may produce, that make a profession. Their thinking may run like this: "Everybody is getting saved, so why not me?" So, they profess, but the indwelling of the Spirit is not there. Along with true believers, they too are received into the fellowship. The years roll by, and most on the oversight have gone home to heaven, but others have taken their position as elders in that assembly. The sad thing is, that some who have entered the oversight are false professors! Time marches on, and now things are being introduced that are unscriptural. Why is that? Simply because those in the oversight that have never been born again are not content with the "old paths." They feel that it is more appropriate to do God's work their way, not God's way. The Scriptures are set aside for more modern ideas. The total dependence of the Holy Spirit as the sole director in the assembly is considered not sufficient. Programs are instituted, ritualism is introduced, and what was once a testimony for God, becomes merely a religious club of so-called Christians.

This is mainly what we see in Christendom, and I am very much afraid that this is what is beginning to rear its ugly head in the assemblies of God. Israel began their journey with a mixed multitude! Well may we cry like David, *"Rid me, and deliver me from the hand of strange children"* (Ps. 144:11).

PARENTS TEACHING CHILDREN

It is interesting to notice how Moses, in detail, instructs parents regarding their children. Let me draw to your attention four verses.

> *(1) "And that thou mayest tell in the ears of thy son, and of thy son's son, what things I have wrought in Egypt, and My signs which I have done among them; that ye may know how that I am the LORD"* (Ex. 10:2).

> *(2) "And it shall come to pass, when your children shall say unto you, What mean ye by this service? That ye shall say, It is the sacrifice of the LORD's passover, Who passed over the houses of the children of Israel in Egypt, when He smote the Egyptians, and delivered our houses. And the people bowed the head and worshipped"* (Ex. 12:26-27).

> *(3) "Unleavened bread shall be eaten seven days; and there shall no leavened bread be seen with thee, neither shall there be leaven seen with thee in all thy quarters. And thou shalt shew thy son in that day, saying, This is done because of that which the LORD did unto me when I came forth out of Egypt"* (Ex. 13:7-9).

> *(4) "And every firstling of an ass thou shalt redeem with a lamb; and if thou wilt not redeem it, then thou shalt break his neck: and all the firstborn of man among thy children shalt thou redeem. And it shall be when thy son asketh thee in time to come, saying, What is this? that thou shalt say unto him, By strength of hand the LORD brought us out from Egypt, from the house of bondage"* (Ex. 13:13-14).

(1) They were to impress their sons with the miracles that the LORD wrought in Egypt, so that they might know that He is the LORD.

(2) They were to keep before the minds of their sons the mighty deliverance wrought by the LORD in Egypt, on their behalf.

(3) They were enjoined to impress their sons with the fact that God imposed principles upon them as a holy people.

(4) The fathers were responsible to educate their sons regarding the requirements of redemption.

If you are a reader that is in assembly fellowship, and a father of children, let me ask you a question. Have you ever sat down with your little ones and explained to them why you and your wife attend the Lord's Supper? Have you ever shown your children why there is only one loaf and one cup, and why brethren pray and give out hymns to sing? Have you ever told them why you wear the best clothes you can afford on that occasion? Their little minds are curious, and certainly they have a right to know. Christian's children are raised in a foreign atmosphere to the earth- dweller's child, and they have the right to know the reason for the big difference. Are they taught reverence and fear regarding assembly gatherings, or do you allow them to march in the assembly with cookies, cereal, coloring books, toys, games, and other amusements?

A FAMILY OF TWELVE CHILDREN

Allow me to make reference again to my friends who raised twelve children. I cannot help but admire them for their godly convictions carried out in the training of their children in the way they should go (Prov. 22:6). Those folks, with all their children, never missed a single meeting any time I was in their area preaching. Some of those gospel meetings lasted over ten weeks. The whole family was always there, and in good time. The only thing the children were allowed in their possession was a hymn book and a Bible during a meeting. They were not allowed to look around or make any noise. If a Bible or hymn book dropped to the floor, it was not recovered. It was an amazing thing to see. The little girls were required to wear hats over their uncut hair. The little boys wore a white shirt, tie and suits tailored by their godly mother. Discipline was strictly enforced with the rod, applied in love, and the fear of God. No running was allowed within the property of the hall. As mentioned before, a little "Sunday school" was held in the home on a daily basis before the children left for school. They never had a T.V., but had hundreds of acres of mountainous land in which to play. The world never captured the attention of any of those twelve children. Sports never interested them, nor the theater or worldly events. A big garden taught them the necessary principles of canning and putting up food for the coming winter. The gun was a necessary tool as well, to bring down deer to provide good, low cholesterol meat. Today, that family is grown. All are saved except two married daughters. Every son in the assembly audibly worships every Lord's day. The two unsaved daughters love God's people, and one of them attends all the meetings on the Lord's Day, with her little one. It is a remarkable family, simply because the father and mother raised their twelve children according to the teachings of Holy Scripture. God said to Israel, *"Thou shalt shew thy son in that day"* (Ex. 13:8).

"And it shall be for a sign unto thee upon thine hand, and for a memorial between thine eyes, that the LORD's law may be in thy mouth: for with a strong hand hath LORD brought thee out of Egypt" (Ex. 13:9).

WEARING THE SCRIPTURES

The manner in which the Jews understood and kept this law readily appears in their practice. Four portions of the Scriptures were written on four pieces of parchment. These Scriptures were: Exodus 13:2-10; then Exodus 13:11-16; followed by Deuteronomy 6:4-9; and Deuteronomy 9:13-21. These parchment slips, with a total of thirty verses inscribed on them, were then rolled up, each by itself, and placed in four compartments that were joined together by one piece of leather. The transcripts were all correct from the Mosaic text, without one unnecessary or deficient letter, otherwise they were not allowed to be worn. Those worn on the head, rested on the forehead. Those for the hand or arm were usually fastened above the elbow on the left arm, thus placing them nearer the heart. According to the commandment in Deuteronomy 6:6 – *"And these words, which I command thee this day, shall be in thine heart."* This practice is still carried on today by strict Orthodox Jews.

AN OVERPAYMENT ADJUSTED

Is there an application of this for Christians of today? Most certainly there is! Are the Scriptures on **MY HAND?** Is my service consecrated to God? Are my dealings with men, whether in business, or in other affairs, controlled and governed by the principles of God?

There was a man who cashed his paycheck at a bank where he had an account. The teller, inadvertently gave him one hundred dollars too much. The transaction took place at a drive-in window. Receiving the envelope, the Christian drove home, but upon opening the envelope he discovered to his surprise the overpayment. At that time wages were less than three dollars an hour. Immediately he drove back to the bank and sought out the clerk who made the mistake. He felt that no one else in the bank should know, lest the teller would be in trouble with the management. When the teller was approached, she could hardly believe what was happening, and told the man that she would have had no way to trace where the one hundred dollars had gone, and that she would have been held accountable. She was profusely thankful and the man gave her a gospel tract, which she gladly received. That, my friend, is wearing the Scriptures on your hand.

The Scriptures were to be worn between **THEIR EYES**, openly displayed on their forehead for all to see. Certainly such a custom would mark them out, would it not? Gentiles would be saying, "Oh, here he comes. That man that is rather odd. He has that thing hanging down, and bouncing on his forehead." Yes, there would be a bit of reproach to it, I would say. But, the Jew would not be ashamed. In fact, he proudly wore it, for it was a public declaration. It was a full manifestation, that he was different from others. He was a child of the God of Abraham, Isaac, and Jacob.

ANTIOCH CHRISTIANS

Now then, my Christian friend, what about you? Are you a walking epistle of the truth? Christ is in you, the hope of glory, but is He publicly manifested in your walk before a godless world? Ah, that's the thing! It is all-important, is it not? Why were the disciples first called Christians in Antioch? (Acts 11:26). It was a new expression, never heard before. What brought it about? The answer is wonderful! These people, when they engaged in conversation with their neighbors, or the merchants, talked about Christ. Whenever they would sing, it would be about Christ. When they held their open air meetings, they preached Christ. Every phase of their life was occupied and permeated with Christ. One couldn't escape them. They were everywhere manifesting Christ. So God put it into hearts of the name-calling Antiochians to mark these disciples of the Lord with this name – **"Christians."** How wonderful! How glorious! What wonderful people they were!

Paul, writing to the Corinthians, exclaimed; *"Forasmuch as ye are manifestly declared to be the epistle of Christ ..."* (2 Cor. 3:3). In other words, the change produced in their lives, from the salvation they had experienced, was as truly the work of Christ as much as a letter dictated and written by a man in his work. Their change was apparent to all. Christ was the Author of the epistle. Paul was the penman, and the Corinthians were the recipients on which the message was written. It was written upon the fleshly tables of their hearts, thus producing an amazing transformation in their lives. Is this not a picture of the Scriptures *"between the eyes"*?

Last of all, God tells Israel, "that the LORD's law may be in **THY MOUTH.** Is this not the outcome of the previous two commands? When the Word of God is in our mouth, that is only the result of it being already in our heart, for out of the abundance of the heart the mouth speaketh. *"A good man out of the good treasure of his heart bringeth forth that which is good* (beneficial); *and an evil man out of the evil treasure of his heart bringeth forth that which is evil* (diseased, harmful): *for of the abundance* (the overflow) *of the heart his mouth speaketh" (Luke 6:45).*

What about our speech? Notice Paul's injunctions. *"Let no corrupt* (worthless) *communication* (speech) *proceed out of your mouth, but that which is good to the use of edifying, that it may minister grace unto the hearers"* (Eph. 4:29). *"But now ye also put off all these; anger, wrath, malice, blasphemy, filthy communication out of your mouth"* (Col. 3:8). Finally, *"Let your speech be alway with grace, seasoned with salt, that ye may know how ye ought to answer every man"* (Col. 4:6).

APPROACHING SINNERS

In other words, let us be wise and prudent in our speech, especially toward unbelievers. Our speech should manifest that the grace of God is in our hearts. The words we employ should manifest that we are governed by the principles of true Christianity, and that we are under the influence of true love to our Saviour. Our speech is to be *"seasoned with salt."* As salt is blended in our food to enhance its flavor, in like manner, we should blend into our speech the spirit of piety. How do we answer inquiring sinners as to the way of life? Are we prepared? Is the Word of God overflowing in our heart? Are we well acquainted with it through personal study and meditation? This is an absolute necessity if we are going to intelligently approach, or answer, a sinner's questions regarding matters of salvation.

Approaching sinners is a challenge. Some are mild, others are violent, and others are haughty. There are the religious, the immoral, the outdoorsman, the hermit, the scholar, the upper society and the lower class, the rich and the poor. How do we approach them with the good news of salvation? Do we need to attend seminars, theological colleges, elocution classes, or go by a set of man-made rules and regulations, to win the lost. Not in any way! To me, all are a waste of valuable time. What the Christian needs to do in order to effectively approach men with the gospel is to have the Word of God embedded within his heart through much study, and meditation, accompanied with much prayer. Not only this, he must live out the Scriptures in his own personal life. He must be a walking epistle of the truth of God. The Word of God was to be seen between the Jew's eyes, publicly displayed. It was to be fastened securely on his arm, near his heart. Then, and not until then would the word of the LORD be in his mouth.

THE LORD AT JACOB'S WELL

The Lord affords us a valuable lesson in approaching a sinner in John 4. First of all, He goes out of His way to meet her. Are we willing to indispose ourselves to speak to people? If we heard that a soul that we knew many years ago, was dying in a hospital sixty miles away, would we indispose ourselves to go and visit that dying sinner? Christ went out of His way to win one soul, a woman who had been married five times and was presently living in sin.

As He sat on the well, He patiently waited for her. He was relaxed and longsuffering. He was also hungry, but the soul of this woman came before His bodily need. This attitude is wonderful to me.

When she finally came in the heat of the day, He gave her a sense of her importance. If a soul has accomplished things in their life, is it wrong to praise them for it? I have told coal miners that I considered them brave men to go into the lower parts of the earth and to risk their lives to dig coal. There is nothing wrong with such a remark, is there? Is it wrong to tell a sinner how good they can play a musical instrument? Is it wrong to compliment people on their dress, or even on certain accomplishments in their life? I don't believe so. It is a way of winning them, first to yourself, and then winning them to the Saviour. The Lord spoke to this woman about something in which she was interested – water. So the farmer is asked about farming and you express to him the intelligence that must be needed in our day to produce crops. The coal miner is asked how they dig coal, what methods do they use? The bearer of good tidings expresses interest in the man's work, and the man likes him for it. That was the Lord's method with this woman.

He asked her a favor: *"Give Me to drink"* (John 4:7). He was humble and wise. Is it wrong to ask a favor of an unsaved person? It all depends on what the favor is. If it is for the purpose of "getting near to them," then by all means, ask the favor. I have asked rough, ungodly men to help me pitch my gospel tent, with the object of influencing them to attend. Pay was offered them, but not once in forty-eight years of erecting gospel tents has any man taken money for helping me. Remember, the Lord asked a favor of the Samaritan woman, thus, I feel absolutely free to ask favors of the unsaved, if the right object is in view.

Then, the Lord told her about something He had that she didn't have. *"Jesus answered and said unto her, If thou knewest the gift of God, and Who it is that saith to thee, Give me to drink; thou wouldest have asked of Him, and He would have given thee living water"* (John 4:10). One of the best avenues along this line is to tell sinners how you were saved. Instead of "getting at them," you simply tell them what you were before you knew the Lord, and how the Lord, in His abundant mercy, reached out and saved you. Try that approach sometime, my witnessing Christian, and you will find it an excellent opening for further witnessing with that individual. The LORD'S law in thy mouth is a valuable tool!

GOD'S CONSIDERATION OF ISRAEL

How kind and considerate God was of His "newly born" people. They had partaken of the Passover in Egypt, and now they were leaving for another way of life altogether. Experiences were before them, never before encountered. They were not trained soldiers, but rather, freed slaves who were now to become pilgrims, journeying on to the promised land. There was a way to their inheritance that would occupy only a seven to nine day journey. That way was where the Philistines dwelt, a way that was under constant surveillance by the Egyptian army. This route lay along the coast of the Mediterranean, and was the usual caravan path from Egypt to Gaza. However, the nearest way is not always God's way. The Philistines were a powerful and warlike nation, but God saw fit to not make a useless display of His miraculous power in bringing the Philistines down in order to bring His people hastily into their promised possession. God knew that His people, at the first onset, would be unable to face a warlike foe. Before any battles would be fought, there must be time consuming training, and this is what the wilderness journey would provide. The conflict with the Philistines at that early date would not be too much for God's strength, but it would be too much for Israel's faith. Even though His omnipotence was pledged to their defense, He did not exempt His people from the necessity of using the ordinary means of avoiding danger. Thus, He led them another way.

Arthur Pink, in his most excellent book on Exodus, has penned it this way:

> "It was God Himself Who led the people round about 'the way of the wilderness of the Red Sea.' It was God's original intention that Israel *should* take exactly the route which they actually followed. Not only is this evident from the fact that the Pillar of Cloud *led* them each step of their journey to Canaan, but it was plainly intimated by the Lord to Moses *before* the exodus took place. At the very first appearing of Jehovah to His servant at Horeb, He declared, 'When thou hast brought forth the people out of Egypt ye shall serve God upon *this mountain.*' God's purpose in leading Israel to Canaan through the wilderness, instead of via the land of the Philistines was manifested in the sequel. In the first place, it was in order that His marvelous power

might be signally displayed on their behalf in bringing them safely through the Red Sea. In the second place, it was in order that Pharaoh and his hosts might be destroyed. In the third place, it was in order that they might receive Jehovah's laws in the undisturbed solitude of the desert. In the fourth place, it was in order that they might be properly organized into a Commonwealth and Church-state (Acts 7:33) prior to their entrance into and occupation of the land of Canaan. Finally, it was in order that they might be humbled, tried, and proved (Deut. 8:2-3), and the sufficiency of their God in every emergency might be fully demonstrated."[9]

We find the same principle in our day. God does not allow babes in Christ to enter into as severe a trial as those that are more mature in the Lord. *"Like as a father pitieth his children, so the LORD pitieth them that fear Him. For He knoweth our frame; He remembereth that we are dust"* (Ps. 103:13-14). Paul assures his children in the faith with these comforting words. *"There hath no temptation* (trial) *taken you but such as is common to man: but God is faithful, who will not suffer you to be tempted above that ye are able; but will with the temptation* (trial) *also make a way to escape, that ye may be able to bear it"* (1 Cor. 10:13).

ABRAHAM'S TRIALS

Consider the patriarch Abraham and his trials and notice how they increased in intensity as time passed. His first crisis came when God called him out of his country, kindred, and father's house. What did he do when called upon to obey this command? Scripture says, *"By faith Abraham, when he was called to go out into a place which he should after receive for an inheritance, obeyed; and he went out, not knowing whither he went"* (Heb. 11:8). At least in this trial of leaving his homeland, God gave him a

---

[9] Arthur W. Pink. Gleanings in Exodus. (Moody Press, Chicago. 1976) P. 104.

wonderful promise. His second crisis came in regards to his nephew Lot. He was told to separate himself from him (Gen. 13).

A more severe trial was to follow, for his hopes were set on Ishmael. He was a son dearly loved. Even though he said unto God *"O, that Ishmael might live before Thee,"* yet God said to him, *"Sarah thy wife shall bear thee a son indeed; and thou shalt call his name Isaac: and I will establish My covenant with him for an everlasting covenant, and with his seed after him"* (Gen. 17:19). Thirteen years later, Ishmael was sent away with the bondwoman to wander in the wilderness of Beer-sheba (Gen. 21:14).

Then, the final and most severe trial befell Abraham. God said unto him, *"Take now thy son, thine only son Isaac, whom thou lovest, and get thee into the land of Moriah; and offer him there for a burnt offering upon one of the mountains which I will tell thee of"* (Gen. 22:2). How wonderful that the Spirit was able to record in Hebrews 11:16; *"By faith Abraham, when he was tried, offered up Isaac: and he that had received the promises offered up his only begotten son."* The previous trials had strengthened Abraham for the greatest trial of all, the offering up of His only son Isaac. *"God led them not through the way of the land of the Philistines, although that was near; for God said, Lest peradventure the people repent when they see war, and they return to Egypt"* (Ex. 13:17). How understanding and gracious is our God!

6

THE PILLAR OF A CLOUD

"*The children of Israel went up harnessed out of the land of Egypt*" (Ex. 13:18). The word *harnessed* seems to be a derivative from *khamesh*, meaning "five." The thought is of five divisions in a military order. George Bush remarks:

> "It is certain that the original term involves the sense of 'five,' but upon what circumstance the allusion is founded it is extremely difficult to determine. Perhaps the most probable supposition is that it includes both the import of their being in some way arranged into *five* grand divisions or squadrons, and of their being well appointed and equipped for expedited traveling, going forth not in a confused and tumultuary manner like timorous fugitives, but every one duly trussed and girded up so as to cause no impediment to others, and the whole body moving on in a style of an orderly and well marshaled army. When viewed in this aspect, the spectacle must have been most imposing, and we can see with what peculiar propriety it is said, that Israel went out *with a high hand.*"[10]

The margin says, of some Bibles, "by five in a rank," but this is hardly right, for if that was the case, a rank being about three

---

10   George Bush. Exodus. (Klock & Klock Christian Publishers, Inc. Minneapolis, Minnesota. 1981 reprint) P. 162-163.

feet apart, 600,000 fighting men would have formed a procession sixty miles long! If we add to that the remainder of the host, the line would have extended, by way of the direct route, from Egypt into the land of Canaan. *"He brought them forth also with silver and gold: and there was not one feeble person among their tribes"* (Ps. 105:37). What a glorious sight that must have been!

JOSEPH'S BONES

There is something that is very touching at this point. *"And Moses took the bones of Joseph with him: for he had straitly sworn the children of Israel, saying, God will surely visit you; and ye shall carry up my bones away hence with you"* (Ex. 13:19). Moses was carrying out the command of Joseph, for you will remember he had said, *"I die: and God will surely visit you, and bring you out of this land unto the land which he sware to Abraham, to Isaac, and to Jacob. And Joseph took an oath of the children of Israel, saying, God will surely visit you, and ye shall carry up my bones from hence."* Israel had a sacred trust to carry out Joseph's desire. In spite of all the haste connected with their departure, Moses did not forget to take Joseph's bones with them. Finally, reaching the promised land, they buried the sacred remains *"in Shechem, in a parcel of ground which Jacob bought of the sons of Hamor"* (Josh. 24:32).

Joseph's insight was tremendous. He clearly saw the godless character of the Egyptian civilization. Even though at that time the Hebrews were but an insignificant handful of shepherds, he saw in them a future greatness and glory that would far surpass Egypt. He was not ashamed to call the humble dwellers in Goshen his brethren and plainly declared that he preferred a grave with them in the promised land, rather than the greatest mausoleum Egypt could erect for him.

Not only this. Solomon remarked that *"the memory of the just is blessed"* (Prov. 10:7), and how true. Joseph was held in deepest reverence and warmest respect by Israel. Can we not say the same today of men of a former generation that we held in high esteem? We carry their memory with us along life's journey. How indebted we are to those who have gone on before.

FOLLOWING MEN

Perhaps you too, have persons in your life who were of a tremendous help to you in your Christian warfare. They advised you with gracious words, and they set a godly example before you by the manner of life they lived. Such memories are to be cherished. It is good that we should still hear their voice, and be grateful for it. We, as it were, carry their bones with us.

Paul, when writing to the Hebrews exhorted them along similar lines. *"Remember them which have the rule over you, who have spoken unto you the word of God: whose faith follow, considering the end of their conversation* (Heb. 13:7). Allow me to give you the 1884 R.V. rendering of that verse. *"Remember them that had the rule over you, which spake unto you the word of God; and considering the issue of their* life (manner of life) *imitate their faith."* Can we not confess, that as the Hebrews had such men among them that passed away, we too can look back to men of a like caliber? These men were models, they were guides, and shepherds to us. These elders had strong convictions of the truth, and were faithful to it. They finished their godly course well, and they became an encouragement to us who persevere in the life of faith. We seek to attain to the standard that they displayed. We try to be followers of them.

You may say, "Is it right to follow men?" Yes! Following certain men is absolutely right. In fact, it is scriptural, for we are told here to follow their faith, which was their convictions of the truth. Did not Paul exhort the Corinthians? *"Be ye followers of me, even as I also am of Christ"* (1 Cor. 11:1). What determines whether it is right or wrong to follow a person, all depends on who that person is. If you are imitating a worldly minded Christian, it is absolutely wrong. However, if you are following a godly saint, it is definitely scriptural. Are you following the example of godly men who are now at home with the Lord?

What were they like? First of all, their lives were simple. They were not covetous, nor interested in the pleasures of this world. The sports, theaters, clubs, and other worldly activities held no place in their agenda. Their homes were modest, their clothing was conservative, they were benevolent to those in need, and they walked a plain path. When they attended conferences, they waited on the Holy Spirit to guide them as to what to speak and when to deliver their message from God. They never condoned a man-made agenda, where speakers were selected and told what subject to preach. They gave us light from the Scriptures, but were never light in their delivery. There was a soberness, yet a softness about them. Their conscience was not for sale, neither were they worried about "political correctness." They preached the word, being instant in season and out of season, faithfully reproving, rebuking, and exhorting, with all longsuffering and doctrine (2 Tim. 4:2).

THE MEMORY OF THE JUST

David L. Roy, William Warke, Archie Stewart, Oswald MacLeod, and George Graham, were men that captured my heart. They took me under their wing. They not only helped me spiritually, but also financially. They gave me solid advice. They taught me and succored me. They counseled me, and they corrected me. They showed an interest in me, and I gladly followed their faith. I feel tremendously indebted to them. God put me into their hearts, and I put them into my heart. I dearly loved them, and greatly miss them. They finished their course well and left a faith to follow. I carry their bones with me!

THE PILLAR OF A CLOUD

> *"And they took their journey from Succoth, and encamped in Etham, in the edge of the wilderness. And the LORD went before them by day in a pillar of a cloud, to lead them the way; and by night in a pillar of fire, to give them light; to go by day and night: He took*

not away the pillar of the cloud by day, nor the pillar of fire by night, from before the people" (Ex. 13:20-22).

Reading Nehemiah 9:19-20, would indicate that the cloud is a picture to us of the Holy Spirit. He is that divine Person Who is the Author of Holy Scripture, instrumental in the humanity of Christ, and the birth of the Church. He teaches, reproves, bestows gifts, makes overseers, selects and sends evangelists to His work, sheds the love of God abroad in the hearts of believers, and seals us unto the day of bodily redemption. The believer's body is His temple. He dwells within us. He makes intercession for us with groanings which cannot be uttered. He reproves the world of sin, and of righteousness, and of judgment. He is indispensable in Christian activity. Paul was quite aware that the demonstration and power of the Spirit must be manifest in his preaching, otherwise his declaration would have no effect.

Israel was to be guided by the pillar of a cloud throughout their journeys on to Canaan. Times have not changed regarding being led. Scripture states, *"For as many as are led by the Spirit of God, they are the sons of God"* (Rom. 8:14). The Pentecostal movement would try to convince people that a sinner, upon trusting Christ, must then pray for, and wait for, the indwelling of the Holy Spirit. This teaching is erroneous. Ephesians 1:13 clearly states; *"In Whom (Christ) ye also trusted, after that ye heard the word of truth, the gospel of your salvation: in Whom also after that ye believed, ye were sealed with that Holy Spirit of promise"* (Eph. 1:13). The word *"after that,"* more accurately translated is, *"upon,"* and should read like this; *"in Whom upon believing, ye were sealed with that Holy Spirit of promise."* Romans 8:9, clearly states; *"Now if any man have not the Spirit of Christ, he is none of His."* In other words, every child of God, brought into the kingdom of God by the new birth, is indwelt with the Holy Spirit of God. He did not have to pray for the Spirit to come and indwell him, nor did he have to wait for the Spirit to come. No, no! Such teaching in nonsensical. It is totally foreign to the teaching of the Scriptures. Charles Wesley had the right idea when he composed a hymn that included these words: "Soon as my all I ventured, on the atoning blood, the Holy Spirit entered, and I was born of God."

THE SPIRIT OF GOD

Some people say that the Holy Spirit is nothing more than a good *influence*. Influence? Well now, He does influence people, but let me say this, He certainly is far more than just a mere influence! He is a divine Person. He is God! You will remember that when Ananias and Sapphira lied, Peter accused them with these words; *"Ananias, why hath Satan filled thine heart to lie to the Holy Ghost? ... Thou hast not lied unto men, but unto **God**."* Notice, Peter addresses the Holy Ghost as God. The word *"Ghost"* is *"pneuma,"* and that is the same word translated *"Spirit"* in your Bible. Notice, *"And Jesus being full of the Holy Ghost (pneuma) returned from Jordan, and was led by the Spirit (pneuma) into the wilderness"* (Luke 4:1). The question arises, why did the translators translate the same word into two different English words? That's a good question, and it can be answered like this. The translators sought to provide a variety of expression in the sacred text. To be honest, the word *"Spirit"* is really more correct. So, in your Bible, when you read of the Holy Ghost, and in another portion you read of the Holy Spirit, it is the same Person.

The Spirit is called, *"the Spirit of God,"* indicating His diety. He is named, *"the Spirit of Christ,"* for He was given to us by Christ. He is termed, *"the Spirit of truth,"* for He gives the truth, establishes it, and defends it. The Scriptures also speak of Him as *"the Spirit of grace,"* simply because He is the bestower of all Christian graces seen in God's people. He is spoken of as *"the Spirit of holiness,"* for through His divine operation in the believer, sanctification in that person's life is the result. He is referred to as *"the eternal Spirit,"* for He never had a beginning, and He will never cease to be. Lastly, He is termed *"the Spirit of promise,"* for the Lord promised to send Him to His own, after He ascended back into heaven (Eph. 1:13).

EMBLEMS OF THE HOLY SPIRIT

There are emblems of the Holy Spirit worthy of notice. In John 1:32, John the Baptist beheld the Spirit descending from heaven like *a dove*, to abide on Christ. John is the only person recorded that ever saw the Holy Spirit. A dove is a bird with no gall, and one that never leaves its mate. It is a bird provided by God to the poor for sacrifice. Thus, we see the guilelessness, and faithfulness of the Spirit, coupled with the fact that through Him, the Lord offered Himself unto God as a sacrifice, for us, poor sinners (Heb. 9:14).

In John 3:8, the Lord likens Him to *the wind*. *"The wind bloweth where it listeth, and thou hearest the sound thereof, but canst not tell whence it cometh, and whither it goeth: so is every one that is born of the Spirit."* No one has ever seen the wind, but they certainly have seen the effects of it. When a strong wind blows, one can see the trees bending and the leaves flying, but he can't see the wind itself that is causing the movement. So it is with the Spirit. A person can see the effects of the Spirit of God when convicting a sinner, but He cannot see the Person behind the movement. Man cannot control or tell the wind where to blow, and man cannot dictate to the Holy Spirit where to operate and who to save. That is His prerogative. That is solely His work. Mortal man has no right to command a preacher where and what to preach. That is the Spirit's work. *"The wind bloweth where it listeth,"* not where man listeth (desires, or, determines).

With the evangelist, the Spirit selects him for the work, endowing him with the gift to preach. The Spirit sends him forth and dictates to the servant where to preach, what to preach, and how long to stay in that locality preaching. Sad to say, little is known of this sort of subjection and guidance of the Spirit in our day. Such subjection to the Spirit was seen in the apostles, and graphically exposed to us in the life of Paul, the maximal of all examples.

The force of the wind can be frightening, but the soft blowing of a summer breeze can be refreshing. The Holy Spirit can cause great spiritual storms in the life of a sinner, toppling his false foundations and bringing him down to the dust in conviction of his sins. On the other hand, He can fill the believer's heart full of the peace of God which passeth all understanding. Christ called Him *"the Comforter,"* that is, One Who draws alongside to help, and we that are saved can attest to the fact that, on many occasions, He has done that very thing to our burdened hearts. We are never told to address Him in prayer as we do to the Father and the Son, but we do thank the Father and the Son for sending Him to indwell us through our pilgrim journey.

God the Spirit was spoken of as *water* by the Lord in John 7. Water can also signify three things. (1) When something is submerged in water it is usually judgment. (2) When used internally we have the thought of spiritual blessing. (3) When water is applied externally, we have cleansing. Thus, the Spirit of God cleanses and refreshes God's people. *"Wherewithal shall a young man cleanse his way? by taking heed thereto according to Thy word"* (Ps. 119:9). And who wrote the Word? The Holy Spirit! He cleanses us through His writings. He also refreshes us through moving others on our behalf. (see 1 Cor. 16:18; 2 Cor. 7:13; 2 Tim. 1:16; and Phmn. 1:7).

Another emblem for the Holy Spirit is *fire*. The coming of the Spirit to give birth to the Church on the day of Pentecost was likened to the sound of *"a rushing mighty wind,"* and *"cloven tongues like as of fire"* (Acts 2:2-3). It was fire that consumed the books of curious arts at Ephesus (Acts 19:19). If a believer is subject to the Spirit, He will "burn up" all the undesirable things in that believer's life. The tobacco will be "burned up." The television will be consumed. The games of sport will go up in smoke. He will "set on fire" and consume all things of the world that are contrary to God. Just as fire purifies metals, so the Spirit will purify the believer. Christ *"gave Himself for us, that He might redeem us from all iniquity, and purify unto Himself* (through the Spirit) *a peculiar people, zealous of good works"* (Titus 2:14).

THE PILLAR OF A CLOUD

How comforting it is, after being in the cold for hours, to enter a cabin with a wood stove burning fervently, and put your back to it, to feel the warming influence of that stove. Fire is warming. How lovely to see believers, fervent in spirit, through the working of the Holy Spirit within them. They are the opposite to icebergs, that when floating by a village, chill the whole village. Warmth! Holy Spirit warmth! How lovely to see, how blessed to experience! The world knows nothing of it.

Apart from experiencing salvation, there is no greater experience than to be in the presence of fervent Christians, happy saints, warm believers! Isn't it a wonderful experience to sit and listen to a believer, on fire for the Lord, preach the gospel? Isn't it elevating to sit in a circle on Lord's Day morning and listen to Spirit-filled believers rise and worship the Father? I wouldn't exchange such a meeting for a private visit with the President of the United States of America, the Queen of England, or any other dignitary on earth. To me, the breaking of bread with fervent believers is the nearest place to heaven on earth! I have heard believers paying good money to visit the "holy land," and talking about it for weeks afterward. Let me tell you, I visit the holy land every Lord's Day, and it's certainly not a commercialized, guided tour of Jerusalem, but rather an entrance into the holiest by the blood of Jesus. I step into the sanctuary of God with fellow believers, and seek to gaze with wonder and awe on my blessed Lord, and to worship the Father in spirit and in truth. That to me is the crown of all experiences. It can never be surpassed!

Not only this, but fire fuses metals together. Ask any welder and he will agree. When it comes to the dispensational Church, Paul writes, *"The whole body fitly joined together"* (Eph. 4:16). When he writes the Corinthians, a local assembly, he enjoins them; *"Now I beseech you, brethren, by the name of our Lord Jesus Christ, that ye all speak the same thing, and that there be no divisions among you; but that ye be perfectly joined together in the same mind and in the same judgment"* (1 Cor. 1:10). Through the activity of the Spirit in each individual believer, He seeks to draw them together. That is seen in Matthew 18:20. *"For where two or three are gathered together in My name, there am I in the midst of them."* The words, "gathered together," is in the "passive voice, perfect participle," meaning that the people coming together are not the actors, but rather the ones being acted on by another. That other Person is none other than the Holy Spirit. It is He that draws the Lord's people together in perfect harmony and unity. Blessed be His name.

Allow me to say one more thing about fire – it illuminates. You will remember the Hebrews that were saved. The Spirit reminds them of their experience with these words: *"But call to remembrance the former days, in which, after ye were illuminated, ye endured a great fight of afflictions"* (Heb. 10:32). There was a power that opened the eyes of their understanding. They were enlightened to see that Jesus was the true Messiah, and that He had died for their sins. Who convinced them of these blessed truths? Why, none other than the Spirit of God! Paul attributes the effectiveness of his preaching of the gospel to the Thessalonians, not to any ability of his own, but to the Holy Spirit. *"For our gospel came not unto you in word only, but also in power, and in the Holy Ghost, and in much assurance"* (1 Thess. 1:5). His desire at Corinth was that the Spirit might accompany his gospel message. *"My speech and my preaching was not with enticing words of man's wisdom, but in demonstration of the Spirit and of power: That your faith should not stand in the wisdom of men, but in the power of God"* (1 Cor. 2:4-5).

Not only this, but the Holy Spirit illuminates the believers regarding divine truths. The Lord told His own, *"Howbeit when He, the Spirit of truth, is come, He will guide you into all truth"* (John 16:13). *"He will guide you."* In other words, He will make an entrance for you into the truth. He will move you toward that destination. To be led into a truth is more than just being acquainted with it. When the Spirit leads into a truth, that person is strongly affected by it. The truth is not merely placed into the head, but rather the power of it abides in the heart, shining more and more, and reflecting itself in that individual's life.

THE PILLAR OF A CLOUD

The "pillar of a cloud" was given by God to lead Israel, and to protect them from the scorching rays of a desert sun. At night, it miraculously turned into a pillar of fire to give them light for the journey, and also to keep wild beasts away when camped. Psalm 121:6 gives us another reason for this pillar of a cloud hovering over the whole camp of Israel. *"The sun shall not smite thee by day, nor the moon by night."* The moon has many strange influences over this Earth. It affects the water levels in wells, it affects the ocean's tides, and it affects the minds of some human beings. Did you ever hear that word, "lunatic?" It is a description of a person that has been abnormally affected mentally. *Luna* is the moon, and *tic* is a quirk, or an idiosyncrasy. It is a proven fact that the moon affects the minds of certain people, and when the moon is full, these people act very strangely. Policemen will verify that on a full moon they receive more domestic violence calls. Mental institutions are plagued with problems during a full moon. Nursing homes, and other institutions can say the same. In fact, it is reported that in the Far East (where Israel journeyed) the moon has a greater influence over the minds of men than in our part of the world. God graciously protected His people from becoming "moonstruck."

Let me add this before closing on this thought of strange behavior. There are movements among us today that promote strange behavior, and attribute it to the Holy Spirit. They talk about being "slain by the Spirit," and losing all control of self. It is even carried to the extent of people falling down and rolling uncontrollably. Thus, we have the term, "holy rollers." Others, losing all control, begin to babble gibberish, as if in a trance. One sensible man told me that he attended such a gathering, but only once, for when, supposedly, the Spirit got a hold of the congregation, all bedlam broke loose. He said to me, "they scared the wits out of me!" He fled from the place. Such behavior is certainly not of God, and to attribute it to the power of the Holy Spirit borders on blasphemy. It is a total disgrace to true Christianity to say the least. No, my friend, the tender Holy Spirit of grace never prompts such idiotic behavior in God's people.

Moses records: "*He took not away the pillar of the cloud by day, nor the pillar of fire by night, from before the people*" (Ex. 13:22). In the days of Ezra and Nehemiah, the Levites stood up on a scaffold and in relating Israel's history to the congregation, they mentioned the pillar of the cloud. "*Yet Thou in thy manifold mercies forsookest them not in the wilderness: the pillar of the cloud departed not from them by day, to lead them in the way; neither the pillar of fire by night, to shew them light, and the way wherein they should go*" (Neh. 9:19). Coming to the New Testament, we find the Lord giving His own a promise relating to the Holy Spirit. "*And I will pray the Father, and He shall give you another Comforter, that He may abide with you for ever*" (John 14:16).

Paul relates to the Thessalonians the activity of the Spirit stating; "*For the mystery of iniquity doth already work: only He* (the Spirit) *who now letteth* (hindereth) *will let* (hinder), *until He* (the Spirit) *be taken out of the way*" (2 Thess. 2:7). Even in Paul's day, the spirit of antichrist was raising its ugly head, and working in the world of mankind. However, the influence of the Holy Spirit in the Church (for all believers are indwelt by Him), is a hindering factor in the progression of evil. Believers, as the salt of the earth, are a hindering factor on total corruption permeating society. The influence of the Spirit in the believers has a hindering factor on the complete breaking out of lawlessness in a corrupt world. However, at the rapture, His restraining influence through believers will be removed, simply because the believers will be removed and caught away to meet the Lord in the air. In that respect, the Spirit of God will be taken out of the way.

When the believers of this dispensation are removed, all lawlessness will break out, and this world will enter into a time of great tribulation. During this period, the Spirit will work through the 144,000 Jewish missionaries mentioned in Revelation 7. They will be sealed for their work of evangelizing. We, of the Church age, have the guarantee that the Spirit will be with us throughout our pilgrimage here, just as Israel had the guarantee that the pillar of the cloud would not be taken away from them. Thank God for His influence among us and for His guidance for us as we journey on to our promised inheritance!

THE GLORY OF THE LORD

As we investigate this pillar of a cloud, many intriguing things come to view. At night there seemed to be an outward rendering of the outer body of the cloud, thus revealing an interior glowing splendor. This splendor, appearing at night was termed, *"the glory of the LORD."* When God displayed His displeasure, or when He would strike them with an awful display of His majesty, this Glory would be manifested. Such was the case in the giving of the Law from Sinai, and also when Aaron's sons, Nabab and Abihu sinned. Notice the following references regarding the displeasure of God and a manifestation of His glory.

> *"And Moses spake unto Aaron, say unto all the congregation of the children of Israel, come near before the LORD: for He hath heard your murmurings. And it came to pass, as Aaron spake unto the whole congregation of the children of Israel, that they looked toward the wilderness, and, behold, the glory of the LORD appeared in the cloud"* (Ex. 16:9-10).

> *"But all the congregation bade stone them with stones. And the glory of the LORD appeared in the tabernacle of the congregation before all the children of Israel"* (Num. 14:10).

> *"And Korah* (in the attitude of rebellion) *gathered all the congregation against them unto the door of the tabernacle of the congregation: and the glory of the LORD appeared unto all the congregation"* (Num. 16:19).

> *"And it came to pass, when the congregation was gathered against Moses and against Aaron, that they looked toward the tabernacle of the congregation: and, behold, the cloud covered it, and the glory of the LORD appeared"* (Num. 16:42).

When the people gathered themselves together against Moses and against Aaron, *"Moses and Aaron went from the presence of the assembly unto the door of the tabernacle of the congregation, and they fell upon their faces: and the glory of the LORD appeared unto them"* (Num. 20:6).

Walking into the Book of Leviticus, we discover numerous offerings being presented to the LORD. A priesthood has been initiated, and a sanctuary for God established. It was a wonderful day. Moses lifted up his hand toward the people and blessed them and came down from offering the sin offering, the burnt offering, and the peace offerings. Then we read,

> *"And Moses and Aaron went into the tabernacle of the congregation, and came out, and blessed the people: and the glory of the LORD appeared unto all the people. And there came a fire out from before the LORD, and consumed upon the altar the burnt offering and the fat: which when all the people saw, they shouted, and fell on their faces"* (Lev. 9:23-24).

Following this joyous occasion, came a very sobering and grieving event. When Nadab and Abihu offered strange fire before the Lord, God's displeasure was immediately manifested when there went out fire from the LORD, and devoured them, and they died before the LORD.

How awesome the sight of the glory of the Lord at Sinai. *"So terrible was the sight, that Moses said, I exceedingly fear and quake"* (Heb. 12:21). On that occasion when God gave the Law, there was thunders, lightnings and a thick cloud on the mount, and the voice of the trumpet exceeding loud, so much so, that all the people trembled.

THE SHEKINAH

From the record of these events, it would seem that the majestic pillar of cloud served as the Shekinah, which was the visible

THE PILLAR OF A CLOUD

representative of Jehovah, Who graciously dwelt in the midst of His redeemed people. Exodus 13:21 reads: *"And the LORD went before them by day in a pillar of a cloud."* It is interesting to note that the Targum reads: *"The Glory of the Shekinah went before them."* In Arabic, it reads: *"The Angel of the Lord went before them."* The last rendering is confirmed by Moses, for he writes in Exodus 14:19: *"And the angel of God, which went before the camp of Israel, removed and went behind them; and the pillar of the cloud went from before their face, and stood behind them."* So we see that what is called the *"pillar of a cloud,"* in one clause of a verse, is called *the "angel of God"* in another. "It appears that the term 'Angel' is employed to denote any kind of agency, personal or impersonal, by which the divine will or working is made manifest."[11]

The visible phenomenon of the burning bush is called "the angel of the LORD" which is another name for the *Shekinah*. (Ex. 3:2). In Exodus 23:20 we read, *"Behold, I send an Angel before thee, to keep thee in the way, and to bring thee into the place which I have prepared."* This appears to be the visible Shekinah in the pillar of the cloud. We find reference to this in Isaiah 63:9. *"In all their affliction He was afflicted, and the angel of His presence saved them: in His love and in His pity He redeemed them; and He bare them, and carried them all the days of old."*

It would seem that this pillar of a cloud was to Israel the Angel-Jehovah, the God of their nation. Gazing upward to that awesome sight above their heads was the visible embodiment of the God that brought them up out of Egypt. Jehovah was ever looking down upon His people. No movement ever missed His all-seeing eye. This thought is verified with what we read in Exodus 14:24. *"And it came to pass, that in the morning watch the LORD looked unto the host of the Egyptians through the pillar of fire and of the cloud, and troubled the host of the Egyptians."*

The word *"LORD"* would convey to the ancient readers of the Hebrew text the idea of the visible phenomenon through

---
11 George Bush. Exodus. (Klock & Klock Christian Publishers, Inc. Minneapolis, Minnesota. 1981 reprint). P.165.

which all the divine attributes were manifested. Notice how Moses relates to this in his account.

> "The LORD your God which goeth before you, He shall fight for you, according to all that he did for you in Egypt before your eyes ... Who went in the way before you, to search you out a place to pitch your tents in, in fire by night, to shew you by what way ye should go, and in a cloud by day" (Deut. 1:30, 33).

The pillar of the cloud was also a visible symbol of the voice of God. You will remember the psalmist relates with these words: *"He spake unto them in the cloudy pillar: they kept His testimonies, and the ordinance that He gave them"* (Ps. 99:7). Another remarkable passage states: *"And it came to pass, as Moses entered into the tabernacle, the cloudy pillar descended, and stood at the door of the tabernacle, and the LORD talked with Moses"* (Ex. 33:9). Notice that *"cloudy pillar,"* and *"LORD,"* were used synonymously. The cloud of the Shekinah was the divine means of communication to the covenant people. When the Shekinah was enthroned within the sanctuary, the holiest of holies, it was from there that the voice of the Lord was uttered.

CHRIST THE WORD

Coming to Christ in John's gospel, we discover sublime and wonderful truths concerning that One Who was termed, "the Word." John identifies Christ with the Jehovah (the oracular presence), the Shekinah of the Old Testament, stating: *"In the beginning was the Word, and the Word was with God, and the Word was God"* (John 1:1). It has been suggested that "the beginning" refers to the former dispensation. Consequently, under the former dispensation *"was the Word,"* the law-giving Shekinah. Following this, John states, *"and the Word was with God, and the Word was God."* This is parallel to what Moses says. *"Behold, I send an Angel before thee ... Beware of Him, and obey His voice, provoke Him not; for He will not pardon your transgressions: for My name is in Him"* (Ex. 23:20-21). All divine attributes were associated with, and dwelling in, this symbol that caused a pronounced stimulation of the senses.

John continues: *"And the Word was made flesh and dwelt among us."* The time had finally come when the symbol of the former economy became very evident in human flesh, as the incarnate Jehovah tabernacled among us. Whenever His Person was seen, they beheld His moral glory, but I wonder if there is not a deeper meaning in John's exclamation: *"(And we beheld His glory, the glory as of the only begotten of the Father,) full of grace and truth"* (John 1:14). John was an eyewitness on the mount of transfiguration, when there was a momentary laying aside of the veil of His flesh, revealing the Shekinah glory of His Godhead. How wonderful! The incarnate Saviour was none other than the Jehovah of the previous dispensation, Who was manifested in the pillar of the cloud! The title Jehovah, in this connection, belongs to Christ. Peter, on the mount of transfiguration, manifested his knowledge of a former dispensation, that in that former time, the Shekinah was associated with the tabernacle. Thus, when that Shekinah was manifested in His Lord, he proposed erecting a tabernacle to receive the Shekinah.

Not only was the cloudy pillar a type of the Holy Spirit, but I trust, that through this exposition, you will be convinced as well that the pillar of the cloud was also a picture of our Lord Jesus Christ, the living Word.

> *"And the LORD spake unto Moses, saying, Speak unto the children of Israel, that they turn and encamp before Pihahiroth, between Migdol and the sea, over against Baalzephon: before it shall ye encamp by the sea"* (Ex. 14:1-2).

"Pihahiroth" means, *"Place of liberty."* Israel was now enjoying their liberty from slavery in Egypt. *"Migdol"* means, *"tower,"* or *"fortress."* It was in such a fashion that God had demonstrated Himself to them. *"Baalzephon"* means, *"Lord of the North,"* which indicates judgment. God was about to show His almighty power in judgment on Pharaoh and his mighty army.

Israel had gone out with "an high hand." Egypt was glad to see them leave. Indeed, they thrust them out (Ex. 11:1). They left their slavery with power and dignity. Jubilance must have prevailed in the camp. They were finally rid of their bondage, free, and redeemed by Jehovah. They had left with the treasures of Egypt, and their flocks and herds surrounded them. Egypt was now behind them and the vast expanse of freedom lay before them. The scene around this overjoyed throng must have been picturesque, as another writer puts it, "the desert itself would have been covered at this season with a thin coat of verdure and thickly jeweled with bright and fragrant flowers."[12]

A STRANGE TURN

In the midst of their abounding happiness, suddenly the voice of God is heard by Moses. *"Speak unto the children of Israel, that they turn."* This particular word *"turn,"* means to *"turn aside."* The direct course would have been due east till they had rounded the upper extremity of the gulf. However, they are now told to deviate from the direct course, which to Israel must have been quite a surprise.

Anyone knowing the topography of that region would consider such a move very strange, and perhaps even threatening. Why would Moses lead 2,500,000 people to a place where they would be hemmed in with mountains surrounding them and the Red Sea before them? A careful reader will find the answer in Exodus 14:3-4. Notice the inspired text. *"For Pharaoh will say of the children of Israel, They are entangled in the land, the wilderness hath shut them in. And I will harden Pharaoh's heart, that he shall follow after them; and I will be honoured upon Pharaoh, and upon all his host; that the Egyptians may know that I am the LORD."*

God was setting a trap for His ultimate and final dealings with Egypt. That trap would also completely free His people

---

12 George Rawlinson. The Pulpit Commentary, Exodus. (Hendrickson Publishers, Peabody, MA). P.315.

from the clutches of the enemy that had held them in bondage so many years.

GOD INDUCING PHARAOH

The LORD was moving Israel to a precarious position to provide Pharaoh an additional inducement to pursue them to his own annihilation. It had been told Pharaoh that the people had "fled." Certainly he knew that they had left Egypt for a three-day journey into the wilderness, but the report came that they were going even farther away from Egypt. They had *fled!* Who brought this report is not recorded, but perhaps some of the mixed multitude among Israel may have turned back to give the report as a result of the nation's seemingly unwise turn toward the south at Etham. Pharaoh and his people's heart turned. They had been glad to be rid of God's people, but having reflected on various issues, they said, *"Why have we done this, that we have let Israel go from serving us?"* (Ex.14:5). Egypt had lost a tremendous population, perhaps 2,500,000, besides the mixed multitude that had gone with Israel. Among that population were skilled workers, valuable to the economy of Egypt. Pharaoh and his host were smarting with injured pride and desperate for vengeance. They had lost their silver and their gold to these fleeing people. They had lost their firstborn because of Israel. Their land lay in ruins because of them. The proud Egyptians were totally humiliated. Why had they let Israel go?

GOD'S TRAP FOR PHARAOH

In Pharaoh's mind, there must be a recovery of his nation. He had been weakened, but his pride convinced him that he must recover his power and be acknowledged as a mighty monarch over his people. To Pharaoh, it was delightful news to hear that Israel had entangled itself in the wilderness. The word *"entangled"* is also translated *"perplexed"* in Esther 3:15. Israel's sudden turn led Pharaoh to conclude that they had lost their way, and that they didn't know what to do. This fully convinced and prompted him to move against them. He may have even thought that it was his vain gods that had placed Israel in such a vulnerable position for an attack. He thought that the time had come to recover all, and thus to be hailed by his nation as a mighty victor. The poor man, little did he know that the divine hand of Almighty was setting the trap for his total destruction, and the elimination of his mighty army.

God had led His people where trouble would assail them. He allows the same in the Christian's experiences. However, there is a divine reason for it, for in the trial, He manifests to us His grace and power, which otherwise we may not have experienced.

Pharaoh's forces were mustered. Six hundred chosen chariots. These vehicles of war were drawn by two horses and were ordinarily occupied by two men, the warrior and the charioteer. It must have taken Pharaoh a day to hear of Israel's journey from Etham, and at least another day for him to gather his army, and then four days to march from Tanis to Pi-hahiroth. Jewish tradition relates that Israel crossed the Red Sea on the night of the twenty-first of Nisan (Abib).

Because of the humiliations they had experienced, and their tremendous loss financially and industrially, hatred burned in the Egyptian's hearts to Israel. They were eager, and felt just, in trying to recover these "fugitives" that they had let go. The Egyptians would be rejoicing when they viewed Pharaoh's glorious cavalcade gallop off into the distance in hot pursuit of Israel. Israel, unprepared and unaccustomed to war, would be weak, and ill fortified to even dream of resisting this splendidly-equipped host of warriors. Pharaoh had the utmost confidence that he had Israel securely in his grasp. There was no doubt in any Egyptian mind that the invasion would be a total success. However, they never suspected that Jehovah, the LORD of hosts, the God of Israel, was looking down, and setting the trap that would annihilate all Egyptian enterprise in driving God's redeemed back into Egypt.

THE CHRISTIAN'S SPIRITUAL CONFLICTS

Can we not relate all of this to ourselves today? The experiences of the Christian life are very similar to Israel's experiences. With a *"high hand"* the LORD brought us out of bondage, but that was not the end of our spiritual conflicts. Being delivered from the power of Satan, we soon found out that various attempts were made by the powers of darkness to reassert their dominion over us. The world with its false ways sought to get its grip upon our souls again. Even our own deceitful heart plagued us, some with doubts of our salvation, and others with unclean thoughts.

With some, even our old companions sought to draw us back to their companionship and way of life. Old habits that we thought we had broken, marched back again seeking for the mastery. With many, temptations come in floods. Like Pharaoh and his chariots, they march upon us and fill us with disquietness and distress.

Alas, some succumb to the enemy and fall back into their former way of life, proving that they never became the possessors of divine life. With the true Christian, even though a babe in Christ, God will deliver him, and his victory over the enemy will undoubtedly prove him to be a genuine child of God.

These thoughts are reflected in the parable of the sower, are they not? As he sowed the seed (God's word), some fell upon a rock. The Lord goes on to explain this with these words. *"They on the rock are they, which, when they hear, receive the word with joy; and these have no root, which for a while believe, and in time of temptation* ('adversity, testing') *fall away"* (Luke 8:13). Ah yes! He had a profession, but the Lord said, *"Whosoever hath not* (salvation), *from him shall be taken even that which he seemeth to have"* (his profession) (Luke 8:18). His faith is dead, not being accompanied by Christian works (Jas. 2:17, 20, 26).

ISRAEL "TRAPPED"

Israel was hemmed in. There was no way of escape, for Pharaoh's army filled the gap by which Israel had entered to encamp on the shores of the Red Sea. Some writers believe that Pharaoh came upon the encamped Israelites through the valley of Bedea, in the plain at the mouth of which they were encamped. However, it is not likely that he would take a course that would deprive him of his purpose to drive the "escaped" nation back into Egypt. If he had come through the valley of Bedea, it would have given Israel the opportunity to escape his onslaught by the way they had entered. Pharaoh was well acquainted with the topography of that land. He came upon Israel the same way they had come, thus shutting up the door of escape. If they had fled from before him, their only route could have been through the valley of Bedea, back to Egypt, before Pharaoh's host. Pharoah had two options: First, to drive them through the valley of Bedea straight back to Egypt, or destroy them if they dared to resist. The Egyptians were satisfied that they had secured their prey, and that it was entirely impossible for Israel to escape. With this in mind and Israel firmly secured in their trap, they felt the liberty to encamp for the night to rest and gain strength for the actual capture of their prey in the morning. Little did they know that this was their last night on earth!

THE CRY OF DESPAIR

As for Israel, impassable mountains surrounded them and the sea lay before them, so what did they do? There are various thoughts on this subject. Let us read the text. *"And when Pharaoh drew nigh, the children of Israel lifted up their eyes, and, behold, the Egyptians marched after them; and they were sore afraid: and the children of Israel cried out unto the LORD"* (Ex. 14:10). The difference of thought is, what kind of a cry was this? Was it a cry for help, or was it a cry of despair? Well, my dear reader, I think that the next verse answers the question. *"And they said unto Moses, because there were no graves in Egypt, hast thou taken us away to die in the wilderness? Wherefore hast thou dealt thus with us, to carry us forth out of Egypt?"* (Ex. 14:11). The sight of their former masters approaching them with a vengeance drove them to despair, and they cried out their complaint. How quickly the joy of their salvation disappeared. Filled with terror, they are brought down and weakened more than ever.

MOSES' MEEKNESS

Israel's attitude changes. They accuse Moses. With their reproach, they add sarcasm. I am sure that they inflicted pain upon Moses with their speech. Their sharp words were like barbed arrows, not easily worked out of the memory. Consider their injustice. Their remarks were false and exaggerated. Moses seemed to manifest pitiful consideration for these unthankful people. There is no retaliation on his part. Truly, he was the meekest man in all the earth. My heart goes out to him. He had given up a luxurious life in the palace of Pharaoh's daughter. He had sacrificed one third of his life in the backside of the desert, living a nomad life, tending a few sheep. He had forsaken the pomp, glory, and riches of Egypt, and had put his life on the line standing before Pharaoh for God, and now this! The people that he loved had no mercy on him. It was the LORD Who had brought them to this hemmed in position, but they had their eyes off of God and rudely blamed Moses for their distressing position. We read of Moses crying to the LORD on this occasion. He immediately replies to the people, *"Fear ye not, stand still, and see the salvation of the LORD, which He will shew to you to day: for the Egyptians whom ye have seen to day, ye shall see them again no more for ever. The LORD shall fight for you, and ye shall hold your peace"* (Ex. 14:13-14).

In other words, he tells them to stand firm in their minds and not to stagger. Do not waver! He notifies them that they will hold their peace, simply meaning that they would cease all action. They would do nothing. The same thought is also in Revelation 8:1. *"And when he had opened the seventh seal, there was silence in heaven about the space of half an hour,"* simply denoting that there was a respite from action. Are not these injunctions similar to the troubled soul seeking salvation? *"But to him that worketh not, but believeth on Him that justifieth the ungodly, his faith is counted for righteousness"* (Rom. 4:5). *"For by grace are ye saved through faith; and that not of yourselves: it is the gift of God: Not of works, lest any man should boast"* (Eph. 2:8-9).

Moses prayed. Let me give you another person's thoughts.

"Moses's silent prayer prevailed more with God, than Israel's loud out-cries. But is God displeased with Moses for praying? No, he asks this question, Wherefore criest thou unto Me? Wherefore shouldst thou press thy petition any farther, when it is already granted? Moses has something else to do besides praying. He is to command the hosts of Israel. Speak to them that they go forward. Some think Moses had prayed, not so much for their deliverance, he was assured of that; as for the pardon of their murmurings, and God's ordering them to go forward was an intimation of the pardon. Moses bid them stand still and expect orders from God: and now orders are given. They thought they must have been directed either to the right hand, or to the left; no, saith God, speak to them to go forward, directly to the sea-side; as if there had lain a fleet of transport ships ready for them to embark in. Let the children of Israel go as far as they can upon dry ground, and then God will divide the sea. The same power could have congealed the waters for them to pass over, but infinite wisdom chose rather to divide the waters for them to pass through, for that way of salvation is always pitched upon which is most humbling."[13]

---

13 John Wesley. Notes on Exodus 14. (MacSword, Bible study software for Mac OS-10).

John Wesley's comment reminds me of Solomon's statement relative to various times in Ecclesiastes 3:1. *"To everything there is a season, and a time to every purpose under the heaven."* There is a time to be still and pray, but there is also a time in which to arise and be going! God as much as said to His servant, "Moses, cease praying and get busy and speak to these people that they go forward!"

PREACHING IN A BALL FIELD

I remember an occasion in a small coal mining village. My gospel tent was pitched at the end of their park's ball field. My travel trailer was beside the tent. It was a beautiful morning and I was on my knees in prayer, when suddenly, there was a banging on my door. Immediately, my praying ceased, and there stood a Roman Catholic resident who happened to be a photographer for a nearby city's newspaper. Three school busses had pulled into the park, full of children working for the state on a clean up program. This photographer happened to know the manager of this operation, and he had persuaded the man to sit about 60 young folks in a circle on the pitcher's mound for me to preach five minutes to them. Answering his pounding on my trailer door, he informed me of the situation. Did I say, "Well, this is great, let me pray about it for awhile?" Most certainly not! I quickly put on a snap-on tie, grabbed my Bible, and was out on the pitcher's mound ready to go. There was no preparation, but God knew the circumstances. It was an instant opportunity!

The state was paying the children the minimum wage and multiplied by sixty or more, five minutes amounted to a fair amount of money in the manager's eyes. What a golden opportunity. I had a captive audience of young minds, pliable and able to absorb. I thought that the simpler the better, so one text was read. *"This is a faithful saying, and worthy of all acceptation, that Christ Jesus came into the world to save sinners; of whom I am chief"* (1 Tim. 1:15).

After my allotted five minutes, the fire was just starting to glow. It was a wonderful opening and experience. Finally, after twenty-five minutes we finished and thanked them all for listening so intently. One more thing was done before they went back to work; each one was given a beautiful framed gospel plaque.

Seeing that this event took place in a ball park on the pitcher's mound, the newspaper placed the following caption over the photograph of me preaching; "Evangelist preaches a sermon on the mound." However, before the newspaper went to print, I was shown the proof, and of course had the headline immediately changed.

DARKNESS AND LIGHT

"And the angel of God, which went before the camp of Israel, removed and went behind them; and the pillar of the cloud went from before their face, and stood behind them: And it came between the camp of the Egyptians and the camp of Israel; and it was a cloud and darkness to them, but it gave light by night to these: so that the one came not near the other all the night" (Ex. 14:19-20).

God now begins to move in a personal way. What astonishment must have been theirs when this unique movement was observed by the fearful nation. The result of a time element in preparing the Red Sea with a strong east wind necessitated the protective movement of the cloud, which in reality, was the angel of God, the LORD Himself. It is not that the LORD appeared as an angel, for the writer to the Hebrews clearly states, *"For verily he took not on Him the nature of angels; but he took on Him the seed of Abraham"* (Heb. 2:16). The reason for employing the word "angel" has already been previously expounded in this book.

The glory of the LORD had become their safeguard. The

Targum reads: "It was a cloud half lucid and half dark; the light gave light unto Israel, and the darkness gave darkness unto the Egyptians." What a difference the cloud made in the two camps! Consider the two great camps of the human race. Those saved and dwelling as the children of light, in spiritual light, and those not saved, dwelling in darkness. Peter exclaims: *"But ye are a chosen generation, a royal priesthood, an holy nation, a peculiar people; that ye should shew forth the praises of Him who hath called you out of darkness into His marvellous light"* (1 Pet. 2:9).

SEPARATION

The cloud also afforded protection through separation. *"The one came not near the other all the night."* Christians are not like Roman Catholic monks, dwelling in isolation from society, in monasteries, or like nuns shut up in convents from the world. Nothing of the sort! Such activities run contrary to the teachings of Holy Scripture. Our Lord sets the example. *"This Man receiveth sinners, and eateth with them"* (Luke 15:2). At the same time, He is spoken of as *"separate from sinners." "For such an High Priest became us, Who is holy, harmless, undefiled, separate from sinners, and made higher than the heavens"* (Heb. 7:26). That word, *"separate from sinners,"* is a perfect participle, which indicates "a present condition resultant from a past act."

In His ministry on earth, our blessed Lord ate with sinners, yet was separate from them in all their ways. We, as the people of God, should emulate Paul who said, *"I am made all things to all men, that I might by all means save some"* (1 Cor. 9:22). Does that sound like a man shut up in some isolated monastery? Most certainly not! Paul mingled with people, associated himself with people, with the object of winning them to Christ. Yet, he was separate from them in their worldly ways. There was no worldly fraternization, and no indulging in their sinful pleasures. There was nothing of that sort, neither should there be anything of that nature seen with us. We may be in the world, but we are certainly not of the world. May the Lord, the Spirit, impress upon our hearts the importance of winning souls, yet the responsibility of being separate from their ungodly ways. The cloud separated the two camps, and protected His people from the enemy. Our separation is a great factor in keeping us from falling into the hands of the enemy, thus losing our testimony.

7

CROSSING THE RED SEA

The time had finally come! Israel had experienced *salvation* through the blood of the Passover lamb, and now they would experience *separation* from Egypt through the Red Sea. They were about to become pilgrims in the wilderness, sanctified unto the LORD. Jewish tradition tells us that it was April 21, when *"Moses stretched out his hand over the sea, and the LORD made the sea go back by a strong east wind all that night, and made the sea dry land, and the waters were divided"* (Ex. 14:21).

This took place seven days after a full moon, consequently, there was no light before them, just the illumination of the cloud behind them. All night, the east wind blew, not only parting the waters, but also drying the sea bed, making the passage a virtual highway! They had been told to stand still and see the salvation of the LORD, and now the command was to go forward! *"And the children of Israel went into the midst of the sea upon the dry ground: and the waters were a wall unto them on their right hand, and on their left"* (Ex. 14:22).

Contrary to all the laws of liquids, the waters were divided and stood erect on either side like walls of solid ice! Moses, in his song of victory, states: *"With the blast* (wind) *of Thy nostrils the waters were gathered together, the floods stood upright as an heap, and the depths were congealed in the heart of the sea"* (Ex. 15:8). Ask any chemist how water can be congealed, and he will tell you that the only way to congeal water is to freeze it, thus turning it into ice. Moses and Aaron advanced together into the unknown, and Israel followed. The psalmist describes it thus.

> *"Who is so great a God as our God? Thou art the God that doest wonders: Thou hast declared Thy strength among the people. Thou hast with Thine arm redeemed Thy people, the sons of Jacob and Joseph. Selah. The waters saw Thee, O God, the waters saw Thee; they were afraid: the depths also were troubled. The clouds poured out water: the skies sent out a sound: thine arrows also went abroad. The voice of Thy thunder was in the heaven: the lightnings lightened the world: the earth trembled and shook. Thy way is in the sea, and Thy path in the great waters, and Thy footsteps are not known. Thou leddest Thy people like a flock by the hand of Moses and Aaron"* (Ps. 77:13-20).

It would seem that the very forces of nature were greatly disturbed on this memorable occasion. That step into the unknown placed the nation in the "Hall of Faith," in Hebrews 11:29. *"By faith they passed through the Red sea as by dry land: which the Egyptians assaying to do were drowned."* On that occasion they were *"all baptized unto* (into) *Moses in the cloud and in the sea"* (I Cor. 10:2), meaning that they were placed into the covenant of which Moses was the mediator. They were brought under obligation of acting according to its precepts.

BAPTIZED INTO CHRIST

We have a similar situation concerning ourselves as Paul relates in Romans 6:3-7.

> *"Know ye not, that so many of us as were baptized **into** Jesus Christ were baptized into His death? Therefore we are buried with Him by baptism into death: that like as Christ was raised up from the dead by the glory of the Father, even so we also should walk in newness of life. For if we have been planted together in the likeness of His death, we shall be also in the likeness of His resurrection: Knowing this, that our old man is crucified with Him, that the body of*

sin might be destroyed, that henceforth we should not serve sin. For he that is dead is freed from sin."

SIN, DEATH, AND SLAVERY

The baptism to which Paul is referring is not by water. One is not placed *into* the body of Christ by water baptism. Paul, in Romans 6, is relating to the saints their present position as being no longer slaves (servants) to sin. They were rather now positioned as slaves (servants) to Christ. By the operation of the Holy Spirit, upon conversion, they were baptized *into* Christ! Sin is personified as a master. We, upon being put *into* Christ, immediately died to sin. Consequently, sin no longer has dominion over us. The Christian is inseparably joined to Christ. We have been baptized into His death. In other words, we died with Christ. When He died unto sin on the Cross, sin consequently had no more dominion over Him (v. 9-10). The only way sin had dominion over Him, was for Him to allow that to take place, by becoming a sin offering for us. *"For He* (God) *hath made Him* (Jesus) *to be sin* (a sin offering) *for us, Who knew no sin; that we might be made the righteousness of God in Him"* (2 Cor. 5:21). He placed Himself under its penalty. Now that He has paid the price, He no longer has anything to do with sin. The work is finished! *"Death hath no more dominion over Him. For in that He died, He died unto sin once: but in that He liveth, He liveth unto God"* (Rom. 6:9-10).

What has happened to Christ in this chapter, has also happened to us. He died unto sin – we died unto sin! He liveth unto God – we are alive unto God! All of this has taken place as a result of being baptized *into* Him by the Holy Spirit.

Paul goes on to say, *"For if* (since) *we have been planted together in the likeness of His death, we shall be also in the likeness of His resurrection* (Rom. 6:5). That statement relates to the present time, not necessarily the future. Notice verse ten and eleven. *"For in that He died, He died unto sin once: but in that He liveth, He liveth unto God. Likewise reckon ye also yourselves to be dead indeed unto sin, but alive unto God through Jesus Christ our Lord."* There it is in a nutshell. We have been planted together, that is, grafted, in union with Him, in the likeness (not identical) of His death. He died to sin on the Cross, and we died to sin upon trusting Him; not identical to Christ, but a likeness, for certainly we didn't actually die on a Cross as He did.

RESURRECTION

Having established this truth, we then see that we are also in the likeness of His resurrection! He rose physically from the tomb and now death has no more dominion over Him. He now lives unto God and is in a new sphere. He has been received back into heaven and crowned with glory and honor! The same has happened to us, in a likeness. We too have nothing more to do with sin. Ephesians 2:5-6 is mercilessly clear on the subject. *"Even when we were dead in sins, hath quickened us together with Christ, (by grace ye are saved;) And hath raised us up together, and made us sit together in heavenly places in Christ Jesus."* In this profound statement, we have the *"likeness of His resurrection."* As stated before, everything that happened to Christ in Romans 6, has happened to us!

Israel was baptized into Moses their mediator, introducing them into a covenant, therefore establishing a unique relationship with Moses and their God. We have been baptized into Christ our Mediator, thus placing us into a new covenant.

At this point, let me quote Arthur Pink regarding the crossing of the sea.

> *"'By faith they passed through the Red Sea as by dry land'* (Heb. 11:29). From this it is very clear that the waters of the Red Sea did not begin to divide until the feet of the Israelites came to their very brink, otherwise they would have crossed by sight, and not 'by faith.' Equally clear is it that the sea was not divided throughout at once. As

another has said, 'It does not require faith to begin a journey when I can see all the way through; but to begin when I can merely see the first step, this is faith. The sea opened as Israel moved forward, so that every fresh step they needed to be cast upon God. Such was the path along which the redeemed of the Lord moved, under His own directing hand.'"

First of all, let me say that I disagree with this explanation. The reasons are manifold. (1) Israel was headed toward the east, and the wind was blowing from the east, which meant that they were heading toward the source of the wind. This meant that the waters were being divided from the east toward the west. Consequently, when Israel stepped into the bed of the sea, it had been completely opened from the east coast on to the west coast where they were encamped. (2) It took the wind *"all that night"* to turn the muck of the sea bed into dry land. (3) Apparently, the wind was so violent as to blow apart the waters. If that wind was at their back, opening the waters before them as they stepped along, what would prevent them from being blown into those opening waters? (4) Since when does it not take faith to step into a sea bottom, knowing that on each side, contrary to nature, there was a wall of water at least eighty four feet high? To walk twelve miles through such circumstances would indeed take faith.

Another writer has put the crossing this way. I leave it for your consideration.

> "'*The Lord caused the sea to go back.*' That part of the sea over which the Israelites passed was, according to Mr. Bruce and other travellers, about *four leagues* across, and therefore might easily be crossed in one night. In the dividing of the sea, *two* agents appear to be employed, though the effect produced can be attributed to neither. By stretching out the rod, the waters were *divided*; by the blowing of the vehement, ardent, east

wind, the *bed* of the sea was dried. It has been observed, that in the place where the Israelites are supposed to have passed, the water is about *fourteen fathoms* or *twenty-eight yards* deep: had the wind mentioned here been strong enough, naturally speaking, to have divided the waters, it must have blown in one narrow track, and continued blowing in the direction in which the Israelites passed; and a wind sufficient to have raised a mass of water *twenty-eight* yards deep and *twelve* miles in length, out of its bed, would necessarily have blown the whole *six hundred thousand* men away, and utterly destroyed them and their cattle. I therefore conclude that the east wind, which was ever remarked as a *parching*, burning wind, was used *after* the division of the waters, merely to *dry the bottom*, and render it passable. For an account of the hot drying winds in the east, see Clarke on Gen. 8:1.

God ever puts the highest honour on his instrument, *nature,* and where *it* can act, he ever employs it. No natural agent could divide these waters, and cause them to stand as a *wall* upon the right hand and upon the left; therefore, God did it by his own sovereign power. When the waters were thus divided, there was no need of a miracle to dry the bed of the sea and make it passable; therefore, the strong desiccating east wind was brought, which soon accomplished this object. In this light, I suppose the text should be understood. '*And the waters* were *a wall unto them on their right and on their left*' (v. 22). This verse demonstrates that the passage was miraculous.

Some have supposed that the Israelites had passed through, favoured by an extraordinary *ebb*, which *happened* at that time to be produced by a strong wind, which *happened* just then to blow! Had this been the case, there could not have been waters *standing on the right hand and on the left*; much less could those waters, contrary to every law of fluids, have stood as *a wall* on either side while the Israelites passed through, and then *happen* to become obedient to the laws of gravitation when the Egyptians entered in! An infidel may deny the revelation in toto, and from such, we expect nothing better; but to hear those who profess to believe this to be a Divine revelation endeavouring to prove that the passage of the Red Sea *had nothing miraculous in it*, is really intolerable. Such a mode of interpretation requires a miracle to make itself credible. Poor infidelity! How miserable and despicable are thy shifts![14]

Before continuing on this subject, let me insert what God said about the crossing of the Red Sea.

> *"For we have heard how the LORD dried up the water of the Red sea for you, when ye came out of Egypt; and what ye did unto the two kings of the Amorites, that were on the other side Jordan, Sihon and Og, whom ye utterly destroyed"* (Josh. 2:10).

> *"For the LORD your God dried up the waters of Jordan from before you, until ye were passed over, as the LORD your God did to the Red sea, which He dried up from before us, until we were gone over"* (Josh. 4:23).

> *"He turned the sea into dry land: they went through the flood on foot: there did we rejoice in Him"* (Ps. 66:6).

> *"Thou didst divide the sea by Thy strength: Thou brakest the heads of the dragons in the waters"* (Ps. 74:13).

---

14   Clark. MacSword, <u>Notes on Exodus 14</u> (Bible study software for Mac OS-10).

"He rebuked the Red sea also, and it was dried up: so He led them through the depths, as through the wilderness" (Ps. 106:9).

"To Him which divided the Red sea into parts: for His mercy endureth for ever" (Ps. 136:13).

"Then He remembered the days of old, Moses, and His people, saying, Where is He that brought them up out of the sea with the shepherd of His flock? where is He that put His Holy Spirit within him? That led them by the right hand of Moses with His glorious arm, dividing the water before them, to make Himself an everlasting name? That led them through the deep, as an horse in the wilderness, that they should not stumble?" (Isa. 63:11-13).

"Moreover, brethren, I would not that ye should be ignorant, how that all our fathers were under the cloud, and all passed through the sea" (1 Cor. 10:1).

"By faith they passed through the Red sea as by dry land" (Heb. 11:29).

Egypt was desperate to recover its prey. One wonders if they were in their right mind. Excitement must have prevailed, and logic was thrown to the wind. Israel was escaping! They must be captured at any cost! Thus Moses records; *"And the Egyptians pursued, and went in after them to the midst of the sea, even all Pharaoh's horses, his chariots, and his horsemen"* (Ex. 14:23). Egypt, with all its worldly wisdom, had now fallen completely into the LORD's trap. They were doomed! *"By faith they* (Israel) *passed through the Red sea as by dry land: which the Egyptians assaying to do were drowned"* (Heb. 11:29). ***"Assaying to do."*** — The Greek reads, *"of which* (Red Sea) *the Egyptians having made experiment."* It was *rashness* and *presumption* on their part. Sadly, imitation Christianity is mistaken by many for *faith.* Consequently, with similar rash presumption, many rush into eternity, only to be forever lost!

THE TIME OF CROSSING

As the Israelites went out of Egypt at the vernal equinox, the morning watch, or, according to the Hebrew, *beashmoreth habboker*, the *watch of day-break*, would answer to our *four o'clock* in the morning. It was at this time, *"the morning watch,"* that *"the LORD looked unto the host of the Egyptians through the pillar of fire and of the cloud, and troubled the host of the Egyptians"* (Ex. 14:24).

> *"'The Lord looked unto.'* This probably means that the cloud suddenly assumed a fiery appearance where it had been dark before; or they were appalled by violent *thunders* and *lightning*, which we are assured by the psalmist did actually take place, together with great *inundations of rain*, The *clouds* POURED OUT WATER; *the skies sent out a* SOUND: *thine* ARROWS *also went abroad. The* VOICE *of thy* THUNDER *was in the heaven; the* LIGHTNINGS LIGHTENED *the world; the earth* TREMBLED *and* SHOOK. *Thy way is in the sea, and thy path in the great waters. Thou leddest thy people like a flock, by the hand of Moses and Aaron*; (Ps. 77:17-20).

Such tempests as these would necessarily terrify the Egyptian horses, and produce general confusion. By their dashing hither and thither, the wheels must be destroyed, and the chariots broken; and foot and horse must be mingled together in one universal ruin; (see Exodus 14:25).

During the time that this state of horror and confusion was at its summit, the Israelites had safely passed over; and then Moses, at the command of God, (Ex. 14:26), having stretched out his rod over the waters, the *sea returned to its strength* (Ex. 14:27); i.e., the waters by their natural gravity resumed their *level*, and the whole Egyptian host were completely overwhelmed (Ex. 14:28).

But as to the Israelites, the waters had been a wall unto them on the *right* hand and on the *left* (Ex. 14:29). This the waters could not have been, unless they had been supernaturally supported; as their own gravity would necessarily have occasioned them to have kept their level, or, if raised beyond it, to have regained it if left to their natural law, to which they are ever subject, unless in cases of miraculous interference. Thus, the enemies of the Lord perished; and that people who decreed that the male children of the Hebrews should be *drowned*, were themselves destroyed in the pit which they had destined for others. God's ways are all equal; and he renders to every man *according to his works.*"[15]

GOD'S WRATH ON PHARAOH

The downpour of rain, the bolts of lightning, the roar of thunder and the trembling of the earth, brought utter terror and confusion to Pharaoh's host. Pharaoh and his commanders were terror-stricken. Panic and dismay pervaded the host of a once-proud and mighty army. Have you ever seen a horse panic? Now that is a sight to behold! Can you imagine what it was like on this occasion? Blazes of light in the prevailing darkness, accompanied with explosions of thunder, and a breath-taking downpour of rain upon a trembling earth. The horses would be wild, the chariots would be furiously clashing together, upsetting, breaking, and tearing the wheels from their axles. Some horses would be floundering and sinking in the rain-soaked muck of the sea bottom. Chariots still maintaining their wheels would be bogged down in the mire caused by the downpour, hardly able to move. I would say that this is perhaps the greatest scene of confusion in the Bible, except for certain events in the Book of Revelation.

---

15   Clark. MacSword, <u>Notes on Exodus 14.</u> (Bible study software for Mac OS-10).

TOO LATE! NO ESCAPE!

When Israel reached the other side, and were safe and sound on solid ground, the LORD spoke again to Moses as the morning appeared, instructing him to stretch out his hand over the sea. The poor Egyptian army was trying to turn back in a vain effort to escape, for it had suddenly dawned upon their darkened minds that the LORD was fighting for Israel. Alas, there was no turning back. They had crossed the final boundary line of God's dealings with them. They were beyond hope, doomed, and lost!

There are people in Scripture that remind me of this condition. Remember Herod? He had the head of John the Baptist taken off, for the sake of an ungodly woman. Later, the Lord Jesus stood before him. Herod had heard of Jesus and was anxious to meet Him for the sole reason that he had hoped the Lord would have worked a miracle in his presence. He questioned the Lord in curiosity, but the Lord answered him nothing. Christ could have preached to him the way of salvation, but no, there was a dead silence on the Lord's part. Why? I believe the reason that Herod had crossed the boundary line of God's dealings with him. He had previously rejected the gospel message, thus, as the hymn writer has put it, God "left him alone in the darkness to dwell, in sight of the heavenly shore."

We almost see the same thing with the *"gays."* In that group of humanity we discover *"women"* changing *"the natural use into that which is against nature; and likewise also the men leaving the natural use of the women"* burning *"in their lust one toward another; men with men working that which is unseemly." "For this cause God gave them up unto vile affections"* (Rom. 1:26-27). Then we read; *"And even as they did not like to retain God in their knowledge, God gave them over to a reprobate mind, to do those things which are not convenient"* (v. 28). There was a day when they heard of God, but they totally rejected Him. Because of their perverse mind, God acted very negatively toward them, thus we read; *"Because that, when they knew God, they glorified Him not as God, neither were thankful; but became vain in their imaginations, and their foolish heart was darkened. Professing themselves to be wise, they became fools"* (Rom. 1:21-22). We have them all around us in our fallen society today. They have rejected God, and God has given them over to a reprobate mind, and to their sinful ways. Their foolish heart has been darkened and God pronounces them *"fools."*

In preaching for so many years, I have come across, decent, clean living people, and I wonder if God has not abandoned them. They seem to draw an absolute blank when the gospel is presented to them. No matter how many times they hear, they remain in sin's darkness. Could it be that somewhere in their lifetime, they crossed the line of God's dealings with them? It could very well be!

Very often, Genesis 6:3 is taken out of its context and used in the gospel, and rightly so. *"And the LORD said, My Spirit shall not always strive with man."* What an awful position to be in, to have crossed the line that has been drawn by rejecting our Lord, where the call of His Spirit is lost. Look at the Pharisees! Notice the condemning remarks of our Lord to them. *"I go My way, and ye shall seek Me, and* **shall** *die in your sins: whither I go, ye cannot come ... I said therefore unto you, that ye* **shall** *die in your sins: for if ye believe not that I am He, ye* **shall** *die in your sins"* (John 8:21, 24). Isn't that fearful? Isn't that sobering?

God's dealing with Pharaoh and all his fighting men were terminated, and the congealed waters of the Red Sea sought their own level. *"The sea returned to his strength ... and overthrew the Egyptians in the midst of the sea. And the waters returned, and covered the chariots, and the horsemen, and all the host of Pharaoh that came into the sea after them; there remained not so much as one of them. ... Thus the LORD saved Israel that day out of the hand of the Egyptians"* (Ex. 14:28,30). Ancient tradition claims, that Pharaoh's magicians, Jannes and Jambres, perished with the rest. How wonderful! How glorious! What a great God!

OUR THREE ENEMIES

Can we relate to this in our present day and experiences? We most certainly can! Before you were saved what kept you from the freedom found in Christ? Was it not a number of things such as the world, the flesh, and the devil? Like the Egyptians to Israel, so these three things were enemies to us. What has happened to them? What has God done to them on our behalf?

(1) The World

First of all, let us consider enemy number one – ***the world.*** We are not talking about the globe, nor its people, but rather its adornment, and its ways. Where does the Christian stand in relation to the world with all its empty pleasures and aspirations? The answer is plain and simple. Notice Paul's exclamation. *"But God forbid that I should glory, save in the cross of our Lord Jesus Christ, by whom the world is crucified unto me, and I unto the world"* (Gal. 6:14). Have you got that? Does it make a deep impression on your mind? It should, for it is a vital truth! As we all know, it is a physical impossibility for a person to crucify one's self. It must be done by another. God accomplished this the moment we trusted Christ. In other words, I now have nothing to do with the vain pursuits of this sin-stricken society. I have ceased to be engaged in things that society covets.

The Runner and the Marathon

Let me present a supposed case as a simple illustration. John was an accomplished runner. However, the day came when he was saved. Shortly after, the world sweetly and subtlety invited him to run in a local marathon. His chances of winning were excellent. The praise of the ungodly awaited him, the glory of winning attracted him. What was he to do? Thankfully, John had been reading his Bible on a regular basis, and the Spirit had informed him how to act under various circumstances. These verses came to mind. *"Be ye not unequally yoked together with unbelievers: for what fellowship hath righteousness with unrighteousness? and what communion hath light with darkness?"* (2 Cor. 6:14).

To run with unconverted people in a united effort, was being unequally yoked together with unbelievers. John frowned. The Spirit then brought to his mind another portion of Scripture. *"Now Jehoshaphat had riches and honour in abundance, and joined affinity with Ahab ... And Jehu the son of Hanani the seer went out to meet him, and said to king Jehoshaphat, shouldest thou help the ungodly, and love them that hate the LORD? therefore is wrath upon thee from before the LORD"* (2 Chron. 18:1; 19:2). Jehoshaphat, a saved man, joined in a common cause with Ahab, an ungodly man. It was wrong in God's eyes!

Other verses seemed to arise and confront John. *"Be not conformed to this world: but be ye transformed by the renewing of your mind, that ye may prove what is that good, and acceptable, and perfect, will of God"* (Rom. 12:2). *"If* (since) *ye then be risen with Christ, seek those things which are above, where Christ sitteth on the right hand of God. Set your affection* (mind) *on things above, not on things on the earth"* (Col. 3:2). *"Ye adulterers and adulteresses, know ye not that the friendship of the world is enmity with God? Whosoever therefore will be a friend of the world is the enemy of God"* (Jas. 4:4). *"Love not the world, neither the things that are in the world. If any man love the world, the love of the Father is not in him"* (1 Jn. 2:15). John, being so forcibly reminded of his position in Christ, realized afresh that the world was crucified unto him, and he unto the world. Thankfully, he changed his course. Instead of using his energy and time to run a marathon, he "ran" from door to door with gospel tracts, witnessing for Christ.

(2) The Flesh

Enemy number two now comes to our consideration, namely, **the flesh.** What is the flesh? Scripture uses this word three ways. (1) A description of the human race (Gen. 6:12; Luke 3:6). (2) Our physical body (John 1:14). (3) Finally, this word "flesh" is used to describe our fallen and depraved nature. Paul exclaimed; *"For I know that in me (that is, in my flesh,) dwelleth no good thing"* (Rom. 7:18). He also states that the flesh and the Spirit are *"contrary the one to the other."* Peter speaks of fleshly lusts that war against the soul (1 Pet. 2:11). Paul also speaks of the *"affections and lusts"* of the flesh. *"Affections"* means, impulses in the passive sense. The innate forces resident in the nature, while "lusts" indicate the active craving forces reaching out to find gratification of the desires. What a sordid position in which the natural man finds himself.

What about the Christian? Let Scripture speak! *"They that are Christ's have crucified the flesh with the affections and lusts"* (Gal. 5:24). Paul exhorts the Galatians: *"This I say then, walk in the Spirit, and ye shall not fulfil the lust of the flesh"* (Gal. 5:16). He does not say, ye shall not *feel* the lust of the flesh. Oh no! I am afraid that many of us are attacked at times by strong desires contrary to God. However, we have the indwelling of the Spirit Who gives us the victory over the flesh so that we do not *fulfil* its lusts.

"All genuine *Christians have crucified the flesh* – they are so far from obeying its dictates and acting under its influence, that they have crucified their sensual appetites; they have nailed them to the cross of Christ, where they have expired with Him; hence says Paul, (Rom. 6:6) *'our old man'* - the flesh, with its affections and lusts, *'is crucified with Him, that the body of sin might be destroyed, that henceforth we should not serve sin.'"*[16]

Unlike the unconverted man, the believer has the power, through the Spirit, to keep the flesh in a state of crucifixion. This enables him to produce the fruit of the Spirit. The believer is an executioner, dealing cruelly with the body of sin. Paul kept under his body, and brought it into subjection (1 Cor. 9:27). God has destroyed this enemy, the flesh. We are no longer dwelling in it. It has no more dominion over us. However, we are no longer in the flesh, but the flesh is still in us, until the redemption

---

16 Clark. MacSword, Notes on Galatians 5. (Bible study software for Mac OS-10).

of the body at His coming (Rom. 8:9).

(3) The Devil

The third enemy which we will now briefly consider is *the devil*. At one time, we were his children. John states:*"We know that we are of God, and the whole world lieth in wickedness"* (1 Jn. 5:19). The correct thought is, *"the whole world lieth* (as a baby) *in the wicked one."* Like a little child cuddled and lulled to sleep by the embrace of its mother, so this world lies in the lap of the devil, embraced, and lulled into spiritual sleep by this vicious foe of God and humanity. Christ refers to him as "a strong man." *"No man can enter into a strong man's house, and spoil his goods, except he will first bind the strong man; and then he will spoil his house"* (Mark 3:27).

Before conversion, we were in the strong man's house, held by Satan's captive chain. Thank God, a stronger man came (Christ), broke the chain, and set us free. *"Forasmuch then as the children are partakers of flesh and blood, He also Himself likewise took part of the same; that through death He might destroy (annul) him that had the power of death, that is, the devil"* (Heb. 2:14).

While held in darkness by the powers of darkness, God intervened. The light of the gospel of the glory shined in our hearts and we were saved. We *"were sometimes darkness, but now are ye light in the Lord"* (Eph. 5:8). John testifies: *"I have written unto you, young men, because ye are strong, and the word of God abideth in you, and ye have overcome the wicked one"* (1 Jn. 2:14.)

God effectually called us out of darkness into His marvelous light (1 Pet. 2:9). Satan may try us as he did Job and Peter, but he will never hold dominion over us. His power over us has been annulled by the death and resurrection of Christ. What a tremendous transaction! What a wondrous deliverance! Nothing on earth can compare with it! Eternally saved and forever delivered from the thralldom of Satan! Hallelujah what a Saviour!

A DROWNED ARMY

When the waters of the Red Sea came together, Israel's enemies were destroyed. When God saved us by His grace, our three enemies lost their power over us! Let us make our calling and election sure (2 Pet. 1:10). That is, let us live in such a way as to prove these facts in our lives before men.

"*And Israel saw the Egyptians dead upon the sea shore*" (Ex. 14:30). Evidently, the violence of the waters cast many of the drowned soldiers up on the shore. Or it may have been the next tide. We do not read of the children of Israel taking any arms with them upon leaving Egypt, but evidently they had military equipment, essential in their wars against the Amalekites and the Amorites. More than likely, these arms were taken off the corpses of the dead Egyptian soldiers. This is only conjecture, but highly possible.

However, Psalm 74:13-14; and passages in Isaiah and Ezekiel, would seem to fortify my thoughts on this subject.

> "*Thou didst divide the sea by Thy strength: Thou brakest the heads of the dragons* (Pharaoh's army) *in the waters. Thou brakest the heads of leviathan* (Pharaoh) *in pieces, and gavest him to be meat to the people inhabiting the wilderness.*"

> "*Awake, awake, put on strength, O arm of the LORD; awake, as in the ancient days, in the generations of old. Art thou not it that hath cut Rahab (Egypt), and wounded the dragon? Art thou not it which hath dried the sea, the waters of the great deep; that hath made the depths of the sea a way for the ransomed to pass over?*" (Isa. 51:9-10).

> "*Speak, and say, Thus saith the Lord GOD; Behold, I am against thee, Pharaoh king of Egypt, the great dragon that lieth in the midst of his rivers, which hath said, My river is mine own, and I have made it for myself*" (Ezek. 29:3).

GOD'S CONTEMPT

The Egyptians were very particular about embalming and preserving the bodies of their great men. However, God pours out His contempt upon them. They sprawled along the shore, like dung upon the face of the earth. There they lay to be food for fowl and beasts of prey, and to rot into wormy dust, with their naked bones to be parched and bleached under the desert sun. What ignominy! What shame! They entered the sea with pride, power, and self-confidence, but the Almighty brought them down to utter disgrace! *"Whatsoever a man soweth, that shall he also reap"* (Gal. 6:7).

It is interesting to notice the divine commentary on Israel and the sea in Psalm 106:7-12.

> *"Our fathers understood not Thy wonders in Egypt; they remembered not the multitude of Thy mercies; but provoked Him at the sea, even at the Red Sea. Nevertheless He saved them for His name's sake, that He might make His mighty power to be known. He rebuked the Red Sea also, and it was dried up: so He led them through the depths, as through the wilderness. And He saved them from the hand of him that hated them, and redeemed them from the hand of the enemy. And the waters covered their enemies: there was not one of them left. Then believed they His words; they sang His praise."*

"The LORD **overthrew** *the Egyptians in the midst of the sea."* (Ex. 14:27). He *"***overthrew** *Pharaoh and his host in the Red Sea."* (Ps. 136:15). The Hebrew word is *"shook off."* The LORD, in speaking to Job concerning the dayspring, uses this word, saying, *"That it might take hold of the ends of the earth, that the wicked might be shaken out of it."* Josephus says that the army of Pharaoh consisted of *fifty thousand* horsemen, and *two hundred thousand* footmen, of whom not one remained to carry tidings of this most extraordinary catastrophe. So complete was the destruction of Egypt's power, even though Israel dwelt within a short distance from them for

forty years in the wilderness, yet Egypt never attempted to pursue them again, or disturb them in any way.

DIVINE OMNIPOTENCE REALIZED

"And Israel saw that great work which the LORD did upon the Egyptians: and the people feared the LORD, and believed the LORD, and His servant Moses" (Ex. 14:31). What a sight for a redeemed nation to behold! The Chaldean language says; *"Israel saw the power of the great hand."* Divine omnipotence was greatly displayed on that occasion. Israel was now fully convicted in their soul of God's power on their behalf, that it caused the whole nation to fear the LORD. This is the first occasion in the Bible where you read of a nation fearing the LORD. I suppose that on this memorable occasion, they would look back with shame on their previous doubting and murmurings. As George Bush remarks,

> "Infidelity and rebellion are, for a time at least, banished from their hearts, and 'while they believe His word, they sing His praise;' although their subsequent demeanor showed that they were still capable of forgetting and slighting their heavenly benefactor."[17]

THE FEAR OF GOD

Having the fear of the LORD is a healthy condition. Scripture says that it *"is the beginning of wisdom"* (Ps. 111:10; that it *"is the beginning of knowledge"* (Prov. 1:7); that it *"prolongeth days"* (Prov. 10:27); that in it *"is strong confidence"* (Prov. 14:26); that it *"is a fountain of life"* (Prov. 14:27); that it *"tendeth to life"* (Prov. 19:23); and *"by humility and the fear of the Lord are riches, and honour, and life"* (Prov. 22:4). Finally, *"by the fear of the Lord men depart from evil"* (Prov. 16:6).

---

17   George Bush. Exodus. (Klock & Klock Christian Publishers, Inc. Minneapolis, Minnesota. 1981 reprint). P.183.

Coming to our dispensation, we discover this: *"Then had the churches rest throughout all Judea and Galilee and Samaria, and were edified; and walking in the fear of the Lord, and in the comfort of the Holy Ghost, were multiplied"* (Acts 9:31).

The fear of God is seen in a few Biblical characters such as; the midwives (Ex. 1:17, 21); Nehemiah's brother Hanani (Neh. 7:2); Job (Job 1:1); the unnamed thief on the cross (Luke 23:40); and Cornelius, who was still unconverted at that time (Acts 10:2).

What a great asset it is to any assembly of "gathered out" Christians, when the fear of God is manifest. Alas though, in our day, in some individuals, and in some assemblies, very little of the fear of God is seen. We wonder at our lack of influence over the lost; our lack of power to bring souls to hear the gospel; our lack of Holy Spirit power in our preaching. In some Christians, their dress, their demeanor, and their desires, display a lack of the fear of God. In some places, Sunday Schools have been turned into craft classes, accompanied with lightness and silly stories. Seriousness has fled through the back door and fluffiness prevails. Books of various sorts are introduced, some composed by men that have no regard for godly principles. There's an old hill-song that goes like this: "Dust on the Bible, dust on the Holy Word," and it would seem in some places that we have come to that heartbreaking condition. What has caused this miserable departure? The answer is simple – the lack of the fear of God!

LACK OF RESPECT

Let me say one more thing on this most unpleasant subject. Where the lack of the fear of God prevails, there will be a lack of respect to those who do fear God. Can you picture a godly servant of the Lord, sacrificing his whole life for the benefit of God's people, being turned away, because his faithful preaching is not desired? It has happened in more than one place. When people lack the fear of God, they can be cruel.

THE REJECTED MISSIONARY

I know a missionary who made great sacrifices to enter full-time work for God. His comfortable way of living was forfeited for a most humble way of life in a foreign land. He toiled, and with sweat and tears brought the gospel to people who had never heard it before. Assemblies were planted as he taught them the right ways of God relative to gathering in assembly capacity. However, the day came, when he was not wanted anymore. His preaching was too straight for them. He was turned away from the people that he labored for and loved. Now to me, nothing could be more heart-rendering, nothing could be more callous and cruel. Such behavior is very capable of breaking one's heart. What was the basic problem? Men had gained control of the assembly who lacked the fear of God.

If your assembly has a Sunday School, is the Bible the sole textbook? If not, then the Bible is considered insufficient. Are the songs scriptural? Will they stand the test of Scripture? Are they frothy, weightless, unprofitable, and perhaps even unscriptural? I have, with dismay, heard children sing, "Jesus wants me for a sunbeam." Where is that in the Bible? Why would Christ want anybody for a sunbeam? There is no sense to it whatsoever. Far better to sing, "I've a soul to be saved, may this truth be engraved, on my heart and on my mind while I'm young. O how awful the cost, if my soul should be lost, and in hell if I die as I am." In the last forty years, God's assemblies have been invaded with Sunday School songs that are unscriptural and to no profit whatsoever. This is a result of the lack of wisdom and knowledge, which is the sad result of the lack of *the fear of God*.

MOSES' SONG

"Then sang Moses and the children of Israel this song unto the LORD, and spake, saying, I will sing unto the LORD, for He hath triumphed gloriously: the horse and his rider hath He thrown into the sea" (Ex. 15:1).

Since we hope, in the will of the Lord, to compose a book on the songs of the saints, we will forbear exposing this lovely chapter to a fuller extent, but will simply give you a "skeleton view" for your consideration. This song of Moses is the first recorded song of a nation in the history of mankind! Never before do we read of any nation lifting their united voices in song. Basically, singing is not for the entertainment of others. Our singing is a form of worship, directed to the LORD. You will notice that the text plainly informs us to Whom they were singing. It was *"unto the LORD."* David exclaimed; *"I will praise Thee with my whole heart: before the gods will I sing praise unto Thee"* (Ps. 138:1).

In Hezekiah's day, that concept had not changed. *"Hezekiah the king and the princes commanded the Levites to sing praise unto the LORD with the words of David, and of Asaph the seer. And they sang praises with gladness, and they bowed their heads and worshipped"* (2 Chron. 29:30).

Coming to Ezra's day, we see the same thing. *"And they sang together by course in praising and giving thanks unto the LORD; because He is good"* (Ezra 3:11).

Come to the church age and what do you find? Choirs? Musicals? Song festivals? If so, I would like to know in what New Testament book and in what chapter and verse such activities are found. What does the Bible say? Well my friend, it is very basic and exceedingly simple. Notice! *"Speaking to yourselves in psalms and hymns and spiritual songs, singing and making melody in your heart **to the Lord**"* (Eph. 5:19). Now please do not get me wrong. I love to hear the saints sing. It thrills my soul. However, that should not be the object of their singing, simply to thrill those about them. Ah no, that is a very low concept of singing. They should be singing to please the Lord. It is a form of worship. It is a sacred occupation.

Israel's song was divinely *inspired*! It came, as it were, down from the sanctuary of God, penetrating the hearts of the redeemed and bursting forth from clay lips to the glory of God.

Not only was the song *inspired*, but it was *intelligent*. In poetic language it gives a graphic description of Israel's mighty deliverance, Egypt's total overthrow, and the omnipotent power of the LORD. However, the song was *invigorating* and *important* too. How it must have thrilled those about the very throne of God in heaven to hear over two million human voices raising such an anthem of praise to the LORD! I am sure that it had a most profitable effect upon the singers as well. There are two recorded songs of Moses, here and in Deuteronomy 32. Then we have the song of Moses mentioned in Revelation 15:3, which seems to be a reference to this song raised on the shore of the Red Sea.

What a tribute to the LORD, Who is mentioned 12 times in this song, and referred to 33 times. Considering the three main sections of this beautiful song, we see from verse 2 to 5 what the LORD was to them. In the second section, verses 6 to 10, we observe what the LORD did to their enemies. Then, from verses 11 to 18, we behold what God would do in a future day to the nations.

8

MARAH AND ELIM

"So Moses brought Israel from the Red sea, and they went out into the wilderness of Shur; and they went three days in the wilderness, and found no water" (Ex. 15:22).

Considering the multitude of people with their flocks and cattle, it is assumed that twelve miles would be a normal days journey for such a company. So, as we open this chapter, we find Israel about thirty-six miles from the place where they raised their tremendous tribute of praise unto the LORD. The scene has drastically changed, and also the attitude of the people.

I have little doubt that when they viewed the waters of Marah afar off, there would have been a "mad rush" to the waters to quench their growing thirst. What an awakening to those who arrived there first! What a rude disappointment! The nitre content in the waters was so great, that it was impossible to drink. They were bitter. Immediately, they murmured against the man that had made great sacrifices on their behalf. Moses became the brunt of their murmurings.

Even today, we live in a strange, and similar society. I have observed men making great sacrifices for others, only to have the people that they have sought to help turn on them with complaints. There have been faithful servants of Christ who have made tremendous sacrifices due to their calling. I have seen those same men seeking to warn and instruct believers, only to be faulted and told that their ministry was not wanted any longer. Christians that are drifting away from the truth do not like to be told of their drifting, neither will they tolerate plain teaching if they happen to be in an oversight position. They will go so far as to tell the preacher that he is not wanted. Of course, such an attitude is only a repeat of history, for we find the same attitude in Isaiah's day. There were those who were saying unto the prophets, *"Prophesy not unto us right things, speak unto us smooth things, prophesy deceits"* (Isa. 30:10).

A NEW WORLD

The excitement of Israel's deliverance is now behind them. All of a sudden they have been positioned in a new world, and an entirely different atmosphere. What joy accompanies God's salvation. There is no joy on earth that can compare to it. But, how often is the case that when the first Christian trial arrives, some saints lose the joy of their salvation. To preach to sinners that if they only trust Christ, all of their earthly problems will vanish, and life will be entirely "a bed of roses," is a calamity indeed! Nothing could be farther from the truth. Sinners should be made aware of the cost of salvation, and I believe that the Word of God would support this thought. Notice how Christ presented salvation to the multitudes in Luke 14, verses 25 to 33. He warns them that to obtain salvation, they must put Him first, even above their own loved ones. He informs them that they must bear their own cross to follow Him. He tells them to sit down and count the cost. He tells them that they must forsake all that they have in order to be His disciple. Does that look like a "rosy picture?" Definitely not! Notice His words in Matthew 7, verses 13 to 14. He exhorts the people to enter in at the strait gate. The word "strait" means narrow. Then he defines that way by saying that it is "narrow." The word narrow is interesting, for it carries the thought of "being pressed down under pressure." It is also translated "tribulation," in your Bible. In other words, the Lord is telling His audience to do all possible to enter in, but when they do, they must experience tribulation for His sake. In no way does He ever suggest that by obtaining salvation all trials will be over.

Ah no! It is quite the contrary; salvation brings trials never before experienced.

You will remember how the apostle Paul went about *"confirming the souls of the disciples, and exhorting them to continue in the faith, and that we must through much tribulation enter into the kingdom of God"* (Acts 14:22). Turning to Peter, we find the same thing. *"Beloved, think it not strange concerning the fiery trial which is to try you, as though some strange thing happened unto you"* (1 Pet. 4:12). Peter tells the saints not to think it strange, for he saw that it was quite a normal thing for God's people to have fiery trials. In fact, you will remember that the Lord said to Ananias concerning Paul; *"For I will shew him how great things he must suffer for My name's sake"* (Acts 9:16). The word "suffer," in relation to the pilgrim and stranger, occurs no less than five times in Peter's first epistle, as if it was a thing to be expected. Paul relates some of his trials in 2 Corinthians 11:23-27, and speaks of them as *"our light affliction"* (2 Cor. 4:17).

THE FIRST WILDERNESS TRIAL

So there they stand with their little ones, and their cattle, and nowhere is there suitable water to be found to alleviate their trial. Sad was their case, for they murmured against the man that loved them the most.

Is it not interesting to notice the reaction of this great man Moses? There is no retaliation. He does not turn to the source of the problem, but rather to the One Who could solve that problem – he cries unto the LORD. The people were giving him a severe problem, and in meekness he turns to the LORD for guidance and immediate help. There is a familiar hymn that many of us sing with seeming wholeheartedness, yet seldom do we live up to its words. That hymn was written by a man who lived in Canada and who had experienced trials. Engaged to be married, the author's sweetheart was accidentally drowned on the eve of their wedding-day. Moving from Ireland to Canada for a fresh start in life he again became engaged, only to see his bride-to-be stricken with a severe illness. Helping her with nursing care, he watched her slowly die. Sometime later, he wrote his ailing mother in Ireland, writing at the top of the page, *"Pray without ceasing"* (1 Thess. 5:17). Underneath those words he wrote a poem which he had composed. He never intended the words to be made public or put to music, but a friend happened to see those beautiful words, and from his efforts, we have a beautiful song to sing. Yes, Joseph Scriven wrote these touching words:

> "Are we weak and heavy-laden,
> Cumbered with a load of care?
> Precious Saviour, still our refuge:
> Take it to the Lord in prayer.
> Do thy friends despise forsake thee?
> Take it to the Lord in prayer;
> In His arms He'll take and shield thee
> Thou wilt find a solace there."[18]

God comforts the psalmist with these assuring words, *"Call upon Me in the day of trouble: I will deliver thee, and thou shalt glorify Me"* (Ps. 50:15). Moses was a man that knew the necessity of seeking the face of God in prayer in a day of distress and trouble.

"Hope deferred maketh the heart sick" (Prov. 13:12). Israel's heart was sick. They had seen the waters afar off. The remedy was at hand, and soon they would be relieved of their present distress. Alas! That did not take place. God allowed a severe disappointment to enter their life. My dear Christian friend, does this sound familiar to you? Everything looks good, and the future looks even brighter, then, all of a sudden, the dark clouds of disappointment form, and the rains of trial pour down upon our head. Without warning, we are immersed in a desperate situation. What do we do? What do YOU do? Complain? Blame another person? Or, do you take it to the Lord in prayer? Every time this subject comes to my pen, I cannot help but think of Paul and Silas lying in a "mud-hole" beneath the prison. Their

---

18   Jack Strahan, <u>Hymns and their writers.</u> (Gospel Tract Publications, Glasgow. 1989 reprint) P. 185.

backs had been beaten, and their feet made fast in the stocks, yet they were praying! It is most unnatural! It is simply amazing! Let me further say, it is a manifestation of godliness! Again, we lay the question at your feet, what do you do in times of severe disappointment and distress? Moses cried unto the LORD.

MOSES AND THE TREE

"And the LORD shewed him a tree" (Ex. 15:25). The tree had been there all along, but it took the Lord to reveal it to Moses. Some writers would have us believe that there was some virtue in the quality of the tree to cause a chemical reaction, thus making the waters sweet. That idea is to be rejected. This event is a supernatural miracle, not a natural cure. The sweetening was not dependent upon the nature or quality of the tree, but in the power of God, just as there was nothing in the wet clay to give the blind man his sight, but rather the power of God (John 9:6).

Having cast the tree into the waters, the waters were made sweet. Thus, the cause of all their frustration and anxiety melted away, and they were able to refresh themselves with an abundant supply of good water. Now brethren, let us pause for a moment and consider the solution to all of our anxieties, frustrations, cares, and trials. There is no necessity to run to the doctor for medication to releave stress, neither to the psychiatrist for any mental problem. Why run to these people when the cure is at your very doorstep? You may say, "Just what is this cure that you are talking about?" Well, my friend, the cure is the Cross! Bring the Cross into your problems and trials. The Lord would encourage us with these words;

> *"Looking unto Jesus the Author and Finisher of our faith; who for the joy that was set before Him endured the cross, despising the shame, and is set down at the right hand of the throne of God. For consider Him that endured such contradiction of sinners against Himself, lest ye be wearied and faint in your minds"* (Heb. 12:2-3).

The Hebrew believers were compassed with trials. With many, the Roman government had spoiled their goods. However, they brought the Cross into their circumstances and took joyfully the spoiling of their goods (Heb. 10:34).

After telling the Hebrews, to *"look unto Jesus,"* the Lord tells them to *"consider Him."* In other words, they were first told to consider attentively ("look"). And they were to estimate, or, contemplate ("consider"). The dictionary tells us that the word *"contemplate,"* means: "to look at something thoughtfully and steadily. To think about something seriously and at length, especially to understand it more fully. To think about something as a possible course of action."

Not bringing the Cross into their trials would produce weariness and faintness in their own minds. The implication was that they would become so discouraged as to quit. Let us ever remember that whatever trials may come our way, God allows them. The reasons vary. A trial may be given so that God will manifest His power on our behalf, or it may be allowed in order to bring us closer in dependence upon Him. It also may be given as a correctional measure to restore us to Himself. As far as the Hebrews were concerned, the reason for their trials was made known to them in these inspired words:

> *"Furthermore we have had fathers of our flesh which corrected us, and we gave them reverence: shall we not much rather be in subjection unto the Father of spirits, and live? For they verily for a few days chastened us after their own pleasure; but He for our profit, that we might be partakers of His holiness. Now no chastening for the present seemeth to be joyous, but grievous: nevertheless afterward it yieldeth the peaceable fruit of righteousness unto them which are exercised thereby"* (Heb. 12:9-11).

Is it not the ultimate goal in the Christian life, to be a partaker of His holiness, and to yield the peaceable fruit of righteousness?

"The cross on which the Saviour died,
And conquered for His saints,
This is the tree by faith applied
Which sweetens all complaints."

Thus Marah figuratively speaks to us of "God allowed" trials, and of God's solution for us in whatever trial may come our way.

A STATUTE AND AN ORDINANCE

It was at Marah that God made for them a statute and an ordinance that is recorded in verse 26. *"If thou wilt diligently hearken to the voice of the LORD thy God, and wilt do that which is right in His sight, and wilt give ear to His commandments, and keep all His statutes, I will put none of these diseases upon thee, which I have brought upon the Egyptians: for I am the LORD that healeth thee."* God now imposes upon the nation a definite decree, a prescribed rule, or course of action. God made known to them the conditions on which they might expect to enjoy His divine favor. They were not to imagine that just because they were the favored people of God that they would be exempt from discipline for any disobedience. Quite the contrary! The warning was very plain that they would experience the same punishment that God inflicted upon the Egyptians for any disobedience on their part. There was given to them a full list of plagues that would befall them for disobedience in Deuteronomy 28:15-68. This declaration at Marah was so important, that Jeremiah made mention of it a thousand years later (Jer. 7:21-23).

GOD'S RESPONSE

Has the day of grace changed the position and attitude of God toward His people, relative to their disobedience? Let the scriptures provide the answer.

> *"If any man defile the temple of God, him shall God destroy; for the temple of God is holy, which temple*

ye are" (1 Cor. 3:17). *"Be not deceived; God is not mocked: for whatsoever a man soweth, that shall he also reap. For he that soweth to his flesh shall of the flesh reap corruption; but he that soweth to the Spirit shall of the Spirit reap life everlasting"* (Gal. 6:7-8). *"For he that eateth and drinketh unworthily, eateth and drinketh damnation to himself, not discerning the Lord's body. For this cause many are weak and sickly among you, and many sleep"* (1 Cor. 11:29-30). *"If any man see his brother sin a sin which is not unto death, he shall ask, and he shall give him life for them that sin not unto death. There is a sin unto death: I do not say that he shall pray for it"* (1 Jn. 5:16).

If you defile God's assembly, God will respond in defiling you. If you sow to your flesh, keeping wrong company, feasting on wrong literature, listening to perverted music, spending your substance totally on self, and intoxicating yourself with the world's pleasures and comforts, in return, God will make sure that you will reap a harvest of disappointment and loss down here. Also, the eternal reward that could have been yours will be forever lost in the glory. With some, the solemn results can even result in death. Taking lightly the importance of the Lord's Supper, resulted in severe sickness, and with some, even death in the Corinthian assembly Yes, there is a sin unto death. Judgment begins at the house of God.

These multiple warnings should put the fear of God into us, lest by any disobedience to His word we find ourselves under His retributive hand. They were to hear "diligently." That word comes from a primitive root, meaning, "to hear intelligently." In other words, God wants us to read His word intelligently. He wants us to understand what we read. But there follows something equally as important. They were to do that which was right in His sight. Now this is an all-important thing. To understand the word of God intelligently, and then to go one's own way, can be disastrous indeed! Understanding God's mind for us brings upon us grave responsibilities! Ignorantly sinning is bad enough, but willfully sinning is far worse.

JEWELRY REMOVED

Let me illustrate. Many years ago I was staying in a home in Nova Scotia while holding ministry meetings with an assembly. The sister who hosted me was young in the faith, and a lovely soul. However, adorning her body were jewels. The dear lady was totally ignorant of God's mind for her relative to her dress. No Christian had ever approached her about her adornment. Carefully, I approached her after breakfast concerning her jewelry. Opening her own Bible, I asked her to read this portion: *"In like manner also, that women adorn themselves in modest apparel, with shamefacedness and sobriety; not with broided hair, or gold, or pearls, or costly array"* (1 Tim. 2:9). Then turning to 1 Peter 3:3-4, she read: *Whose adorning let it not be that outward adorning of plaiting the hair, and of wearing of gold, or of putting on of apparel; But let it be the hidden man of the heart, in that which is not corruptible, even the ornament of a meek and quiet spirit, which is in the sight of God of great price"* (1 Pet. 3:3-4).

Laying her Bible on the sink counter, she quietly took off her earrings and her expensive necklace, and laid them on the counter, and carefully said, "I will never wear these again." What a lovely attitude! I was thrilled at the godly response of this dear sister. One might say, she had been ignorantly sinning, but upon being shown the word of God, she was not about to be a willful sinner. Can you see the difference? Many untaught saints are ignorantly sinning, but that is far different than willfully sinning. How grievous to see willful sinning on the part of a redeemed soul, knowing that they are putting themselves in a most unfavorable position with their Father in heaven, and losing an eternal reward in the glory.

KEEPING ALL HIS WORD

Israel was to *"give ear to His commandments, and keep all His statutes."* In other words, after being told, they were to guard and preserve what they had heard. Not just part of what they had heard, but ALL that they had heard. There is to be no half-heartedness when it comes to keeping the doctrines of God's word.

Paul, when nearing the end of his life, said, *"I have kept the faith."* Paul was never guilty of watering down what God had taught him, nor changing the truth, nor removing the ancient landmarks. In fact, he told Timothy, *"The things that thou hast heard of me among many witnesses, the same commit thou to faithful men, who shall be able to teach others also"* (2 Tim. 2:2).

Are we changing? Are we introducing human programs, thus displacing the Holy Spirit's movements among us? Are we employing the world's tactics to attract people to our gospel meetings? Are we humanly-programming our conferences, dictating who speaks, and in some cases, even dictating the subject to be spoken? Ask yourself the question today, are we guilty of departing from the faith once for all delivered unto the saints, or not? There is a verse that has been quoted perhaps more than any by brethren that are seeking to maintain divine principles, and it is this: *"Thus saith the LORD, Stand ye in the ways, and see, and ask for the old paths, where is the good way, and walk therein, and ye shall find rest for your souls"* (Jer. 6:16). However, sad to say there are some today that have the same reply as in Jeremiah's day. *"But they said, We will not walk therein."*

Israel was commanded to **diligently hearken, do, give ear, and keep all His statues.** We are commanded to do the same.

THE SILVER LINING

The road to Elim was perhaps eight to ten miles from Marah. It was close by. You will notice that the Scripture uses 140 words to describe Marah, while only 24 words are employed to tell us of Elim. There is almost six times more said about Marah than Elim. The Scripture at this point was written in the same pattern as the human mind thinks. Be honest, don't we dwell more upon our problems and trials than on our times of refreshing and blessing? Elim was a place provided by God for Israel's rest and refreshment along their pilgrim way. There is an old saying, that every dark cloud has a silver lining, and how often we have experienced that with every trial. There is divine relief nearby. How tender, thoughtful, and loving is our God, Who has a refreshing Elim for us alongside the bitterness of a Marah. For an example, consider Peter and John being brought before the authorities and threatened – that's Marah. Yet, being let go, we see them with their own company, filled with the Holy Ghost and with great power giving witness – that's Elim! Look at Paul in the prison at Philippi, that was a Marah. However, before the chapter closes, we find him and Silas in the Jailor's house feasting in the midst of rejoicing. That's Elim!

One is reminded of what Paul said to the Corinthians: *"There hath no temptation taken you but such as is common to man: but God is faithful, Who will not suffer you to be tempted above that ye are able; but will with the temptation also make a way to escape, that ye may be able to bear it"* (1 Cor. 10:13). How good is the God we adore!

It is interesting to notice that Elim had 12 wells (springs) of water and 70 palm trees. Israel was composed of 12 tribes and had 70 elders. Christ chose 12 to accompany Him in His ministry, and soon after appointed 70 to go before His face (Luke 10:1).

9

THE MANNA

Ah, how lovely it would have been to just settle down and dwell at Elim. It was an ideal place, a place of refreshment and comfort, with provision for themselves and for their cattle. Why move on? Well, the reason is that they were the heirs of promise, and Elim was not to be their home, but rather Canaan. At this point they were strangers and consequently, pilgrims, on the march through a waste howling wilderness to possess their inheritance.

Brethren, we too are strangers and pilgrims in a desert world, and whether we want to admit it or not, God cannot trust us with too many Elims. This world is not our portion in which to settle down and relax. No, no, that will never do. That is not the divine program for us. Occasionally, He allows Elims to come our way that we may be better able to walk in the paths of righteousness. We may rest in Elim, but we are never to ungird our loins. We must be ever ready for the march and the battles of the Lord.

I have never cared for that popular expression, "Take it easy." Since when is the Christian supposed to "take it easy"? We are told to put on the whole armour of God that we might be able to withstand in the evil day. In our pilgrim journey, evil days lie ahead. How suddenly they come upon us. If I am "taking it easy" I will collapse, but if I am alert, having on the armour of God, I shall withstand. *"Therefore let us not sleep, as do others; but let us watch and be sober"* (1 Thess. 5:6). Perhaps the hymn writer had this in mind when he penned those words:

"Heed we the steward's call,
Work, brethren, work!
There's room enough for all;
Work, brethren, work!
This vineyard of the Lord
Constant labour doth afford;
Yours is a sure reward;
Work, brethren, work!"[19]

GOING BACK

Between Elim and the Wilderness of Sin, the LORD directed their way back to the shores of the Red Sea. This move is recorded for us in Numbers 33:10. Why back to the Red Sea? The reason seems to be that God wanted them to have another final look to bring to their remembrance the tremendous deliverance that they had experienced through the omnipotence of their God. I can just picture this vast multitude standing in silence, looking out over the waters that buried all their foes. Would it not produce much reflection within their bosom? Would it not cause renewed thanksgivings to well up in their hearts?

Brethren, it is good to stand still and look out over the shores of the Red Sea, but you don't have to fly to the other side of the world to accomplish this. Just sit quietly in the circle on Lord's Day morning with the emblems, and the Lord Himself in the midst, and lo and behold, you will be at the shores of the Red Sea! How often have you sung these words at such a gathering?

"Sweet the moments, rich in blessing,
Which before the Cross we spend,
Life and health, and peace possessing
From the sinner's dying Friend.

Here we rest, in wonder viewing
All our sins on Jesus laid,

---

19   Author unknown. The Believer's Hymn Book. (John Ritchie Ltd. Kilmarnock, Scotland). P. 55.

And a full redemption flowing
From the sacrifice He made."[20]

There, at the Lord's Supper, we see the great sacrifice made for us! We view our tremendous deliverance from the enemy, and we are reminded of our separation from an Egyptian world. There we are reminded that our Saviour, *"having spoiled principalities and powers, He made a shew of them openly, triumphing over them in it"* (Col. 2:15). The Lord's Supper is the nearest place to heaven on earth. Truly, the moments are sweet and rich in blessing!

THE WILDERNESS OF SIN

Leaving the shores of the Red Sea, the pillar of the cloud led them to the wilderness of Sin, which is between Elim and Sinai. This took place exactly one month after departing from Egypt. The reflections gained at the shores of the sea seemed to be very temporary indeed, for we read, *"the children of Israel murmured against Moses and Aaron in the wilderness"* (Ex. 16:2). Such behavior exposes to us a sad fact. The impression made at the sea was not long lasting. Like the morning dew, it soon evaporated and was gone.

Now let us be slow to criticize these people, for do we not see the same thing today amongst us? We rise from the supper, a solemn occasion, and the vicarious death of our blessed Lord permeates our mind. But how long do the impressions last? Is it not true that our meditation of Him soon evaporates and we act in a giddy, frivolous way? Israel's lack of contemplation produced murmuring, while our lack of contemplation produces undue merriment. I am not for one minute endorsing unhappiness and depression, but what I am saying is that giddiness and lightness has no place in our behavior, especially after such an occasion as the Lord's Supper.

---

20   Walter Shirley. The Believer's Hymn Book. (John Ritchie Ltd. Kilmarnock, Scotland.) P. 222.

A so-called "coffee break" immediately following the Lord's Supper, in most cases, erases sobering thoughts concerning His suffering for our sins. Our older brethren never condoned it, and God's assemblies never practiced it. Hovever, we are living in "modern times" when levity seems to be the norm. Conversations turn to temporal things, laughter prevails, and thoughts concerning our blessed Lord diminish. Some assemblies have never subscribed to such an addictive practice for that very reason.

THE FIRST OCCASION

Many years ago, I sat at the Lord's Supper with a group of believers. It was the planting of a scriptural assembly, and this was the first time any of them had ever broken bread. One by one all the men rose to thank God for His Son. A word was given at the close of the gathering, and the solemn occasion was closed in prayer. Then, the saints rose, and standing in the circle, they all began weep as they looked upon the broken bread and the empty cup. I shall never forget that memorable occasion. It was one of the most precious, and rewarding events in my lifetime.

Let me ask you, how often do you see saints weeping after rising from the supper? Let us be slow in our criticism of the children of Israel. Can we heartily sing the following words of Isaac Watts?

> "Alas! And did my Saviour bleed?
> And did my Sovereign die?
> Would He devote that sacred head
> For such a worm as I?
>
> Thus might I hide my blushing face,
> While His dear cross appears;
> Dissolve my heart in thankfulness,
> And melt my eyes to tears."[21]

---

21   Isaac Watts. <u>The Believer's Hymn Book.</u> (John Ritchie Ltd. Kilmarnock, Scotland). P. 7.

Isaac Watts deeply appreciated the value of the cross, and I have no doubt that it was his meditation day and night. I'm afraid, I must say, that the singing of many of our godly hymns makes us proclaimers of falsehood. Let every one of us search our own heart and ask ourselves the question, "Where do I stand in relation to all of this?"

DIMINISHED FAITH

> *"And the children of Israel said unto them* (Moses and Aaron), *would to God we had died by the hand of the LORD in the land of Egypt, when we sat by the flesh pots, and when we did eat bread to the full; for ye have brought us forth into this wilderness, to kill this whole assembly with hunger"* (Ex. 16:3).

Over two million people had their stock of food, nearly, or altogether exhausted. The horrors of coming famine had overtaken them. Their faith had greatly diminished, and with impatient spirits they pour out their complaint, murmuring against Moses and Aaron. Their blighted minds turned back to Egypt and the provision that they enjoyed there. However, they conveniently forgot the slavery, the groaning and crying that was theirs under the taskmasters of a cruel Pharaoh. How perverse and ungrateful human nature is! I am amused when I hear older people talking about "the good old days." Ah yes, but they forget the bread lines, the hard times of a severe depression, and many other grievous conditions connected with "the good old days."

Not only this, these murmurers blamed Moses and Aaron for leading them to their present position. One wonders if they had never realized that Moses and Aaron were in the same circumstances. They too had no more to eat than the rest. Seemingly, these people had forgotten that the pillar of the cloud had led them there. They had been divinely directed into their present circumstances, not humanly led. Furthermore, their faith in the omnipotence of God had diminished, being replaced with unbelief. They had forgotten all that the LORD had previously wrought on their behalf. He had brought Egypt to total ruin on their behalf. He had annihilated all the forces of their enemy in the depths of the sea. He had provided abundance of water for them at Marah, making the waters miraculously sweet. He had graciously comforted them as they rested at Elim, with its twelve springs and seventy palm trees. But now, all that the LORD had accomplished on their behalf had evaporated from their memory. How ungrateful, how perverse, and how impious these people had become.

Does not the devil work the same today with God's people when trials come their way? He reminds them of the "fun" they had in their unconverted days, and seeks to instill in their minds that God has forgotten them, and that He has left them, not caring about their present affliction. Oh the flesh! The world! The devil! What cruel tyrants they are in seeking to influence us to lose our confidence in the LORD God, our blessed Redeemer, Saviour and Guide! The children of Israel murmured!

GOD'S GRACIOUS RESPONSE

At this point, it is very interesting to notice the response of the LORD regarding this perverse and wicked behavior. There was no severity on His part, but rather grace, and the question arises, why? In the very next chapter, the contrast in the LORD's response to their murmurings is very evident. The judgment of God fell in severity, and many died.

Let us remember, that the LORD had just brought Israel into His school of learning. They were, as it were, but babes. Thus, the tenderness and grace of God is manifested in chapter 16. The LORD acted in such a way to overcome their evil with good. He graciously gave them *"bread from heaven."* In chapter 17, they had experienced more of God's ways with them than previously, thus, more was expected of them. Consequently, their murmuring at a later period, brought severe judgments.

One could aptly apply their situation to God's dealings with sinners by the following verses. *"Or despisest thou the riches of His goodness and forbearance and longsuffering; not knowing that the goodness of God leadeth thee to repentance? But after thy hardness and impenitent heart treasurest up unto thyself wrath against the day of wrath and revelation of the righteous judgment of God"* (Rom. 2:4-5). God spares sinners, and the extent of His longsuffering is amazing. They can raise their little fist in defiance against God, and wantonly go their own way, heeding not His call. Yet in spite of it all, He fills their houses with good things. However, the day for them is coming, when the boundary line of His forbearance will be passed, and His wrath shall fall upon them. *"A prudent man foreseeth the evil, and hideth himself: but the simple pass on, and are punished"* (Prov. 22:3; 27:12).

BREAD FROM HEAVEN

"Then said the LORD unto Moses, Behold, I will rain bread from heaven for you; and the people shall go out and gather a certain rate every day, that I may prove them, whether they will walk in My law, or no" (Ex. 16:4).

What unusual bread it was! Enough to feed over two million people, and sustain them throughout their forty years of wandering in the wilderness. Needless to say, some so-called intelligent and scientifically minded people have tried to explain this miracle away. Without any hesitation, they tell us that this food came from the tamarisk tree that was found in certain places in the wilderness. In the month of June, a substance called *mann* by the Bedouins, drops from the thorns of this tree upon the fallen twigs, thorns, and leaves which always cover the ground beneath this tree. This substance is white and flakey, and as soon as the sun shines upon it, it dissolves. The Arabs clean away the leaves and dirt of this substance, then boil it, strain it through a piece of cloth, and store it in leathern bottles, preserving it until the following year. They then pour it over unleavened bread as we would use honey. History never describes it as being made into cakes or loaves. It was only found in years when abundant rains had fallen. Consequently, there were years when none was to be found. It never acquired a state of hardness to allow it to be pounded as Israel did to God's manna in Numbers 11:8. The quantity of manna collected in an abundant year only amounts to a total of about six hundred pounds. The harvest being in June, lasts only about six weeks. In contrast, God's manna fell six days a week for forty years, and amounted to about three hundred boxcar loads holding 15 tons each. This was on a daily basis, six days a week, with twice as much on the sixth day! In other words, there were 12 million pints, totaling 4,500 tons per day! This definitely amounts to the greatest of all miracles recorded in the Holy Scriptures as to provision and duration!

THE MANNA DESCRIBED

The manna certainly was not simply the product of nature as some historians would say. The facts narrated definitely prove otherwise. No natural cause produced the manna. To those who would claim that it was the product of the tamarisk tree, or some species of a vegetable gum found in that area, let me ask you this. Why was the supply more abundant than anything ever seen before? Why was it only found on top of the dew in the morning? Why did twice as much fall on Friday, and none on Saturday? Why, if kept over, did it breed worms and stink, but not the manna gathered on the sixth day when kept until the seventh day? Why did one omer of it never corrupt when placed in the golden pot, but was instead preserved for forty years? Why did it suddenly cease the moment they entered into the land of Canaan? No, my friend, the giving of the manna was the greatest sustained miracle of all time!

The God-given manna had definite characteristics, all of which typify Christ. Let me name them, one by one.

(1) Verse 14. **The manna was small.** Our blessed Lord was small in that *"He made Himself of no reputation,*

and took upon Him the form of a servant, and was made in the likeness of men" (Phil. 2:7).

(2) Verse 14. **The manna was round.** Something that is round has no end. Our Lord is eternal. *"In the beginning was the Word"* (John 1:1). The word *was* means that in the beginning, He was already there. *"Having neither beginning of days, nor end of life"* (Heb. 7:3). *"Before Abraham was I am"* (John 8:58). God used that expression *"I AM"* in Old Testament times to manifest Himself as Jehovah, the everlasting One. Our Lord uses the same expression to convey the same thought, that He is the everlasting God, and that irrespective of time, He exists!

(3) Verse 31. **The manna was white.** Christ was without blemish and without spot. He was holy before He came into this world. He was holy at His birth. He was holy during His ministry. He was holy in His death. He was holy in His resurrection. He is forever holy in heaven.[22]

(4) Verse 31. **The manna was sweet.** *"O taste and see that the LORD is good* (sweet): *blessed is the man that trusteth in Him"* (Ps. 34:8).

(5) Verse 31. **The manna was like coriander seed.** It was a round aromatic seed, beautiful to behold. There is an intricate design to this little seed. It is beautifully engraved by the Creator's hand. It is one of the wonders of God's reproductive creation. Beautiful to behold and fragrant to smell. How wonderfully it portrays that One Whose intricate pathway down here was under the complete "engraving" of His Father. Every step, every movement was divinely planned in the heart of God and fully displayed in our blessed Lord.

---

22   Isa. 6:3; Luke 1:35; Mark 1:24; Lev. 6:25; Acts 13:35; Rev. 3:7.

"O Lord, when we the path retrace
Which Thou on earth hast trod,
To man Thy wondrous love and grace,
Thy faithfulness to God.

O Lord, with sorrow and with shame,
We meekly would confess,
How little we, who bear Thy Name,
Thy mind, Thy ways express."

– James G. Deck

(6) Verse 21. *"When the sun waxed hot, it melted."* This portrays the fact that we are to seek Him early. *"Seek ye the LORD while He may be found, call ye upon Him while He is near"* (Isa. 55:6).

THE MANNA GIVEN

The manna was given on a daily basis to prove them. They were never allowed to possess a "bank account" of manna. The supply given at an every day raining was only a one-day supply, except on Friday when a double amount was provided. God was going to see if they were willing to simply trust Him and to walk by faith in the absence of all human means of provision or not. Are we willing to trust our God on a daily basis? Are we fully assured of His words; *"Take no thought for your life, what ye shall eat, or what ye shall drink; nor yet for your body, what ye shall put on"* (Matt. 6:25). *"Consider the ravens: for they neither sow nor reap; which neither have storehouse nor barn; and God feedeth them: how much more are ye better than the fowls?"* (Luke 12:24).

RESPONSIBILITIES

God would have us in a constant state of dependence upon Himself. The world, without God, lives in a perpetual state of uncertainty and anxiety. They worry about the future. Now that is not to say that we are to be totally indifferent to the everyday responsibilities of life. No, no, we are to be diligent with our substance. Solomon, in his wisdom advises us. *"In the day of prosperity be joyful, but in the day of adversity consider: God also hath set the one over against the other, to the end that man should find nothing after him"* (Eccl. 7:14). In days of abundance, perhaps we receive more than we really need. What do I do with the excess? I can do one of three things. I can squander it, I can save it for the day of adversity, or I can give it to others in need. God never intends for us to live above our means, like the credit people advocate, neither does He advocate wasting our substance on nonessentials. So that leaves us with two choices. If we acquire more than we need, we can set it aside for a "rainy day," or we can give it to the Lord over and above our regular portion. The choice is ours. The Philippian assembly gave of their substance, time and time, again to Paul. He assured them, that even though they had given of their substance, that God would supply all their need according to His riches in glory by Christ Jesus (Phil. 4:19). A person never becomes poorer through giving his substance to God. Rather his giving becomes fruit abounding to his account.

THE MANNA GATHERED

The head of the house was to gather and distribute the manna to those that were in his tents. Some gathered more, and some less. Nevertheless, *"he that gathered much had nothing over, and he that gathered little had no lack; they gathered every man according to his eating"* (Ex. 16:18). Paul refers to this in 1 Corinthians 8:13-15, "from which it is inferred by some that when any one had gathered more than his due share, he gave the surplus to those who had gathered less. Others, however, suppose that the whole quantity gathered by any one family was first put into a common mass and then measured out to the several individuals composing the household."[23] One author says: *"He that gathered much had nothing over"* because his gathering was in proportion to the number of persons for whom he had to provide. And

---

23 George Bush. Exodus. (Klock & Klock Christian Publishers, Inc. Minneapolis, Minnesota. 1981 reprint). P. 210.

some having fewer, others more in family, the gathering would be in proportion to the persons who were to eat of it. Therefore *he that gathered much had nothing over, and he that gathered little had no lack.* Probably, every man gathered as much as he could; and then, when brought home and measured by an omer, if he had a surplus, it went to supply the wants of some other family that had not been able to collect a sufficiency, the family being large. Thus there was an *equality*, and in this light the words of Paul, in 2 Corinthians 8:15, lead us to view the passage."[24]

None of the manna gathered for the day was to be left till the morning. *"Notwithstanding they hearkened not unto Moses; but some of them left of it until the morning, and it bred worms, and stank: and Moses was wroth with them"* (Ex. 16:20). What was their problem? It seems very evident that they placed very little faith in the promise of the LORD. What other reason could there be? Their unbelief produced the frown of God, and their hoard was turned to worms and stank. I have seen people hoard possessions for fear of what they term, an uncertain future, only to lose it all.

We certainly agree with prudent people that some provision for the future is required of us. We are told to go to the ant and consider her ways and be wise, for she lays up in store for coming days of want (Prov. 6:6). Paul says that he that provides not for his own household is worse than an infidel (1 Tim. 5:8). However, to hoard everything in fear of the future, to make an accumulation of wealth our object in life, is wrong. When one becomes obsessed with "making money" to the expense of godly living, God frowns on such behavior, and mind you, He can swiftly remove one's lifetime of labor, leaving them totally dependent upon Him. Solomon was led to see this, for he said, *"Wilt thou set thine eyes upon that which is not? for riches certainly make themselves wings; they fly away as an eagle toward heaven"* (Prov. 23:5). Again, I emphasize, lest you get the wrong idea, that I am not for one moment endorsing laziness, neither am I promoting carelessness. What I am saying is simply, that Chris-

---

24 Clark. Notes on Exodus 16. (MacSword, Bible study software for Mac OS-10).

tians will be provided for by God, but at the same time, the Lord expects us to be prudent with what we presently possess. We aren't to be so lazy that we will just sit back with no desire to work, and say, "The Lord will provide."

"And they gathered it every morning, every man according to his eating: and when the sun waxed hot, it melted" (Ex. 16:21). Each man was allowed six pints, a suitable and satisfying portion indeed. However, there was one danger, *"when the sun waxed hot, it melted."* There was an urgency to give the gathering of the manna first place in the day's schedule. This suggests to me the importance of giving Christ the first place in my life. How often the cares and responsibilities of the day crowd in around us, and we neglect one important and vital thing – the gathering of the manna. How profitable it is to start the day with thoughts gleaned from the word of God concerning our blessed Lord. Have you not found, that when you give Him His rightful place, that things seem to run more smoothly through the day?

THE DEW

Nature produced something in connection with this bread from heaven. It was dew. *"And when the dew that lay was gone up, behold, upon the face of the wilderness there lay a small round thing, as small as the hoar frost on the ground"* (Ex. 16:14). *"When the dew was gone up,"* does not necessarily mean "when it evaporated." The expression is the same as applied to the quails in verse 13, *"the quails came up,"* simply meaning, "they made their appearance." So, the thought is, when the dew appeared on the surface of the ground, the manna was found on top of it. We find a more explicit description in Numbers 11:9. *"And when the dew fell upon the camp in the night, the manna fell upon it."* The dew did not vanish away before the manna was seen. Quite the opposite. The manna lay upon the dew. In other words, it was gathered totally free from the dust or soil of the desert floor. Where the people encamped there was contamination, thus, it fell outside the camp, *"upon the face of the wilderness."*

EGYPT TO CANAAN

A photograph of individual faces as they first looked upon this mysterious substance would have made a very interesting photo album indeed. The whole thing was absolutely amazing. It was phenomenal! Such a thing had never been seen before! Tons of this beautiful and delicate substance lying on top of the glistening dew as the sun made its orbit over the eastern horizon. The glory of the LORD appeared in the cloud. One cannot but be reminded of the coming of the Bread of life into this world. The glory of the Lord shone round about.

> *"And when the children of Israel saw it, they said one to another, It is manna: for they wist not what it was. And Moses said unto them, This is the bread which the LORD hath given you to eat"* (Ex. 16:15).

THE MANNA – A PORTION

Without wearying you with the etymology of Hebrew words, we will simply say that the expression *"manna"* could have easily been translated, *"portion."* The most learned of the Rabbis say that the Hebrew word *"man"* signifies the food appointed, prepared for, and doled out to the children of Israel as their portion. Prior to receiving their portion, they had been informed by Moses that food would be given to them that would satisfy all of their need in their journey (Ex. 16:12). Consequently, when they went out and saw this substance for the first time, they immediately recognized it as God's portion for them, thus calling it *"manna,"* which rightly translated is, *"portion."*

Dear Fanny Crosby recognized Christ, the living bread from heaven, as her portion, and wrote:

> "Thou my everlasting portion!
> More than friend or life to me,
> All along my pilgrim journey,
> Saviour, let me walk with Thee."

I trust that it can be said of all of us, that the world has lost its charm, that it cannot satisfy, and that it is all vanity. Can we sing heartily, "Now none but Christ can satisfy, none other name for me"? The world stoops at its broken cisterns, only to be disappointed, while the true saint of God quietly eats the living Bread and finds in that Bread, true and lasting joy, and satisfaction.

"Man earthy of the earth, an hungered, feeds
On earth's dark poison tree.
Wild gourds and deadly roots and bitter weeds,
And as his food is he.
And hungry souls there are, that find and eat
God's manna day by day,
And glad they are, their life is fresh and sweet,
For as their food are they."[25]

THE MANNA AND THE SABBATH

At this point in Israel's journey the Law had not yet been given, but the Sabbath was recognized and had been previously observed. It may have fallen into much neglect among the Israelites, but now there rises a very suitable occasion for its observance. They were told that on the sixth day (Friday) a double portion would be provided by the LORD. They were to gather twice as much and lay up half of their gathering for Saturday's portion. *"And he said unto them, this is that which the LORD hath said, to morrow is the rest of the holy sabbath unto the LORD: bake that which ye will bake to day , and seethe that ye will seethe; and that... until the morning"* (Ex. 16:23). If they desired, they were allowed to bake or boil the next day's portion for their provision. What was kept over for the next day bred worms and stank when gathered on other days, but when Saturday's portion was gathered on Friday, it remained pure and sweet. This miracle alone proves that the manna was not some sort of natural food to be found in the wilderness.

Having gathered Saturday's portion on Friday, allowed them to cease all work on the Sabbath. Is there not a lesson in

---

25 Ter Steegen

this for us? Christians do not observe the Sabbath (Saturday), but they certainly should observe the Lord's Day, rightly termed "The Lordly Day." It is the appointed day when we remember the Lord in the breaking of the bread (Acts 20:7). It is a special day, when more attention is given to the things of God. It is a day to be reverently observed. Would you go shopping on the Lord's Day? Would you wash your car or do the laundry on the Lord's Day? What are your activities on the Lord's Day? Do you consider the day distinct from other days, or do you reckon it to be just another day? I remember seventy years ago when it would be a rarity to see an unsaved farmer making hay on the Lord's Day. The fear of the Lord seemed to prevail. Not so now. The ungodly use the Lord's Day as an occasion for all sorts of fleshly activities, from sports to picnics, from plowing the ground, sowing the seed, and harvesting their crop, to running to various festivals. Among the ungodly, the fear of the Lord has greatly departed.

THE LORD'S DAY

What should the attitude of the Christian be? Consider John on the Isle of Patmos. *"I was in the Spirit on the Lord's day."* Need I say more? Two times the word *"Lord's"* as denoting *character*, not necessarily *possession*, is found in your New Testament. *"The Lord's supper,"* (1 Cor. 11:20), and *"the Lord's day"* (Rev. 1:10). Thus, the *day* and the *supper* are both considered *"lordly."* That is, their character is different than the usual. The supper is not an ordinary meal, it is something very special, it is *lordly*. In like manner, the first day of the week is a very special day, it is *lordly*. It is not like other days.

C. H. MacIntosh related in one of his books that Christians should be more tired at the end of the Lord's Day than any other day. That is, tired as a result of laboring for the Lord. Years ago, it was a common thing for Christians to be very busy for the Lord on that special day.

A BUSY DAY

I remember being in one place, and the activities for the day were, first, the breaking of bread, followed by a ministry meeting, followed by a children's meeting, followed by an open air gospel meeting downtown, followed by another ministry meeting, then a prayer meeting, followed by door to door visitation, followed by a prayer meeting, finally, followed by a gospel meeting. Needless to say, I had no trouble sleeping that night! Oh yes, I must add that on two occasions during that busy day, we nourished our working bodies with good food!

The Lord's Day is unique, it is vastly different than other days. However, in our modern society, the fear of God has departed. The "blue law," has been abolished. Consequently, gas stations, grocery stores, department stores, and a host of other business places are open for business on the Lord's Day. Some Christians are under contract with their employer to work shifts. That is a hard situation to avoid. Consequently, some saints are called upon to work on the Lord's Day. Slaves, at the commencement of the day of grace, very often were not free from their masters until the evening of the day, including the Lord's Day. Because of this imposition upon them, many assemblies broke bread at night to accommodate brethren that were slaves. That consideration was only using common sense. Let us be realistic. A farmer with a herd of milk cows could hardly neglect them on the Lord's Day. Anybody familiar with such cattle fully understands that cows must be milked twice a day, seven days a week. It is unavoidable, it is an absolute necessity.

LORD'S DAY – A HOLY DAY

There is even another area to consider, and it is that which concerns our modern educational system. In past years, the Lord's Day was honored by the school system. Not anymore! To accommodate the ungodly, graduations in many places are scheduled for the Lord's Day. So the graduating child has preeminence over the Lord. Are such occasions really that vital? I personally do not think so. If the child was sick it wouldn't be able to attend. If the parents were sick, they wouldn't be able to attend. I am speaking now of Christian families, not the ungodly. However, it is strange to me that if good health prevails in the family, and the graduation is scheduled for the Lord's Day, that parents will attend at the expense of missing an assembly meeting. In other words, the Lord is in the midst at the assembly gathering, but this is not as important as honoring their child. I consider this giving the Lord second place, a dishonoring move that brings displeasure to His heart.

One hundred and ten years ago, when my mother was a little girl in England, on the Lord's Day, she was required to sit on the porch in her "Sunday best." She was not allowed to play in the yard. Her parents were not even saved, but very religious. I will admit, they went a bit far with rules and regulations for that special day, but in it all, my mother was made to realize that Sunday was not just another ordinary day. Ah yes, we have toned things down quite a bit. We are not legal, but on the other hand, have we not drifted to the place of "illegal" conduct in some areas? We arrive home from the Lord's Supper, change our clothes and tear about here and there for our own pleasure. Up and down the trail we blaze on a four-wheeler, or, out for a sightseeing tour in our automobile. Perhaps even a relaxing boat ride, or some other empty amusement captures our mind, and "away we go." Ah yes, those fleshly lusts do war against the soul, don't they? (1 Pet. 2:11).

No my beloved brother or sister, it is far better to be weary at the close of the Lord's Day from doing His bidding, from laboring for Him, whether visiting shut-in saints, or seeking to reach the lost, or even spending the time in fasting and prayer. Also, if there are no assembly activities for a few hours, tell me, what is wrong with sitting down quietly with your Bible and reading what He has to say to you? Remember, *"Only one life, 'twill soon be past. Only what's done for Christ will last."* There was no work to be done on the Sabbath. It was a different day. The Lord's Day is different!

JOE'S DELI

In closing our thoughts on this subject, allow me to relate to you the convictions of a man named "Joseph." He is a Lutheran, and professes to be born again. He owns a restaurant in our locality named, "Joe's Deli." His prices are very reasonable, and his food is of the highest quality. No matter what time of the day you go to Joe's, the place is packed. Folks simply flock to Joe's for a delicious meal, and the portions are so large that folks nickname Joe's as the "doggie-bag restaurant," for most folks walk out with a good portion of their meal in a little styrofoam box. The interesting thing is, Joe's is closed every Lord's Day. He was interviewed by the Cleveland newspaper and asked why, with such a good business, he closed on Sunday. His reply was something to this effect: "I honor the Lord Who gave me this business. I lose no money by closing, for if I opened on Sunday, the Lord could give me less business the rest of the week, and I would be the loser." This man had his perspectives right. Yes, *"Them that honour Me, I will honour,"* is still in our Bible (1 Sam. 2:30).

"And it came to pass, that there went out some of the people on the seventh day for to gather, and they found none" (Ex. 16:27). This is evidence that there were some who did not take the prohibition very seriously. They made no difference over the Sabbath than any other day. Of course, in this world, where the fear of God has mostly evaporated, we observe this attitude every Lord's Day as we see people running here and there, pulling their campers, boats, skidoos, and other pleasure paraphernalia. God is not in all their thoughts.

"Room for business, room for pleasure.
But for Christ the crucified,
Not a place that He can enter,
In that heart for which He died."

The godly Christian is far different. He sets aside the Lord's Day entirely for the Lord if at all possible. And as he rides his "faith-mobile" toward the celestial city, he sings;

"Lord Jesus, Thou who only art
The endless source of purest joy,

O come and fill this longing heart;
May naught but Thee my *thoughts* employ
Teach me on Thee to fix my eye,
For none but Thee can satisfy.

The joys of earth can never fill
The heart that's tasted of Thy love;
No portion would I seek until
I reign with Thee, my Lord, above,
When I shall gaze upon Thy face,
And know more fully all Thy grace.

O what is all that earth can give?
I'm called to share in God's own joy;
Dead to the world, in Thee I live,
In Thee I've bliss without alloy:
Well may I earthly joys resign;
All things are mine, and I am Thine!"[26]

An *ungrateful* heart is always associated with an unbelieving mind and an unholy life.

A GOLDEN POT OF MANNA

"And Moses said, This is the thing which the LORD commandeth, Fill an omer of it to be kept for your generations; that they may see the bread wherewith I have fed you in the wilderness, when I brought you forth from the land of Egypt. And Moses said unto Aaron, Take a pot, and put an omer full of manna therein, and lay it up before the LORD, to be kept for your generations. As the LORD commanded Moses, so Aaron laid it up before the Testimony, to be kept" (Ex. 16:32-34).

Knowing the frailness of the human mind, and its proneness to forget, God, in His infinite wisdom, has on various occasions, instituted memorials. In our dispensation, He has ordained the Lord's Supper which involves two memorials, namely a loaf of

---

26   Anonymous. The Believer's Hymn Book. (John Ritchie Ltd. Kilmarnock, Scotland). P. 124.

bread and a cup of wine. Thus, we are held in constant remembrance of our Lord's body given and His precious blood shed for our sins at Calvary.

God would have Israel to be held in constant remembrance of His gracious and provisional dealings with them as they journeyed through a waste-howling wilderness. The bread from heaven was a daily provision that lasted on their whole journey to Canaan. For forty years it was given to a hungry people daily.

Generations come and go, and memorable things have the habit of evaporating in the mind from generation to generation. The LORD was now going to institute something to prohibit, or at least help stay that failure. They were to lay up before the LORD an omer of manna in a pot to be kept for *their generations*.

It is easy to observe how interested the LORD was in the generations to come. God's assemblies are only one generation away from complete departure. Brethren may faithfully hold to the divine pattern, but the day comes when they are called up to glory, thus leaving the next generation to carry on the testimony. If the next generation does not have the same conscience as the former generation, and if they do not hold the same convictions, the testimony will suffer severely and departure will be the sad result. When this takes place, the testimony will soon drift back into Christendom.

It is essential that we be held in constant remembrance of the teachings of older brethren. Peter saw the need of repetition, stating, *"Wherefore I will not be negligent to put you always in remembrance of these things, though ye know them, and be established in the present truth"* (2 Pet. 1:12). *"Yea, I think it meet, as long as I am in this tabernacle, to stir you up by putting you in remembrance"* (2 Pet. 1:13). *"Moreover I will endeavour that ye may be able after my decease to have these things always in remembrance"* (2 Pet. 1:15) *"This second epistle, beloved, I now write unto you; in both which I stir up your pure minds by way of remembrance"* (2 Pet. 3:1).

THE FACULTY OF MEMORY

Paul exhorts the Hebrews to remember their former elders, and to imitate their manner of life, remembering how well they finished their course down here (Heb. 13:7). He exhorts Timothy, writing; *"The things that thou hast heard of me among many witnesses, the same commit thou to faithful men, who shall be able to teach others also"* (2 Tim. 2:2). Jude gives a similar expression, stating; *"Beloved, when I gave all diligence to write unto you of the common salvation, it was needful for me to write unto you, and exhort you that ye should earnestly contend for the faith which was once* (once for all) *delivered unto the saints"* (Jude 1:3).

The faculty of memory is a valuable tool in the hands of a child of God. The pattern has been set, the form of doctrine never changes, and we are obligated to comply, without any question, to its dictates. Alas, in these last days, how different things are becoming. Changes are taking place, we are drifting farther and farther from the divine blueprint, and if this situation continues, we the separated and gathered out companies of the Lord's people will be blended into the quagmire of Babylonish Christendom.

THE MANNA IN THE ARK

Not until we come to Hebrews 9:4 does the Spirit reveal the quality of the pot in which the omer of manna was to be placed. The Spirit mentions it while describing the most holy place on the great day of atonement, stating; *"Which had the golden censer, and the Ark of the covenant overlaid round about with gold, wherein was the golden pot that had manna, and Aaron's rod that budded, and the tables of the covenant."* The reason we believe that the Spirit is referring to the great day of atonement is that this day was the only time that the golden censer was carried into its holy confine. The careful reader will notice that it was *inside* the Ark that the pot was placed. The word, *"wherein"* does not refer to the holy place, as some erroneously teach, but rather to the Ark itself. The golden pot containing the manna was *inside* the Ark.

However, when we come to Exodus 16:34, we read that it was to be laid up *before* the testimony to be kept. So how does one reconcile these two seemingly contradictory verses? Hebrews 9:4 says that the pot was *inside* the Ark, while Exodus 16:34 says it was *before* the Ark. The solution is very simple. Carefully notice these words. *"So Aaron laid it* (the pot) *up before the Testimony, to be kept."* Consider the fact that the word *"the Ark"* is not found. This could very well indicate that the *testimony* mentioned here was not the *Ark*, but rather *the tables of stone*. Notice further; *"And thou shalt put the mercy seat above upon the Ark; and in the Ark thou shalt put the testimony that I shall give thee"* (Ex. 25:21). True, the Ark is called *"the Ark of the testimony,"* but remember also that the word *"the testimony"* when found without the word *"ark"* joined to it, always seems to indicate simply the two tables of stone. Thus, Exodus 16:34, and Hebrews 9:4, perfectly agree with each other. The golden pot containing the manna was carefully placed inside the Ark in front of the tables of stone that also were therein. The instructions are here, but the actual placing of these items had to await the day when the Ark was completed and the tabernacle pitched.

THE MANNA – TYPE OF CHRIST

Allow me to give a practical application to this historic event. The manna speaks of Christ in His unblemished and unspotted humanity. The four gospels give us much to eat and digest relative to the living Bread from heaven. His perfect manhood is graphically portrayed before our wondering eyes. But let me say this. Not all was written of His majestic, yet humble movements. Ah no, for you will remember what John exclaims at the closing of his glorious gospel. *"And there are also many other things which Jesus did, the which, if they should be written every one, I suppose that even the world itself could not contain the books that should be written. Amen"* (John 21:25). This is what is termed a hyperbole, meaning, "a deliberate and obvious exaggeration used for effect."

What John is telling us is, that concerning the life of Christ on Earth, there is much that has never been revealed. So much so, that no amount of writing could ever cover the whole subject! That alone is absolutely tremendous! The biography of men has a length-limit, but the Sprit's knowledge of the Man Christ Jesus is limitless. There is no end to it, but presently it is hidden.

Now then, come with me to 1 Kings 8:9, where we read; *"There was nothing in the Ark save the two tables of stone, which Moses put there at Horeb, when the LORD made a covenant with the children of Israel, when they came out of the land of Egypt."* On that occasion, Solomon's temple was complete, and the Ark was positioned therein on a solid gold floor as its final resting place.

This is a picture of Christ in heaven and His bride associated with Him there. The manna was no longer hidden. Can you see the truth in this? It is simply beautiful! When we reach the other side, and all the redeemed are in the glory, the Lord will unfold to us the hidden things concerning Himself, things that the Holy Scriptures have never revealed.

This teaching and learning session will be for the endless ages of eternity. That is exactly what is meant in Revelation 2:17, when the Spirit says; *"He that hath an ear, let him hear what the Spirit saith unto the churches; To him that overcometh will I give to eat of the hidden manna."* The true believer is the overcomer, and praise the Lord, we shall sit at His feet in rapt attention as He unfolds to us the exceeding greatness and eternity of His glorious Person!

10

REPHIDIM
THE SMITTEN ROCK

In considering this episode, we want to consider first the geographical and historical side of the account and then apply this significant event to a few spiritual truths.

In their journey from the wilderness of Sin to Rephidim, two stopping places of refreshment are recorded in Numbers 33:12-13, namely Dophkah and Alush. They journeyed *"according to the commandment of the LORD."* The commandment of the Lord was simply the moving of the *"pillar of the cloud."* When it began to move, Israel was to break up camp and move. When it rested, Israel was to set up camp and dwell in that location until the *"pillar of the cloud"* moved again." In other words, the commandment of the Lord was signified by the movement of the *"pillar of the cloud."*

As far as the two recorded stopping places are concerned, they cannot be exactly located today, but it is generally believed that the first was Wady Naszeb, still a favorite stopping place for travelers because of the good water found there and the shelter of a huge looming rock which provided ample shade at certain times of the day. As Isaiah describes a similar situation with these words; *"And a man shall be as an hiding place from the wind, and a covert from the tempest; as rivers of water in a dry place, as the shadow of a great rock in a weary land"* (Isa. 32:2).

The second stopping place may have been at Wady Boodra

where there is found a spring of good water. The terrain was sandy and stony, with narrow passes between rising peaks displaying various form and colors. Finally, they reached Rephidim, where there was no water. The *"pillar of the cloud"* had now brought them to another place of testing.

The name "Rephidim" means "resting-places," and more than likely, due to the name, the people would have been looking forward to reaching such a place. However, if they did have happy expectations, they were soon gone, for upon reaching Rephidim there was no water! The cattle were in dire need of water. The heads of families would be in great straights as they beheld their wives and little children at the point of death from severe thirst. Why would a loving God cause such circumstances to come their way? Why was He not interposing? Was He not conscious or concerned about their desperate need? There is no doubt in my mind that such thoughts were crossing the minds of most. Could it be that you too wonder why? Well, the reasons for it all were numerous.

First of all, God wished to reveal to them just what their heart was like. He wanted them to know themselves. He also brought them into such a trial that they might learn to rely on God. Also, we may say, that the LORD allowed this trial to show them His almighty power and provision for them. Last of all, this trial was intended to strengthen them for future trials that would cross their path.

QUESTIONINGS

The questionings of men in regards to Gods ways are the same today. Many of us have heard these expressions: "If there is a God, why does He allow suffering and sorrow?" Or, "Why did God allow my loved one to contract cancer?" "Why? Why? Why" comes the cry of ignorance from the lips of thousands. Sometimes even saints get carried away with the spirit of unbelief. The sick are heard to say, "Doesn't the Lord love me, doesn't He care?" Those who are in dire circumstances cry out, "Things are so dreadful, I think that the Lord has left me."

If only people knew God in an intimate way, their attitude would be far different. Perhaps they would be saying like C. H. MacIntosh once said, "God's presence in the trial is far more rewarding than God's exemption from the trial." Peter speaks of the Christian's trials as strange and fiery. We are exhorted to rejoice when they come. Alas, how often it is far different. When our great expectations crash, we cannot understand why God, if He is so loving, would ever have allowed it. Our wonderings are the result of our ignorance of God's infinitely wise ways. Oh dear saint, may the Lord give us the needed wisdom regarding His ways, and the grace to thankfully sing;

> "In seasons of grief to my God I'll repair
> When my heart is o'erwhelmed
>   with sorrow and care,
> From the ends of the earth to Thee will I cry,
> Lead me to the Rock that is higher than I." [27]

"Give us water that we may drink," was their impudent and impatient demand of Moses as if he had the powers to produce water that only omnipotence possessed. Only God was equal for the occasion, but to listen to these people one would think that Moses was omnipotent. They had seemingly turned brutal, for the man that forfeited all the treasures of Egypt, and a life of royalty, all on their behalf, now stood in jeopardy of his life by the very people he had so befriended. However, the eye of Moses was not resting on the children of Israel, but rather on God, *"the Father of lights, with Whom is no variableness, neither shadow of turning"* (Jas. 1:17).

> "One there is above all others;
> O how He loves!
> His is love beyond a brother's;
> O how He loves!

---

[27] John Price. The Believer's Hymn Book. (John Ritchie Ltd. Kilmarnock, Scotland). P. 88.

Earthly friends may fail or leave us;
One day soothe, the next day grieve us,
But this Friend will ne'er deceive us;
O how He loves!²⁸

MOSES AND THE ROCK

"And Moses cried unto the LORD, saying, What shall I do unto this people? they be almost ready to stone me" (Ex. 17:4). Immediately the LORD gave His servant instructions and the solution to the problem. A miracle was about to take place, but God would have it hidden from the eyes of the complainers, except the elders of the people. These chosen elders were to accompany Moses to the flinty rock. This would enable them to be formal witnesses to the miracle about to be performed. Just as the wise men were guided to the house in Nazareth to present their gifts, not to Mary, but to the Christ child, so Moses, and the elders, were guided by the cloud to the rock. That cloud stationed itself on the very spot where the miracle was to be performed.

The observing reader will notice that Moses was instructed to carry only one thing in his hand and that was his rod. However, notice how the rod is defined. The LORD doesn't speak of it as the rod that turned into a serpent, but rather the rod that was employed when the LORD turned the river Nile into blood. On that particular occasion, Moses smote the river, a picture of judgment. Thus we have the same thing at the rock. He was to smite it, conveying the thought of judgment inflicted. This thought carries us still further, on to Calvary, where Christ the Rock was *"stricken, smitten of God, and afflicted"* (Isa. 53:4). Just as the elders of Israel viewed the rock being smitten, so also, the elders of Israel were present at the smiting of Christ at Calvary.

Equally interesting is the fact that upon revealing Himself as the Rock to Peter in Matthew 16:18, His next revelation

---

28 Marianne Nunn. The Believer's Hymn Book. (John Ritchie Ltd. Kilmarnock, Scotland). P. 213.

to His own is found in verse 21, where it is recorded; *"From that time forth began Jesus to shew unto His disciples, how that He must go unto Jerusalem, and suffer many things of the elders and chief priests and scribes, and be killed, and be raised again the third day."* Thus, we have the Rock smitten at Jerusalem. Zechariah speaks of this over 480 years prior to it taking place. *"Awake, O sword, against My Shepherd, and against the Man that is My Fellow, saith the LORD of hosts: smite the Shepherd, and the sheep shall be scattered: and I will turn Mine hand upon the little ones"* (Zech. 13:7). It is interesting to note that the word *"Fellow,"* is *"comrade,"* a person on equal footing, which is but another proof of the deity of our Lord, for only He is on equal footing with God the Father.

THE SMITTEN ROCK

As Moses smote the rock, God stood before Him, a divine witness to it all. In like manner, our blessed Redeemer was *"delivered by the determinate counsel and foreknowledge of God,"* and taken by wicked hands and crucified and slain (Acts 2:23).

Notice, Moses never writes about the abundance of the supply on that occasion, but when we turn to the Psalms, the Spirit gives us a more detailed picture. *"He clave the rocks in the wilderness, and gave them drink as out of the great depths. He brought streams also out of the rock, and caused waters to run down like rivers ... Behold, he smote the rock, that the waters gushed out, and the streams overflowed"* (Ps. 78:15-16, 20). *"He opened the rock, and the waters gushed out; they ran in the dry places like a river"* (Ps. 105:41). Isaiah also speaks out. *"He caused the waters to flow out of the rock for them: He clave the rock also, and the waters gushed out"* (Isa. 48:21).

What a tremendous sight that must have been, when the waters arrived where they were. I would have liked to have seen the faces of these impious people as the waters rushed down upon and around them, fully supplying the grumblers above all expectations! They had doubted the very presence of God with them, crying out, *"Is the LORD among us or not?"* What a glaring display of unbelief! Yet, in spite of it all, the LORD didn't smite them, but rather gave to them abundantly and that above measure! What a marvelous display of the grace, the kindness, and the longsuffering of God! It far surpasses all human comprehension, does it not?

AMALEK

As soon as satisfaction filled the camp, another ominous cloud arose on the horizon. It is described in these terse words; *"Then came Amalek, and fought with Israel in Rephidim"* (Ex. 17:8). Who was Amalek? His history is perverse and provoking. Nothing good is to be said. You will remember Esau, won't you? He is the fellow that sold his birthright for a mess of pottage. He thought very lightly of spiritual things. He was a man of the earth, and could be termed a true earth-dweller. Esau had sons. One of them was named Eliphaz (Gen. 36:10). This son had a concubine and she bore to him Amalek. The whole affair is an exposure of degenerate flesh. Eliphaz went beyond the bond of matrimony to produce Amalek, who consequently is a picture of degenerate flesh.

Amalek was the first of the nations, and the most powerful race in the peninsula. He was warlike, unsuspecting in his movements until his outright attack. He was cunning, and he feared not God. Balaam prophesied that Amalek's latter end would be that he perish forever.[29] This nation is a vivid picture of the flesh (that depraved nature) that dwells in mortal man. Our application of this fact will be made later in our commentary of this incident. Presently, we just want to look at the episode as Moses recorded it. In other words, we want to consider the history of this first war in which Israel was engaged.

---

29 Numbers 24:20; Deuteronomy 25:17-18; 1 Samuel 15:2.

JOSHUA

Immediately upon being attacked, Moses sought out Joshua. Joshua had commended himself in many ways to Moses, thus Moses had the utmost confidence in him. Isn't it wonderful that when problems arise in our lives, there are persons that we can turn to for help and advice? God's assemblies are in need of help today. Many godly brethren have left us for heaven, and a few still remain. The question arises, in how many young men in God's assemblies can godly older men place their confidence. How many men are of the caliber of Timothy, of whom Paul said, *"I have no man like minded."* If you happen to be among the younger of the brethren, let me ask you, do the older, godly brethren, see a quality in you that encourages them? Can they safely place their confidence in you? Or are you one of those who have new ideas and would like to "improve" things in God's assembly? Are your interests at variance with the interests of older and godly saints? Are you a devout learner? Are your delights found in the Holy Scriptures, or in the vain world? Well may we who are nearing the end of the journey pray earnestly for young Joshuas in our gatherings. They are becoming exceedingly rare.

THREE MEN ON A HILL

What a sight that must have been; three men on the top of a hill, engaged in prayer, and an army, led by Joshua, in the valley fighting the enemy. Moses has "the rod of God" in his had, a symbol and pledge of God's presence and working. When Moses held up his hand, Israel prevailed. When he let down his hand, Amalek prevailed. It would seem that which way the battle would go depended on that rod being held high by Moses. You will notice that we do not read of the expertise of Joshua, of his ability to fight, or of his greatness in any way. Oh no, all depended on that upheld hand holding the rod of God! The whole proceedings were miraculous. There is no thought of human ability, or human prowess producing a great victory. Joshua's victory was the result of an outside source, namely three men on the hill.

MOSES' BOOK AND ALTAR

"And Joshua discomfited Amalek and his people with the edge of the sword" (Ex. 17:13). That expression, *"the edge of the sword,"* always denotes a great slaughter of the enemy. So great was this memorable event that the LORD told Moses to write it in a book for a memorial, and to rehearse it in the ears of Joshua, that He would utterly put out the remembrance of Amalek from under heaven. In connection with this, Moses built an altar, and called the name of it Jehovah-nissi, meaning, "the LORD is my banner." It seems that the naming of this altar came from the fact that God told Moses that He would have war with Amalek from generation to generation. More is said in Deuteronomy 25:19; *"Thou shalt blot out the remembrance of Amalek from under heaven; thou shalt not forget it."*

In connection with this, Psalm 83:4 comes to mind. *"They have said, Come, and let us cut them off from being a nation; that the name of Israel may be no more in remembrance."* This was Amalek's intent. Scripture says, *"Be not deceived; God is not mocked: for whatsoever a man soweth, that shall he also reap"* (Gal. 6:7). Amalek sought to sow the seeds of annihilation regarding Israel, but reaped the bitter fruit of being annihilated themselves! The sentence from God had gone forth and they were a doomed people. This sentence was executed in part by Saul,[30] and completely by David.[31]

There is a good reason why the LORD told Moses to put the events of the battle in writing and to rehearse it in the ears of Joshua. Since he was to be the successor of Moses, and the man in charge of Israel's army when they went into the land to war against the enemy, it was very important that he be constantly reminded of God's power to give the victory, manifested at Rephidim.

The building of an altar on that occasion certainly indicates that Moses offered a sacrifice unto Jehovah, expressing deep ap-

---
[30] 1 Samuel 15.
[31] 1 Samuel 30; 2 Samuel 1:1-8.

preciation for the LORD'S intervention on their behalf, not only in supplying the nation with refreshing, and much needed water, but also for giving them the victory over their foe. This is the first occurrence where scripture informs us that Moses built an altar. It is also the first time where we read of Moses writing *"the book,"* the definite article being used indicating that the book however had been used previously to record events.[32]

THE APPLICATION

Now then, having taken you through this historical event, what profit would the mere history of it accomplish, except to fill your head with facts? I should think that books should be written to accomplish far more than that. So let us now apply this memorable event to spiritual truths relative to ourselves. By doing this, these writings will become profitable to you. In this event we have warnings, exhortations, comfort, and last, but not least, Christology.

THREE GREAT ENEMIES

The Christian has three great enemies, the world, the flesh, and the devil. The world is all around us, the flesh is within us, and the devil, at times, comes upon us. As for the word *"flesh,"* it is used in multiple ways in Scripture. It can mean the human body, mankind, the humanity of Christ, the weaker element in human nature, the unregenerate state of men, and the lower element in a Christian. The meaning is determined by the context in which it is found. Take for example these verses: *"And the Word was made flesh, and dwelt among us"* (John 1:14). *"And without controversy great is the mystery of godliness: God was manifest in the flesh"* (1 Tim. 3:16). *"Every spirit that confesseth that Jesus Christ is come in the flesh is of God"* (1 Jn. 4:2). Undoubtedly, any sensible person can see that the word "flesh" here, relates to the body of our Lord. Also, you will read these words elsewhere: *"And God looked upon the earth, and, behold, it was corrupt; for all flesh had cor-*

---

32 See the Newberry Bible margin on Exodus 17:14

rupted his way upon the earth" (Gen. 6:12). It is easy to see by this, that here the word "flesh" simply refers to all mankind, that is, the human race. Then again we consider that word "flesh" in Romans 8:3 and we see it employed to express the weaker element in human nature. Notice. *"For what the law could not do, in that it was weak through the flesh."*

THE FLESH

Now at this point we are not concerned about the word *"flesh"* being used in the ways we have described. What we want to consider is the word "flesh" as a description of the fallen and depraved nature of the natural man. This is what Amalek represents. This lower element in the Christian often raises its ugly head and would have God's people act as badly as an unregenerate person would act. The unregenerate are classified as being *"in the flesh."* Thus, *"they that are **in the flesh** cannot please God"* (Rom. 8:8). The Christian is different. He is not in the flesh, and that is not his standing before God. However, the flesh is in him! So Paul goes on to say; *"But **ye are not in the flesh**, but in the Spirit, if so be that the Spirit of God dwell in you. Now if any man have not the Spirit of Christ, he is none of his"* (Rom. 8:9).

THE FLESH – A CONSTANT PROBLEM

Consequently, if you are a true child of God, you still possess your old nature, namely, "the flesh." He is a constant problem to the believer. Paul informs the Galatians with these enlightening words: *"For the flesh lusteth against the Spirit, and the Spirit against the flesh: and these are contrary the one to the other: so that ye cannot do the things that ye would"* (Gal. 5:17). Have you ever been constrained by the Spirit to hand a soul a gospel tract, only to suddenly have a fear of some possible unpleasant consequence, thus failing to accomplish your desire? How do you explain that? Well, it is simple. The flesh within you went to war and discouraged you from fulfilling the desire that the Spirit put into your soul.

Have you ever bent the knee in prayer, only to have a wave of ungodly thoughts invade your mind, thus vexing your soul? What happened? The solemn fact is that your flesh rose up and sought to distract you from that holy activity of prayer.

Have you ever uttered a lie to cover a sin? Have you ever lost your temper? Have you ever had unholy thoughts of the opposite sex? Have you ever harbored enmity or hatred to another? Have you ever had an outburst of anger? Have you ever sought your own things above everything else? Are you proud of your attainments? Do you look down on others? Do you enjoy the amusements of the world, its sports, theaters, and parties? You see, all these are but the works of the flesh. The only thing that the ungodly can produce is the works of the flesh, for they *are "in the flesh."* This is their standing, consequently their state before a holy God.

THE FLESH – CRUCIFIED

Paul relates this truth; *"They that are Christ's have crucified the flesh with the affections and lusts"* (Gal. 5:24). The word *"affections"* is passive, and indicates the inborn forces permanently dwelling in the evil nature, our impulse and affections. The word "lusts," (a strong craving, or desire) is in the active, pointing to the fact that those indwelling forces reach out to find full gratification of those indwelling desires.

Paul exhorts the Galatian saints; *"This I say then, Walk in the Spirit, and ye shall not fulfil the lust of the flesh"* (Gal. 5:16). You will notice that he doesn't say, "ye shall not *feel* the lust of the flesh." No, no! He says that we *"shall not **fulfil** the lusts of the flesh."* There is a vast difference, isn't there? Walking in the Spirit simply means living a life dictated by the Spirit, and being under His supervision and control. When a godly life of this nature is lived, then the Christian will not have the flesh imposing God-dishonoring things upon him. Why no! He will, in the Spirit, order his life in such a way that he will not *fulfill* the desires of the flesh. However, this will not necessarily exempt him from *feeling* the strong desires of the flesh.

THE FLESH – WARLIKE

Peter exposes the nature of the flesh. Like Amalek, it is warlike. Thus this timely warning: *"Dearly beloved, I beseech you as strangers and pilgrims, abstain from fleshly lusts, which war against the soul"* (1 Pet. 2:11). When God saves a sinner, the flesh deeply resents it, and sets up a war campaign to battle the saint of God. We see this exposed by Paul when he writes of Ishmael and Isaac. Ishmael was the son of the bondwoman and is a picture of the flesh. Isaac was the son of the free, and is a picture of a Spirit indwelt saint. In that family, Ishmael was born first, and later, when Isaac was born, he was resented by Ishmael, for he no longer had the preeminence.

Paul says; *"Now we, brethren, as Isaac was, are the children of promise. But as then he that was born after the flesh persecuted him that was born after the Spirit, even so it is now"* (Gal. 4:28-29). We that are saved have all experienced this, have we not? The moment we were saved, all seemed so wonderful, but it wasn't long until our old, depraved nature, made its attack on us. So much so, that we began to wonder if we were really saved after all. What was happening? Well, upon conversion, we were immediately indwelt and possessed with the Holy Spirit. For the first time in our life, we now possessed a new nature that would thirst after spiritual things. Naturally, our old nature deeply resented this, and it immediately declared war on us! Then it made its attack in various form and ways. This campaign of the flesh against us will continue until we are taken home to heaven. Our only recourse is to "walk in the Spirit," and to reckon the flesh as crucified.

THE FLESH – CUNNING

Like Amalek, the flesh within us does not fear God, and it is always ready to make a "sneak attack" upon us. It is cunning.

You will remember that it was the faint and weary ones upon which Amalek made his surprise attack. What a warning to us! Let us be very careful to maintain a healthy spiritual state before the Lord, for in doing so, this will enable us to resist this persistent foe – the flesh! Remember this; the flesh can never be eradicated, absorbed by the Spirit, expelled, improved, or destroyed. It is with us until our homecall.

Paul exhorted the Colossian saints with these words: *"If (since) ye then be risen with Christ, seek those things which are above, where Christ sitteth on the right hand of God. Set your* affection (mind) *on things above, not on things on the earth … Mortify* (put to death) *therefore your members which are upon the earth; fornication, uncleanness, inordinate affection, evil concupiscence, and covetousness, which is idolatry"* (Col. 3:1-2, 5). Thus, we see that the flesh acts in the opposite way. It seeks the things which are on earth, of which some are listed above.

Paul instructs the Roman saints; *"Put ye on the Lord Jesus Christ, and make not provision for the flesh, to fulfil the lusts thereof"* (Rom. 13:14). Another has said; "Direct none of your attention to the cravings of your corrupt nature, how you may provide for their gratification." There is a danger of making provision for the flesh. That is, placing ourselves in a position where we will be tempted more readily, by the flesh, to fulfill its lusts. Let me give you some examples.

PROVISION FOR THE FLESH

John was newly saved. He had been a drunkard. One day he decided to revisit his old environment. Walking into the bar room he had a look around, just for memory's sake. Of course, some of his old companions were there, and they enticed him to sit with them. The next thing John knew, he was intoxicated. What had happened? He had made provision for the flesh, and consequently, succumbed to it.

Nancy loved the dance floor and the bowling alley. Her

salvation completely severed her from such follies. She was happy in the Lord. However, the day came when she received an invitation to attend, as a spectator, a dancing show. Her old passions for the dance floor immediately made their attack. She attended, thus making provision for the flesh. The old desire to dance flooded her soul, and she succumbed.

COMPUTERS – SUBTLE DANGERS

The stories could go on and on, but by now I think that you have the import to the scriptural warnings regarding the flesh. Let me state one more thing. Many of us own computers. They are wonderful pieces of equipment, and very helpful in composing gospel tracts and books. They excel any normal encyclopedia as far as ferreting out information is concerned. They are a vital asset in many fields, and most valuable in the commercial and business world. The fact that they have become a most needed machine makes them exceedingly dangerous, for if used improperly, they can devastate a Christian's well being and testimony. Most of us are fully aware of the subtle dangers that lurk in the keys of the computer. By typing certain words into the computer's search engine, one can project on its monitor the most vile and corrupt sexual scenes imaginable. Thus, the computer, that is so essential in today's society, provides a very accessible provision for the flesh. The temptation lies before the operator. One brother recently expressed to me grave concern for young Christians with such a temptation before their eyes. With very little effort, they can behold on their computer, pornography at its vilest. Older saints are not exempt either, but the temptation seems to be greater when one is in their youth. Paul uses that very word *"youthful"* doesn't he? *"Flee also youthful lusts: but follow righteousness, faith, charity, peace, with them that call on the Lord out of a pure heart"* (2 Tim. 2:22).

JOSHUA, MOSES, AARON, AND HUR

Joshua battling Amalek, is pictured as a saint fighting the

flesh. As the battle rages in the valley, on the top of the hill are three men, Moses, Aaron and Hur. These are representative men, that speak of others. Moses is a picture of a praying saint. Hur, means "light, pure," and is emblematic of the Holy Spirit. Aaron, means "exalted," pointing us to Christ, our High Priest.

Now let us tie these names together. Perhaps there are many saints like Epaphras, praying for you. It was recorded of him; *"Epaphras, who is one of you, a servant of Christ, saluteth you, always labouring fervently for you in prayers, that ye may stand perfect and complete in all the will of God"* (Col. 4:12). Moses had two helpers, Aaron and Hur, who held up his weary hands that he might be effective. Let me explain it this way. When in my youth, there were older, godly saints who prayed for my survival, testimony-wise. Their prayers for me were made effective through the aid of two Persons.

(1) The Holy Spirit, of Whom it is said; *"Likewise the Spirit also helpeth our infirmities: for we know not what we should pray for as we ought: but the Spirit itself maketh intercession for us with groanings which cannot be uttered"* (Rom. 8:26).

(2) The Lord Jesus Christ, of Whom the Scripture declares; *"Wherefore He is able also to save them to the uttermost that come unto God by Him, seeing He ever liveth to make intercession for them"* (Heb. 7:25).

In the historical event of Rephidim we have pictured for us the truth of saints praying for us through the aid of the Holy Spirit and our High Priest, the Lord Jesus Christ. These two divine Persons facilitate and make effective the prayers of the godly.

Some have likened Moses to Christ our Priest on this occasion, but that is a very faulty application for this very reason; that the hands of our Great High Priest ***never*** grow weary! Thus, we have praying saints, the Holy Spirit, and the Lord Jesus Christ, all on our behalf, to help us keep the flesh in the place of death.

Let me finish this section with Paul's inspired warning. *"Therefore, brethren, we are debtors, not to the flesh, to live after the flesh. For if ye live after the flesh, ye shall die: but if ye through the Spirit do mortify the deeds of the body, ye shall live"* (Rom. 8:12-13). What does *"ye shall die"* mean? Perhaps the thought is, if such a life in an unbeliever ultimately leads to eternal death, why should a believer tamper with that which has such solemn consequences? The statement is a general statement. Paul states that we are not debtors to live after the flesh, because such people who do live after the flesh belong to the realm of death, they are not saved. Paul is awakening the saints to realize that this is not true of them, thus, in no sense can they go on living that kind of life. What does *"ye shall live"* mean? Simply this; *"ye shall live as sons,"* a life of faith and holy obedience. The *"deeds of the body"* are its doings, its aspirations, impulses, desires, and works.

May the Lord, the Spirit, help us daily to cast *"down imaginations, and every high thing that exalteth itself against the knowledge of God, and bringing into captivity every thought to the obedience of Christ"* (2 Cor. 10:5).

11

MOSES AND JETHRO

> *"And Jethro, Moses' father in law, came with his sons and his wife unto Moses into the wilderness, where he encamped at the mount of God"* (Ex. 18:5).

The events in this chapter are very interesting, and so, for a few pages, let us look together at the memorable meeting of these two great men, Moses and Jethro. Some have argued that Jethro was the brother-in-law to Moses, and others would claim that he was Moses' father-in-law. The Hebrew text could read either way. The word is *"chothen,"* meaning, *"a relative by marriage."* Personally, I feel more comfortable with the rendering given by the King James translators, that he was the father-in-law to Moses and the father of Zipporah, Moses' wife.

Another question arises; was this man Jethro a saved man or not, and if so, when was he saved? Then, we want to consider if the events related in chapter 18 in chronological order? That is, did they take place between the events recorded for us in chapters 17 and 19? One more thing that we wish to address is this; was the advice received from Jethro of God, or not? Did Moses make a grave mistake in following his father-in-law's advice? The reason that I have raised these questions is for the simple fact that all writers do not agree on the points that I have brought to your attention. After reading this chapter, you also, like some other authors, may not agree with me, but that certainly will not make us disagreeable with each other, will it? The differences are not vital, and they do not change in any way the truths that I wish to propagate in this chapter.

EGYPT TO CANAAN

The first thing that we want to consider is the nature of this meeting. Before going back into Egypt to represent God and to withstand Pharaoh, one thing was necessary. Moses sent his wife and two sons back to her father's house (Ex. 4:20). The fact that he set them upon an ass indicates that the sons were still young. Perhaps he was considering their safety. Also, we may consider, that a battlefield is no place for a woman with children. They would be a hindrance to his activities for God in Egypt. We are reminded of the words of our Lord when He said: *"Verily I say unto you, there is no man that hath left house, or brethren, or sisters, or father, or mother, or wife, or children, or lands, for My sake, and the gospel's, but he shall receive an hundredfold now in this time, houses, and brethren, and sisters, and mothers, and children, and lands, with persecutions; and in the world to come eternal life"* (Mark 10:29-30).

Let us give honor to men who have bidden "goodbye" to their wives and little families in the United States, where distances are great. On many occasions they have committed their family to the Lord, and have launched out, many miles from home, to labor for God in new ground and also with distant assemblies. Years ago, when money was scarce, and travel burdensome, some men labored for many months away from their loved ones for the sake of Christ and His gospel. Such activities placed the total burden of the home upon the wife. Leaving wife and children can be a heart-rendering experience. Years ago, I remember a man coming over from Scotland to labor in the United States. It was one year before his wife and four little children could join him. On more than one occasion, while alone in a little room provided for him, he wept. No one but the Lord knew the sorrow of his heart.

On the other hand, I have seen men leave the Lord's work as full time servants, because their wives could not endure the lifestyle required. I remember one man, when away from home, he had to phone his wife on a daily basis and she would weep and complain over the situation. Also, she couldn't manage the children. She didn't believe in spanking the children when needed, so consequently, they gave her a horrible time. It wasn't too long before that poor man had to lay down the gospel plow and return to his secular labor and a fretting wife.

I believe that before an assembly commends a man to the work of the Lord as an evangelist, that his wife should be questioned as well as he. That might prevent disaster and embarrassing moments further down life's road. Is she in agreement with her husband's desire to launch forth? Is she emotionally stable for such a change in lifestyle? Can she handle finances? Is she able to live with very little of this world's goods? Far better to address these things before they happen, than to have them happen, and then fall under the burden of them in failure and disgrace.

JETHRO – A GOOD EXAMPLE

In considering the meeting of Jethro with Moses we want to remember two important things. First, both men were great men. Jethro was the priest of Midian, possibly the high priest of that nation, and Moses had been a prince in Egypt, but was now a prophet, judge, and leader of Israel. There are lessons for us in this narrative, regarding courtesy and the reception of guests. The setting is Oriental in nature, but nevertheless affords us a healthy pattern for our day. Notice first, that Jethro went beyond what was required, in the fact that he sent word ahead to Moses of his coming. Verse six in Darby's rendering reads: *"And he sent word to Moses: I, thy father-in-law Jethro, am come to thee, and thy wife, and her two sons with her."* Young's Literal Translation reads: *"I am coming unto thee."* In the country it seems to be more acceptable than in the city to just drop in for a little visit. However, to just drop in unexpectedly for a visit involving an overnight stay, with no warning to the expected host, is most inappropriate indeed, whether it be country or city. The Lord would never impose Himself in such a way. In fact, you will remember that when He walked with those on the road to Emmaus, as they drew near to the village, whither they went, He would have gone further. He would not impose Himself upon them. *"But they constrained Him, saying, Abide with us: for it is toward evening, and the day is far spent. And He went in to tarry with them"* (Luke 24:29). The Lord was a perfect Gentleman. Do we imitate Him?

Jethro had been a good steward of "another man's goods." Moses had entrusted the care of his little family to his father-in-law, and now, after a period of time, Jethro could faithfully return the sacred deposit with no loss to Moses. Zipporah and her two sons were well and healthy. No disease had ravaged their well-being, they had been spared death, and all was well with them in a temporal way. Let me ask you a pertinent question. If you have a full time worker in the gospel in your assembly who has a wife and little ones – in his absence, what attention do you give to his wife and children? Do you inquire of their welfare? Do you take an interest in his children? Have you ever invited his little family over for a meal, or taken them to a restaurant? Brethren, let us not be simply theological Christians. Let us be practical and practicing Christians! Jethro took good care of his trust in the absence of Moses.

MOSES – A GOOD EXAMPLE

Upon hearing of the coming of Jethro, Moses went out of his way in politeness, and respect, by going out to meet his father-in-law, doing obeisance and kissing him. Moses himself wrote under God's direction; *"Thou shalt rise up before the hoary head, and honour the face of the old man, and fear thy God: I am the LORD"* (Lev. 19:32). Moses was very conscious to observe this very precept. Such an attitude is not very popular today due to humanistic views propagated by ungodly men. Children are taught in our school system the fallacy of "high self-esteem," which of course, pumps ungodly pride into the victim of such unscriptural teaching. Let us be very careful to give proper due to the hoary head, and honor the face of the old man. Paul exhorted Timothy to *"rebuke not an elder* (an older person), *but intreat him as a father"* (1 Tim. 5:1). Moses is found bowed down to the ground before the feet of Jethro. What a manifestation of grace, lowliness, and meekness, reminding us of the exhortation of Paul; *"Let nothing* be done through strife or vainglory; but in lowliness of mind let each esteem other better than themselves"* (Phil. 2:3). If this were true of us, there certainly would be far less problems in the assemblies of God today.

WAS JETHRO SAVED?

The question arises, was Jethro a child of God? Well now, consider the following facts. Would an unbeliever rejoice upon having related to him all the goodness which the LORD had done unto Israel? Would a sinner say; *"Now I know that the LORD is greater than all gods: for in the thing wherein they dealt proudly He was above them"* (Ex. 18:11)? Would an unconverted man take a burnt offering and sacrifices for God, and in so doing, would Moses, Aaron, and all the elders freely fellowship with him in such an occasion if he was a sinner? Jethro says, *"Now I know."* "He knew it before, but now he knew it better; his faith grew up to a full assurance, upon this fresh evidence."[33] As Matthew Henry aptly states, "Their mutual friendship was sanctified by joint-worship."

A GODLY GATHERING

Consider for a moment the character of the gathering in Moses' tent. What was their attitude toward each other? What was the theme of their conversation? The answers to these questions will afford us good examples to follow in our engagements with others. Moses and Jethro showed the utmost respect for one another, and showed a keen interest in each other's affairs. *"They asked each other of their welfare"* (Ex. 18:7). Jethro heard all that God had done for Moses, but he desired to know more. He was interested in the details. What was the major theme of their conversation? The theme was God, and His wondrous workings on behalf of His people.

---

33   Matthew Henry. <u>Matthew Henry's Commentary.</u> (MacDonald Publishing Company, McLean, Virginia 22102. Vol.1). P. 351.

Jethro and Moses' friendship was sanctified by joint-worship. They joined each other in a feast of rejoicing, based upon the offering of a sacrifice. Jethro, Moses, Aaron, and all the elders, came together and ate the bread of God from heaven – the manna. The gathering was godly.

DIRT-BIKES AND ATV FOUR-WHEELERS!

Let us examine ourselves. When we invite guests to our home, do we treat them with the utmost respect? When the meal is spread and all are sitting at the table, what is the nature of our conversation? Does it center around Christ the true manna? Some time ago I sat at dinner with some young men. The conversation became quite active, the topic being dirt-bikes, and ATV 4-wheelers. Suddenly, I interjected and said, "What do you men think of Hebrews chapter one? What is the last thing mentioned in that chapter?" There was a dead silence, so I asked them to give me their thoughts on the beginning of the chapter – silence. They could intelligently talk about carburetors, doing "wheelies, " how to get more power out of the motor, and so on. However, Hebrews chapter one seemed to be a mystery to them. They were not acquainted with the scriptures, consequently the conversation came down to the level of their expertise, namely ATVs and dirt-bikes. Ah brethren, let us measure ourselves and ask the question, where do my major interests lie? With Moses and Jethro it seems very evident that their interests were in the things of God. We all would do well to emulate them. Is our communion in the home with guests, after a godly sort? Do we eat before God soberly with thanksgiving and godly fear? Do we eat and drink to the glory of God, with our conversation being as becometh saints? Do we consider that Christ is the silent and unseen guest and that the eye of God is upon us, and thus act accordingly? *A good man out of the good treasure of his heart bringeth forth that which is good; and an evil man out of the evil treasure of his heart bringeth forth that which is evil: for of the abundance of the heart his mouth speaketh"* (Luke 6:45). What kind of treasure is being stored in my heart? What kind of behavior is seen in my life?

MOSES AND JETHRO

Some have stated that it was at their meeting that Jethro was converted. However, I cannot picture Moses, Aaron, and the elders of Israel allowing a new convert to the faith to officiate for them in offering a burnt offering. To assume the lead in sacred matters when new to the faith certainly would be out of order, neither would Moses have condoned it. No, all indications are that Jethro was a seasoned believer in the one and only true God, the same God that had made Himself known to Moses and to Israel.

Jethro was a man that naturally would command the respect of Moses, for after all, was not Moses totally dependent upon him for forty years? Also, in taking a wife, do you suppose Moses would take a partner in life from a heathen home? I personally do not think so. Jethro was a great man in his country who knew God, and he took in Moses, the fugitive from Egypt. Now things have changed, and it is Moses who has become the greater man. However, notice that in Jethro there is no animosity, there is no jealously, but rather the utmost respect and friendliness.

MY ATTITUDE TO YOUNG MEN

Ah, what lessons we have here, my brethren. Have you ever observed a young man advance in the things of God, and eventually surpass some older brethren in his wisdom, knowledge, grace, and speaking ability? If the answer is, "Yes," then what was your attitude toward him? Did you term him a young upstart, proud, too forward, and looked upon him with contempt? Or, were you thankful to see young gift developing in your midst? Did your friendship with the younger and gifted man become even greater? Now be clear about this, I am not referring to proud, self sufficient, pushy people at all. I am talking about genuine, godly, and gifted people. It is a shame when an older, untaught brother, cannot say anything good about a younger man that manifests a superior gift. King Saul was a man that could not stand anyone to be praised more than he, thus David, the greater man, instead of being loved and appreciated, was hunted and hated. I am afraid that we have "Sauls" among us today.

WHEN DID MOSES AND JETHRO MEET?

The next question arises; when did this meeting actually take place? Authors are at variance on this issue. Some believe that the narrative is in chronological order, while others feel that it took place between the tenth and the eleventh verses of Numbers 10. Verses 11 and 12, which took place after Jethro's meeting with Moses reads thus:

"And it came to pass on the twentieth day of the second month, in the second year, that the cloud was taken up from off the tabernacle of the testimony. The Tabernacle at this point had been reared up one month and twenty days before (Ex. 40:17). *And the children of Israel took their journeys out of the wilderness of Sinai; and the cloud rested in the wilderness of Paran."*

Our text in chapter 18 reads; *"And Jethro, Moses' father in law, came with his sons and his wife unto Moses into the wilderness, where he encamped at the mount of God."* However, the next chapter states in the first two verses, that they were not yet come to Horeb, the mount of God, and that it was not until the third month of the second year after their departure from Egypt, that they arrived there.

Comparing this with Numbers 10:11, we see that they stayed at Horeb (Sinai) until *"the twentieth day of the second month, in the second year,"* so that their encampment at mount Sinai lasted almost one year. It was during this time that the Law was given. It was during this time that Moses complained that he was not able to bear alone the burden of governing so many people. It was at that time that he established judges and captains over the people. This fits in perfectly with Exodus 18, where Jethro advises this very thing, and Moses acts according to his advice.

MOSES' PLEA TO JETHRO

The Jethro of chapter 18, and the Hobab of Numbers 10, are the same person (Judg. 4:11). As the camp is about to move out of the wilderness of Sinai, we read in Exodus 18:27; *"And Moses let his father in law depart; and he went his way into his own land."* However, coming to Numbers 10, we discover a detailed account of Moses' pleading with his father-in-law to go with them (verses 29-32). He assures Hobab that by coming with them, they would do him good, simply because the LORD had spoken good about Israel. Hobab was well acquainted with the desert, and would be able to point out watering places and direct them to fountains. What a tremendous asset this man would be to Moses (so he thought) having such an accurate knowledge of the wilderness. Notice the plea of Moses. *"And he said, Leave us not, I pray thee; forasmuch as thou knowest how we are to encamp in the wilderness, and thou mayest be to us instead of eyes"* (Num. 10:31). What a shame! What a departure from true faith! The divine guidance of the cloudy pillar seems to have been forgotten. The expertise and cunning planning of man seems to supersede the leading of Jehovah. Moses desired Hobab to be their eyes! Only faith can rest on an unseen arm. Moses' faith had dwindled, his eyes had turned from God to man. Consequently, we see the Ark of the covenant of the LORD going before them in the three days' journey, to search out a resting place for them. This is the only occurrence of the Ark going first in the march, while they were in the wilderness. It went first at the crossing of Jordan, but the wilderness journey was over. The reason being, that God cannot be replaced by man. He was their eyes, and he was their sole guide! God is jealous of His people's affections and dependence on Himself!

REPLACING THE HOLY SPIRIT

Coming to our own day, what do we find? When the assemblies of God, gathered unto the name of our Lord Jesus Christ (as we know them today) commenced their pilgrim testimony and journey in 1859, there was a total dependence on the Holy Spirit as to their guidance. It was the Holy Spirit that made overseers (Acts 20:28); it was the Holy Spirit that sent forth evangelists (Acts 13:4). They were directed where to go, how long to stay, and what to preach (Acts 16:10; Acts 18:9-11; 1 Corinthians 2:4). We have come down the road 150 years since then, and what do we find? Sad to say, in some areas (thank God, not all) we see human planning replacing the divine guidance of the Spirit. We are thankful for those who have been placed in various assemblies by the Spirit as overseers. However, is it not true that some have been positioned as overseers by man? Was it not perhaps because they were related to an existing overseer, or perhaps because they were successful businessmen? As for evangelistic work among us, is there the careful consideration of the Spirit where to preach? Is there the "assuredly gathering" of the Lord calling one to a certain field? Would you say that programmed efforts in the gospel, with a set closing date, is the leading of the Spirit? To engage thus in a gospel effort, can hardly be termed the leading of the Holy Spirit. In some areas, the Holy Spirit has been put, as it were, into a little box, and we do what we want to do, regardless of what the Spirit wants done.

SPIRIT CONTROLLED, OR, MAN CONTROLLED CONFERENCES?

You will search in vain in the New Testament teachings for "conferences," yet at the commencement of such activity, there was blessing. Servants would come with a message on their hearts from God. The Spirit was the "Master of ceremonies," if I may so put it that way. He controlled from the commencement of every conference, unto its conclusion. Spirit-controlled men would pray, and Spirit-guided men would minister the word. The Spirit would guide, not only as to the message to be delivered, but also just when to rise and deliver that message. There was no such thing as pre-arranged subjects, pre-chosen speakers, and set time limits. This business of announcing that there are three hours and if each speaker would take no more than 30 minutes that there would be enough time for six speakers is foreign to New Testament teaching. No chapter and verse can be produced to uphold such an announcement. This is the modern way of limiting the Holy Spirit. We have become quite proficient is dictating to the Spirit, rather than letting the Spirit dictate to us.

TWO SPEAKERS

Let us just suppose that two men have a word from the Lord. The first man is highly gifted, and his subject requires 45 minutes. The second man is not as gifted as the first man, but he has a message that would take no more than 15 minutes. Oh no, such activity will not do. Each man is allotted 30 minutes. So the gifted man is forced to cut his message down and the other man is urged to stretch his message out to the point of wearying his listeners. Where is the Holy Spirit? Why, He has been put into a box! He has not been allowed to control the meeting.

Moses said, *"Thou mayest be to us instead of eyes."* So in some areas, human planning has displaced the Holy Spirit. Consequently, speakers are chosen to the exclusion of others, subjects are given to preach, and time limits are set for the delivery of the man-appointed subject.

God overruled in the case of Moses' weakness. The Ark went before them, for without it they could have neither rest, comfort, or guidance. The Ark was their defense. May the Lord help us to see the absolute need of totally waiting upon God as to guidance, and not look to man saying, *"thou mayest be to us instead of eyes."*

> "Rise my soul! Thy God directs thee;
> Stranger hands no more impede;
> Pass thou on; His hand protects thee,
> Strength that has the captive freed.
>
> Is the wilderness before thee?
> Desert lands where drought abides?
> Heavenly springs shall there restore thee,
> Fresh from God's exhaustless tides.

Though thy way be long and dreary,
Eagle strength He'll still renew;
Garments fresh and foot unweary
Tell how God hath brought thee through."[34]

In the discourse between Moses and Jethro, mentioned in Exodus 18, we find that Moses speaks of *the statutes and laws of the Lord* as things already revealed and acknowledged, which necessarily implies that these laws had already been given. This is quite evident from the fact that giving of the Law did not take place until several months after the events mentioned in the preceding chapters. In other words, as chapter 18 opens, the Law stated in chapter 20, had already been given. Thus we conclude, that chapter 18 is not in chronological order, but rather fits between verse 10 and verse 11 of Numbers chapter 10.

Another point to notice is the fact that when Jethro took a burnt offering and sacrifices for God, and Aaron came, and all the elders of Israel, that they ate bread with Moses' father-in-law *"before God."* That same form of speech is used, and plainly refers to God's manifested presence in the tabernacle. See Deuteronomy 12:5-7, and 1 Chronicles 29:21-22. *"Before God"* simply means, *"before the tabernacle,"* showing that at that point, the tabernacle was already erected, that date being the first month in the second year, on the first day of the month (Ex. 40:17).

MOSES – RIGHT OR WRONG?

The next question arises; was Moses in the mind of God by following the advice given to him by his father-in-law? Again, we come across disagreements from various writers. Some believe that Moses did the wrong thing, and that God was able to give him the needed grace to carry on as he had in the past. Others believe that the advice was not only timely, but that it was of the LORD.

---

34 John Nelson Darby. The Believer's Hymn Book. (John Ritchie Ltd. Kilmarnock, Scotland). P. 206

MOSES' PRIORITIES

With these thoughts in mind, let us examine the facts. Notice the divine record. *"And it came to pass on the morrow, that Moses sat to judge the people: and the people stood by Moses from the morning unto the evening"* (Ex. 18:13). The first thing that we want to notice is this; Moses had received into his home important company, but that in no way deterred him from his sacred duties to Jehovah and Israel. He didn't say, "Well, I have company and will have to set aside my spiritual duties until they leave. After all, my father-in-law has come a long way to bring my wife and sons back to me, and out of respect, I must give them some time." Not a bit of it! Such foolishness never entered his head. "Though Jethro, his father-in-law was with him, which might have given him a good pretense for a vacation (he might have adjourned the court for that day, or at least have shortened it), yet he sat, even the next day after his coming, *from morning till evening*. Note. Necessary business must always take place of ceremonious attentions. It is too great a compliment to our friends to prefer the enjoyment of their company before our duty to God, which ought to be done, while yet the other is not left undone."[35]

UNEXPECTED COMPANY

It reminds me of an incident many years ago in our assembly. Some relatives happened to drop in to an older Christian couple's home, just for a visit. They were from out of town. Now the proper thing to do would be not only to warmly welcome them, but to also carefully entertain them. However, there was a problem, for the older couple was just getting ready to go to the weekly prayer meeting of the assembly. What now? Well, there was no problem as far as the godly couple was concerned. They gave their relatives a warm welcome, invited them in, and then said to them, "We are just going to the prayer meeting, will you come with us, or would you rather sit here in our home until we return?" The unsaved relatives declined to go, so the old couple

---

35 Matthew Henry. <u>Matthew Henry's Commentary.</u> (MacDonald Publishing Company, McLean, Virginia 22102. Vol.1). P. 351.

left their guests sitting alone in their home until they returned. You may say, "That was inconsiderate and rude!" Is that so? Well, let me say this, that it would have been inconsiderate and rude to the Lord for them to have stayed at home, and thus place their relatives above the Lord. As far as the older couple was concerned, Christ took first place in their life. This was the character of Moses, was it not? What about you? Do you give Christ first place in your life? *"He that loveth father or mother more than Me is not worthy of Me: and he that loveth son or daughter more than Me is not worthy of Me"* (Matt. 10:37).

Now comes the question whether Moses was right or wrong in following the advice of his father-in-law, Jethro. Having been in Pharaoh's court, Moses would have been well acquainted with the most efficient procedure in governing people. Egyptian kings usually decided cases by nominated judges. To have a well-ordered community, as practiced in Egypt, judicial functions were separated from legislative and administrative, and entrusted to a large number of persons, not monopolized by a single individual.

Considering the children of Israel, they had just been released from hard slavery, they had no education, and certainly possessed no knowledge of the principles of law, or experience in court procedure as Moses knew it in Egypt. Moses felt that he alone was the only one equal to the task of discharging the office of judge in a community consisting of over two million people, for he alone was learned in all the wisdom of the Egyptians (Acts 7:22). Consequently, Moses sat from morning to evening, day after day, listening to the people's problems, and passing judgment on their varied cases. Even though *"his eye was not dim, nor his natural force abated"* (Deut. 34:7), yet Moses had to admit, *"I am not able to bear this people alone, because it is too heavy for me"* (Num. 11:14). *"I am not able to bear you myself alone. How can I myself alone bear your cumbrance, and your burden, and your strife?"* (Deut. 1:9,12). Jethro, immediately upon observing Moses' "work day," perceived his son-in-law's problem, and with love and wisdom offered him his timely advice.

MOSES' "WORK DAY"

Can you picture "the work day" for this great man Moses? Let us draw near and observe. There is a backlog of cases, some of them mere trivial cases. *"The people stood by Moses from the morning to the evening."* A long wait never calms a person, but rather aggravates them. I remember taking some folks to a restaurant and we were told that there would be an hour wait before being seated. I took a walk until the seating time came. The place was packed with customers. We were seated, given a glass of water, and then we waited. Twenty minutes later, the waitress came with a smile and took our order. By this time, all of us were very hungry. It was past 7 PM. We waited for our meal, and we waited, and we waited. Forty minutes later, the meal arrived, two hours after our arrival to that restaurant! Was I aggravated? Please don't ask!

Have you ever gone to a post office where only one clerk is taking care of a multitude of people? When you see four wickets, thirty people in line, and only one clerk, does it upset you? Some people have a great amount of patience, while others do not. I can just picture some of these Israelites standing and waiting, waiting, waiting, in order to have their case processed by one man – Moses. It must have been trying for them. Basically, it was not fair. It was an inconvenience, and it certainly did not calm one's temper. Basically, the people Moses was called upon to judge were stiffnecked, obstinate, stubborn, and rebellious. They are called "stiffnecked" seven times by Moses, and 765 years later in Hezekiah they are still termed "stiffnecked." That is why I believe that most of them were in a miserable state by the time they stood before Moses to judge their case.

The sun makes its appearance over the eastern horizon. Moses hastens to his judgment seat. Crowds are waiting, people are expecting to be heard. One after another presents his case. Some very serious, others very trivial. Moses is burdened with them all. The day rolls on and the sun begins to sink low in the west. There is still a line of grumbling people waiting for justice. However, it is time for bed and they are turned away and told to return on the morrow. Can you picture such a situation? Can you envisage the countenance of those who were turned away for that day?

From Moses' own words in Numbers 11, and Deuteronomy 1, the responsibility of being the sole judge of such a multitude was producing a mental strain so injurious that it was impairing his faculties, rendering him unfit to perform the delicate duties of a judge, especially as the day wore on. Had there been no one else among the Israelites competent to perform any part of the work, he would have been right in continuing in his present course, even though it was impairing him in various ways. But that was not the case, for there were to be found in Israel men qualified to help, by performing minor judicial functions. Jethro seemed to immediately perceive this, while Moses seemingly was oblivious to the fact. Moses was exhausting himself unnecessarily, a course of action that could not be justified.

As stated before, this action was unduly taxing the patience of a stiffnecked people. There was a delay of justice. It was inconvenient to have to wait from morning to evening before obtaining a hearing, or perhaps even to be turned away to return the next day. The inconvenience would even be greater if Israel was called upon to go forward under the moving of the pillar of the cloud. That would delay the person's case for days, until the cloud rested, and the camp pitched.

Take the case of Absalom. He had, so he thought, a case to be heard by the king, but he was put off. We are not given the reason for David's continual delay in listening to his son, but nevertheless, the fact that Absalom felt slighted, produced far greater problems for David later.

I cannot but help to thank God for His sending Jethro when he did, with wise, timely, and "common sense" advice. I am also thankful for the attitude of Moses for humbly taking that advice. Some writers hastily accuse Moses of sinning against God by receiving his father-in-law's advice and acting upon it. If you are among that accusing group, let me ask you, would you con-

MOSES AND JETHRO

done a one-man operation in the assemblies today? Would you advise that one man should do it all? Is this the mind of God today, for His gathered-out people? You will have to admit that, no, this is not the mind of God to the government of a scriptural assembly. Even at the commencement of the Church, when the apostles were still living, a one-man ministry was not the mind of God. You will remember that the apostles ordained them elders in every church (Acts 14:23). *"Ordained,"* simply means that in their wise observation of brethren in various churches, they pointed out to the congregation those in each particular church that filled the requirements of an elder. With that made known, those who were pointed out began to function as such. You will find a similar situation in the Jerusalem Church. Notice.

> *"And in those days, when the number of the disciples was multiplied, there arose a murmuring of the Grecians against the Hebrews, because their widows were neglected in the daily ministration. Then the twelve called the multitude of the disciples unto them, and said, It is not reason that we should leave the word of God, and serve tables. Wherefore, brethren, look ye out among you seven men of honest report, full of the Holy Ghost and wisdom, whom we may appoint over this business. But we will give ourselves continually to prayer, and to the ministry of the word. And the saying pleased the whole multitude"* (Acts 6:1-5).

The church in which Gaius was in fellowship was in a deplorable condition. There was a dictator there named Diotrephes who loved to have the preeminence. There seemingly was no consideration on his part of his other brethren. He did it all! He was the last and only word. Paul, in writing to the church at Corinth, uses the illustration of a human body to convey the spiritual truth of the Spirit's operation in a local assembly.[36] He emphasizes the fact that there are diversities of gifts, and that these gifts are divided to every man severally as He will. He points out that even though the human body is one, that it has

---

36   Read 1 Corinthians Chapter 12, carefully.

many members, all working together for the functioning of that body. All have their particular part to perform, and failure to do so produces a negative effect upon the whole body.

> *"If the foot shall say, Because I am not the hand, I am not of the body; is it therefore not of the body? And if the ear shall say, Because I am not the eye, I am not of the body; is it therefore not of the body? If the whole body were an eye, where were the hearing? If the whole were hearing, where were the smelling? But now hath God set the members every one of them in the body, as it hath pleased Him"* (1 Cor. 12:15-18).

JETHRO'S ADVICE

The advice of Jethro is profitable to notice. Consider his rational thinking, and his proposed solution to Moses' problem. After careful observation of Moses' "work day," Jethro said, "The thing that thou doest is not good." Then he gives the reason why it was not good. *"Thou wilt surely wear away, both thou, and this people that is with thee: for this thing is too heavy for thee; thou art not able to perform it thyself alone"* (Ex. 18:18). Writers that oppose Jethro's advice seek to explain the circumstance by saying that if Moses had looked to God, that He would have empowered him for the task, to perform it alone. The problem with such conjecture is that it implies that prior to Jethro's advice Moses had not been looking to God for that "extra boost," to perform all the work alone. I cannot accept that sort of reasoning, and consider it a slur on the character of this godly and mighty man. No, I am afraid that if our minds are not filled with preconceived notions, that we will have to admit that Moses did the right thing in acting upon Jethro's advice.

It is pleasing to see the first consideration regarding his advice is God.

> *"Hearken now unto my voice, I will give thee counsel, and God shall be with thee: Be thou for the people*

> to God-ward, that thou mayest bring the causes unto God" (Ex. 18:19).

"God shall be with thee," that is, by following my counsel you may anticipate the divine blessing. *"That thou mayest bring the causes unto God."* That is, he was to act as a mediator and interpreter with God, bringing the causes of the people before Him, and in turn, also reporting "the ordinances and laws" which would constitute his decisions in the cases referred to him as we see in the following verse.

> *"And thou shalt teach them ordinances and laws, and shalt shew them the way wherein they must walk, and the work that they must do"* (v. 20).

Thus, in Jethro's opening statement he declares the two-fold office Moses was to sustain, namely, that of an advocate on behalf of the people, and an interpreter on the behalf of God.

> *"Moreover thou shalt provide out of all the people able men, such as fear God, men of truth, hating covetousness; and place such over them, to be rulers of thousands, and rulers of hundreds, rulers of fifties, and rulers of tens"* (Ex. 18:21).

FOUR REQUIREMENTS

The next step in Jethro's advice was to bring before Moses the character of the men that were to be chosen to help him in administrating justice in Israel. The requisites are four.

(1) They were to be *"able men."* That is, active and energetic in character. The same word is translated *"men of activity"* (Gen. 47:6), *and "mighty men of valor"* (1 Chron. 26:6). These would be men of good sense regarding judgment and resolution. Men that would not be swayed by the frowns, or loud demands and protests of their clients. It has been said that *"clear heads and stout hearts make good judges,"* and rightly so. Men that can righteously pass "judgments" in an assembly for God, regardless of friends

or relatives, are *"able men"* indeed, and valuable men! As we see the older generation passing off of the scene and younger men taking the place of responsibility in the assemblies of God, well might we pray for the Lord the Spirit to raise up *"able men."* Men that possess sufficient intelligence and discrimination to judge even the lowest cases. Men that know their Bible, and that can "pull out of the Holy Book," without hesitation, the answer needed. Any man assuming the place of an overseer, if not an "able man," will not be respected, no confidence will be felt in him, his decisions will carry no weight, and he will injure rather than benefit the community.[37]

(2) The second requirement was; *"men, such as fear God."* These would be men that were very conscious of God, that His eye was upon them, and that He was just and holy. They would be men that were very much aware that they would have to give an account unto God for all their doings. Any base temptation in their heart would be suppressed by the fact that they feared God. Thus, they would be men, holy in character. Luke 18:2 reveals what the danger can be if there is no fear of God. *"There was in a city a judge, which feared not God, neither regarded man"* (Luke 18:2). The Lord speaks of him as an *"unjust judge"* (v. 6).

(3) The third essential was that they were to be, *"men of truth."* Such men would never betray a trust. You could confide in them, knowing that what you had told them would go no further. One could rely on what they said. Men that would never utter a falsehood, or act an insidious part. I have seen people bring their problems to another in total confidence, only to have that person in whom they confided betray their trust, by telling others. What a betrayal of trust! If any person comes whispering to you saying, "Let me tell you a secret that so-in-so told me, but don't tell anyone that I told you;" tell them plainly that you don't want to hear it! Such whisperers are not *"men of truth,"* and they need to be rebuked. Solomon describes it thus: *"Confidence in an unfaithful man in time of trouble is like a broken*

---

[37] See J. Orr. Exodus 18:21 (Vol. II). (The Pulpit Commentary, Vol. 1. Hendrickson). P. 94.

tooth, and a foot out of joint" (Prov. 25:19).

(4) *"Hating covetousness,"* is the next requisite proposed by Jethro. Men who would have a noble contempt of worldly wealth, and a positive abhorrence of taking bribes. This is the characteristic of men who will dwell with the devouring fire, who will dwell with everlasting burnings. Those expressions are descriptive of a righteous and holy God. Then Isaiah follows with these words. *"He that walketh righteously, and speaketh uprightly; he that despiseth the gain of oppressions, that shaketh his hands from holding of bribes, that stoppeth his ears from hearing of blood, and shutteth his eyes from seeing evil"* (Isa. 33:15). In the days of the judges, when Samuel ruled, this quality was sadly missing in his sons, for we read of them; *"And his sons walked not in his ways, but turned aside after lucre, and took bribes, and perverted judgment"* (1 Sam. 8:3). In Isaiah's day, 360 years later, we find the same condition. *"Thy princes are rebellious, and companions of thieves: every one loveth gifts, and followeth after rewards: they judge not the fatherless, neither doth the cause of the widow come unto them"* (Isa. 1:23). Coming farther along in Israel's history, we discover the same corruption in Micah's time. *"The heads thereof judge for reward ... the judge asketh for a reward"* (Mic. 3:11; 7:3).

In many ancient kingdoms, corruption, when detected in a judge, was punished by instant execution. Today, in the East, it is hardly possible to find a judge who is not anxious to receive bribes. What about the assemblies of God? Do we not discover the same required qualities in overseeing brethren? Turning to 1 Timothy 3, we find 16 qualities given to us of an elder. These qualities closely correspond to the qualifications laid down by Jethro to Moses.

JETHRO'S INSIGHT

Jethro evidently perceived looming dangers to which Moses was oblivious. He saw that Moses had taken upon himself a task for which he was not equal. He perceived that the work, as devoted as Moses was, was not being properly done. He understood that the time and energy which Moses was using could be put to more valuable and profitable use. Finally, he saw that there were men in Israel who were gifted enough to do much of the work that Moses was seeking to accomplish. Through the advice of Jethro, many men in Israel who were gifted, were given the opportunity to exercise their gift by being appointed to judge various cases, leaving the most serious and complex cases to Moses. Thus, in military fashion, we have grades of appointment and levels of authority formed. I am reminded of a verse. *"Let all things be done decently and in order"* (1 Cor. 14:40). Consequently, we have instituted in Israel rulers over thousands, hundreds, fifties, and tens. How wonderful! It was not until then that every man could have his cause considered by a judge, without waiting, waiting, and waiting. The most difficult cases were to be brought to Moses, who, as a result of manifold help from minor judges, would have ample time to carefully deliberate the most difficult cases of various clients.

After laying down the plan for Moses, Jethro said, *"If thou shalt do this thing, and God command thee so, then thou shalt be able to endure, and all this people shall also go to their place in peace"* (Ex. 18:23). The fact that Jethro insisted on men being appointed that possessed the qualities he listed, shows him to be a man of true piety, and one who had the true interests of Israel and Moses upon his heart. Notice carefully, that his plan, before being adopted, was to be submitted for God's approval (*"and God command thee so"*). So it should be today in every assembly of God. Every scheme introduced should first be with God's approval. That approval can only be known by an intimate knowledge of the Holy Scriptures.

12

MOSES AND THE LAW

"In the third month, when the children of Israel were gone forth out of the land of Egypt, the same day came they into the wilderness of Sinai" (Ex. 19:1).

There is a striking coincidence in this verse when compared with Acts 2:1, which reads, *"And when the day of Pentecost was fully come, they were all of one accord in one place."* On that day the Church was born! "Pentecost," means "fifty," and it was fifty days after the Jewish Passover (when Christ was offered as our Passover), that the Holy Spirit came down and indwelt the believers, giving them power to witness. It was a memorable day indeed!

Coming to Exodus 19, we see the LORD God coming down and giving the Law to Moses, exactly fifty days after Israel's first Passover and departure from Egypt! According to Jewish usage, the expression, *"the same day"* means the first day of the month. This was just forty-five days after Israel's departure from Egypt. They departed on the fifteenth day of the first month (Num. 33:3), leaving sixteen days until the second month. The second month involved twenty-nine days, making a total of forty-five days. To these days we must add the day Moses went up to God (v. 3), then the following day when he returned Israel's answer to God (v. 7–8), and three days more mentioned in verses 10, and 11. Adding these days up, we come to a total of 50 days from the Passover to the giving of the Law on Mount Sinai. These two date-corresponding events, namely the giving of the Law, and the giving of the Spirit, are similar, yet also strikingly different. In both incidences, God established a covenant with His people. Yet under the first covenant we sadly observe the slaying of about three thousand men because of their idolatry (Ex. 32:28). While under the second covenant we joyfully see the salvation of about three thousand souls, because of their faith in Christ (Acts 2:41). Thus, we see subtraction under the Law, but addition under grace.

SINAI – LOCATION

There is much conjecture as to the exact location of Mount Sinai. The word *"Sinai"* is mentioned 34 times in the Old Testament and twice in Galatians by Paul. Connected with this word is also the word *"Horeb,"* being mentioned seventeen times, exclusively in the Old Testament.

In the writings of Moses, the Law is described as having been given from Mount Sinai, and in other portions as having been given from Mount Horeb. Of course, skeptics immediately take this up to prove that the Bible contradicts itself. However, these ignoramuses don't understand that Horeb and Sinai are not distinct summits of the same range. *"Horeb"* is the name of the whole mountainous region generally, while *"Sinai"* is the name of a particular summit. So let us be clear on this, that, *Horeb* is usually spoken of as *a region,* and Sinai is spoken of as *a distinct mountain.*

There seems to be no instance in which the name *"Horeb"* occurs to convey the thought of descending, or ascending, or standing upon it as a mountain, as we have associated with the word *"Sinai."* There are two instances that would seem to contradict this statement, but a careful observation of the two following verses, only confirms what has been said.

> *"Now Moses kept the flock of Jethro his father in law, the priest of Midian: and he led the flock to the backside of the desert, and came to the mountain of God, even to Horeb"* (Ex. 3:1). *And he* (Elijah) *arose, and did eat and drink, and went in the strength of that meat forty days and forty nights unto Horeb the mount of God"* (1 Kgs. 19:8).

MOSES AND THE LAW

In both of these places, it can be plainly seen that Horeb denotes the whole range, while the mount of God denotes only Sinai. This thought is further confirmed in the fact that the actions are mentioned as having taken place in Horeb, which were certainly not on any particular mountain, but rather in the surrounding valleys and plains. The psalmist says: *"They made a calf in Horeb"* (Ps. 106:19). This didn't take place in the mountain of Sinai, but rather in the wilderness of Sinai, while Moses was in the mountain. Moses smote the rock in Horeb (Ex. 17:6). This certainly was not up the mount of Sinai, but in the same mountainous range called Horeb, which covered that area termed Rephidim. It is informing to note, that the famous historian, Josephus, does not mention any mount called Horeb. He speaks exclusively of Mount Sinai, and writing about the incident at Rephidim, notes that Israel, upon leaving that place, journeyed on until they arrived at Sinai. Thus, as already observed, on the *fiftieth day* from the celebration of the Passover, the glory of God appeared on the mount, in commemoration of which the Jews celebrate the feast of *Pentecost*.

SINAI DESCRIBED

Approaching the central granite mountains of Sinai from the N.N.W., through a steep, and rocky pass, between blackened cliffs of granite up to 1,000 feet high, one would come to a plain over two miles in length and nearly two-thirds of a mile broad. This plain is wholly enclosed by dark black and yellow granite mountains composed of splintered peaks and ridges, from 1,000 to 1,500 feet high, named Er Raheh, "the Palm of the Hand." At the south end there is a sheer precipice 1,500 feet, which has been called, "The Mount of God – God's Pulpit." It is generally believed that this is the area where Israel encamped while receiving the Law from God.

The subject of God giving the Law is vast, and would more than fill an ordinary book. However, in dealing with this tremendous subject, we will only be giving you the highlights of this memorable event, so that you will be somewhat aware of what took place. The first thing that we want to notice is:

MOSES' UPS AND DOWNS

In the beginning and the end of each of the following four sections we read these words: *"Moses went up,"* or, *"then went up Moses,"* followed by, *"Moses went down,"* or, *"he came down."*

(1) Exodus 19:3–14. Moses told what God had done.

(2) Exodus 19:20–25. Moses warned, and told to bring Aaron.

(3) Exodus 24:9–32:7, 15. Moses given tables of stone. The sin of Israel.

(4) Exodus 34:2–29. Moses hews two tables of stone.

Having ascended the mount, the LORD called unto Moses out of the mountain, saying; *"Thus shalt thou say to the house of Jacob, and tell the children of Israel."* Thus, we have one assembly of people defined two ways. First, *"The house of Jacob."* God was the God of Jacob, thus indicating His presence and His preservation (Gen. 28:15). Second, *"the children of Israel,"* indicating God's provision and power. God Almighty, the All-Sufficient One (Gen. 35:10–11). Another author's comment is worthy of note.

> "This twofold denomination of the chosen people is rather remarkable and no doubt was intended to carry with it some special emphasis of meaning. As the mercies conferred upon them as a people extended back into the history of the past, it was perhaps designed, by the use of these two names, to remind them of their humble beginnings and their subsequent increase; to suggest to them that they, who were once as lowly as *Jacob* when he went to Padan-aram, were now grown as great as God made him, when he came

from thence and was called *Israel*. The mention of the twofold appellation of their ancestor, would tend also to excite them to obedience in conformity to his example."[38]

On the mount, the LORD brings before Moses, eight things worthy of consideration.

(1) DEVASTATION. *"Ye have seen what I did unto the Egyptians."* He would have them to remember His divine power on their behalf, bringing the powerful nation of Egypt to total ruin. One is reminded of Paul's exposing words regarding Christ and the powers of darkness, which, at one time, held us captive. *"And having spoiled principalities and powers, He made a shew of them openly, triumphing over them in it"* (Col. 2:15). *"Forasmuch then as the children are partakers of flesh and blood, He also Himself likewise took part of the same; that through death He might destroy* (annul) *him that had the power of death, that is, the devil"* (Heb. 2:14). What God told Satan in the garden of Eden, was fulfilled at Calvary. *"And I will put enmity between thee and the woman, and between thy seed and her seed; it shall bruise thy head, and thou shalt bruise His heel"* (Gen. 3:15).

(2) ELEVATION. *"I bare you on eagle's wings."* Birds carry their young in their talons while in flight. No so the eagle. This unique bird caries its young on top of its wings. Unlike other birds, for an archer to shoot a baby eagle, he would have to kill the mother first. Here we have a picture of God's tender care for His people, swiftly transporting them from the house of bondage to His desired rest. This truth is amplified in Deuteronomy 32:11–12. *"As an eagle stirreth up her nest, fluttereth over her young, spreadeth abroad her wings, taketh them, beareth them on her wings: So the LORD alone did lead him, and there was no strange god with him. He made him ride on the high places of the earth, that he might eat the increase of the fields."* "In all their affliction He was afflicted, and the angel of His presence saved them: in His love and in His pity He redeemed them; and He bare them, and carried them all

---

38   George Bush. Exodus. (Klock & Klock Christian Publishers, Inc. Minneapolis, Minnesota. 1981 reprint). P. 237.

the days of old" (Isa. 63:9). "Eagles wings!" Not only are they symbolic of tender care, and elevating power, but they are also a symbol of divine protection! What an elevated people are God's people! Do you understand this my dear brother, sister? You are an elevated person! You are not only a child of God (relationship), but also a son of God (responsibility and dignity). As such, how could you ever be ashamed of the gospel of Christ? How could you dare cringe as a coward before the ungodly? You are the nobility of heaven! Hold your head high! Manifest the dignity of an ambassador from heaven! Act so as to create in the minds of the spiritually blind, that you have something that they do not possess. How dare we be discouraged when things look dark. Lift up your heads brethren, for our redemption draweth nigh. The day is very near, when we shall all stand before the Judgment Seat of Christ, to receive a reward, for every little thing that we have accomplished for the Master, while in our body down here.

> Let us love the Lord that bought us,
> Pitied us when wand'ring far;
> Called us by His grace, and taught us
> Where our joys and blessings are;
> He has washed us in His blood,
> He presents our souls to God.
>
> Let us sing, though fierce temptation
> Threaten hard to bear us down;
> For the Lord, our strong salvation,
> Holds in view the conq'ror's crown;
> He who washed us in His blood,
> Has secured our way to God.
>
> Let us wonder; grace and justice
> Join, and point to mercy's store;
> When through grace in Christ our trust is
> Justice smiles, and asks no more;
> He who washed us in His blood
> Soon will bring us home to God.[39]

---

[39] John Newton. The Believer's Hymn Book. (John Ritchie Ltd.

(3) SEPARATION. "And brought you unto Myself." It has been rightly said that this is the ultimate aim of all the gracious methods of God's providence and grace, to bring us back to Himself, to reinstate us in our lost favor, and to restore us to that relationship, in which alone we can be happy. God had delivered His people from cruel bondage, and now He was going to bring them into a covenant relationship with Himself. This would ensure them of the enjoyment of His special protective favor.

What about us? Can we not relate this to our own salvation experience? Consider, and enjoy these precious words: *"But now in Christ Jesus ye who sometimes were far off are made nigh by the blood of Christ"* (Eph. 2:13). *"For Christ also hath once suffered for sins, the Just for the unjust, that He might bring us to God"* (1 Pet. 3:18). This most-blessed truth is amplified in the words of the poet:

> Nearer to God I could not be.
> For in the Person of His Son,
> I am as near as He.

(4) OBSERVATION, OBEDIENCE. *"Now therefore, if ye will obey My voice indeed, and keep My covenant, then ... "* Notice that word "therefore." What does it mean? Simply this. That because of what has already taken place (His mighty deliverance, protection, power, and bringing them unto Himself), He expected something in return. He expected explicit obedience to His voice, and faithfulness to His covenant. He informs them that they are obligated thus to Him. There was to be no deviation from His prescribed ways. He promises them temporal and spiritual blessings, on one condition, and that was, that they faithfully obey and keep His commandments.

SERVANT – SLAVE

Now then, have things changed from the days of Sinai? Are the days following the birth of the Church at Pentecost any different? Most certainly not! Time and time again, you read

---

Kilmarnock, Scotland). P. 111.

of Paul being a servant of Jesus Christ. The word "servant" is "slave." What is a slave? Why, he is a person that has been purchased by his master. He is not his own. He has no will of his own. All that he possesses, belongs to his master. His welfare depends on his obedience to his master's every whim, or command. He is absolutely obligated to obey, with no questions asked. Let me ask you, are you a servant of the Lord Jesus Christ? Are you saved? If so, then the Saviour has positioned you as His servant, or, in other words, you are His bondslave. The Lord God's Servant was Christ (Isa. 42:19). As such, what did He say? Notice! "Father, if Thou be willing, remove this cup from Me: nevertheless not My will, but Thine, be done" (Luke 22:42). "The Father hath not left Me alone; for I do always those things that please Him" (John 8:29). There you are, my friend. The Lord Jesus was a slave to His Father. He perfectly kept the covenant. He treasured it up in His heart. He was the blessed Man of Psalm one. He never deviated from the truth. He never faltered, for how could He? He was intrinsically sinless.

CHRIST – OUR EXAMPLE

Take notice of this: "For even hereunto were ye called: because Christ also suffered for us, leaving us an example, that ye should follow His steps" (1 Pet. 2:21). We can't follow in His steps, for He was sinless. A little child walking with his father in the snow, cannot place his feet in the same imprint of his father's steps, for they are too far apart. However, he certainly can follow the trail left by his father, and that is the thought here. We are not perfect, but we are pardoned. Let us follow Him. Let us keep His commandments, for they are not grievous. Doing so will ensure us of the rich blessings of God. We will be given divine comfort, divine guidance, divine power, and divine peace.

Some Christians seem to stand at "wit's end corner." They don't know which way to turn. Their lives have become one hectic mess. They are running to psychiatrists for solutions to their manifold problems. What is the problem? Could it be, that if they were to trace back in their lifetime, they would find a deviation from obeying the commandments of God? It very well could be. What is the cause of spiritual ignorance? Or what is the cause of so much unrest among the people of God? Cannot the problems be traced back to a lack of faithfulness in keeping all the commandments of the Lord? I think that it would be well for all of us to exclaim, *"Search me, O God, and know my heart: try me, and know my thoughts: And see if there be any wicked way in me, and lead me in the way everlasting"* (Ps. 139:23–24).

CHRIST'S DEMAND

Proof that the Lord Jesus demands first place in our lives is found in a number of His sayings. *"Whosoever he be of you that forsaketh not all that he hath, he cannot be My disciple"* (Luke 14:33). *"He that loveth father or mother more than Me is not worthy of Me: and he that loveth son or daughter more than Me is not worthy of Me"* (Matt. 10:37). Then He gives us proof of that love to Him by saying, *"He that hath My commandments, and keepeth them, he it is that loveth Me"* (John 14:21). *"If a man love Me, he will keep My words"* (John 14:23).

This is simple, yet searching ministry, from our Lord. There is no side-stepping it, no altering it, and no watering-down of its plain teaching. The words are so plain that a ten-year-old could understand them. True, Satan can attack the child of God with fears, depression, and even sickness. However, take a keen look at your past, and ask yourself, have I disobeyed His commandments? If so, that may be the answer to your manifold problems dear child of God.

Before closing this subject, let us remind ourselves of the salient truths found in the first Corinthian epistle. In chapter three, we are warned not to defile the assembly with unprofitable teaching. In chapter five, we are warned against fornication, and a lax attitude in dealing with various sins. Chapter six warns us against going to law with another brother, and that God's assembly should have a court system to judge cases.

Various rules regarding marriage are afforded us in chapter seven, and chapter eight warns against defiling the conscience of a weak brother. Chapter ten brings before us prohibitions regarding fellowship with the idol's temple, which today could be applied to Christendom.

Chapter eleven tells sisters that their hair is not to be tampered with by a cutting instrument, for their *"long"* hair is given to them for their glory, and that in the assembly gathering, she is to have her head covered with a vail. Also, the Lord's Supper is "blueprinted" for us, namely, one loaf of bread, and one cup of wine, to be partaken of by all in the fellowship. Finally, the saints are instructed as to the giving of their substance to the Lord in chapter sixteen.

Notice the classification of all these exhortations and warnings: *"If any man think himself to be a prophet, or spiritual, let him acknowledge that the things that I write unto you are the commandments of the Lord"* (1 Cor. 14:37). The question remains, if we flagrantly disobey the commandments of the Lord, how then can we expect the blessing of the Lord? We can't!

(5) APPRECIATION. *"Ye shall be a peculiar treasure unto Me."* In the Chaldee language, this expression signifies *"to gain, to acquire to one's self, to make one's own, to appropriate."* It conveys the thought that to God, Israel was a treasure which He made of His own peculiar choice. A treasure that He had set His heart on, and would not be willing to share with anyone else, nor resign to the care of any other. Other Scriptures attest to this wonderful fact. *"For thou art an holy people unto the LORD thy God: the LORD thy God hath chosen thee to be a special people unto Himself, above all people that are upon the face of the earth"* (Deut. 7:6). *"For the LORD's portion is His people"* (Deut. 32:9). *"For the LORD hath chosen Jacob unto Himself, and Israel for His peculiar treasure"* (Ps. 135:4).

Coming to the New Testament, we find the same association with the Lord and His redeemed people. Notice: *"Who gave Himself for us, that He might redeem us from all iniquity, and purify* *unto Himself a **peculiar** people, zealous of good works"* (Titus 2:14). The word *"peculiar"* in this passage means, *"precious."* However, the phraseology in 1 Peter 2:9 is a little varied, the word *"peculiar"* being translated in the Septuagint as *"jewels." "But ye are a chosen generation, a royal priesthood, an holy nation, a **peculiar** people; that ye should shew forth the praises of Him who hath called you out of darkness into His marvellous light."* The sense is the same, being that of a people who are select, precious, endeared, something exceedingly prized and sedulously preserved. The world, with all its accomplishments, and advances in various fields, means nothing to God in comparison to His precious treasure, His most prominent and valuable jewel, namely, His bought people. We are His prized possession! What a wonder of manifold, and divine grace!

(6) EXALTATION. *"Above all people."* God's redeemed people are on a higher plane than the rest of humanity. The world has the devil as their father, and they are the slaves of sin. Christians have God as their Father and are the servants of Christ. Men grope in darkness due to the blindness of their mind. Believers have been enlightened to divine truths and possess the Holy Spirit of truth within, who unfolds to them the sacred things of God written in the Holy Scriptures. The unsaved have a fearful looking for of judgment and fiery indignation, while the child of God looks for a celestial city, the New Jerusalem, as his future abode. What dignity, what elevation, has been bestowed upon us dear child of God! We are the sons of God! We have an inheritance incorruptible, undefiled, and that fadeth not away, for it is reserved in heaven for us. We are heirs of God, and joint heirs with Jesus! Truly, we are above all people. Unconverted kings, presidents, dictators, and the richest monarchs of earth, are beneath us! Our link, our association, is with the King of kings, and the Lord of lords. Blessed be His holy name!

(7) PARTICIPATION. *"And ye shall be unto Me a kingdom of priests."* It was God's intention that those of that redeemed nation would be priests. They would be called upon to minister to the nations the things that be of God. Teaching the heathen the ways of God, His will, and leading them into His presence. What a promise of high honor! They were to be a commonwealth of spiritual sovereigns, hallowed, and set apart for God. However, their right to become so positioned before the nations, was forfeited through their idolatrous activity while Moses was on the mount receiving the Law.

(8) SANCTIFICATION. *"A holy nation."* That is, they were to be a nation hallowed, set apart, and consecrated for God. Immediately, the mind of any intelligent reader of the Scriptures, is drawn to the counterpart of these truths to 1 Peter 2:4-5, 9.

> *"To Whom coming, as unto a living stone, disallowed indeed of men, but chosen of God, and precious, Ye also, as lively stones, are built up a spiritual house, an holy priesthood, to offer up spiritual sacrifices, acceptable to God by Jesus Christ."*

> *"But ye are a chosen generation, a royal priesthood, an holy nation, a peculiar people; that ye should shew forth the praises of Him who hath called you out of darkness into His marvellous light."*

The expression, *"to Whom coming,"* carries the thought of an habitual coming. It is not the thought of coming to Him for salvation, which is a one-occasion experience. No, no, that is not the thought. We are dealing with priests here, coming before the Lord to worship, to offer up spiritual sacrifices. Such sacrifices are the fruit of our lips, giving thanks to His name, as Hebrews 13:15 implies. As living stones, believers have been incorporated into a spiritual house, an holy priesthood. That priesthood is not the local assembly of believers, but every soul on earth that has experienced redemption through His blood. They may be a Pentecostal, a Methodist, a Lutheran, a Presbyterian, a Baptist, a Roman Catholic, or may not attend any church. If they are born again, they are in the priesthood of all believers. A scriptural gathering of believers to worship in an assembly, does not constitute a priesthood. I knew a man, many years ago, that tried to convince certain believers, that we only became priests as we entered the door of a Gospel Hall to break bread. What utter nonsense! What a perversion of the truth! God's people were made priests the moment they were born again. We gather as priests, but in gathering, we are not forming a priesthood. Please put such nonsense out of your mind. However, the corporate worshipping of priests is a very precious privilege. Denominationalism, as a rule, does not allow such functioning. They have their salaried preacher, who performs most of the local "church's" functions. He is active and the congregation is passive. Such activity is odious to God. Gifted men stand up to preach, and others rise to teach. This activity is not given by the Spirit to every man. However, when it comes to worship, all are on the same level. Sisters maintain silence (1 Tim. 2:11–12; 1 Corinthians 14:34), and brethren rise to audibly worship as the Spirit guides. Such godly activity is beautiful to behold.

The sacrifices are spiritual. The old order of bringing an animal to be slain and burned on an altar has passed away. We offer the sacrifice of praise, the fruit of our lips. We are "fruit-gatherers" during the week, filling our baskets (our hearts) with precious thoughts concerning Him. Then, when we as holy priests gather together, we enter the sanctuary through the veil, that is to say His flesh, and we worship, presenting our thoughts of Christ to the Father, through His Son.

"TO WHOM COMING"

The One to Whom we come has been *"disallowed indeed of men."* This carries the thought of *"being examined and deemed useless after testing."* The world's appraisal of Christ is very low. Their blinded mind cannot detect any beauty in Him. To them, He is of no use. How different He is to God! *"Chosen of God, and precious."* The word *"chosen,"* is a noun, which means that He is the *Chosen One*. Christians driving down the road to the assembly gathering could rightfully say, "We are going to meet the Chosen One!" Out of all the myriads of celestial angels, out of the numberless throng of the nobles of earth, He alone in the Chosen One. Thus, to God He is precious. Yes, and to us also,

He is precious (1 Pet. 2:7).

> "Precious Saviour, we adore Thee.
> Thine own blood hath made us nigh.
> Thanking Thee, with tears we worship.
> All for us, Thou came'st to die.
>
> This dark world hath Thee rejected,
> Disallowed of men art Thou.
> But to God exceeding precious.
> Once despised, we worship now."[40]

Not only are we in a *holy priesthood,* affording us liberty into the sanctuary to worship, but Peter also informs us that we are in a *royal priesthood.* In this particular function, it is not so much entering the sanctuary to worship, but rather entering the streets to witness. As such, we show forth the praises, or virtues, of God. He has called us out of spiritual darkness, and transported us into His marvelous light. As children of the light, we let our light shine. We sing of Christ! We speak of Christ! We preach Christ! We live Christ! He is our motivation. He is our message. We make Him known to others in no uncertain terms. We are not ashamed of the gospel of Christ, for we recognize that it is the power of God unto salvation unto all that believe. Are you living up to this responsibility, dear redeemed one? Are you a faithful witness as He was? Are you telling the story abroad?

WOMEN PRIESTS

Are women priests? Absolutely! I remember preaching the gospel with an assembly a few years ago. Christians children attended nightly, but occasionally, a sister in that assembly would bring a total stranger in to hear the gospel. In meeting people, she invariably would approach them about their soul, and the need of salvation. What most of the brethren in that assembly could not accomplish, she did! That accomplishment was,

---

40 Robert E. Surgenor (September 2, 2008)

bringing sinners into the gathering to hear the gospel. She was a true royal priest, was she not? You may not have "platform ability" to preach the word, but do you "gossip" it? Do you witness privately? When is the last time (if ever) that you brought a stranger to a gospel meeting? When is the last time that you pressed a gospel tract into the hand of a sinner? You are a royal priest. Are you functioning? May the Lord of the harvest exercise all of us to function more faithfully as royal priests. Israel forfeited their privilege of being a priestly nation, but Christians, through the new birth, have been brought into a life-long priesthood to function as holy and royal priests.

MOSES' RETURN – ISRAEL'S VOW

Coming down from the mount, Moses called for all the elders and laid before them all these words which the LORD commanded him. It would seem in turn that they relayed these God-given words to the people, who in return inadvertently exclaimed, *"All that the LORD hath spoken we will do."* Do we not see a spirit of self confidence in their hasty reply? They really knew very little of their own spirits, and rushed hastily, assuming obligations of which they had little knowledge.

"And Moses returned the words of the people unto the LORD" (Ex. 19:8). This incident of the giving of the Law and the relation of Moses to God and to the people, is described in Galatians 3:19: *"The law ... it was ordained by angels in the hand of a mediator."* The word "mediator," means, "a go-between," and that is exactly the role Moses fulfilled. Coming to the new testament we find that word related to Christ on five occasions.

> *"For there is one God, and one Mediator between God and men, the Man Christ Jesus"* (1 Tim. 2:5).

> *"But now hath He obtained a more excellent ministry, by how much also He is the Mediator of a better covenant, which was established upon better promises"* (Heb. 8:6).

"And for this cause He is the Mediator of the new testament, that by means of death, for the redemption of the transgressions that were under the first testament, they which are called might receive the promise of eternal inheritance" (Heb. 9:15).

"And to Jesus the Mediator of the new covenant, and to the blood of sprinkling, that speaketh better things than that of Abel" (Heb. 12:24).

In the first quotation, we see the uniqueness of Christ as the Mediator. Second: Through Christ, the establishing of a better covenant with better promises. Third: Christ's mediatoral work involving death, to redeem old testament saints. Fourth: The superiority of His blood compared to Abel's offering. In over one hundred ways, Moses was a type of Christ. This was one of them. Both were mediators.

THE VOICE OF GOD

The presence of God was in the cloud, but it would seem on this unique occasion, that the cloud became increasingly thick, meaning dense, or dark. "Lo, I come unto thee in a thick cloud" (Ex. 19:9). It was accompanied with lightnings and thunder as the cloud descended upon the top of the mount. *"So terrible was the sight, that Moses said, I exceedingly fear and quake"* (Heb. 12:21). On this most solemn occasion, Israel actually heard the voice of God speaking to His servant Moses. This would eliminate all future excuse for accusing Moses of tricking them in accepting a system of laws and ordinances of his own making. Upon hearing the voice of God, they would plainly see that Moses was merely the mediator between them and God, Who was the highest authority in all the universe.

That is why, when an elder, or teacher of the Word ministers to us, if He is expounding the Word of God to our hearts, are we not obligated to acknowledge that it is the voice of God speaking to us, the voice of the highest authority in the Universe?

Are we not obligated to obey? I have heard elders say to me, "I am glad that you ministered as you did, for they will be more likely to hear you, than to listen to us." Now let me say this. This situation is a sad state of affairs. What has an assembly come to, when faithful men minister against departure, only to be ignored by those in that assembly who are departing from the faith? It is not a matter of a lack of knowledge that is destroying some testimonies, it is rather a rebellious spirit against the Word of God that is bringing some assemblies down. Israel hastily said, "All that the LORD hath spoken, we will do." However, we have Christians today that blatantly say, by their actions, "All that the Lord hath spoken we will NOT do!"

Since this book is primarily dealing with the journey of Israel, we will not abide at Sinai for a full exposition of this event. However, we will pass on some basic, and simple observations, for you to beat out more fully in the sanctuary of God if you desire.

THE LAW – A GUARDIAN

Some have inquired, why was the Law given? It was primarily given to show man what he ought to be, and to show the exceeding sinfulness of sin. The Law also revealed the holiness of God. It was also a guardian until Christ came. Let me explain that last statement. Paul, in addressing the Jews by the Spirit, writes:

> *"But before faith came, we were kept under the law, shut up unto the faith which should afterwards be revealed. Wherefore the law was our schoolmaster to bring us unto Christ, that we might be justified by faith"*(Gal. 3:23-24).

"Before faith came." That is, before Christ died, and faith as a principle of blessing, was made known. They were kept under, they were shut up, as long as the dispensation of Law existed. They were like fish enclosed in a net. A middle wall of partition was erected between Israel and the nations (Eph. 2:14). They were like sheep in a fold (John 10:1). The Law was intended, through its moral and religious codes, to protect Israel from the

sins and vices of the nations, by separating them completely from the heathen. They were thus, "kept under the law, shut up unto the faith."

Paul goes further with his explanation. "The law was our schoolmaster to bring us unto Christ." The word in our day is, "pedagogue, or guardian." Let me illustrate it like this. Say that you are a rich person, and the day comes when you send your child to school. You hire a guardian to accompany that child. He walks to school with your child, and sits with him in class. Returning home, he still abides with the child. You see, he is protecting that child from possible outside influences, or perhaps even harm. Also, he prevents that child from getting into trouble. He is a pedagogue, he is the child's guardian. Now that is what the Law was to Israel, unto Christ. That expression "to bring us" is in italics in your Bible, denoting the fact that those words are not in the original text. In other words, that Law hemmed Israel in, until Christ came, Who freed them from the Law.

Then Paul goes on to say: "But after that faith is come, we are no longer under a schoolmaster" (tutor, or guardian) (Gal. 3:25). Guardians, in Paul's day, guarded children from 6 to 16 years of age. After reaching 16 years, they were no longer needed. So we see that they were temporary. The Law was the same thing! It was a temporary institution. Christ led them out from the fold, and delivered them from being under the Law. Blessed be His name!

THREE KINDS OF LAW

In the giving of the Law, God was going to assure them of their unique relationship to Himself, by entering into a covenant with them. The Law would lay down the fundamental principles of His government, impressing on them truths that they were to communicate, at a later date, to mankind. From Exodus 20:1, to verse 17, God gives His MORAL LAW, which would govern their individual life. Then from chapter 21 to chapter 23, He unveils His CIVIL LAW, which would govern their national life. Finally, in chapters 25 and 28, and also in the Book of Leviticus, we have presented Israel's CEREMONIAL LAW, which would guide them in their religious life. The civil and ceremonial law was put into a book, and placed beside the Ark (Deut. 31:24-26).

Considering God and His various dealings with Israel, we gain an insight into His Judgments in Egypt. At the Red Sea, we behold with wonder and awe His Power. Viewing the pillar of the cloud, we learn to appreciate His Guidance. In the giving of the manna, we readily see His Grace and Mercy. However, in His giving of the Law to Israel, we stand afar off with reverence and godly fear and behold His Majesty and Holiness.

GOD'S MORAL LAW

Regarding God's moral law, it was first delivered orally. In the first section presented, we have man's duty to God (Ex. 20:1-11). (1) His Person was to be supreme in the heart. They were to have no other gods before Him. (v. 3). (2) His worship was to be by faith. There would be no graven image or likeness of anything in heaven or earth to facilitate their worship (v. 4). (3) They were to be controlled in their speech, being careful not to take His name in vain (v. 7). Compare this with Ecclesiastes 5:1-2. (4) Finally, they were to remember His day, keeping the Sabbath holy.

In the second section, we have man's duty to man (Ex. 20:12-17). (1) They were to honor their father and their mother (v. 12). (2) They we not allowed to kill (v. 13). (3) They were not to commit adultery (v. 14). (4) They were not to steal (v. 15). (5) They were not to bear false witness (v. 16). (6) They were not to covet (v. 17).

God commands offspring to honor their parents, for if that is lacking, there consequently will be no reverence for God. Liberals advocate a "no spanking" agenda, and have imposed it upon our society, even the public school system. That is why youth today are rebellious to their parents, and have no reverence nor regard for God.

OFFENCE – PENALTY

Liberals fiercely oppose the death penalty, and in their total ignorance of the Bible, quote "thou shalt not kill," to support their belief. In most countries, laws are based on the Law given to Moses. What the liberals fail to see is, that there are two sections to the criminal code. The first section deals with the offence. "Thou shalt not kill." The word is "murder" (Heb. "la tirtzaha"), the violent, unjust taking of a life. It is distinguished from "harag," also translated, "to kill," but which is more legitimately employed to designate that kind of legal killing which is the result of the sentence of a magistrate. Murder (la tirtzaha) is an offence, consequently God says, "thou shalt not." The second section deals with the penalty. Read into the next chapter and you will find what it plainly says. "He that smiteth a man, so that he die, shall be surely put to death." "And he that smiteth his father, or his mother, shall be surely put to death" (Ex. 21:12, 15). Notice the repetition in Numbers 35. "The murderer shall surely be put to death" (verses 16, 17, 18, 30, 31). Furthermore, the failure to carry out the penalty section of the law has serious consequences.

> "Whoso killeth any person, the murderer shall be put to death by the mouth of witnesses: but one witness shall not testify against any person to cause him to die. Moreover ye shall take no satisfaction for the life of a murderer, which is guilty of death: but he shall be surely put to death … So ye shall not pollute the land wherein ye are : for blood it defileth the land: and the land cannot be cleansed of the blood that is shed therein, but by the blood of him that shed it" (Num. 35:30-31, 33).

Can we not rightfully gather by this, that our country, through lack of putting convicted murderers to death, is defiled in the eyes of Almighty? Sitting quite comfortably in their cells, they are contributing to the corruption of this great nation. If you disagree with this, it is not the author you are disagreeing with; it is God. I have only quoted to you what God has plainly said.

ADULTERY

The next sin is adultery. God is very plain regarding the penalty. "The man that committeth adultery with another man' wife, even he that committeth adultery with his neighbour' wife, the adulterer and the adulteress shall surely be put to death" (Lev. 20:10). What called for the death penalty under the Law, calls for excommunication under grace. Thus, the fornicator (a comprehensive word embracing married and single folk), is to be put away from God's assembly as a "wicked person" (1 Cor. 5:11-13). If that person is restored to the assembly at a later date, he carries a mark the rest of his days. He is a priest with a blemish. He is branded with the mark of "blame." One of the qualifications of an overseer is that he be "blameless" (1 Tim. 3:2). Thus, one having been guilty of fornication, is disqualified from the office of an overseer. Would not this restriction also embrace one being commended by an assembly to the full-time work of the Lord as an evangelist?

STEALING

The next disorder is stealing. Robbery involves taking by force, something not rightfully yours. Stealing involves taking, but not employing force. So the little child opens the cookie jar when the parent is absent, and takes a cookie that is not his. That is stealing. Workers can steal their employer's time, by loafing on the job. People can steal from the credit card company by not paying the bills they have accumulated. One can steal from the government on his tax return. Borrowing, with no intention of returning, is stealing. If two preachers agreed to 30 minutes each, and the first preacher took 40 minutes, leaving the other only 20 minutes, I suppose one could charge the first preacher with stealing ten minutes of the second speaker's time.

Fraudulent "bargains," imposed on the ignorant, taking unjust advantage of insolvent laws, exacting usurious interest for money, defrauding the public, keeping back the wages of hirelings, using false weights and measures, and removing ancient landmarks, are all considered stealing. The simple description would be, taking something unlawfully that is not rightfully yours.

BEARING FALSE WITNESS

Regarding bearing false witness against one's neighbor, God told them, "thou shalt not." Such activity can take on various forms, of which we will mention just a few. The former injuries mentioned, involved deeds, or actions. Bearing false witness involves words. The word "neighbor" in this instance would involve more than a narrow circle. It embraces not only an acquaintance, but also a stranger, friend or foe.

> *"Thou shalt not go up and down as a talebearer among thy people: neither shalt thou stand against the blood of thy neighbour: I am the LORD"* (Lev. 19:16).

They were not to stand as a false witness against their neighbor, whereby his blood (his life), may be endangered. James has much to say about our little member, the tongue.

> *"The tongue is a fire, a world of iniquity: so is the tongue among our members, that it defileth the whole body, and setteth on fire the course of nature; and it is set on fire of hell"* (Jas. 3:6).

Thousands upon thousands have been led to death from the testimonies of lying tongues. Wars have been born, as the result of lying tongues. Millions are religiously deceived today as the result of false ministers, twisting the Holy Scriptures, with perverted tongues (2 Pet. 3:16). Even the silence of a witness during a false report bears the imprint of being a false witness. When a false report is given, if he keeps silent, not rebuking it, in reality, he is giving the impression that he agrees with the report. Many people conducting funerals are guilty of bearing false witness. Perhaps the departed one has been a rogue, but at the funeral, the speaker tells the audience how wonderful that departed one was. He paints a beautiful picture over a wicked life, thus bearing false witness. It all comes to this, that, "lying lips are abomination to the LORD: but they that deal truly are his delight" (Prov. 12:22).

Thus, in verse 12, we see respect for authority; in verse 14, respect for one's marriage; in verse 15, respect for a person's private property; in verse 16, respect for a person's reputation.

It is very noticeable that in the first section, regarding man's duty to God, we have regulations regarding, thoughts, words, and deeds. While in the second section, regarding man's duty to man, the order is reversed. We have regulations regarding, deeds, words, and thoughts.

Coming to Exodus 24:12, we find Moses returning up the mount to receive the Law in written form, on two tables of stone. The writing was done with the finger of God. The fact that the commandments were written on both sides (Ex. 32:15), provides us with the thought that the Law cannot be evaded. It faces up to all.

Allow me to move on to Exodus chapter 32.

> "And when the people saw that Moses delayed to come down out of the mount, the people gathered themselves together unto Aaron, and said unto him, Up, make us gods, which shall go before us; for as for this Moses, the man that brought us up out of the land of Egypt, we wot not what is become of him. And Aaron said unto them, break off the golden earrings, which are in the ears of your wives, of your sons, and of your daughters, and bring them unto me. And all the people brake off the golden earrings which were in their ears, and brought them unto Aaron. And he received them at their hand, and fashioned it with a

graving tool, after he had made it a molten calf: and they said, These be thy gods, O Israel, which brought thee up out of the land of Egypt. And when Aaron saw it, he built an altar before it; and Aaron made proclamation, and said, To morrow is a feast to the LORD. And they rose up early on the morrow, and offered burnt offerings, and brought peace offerings; and the people sat down to eat and to drink, and rose up to play" ... *"And Moses turned, and went down from the mount, and the two tables of the testimony were in his hand: the tables were written on both their sides; on the one side and on the other were they written. And the tables were the work of God, and the writing was the writing of God, graven upon the tables. And when Joshua heard the noise of the people as they shouted, he said unto Moses, There is a noise of war in the camp. And he said, It is not the voice of them that shout for mastery, neither is it the voice of them that cry for being overcome: but the noise of them that sing do I hear. And it came to pass, as soon as he came nigh unto the camp, that he saw the calf, and the dancing: and Moses' anger waxed hot, and he cast the tables out of his hands, and brake them beneath the mount. And he took the calf which they had made, and burnt it in the fire, and ground it to powder, and strawed it upon the water, and made the children of Israel drink of it."*

What an experience! Could this be the people that had just recently said, "All that the LORD hath spoken we will do"? Yes. It is the same people! Forty days had passed since Moses had been in their presence. He had gone up into the mount to meet with God, and to receive the commandments written with the finger of God upon the two tables of stone. During this period of time, the flesh was working in the people. Where was Moses? Was he consumed in the fire? Had he perished, never to return? These fleshly thoughts may have permeated their mind. They could wait no longer.

"The people gathered themselves together unto Aaron." The word "unto," carries the thought of, "against." These people gathered themselves against Aaron. The Hebrew words employed, seem to convey the idea that the people beset Aaron in a violent, unrestrained and emotional manner. They clamored, demanding of him that he bow to their desires. It probably was a fearful scene for Aaron. I am inclined to believe that at first he opposed, but as the crowd's frenzy continued to rise, he succumbed to their fleshly desire.

PILATE AND CHRIST

Considering this event, I am reminded of Pilate. Any careful reader of the Scriptures knows that Pilate tried in various ways to release Jesus from the angry mob that was clamoring for His death. One of those ways was that he delivered Jesus to be scourged. He hoped that after the Lord received such a brutal plowing upon His back, that it would arouse the sympathy of the crowd, and they would consider that the Lord had received enough punishment, thus allowing Pilate to release Him. Bringing the scourged Saviour out before the multitude, Pilate announced, "Behold the Man." What was the reaction? Why it was just the opposite to what Pilate expected! Instead of them crying out, "Release Him, He has suffered enough," "they cried out, saying, Crucify Him, crucify Him" (John 19:1-6). Pilate's fleshly scheme had failed

AARON AND THE PEOPLE

Aaron was in a similar predicament. How could he suppress this movement? His solution was this; he asked them to part with something that was very valuable to them. He requested of them to give up their wealth, to forfeit their gold treasures, contained in the earrings worn by the women. Certainly, he thought, their vanity wouldn't allow them to part with their adornment and wealth. Aaron didn't have the courage to just plainly rebuke them for their sin. Ah no, perhaps his life was at stake! He had devised a fleshly means of perhaps discouraging them through his suggestion of forfeiting their gold. How fearful to see a prominent man succumbing to the fleshly desires of an impious mob! He failed to take a firm stand. He failed to place humble trust in God, regardless of the consequences. Aaron was a weak man. They say, "silence is golden." Yes, even to the disobedient, silence can be golden. Let me explain.

Many years ago at a conference, a younger man approached me very much disturbed. He was very exercised to give a word of correction in the spirit of love, and by looking at some of the Christians, I thought it would be proper. However, an older and prominent preacher made a remark from the platform that we didn't need any corrective ministry, that the Lord's people were living in difficult times and that all needed words of encouragement. What caused this remark? Was the man afraid that if he rebuked the Lord's people, that he would lose his popularity? Would negative remarks affect his "income?" One cannot judge, but we can say this, that political correctness is not spirituality, but rather carnality.

THE GOLDEN CALF

Like Pilate, Aaron miscalculated. Upon requesting their jewelry, immediately there was a tremendous response! Notice the inspired record. "And all the people brake off the golden earrings which were in their ears, and brought them unto Aaron" (Ex. 32:3). Aaron was now obligated to act, and in doing so we notice two things about this idol. "And he received them (their golden earings) at their hand, and fashioned it with a graving tool, after he had made it a molten calf: and they said, These be thy gods, O Israel, which brought thee up out of the land of Egypt" (Ex. 32:4). If Aaron followed the pattern of making idols as he had seen done in Egypt, this probably was his procedure. First, he fashioned it with a graving tool. That is, with a tool he formed the calf out of wood. The literal rendering is this. "He fashioned it with a graving-tool, and made it a calf of molten work." After making the calf out of wood with the graving tool, he then melted the gold, and cast the metal into a flat sheet, then hammered it out, and spread it over the wooden idol thus covering it with gold plate.

The way in which this idol was destroyed by Moses substantiates this interpretation. "And he took the calf which they had made, and burnt it in the fire, and ground it to powder, and strawed it upon the water, and made the children of Israel drink of it" (Ex. 32:20). "And I (Moses) took your sin, the calf which ye had made, and burnt it with fire, and stamped it, and ground it very small, even until it was as small as dust: and I cast the dust thereof into the brook that descended out of the mount" (Deut. 9:21). The idol was first of all burnt. That is, the wooden center was burnt into charcoal. Then the golden covering was ground into powder.

The golden calf (a young bull), was to be a visible representation of an invisible Jehovah. However, God looked upon this differently. He saw that this humanly created image was a likeness of their idolatrous and sensual hearts. One can hardly imagine those who fashioned the image, who had experienced such tremendous dealings with God, who had witnessed His glorious power and divine majesty, crying out; "These be thy gods, O Israel, which brought thee up out of Egypt" (Ex. 32:4). The word "gods," is "'elohiym." It is in the plural, but even so, Scripture uses it for God about 7,600 times, its first occurrence being in Genesis 1:1.

AARON'S ALTAR

Even Aaron, in his giving way to their demands, sought to ease his conscience by building an altar before the image, making a proclamation; "Tomorrow is a feast to the LORD." He followed a multitude to do evil (Ex. 23:2), thus encouraging the idolatry that he found impossible to restrain. It would seem that he did not intend for the people to drift away from worshipping Jehovah, or to view the calf as anything but a symbol of Jehovah. However, his thoughts were not their thoughts! How anxious they were to try out their new object of worship. They could hardly wait for the breaking of the sun the following day. "They rose up early on the morrow, and offered burnt offerings, and brought peace offerings." What zeal, what earnestness, but sadly, in a wrong thing!

ZEAL WITHOUT KNOWLEDGE

Look at the worshippers of Allah. At certain times of the day, they will lay down their little prayer mat, and bow their foreheads to the earth, facing the East, chanting a mechanical prayer to their god. They are sincere, and earnest!

Some devout Roman Catholics in Europe, rise very early on a daily basis, and trudge to their chapel to bow down and count their rosary, chanting repetitious prayers to Mary, who, in heaven, is oblivious to all that is transpiring on earth. These so-called devout worshippers, are as sincere as one could possibly be. How sad, for they are sincerely wrong!

Then, consider true saints today. Do you see the same devotedness? Do you observe the same zeal? Are we really sincere? Do we thirst after the Word of God morning after morning? Can we hardly wait until the day and the hour comes when the assembly is to be gathered together? You answer the question.

ROME'S IDOLATRY

Rome has introduced its images. They claim that these various images are helps to worship. What really takes place is that these images soon become little idols in the heart of the worshipper. They bow down before them, and they actually speak to them. There are no tangible items involved in Christian worship, except one loaf of bread, and one cup of wine at the Lord's Supper. No images of departed saints, no prayer beads, no crosses, no "holy" water, no relics of any kind, no incense, no candles, are to be thus employed. God hates it, for all of these contraptions used by the heathen, and in parts of Christendom, are idolatry!

Apostate Rome has incorporated three "elements" to constitute what she truly is. She has drawn into her skirts, Jewish ritual, pagan idolatry, and a smattering of Christian truths. These three things blended together, form the doctrines of Rome, the mother of harlots. She professes to be a Christian organization, but is guilty of brutally murdering over ninety million Christians who refused to bow to the blasphemous doctrines of Rome. That "Holy Inquisition" lasted for eight hundred years.

WYCLIFFE AND TYNDALE

Men who translated the Holy Scriptures for us in English, John Wycliffe (1320?-1384), and William Tyndale (1494-1536), were brutally murdered by Rome. Rome sought to keep the Bible away from the public, knowing that if the common man read it, he would discover the errors of her religious system. Wycliffe was so hated by the Church of Rome for translating the Bible into English, that the Pope demanded that Wycliffe's bones be dug up, burned and thrown in the River Swift, 44 years after his death.

"And they rose up early on the morrow, and offered burnt offerings, and brought peace offerings; and the people sat down to eat and to drink, and rose up to play"(Ex. 32:6). Many in Israel were delighted with their new golden calf. It was a new way to worship. They gathered around it, bright and early, with great enthusiasm. "To play," means "to sport, be merry," and to "dance and sing."

This whole affair was not the result of spiritual ignorance, but a willful turning away from the spiritual worship and true knowledge of Jehovah. Right before their eyes, He had made known His supreme majesty, power, and glory. It was in the very face of the mount that these people turned willfully aside. They had actually heard the voice of Almighty speaking to Moses, and with wondrous awe, they had beheld the lightning, heard the thunder, and had felt the trembling of the whole mount. Yet, in spite of all their revelations, they turned from God. What a contrast the preaching of the gospel accomplished in Thessalonica, where it was said of those who heard Paul, "ye turned to God from idols to serve the living and true God" (1 Thess. 1:9). The Thessalonians turned to God and left their idols, while in contrast, the Israelites turned to an idol, and left their God.

A SORDID REPORT

It seems that idolatry and licentiousness go hand in glove. Those who bow to idols, invariably bow to sexual lust. In our day, the news media has exposed the covert activities of the Roman Church. Thousands of little children have been sexually abused by Roman Catholic priests. Let me quote another author.

> "Rome has more prostitutes than any other city because she has the most celibates.' Pius II declared that Rome was 'the only city run by bastards' [sons of popes and cardinals]. Catholic historian and former Jesuit Peter de Rosa writes: 'Popes had mistresses of fifteen years of age, were guilty of incest and sexual perversions of every sort, had innumerable children, were murdered in the very act of adultery [by jealous husbands who found them in bed with their wives].' As for abominations, even Catholic historians admit that among the popes were some of the most degenerate and unconscionable ogres in all of history. The numerous outrageous crimes, many of which are almost beyond belief, have been recited by many historians from preserved documents that reveal the depths of papal depravity. To call any of these men 'His holiness, Vicar of Christ' makes a mockery of holiness and of Christ. Yet the name of these unbelievably wicked popes - mass murderers, fornicators, warmongers, some guilty of the massacre of thousands - is emblazoned in honor on the Church's official list of popes. These abominations that John (the

MOSES AND THE LAW

apostle) saw not only occurred in the past but continue to this very day."[41]

This sordid report is only further evidence that idolatry leads to licentious behavior. How different from true Christianity. What a vast difference between the apostle Paul and the many Popes in history. Paul could truthfully say, *"Ye are witnesses, and God also, how holily and justly and unblameably we behaved ourselves among you that believe"* (1 Thess. 2:10). What a challenging standard for all of God's people today, whether a teacher, an overseer, and evangelist, or just an ordinary "rank and file" Christian. The injunction still remains, indelibly written on the holy page of Scripture; *"But as He which hath called you is holy, so be ye holy in all manner of conversation,"* meaning, behavior in life. (1 Pet. 1:15).

IDOLATROUS ACTIVITY

"The people sat down to eat and to drink, and rose up to play." The word "play,"(letzahek) is looked upon in different ways. The word is first employed with Abraham and Sara and is translated "laughed" (Gen. 17:17; 18:12, 13, 15). Its next occurrence is with Lot, and there it is translated "mocked" (Gen. 19:14). When used with Isaac, it is translated, "sporting" (Gen. 26:8). In the case of Abraham, it was joy, but in the case of Sarah, it was doubting God's word. Regarding Lot, it would seem that his relatives considered him to be delirious, and in the case of Isaac, it was merriment. In Israel's case, this same word seems to carry a more sinister meaning. There seems to be licentiousness connected with it, for we read that they had made themselves naked to their shame. So the affair was not merely the sports of singing, dancing, and merry-making, but also a conduct of voluptuous reveling and drunkenness.

The word "dancing," (Ex. 32:19) exposes more of the nature of their conduct. Dancing among Oriental nations, were

---

41   Dave Hunt. A Woman Rides the Beast. (Harvest House Publishers, Eugene, Oregon 97402). Page 78-79.

of a sexually immoral character. In Egypt, professional dancers catered to the baser lusts, being always sensual and indecent; while dancing in Babylon, Syria, and Asia Minor was nothing more than a wild orgy to the point of frenzy. It would seem that it was this sort of dancing in which the Israelites were engaged. As stated before, Idolatry always leads to shameful behavior.

To make matters even worse, this wicked activity was possibly being observed by the surrounding enemies. "Aaron had made them naked unto their shame among their enemies" (Ex. 32:25). The Hebrew word for "naked," is "parua," and can mean, "to fall into disorder, confusion, and exposedness, a state in which one is naked of defense." This may be the leading idea, not so much as being denuded of their garments, but rather that they were now deprived of the favorable presence and protection of heaven. They now stood as naked and unarmed men, subject to flight even by the weakest enemy.

ARE WE NAKED?

Brethren, does this not ring a note in our hearts? Are we aware of the fact that our power with God and with men, lies in our obedience to His every command? How can one expect the power of God to be with them, while living a hypocritical life? It is impossible. Why do churches fail? Have we left (divorced) our first love, like Ephesus? Or have we resorted to Nicolaitanism, as Pergamos? Or do we simply have a name to live, while being dead, like Sardis? Or is it that we are rich and increased with goods, and feel the need of nothing, like Laodicea? Is it true that we are "naked?" That we have lost our defence? Is it true, that we have resorted to human engineering and planning for our conferences, rather than let the Holy Spirit be the sole Controller in such activities? Our enemies beset us round about, but we have little, if any, power over them. Our nakedness is upon us, but rather than admit it and repent with tears, we have resorted to human devices to "stay afloat." Israel, through their departure, had lost God's presence, and God's defense.

ISRAEL CORRUPTED

God told Moses, "The people have corrupted themselves" (Ex. 32:7). That word "corrupted" (shachath), can mean, "to decay, ruin, destroy, or utterly waste." In other words, Israel had ruined themselves. In Genesis 6:13, the word is translated, "destroy." What relationship they had with Jehovah was now destroyed. Their protection, their blessings, their power, and their true peace had now melted away.

You will notice how God speaks of them on this occasion. "And the LORD said unto Moses, Go, get thee down; for thy people, which thou broughtest out of the land of Egypt, have corrupted themselves" (Ex. 32:7). Notice, God did not say that it was His people which He brought up out of Egypt. Ah no, it would almost seem as if He had disowned them! He says to Moses, that they are his people which he brought up out of Egypt. God leaves Himself out of the picture. Now this is very serious, is it not? These people are now out of touch with God. It seems that He now would have nothing to do with them. In fact, He was ready to wipe them off the face of this earth. Imagine God saying to Moses, a mere man, "Let Me alone, that My wrath may wax hot against them, and that I may consume them: and I will make of thee a great nation" (Ex. 32:10).

MOSES' INTERCESSION

The intercession of Moses reveals the excellent quality of the man. God had said to him, "Now therefore let Me alone, that My wrath may wax hot against them." However, this was not a command, as it may seem. No, the words were intended rather to encourage Moses in his case of bringing his request before God. What God was indicating, was if Moses interceded for Israel, then God's hands would be stayed from punishing Israel. God would be unable to act in His wrath. Of this hint, Moses was not slow in availing himself to immediately intercede for Israel. What a graphic picture we have of our Great High Priest! Where would we be without Him? There is not a day that goes by, but in some way, in some measure, we sin against God. However, there is no divine hand moved against us in wrath. What a wonderful Saviour is ours! *"Who is he that condemneth? It is Christ that died, yea rather, that is risen again, Who is even at the right hand of God, Who also maketh intercession for us"* (Rom. 8:34). *"Wherefore He is able also to save them to the uttermost that come unto God by Him, seeing He ever liveth to make intercession for them"* (Heb. 7:25). In other words, there is One at God's right hand Who lives on our behalf. He, through His intercession on our behalf, saves our testimony day by day, yes, even to the completion of our journey here. That is what is meant in those comforting words, "He is also able to save them to the uttermost." Moses made earnest intercession for the people. He was heard, and the people were spared.

MOSES' APPEAL

Moses was quick to bring before God that Israel was not his people, but rather they were the LORD'S people, and that it was Jehovah that had brought "forth out of the land of Egypt with great power, and with a mighty hand" (Ex. 32:11). There are four salient things Moses presents to God in his intercession that are worthy of notice. First, he appeals to the LORD that these people were the LORD'S. Second, he mentions the great care that God exercised in bringing them up out of Egypt. Third, he brings humbly before the LORD, that if they were consumed by divine power, that the Egyptians would gloat over the judgment inflicted, accusing God of bringing them into the wilderness for the purpose of slaying them. Lastly, he appeals to God of the fact that he had made a promise to Abraham, Isaac, and Jacob, to multiply their seed as the stars of heaven, and that God must be true to His covenant. What an intelligent appeal! What a masterpiece! His words were selected carefully, and presented humbly, and in earnest. Little wonder he is called a man of God. What was the end result? Read on! "And the LORD repented of the evil which He thought to do unto His people" (Ex. 32:14). Let me say this, the God of Moses, is also our God. Do we have this power with Him? If not, is it available? I believe it is, if we are in the right condition of soul. The problem that many of us experience today of a silent heaven is not that God has changed. Oh no! Perhaps the problem is, that we need to change!

> "If I regard iniquity in my heart, the Lord will not hear me" (Ps. 66:18).

> "The effectual fervent prayer of a righteous man availeth much" (Jas. 5:16).

THE TABLES BROKEN

"And Moses turned, and went down from the mount, and the two tables of the testimony were in his hand: And it came to pass, as soon as he came nigh unto the camp, that he saw the calf, and the dancing: and Moses' anger waxed hot, and he cast the tables out of his hands, and brake them beneath the mount" (Ex. 32:15, 19).

As meek as Moses was, he could not tolerate anything that cast a blot on the divine glory, or anything that took away God's prominence in the heart. He could easily pass by insults hurled against him, but not so regarding any offence against Jehovah. He cast the God-made tables at his feet, breaking them. This significantly showed the covenant that had been made was now annulled, and consequently, all their expectations from God were entirely destroyed. Moses deliberately broke the tables, not simply because of his anger, but as an action to show that their covenant with God no longer existed. What Moses did was perfectly lawful and right, for he was under divine dictation. God willed it so.

"And I took the two tables, and cast them out of my two hands, and brake them before your eyes" (Deut. 9:17). What a solemn demonstration, and announcement to Israel as a witness to what they had done. Never do we read of God rebuking Moses for breaking the tables. In fact, Moses relates his action with no remorse whatsoever. Because of these facts, we conclude that Moses, in breaking the tables, was acting according to the will of God.

One can see righteous indignation on the part of Moses in breaking the stones, but as previously stated, his action goes far deeper than mere anger. It was an act, symbolic of the breaking of the covenant. The tables of stone was all that remained of that covenant, and breaking them was the final act in its rupture.

DRINKING THE IDOL

After destroying the golden calf, and grinding it to powder, he "strawed it upon the water, and made the children of Israel drink of it" (Ex. 32:20). The question arises, why? The answer is, that his action was intended to set forth, in a visible way the sin, and its dire consequences. Their sin was ingested into their bowels along with the water. This would be a sign, that they would have to bear their sin. This act can also be seen in Numbers 5:24, where the woman suspected of adultery was required to drink the curse-water.

AARON'S ACCOUNT

When Aaron gave an account unto Moses regarding the taking of the gold calf he said, "And I said unto them, Whosoever hath any gold, let them break it off. So they gave it me: then I cast it into the fire, and there came out this calf" (Ex. 32:24). Let me give you the comment of this report from different authors.

"He had been overcome by the urgency of the people and had thrown the gold they handed him into the fire, and that this calf had come out, as if the image had come out of its own accord, without his intention or will."[42]

"Aaron's excuse - it just happened. He put the gold, poor

---

42 C. F. Keil, F. Delitzsch. Commentary on the Old Testament. (W. B. Eerdmans Publishing Company, Grand Rapids, MI.). Volume 1, Page 226.

MOSES AND THE LAW

man, into the fire, and 'there came out' this calf! It came out. He did not make it; it just came out."[43]

"Aaron childishly insinuates that when he cast the gold into the fire it came out, either by accident or by the magic art of some of the mixed multitude (as the Jewish writer's dream), in this shape; but not a word of his graving and fashioning it."[44]

"There came out this calf. Aaron speaks as if he had prepared no mould, but simply thrown the gold into the hot furnace, from which there issued forth, to his surprise, the golden calf. Having even no plausible defense to make, he is driven to the weakest of subterfuges."[45]

"They gave me this gold, I put it into the furnace, and there came out this calf. I did not do it; it was the furnace that did it. Pity me, I am the unlucky creature of circumstances."[46]

Are these accounts accurate? If so, then Aaron was a colossal deceiver and liar. Also, he did not credit Moses with much intelligence, if he expected him to believe what these writers say he concocted. Can we lay such charges to Aaron. I don't believe so! Let me explain what I believe actually took place. First of all, any student of the Holy Writings recognizes this, that the Holy Spirit does not always give us a complete and graphic report of a particular incident.

I find it hard to accept what many teach, that Aaron resorted to a stupid and ridiculous subterfuge, to convince Moses of his innocence. He was not trying to convince Moses that the calf was produced by accident, or by some magical operation. The Jewish

---

43 J. Orr. The Pulpit Commentary, Exodus. (Hendrickson Publishers, Peabody MA) Volume 1, Page 337.
44 Matthew Henry. A Commentary on the whole Bible, Exodus. World Bible Publishers, Iowa Falls, Iowa. Page 414.
45 George Rawlinson. The Pulpit Commentary, Exodus. (Hendrickson Publishers, Peabody MA) Volume 1, Page 339.
46 F. B. Meyer. Devotional Commentary on Exodus. (Kregel Publications, Grand Rapids, MI.) Page 421.

Targum goes so far as to say that Aaron tried to convince Moses that he merely cast the gold into the fire, and Satan entered it and it came out in the form of a calf. What a wild interpretation!

Here is what I believe happened. Aaron's words were simply a brief and muddled account of the process of the formation of the calf, of which details he did not wish to dwell. He did not deny his agency in the affair. He readily confessed that he took the gold and melted it, and that the calf was the result; but in shame, he does not recite all the particulars of the process. Aaron sinned in what he did, but I refuse to charge him of being a deceiver.

THE CLAIRON CALL

After severely rebuking Aaron, the clarion call is made: "Who is on the LORD'S side? let him come unto me" (Ex. 32:26). Immediately, the sons of Levi responded. The judgment was to be inflicted by the hands of men acting for God. On other occasions, we see God Himself inflicting the judgment, but on this occasion, a test was being offered unto the nation - who is faithful, who is willing, to execute the judgment of God on one's own brethren? This was a test as to fidelity to the LORD. Even some of the tribe of Levi were slain on this occasion as Deuteronomy 33:9, reveals. Of those who executed the judgment it was said, "neither did he acknowledge his brethren, nor knew his own children."

Now this is very severe, is it not? If your own kin, whether son or grandson came under the judgment, they were to be slain! The sin was so vile, it had tarnished the name of Jehovah, and retribution must be swiftly administered. If you cannot agree with this, it is because you have a very low estimation of the holiness of Almighty. You are not looking at the whole situation through divine eyeglasses, but through the carnal eyeglasses of the flesh. That was the problem at Corinth. The assembly had become very tolerant of sin. They had lost sight of the holiness of God. Consequently, the judgment of God fell upon them and many were weak and sickly, and many had died. *"Be not deceived, God is not mocked, for whatsoever a man soweth, that also shall he reap"* (Gal. 6:7). Carry this truth into God's assembly and what do you find? Or, what should you find? Well, sin must be dealt with, no matter what the cost. Sentimental feelings must be laid aside, and the "wicked person," righteously judged. Whether husband, wife, son, daughter, grandson, or granddaughter, all must be accordingly dealt with, that the name of the Lord Jesus be vindicated, and the assembly cleansed. The solemn command remains, *"Therefore put away from among yourselves that wicked person"* (1 Cor. 5:13).

There seemed to be no resistance on the part of those who were slain. Only the chief offenders were marked out for the death penalty. The divine hand would be pointing them out to the executioners. So brought down by conscious guilt, and confounded and intimidated by the authority of Moses, they submitted to the righteous judgment.

Levi had been informed by Moses that their action for God would, in return, secure for them a blessing, by being brought into the priestly office. This seems to be the thought in Deuteronomy 33:8-10. Compare this with Exodus 32:29. The truth still stands; *"them that honour Me I will honour"* (1 Sam. 2:30).

GOD'S STONES – MOSES' STONES

It is well to note the difference in the first and second giving of the written law. On the first occasion, God provided the tables of stone, and wrote on them. The second time, Moses hewed the tables of stone for God to write on. After Moses, received the Law on the first occasion, we read, *"And He gave unto Moses, when He had made an end of communing with him upon mount Sinai, two tables of testimony, tables of stone, written with the finger of God"* (Ex. 31:18). On the second occasion, we read, "And the LORD said unto Moses, Hew thee two tables of stone like unto the first: and I will write upon these tables the words that were in the first tables, which thou brakest." And he hewed two tables of stone like unto the first; and Moses rose up early in the morning, and went up unto mount Sinai, as the LORD had commanded him, and took in his hand the two tables of stone (Ex. 34:1, 4).

Now, there is a reason for this, and if you ask your fellow brethren what it is, it will be a rare thing if you receive an explanation. It took me over twenty years of reading the Scriptures to discover what I believe to be the solution to the mystery. The answer is found in the New Testament in Paul's second epistle to the Corinthians. First of all, you will recognize the fact that the Holy Scriptures liken the human heart to a "stony heart" (Ezek. 36:26). Moses fashions two tables of stone suitable to be divinely written on. Moving to 2 Corinthians 3:3, we read; *"Forasmuch as ye are manifestly declared to be the epistle of Christ ministered by us, written not with ink, but with the Spirit of the living God; not in tables of stone, but in fleshy tables of the heart"* (2 Cor. 3:3). In other words, we receive divine impressions and answer to them. The Spirit wrote on their hearts, using Paul as the pen.

Moses now holds in his hands two tables of stone. He hewed them himself. To him, they are personal, and would speak to us of Moses' heart. Typically, one could say that God was now going to write the holy Law on the tables of his heart. Another author has suggested the following thought:

> "As Moses had restored the covenant through his energetic intercession, he should also provide the materials for the renewal of the covenant record, and bring them to God, for Him to complete and confirm the record by writing the covenant upon the tables."[47]

There are other Scriptures worth noticing in connection with the tables of stone.

"For this is the covenant that I will make with the house of Israel

---

[47] C. F. Keil, F. Delitzsch. <u>Commentary on the Old Testament.</u> (W. B. Eerdmans Publishing Company, Grand Rapids, MI.). Volume 1, Page 240

after those days, saith the Lord; I will put My laws into their mind, and write them in their hearts: and I will be to them a God, and they shall be to Me a people" (Heb. 8:10).

"This is the covenant that I will make with them after those days, saith the Lord, I will put My laws into their hearts, and in their minds will I write them" (Heb. 10:16).

"But this shall be the covenant that I will make with the house of Israel; After those days, saith the LORD, I will put My law in their inward parts, and write it in their hearts; and will be their God, and they shall be My people" (Jer. 31:33).

WRITTEN ON THE HEART

Paul, in writing to the Hebrews, is not only reminding them of the future blessing of the nation of Israel during the Millennium, but also refers to this present dispensation, where the writers of the New Testament epistles, as it were, prepared the stones. But it was the finger of God that wrote on their hearts His commandments for the Church. Thus, through human instruments, we have the Holy Scriptures written with the finger of God, for our benefit. Christians have the Holy Spirit, Who is the Author of the Word, dwelling within them. We no longer walk after the flesh, but after the Spirit. God has written on our minds and hearts His desires for us regarding godly living. Israel's laws were rules and regulations. They were inscribed on stone tablets. Our incentive to live for God is far different. His desires for us are written on the fleshly tables of our heart. Instinctively, our desires are to please God, and fulfill His will for us, by living a holy life. Moses hewed the second set of stones, thus painting a most blessed picture for us.

13

PROVIDING FOR THE TABERNACLE

Coming to the thirty-fifth chapter of Exodus, we have presented to us a far different scene. It is a lovely scene to behold, and presents to us the results of restored and devoted hearts to Jehovah. There is now going to be much activity for the glory of God. One thing is emphasized before the activity commences and it is this; the keeping of the Sabbath is mentioned. Man works, then rests. But God's thoughts are not man's thoughts, for God says that rest comes before work.

The lesson is, that before one can do one ounce of work for God, he must enter into His rest, he must be saved. Prior to entering into God's rest (salvation), he is spiritually dead in trespasses and sins. What can a dead man accomplish for God? Nothing! In the New Testament, the Hebrews were exhorted to *"labour therefore to enter into that rest"* provided by God through the death of His Son (Heb. 4:11). The Hebrews in Paul's day were reminded of their brethren of a former day who failed to enter into God's rest through unbelief. They never entered the promised land, but fell in the wilderness. Keeping this before them, Paul then exhorts them with these solemn words; *"lest any man fall after the same example of unbelief."*

THE SABBATH

"Ye shall kindle no fire throughout your habitations upon the Sabbath day" (Ex. 35:3).

Now this is interesting. How would we apply it to today's teaching? What about a cold morning? What about a cooked meal? One can readily see that on the Sabbath they would be deprived of catering to their flesh. There would be the setting aside of the desires of the flesh. There would be the absence of any consideration for one's own comfort in a natural way. In other words, the Sabbath involved sacrificing some of the comforts of life.

Coming to our day, there we read of men who have left a good income, comfortable home, pleasant surroundings, and launched forth into darkened lands with the Gospel of Jesus Christ. Some have gone into the jungles to exist in grass huts, while others have been brutally murdered in their endeavors to reach the lost. Their reward is in heaven. We have entered into God's Sabbath as it were, but are we willing to make sacrifices that will be against our flesh?

You will notice that with any dealing of God in Exodus, the Sabbath is always introduced. You find this in the giving of the manna in chapter 16; in chapter 20 at the giving of the Law; then again in chapter 31, where Bezaleel and Aholiab are selected for the devising of cunning works with gold, silver, and brass for the tabernacle; then finally in chapter 35, where we observe the donations and building of the tabernacle.

At this point, allow me to insert the sacred text for your convenience.

> *"And Moses spake unto all the congregation of the children of Israel, saying, This is the thing which the LORD commanded, saying, Take ye from among you an offering unto the LORD: whosoever is of a willing heart, let him bring it, an offering of the LORD.*
>
> *And all the congregation of the children of Israel departed from the presence of Moses. And they came, every one whose heart stirred him up, and every one whom his spirit made willing, and they brought the*

LORD'S offering to the work of the tabernacle of the congregation, and for all his service, and for the holy garments.

And they came, both men and women, as many as were willing hearted, and brought bracelets, and earrings, and rings, and tablets, all jewels of gold: and every man that offered offered an offering of gold unto the LORD. And every man, with whom was found blue, and purple, and scarlet, and fine linen, and goats' hair, and red skins of rams, and badgers' skins, brought them. Every one that did offer an offering of silver and brass brought the LORD's offering: and every man, with whom was found shittim wood for any work of the service, brought it.

And all the women that were wise hearted did spin with their hands, and brought that which they had spun, both of blue, and of purple, and of scarlet, and of fine linen. And all the women whose heart stirred them up in wisdom spun goats' hair.

And the rulers brought onyx stones, and stones to be set, for the ephod, and for the breastplate; And spice, and oil for the light, and for the anointing oil, and for the sweet incense. The children of Israel brought a willing offering unto the LORD, every man and woman, whose heart made them willing to bring for all manner of work, which the LORD had commanded to be made by the hand of Moses.

And Moses said unto the children of Israel, See, the LORD hath called by name Bezaleel the son of Uri, the son of Hur, of the tribe of Judah; And he hath filled him with the Spirit of God, in wisdom, in understanding, and in knowledge, and in all manner of workmanship; And to devise curious works, to work in gold, and in silver, and in brass, And in the cutting of stones, to set them, and in carving of wood, to make any manner of cunning work. And he hath put in his heart that he may teach, both he, and Aholiab, the son of Ahisamach, of the tribe of Dan. Them hath he filled with wisdom of heart, to work all manner of work, of the engraver, and of the cunning workman, and of the embroiderer, in blue, and in purple, in scarlet, and in fine linen, and of the weaver, even of them that do any work, and of those that devise cunning work" (Ex. 35).

HEARTS

Moses had received the pattern of the tabernacle on the mount, and now he speaks to all the congregation of the children of Israel saying, *"This is the thing which the LORD commanded saying. Take ye from among you an offering unto the LORD: whosoever is of a willing heart, let him bring it, an offering of the LORD."*

Notice that in the sacred text, I have highlighted the word **"heart."** This whole affair was not mere duty, nor was it brainy intellectualism. Ah no, it was heart-work from the very start to the finish. We read *of wise hearts, stirred hearts,* and *willing hearts.* Where you have people with these qualities, you will see happiness, success, endurance, expertise, and any other thing needed to make an undertaking for God, a tremendous success. It takes a *stirred* heart to motivate a soul for the glory of God. Not only to motivate, but to endure in labor for Him. It takes a *willing* heart to bring something for God, and a *wise* heart to make something for God that will last. The response and quality of these people is amazing!

Now then, let me ask you, how many Christians do you see today with these qualities? How many have stirred hearts? We seem full of intellectualism, don't we? We are very smart in material things. But what about our hearts? Are we stirred? Years ago, Lord's Days were very busy days for some saints. Were they relaxing in their comfortable homes? Not at all. They were out in the street with gospel tracts, or visiting a contact in view of getting them to the gospel meeting that night. Here and there, one would find a group of saints standing on a street corner singing hymns, and brethren taking turns in preaching the gospel. They called this activity, "open-air meetings." Are you acquainted with such activity? Many brethren rarely engaged in conversation with an individual without giving them a gospel tract. Activity abounded for the furtherance of the glorious gospel of God. How do we measure up to this in our modern and intellectual day? Are we *stirred-hearted?*

Are we *willing-hearted?* What is our attitude to the assembly of God in which we are supposedly in fellowship? What do we bring? What do we sacrifice? Are we willing to give of our substance for the testimony, and for the work of God in the spread of the gospel? One old and godly brother said to me many years ago, "When God converts a man, He also converts his pocketbook." Well, that is the ideal, but that is not always the case.

The willing-hearted are very exercised to bring their thank offerings. They rise at the Lord's Supper and offer the sacrifice of praise to God, that is the fruit of their lips, giving thanks to His name. This is a continual activity (Heb. 13:15). They willingly praise God in their homes as well as publicly in assembly. The willing-hearted saint lays by him in store as God hath prospered him, and cheerfully gives part of his monetary income to the Lord (1 Cor. 16:1–2). But that is not all. He prays for God to lay upon his willing heart, the need of others. He seeks to be aware of other people's circumstances. There are widows, evangelists, aged saints, sick saints, missionaries, and tried and troubled saints that would welcome help in a material way. The willing-hearted Christian is aware, and moves with compassion, ministering unto them in the Lord's Name. It didn't take Zacchaeus long to become willing-hearted. Immediately, upon receiving the Saviour we hear him say; *"The half of my goods I give to the poor"* (Luke 19:8). It didn't take any persuasion for the widow to cast into the treasury all of her living. She was poor, but what little she possessed was willingly given to her God (Mark 12:42). Let us search our own hearts, and ask ourselves the pointed question, am I truly willing-hearted?

Sometimes, little children can put us to shame. Let me illustrate.

> "There was a missionary meeting in a church in Scotland. The people were greatly moved. They gave generously to send missionaries into God's worldwide vineyard. Little Alexander Duff, just ten years old, sat in a pew. His heart was strangely moved. But he had nothing to give. After the offering was taken, the ushers returned to the rear of the church. Little Alexander followed them. Looking into the face of one of the collectors, the lad said, 'Please, Sir, put the basket low!' The usher, catering to what he thought was a childish whim, put the basket on the floor. 'There you are, my boy,' he said, smiling. How surprised all were when the boy stepped into the basket and said, 'O God, I have no money to give, but I give myself in the offering!'"   –W. B. K.

> "Not what I get, but what I give
> This be the gauge by which I live.
> Not merely joys that come my way,
> But the help I give to those astray.
> Not the rewards of money and fame,
> But the loads I lift in Jesus' name.
> This be the pay at the end of the day,
> Not what I keep, but give away."
> – Selected

Are we "wise-hearted?" The Corinthian saints came behind in no gift, yet Paul asks, *"Is there not a wise man among you?"* (1 Cor. 6:5). How extremely valuable are wise-hearted men! Moses, in relating the choosing of men as rulers over the people, stated, *"Take you wise men, and understanding, and known among your tribes, and I will make them rulers over you"* (Deut. 1:13). Moses saw the value of wise men of understanding. Regarding the construction of a sanctuary for God, wisdom was needed, and the LORD provided those qualities to certain men. Thus we read, *"Then wrought Bezaleel and Aholiab, and every wise hearted man, in whom the LORD put wisdom and understanding to know how to work all manner of work for the service of the sanctuary, according to all that the LORD had commanded"* (Ex. 36:1).

Solomon relates to this by writing, *"Through wisdom is an house builded; and by understanding it is established"* (Prov. 24:3). Ezra saw a need on the way back from Jerusalem, when they encamped eighty miles and nine days from Babylon, by the river that ran to Ahava. He viewed the people, and the priests, and found there none of the sons of Levi. He saw the need of men that could minister for the house of their God. Word was sent back to brethren still in Babylon. This involved hundreds of miles of travel. Then we read, *"And by the good hand of our God upon us they brought us a man of understanding, of the sons of Mahli, the son of Levi, the son of Israel; and Sherebiah, with his sons and his brethren, eighteen"* (Ezra 8:18).

WISE-HEARTED MEN

A scriptural assembly cannot properly function without wise-hearted men. Stephen was a man of wisdom. His words were appropriate, and they carried weight. He said the right thing, at the right time, and in the right way. He was a wise, and fearless man. He knew the Scriptures and knew how to apply them. The haters of Christ, the religious leaders of his day, *"were not able to resist the wisdom and the spirit by which he spake"* (Acts 6:10). A wise man has not only knowledge, but he also knows how to effectively apply his knowledge to the benefit of the saints, and the assembly of God. Such men are worth more than their weight in gold! Oh, that we had more wise men among us! Our testimonies would be shining far brighter! Perhaps even our gatherings would be far greater. Unbelievers would more readily see reverence in our gatherings. They would be acknowledging, with little difficulty, that God is in us of a truth. Wisdom! Wisdom! Seek it my dear saint! Do you realize your lack of it? Does your autobiography contain many mistakes? Then by all means come to the throne as a needy supplicant, and ask of God. Remember the promise! *"If any of you lack wisdom, let him ask of God, that giveth to all men liberally, and upbraideth not; and it shall be given him"* (Jas. 1:5).

The first mention of a woman's hand was in Eden. Disobediently, *"she took of the fruit thereof, and did eat"* (Gen. 3:6). In Exodus 35, we have the opposite. Women, in devotion, are not taking, but giving. With heart's stirred up, and willing, and with wisdom they worked in their homes to make God's sanctuary a beautiful place. Notice the sacred report.

> *"And they came, both men and women, as many as were willing hearted, and brought bracelets, and earrings, and rings, and tablets, all jewels of gold: and every man that offered offered an offering of gold unto the LORD ... And all the women that were wise hearted did spin with their hands, and brought that which they had spun, both of blue, and of purple, and of scarlet, and of fine linen. And all the women whose heart stirred them up in wisdom spun goats' hair"* (Ex. 35:22, 25-26).

LIKEMINDEDNESS

In the giving of their gold, we see the sacrificing of personal wealth for the beautification of God's dwelling place. Their *"heart stirred them up."* That word *"stirred"* means, *"to be carried away."* They were totally engrossed with the house of God. They had a "one-track mind." All for God, nothing for self! The word *"women"* in verse 25 is in the singular, signifying that all these women were working together as one. This reminds me of Paul's exhortation to the Philippians, *"Fulfil ye my joy, that ye be likeminded, having the same love, being of one accord, of one mind ... I beseech Euodias, and beseech Syntyche, that they be of the same mind in the Lord"* (Phil. 2:2; 4:2). The same exhortation falls upon the saints in Rome. *"Be of the same mind one toward another. Mind not high things, but condescend to men of low estate. Be not wise in your own conceits"* (Rom. 12:16). Likewise, he writes the assembly at Corinth. *"Now I beseech you, brethren, by the name of our Lord Jesus Christ, that ye all speak the same thing, and that there be no divisions among you; but that ye be perfectly joined together in the same mind and in the same judgment"* (1 Cor. 1:10). There is a saying in the world that holds a bit of practical truth, and it is this: "United we stand. Divided we fall." Where there is humility, prayerfulness, a thorough knowledge of the Scriptures, a bowing to Christ's lordship, and the fear of God, there will be one-mindedness among the saints. There is no doubt about it!

You may counter this remark and say, "Why then is there discord among us? Why do we not all agree on certain matters?" The answer is simple. The reason for any discord can be found in the fact that all of the qualities mentioned above are not found.

WOMEN SPINNING

The women, in their tents, were busy, not spinning with their tongues, but busy spinning with their hands, weaving threads of goat's hair together. My father, at the age of seven or nine, worked in a woolen mill in Kells, Northern Ireland. He related to me that when they worked with goat's hair, it left a smell on them. Returning home, that smell remained, so that those in the house knew immediately that he had been working with goat's hair that day. Sisters weaving together thoughts of Christ in the quietness of their homes, when coming to God's assembly, they carry the fragrance of Christ with them. It is wonderful to behold. Their meekness, their modest apparel, combined with shamefacedness and sobriety, all reveal the fact that they have been, as it were, spinning the goat's hair in their home.

HOME – THE WOMAN'S SPHERE

There is a spiritual truth to be gleaned from the labors of these women, which we can relate to today. The first thing to notice is that the woman's sphere of activity is in the home. The world thinks otherwise, and our society encourages married women to go out into the vast workforce and make something out of themselves. To forge ahead, and climb the ladder of independence, fortune, and success. Following this concept of life has produced poison fruit. One of those fruits is divorce. When married women were keepers at home, as the Bible commands (Titus 2:5), the divorce of married couples was very rare. However, with our sophisticated, intellectual, and modern way of thinking, we have produced divorces in over 52% of all marriages in the USA.

Sister, be careful to obey the Word of God (especially if God has given you children), and fill the sphere that God has given you as a *"keeper"* (guard) at home. Women have been appointed by the Lord to *"guide the house"* (1 Tim. 5:14). That word means *"rule, management and direction of household affairs."* It would be a strange thing to enter a Walmart store and ask for the manager, only to be told that on a daily basis he went to work for K-Mart, but that he would be back that evening. Can you see the analogy? What if you were to go to a Christian home that has little children. Knock on the door, only to find out, that the sister has shuffled off her children to a nursery, or to her parents, and that she has gone to another place to work for the day. Is this normal in our society. Unfortunately, it is. Is it scriptural? Absolutely not! But the argument arises, that one cannot live on just the income of the husband. Was that considered before the marriage? Evidently not. But now that they are married, they feel the need of two incomes, as one income is not sufficient to meet their **needs**. Let me rephrase that last statement. They feel the need of two incomes, as one income is not sufficient to meet their **wants**.

There is a common saying among older folk about young couples. "When young folks get married today, they expect to have all the things that it took us years to accumulate in our marriage. Some have more than we did after we were married twenty years!"

This is the reason why both couples are working. Their wants exceed the husband's income, so the wife leaves her God-appointed sphere in order to supplement her husband's income. Instead of one old car, they must have two newer vehicles. Instead of living in a humble little dwelling, they must have a spacious, well-designed home, which, of course, demands "spacious" monthly payments. The marketing world contributes to their thirst and allows them to purchase home commodities "on time" with no payments until next year. The credit card enables them to "satisfy" the lust of the eye, but the truth of the matter is, *"the eye is not satisfied with seeing"* (Eccl. 1:8). It is not morally right to purchase commodities through a credit card, and not have the means to pay already in your purse. *"Owe no man anything"* can still be found in your Bible (Rom. 13:8), and if we are scripturally wise, we will abide by God's advice.

The women spun the goat's hair at home, preparing it for use in God's sanctuary. There have been women who have accomplished mighty deeds for God by working in their home.

A MOST UNUSUAL WOMAN

In 1952, I met a most unusual woman. She did much to relieve the afflicted, and helped the poor as much as she was able. Her days were spent at home busy with cloth, thread, and needle, as she made coats and garments for those in need. Everybody in town knew and highly respected her. One day, she fell sick and died. Let me say, her death did not pass unnoticed, for many came to the viewing. There were a number of widows that she had befriended, and they stood reverently before her casket and wept. I never did find out her last name, but she lived in a town called Joppa, and her name was Dorcas. I met her in the Book of Acts, when I came to chapter nine. She made quite an impression on me. She worked in her home for God.

ABRAHAM AND SARAH

One day, on the plains of Mamre, Abraham experienced three unannounced visitors, as he sat at the tent door in the heat of the day. His immediate desire was to host his guests. He offered them meat and drink. So what did he do? The solution was simple. He *"hastened into the tent unto Sarah, and said, Make ready quickly three measures of fine meal, knead it, and make cakes upon the hearth"* (Gen. 18:6). Where was his wife? Naturally, she was in the tent, her God-given sphere.

LOT AND HIS FAMILY

Even though Lot was carnal, you will notice where his wife was when the warning to flee Sodom came. *"And when the morning arose, then the angels hastened Lot, saying, arise, take thy wife, and thy two daughters, which are here"* (Gen. 19:15).

QUALITIES OF A GODLY SISTER

Notice the six qualities of a godly sister who had become a widow in 1 Timothy. **First**: *"Well reported of for good works."* This was the commendation of Dorcas, *"full of good works."*

Second: *"She hath brought up children."* The word is, *"nourish."* That is, she gave her children everything required to live, grow, and remain healthy. She helped them to develop. She would encourage and strengthen them for their life that lay before them. All these things can also be reckoned to the spiritual side of a child's life. She trains them in the way they should go, and constantly brings before them the Holy Scriptures. No mother can fulfill these duties working an eight-hour day elsewhere, away from her home.

Third: *"She lodged strangers."* Evangelists who travel among the gathered-out saints can attest to the fact that such sisters are most valuable. There is something wonderful, beautiful, and fragrant, about the presence of a godly woman in her home. She attends to her guests, guides her children, and seeks to be a blessing to all that come in contact with her. King Lemuel exclaimed, *"Who can find a virtuous woman? For her price is far above rubies"* (Prov. 31:10).

ELISHA'S HOST

You remember when Elisha passed to Shunem, it seems that every time he passed a certain dwelling, the woman of the house constrained him to eat bread. As this continued, this great woman perceived that her oft repeated guest was a holy man of God. So she consulted her husband, who gave her permission to accommodate her frequent guest more adequately. She provided for Elisha a little chamber with the bare essentials, a bed, a table, a stool and a candlestick (2 Kgs. 4:8–10). She was aware of a need, and acted accordingly. Needless to say, she was a woman who managed her house twenty four hours a day.

ENTERTAINING STRANGERS

In New Testament times, the Hebrew believers were exhorted to *"not forget to entertain strangers"* (Heb. 13:1). The word *"entertain,"* is *"hospitableness."* Is not this a gift to be cultivated? *"Distributing to the necessity of saints; given to hospitality"* (Rom. 12:13*).* *"Use hospitality one to another without grudging"* (1 Pet. 4:9). In other words, don't be thinking, "Oh my, taking in these guests will increase my food bill. It means more work. It hinders my plans." No, no, that kind of thinking will never do my beloved. Remember this, *"God is not unrighteous to forget your work and labour of love, which ye have shewed toward His Name, in that ye have ministered to the saints, and do minister"* (Heb. 6:10).

A COLD HOUSE

I have stayed in homes where people do not have much, yet they provide their best. What wonderful people! On the other hand, about forty years ago, I stayed in a home one winter, where both the husband and wife worked. At least they took me in while I visited the assembly where they were in fellowship. However, when they went to work at 7:30 A.M., they turned the thermostat down to 59 degrees! They were very frugal, which I wouldn't find fault with, but as I sat in my room with my overcoat on, I didn't appreciate nature's air conditioning!

Fourth: She *"washed the saints' feet."* In Oriental lands, this is a custom that ministers cheer and refreshment. This carries the thought of service that is menial, the sister not being too proud to stoop. The husband invites the guests, but the task of preparing the meal, serving it, and then clearing the table and washing the dishes is left to the wife. It is quite an accomplishment for a sister to minister in such a way, that when her guests leave her well-attended home, they can say to one another, *"My, but I was greatly cheered and refreshed in that home."*

A WARM HOUSE

Last Lord's Day I visited an assembly. Through the years, they had become very small. The location of the hall had so deteriorated that it was almost impossible to get people in to hear the gospel. Shootings and killings were quite common in the neighborhood. My visit was intended to encourage them. However, before the day was over, it was the visitor that was greatly encouraged. Hospitality was shown without grudging. I was invited to one family's home for dinner. Two other couples were also invited. The meal was spread, the food was delicious and enjoyed. After dessert (home-made blueberry pie!), the men retired to the living room, and we conversed over the Scriptures one with another. I left that evening happy in soul. It could even have been said of me like the eunuch, I went on my way rejoicing!

Fifth: She *"relieved the afflicted."* That is, the widow mentioned had ministered unto others, relieving them of mental, or physical pressure. Mature sisters counseling young sisters, visiting sick saints, and sympathizing and offering solutions to mentally disturbed saints is a privileged work, and labor of love. A sister working outside of her home would hardly have time for such wholesome activity. One cannot leave a job to visit a sick soul, or to encourage a despondent saint, or to advise a young sister. But if she is a keeper at home, she will have the liberty to function in this capacity.

Sixth: She *"diligently follows every good work."* The married woman has an occupation, and it is not an office worker, a factory worker, a restaurant worker, or any kind of a worker for an employer. Her occupation surrounds her home, and we have just enumerated five things relative to that very thing. These are beneficial (*"good"*) works. Notice, she is to diligently follow them. She "runs after them." She seeks them, finds them, and then continues in them. Her work is not spasmodic. She is not a "roller-coaster" Christian. No, no! She endures in her daily labor for God, using her home as a base for all her godly activity! The women spun goat's hair in their tent.

SPONTANEOUS LIBERALITY

None were excluded. They all brought what they had. *"Every man, with whom was found blue, and purple, and scarlet, and fine linen, and goats' hair, and red skins of rams, and badger's skins, brought them"* (Ex. 35:23). Even the rulers, who possessed more material goods than others, freely brought. Gladly, they contributed their onyx stones, spice and oil. There was no questioning, no debating, no holding back. Ah no, they were all wholehearted! God's sanctuary must come first!

Christendom has invented pledges, grand-prize drawings, earnest appeals for money, and other devices to extort money from people. Not so here! All was spontaneous, all was liberal, and all was given joyfully. If God has a work to do, He will lay it upon the hearts of His people to further His work. No gifts were procured by human means. This is one of the most wonderful scenes in Holy Scripture depicting love to Jehovah, and holy giving. There was nothing like it before, and seldom has there been anything like it since. Perhaps the Church at its commencement would come close to it, for it was said of them; *"And all that believed were together, and had all things common; And sold their possessions and goods, and parted them to all men, as every man had need"* (Acts 2:45). In reality, even though they were giving their goods to other saints, they were giving to the Lord.

Perhaps I might add another fairly similar occasion. When the temple was about to be built, David, at the end of his life's journey raised the question to all the congregation. *"Who then is willing to consecrate his service this day unto the LORD?"* (1 Chron. 29:5). He realized that the work was great and that the palace was not for man, but for the LORD God. He told them that he had prepared with all of his might, and that he had set his affection to the house of his God. The response was tremendous. We read, *"Then the people rejoiced, for that they offered willingly, because with perfect heart they offered willingly to the LORD: and David the king also rejoiced with great joy"* (1 Chron. 29:9).

THE MISER AND HIS DOLLAR

The late Archie Stewart, a witty Irish evangelist, once told the story of a miser who attended the Lord's Supper. In his coat pocket he had two bills. One was a one-dollar bill, the other was a twenty-dollar bill. The miser had the one-dollar bill folded differently than the twenty-dollar bill. When the offering was passed in the circle, the miser reached into his pocket and slipped what he thought was the one dollar bill into the basket. That was for the Lord. Of course, the twenty dollars remained in his pocket for himself. However, to his dismay, upon returning home after the meeting, when he reached into his pocket for his twenty dollar bill, instead, he pulled out the one dollar bill. Inadvertently, he had put the wrong bill into the offering. He had placed the twenty dollars into the basket instead of the intended one dollar. Poor fellow, for I am sure that the Lord gave him credit for only one dollar, for that is what he had purposed in his heart to give. In other words, he lost nineteen dollars in the transaction!

MORE THAN ENOUGH

The people brought unto Moses their free offerings every morning. Finally, the workers *"spake unto Moses, saying, The people bring much more than enough for the service of the work, which the LORD commanded to make"* ... *So the people were restrained from bringing. For the stuff they had was sufficient for all the work to make it, and too much"* (Ex. 36:5–7). Have you ever heard the like of this before? Did you ever hear of a radio, or a television preacher, begging his audience to please refrain from giving more, because he had more than enough? Hardly! There was something real about this giving. There was no pushing, pleading, or begging for donations. Not at all! The opposite was true, for they had more than enough! What an abundance the early Church had! They had an abundance of gifts, teachers, evangelists, shepherds, and divine power! God was in them of a truth. Thousands, who had experienced the new birth, walked the streets of Jerusalem. The message of the gospel rolled forth with dignity, and with Holy Spirit power! God was working mightily, and souls were being saved on a daily basis. It truly must have been a sight to see. We shall meet these souls in heaven, and I often wonder, if through the eternal ages, they will be permitted to relay to us the details of that wondrous occasion in the Church's history.

ISRAEL'S NEW YEAR'S DAY

The LORD had spoken to Israel through Moses saying; *"Let them make Me a sanctuary; that I may dwell among them"* (Ex. 25:8). It was the third month after their departure out of Egypt that the Lord commenced His dealings with them concerning the Law, and His blueprint for the tabernacle was given (Ex. 19:1). Nine months later, on Israel's religious New Year's day, the tabernacle was reared up. The work of making God a dwelling place was complete. Thus we read, *"According to all that the LORD commanded Moses, so the children of Israel made all the work. And Moses did look upon all the work, and, behold, they had done it as the LORD had commanded, even so had they done it: and Moses blessed them ... And it came to pass in the first month in the second year, on the first day of the month, that the tabernacle was reared up"* (Ex. 39:42–43; 40:17).

What a wonderful New Year's day this was for the nation of Israel. It was the anniversary of their departure from Egypt.

The spiritual implication is this. The beginning of spiritual life, known and enjoyed, and becoming a temple of the Holy Spirit, coincide. *"In Whom also after that ye believed,* (upon believing) *ye were sealed with that Holy Spirit of promise"* (Eph. 1:13).

For one month and twenty days, the pillar of the cloud hovered over the tabernacle, and the Aaronic priesthood began to function. The brazen altar's fire burned continually, as lamb after lamb was offered as a sweet smelling savor to Jehovah. Israel became a worshipping nation, as various animals were brought on a daily basis and sacrificed unto God, according to ceremonial law.

Never before, in the history of man, had there ever been a nation so privileged as Israel. The LORD was in their midst. They were His gathered-out people. He was their object of worship. He was also their sole guide, and Protector, and His purpose for them was to bring them into a land flowing with milk and honey.

14

ISRAEL LEAVES SINAI

> *"And it came to pass on the twentieth day of the second month, in the second year, that the cloud was taken up from off the tabernacle of the testimony. And the children of Israel took their journeys out of the wilderness of Sinai; and the cloud rested in the wilderness of Paran. And they first took their journey according to the commandment of the LORD by the hand of Moses"* (Num. 10:11-13).

The cloud began to move. The trumpets were blown, and Israel broke camp. The task of dismantling and preparing the tabernacle was done decently and in order. The sons of Merari were responsible for the transporting of the boards, the pillars, the sockets, and all the vessels thereof. Their burden was far heavier than the sons of Gershon and Kohath. Consequently, to them had been allotted four wagons and eight oxen. As for the sons of Gershon, they were only given two wagons and four oxen. Their responsibility was to bear the curtains, the tabernacle coverings, the hangings of the court, their cords, and all the instruments of their service. Last, but not least, we have the Kothathites. Their ministry was the most unique, in that they lacked wagons or oxen to help them in their labor. Their ministry was to transport the sacred vessels of the sanctuary after they had been properly prepared by Aaron and his sons. The Ark ws adorned with its final covering of blue. The table of shewbread, the golden altar, and the brazen altar, were all covered with badger's skins. These burdens would be humanly felt by the sons of Kohath, as they moved with divine guidance through a waste-howling wilderness.

EVANGELISTS

These three types of service for the LORD have been likened to three offices among us today. First: The heavy burden bearers, the sons of **Merari**, would remind us of the ***evangelist***. They carried the basic essentials of the structure in which the following items would be employed. The evangelist's work is extremely basic. He works with raw material. He reaches out to people that do not know their right hand from their left when it comes to spiritual things. He speaks to those who sit in darkness, bound by Satan's captive chain. His endeavors can bring him into dangerous circumstances. He has heard the call, *"Go ye into all the world and preach the gospel."* His sights are in the regions beyond. To the weak he becomes weak, that he might gain the weak: he is made all things to all men, that he might by all means save some (1 Cor. 9:22). He is constantly looking to God to supply his need, both spiritually, physically, and temporally. I would say that there is a more "rough and readiness" to his labors than that of a shepherd or teacher.

If all this sounds strange to you, then perhaps it is because you are looking at a different kind of evangelist than what we find in the Scriptures. Perhaps you are looking at a man that constantly travels in a circuit among the assemblies. He stays in Christian's homes, is well fed and taken care of on a daily basis. Being with an assembly, he always has a ready-made audience, and sinners in his audience are mostly the children of Christian parents. Assemblies need gospel meetings. True! However, I am talking about pioneer evangelists, men that have no one to wait on them "hand and foot." They are men that are in the regions beyond, far away from the joyful singing of the saints, and the luscious meals of sisters. I am speaking of evangelists in the true sense of the word.

SHEPHERDS

The sons of ***Gershon*** come next. They portray to us the ***shepherds*** of the flock. The word "shepherd" is common among us, but do we really understand all the implications that this word conveys? I think, at this point, that it would be very profitable to scrutinize its meaning. The word is found 18 times in the N.T., but its first occurrence in Hebrew is in Genesis 4:2. *"Abel was a keeper of sheep."* The first time it is translated *"shepherd"* is in Genesis 46:32. *"And the men are shepherds, for their trade hath been to feed cattle; and they have brought their flocks, and their herds, and all that they have."* It is easy to see from these two texts alone that the words convey to us, that a shepherd is one that keeps and feeds sheep.

In Isaiah 40:11, we have a graphic description of a shepherd's activity. The Lord God speaks of a coming day for the nation, when Christ will shepherd His people.

"He shall feed His flock like a shepherd: He shall gather the lambs with His arm, and carry them in His bosom, and shall gently lead those that are with young." Notice first, the shepherd *feeds*. He is a person that can satisfy the hunger of his flock. Shepherds in a local assembly accomplish this in Bible readings, and ministry meetings. They may not be teachers, in the full sense of the word, but they certainly have an aptness to teach (1 Tim. 3:2). They feed the flock.

The next thing we see about a shepherd is that he *gathers* the lambs with his arm. In other words, he protects them from evil influences and makes them feel secure. The shepherd counsels young and old with sound advice. It is the shepherd's responsibility to sit with an engaged couple and give them good counsel regarding marriage and its responsibilities. "Marriage and the family" specialists are not really needed if shepherds are doing their work.

The third activity we notice is, he will *carry* the lambs *in his bosom*. He supports them. How wonderful to receive support from shepherds when enduring a trial. They support the weary and tried with their comforting words and with their money. That is, if financial aid is needed.

Last of all, the shepherd will *gently lead* those that are with young. Having just given birth, the mother is physically weak, and there is a journey to take to greener pastures. The shepherd is able to sympathize with the infirmed. He does not drive the sheep. Ah no, he leads them, and he does it gently. These are the markings of a true shepherd. How many fill these qualifications in your own assembly?

Coming to Ezekiel 34:15, we read these words:

"I will seek that which was lost, and bring again that which was driven away, and will bind up that which was broken, and will strengthen that which was sick." Again, we come across that word *"feed."* The following quality is he causes the sheep to lie down. Disturbed or frightened sheep will not lie down. However, a shepherd is a person, that can bring peace and tranquility to the flock.

Not only this, he seeks that which was lost. The backslider needs a shepherd to come to him in the spirit of meekness, with the purpose of restoring that wayward one back to the fellowship of the Lord and the assembly.

Another thing to notice is that he will bring again those who were driven away. He seeks to recover saints that have been stolen by another. He will also *"bind up that which was broken."* He is a skilful, spiritual surgeon. He sets the broken bone, so that the saint will be able to walk correctly for the Lord again. This thought is conveyed in Galatians 6:1. *"Brethren, if a man be overtaken in a fault, ye which are spiritual, restore such an one in the spirit of meekness; considering thyself, lest thou also be tempted."* The word *"restore"* means *to "set a broken bone."*

Last of all, we see the true shepherd as one that will *"strengthen that which was sick."* He is a successful physician. He has cures for various spiritual ills. Men like this are very valuable, and they are rare. How many are in your assembly?

TEACHERS

Leaving the Gershonites we come lastly to the sons of Kohath. To these men were entrusted the transportation of the holy vessels. They represent those who are teachers in the local assemblies of God's gathered out people. They handled very sacred things, namely, the vessels that were used in approaching unto God. Those vessels were to be carried by themselves, no human mechanism was to be employed as in the case of the Merarites, or the Gershonites.

What is a teacher in the scriptural sense of the word? A teacher is a man that can take a portion of Scripture and unfold to his audience the exact meaning of what the text is conveying. He makes complicated portions of Scripture simple, so that you can easily understand them. He is a man that can bring things out of well-known Scriptures, that you never saw before. He may not be an exhorter, or an evangelist, but one thing he has the ability to do, and that is to make plain the Word of God so that saints can understand it. He may be an overseer, or he may not. He may not even be a visitor of the saints, or a sociable type of person, or, he might be. One thing he does have, and that is the ability to teach. This Spirit-given gift is carried out in a local way. Remember the favored church at Antioch? It had a number of teachers (Acts 13:1).

The evangelist is a man that is released from his responsibilities in the assembly, but one never reads of this release for one that teaches. His sphere, scripturally, seems to be in a local setting. Here is a searching question for you. Where are the teachers today among the gathered-out companies of the Lord's people? If you can name a few, why then are they not being encouraged to rise at our conferences to teach, while evangelists are allowed to dominate the teaching platform? True, some evangelists have the gift of a teacher, but in most cases, like the shepherds, they only have an aptness to teach. That is, their teaching does not reach the same level as that of a God-gifted teacher. I hope that you recognize that fact. All you have to do is read 1 Corinthians 12 to see that what I am projecting to you is Scriptural truth.

THE HOLY SPIRIT DIVIDES

The Scripture plainly states that there are "diversities of gifts." Whether it is the gift of shepherding, evangelizing, or teaching, they are distributed by one Spirit for the profit of all. Who determines who gets any particular gift? Why the answer is simple! It is the Holy Spirit that divides to every man severally as He will (v. 11). In some cases he gives one man more than one gift. But the giving of these various gifts is solely up to Him. Let us remember that, and let us start to recognize that. I say, *let us **start** to recognize that,* for the simple reason being that we presently are not recognizing it. Our conferences openly prove that!

Take your own poll. At the last conference you attended, of all the men that spoke, how many were full-time workers in evangelism, and how many were common men in some local assembly that were teachers? Answer me, how many? What was the percentage? If you answer, "One hundred percent were evangelists," then by your answer, you have supported my point. Let us earnestly pray that the Lord, the Spirit, will raise up teachers among us, and that God will give overseers who are responsible for their own conference platforms the courage to encourage teachers to rise with a word for God's listening people.

CHRIST – THE PERFECT EVANGELIST

Before closing this chapter, let me point you to One that filled all three of these offices that we have been considering. Our blessed Lord was an *evangelist*, a *shepherd*, and a *teacher*. You will remember His first recorded message in the Gospel of Luke. In chapter four, we find Him in the town where He grew up – Nazareth. Luke's pen takes us to the synagogue, and there we see the Lord with the book of Isaiah in His hand. He quotes from chapter 61 regarding the coming Messiah, and refers it to Himself. In that portion, two great things are revealed, namely, *"the Spirit of the Lord is upon Me, because He hath anointed Me to preach the gospel to the poor"* (v. 18). In other words, His power was from above, and His presentation was the gospel. What characterized His preaching? Well, let me say candidly, that what characterized His preaching is not seen too often today in preachers. First of all, this abominable thing called "political correctness" was never seen. No! Not so much as once! He never sought the favor of people by manipulating His words. His preaching was very narrow. By that I mean it was always about the soul. He was very personal, and if you don't think so, ask the woman in John four who had been married to five husbands, and was, at the present, living with a man that was not her husband. He exposed her wicked lifestyle right to her face.

Look at the religious leaders. Did He court their favor? Did He compliment them? Did he seek to amuse them, and make them feel important? If you think that He did, you certainly do not know your Bible too well! No! He used none of those tactics that sadly we see among prominent preachers in this world today. Notice His words to the men that fancied themselves, and that considered themselves holier that the rest. *"Woe unto you, scribes and Pharisees, hypocrites! for ye are like unto whited sepulchres, which indeed appear beautiful outward, but are within full of dead men's bones, and of all uncleanness"* (Matt. 23:27). Now how could you be more blunt than that? Tell me, how could you? Was He rude? No! He was never rude! The fact of the matter is that He simply told it as it was. He didn't preach to make people feel self-satisfied, or important. Quite the contrary! He preached with divine power to convict men of their sins that they might repent. He was exceedingly strong on repentance. In fact, His first recorded words to sinners were; *"Repent: for the kingdom of heaven is at hand"* (Matt. 4:17). He preached more about hell, and hell fire, than any other preacher in the Bible. What do you think of that? How many evangelists today preach sin, repentance, hell, the judgment, and the lake of fire? Not one mega-church builder would ever dare to preach along those lines. He would never be able to build a mega-church if he did. Ask him, and he will even admit to this!

Ah, my friend, but there is more to His preaching than what I have just stated. To sincere people, searching people, and souls that were humble, He preached with divine compassion. Look at Him in Capernaum. It was there that He healed the centurion's servant. It was there that He raised Peter's mother-in-law from a bed of sickness. It was there that He also healed the sick of palsy, and the nobleman's son. It was there that He preached about Himself as the Living Bread from Heaven (John 6). He walked their streets, He performed many miracles before their eyes, and He preached, in love, to them. What was the general result in that city? They refused to repent. They absolutely would not heed His call. They wanted nothing to do with Him. He was despised and rejected. So what did He do? Consign them all to hell immediately? Nothing of the sort! Here is what He said to them. *"Woe unto thee"* (Matt. 11:21).

Now just what does that mean? Simply this. *"Woe,"* is an exclamation grief. Why the grief? Because He knew what the dire consequences would be of those who rejected His message. He even told them so. Notice His powerful words. *"And thou, Capernaum, which art exalted unto heaven, shalt be brought down to hell: for if the mighty works, which have been done in thee, had been done in Sodom, it would have remained until this day. But I say unto you, That it shall be more tolerable for the land of Sodom in the day of judgment, than for thee"* (Matt. 11:23-24).

As a Preacher, he fully recognized their need of salvation. He fully understood their latter end. Thus, He was faithful to them in every aspect of the word. But, as said before, in return, He was despised and rejected. So, what did He do? The end of Matthew 28, gives us the heart-touching answer. He made His final appeal to them, in love to their souls. *"Come unto Me, all ye that labour and are heavy laden, and I will give you rest."* What a wonderful example He was for every evangelist today!

CHRIST – THE PERFECT TEACHER

Not only did the Lord preach, but He also taught. Nicodemus recognized this and even confessed it openly when he came to Him. *"We know that Thou art a Teacher come from God:*

for no man can do these miracles that Thou doest, except God be with him" (John 3:2).

He was a marvel to those who heard Him. *"When He was come into His own country, He taught them in their synagogue, insomuch that they were astonished, and said, Whence hath this Man this wisdom, and these mighty works?"* (Matt. 13:54). Entering the synagogue at Capernaum He taught. Here is the result, recorded by the Spirit. *"They were astonished at His doctrine: for He taught them as One that had authority, and not as the scribes"* (Mark 1:22). You will remember in the temple at Jerusalem, on the last day of the feast, it was said of Him by the officers, *" Never man spake like this Man"* (John 7:46).

The Lord was the most profound teacher that mortal ears ever heard. He always said the right thing, at the right time, and in the right way. He frequently referred to, and quoted, the Old Testament Scriptures. However, be sure of this, that if a preacher's audience rejects His message, and even may become angry, this does not necessarily imply that his preaching was faulty. For when the Lord preached in the Synagogue at Nazareth, before He was finished, His audience was filled with wrath, so much so, that they attempted to murder Him.

Any teacher who is afraid of wounding his audience with the truth, is unlike his Lord. If a teacher has true love for God's people, is wise in his selection of words, and preaches what the Holy Spirit lays upon his heart, he may wound certain people. However, like Jonah, he realizes God's mind for those who proclaim His Word, and it is this. *"Arise ... and preach ... the preaching that I bid thee"* (Jon. 3:2).

Not only this, the Lord's teaching was very interesting. He used illustrations common to everyday life. Mark tells us that, *"He taught them many things by parables"* (Mark 4:2). Thus, we have the story of the sower.

People understood His words. His preaching was plain, powerful, piercing, purposeful, and perfect! His teaching was negative and it was also positive, depending on the situation. He fully knew the Scriptures, and He fully knew His audience. He was *"the Amen, the faithful and true Witness, the beginning of the creation of God"* (Rev. 3:14).

To His disciples, He taught them how to act, what to say, and what to expect. He fully informed them. He equipped them for the battles of God that lay before them.

There is one more thing about His teaching, that is very precious indeed. As Cleopas and a companion journeyed from Jerusalem to Emmaus, a seven-mile journey, the Lord drew near and went with them. As they walked, *"beginning at Moses and all the prophets, He expounded unto them in all the Scriptures the things concerning Himself"* (Luke 24:27). Isn't that precious? Isn't that delightful? What more wonderful thing could a person do than to spend time in the presence of the Lord, expounding things concerning Himself? So we see that His teaching was always Scriptural, yet varied. It could challenge the soul, it could exhort the mind, and it could warm the heart. What a perfect example for any teacher of God's Word today.

CHRIST – THE PERFECT SHEPHERD

Having considering the Lord as the perfect Evangelist and Teacher, let us now consider Him as the perfect Shepherd. Much has been said already about our Lord as a Shepherd, but we have a few more thoughts to project to you.

There were five Old Testament men that remind us of Christ as a Shepherd.

(1) ABEL, THE RIGHTEOUS SHEPHERD.

(2) JACOB, THE RESOURCEFUL SHEPHERD.

(3) JOSEPH, THE REJECTED SHEPHERD.

(4) MOSES, THE RETURNING SHEPHERD.

(5) DAVID, THE ROYAL SHEPHERD.

(1) Abel, in his death. He is spoken of as righteous (Matt. 23:35).

(2) Jacob, in his care for the sheep, was resourceful. The Lord enables His sheep to overcome difficulties.

(3) Joseph, fed the flock, but was rejected of his brethren. The Lord experienced the same, only to a far greater degree.

(4) Moses, was rejected of his brethren, guided a flock in the backside of the desert, but then returned to his people as a mighty deliverer. In like manner, Israel has rejected her Messiah, but the day is coming, when He will return and deliver His people and will shepherd them.

(5) David, jeopardized his life for the sheep, even to the point of confronting a lion and a bear.

Coming to New Testament Scripture, we discover four qualities of our Lord as a Shepherd. First; He is the **GOOD SHEPHERD**, that gave His life for the sheep (John 10:11). Second; He is the **GREAT SHEPHERD**, Who makes us complete in every good work (Heb. 13:20-21). Third; He is the **CHIEF SHEPHERD**, Who soon shall appear with crowns of glory for those worthy to receive them (1 Pet. 5:4). Fourth; He is spoken of as **ONE SHEPHERD,** emphasizing the fact that He has created one fold, composed of Jew and Gentile (John 10:16).

How thankful we should be to the Holy Spirit, Who in His divine wisdom and sovereignty, has supplied the Church will all the necessary gifts to function as a living organism to the honor of Christ, and to the glory of God.

"And He gave some, apostles; and some, prophets; and some, evangelists; and some, pastors and teachers; For the perfecting of the saints, for the work of the ministry, for the edifying of the body of Christ" (Eph. 4:11-12).

The apostles and prophets no longer exist. They ceased when the canon of Scripture was complete. Remaining are **evangelists**, not pastor-teachers, but simply, **pastors** and **teachers** (two separate gifts). The word *"pastors,"* is literally *"shepherds."*

> "To God be the glory, great things He hath done,
> In every assembly, a gift for each one.
> The evangelists, to preach the gospel so pure.
> The pastors to feed, that the sheep may endure.
> The teachers to enlighten the mind
> with good thought.
> We thank God the Spirit,
> Who these gifts hath brought."[48]

---

48 Robert E. Surgenor. September 26, 2008

15

THE CONSECRATION OF THE PRIESTS

> *"And take thou unto thee Aaron thy brother, and his sons with him, from among the children of Israel, that he may minister unto Me in the priest' office, even Aaron, Nadab and Abihu, Eleazar and Ithamar, Aaron' sons"* (Ex. 28:1).

It was the desire of Jehovah for His people to have access to their God. The way of access was made possible through the priests ordained of God to minister unto Him and to His people. There were two main functions of this office, and they are explained in the following text. *"The sons of Amram; Aaron and Moses: and Aaron was separated, that he should sanctify the most holy things, he and his sons for ever, to burn incense before the LORD, to minister unto Him, and to bless in His name for ever"* (1 Chron. 23:13). Mr. Darby renders it, *"that he should be hallowed as most holy, he and his sons."* In other words, these priests were required to minister unto God, and also unto men. In ministering unto God, they burned incense on the golden altar. In ministering unto men, after ministering unto God, they came out of the sanctuary and blessed their fellow men. As noted before, we have the same function in 1 Peter 2:5,9, where believers are holy priests ministering unto God in their worship, and then royal priests ministering unto men in their witnessing.

THE DEATH PENALTY

There were many rules and regulations imposed upon the priests. Some of these rules, if broken, called for the death penalty! In other words, God was extremely particular that His commandments be carried out. In our modern, and liberal day, I am afraid that many Christians have completely lost sight of the absolute holiness of God, and have no qualms about breaking His commandments, that are laid down in New Testament truths. In some cases, the death penalty lies hidden in the shadows. It is not as abrupt as under the Law, nevertheless it is there, and to back this statement up, all I have to do is turn you to 1 Corinthians 11:30. *"For this cause many are weak and sickly among you, and many sleep"* (they died). You may ask, "for what cause?" The answer is, that they were not rightly discerning the body and blood of the Lord in the partaking of the emblems. Then we have the apostle John's words: *"There is a sin unto death: I do not say that he shall pray for it"* (I John 5:16). The fact that we are not under Law, but under grace, is no excuse for willfully breaking His commandments.

INTERPRETATION – APPLICATION

Entering the subject of the Aaronic priesthood, we want to give you the *interpretation* of the stated verses that we will be considering. Then, from that exegesis, we will give you some sensible *applications*. There is no sense in just filling your brain with information, and leaving you there. Something more is needed, and it is the *application* of divine truths to the soul. There is no sense holding a wet, soapy mop, over a dirty floor, and expect the floor to be made clean. Why no! There must be the *application* of the mop to the floor's dirty surface to produce the desired result, namely, making the floor clean. So we will be *applying* some vital Scriptures to your soul that, we hope, will have a purifying effect upon you. I do not intend to go overboard, but in a sane and sensible manner convey to you the mind of God relative to our lifestyle as holy, and royal priests.

Now before we start, let me say this. Scripture plainly states that *"whatsoever things were written aforetime were written for our learning"* (Rom. 15:4). So, as we commence this vital subject of priesthood, let us settle back and say, *"Lord, what wilt thou have me to do"* (Acts 9:6). That is a good attitude, isn't it? Paul said it, and I hope that you can say it too!

THE PRIEST'S DRESS

The first thing that we want to consider about these men who were to be consecrated into the priesthood, is what the Lord demanded of them concerning their dress. To avoid wearying you, we won't consider Aaron's garments, but just his son's garments.

> *"And for Aaron's sons thou shalt make coats, and thou shalt make for them girdles, and bonnets shalt thou make for them, for glory and for beauty. And thou shalt put them upon Aaron thy brother, and his sons with him; and shalt anoint them, and consecrate them, and sanctify them, that they may minister unto Me in the priest's office. And thou shalt make them linen breeches to cover their nakedness; from the loins even unto the thighs they shall reach: And they shall be upon Aaron, and upon his sons, when they come in unto the tabernacle of the congregation, or when they come near unto the altar to minister in the holy place; that they bear not iniquity, and die: it shall be a statute for ever unto him and his seed after him"* (Ex. 28:40 – 43).

This is one of the many requirements, which, if broken, brought the death penalty. God was extremely particular how they were to dress when officiating for Him. There was no nakedness to be seen, thus, they were required to wear linen breeches. The practical application is this, that God hates to see the flesh, that is, the characteristics of the old man. There can be much flesh in pretending to serve God. Do I preach to be noticed, or to be looked up to? If that is the inner motive, then it is the working of the flesh! Do I minister to others for recognition?

Do I seek a name? If my motives are not right, then all my efforts in the eyes of others are only a public display of the flesh.

COATS

Their coats were to be made of fine linen (Ex. 39:27). White, fine linen speaks of purity and righteousness of character. You may say, "where do you get that?" Well I have the answer, and it is found in Revelation 19:8. *"And to her was granted that she should be arrayed in fine linen, clean and white: for the fine linen is the righteousness of saints"* (Rev. 19:8). There it is! Simple, isn't it? The coat relates to character. God expects purity and righteousness of character in those who function as priests. You may be a priest, but if your character doesn't measure up to righteousness, you cannot serve the Lord.

GIRDLES

The next item was a girdle made of *"fine twined linen, and blue, and purple, and scarlet, of needlework"* (Ex. 39:29). The girdle was employed when work had to be done, so it speaks of active service. The long flowing garment of the priest would hinder vigorous movement in preparing sacrifices, so they pulled up their garment and tucked it under the girdle that was around the middle of their body. This gave them more freedom of movement. Notice the colors. **White** speaks of the purity of the Man Christ Jesus. That's Luke's gospel. **Blue** speaks of that which is heavenly, the Son of God from heaven. This is John's theme in his gospel. **Scarlet** is the color of blood. Christ was the lowly Servant, obedient all through His life, up to the death of the Cross. Mark portrays Him as God's Servant. The last color is ***purple*** which is the color of royalty, and it is Matthew that portrays our Lord as the King. As royal priests, we tell forth His virtues (1 Pet. 2:9). In our service as heralds of the Cross, we hail Him as the perfect Man; as the Son of God from heaven; as the obedient Servant, and as the King of kings. God was particular that the priest's girdles were four-colored. God is very particular how we preach Christ!

BONNETS

The last item mentioned was fine linen bonnets. Any intelligent saint recognizes that the head covering denotes subjection. Sisters display this truth when veiling their heads in all assembly gatherings. We, as functioning priests, are to be in total subjection to our Lord, and to the Word of God. In assembly gatherings, priests are subject to the leading of the Holy Spirit. Now what does the Spirit tell sisters in such gatherings? Why, He tells them to be in silence. *"Let your women keep silence in the churches: for it is not permitted unto them to speak; but they are commanded to be under obedience, as also saith the law ... Let the woman learn in silence with all subjection. But I suffer not a woman to teach, nor to usurp authority over the man, but to be in silence"* (1 Cor. 14:34; 1 Timothy 2:11-12). What does He tell the men? *"I will therefore that men pray every where, lifting up holy hands, without wrath and doubting"* (1 Tim. 2:8). What does He tell public speakers? *"Let the prophets speak two or three, and let the other judge"* (1 Cor. 14:29).

Let me say that it is He alone Who chooses the speakers! It is He alone Who gives them the message to speak. Yes, in a completely God-controlled conference, or at the Lord's Supper, the Holy Spirit is the President. He is the sole Director of operations. When this is practiced, it will produce much fruit to the glory of God, and manifold blessings to the saints of God.

THE SAINT'S DRESS

If God was so particular how the priests dressed under Law, do you think that He is less concerned how saints dress under grace? Does he care? He most certainly does! So, the question arises, how are we to dress in assembly gatherings? The simple answer would be that we are to dress properly. You may ask, "what is proper?" The answer is, "what society demands." We conform to that which society recognizes as proper. Take men of importance, men that represent some corporation. When they make public appearances for their company, how do they dress?

Are they sloppy? Are they casual? Hardly! They dress according to the rules that society demands. They wear a white shirt and conservative suit and tie. As representatives of their corporation do they appear in public with their suits and running shoes or sandals? Not at all! They wear polished dress shoes. Study the President of the United States as he appears in a high-level meeting. Or, observe any dignitary at an important event. How are these people dressed? They are dressed according to the rules of society. What do you see? You see a man adorned in a conservative suit, white shirt, and tie, and polished dress shoes. That's what you see!

THE MURDERER

Consider the cold-blooded murderer. He comes to trial. His lawyer is cunning, he knows a few tricks, and here is one of them. His client is given a gentleman's haircut. He is given a conservative suit to wear, he sits in the defendant's chair and the jury looks at him and says to themselves, "my, but he is a fine looking, clean-cut young gentleman." What is the lawyer's ploy? He is trying to fool the jury into thinking that his murderous defendant is a very respectful person, and that he has respect for the jury that is to deliberate his case.

THE EXECUTIVES

In our newspaper there was an article on the Smucker's Jelly Company. They interviewed the two Smucker brothers that owned and operated that corporation. Do you think that the photo of these men showed them in a sport shirt, or casual pants, and running shoes? Absolutely not! These men were the picture of dignity. The interview was an important occasion to them. They were representing their famous company. Consequently, they dressed accordingly. They dressed in accordance to what proper society demanded. They wore conservative suits.

THE KING OF KINGS

Let us now consider the assembly gathering for Bible study and prayer. How important is that meeting? Well, it is important enough for the Lord to be there. Imagine! In that humble building stands the King of kings, and the Lord of lords! He is the Creator! He is the Sustainer and Upholder of all things! He is the Chief Justice of the Supreme Court of the Universe! There is no dignitary as high or as important, as He! This is tremendous! What an occasion for the sons of God. They are actually going to have a meeting with Him present. Not only this, as sons of God, upon coming together, they are going to represent Him unto all that look upon them. So, how should they dress? What does society say? It says, wear your very best. Leave your sandals, your running shoes, your sweaters, your casual pants, and sporty shirts at home, and display your respect for the Person that you are meeting, and also representing. Society says, "men, wear that which fits the occasion, wear that which is appropriate, and that means, wear your best."

THE BANK MANAGER

At our bank, we have a new manager, a Puerto Rican lady. Does she flit about the bank in a house dress, or a blue-jean skirt? I should say not! Is she shod with sandals, so everyone can see her big toes and little toes? How undignified. Absolutely not! The bank would not stand for such foolishness, or should I say, sloppiness. Her long dress is beautiful, her fine leather shoes match, and there is a dignity about her that commands respect. She beautifully represents the bank. Sister, how do you represent Christ with your dress? Remember this. The attire that adorns my body is a declaration of the value of my appreciation regarding the occasion.

THE TRAMP

Let me consider one more thing with you. Say that there was a man that wandered into an assembly gospel meeting.

He was a tramp, destitute, and a "good-for-nothing," as the world would say. Upon hearing the gospel, he was reached and saved. He continued to attend the assembly gatherings, and learned the truth of gathering unto His name. So, he applied for fellowship. The brethren were satisfied with his conversion, and his change in life style. Yet, he remained poor, and his clothing was anything but commendable. His old overalls were filthy, and his plaid shirt was well worn. Could an assembly refuse the man the right to the fellowship of the assembly? His dress was not very becoming, but could they say to him, "no, you are not going to be received here." If they were spiritual Christians, how could they ever turn such a one away? They couldn't! But what about the way he was dressing? Ah, the solution is simple. Out of love to the poor soul, the elders would take him to a clothing store and buy him a suit, dress shirt, tie, and a decent pair of dress shoes. It is as simple as that. Not only that, they would seek employment for the dear fellow, and help him all they could to get his life back in order. Let us use common sense brethren. This is the solution for the poverty-stricken applicant to God's holy assembly. God was particular what Aaron and his priestly sons wore. God is particular in what we wear.

COLORS

You will also notice the various colors associated with the clothing of the priests. These colors apply to precious, Biblical truths. **BLUE:** This points to a HOLY PRIESTHOOD. **PURPLE**: This associates itself with a ROYAL PRIESTHOOD. **SCARLET**: The blood of Christ is my only ACCESS, as a holy priest, into the holy place to function. Also, it is my THEME in telling forth the virtues of God as a royal priest.

BATHED PRIESTS

On the day of their consecration, they were to be *washed* by another. The word is really *"bathed."* Moses performed the ceremony, and it was only carried out once (Ex. 29:4). From this physical ceremony, allow me to give you the spiritual application. When the Lord sat with His own in that large upper room, He made a very important statement. *"Peter saith unto Him, Thou shalt never wash my feet. Jesus answered him, If I wash thee not, thou hast no part with Me ... Jesus saith to him, He that is washed needeth not save to wash his feet, but is clean every whit: and ye are clean, but not all"* (John 13:8, 10). In the Greek text, the word *"wash,"* and the word *"washed"* are two completely different words. The first word *"wash,"* means, *"to cleanse (especially the hands or the feet or the face), to wet a part only."* However, the word *"washed,"* means, "to bathe (the whole person)." The first word "wash" indicates a continual thing, accomplished by the person himself. He must keep himself clean if he is to enjoy communion and fellowship with the Saviour. If he fails to do so, then, as the Lord states, he will have no part *with* Christ. Notice, the Lord doesn't say, "thou has no part IN Me," meaning salvation. No, no! He says, *"thou hast no part WITH Me,"* meaning communion.

However, the word *"washed,"* or *"bathed,"* has an entirely different meaning. You will find it in Titus 3:5. *"Not by works of righteousness which we have done, but according to His mercy He saved us, by the **washing** of regeneration, and renewing of the Holy Ghost"* (Titus 3:5). This *"washing of regeneration,"* is the new birth, namely, that person being washed from sin, in the death of Christ. The hymn writer had this in mind when he wrote, "Are you washed in the blood of the Lamb?" The *"renewing of the Holy Ghost,"* is the complete change that takes place for the better. It speaks of the convert's new existence through the action of the Spirit. In other words, fellow-believer, the moment you were saved, you were washed (bathed) by Another (that Person being God). This corresponds exactly to what took place on the day of Aaron and his son's consecration. They were bathed by Moses, only once. You were bathed by God, only once.

DAILY WASHING

However, there is the washing, that is a daily thing, performed by our own effort. That is what the Lord indicates in John 13:10. We need to wash our feet on a daily basis. Not only this, we are to wash one another's feet. How is that done? Why, that is the work of the shepherd and the teacher. Through the ministered Word of God, we are cleansed. Going to a conference should not primarily be just a social event. Oh no, it should be a time of cleansing and restoration. On a daily basis, we are in contact with a corrupt and defiling world (our feet), and we need to be washed, we need to be cleansed, so that we can have a part with Christ. We cannot enjoy Him, nor can we commune with Him, if we are defiled. May God help us to realize, that apart from holiness, no man shall see the Lord! Are you defiled? Has this world drawn you away from the Saviour's side? Have you lost the joy of your salvation? Are you unhappy, distressed, and not content? Then by all means dear saint, wash yourself! And, how can this be accomplished? Ah, the answer is found in the Holy Scriptures. Let me quote them.

> *"Wherewithal shall a young man cleanse his way? by taking heed thereto according to Thy Word"* (Ps. 119:9).

> *"Thy Word have I hid in mine heart, that I might not sin against Thee"* (Ps. 119:11).

> *"Now ye are clean through the word which I have spoken unto you"* (John 15:3).

> *"That He might sanctify and cleanse it with the washing of water by the Word"* (Eph. 5:26).

> *"Now ye are clean through the Word which I have spoken unto you"* (John 15:3).

There is your answer! Forget the psychiatrist's books. These people need help themselves. They are off base. Many of them are far removed from reality. Do you need advice? Do you need strength to keep from sinning? Well, let me say this, that is one of the reasons why God wrote the Bible, and indwelt you with the Holy Spirit – that you may be made wise and clean. Go to your Bible, read your Bible, study your Bible, and meditate upon its truths, and you will come out of the mire of confusion, uncleanness, and uncertainty, a mighty and fortified saint for God! I do not have much sympathy for saints that wring their hands and cry, "I just don't know what to do!" If you are in that class, listen to me. Get before your Father in prayer, pour out your heart before Him. Turn to His Holy Word. Let your eyes feast upon it, in total dependence on Him to direct your way. Try that, and see what happens!

However, let me state one more thing. I am not referring to dear souls that have, what is termed, "Clinical Depression." That is another subject altogether. That is where expertise, medical evaluation, and the prescription of certain chemicals may help such a grievous situation. No, I have been referring to saints that do not have a chemical imbalance in their system. I hope that I have made myself clear on this subject.

THE SIN OFFERING

The sons of Aaron were brought before the door of the tabernacle of the congregation and there the beasts that they brought were offered. The first one was a bullock for a sin offering (Ex. 29:10–14). One has to commence with the righteous dealing with sin, before he can advance in any way to the service of God. It is impossible for a sinner to please God. He must be born again if he is ever to serve God. I'm sure that we are all aware of that plain truth. *"They that are in the flesh cannot please God"* (Rom. 8:8). They were to put their hands upon the head of the bullock. The word *"put"* means *"to lean hard upon. To support or brace oneself upon."* As these men leaned hard upon that animal's head, it would feel the burden, it would feel the pressure, as they identified themselves with the bullock. Do you get the picture?

> "All my sins were laid upon Thee,
> All my guilt was on Thee laid,

And the blood of Thine atonement
All my utmost debt has paid.
Gracious Saviour,
I believe, for Thou hast said."[49]

The blood of the sin offering was to be placed upon the horns of the altar, and the rest poured out *"beside the bottom of the altar"* (Ex. 29:12). This reminds us of the fact that the blood of our blessed Lord shed on the Cross, forms the basis of all our approach to God. Also, as the blood on the horns of the altar was ever before the approaching priest, we also, in heaven, will view His wounds, forever reminding us of His love for us, expressed in His death. The bullock for a sin offering was the largest of the sacrifices offered on the day of the consecration of the priests. The lesson is, that the sin offering of Christ was large enough to save the whole world.

The fat and inwards of the sin offering were to be burnt as incense upon the altar, reminding us of the truth declared in Ephesians 5:2: *"Christ also hath loved us, and hath given Himself for us an offering and a sacrifice to God for a sweetsmelling savour."* Then the flesh and the dung were to be taken outside the camp and burned (not as incense, but consumed). The first word *"burn"* in the Hebrew language, is different from the second word *"burn."* This brings to our attention the words of Paul to the Hebrews. *"Wherefore Jesus also, that He might sanctify the people with His own blood, suffered without the gate"* (Heb. 13:12).

THE BURNT OFFERING

The next animal brought to our attention is the ram for a burnt offering (Ex. 29:15–18). The animal was to be slain, and then its blood sprinkled *"round about, upon the altar."* This animal also experienced the weight of the priest's hands upon its head. These men were now going to identify themselves with the burnt offering. We noticed the bigness of the sin offering,

---

49 Mrs. Thompson. The Believer's Hymn Book. (John Ritchie Ltd. Kilmarnock, Scotland). P. 101.

THE CONSECRATION OF THE PRIESTS

but in the burnt offering, our attention is turned to its parts, and to its dividing. *"And thou shalt cut the ram in pieces, and wash the inwards of him, and his legs, and put them unto his pieces, and unto his head."* Thus, we have portrayed in the *inwards*, the motives of Christ; in the *legs*, the movements of Christ; and in the *head*, the mind of Christ, all offered unto God as an offering of a sweet-smelling savour. Corresponding to this we quote three verses: **(1)** His inwards: *"In Him is no sin"* (1 Jn. 3:5). **(2)** His legs: *"Who did no sin"* (1 Pet. 2:22). **(3)** His head: *"Who knew no sin"* (2 Cor. 5:21). The parts to be offered on the altar were first to be washed, typifying the intrinsic purity of our Saviour, the ultimate burnt offering for God. When I muse upon the perfections of Christ, it utterly thrills my soul to think, that in a coming day, I shall be like Him, for I shall see Him as He is! (1 Jn. 3:2).

THE HEAVE OFFERING

Our next consideration is the ram of consecration (Ex. 29:19–34). The offering of this animal would conclude the ceremony of consecration to the priesthood. Again, they were to press their hands heavily upon the head of the animal, thus identifying themselves with it. This ram was to be offered as a heave offering. That is, it was to be physically waved before the Lord. Also, parts of it were to be eaten before the Lord. However, what interests me the most is the application of the blood of the ram of consecration. Consequently, we are going to consider what they were instructed to do. *"Then shalt thou kill the ram, and take of his blood, and put it upon the tip of the right ear of Aaron, and upon the tip of the right ear of his sons, and upon the thumb of their right hand, and upon the great toe of their right foot, and sprinkle the blood upon the altar round about"* (Ex. 29:20).

Consequently, these men were to have consecrated ears, hands, and feet. What does this imply? It projects a New Testament lesson to us, namely, that we as priests, should also have our ears, hands, and feet consecrated to God. The word *"consecrate,"* means, *"to have your hands full."* The thought of *activity* and *devotion* are implied.

BLOOD ON THE EAR

What goes in my ear? The vain music or the unprofitable conversations of the world? Or perhaps, sound speech, which cannot be condemned? Is my ear open to the Word of God? Mary of Bethany comes into view. It was said of her, that she *"sat at Jesus' feet, and heard His word"* (Luke 10:39). What a blessed and profitable occupation for this dear saint. The Lord said that she had chosen that good part. Martha was cumbered with much serving. Busy, busy, busy! However, quietly and with eagerness, Mary sat at the Lord's feet, having her ear filled with His word. Later, in John 11, the great difference between these two sisters was made very evident. Mary's discernment was superior, her compassion was greater, and her humility was more evident. All this was the result of having a consecrated ear.

BLOOD ON THE THUMB

Next, we find the blood applied to the thumbs of their right hands. The anatomy of the hand requires a thumb in order to accomplish a firm grasp. A man who has no thumbs would find it very difficult, if not impossible, to grasp a sledge hammer effectively enough to swing it. Try holding anything firmly without employing your thumb, and you will understand how important the thumb is to accomplish a firm grasp. Man is naturally born a grasping creature. Place your finger in the palm of a newborn child, and it will instinctively grasp your finger. The baby does not have to be taught to do this. No, it is natural.

The marketing world realizes the fact that *"the eye is not satisfied with seeing, nor the ear filled with hearing"* (Eccl. 1:8). People have their own peculiar weaknesses. A man may have a weakness for ties. He may have a hundred ties in his wardrobe, yet displayed in the stores he frequents, there are many beautiful ties on display. Does he need more ties? Not really. However, the lust of the eye motivates him to purchase more. In other words, he grasps them. A lady may have a weakness for hats. She has only one head, but in her closet are numerous hats. The merchant knows how to display his merchandise in such a way that it attracts her eye. Consequently, she purchases a few more hats to crowd her wardrobe. Man is never satisfied, for he is born with a grasping spirit.

I have seen multi-million dollar homes occupied by childless couples. What do they need with a multitude of bedrooms, a few family rooms, an enormous kitchen? Why do they need 15,000 square feet, or more, to house their little bodies? They don't. What has taken place? Why they are affluent. Prestige is very important to them, and so they have grasped.

CREDIT

The invention of the credit card has fueled the inborn trait of grasping. People see, people purchase, and then the bills come due, and many do not have the means to clear their debt. They have grasped what was not rightfully theirs. Such activity is sinful. Often, the creditor has to reclaim his merchandise that the grasping person has acquired. Solomon said, *"If thou hast nothing to pay, why should he take away thy bed from under thee?"* (Prov. 22:27). A credit card can prove to be a real blessing to conservative people, that is, folks that know how to handle their money. I am primarily talking about the flagrant abuse of the credit card system, by foolish, self-indulgent folk.

Approximately five years ago, our liberal Congress, over the objections of the President, passed the Lending Reform Act. The banks objected, but were obligated to conform to the new law. Our country's liberal legislators insisted that poor people needed a break, and they had as much right to live in expensive homes as people with high incomes. Consequently, people who could not afford homes that were far beyond their means, purchased them, through this act passed by Congress. When our economy drastically dropped, the result was, that these people lost their homes. Banks were left holding empty property, with very few buyers in sight, thus putting them in a dangerous financial bind. As this page is being written, as a result of a liberal

Congress and the tendency of man to grasp, our country is on the verge of a total economic collapse.

As priests of God, let us ask the question, is the blood of consecration on my thumb? Do I consider my purchase before my thumb grasps what I want? Do I bring my desire before the Lord? Do I search for His mind in the matter? Hudson Taylor, a famous missionary to China, once remarked, "Oh the joy of having little to care for." The value of my sacrifice is not so much the quantity of my giving, but rather, how much have I retained for myself after giving. The widow of Luke 21 didn't give much, only two mites. The rich gave far more than that. However, when we take these offerings into the sanctuary of God and weigh them, we find that the widow's two mites far outweighed the multitude of gold and silver that the rich gave. Why? Well, the Lord weighed what they had kept for themselves. She gave all while they only gave a little of their substance. The value of her sacrifice soared far above all the rest.

THE RICH MAN – THE POOR WIDOW

Let me explain it this way. Let us say that at the Lord's Supper sits a rich man. This man's bank account is bulging, and his belly is always full. He lacks nothing of this world's goods. Also at the gathering is a poor widow. She lives, dependent on God, from day to day. Her Social Security income limits her drastically as to purchases necessary to sustain her fragile life. The basket is passed. The rich man puts a one hundred dollar bill into the offering. The widow places twenty dollars into the basket. Who gave the most? If you say the rich man gave the most, you are wrong. No, it was the poor widow that gave the most, for she only kept enough to last her until the next Social Security payment. The rich man had a $100,000 car, an $850,000 house, and money in the bank to spare. That measly $100 he placed in the offering, never altered his lifestyle one iota. However, the widow could have used her $20 very profitably to add a little comfort to her lifestyle, but she cheerfully gave it to the Lord. I think by now that you have my point. One could describe this widow as a woman with the blood of consecration on her thumb.

Referring to the New Testament, we notice a man called Barnabas, *"having land, sold it, and brought the money, and laid it at the apostles' feet"* (Acts 4:37). He was a man with a consecrated hand.

We can also apply the blood being on the thumb in this way. Those priests' hands were to be consecrated, that is, they were to be full. On a daily basis, their hands were handling sacrifices to be offered upon the brazen altar. They were busy men. Brethren, as priests, let us be diligent to offer the sacrifice of praise to God continually. May the Lord give all of us grace to handle to a greater degree, the things of God, more than the things of this materialistic world. The blood was put upon the thumb of their right hand.

BLOOD ON THE TOE

The last consideration is the blood put upon the great toe of their right foot. If you were missing your big toes, you would have no balance. Have you, in a standing position, ever leaned forward? If you have, why didn't you fall flat on your face? The reason is, your big toes sprang into action and prevented that. Without big toes, you would have fallen. In speaking on this subject once, a man approached me after the meeting and said, "You were absolutely right. I have proven that for I don't have any big toes."

THE CHRISTIAN'S WALK

So, examine yourself as to your spiritual balance and your walk. There are no less that 22 different ways in which we are exhorted to walk in the New Testament. Of that number, let us confine ourselves to one epistle, the letter of Paul to the Ephesian Assembly. In that epistle, there are six references regarding the Christian's walk. The word *walk* in the following quotations is used to denote one's life, and conduct. The way one behaves himself.

"For we are His workmanship, created in Christ Jesus unto good works, which God hath before ordained that we should walk in them" (Eph. 2:10).

Thus, we see that the believer is the handiwork of God. He is a finished work of art. The word "poem" is derived from this expression, so we can safely say that regarding God's handiwork, everything rhymes. It was God's previous arrangement that we should lead holy lives.

> "Being saved from sin we are made partakers of the Spirit of holiness; and it is natural to that Spirit to lead to the *practice* of holiness; and he who is not holy in his life is not saved by the grace of Christ. The *before ordaining*, or rather *preparing*, must refer to the time when God began the new creation in their hearts; for from the first inspiration of God upon the soul it begins to love holiness; and obedience to the will of God is the very *element* in which a holy or regenerated soul lives."[50]

"I therefore, the prisoner of the Lord, beseech you that ye walk worthy of the vocation wherewith ye are called, ... with all lowliness and meekness, with longsuffering, forbearing one another in love" (Eph. 4:1–2).

We, as God's people, have been effectively called by the Spirit to a vocation, that is, a trade, or occupation. We have become sons of God, but even more than that. We have a very important occupation, and that is, we are priests! Let us then walk worthy of our priesthood. We are on earth to intercede, and make supplications for our fellow men. As priests, we are obligated to tell forth the gospel to the lost. By all means then, let us walk worthy of this tremendously high calling. Lightness and frivolity are not becoming to a holy priest. A lust for mate-

---

[50] Clark. Notes on Ephesians 2. (MacSword, Bible study software for Mac OS-10).

THE CONSECRATION OF THE PRIESTS

rial possessions and gain are not befitting the walk of a priest, ordained of God. No, no! Let us then be very careful in our walk before saint and sinner. Remember, the blood of consecration is on the great toe of the right foot.

"This I say therefore, and testify in the Lord, that ye henceforth walk not as other Gentiles walk, in the vanity of their mind, having the understanding darkened ..." (Eph. 4:17-18).

There is an emptiness to the Gentile mind. Their understanding has been darkened by sin and Satan. They cannot perceive anything of a spiritual nature, thus, they walk after the flesh. Whatever their blinded heart dictates, that is the way they walk. The lust of the flesh, the lust of the eye, and the pride of life motivate their walk. Solomon said that they walk in the ways of their heart, and after the sight of their eyes. Consequently, nothing but God's judgment lies ahead for them (Eccl. 11:9).

We are to strongly avoid such behavior. When godless society observes me, do they see something different? Does my lifestyle condemn their loose living? Is my dress becoming to a Christian. Do I "stand out" in the crowd. Observe the godly woman in public. She is different. She is lacking in worldly behavior.[51] She lacks jewelry.[52] She lacks makeup.[53] She lacks clothing that pertains to a man.[54] She lacks immodest apparel.[55] She lacks cut hair.[56] She lacks a loud and boisterous spirit.[57] There is something very strange about her in the eyes of the ungodly, for she is godly.[58] She is not walking in the vanity of a darkened mind. She is walking according to the divine precepts of God. Consider her. You won't see many like her in today's society.

---

51 1 Timothy 2:9; Titus 2:3.
52 1 Timothy 2:9; 1 Peter 3:3.
53 2 Kings 9:30.
54 Deuteronomy 22:5.
55 1 Timothy 2:9.
56 1 Corinthians 11:15; John 12:3.
57 1 Peter 3:4; Contrast - Proverbs 7:11.
58 1 Peter 4:4.

As God looks down upon mankind, how it must please Him to view a godly woman in the midst of a perverse, and ungodly multitude. She is exceedingly rare. Lift up your heart and thank God for her. The blood of consecration governs her walk.

"And walk in love, as Christ also hath loved us, and hath given Himself for us an offering and a sacrifice to God for a sweetsmelling savour" (Eph. 5:2).

The god-like grace of love should influence our whole manner of life. Love should be the foundation from which we conduct ourselves. We should love the saints. That will be evident if we have a genuine care for them, and diligently seek to help those who are in need. I could tell you of a sister confined to an assisted-living facility. She has been confined there for two years, and not once has a brother, or sister, from the local assembly, phoned or visited her! They lack the blood of consecration on their toe.

What about our love to the sinner? Do we approach them? Do we love their souls enough to make it our aim to get them under the sound of the gospel? The Lord loved the souls of men. He came to seek and to save that which was lost. Are we like Him? I know that we cannot save a soul, but do you seek them out so that possibly they will be saved? Is the blood on your toe?

"For ye were sometimes darkness, but now are ye light in the Lord: walk as children of light" (Eph. 5:8).

We have been enlightened to see the evil of sin, and the beauties of Christ. We have been illuminated, and brought out of darkness into His marvelous light. Let us walk accordingly.

"See then that ye walk circumspectly, not as fools, but as wise" (Eph. 5:15).

The word *"circumspectly,"* is very interesting. It means *"cautiously, watchfully, or, with awareness."* I remember an old servant of the Lord explaining it to me this way. Place bits of glass on top of a cement wall. Along comes a cat that must get to the other side of the wall, by walking along the top of it. The cat proceeds very cautiously. He carefully places his paws on the top of the wall, avoiding the glass. In other words, he is walking circumspectly.

We are to be very careful in our walk, namely, our manner of living. God is watching, angels are watching, demons are watching, the ungodly are watching, and the saints are watching. Let us be careful where we travel. Let us be careful of the company we keep. Let us think before we speak, lest we sin with our tongue. Let us be careful how we treat the saints and God's assembly. Remember, the blood of consecration is on the toe.

The blood on the ear, will affect our **personalities.**

The blood on the thumb, will affect our **possessions.**

The blood on the toe, will affect our **path.**

In Exodus 29:21–37 we have the closing instructions regarding the consecration of Aaron and his sons to the priesthood. We shall mention just a few highlights of this portion for your spiritual benefit.

ABIDE SEVEN DAYS

These men were called upon to abide at the door of the tabernacle of the congregation seven days, until the days of their consecration were at an end. Thus, they kept the charge of the LORD that they died not (Lev. 8:33, 35).

The number seven is referred to among the Hebrews as a number of *perfection,* and is often used to denote *completion, accomplishment, or fullness.* Thus, we have signified that these men experienced a *perfect* consecration. Their whole being, body, soul, and spirit were to be consecrated, and devoted to Jehovah, and to His people. I remember a servant of the Lord, named Clay Fite, ministering to a small assembly of about ten people. They apologized for the fewness of number. He replied that it wasn't the number of people at his meetings that mattered. What mattered was the percentage that were there. He was so happy to minister to only ten people, because they turned out to the meeting 100%. These were saints that were completely, and fully consecrated.

OFFERING THE RAM OF CONSECRATION

Another thing worthy of notice is what was done to the ram of consecration. Parts of it were to be offered upon the altar, wholly for God, and parts of it were to be eaten by the new comers into the priesthood. Also associated with this offering were three kinds of unleavened bread. There was one loaf of bread (*matstsoth*, no matter in what shape), one cake of oiled bread (*challoth*, cakes pricked, or perforated), and one wafer (*rekikey*, an exceeding thin cake). These breads all typify Christ in His spotless humanity. They were waved before the LORD, not only reminding us that the bread that sustains our body comes from God alone, but also that we have the responsibility to wave before the LORD, the impeccable humanity of our beloved Lord Jesus. In our adoration, worship, and praise, we should ever be careful to bring to the eye of God our appreciation and thoughts about the Man, Christ Jesus.

After waving the various breads, they were to be placed upon the altar for a burnt offering. How mindful we are of our Lord's words when He instituted the Supper. Taking the bread, He *"gave thanks, and gave unto them saying, 'This is My body which is given for you.'"* The word "given," denotes, *"to give what is due. To furnish. To give over"* (Luke 22:19). Payment for our sins must be met. The offering up of the Lord Jesus in His body on the Tree, satisfied that payment. When all was paid, He cried, *"It is finished"* (paid in full).

They were to sanctify the breast of the wave offering, and the shoulder of the heave offering, which were to be waved, and heaved up and down. It has been conjectured that the moving back and forth horizontally in the wave offering, and the vertical heaving up and down of the heave offering, symbolized the figure of a cross on which the great Peace-offering between God and man was offered in the sacrifice of Christ. I would hesitate to build an application on that, but leave it for your sensible consideration. The *breast* naturally speaks to us of the tenderness of Christ, and the *shoulder* tells us of His strength. Perhaps also, it would indicate to the priests how that with all their heart, and with all their strength, they should give themselves to the priestly work of God.

> *"And thou shalt take the ram of the consecration, and seethe his flesh in the holy place. And Aaron and his sons shall eat the flesh of the ram, and the bread that is in the basket, by the door of the tabernacle of the congregation. And they shall eat those things wherewith the atonement was made, to consecrate and to sanctify them: but a stranger shall not eat thereof, because they are holy. And if ought of the flesh of the consecrations, or of the bread, remain unto the morning, then thou shalt burn the remainder with fire: it shall not be eaten, because it is holy. And thus shalt thou do unto Aaron, and to his sons, according to all things which I have commanded thee: seven days shalt thou consecrate them"* (Ex. 29:31–35).

FOOD AND THE ALTAR

Priestly food must be eaten in connection with the altar. We cannot feed on Christ, apart from the Cross. Eating at the door of the tabernacle of the congregation indicates that they were enjoying what God was enjoying. With one mind and one spirit, they were experiencing fellowship with the LORD. No stranger was allowed to partake. Ah, my friend, take the highest intellectual person in this world, and join him with the richest person in this world, and what do we see? We see that if they are not saved, in no way can they understand, or have any fellowship with God. The mightiest religious leader of humanity, if not born again, no matter what his credentials may be (even a pope), will find it absolutely impossible to enter into holy fellowship with

God. Only those who are saved and indwelt by the Holy Spirit of God, can appreciate the Person of Christ and His vicarious sacrifice on the Cross. Only a born again person can enter the sanctuary of God and commune with his Father in holy fellowship. If saved, you are a most highly privileged person!

SELF – CLEANSING

Let me draw your attention to one more significant thing before we pull our stakes and take our journey in the wilderness to the next appointed encampment.

You will remember how we emphasized the fact that these priestly men were bathed only once, and that by Moses. That bathing, as noticed, denotes our salvation. When we step into Exodus 13, we find another kind of cleansing, and it is rightfully translated *"wash,"* which does not mean *"bathe."* This washing was continual, and was to be done by the defiled individual himself.

> *"And the LORD spake unto Moses, saying, Thou shalt also make a laver of brass, and his foot also of brass, to wash withal: and thou shalt put it between the tabernacle of the congregation and the altar, and thou shalt put water therein. For Aaron and his sons shall wash their hands and their feet thereat: When they go into the tabernacle of the congregation, they shall wash with water, that they die not; or when they come near to the altar to minister, to burn (an) offering made by fire unto the LORD: So they shall wash their hands and their feet, that they die not: and it shall be a statute for ever to them, even to him and to his seed throughout their generations"* (Ex. 30:17–21).

The laver was made from the highly polished copper mirrors of the women of Israel. Consequently, when the priest approached the laver, he saw his defilement. Drawing water from the laver, he would wash his hands and his feet, possibly in the laver's foot, to cleanse himself from defilement. This was a requisite before officiating before God as a priest. You will be careful to notice, that any failure on his part to cleanse himself, called for the death penalty! Who could ever be so foolish to say that God was not particular?

Coming to the Church of our dispensation, what do we find? We discover that God's principles have not changed, but the awful consequences for failure have been greatly diminished. You don't find people dropping dead while trying to minister unto God in their uncleanness. Nevertheless, this does not absolve us from the fact that God expects us to be very particular as to our condition, ere we seek to accomplish anything for Him. Paul addresses this to the Corinthian saints with these abrupt words. *"Dearly beloved, let us cleanse ourselves from all filthiness of the flesh and spirit, perfecting holiness in the fear of God"* (2 Cor. 7:1). Let us be clear about this: *"If I regard iniquity in my heart, the Lord will not hear me"* (Ps. 66:18). You cannot have an audience with God, apart from holiness. *"Follow peace with all men, and holiness, without which no man shall see the Lord"* (Heb. 12:14).

16

VARIOUS ORDINANCES AND HAPPENINGS

NUMBERS 5

Entering into the book of Numbers, we find the numbering of the people of Israel, and allotted to the various tribes their positions in relation to the tabernacle, and to one another. They are about to set forth on their journey from the wilderness of Sinai. Before the signal was to be given, there were certain ordinances and adjustments to be made known for the regulation of the camp. Since there are hardly any Old Testament incidences or truths that cannot be applied to present day truths, we want to draw to your attention to a few incidences worthy of notice.

Coming to Numbers 5, there is something that immediately strikes us, and it is this; God cannot condone uncleanness in His gathering. This is a truth that runs through the whole Bible from Genesis to Revelation. When we come to this Old Testament portion, we have no problem applying it to church truths. For your convenience I have placed the text to be considered below.

> "And the LORD spake unto Moses, saying, command the children of Israel, that they put out of the camp every leper, and every one that hath an issue, and whosoever is defiled by the dead: Both male and female shall ye put out, without the camp shall ye put them; that they defile not their camps, in the midst whereof I

dwell. And the children of Israel did so, and put them out without the camp: as the LORD spake unto Moses, so did the children of Israel" (Num. 5:1–4).

REASONS FOR EXCOMMUNICAION

There were three conditions listed that called for excommunication from the camp; those who had contracted leprosy, persons affected with issues of various kinds, and persons who had come in contact with the dead. The question arises, why excommunication from the camp? The answer is threefold; physical, spiritual, and typical.

The *physical* reason for excommunication would be to maintain a sanitary condition in the camp, especially with leprosy, which is a very contagious disease. The *spiritual* reason for maintaining purity was because of the character of God. He is holy! *"Thou art of purer eyes than to behold evil, and canst not look on iniquity"* (Hab. 1:13). *"Holiness becometh Thine house, O LORD, for ever"* (Ps. 93:5). The *typical* reason would be, that in these problems and prohibitions, we have a picture of a local assembly of God, and what is expected to maintain its purity.

DIFFERENT SINS

Coming to the New Testament and its commandment relative to a local assembly, we plainly see the necessity of dealing with sin. Different sins call for different actions of correction. **The heretic** was to be rejected. That is, he was to be avoided, and shunned. Restraints were to be imposed upon him (Titus 3:10–11). **The unruly,** those out of step, even those that were idle, refusing to work, were to be warned (1 Thess. 5:14). **The disorderly,** namely those who were insubordinate, and walking not after the tradition received by the apostles, the saints were to withdraw from such (2 Thess. 3:6). Those **elders who dishonored the testimony** through inappropriate behavior, were to be rebuked before all (1 Tim. 5:20). **Those that caused divisions and offences,** contrary to the doctrine, were to be avoided (Rom. 16:17). *Those that were overtaken in a fault* were to be restored in the spirit of meekness by spiritual men (Gal. 6:1). These offences cannot be applied to what lies before us in Numbers 5:1–4, for none of them called for putting away from God's assembly.

SINS OF EXCOMMUNICATION

However, there are a few sins that do call for excommunication, and it is these that we want to consider. In Matthew 18, we have instructions from the Lord concerning an obstinate person. He has trespassed against another brother. The one who has been trespassed against, seeks to tell the other brother his fault, on a one-to-one basis. However, the trespassing person will not listen. The offended one then returns with witnesses to address the problem. The one at fault refuses to hear. Consequently, the matter is then brought before the assembly, but the offender is so pugnacious, and stubborn that he will not hear the government of the church. The Lord said, *"Let him be unto thee as an heathen man and a publican."* In other words, heathen men, and publicans, are not in God's assembly. Consequently, this man is not to be in the assembly. He is to be put away, not for the offence to his brother, but because of *a rebellious spirit* toward the government of the church.

The next portion of Scripture that deals with excommunication from the assembly is 1 Corinthians 5.

> *"But now I have written unto you not to keep company, if any man that is called a brother be a fornicator, or covetous, or an idolater, or a railer, or a drunkard, or an extortioner; with such an one no not to eat. For what have I to do to judge them also that are without? Do not ye judge them that are within? But them that are without God judgeth. Therefore put away from among yourselves that wicked person"* (v. 11–13).

First on the list is *the fornicator.* This is a generic term, thus it includes all kinds of unlawful gratification of the passions of the flesh, whether single, or married. Following this is ***the covetous,*** one greedy of gain. This can be a hard sin to define in the activities of some saints. Certainly, playing the lottery would constitute covetousness. One necessarily would not have to win the lottery to be a covetous person. Why no! All one would have to do is purchase a lottery ticket, and right away he has manifested covetousness. Gambling is covetousness. Playing the stock market is a form of gambling. Running one's self into debt that cannot be paid, is covetousness. Conniving to gain something that is not rightfully yours is covetousness. The list is long, but the fact remains, that the person convicted of this sin is to be put away from the assembly in which he is in fellowship. Shamefully I admit, that assemblies are very slow to deal with this subtle sin.

The third listed sin is ***idolatry***. There were many idolators in the assembly being addressed. To bow before an idol, would be a definite denial of the only God, the God and Father of our Lord Jesus Christ.

The fourth disorder was the person who had ***become a railer***. Such a person is one who seeks to discredit another. He may be a whisperer among brethren, assiduously blackening the name of the one he is attacking. Or, he may even proclaim his railing remarks in a public way. God says that such misbehavior cannot be tolerated in His assembly. The source of it must be put away.

Coming to the fifth sin, we see ***the drunkard.*** Did Noah become drunk? Yes! Was he a drunkard? Hardly! Then, what constitutes a drunkard? It is a person that is a slave to drink. They cannot overcome it, and they display it to the disgrace of themselves and to the testimony of God's assembly. Such ones must be *"put away."*

Finally, ***the extortioner*** comes to view. He is not only greedy of gain, but he will connive, or even rob to enrich himself. He has the expertise of extorting money or material from beguiled folk, by using unacceptable methods. Such a person cannot be tolerated in a holy gathering. He must be put out of the fellowship.

Such discipline is applied with hopeful results. First of all, the name of Christ is vindicated. Second, to maintain the purity of the assembly. Third, the hopeful restoration of the offender. Fourth, to furnish a solemn warning to all the saints, lest they also sin.

The offender is termed *"that wicked person."* The word *"wicked,"* is *"poneros,"* meaning, bad in character and effect. No fellowship is to be extended to him, not even to the extent of eating a meal. *"With such an one no not even to eat."*[59] Some seek to minimize this blunt statement by conjuring up the idea that the word "eat" only refers to the Lord's Supper, but nothing could be farther from the truth. This particular word *"eat"* (*sunesthio*) is used in eating a normal meal. In fact, it is only found in five verses; Luke 15:2; Acts 10:41; 11:3; 1 Corinthians 5:11; and Galatians 2:12. It is never used when referring to the Lord's Supper.[60]

Defilement certainly has dire consequences. To be put out of the camp would be a very humiliating experience. They would suffer the loss of privileges, both ceremonial and spiritual. They would be isolated from the people of God, shut up to dwell alone.

JESUS' MINISTRY

It is interesting to note that the three conditions that called for excommunication from the camp are mentioned and dealt with in the ministry of our Lord. He sought occasion to put Himself in contact with every one of the listed causes of defilement under the law. When reaching forth His hand and touching the leper He said, *"'I will; be thou clean.' And as soon as He*

---

59 J. N. Darby translation.
60 For a fuller exposition on this subject consult my book, The Plagues of Corinth, Gospel Folio Press.

had spoken, immediately the leprosy departed from him, and he was cleansed" (Mark 1:40–41). Mark then refers to the woman with an issue of blood. When she heard of Him, she came and touched the hem of His garment, and immediately the fountain of her blood was dried up. *"And He said unto her, Daughter, thy faith hath made thee whole; go in peace, and be whole of thy plague"* (Mark 5:34). In both cases, the cure was complete, immediate, lasting, and free. Immediately following this, Mark gives us another incident. Jairus' daughter lay cold and still in death. Going into the house where she lay, He took her by the hand, and bid her to arise. *"And straightway the damsel arose and walked."* In none of these wondrous works did the Lord contract defilement. Quite the opposite. His divine power overcame the defilement experienced by those cured.

LEPROSY

In closing this subject, it is interesting to note that even though He healed people with various diseases, the New Testament Scriptures never states that He *"healed"* a leper. You won't find it! However, this is what you will find seven times – He *cleansed* the leper. Consider that for a moment. Jesus commanded His apostles to *"**heal** the sick, **cleanse** the lepers, raise the dead, cast out devils: freely ye have received, freely give"* (Matt. 10:8). What is the difference? Through the ages, the idea became fixed in the Jewish mind, that the cure of leprosy was considered to be a cleansing. It was not a common disease, but it impressed the fact that the ultimate cause that produced it was a polluting thing. Thus, it became one of the great types in the body of the defiling effect of sin upon the soul.

17

THE LAW OF JEALOUSY

NUMBERS 5

The next thing that Moses was called upon to consider, was a marital problem. What was to be done if a husband suspected his wife of committing adultery? Adultery was punishable by death, but one certainly could not be put to death for only being suspected of the act. If the woman was guilty of unfaithfulness, but denied the charge, what was to be done? There were no witnesses, consequently, there could be no penalty inflicted. If she was guilty, her sin was cleverly hidden. If she was innocent, she was being falsely accused. God provided a solution to the whole incident. The husband was to bring his suspected wife unto the priest, along with *"her offering for her."* Evidently, a woman thus suspected of her husband, could hardly be termed a woman living above reproach. Her behavior drew out his suspicion.

Now, let us stop right here and apply this case to ourselves. If a sister adorns her body in such a fashion as to attract the lower nature of the opposite sex, she certainly is not living above reproach. If she is flirty, and light with other men, or often in the company of other men without her husband, she very easily could arouse suspicions in his mind. Sister, be very careful about placing yourself in an environment, or in a position, where suspicions could be raised against you. Be careful to *"walk honestly toward them that are without"* … and to *"abstain from all appearance of evil"* (1 Thess. 4:12; 5:22). Shamefacedness and sobriety are rooted in the godly woman, and always displayed (1 Tim. 2:9). Shamefacedness carries the thought of humility rooted in the character.

THE OFFERING OF JEALOUSY

The offering was to be composed of *"the tenth part of an ephah of barley meal; he shall pour no oil upon it, nor put frankincense thereon; for it is an offering of jealousy, an offering of memorial, bringing iniquity to remembrance"* (Num. 5:15). You will notice the absence of blood. If she was innocent, there would be nothing to expiate. If guilty, there was no offering for her crime. The offering was composed of barley meal, not fine flour. Barley meal was only eaten by the poor, and was half the price of fine flour (2 Kgs. 7:1). This was a picture of her vile and low estate. The offering was dry. No oil or frankincense was upon it. What she had brought revealed how she was living. She was dabbling in earthly things, living a suspicious life that was dry to God. No influence of the Spirit, and no fragrance of godliness had been seen in her life, and this is suggested by the absence of the oil and the frankincense.

The priest was to take *"holy water in an earthen vessel,"* and put the dust from the tabernacle floor into the water. An earthen vessel is cheap and coarse, and would correspond to the offering. Her head was to be uncovered, thus, she was required to publicly display her lack of subjection to her husband. Her uncovered head intimated that her intimate relationship with her husband had been broken, and that if she was guilty, it would be useless to hide her sin any longer. The LORD Himself would then disclose the facts whether she was unjustly accused or not. This ritual was to be carried out before all the eyes of Israel. It would be a humiliating event for her. The priest was to set the woman *"before the LORD."* That means that she was to be placed either before the brazen altar, or the door of the tabernacle with her face toward the Ark, where the divine presence of Jehovah was manifested.

THE JUDGMENT SEAT OF CHRIST

Have you ever considered the *"Judgment Seat of Christ"* (Rom. 14:10; 2 Corinthians 5:10) ? Every action in our lifetime will be exposed. Hidden sins in one's life will be brought to light. I say, that for some it will be very humiliating. The Corinthian saints were told: *"Therefore judge nothing before the time, until the Lord come, who both will bring to light the hidden things of darkness, and will make manifest the counsels of the hearts: and then shall every man have praise of God"* (1 Cor. 4:5). Yes, there will be something in the life of every believer that God will be able to praise them for, but alas, with many, there will be things that will detract from a fuller reward. *"We shall all stand before the Judgment Seat of Christ ... so then every one of us shall give account of himself to God"* (Rom. 14:10, 12). It would be well for all of us to live in view of that great event. I believe that if we set it more graphically before us, that it would tend to holier, and more devoted living.

> *"And the priest shall take holy water in an earthen vessel; and of the dust that is in the floor of the tabernacle the priest shall take, and put it into the water: And the priest shall set the woman before the LORD, and uncover the woman's head, and put the offering of memorial in her hands, which is the jealousy offering: and the priest shall have in his hand the bitter water that causeth the curse"* (Num. 5:17-18).

This is the only time in the Scriptures that the floor of the tabernacle is mentioned. The dust from the tabernacle floor was impregnated with the holiness of God Who dwelt therein. In this case, it was the only thing that was used that belonged to the tabernacle. It was to be put into the holy water and ingested by the suspected wife. Thus, this mixture of dust and water was given a supernatural ability to slay the guilty and to leave the guiltless one untouched.

The jealously offering, consisting of the barley meal, was to be placed in her hands. Thus presenting her life before God, and inviting an investigation of her conduct. The lack of leaven in her offering would be a pledge that her life had been one of fidelity to the law. If the offering called for leaven, then that would have implied before the test, her guilt. Thus, no leaven was connected with the barley meal. The lack of oil and frankincense also indicates that there was no joy, or worship, connected with this offering.

I suppose that you could refer to the priest as an attorney for the man. But, in taking the meal offering from her hand, he acted as her attorney as well. By going through with this ceremony, the woman was seeking to proclaim, or prove to her husband and to all those watching, that she was innocent of her husband's suspicions. What a traumatic ordeal for an innocent wife! What an awful curse for a guilty wife!

Having been set before the LORD by the priest, he was to charge her by an oath, saying unto her:

> "The LORD make thee a curse and an oath among thy people, when the LORD doth make thy thigh to rot, and thy belly to swell; And this water that causeth the curse shall go into thy bowels, to make thy belly to swell, and thy thigh to rot: And the woman shall say, Amen, amen. And the priest shall write these curses in a book, and he shall blot them out with the bitter water: And he shall cause the woman to drink the bitter water that causeth the curse: and the water that causeth the curse shall enter into her, and become bitter. Then the priest shall take the jealousy offering out of the woman's hand, and shall wave the offering before the LORD, and offer it upon the altar: And the priest shall take an handful of the offering, even the memorial thereof, and burn it upon the altar, and afterward shall cause the woman to drink the water. And when he hath made her to drink the water, then it shall come to pass, that, if she be defiled, and have done trespass against her husband, that the water that causeth the curse shall enter into her, and become bitter, and her belly shall

swell, and her thigh shall rot: and the woman shall be a curse among her people. And if the woman be not defiled, but be clean; then she shall be free, and shall conceive seed. This is the law of jealousies, when a wife goeth aside to another instead of her husband, and is defiled; Or when the spirit of jealousy cometh upon him, and he be jealous over his wife, and shall set the woman before the LORD, and the priest shall execute upon her all this law. Then shall the man be guiltless from iniquity, and this woman shall bear her iniquity" (Num. 6:21–31).

At this point, if the woman was truly guilty, and confessed to her guilt before drinking the water, then, according to Hebrew tradition, she would be separated permanently from her husband, and given no dowry.

THE BITTER WATER

The bitter water contained the written curses. Writing the curses in a book (on a scroll, or probably a tablet of wood, especially prepared), they then were to be wiped out into the bitter water. Perhaps the words written with a thick non-permanent ink, were scraped off into the water. She then was to drink that water! There is an expression used today, "I had to eat my own words." This literally could be said of the suspected wife. What a humiliating experience!

Connected with drinking the bitter water, the priest would take her offering out of her hand and wave the offering before the LORD, and offer it upon the altar. Thus, we have a solemn acknowledgment that the whole affair was to be conducted under the LORD'S supervision, and also an acknowledgment that He sees and knows all.

Jewish tradition states that the adulterer died the same day and hour that the adulteress did, and in a similar manner. Jewish doctors state that the bitter water had this effect on the woman only in the case that her husband had not committed adultery himself. However, this is only conjecture, for the Scriptures are silent on those matters.

The law of jealousy suggests many things. You will notice that in the case of the husband and wife, the inquest was not left to the scrutiny of human judges, but was presented to the court of God Himself, for Him to judge, and pronounce the verdict of guilty, or not guilty. There was nothing in the water itself to cause the effect described. The whole thing was supernatural. If the woman was guilty, but unbelieving in what drinking the bitter water would cause, upon being brave enough to drink, she would soon find out, to her dismay, that there was a God in Israel who would pronounce her guilty by the destruction of her reproductive organs. Perhaps the sin was committed in the utmost secrecy, and there was no clue that any possibility of discovery could be possible. However, this law would bring all to the light as if the sin had been committed before all in noonday. Only God's hand in the detection of the crime could effect this revelation. Would not this be a warning to all? It most certainly would! It would reveal that *"neither is there any creature that is not manifest in His sight: but all things are naked and opened unto the eyes of Him with whom we have to do"* (Heb. 4:13). It would make Israel aware of the fact that the Most High God ruled among them, and that sin would not be tolerated. What a preservative of public morals this law would produce among the people. It is the hope of concealment that gives power to temptation, which then results in sin. A thief will not steal if he knows that he is being videotaped while stealing, and as a result, will certainly be brought to justice. If one knows that they will, with no doubt, be detected in a crime, he certainly will not make plans to fulfill that particular crime. What a horrible death the guilty woman would experience upon drinking the bitter water. All the wives in Israel would behold it, and would naturally fear, with a resolve never to commit adultery.

On the other hand, what a triumph for the innocent woman suspected of being an adulteress by her husband. She would drink the bitter water with full confidence in Him Who searches the hearts, knowing that He would absolve her from the accusation, and completely clear her name. What triumph would be hers as she departed from the tabernacle, when the LORD had borne a public testimony to her innocence.

A LESSON FOR US

What is the lesson for us in the jealously offering? For any of you guilty of secret sin, the lesson can be declared in two verses: *"Neither is there any creature that is not manifest in His sight: but all things are naked and opened unto the eyes of Him with whom we have to do"* (Heb. 4:13). *"Behold, ye have sinned against the LORD: and be sure your sin will find you out"* (Num. 32:23). For those who have been unjustly blamed, and have no present means of clearing yourself, let me say this. The truth will eventually come to light in God's own way, and in His own time. Meanwhile, in the interval, *"commit thy way unto the LORD; trust also in Him; and He shall bring it to pass"* (Ps. 37:5). *"Say not thou, I will recompense evil; but wait on the LORD, and He shall save thee"* (Prov. 20:22).

18

THE LAW OF
THE NAZARITE

NUMBERS 6

Stepping from the suspicion of a husband, we come to separation, namely, the vow of a person who desired to be totally separated unto God. Either man or woman could take the vow of a Nazarite. There was no allotted time. It could be for a few days, or it could be for a much longer time, depending on the person. Almost all the Nazarites of Scripture appear to have been Nazarites for their whole life. Such was the case of Samson, Samuel, and John the Baptist, although Samson broke all three of the Nazarite vows. In all of them, the vow was made for them before their birth. Thus, thay had no choice in the matter. The word *"Nazarite"* means *"separated, or, set apart,"* and indicates the thought of total consecration.

Scripture tells of three orders of men that were separated to the service of God. First were **the priests.** Their office was hereditary. Second were **the prophets.** They came into this office by an individual call of God. Third were **the Nazarites.** Their separation was not hereditary like the priests, nor was it a divine call, like the prophets, it was a personal exercise. As stated, Samson, Samuel, and John the Baptist, were exceptions to the general rule.

THE NAZARITE AND GRAPES

If they desired to enter this vow, the restrictions were three. First, they were to abstain from everything related to the grape, whether moist or dried, or made into wine. How can we apply this act of self denial to our behavior today? Well, there was nothing wrong with eating grapes, or drinking wine. It was one of the joys and luxuries of life, yet we have the privilege of restricting ourselves from certain joys and luxuries, as we shall see.

LEGITIMATE THINGS

Come to our day. There are a lot of legitimate things in life that we can lawfully enjoy. Marriage is one of them. God says that marriage is honorable. However, there have been persons who have forfeited this benefit of life in order to devote more time to the things of God. *"For there are some eunuchs, which were so born from their mother's womb: and there are some eunuchs, which were made eunuchs of men: and there be eunuchs, which have made themselves eunuchs for the kingdom of heaven's sake"* (Matt. 19:12). You will remember Paul's inspired words. *"But I would have you without carefulness. He that is unmarried careth for the things that belong to the Lord, how he may please the Lord: But he that is married careth for the things that are of the world, how he may please his wife"* (1 Cor. 7:32-33). Regarding true discipleship, the Lord says, *"If any man will come after Me, let him deny himself, and take up his cross daily, and follow Me. For whosoever will save his life shall lose it: but whosoever will lose his life for My sake, the same shall save it"* (Luke 9:23-24). The words quoted express self denial. Paul states concerning himself, *"All things are lawful unto me, but all things are not expedient: all things are lawful for me, but I will not be brought under the power of any ... I keep under my body, and bring it into subjection* (1 Cor. 6:12; 9:27). *"No man that warreth entangleth himself with the affairs of this life; that he may please Him Who hath chosen him to be a soldier"* (2 Tim. 2:4).

There is nothing sinful in taking a vacation. Some vacations involve traveling great distances to see the handiwork of God, and the various cultures of foreign people. Yet, I could point you to a few married couples who have never taken the time, nor spent the money on such lawful entertainment. With a purpose of heart, they would rather devote that money and time spent on self, by laboring in a more productive way for the furtherance of the kingdom. You see, it is all an individual matter. This is what the Nazarite did, he voluntarily submitted himself to the restriction of enjoying something that was perfectly legitimate. He refrained from the fruit of the vine.

THE NAZARITE'S HAIR

The next restriction was that he was not to cut his hair. Scripture states; *"There shall no razor come upon his head ... He shall be holy, and shall let the locks of the hair of his head grow"* (Num. 6:4-5). J. N. Darby renders it, *"grow freely."* The R.V. says, *"grow long."* Thus we see that the inspired statement in 1 Corinthians 11:15 indicates hair that has never had a cutting instrument applied to it; *"But if a woman have long hair, it is a glory to her."* Trimming, or cutting the ends is a violation, and eliminates her hair as being classified as *"long,"* or *"uncut."*

The import of this is that long hair was a sign of subjection. The Nazarite would fully display his subjection to Jehovah. I suppose that his long hair could possibly be a reproach to him, providing a measure of embarrassing moments. Of course, if saints are totally in subjection to the Word of God today, such behavior could, at times, provide very embarrassing situations. Take, for example, a maiden employed in a business office. All the women employed are worldly, and some are scoffers. They dress to please their flesh. Some are immodest in their dress, others are flamboyant in their demeanor. They flirt with the men, and their language is unclean. However, at one desk is a heavenly jewel, a god-fearing sister in Christ. Her adornment is modest. There are no jewels hanging about her body. She is wearing a modest dress. Her long hair is neatly put up about her head. She is shy, quiet, and sweet. The godless crowd is wearing that which pertaineth to a man (Deut. 22:5), and they ridicule the sister in her long dress. They tell her that she is out of date, an old maid, and odd. She is a reproached woman, simply because she is not hiding her life of separation unto God. She remembers the words of her Lord; *"Blessed are ye, when men shall hate you, and when they shall separate you from their company, and shall reproach you, and cast out your name as evil, for the Son of man's sake. Rejoice ye in that day, and leap for joy: for, behold, your reward is great in heaven: for in the like manner did their fathers unto the prophets"* (Luke 6:22-23). *"If ye be reproached for the name of Christ, happy are ye; for the spirit of glory and of God resteth upon you: on their part He is evil spoken of, but on your part He is glorified"* (1 Pet. 4:14).

THE NAZARITE'S DIFFERENCE

The male Nazarite was made manifestly different in the sight of men. He manifested to everyone he met a vast difference. Is not the godly Christian different in the eyes of the ungodly? He certainly is! He is an ambassador of Christ. He is a son of God. He is a joint-heir with Christ, the Possessor of unsearchable riches. His kingdom is not of this world. His reserved inheritance is in heaven. He is not just different – he is vastly different. He is not slovenly in his dress, neither is he over-stylish. He presents himself in public as a modest, well-dressed gentleman. He certainly is not half-naked as you see some men on the streets. Ah my friend, there is a vast difference! Worldliness is absent. Immodesty is not there. Flamboyancy is not seen. What you do see is, Christ-likeness. The result of such godly behavior brings scorn and ridicule from the ungodly.

Ask yourself the question; how much reproach do you bear? Remember, *"All that will live godly in Christ Jesus shall suffer persecution"* (2 Tim. 3:12). The Nazarite was not to cut his hair.

THE NAZARITE AND DEATH

The final restriction involved death. *"He shall not make himself unclean for his father, or for his mother, for his brother, or for his sister, when they die: because the consecration of his God is upon his head"* (Num. 6:7). In other words, he was to put the LORD above his nearest of kin. Death was uncleanness, and the Nazarite was to always be found among the clean and the living. My associations – what are they, and who are they? No separated Christian could ever be associated with a secret society, such as the Masons, Odd Fellows, and other such orders. Ah no! There is no scriptural support for being unequally yoked together with unbelievers (2 Cor. 6:14). They are among the congregation of the dead.

BROTHER "AGGRESSIVE"

Let us take "brother Aggressive" for an example. He joins a sports team. The first mistake is, he has linked himself with the congregation of the dead. The other players are earth-dwellers, men of the world, and essentially haters of Christ. They are dead in trespasses and sins (Eph. 2:1). His second mistake is, that he receives instruction from the team's coach how to win the game, and how to go out and beat the other fellow. He is led to believe that his team is better than the opposition. However, the Lord says; *"Let nothing be done through strife or vainglory; but in lowliness of mind let each esteem other better than themselves"* (Phil. 2:3). He has completely forgotten about the Lord's yoke, and His advice. *"Take My yoke upon you, and learn of Me; for I am meek and lowly in heart: and ye shall find rest unto your souls"* (Matt. 11:29). Ah yes, "brother Aggressive" is out there with his ungodly companions, his worldly teammates, opposing them with all the aggressiveness he can muster. What has happened to the yoke of meekness and lowliness? Why, he has totally discarded it to the dishonor of that blessed Name to which he has been called. He is not a Nazarite. He is not a disciple.

CLOSE RELATIONSHIP

Come again with me for another thought. Consider our father, mother, brother, or sister. The Nazarite was to put the Lord above all of these close relationships. Does he expect the same today? Absolutely! I know a professing Christian who has an unsaved wife. Many years ago, she threatened him that if he ever came into the fellowship with believers gathered unto the name of our Lord Jesus Christ, that she would divorce him. He succumbed to her threat. They are now both old. She is a total invalid, and their son is a scoffer of the Bible. Poor fellow. If only he had given God first place by obeying the Lord's command above the dictates of his wife, things may have been far different today. He may have experienced a saved and happy family.

Listen to our Lord's words. *"He that loveth father or mother more than Me is not worthy of Me: and he that loveth son or daughter more than Me is not worthy of Me"* (Matt. 10:37). *"If any man come to Me, and hate not his father, and mother, and wife, and children, and brethren, and sisters, yea, and his own life also, he cannot be My disciple"* (Luke 14:26). The word *"hate"* simply means *"to love less."* Consequently, the true disciple loves his father, his mother, his wife, and his children LESS than Christ. May the Lord help all of us not to cater to loved ones at the expense of one's holiness and separation. The Nazarite, *"shall come at no dead body"* (Num. 6:6).

THE NAZARITE DEFILED

"And if any man die very suddenly by him, and he hath defiled the head of his consecration; then he shall shave his head in the day of his cleansing, on the seventh day shall he shave it. And on the eighth day he shall bring two turtles, or two young pigeons, to the priest, to the door of the tabernacle of the congregation: And the priest shall offer the one for a sin offering, and the other for a burnt offering, and make an atonement for him, for that he sinned by the dead, and shall hallow his head that same day. And he shall consecrate unto the LORD the days of his separation, and shall bring a lamb of the first year for a trespass offering: but the days that were before shall be lost, because his separation was defiled" (Num. 6:9-12).

Now notice carefully. Unexpectedly, the Nazarite became defiled. It happened suddenly. It was an unforeseen event. It certainly was not his fault that a person next to him died suddenly. He certainly couldn't help that, nor would he even have desired that such a calamity befall his neighbor. Nevertheless, the Nazarite immediately lost his separation! What dismay that would have inflicted upon his soul. Defilement was imputed, and purification enjoined. God provided a way back. After defilement, he was to wait seven days, and then shave his head. That would give him time to reflect on the whole incident, would it not? The import of this is, that since *"the consecration of his God"* upon his head was desecrated by the pollution of death, it must be removed in order to commence a new beginning. Ah yes, even the sins of our infirmity, or even little faults in which we are overtaken by surprise, call for repentance and a humbling on our part. How solemn also, that we can sin unknowingly, not realizing it until later down life's pathway. The hair was to be removed.

THE NAZARITE REINSTATED

Following this humiliating experience, he was to bring his offering of *"two turtles"* (*turtle-doves*), or *"two young pigeons"* to the priest, before the tabernacle door. One offering was a sin offering, and the other a burnt offering. Thus, his head would be hallowed (*make holy, consecrate*) that same day. He then was to bring a lamb of the first year for a trespass offering which would be a proper offering for involuntary sins (Lev. 22:14). Thus, the victim of circumstances was reinstated as one holy. However, these sobering words follow: *"But the days that were before shall be lost, because his separation was defiled."*

Time lost! How solemn! Many of us can look back with regret over the time we have lost. Perhaps getting involved in some insignificant thing, only to find out later, that it was sin.

To suddenly realize, that all the hours spent on such frivolities was forever lost, hours that could have been used more wisely. Wasted time, which if it had been used properly, could have reaped for us a greater reward at the Bema of Christ. That is the lesson that I see in the Nazarite's lost time. Let us be ever careful how we employ our precious and fleeting time.

THE NAZARITE'S DAYS FULFILLED

When the days of the Nazarite's separation were fulfilled, he was to be brought before the door of the tabernacle of the congregation. There he was to offer unto the LORD *"one lamb of the first year without blemish for a burnt offering, and one ewe lamb of the first year without blemish for a sin offering, and one ram without blemish for peace offerings, and a basket of unleavened bread, cakes of fine flour mingled with oil, and wafers of unleavened bread anointed with oil, and their meat offering, and their drink offerings"* (Num. 6:14-15). The burnt offering would indicate that total surrender of himself to the LORD. The sin offering was offered as an expiation for any involuntary sins committed during his period of consecration. The Nazarite certainly didn't come before the LORD empty, did he? He came fully furnished, and prepared to meet his God on that solemn day.

OUR OFFERINGS

One cannot help but think of the attitude that separated believers should manifest as they come into the presence of God at the Lord's Supper. Do we come fully prepared to offer unto our God that which speaks of Christ? It is our privilege. It is our responsibility! We bring our unblemished Lamb of the first year to the Father, to offer Him as the perfect burnt offering. As the burnt offering was offered on the altar totally for God and sent forth a sweet smelling savor, so we express to God the same concerning His beloved Son, the Lamb of God. Unreservedly, unhesitatingly, and with great joy, He gave Himself unto God as the unblemished burnt offering at Calvary. *"Christ also hath loved us, and hath given Himself for us an offering and a sacrifice to God for a sweetsmelling savour"* (Eph. 5:2). It is important to grasp this.

True, it is wonderful what the Saviour accomplished for us through His sacrifice, but let us ever be aware of what He accomplished for His God, through His death. I heard a man once teach that we should not be occupied at the Supper with what the Lord has done for us, but that we should be wholly engrossed in what He did for God. To me that was a lot of nonsense! That was the unsanctified theology of an intellectual brain. On the other hand, we have the other extreme, and that is, brethren thanking God for what Christ did for them, and not even mentioning what the Lord did for His God. Let us be balanced in our worship, thanking God for what the Lord accomplished for His God, then secondly, thanking God for what the Lord did for us. That, to me, seems to be the order of importance in intelligent worship.

Following the burnt offering, the ewe lamb is mentioned for a sin offering. Thank God for the sin offering at Calvary! Let us revel in it. Let us rejoice greatly in it! Where would we be without it? Why, we would have been in hell, weeping and wailing forever! Oh, the sin offering of our blessed Lord! How precious! How valuable! It will be our theme throughout the eternal ages as we gather around the rainbow throne, singing praises unto Him who has washed us from our sins in His own precious blood! Ten thousand times ten thousand, and thousands of thousands, shall raise that anthem unto the Faithful Witness in that glorious, soon-coming day! (Rev. 1:5-6; 5:11). *"This Man, after He had offered one sacrifice for sins for ever, sat down on the right hand of God"* (Heb. 10:12). Thank God for the Sin Offering!

The Nazarite also brought a ram for a peace offering, with a basket of unleavened bread. Also offered were his meat (meal) offering, and his drink offering. Here we find a token of thankfulness that he had been successful in accomplishing his vow. It was also a festival of rejoicing before the LORD.

The pattern is this. When our sins are put away, immediately we are brought into a unique relationship. *"Our fellowship is with the Father, and with His Son Jesus Christ"* (1 Jn. 1:3). We become associate-companions, having communion with God. *"Therefore being justified by faith, we have peace with God through our Lord Jesus Christ"* (Rom. 5:1). We are made nigh unto God, constituted His children and sons. What a tremendous relationship this is!

Not only this, we have *"the peace of God, which passeth all understanding,"* which keeps (with a garrison) our hearts and minds through Christ Jesus. (Phil. 4:7). I will tell you, this divine association is most wonderful. The abundant grace of God bestowed upon us, mere worms of Adam's fallen and depraved race! It never ceases to amaze me. To be wondrously brought into such favor and blessing by the Most High God, the Possessor of heaven and earth, simply surpasses all human perception!

THE NAZARITE'S BASKET

Accompanying these offerings was *"a basket of unleavened bread, cakes of fine flour mingled with oil, and wafers of unleavened bread anointed with oil, and their meat offering, and their drink offerings"* (Num. 6:15).

> *"And the priest shall bring them before the LORD, and shall offer his sin offering, and his burnt offering: And he shall offer the ram for a sacrifice of peace offerings unto the LORD, with the basket of unleavened bread: the priest shall offer also his meat offering, and his drink offering. And the Nazarite shall shave the head of his separation at the door of the tabernacle of the congregation, and shall take the hair of the head of his separation, and put it in the fire which is under the sacrifice of the peace offerings. And the priest shall take the sodden shoulder of the ram, and one unleavened cake out of the basket, and one unleavened wafer, and shall put them upon the hands of the Nazarite, af-*

ter the hair of his separation is shaven: And the priest shall wave them for a wave offering before the LORD: this is holy for the priest, with the wave breast and heave shoulder: and after that the Nazarite may drink wine"* (Num. 6:16–20).

You will observe that along with these prescribed offerings, the Nazarite also had to shave his consecrated head, and place the hair into the fire of the altar under the peace offering. He had worn the hair of his head in honor of the LORD, and now he was to offer it unto Him. Following this, the priest then took the boiled shoulder of the ram, with an unleavened cake, and wafer, out of the basket, and placed them in the hands of the Nazarite, and waved them before the LORD. Following this, these portions were to be eaten and enjoyed in fellowship with Jehovah.

THE NAZARITE'S LAW COMPLETED

Let us carefully consider this and make the practical application relative to ourselves. We are considering the Nazarite ending the days of his vow, to return to a less restricted way of life, for after the law of the Nazarite was completed, he was allowed to drink wine. My dear brother and sister, I do trust that you are living a life of separation. However, the day you die, or the Lord comes, that will terminate your days of separation on earth. You will then drink the wine of the joys of heaven, never to be reproached again for your devotedness to your LORD. Your earnest desire to serve the LORD with single purpose of heart, typified in the Nazarite's shorn hair, will be presented at last when your life's work on earth is done. As another has so aptly put it – It will be "simply laid upon the altar of the love of God. ... Not being anything worthy in itself, but only as being part of our gratitude to God."

Let us seek daily to discover what God would have us to be, not falling into the trap of simply following the "Christian crowd." What do we accomplish for God more than others? Let us avoid the disastrous question which unblushingly reveals the carnality of the one who asks it, namely, "What is the harm in it?" *"I beseech you therefore, brethren, by the mercies of God, that ye present your bodies a living sacrifice, holy, acceptable unto God, which is your reasonable service. And be not conformed to this world: but be ye transformed by the renewing of your mind, that ye may prove what is that good, and acceptable, and perfect, will of God"* (Rom. 12:1–2). *"Brethren, I count not myself to have apprehended: but this one thing I do, forgetting those things which are behind, and reaching forth unto those things which are before, I press toward the mark for the prize of the high calling of God in Christ Jesus. Let us therefore, as many as be perfect, be thus minded"* (Phil. 3:13–15).

> "What will it be to dwell above,
> And with the Lord of glory reign!
> Since the blest knowledge of His love
> So brightens all this dreary plain;
> No heart can think, no tongue call tell
> What joy 'twill be with Christ to dwell."[61]

---

61 Joseph Swain. <u>The Believer's Hymn Book.</u> (John Ritchie Ltd. Kilmarnock, Scotland). P. 302.

19

THE OFFERING OF THE PRINCES

NUMBERS 7

"And it came to pass on the day that Moses had fully set up the tabernacle, and had anointed it, and sanctified it, and all the instruments thereof, both the altar and all the vessels thereof, and had anointed them, and sanctified them; That the princes of Israel, heads of the house of their fathers, who were the princes of the tribes, and were over them that were numbered, offered: And they brought their offering before the LORD, six covered wagons, and twelve oxen; a wagon for two of the princes, and for each one an ox: and they brought them before the tabernacle" (Num. 7:1–3).

Numbers 7 introduces us to the presentation of dedicatory gifts by the princes of the twelve tribes. These gifts were twofold. The first gifts offered were materials that were indispensably necessary for the transport of the tabernacle while marching through the desert. Second, there were gifts given that were to be used by the priests in their various functions related to the tabernacle when it was set up. The expression, *"on the day,"* could more correctly be read, *"about that time,"* for before the priests offered, the anointing process of the tabernacle occupied seven days (Lev. 8:35). It was after the priests were anointed, their services defined, the tribes registered and arranged under their various standards, and the Levites positioned into various classes, that the princes offered. This was the final, and necessary accompaniment to the tabernacle before it was taken down to experience its journey to the first cloud-appointed resting place on the way to Canaan.

This event is not recorded in chronological order. These presentations took place at the time when Moses, after the tabernacle was erected, anointed and sanctified the altar, the tabernacle and its furniture. The princes offering their gifts took place *before* the departure of the nation from Sinai. That is readily seen, for the materials presented were indispensably needed for the transport of the tabernacle during Israel's march through the desert. Consider the fact that there was an interval of about forty days between the anointing of the tabernacle (the first day of the first month, Exodus 40:16), which lasted eight days, and their departure from Sinai, on the twentieth day of the second month (Num. 20:11). During this period, the Passover would have taken place, occupying six days (Num. 9:1–5). The presentation of the princes' gifts would occupy at least twelve days, and did not entirely precede the publication of the laws referred to, but was carried on partly at the same time.

The individual presentation of the princes, on their appointed days, would perhaps take only a few hours. The remainder of each day would involve Moses publishing the laws. Everything that took place could easily be fitted into the space of one month.

Numbers 7 may be the longest chapter in the Bible. The reason is, that we have much repetition, for even though each prince offered the same gifts, yet each offering is described. The Spirit could have easily written, "And each prince's offering was one silver charger, the weight thereof was an hundred and thirty shekels, one silver bowl of seventy shekels, after the shekel of the sanctuary; both of them were full of fine flour mingled with oil for a meat offering: One spoon of ten shekels of gold, full of incense: One young bullock, one ram, one lamb of the first year, for a burnt offering: One kid of the goats for a sin offering: And for a sacrifice of peace offerings, two oxen, five rams, five he goats, five lambs of the first year." But this is not what took place. No, no! God was interested in the contribution of every person, and He carefully lists all twelve princes and describes their individual gifts. So interested was God in their offerings, that he took 89 verses to record it. I think that it would be profitable to consider these princely men, and their contributions to the sanctuary of God. I know that this book is primarily concerned with the journeys of Israel to Canaan, but after all, if God sees fit to interject a chapter that is 89 verses long during that journey, I think that it would be well to stop for a few moments, and consider this monumental occasion. One thing this presents to us is the good attitude of the people as they were about to journey from Sinai into the wilderness under the direction of Jehovah, by way of the cloudy pillar.

DEDICATION – UNSELFISHNESS – WILLINGNESS

In this whole episode, I can plainly see overflowing hearts. I see absolute dedication to the LORD. I observe complete unselfishness, and a willingness to give God, one's very best! I see wholehearted devotion to God's dwelling place.

Now, let us stop right here and reflect on our own past. Remember the moment that you were saved? How could you forget it? On that occasion, you commenced your pilgrim journey. What was your attitude to the Lord? Was it not one of devotion to Him? Would you not have given Him all? Did not the fire burn in your bosom? Were you not completely pliable in the hands of the Holy Spirit? Did you not lay yourself upon the altar for God and say, "Here I am Lord, I give myself to Thee. What wilt Thou have me to do?" Ah, that was a wonderful occasion, was it not? There was nothing like God's people. You loved them all. There was nothing like God's assembly, when you found it. It was a delightful place indeed! Was it not? Your soul was enraptured with everything connected with holy ground. You would have gladly died for Christ if called upon to do so.

Nothing mattered at all except the things of God. All of a sudden, the vain world, with all its hypocritical and empty pursuits and pleasures, seemed like scum, and like dross to you. You reveled in the fact that you would never be in hell. You rejoiced in your newly-gained eternal salvation. The Holy Spirit was now inside of you, setting you on fire for God. Oh, how absolutely wonderful the day of salvation was! To be taken out of darkness, and translated into divine light, and into the kingdom of the Son of His love. It is indescribable! It is beyond human intellect! The princes offered their very best!

WAGONS AND OXEN

The first thing brought to our attention is the offerings the princes brought for help in the transportation of the tabernacle – six covered wagons, and twelve oxen. Two princes were responsible for one wagon, and one prince responsible for one ox. They brought them joyfully, and willingly, before the tabernacle. God instructed them to give these offerings to the Levites, to assist them in their service in transporting the tabernacle. The sons of Gershon were responsible for the curtains of the tabernacle which was termed, "their burdens" (Num. 4:27). To these Levites were given two wagons and four oxen to pull the wagons.

However, the sons of Merari had greater burdens to bear. Their responsibility was to transport the boards, the bars, the pillars, the sockets of the tabernacle, the pillars of the court, their sockets, and their pins. When you consider the forty eight boards of dense and heavy shittim wood, overlaid with gold, measuring at least two and one half feet wide, by fifteen feet high and ten inches thick, you have a tremendous weight in just one board. The ninety-six sockets of silver weighed four tons! The pillars of the court numbered sixty and stood almost eight foot high. Then we read of the brass sockets for the pillars, and the five pillars of the tabernacle door with their brass sockets. Also included in these tremendous burdens would be the four pillars, and their silver sockets that held the vail. God considered the sons of Merari by giving them four wagons and eight oxen to facilitate them in transporting such a tremendous load. In other words, the princes provided essential help to those who were appointed of God to bear the burden of holy things. What a relief their offering would bring to the burden-bearers!

COMMON SENSE

> "Though God's wisdom had ordained all the essentials of the tabernacle, yet it seems these accidental conveniences were left to be provided by their own discretion, which was to set in order that which was wanting (Titus 1:5), and these wagons were not refused, though no pattern of them was shown to Moses in the mount. Note, it must not be expected that the divine institution of ordinances should descend to all those circumstances which are determinable, and are fit to be left alterable, by human prudence, that wisdom which is profitable to direct."[62]

What has been just stated is that there is such a thing as common sense. There are things we do in scriptural assemblies that are not mentioned in the divine pattern such as, the use of The Believer's Hymn Books. Common sense sees the advantage in using hymn books, however, where do you find them mentioned in the New Testament Church pattern? True, we are exhorted to sing, but no mention is made of hymn books. However, I find it not only sensible, but also permissible to use them. I remember forty five years ago, the late William Williams related to me an amusing, yet pathetic, incident. He arrived at a hall in Venezuela one Lord's Day morning rather early, only to find a brother there with "good news." "Senior Williams," said the man, "I discovered that hymn books are not found in the Bible, so I took them all into the back yard and burned them." The brother was an extremist. So much so, that at a later date, he left the assembly altogether.

---

[62] Matthew Henry

Come with me again to another point. Are conferences beneficial to God's people? In most cases, yes, they are. However, show me a chapter and verse where we have saints traveling hundreds of miles for a weekend to attend a conference? Where in the Scriptures do you find evangelists coming, even from another country overseas, to help at a conference? You can search the Scriptures from dawn to dusk, and you won't find one incidence. Yet, through the years, they have proved to be a real blessing to many of the Lord's people.

One has the same thought regarding chairs. They didn't use chairs at the institution of the Lord's Supper. Why no! They sat on the ground and reclined on one another. So, does that say that we cannot use chairs? You can see the folly in such a way of thinking, or should I say, "with such a way of not thinking!" You see, it is like Matthew Henry said, *"accidental conveniences were left to be provided by their own discretion."*

ARE YOU A PRINCE?

Let me apply the bringing of the wagons for the service of God, for what profit is there in the exposition of divine truths, if there is no practical application? The application is, do you behave like a prince of Israel? What is your attitude toward the burden-bearers among God's people? When is the last time you helped an evangelist? When have you enquired as to the labors of men out in the harvest field. You say, "I pray for them." All well and good, but let me tell you something. When a man is working new ground, do your prayers fill his vehicle with fuel? Do they fill his stomach with food? Do they help him pay his motel bill? Do they help him pay his preaching-room rent? Do they help him pay his home expenses? Let me be candid and say – "No, they don't!" You can pray all that you like, but that will never meet his needs. Now do not get me wrong. Please don't accuse me that I am stating that prayer is not a vital thing, for it is. Evangelists need the prayers of God's people in a vital way. All I am saying is that you may pray that the preacher will be preserved from discouragement. You may pray that God will give him favor with the people, and that he will see souls saved. All this is well and good. But your fervent prayers will not help him in a materialistic way. What would you think of a prince coming to the Merarites and saying. "Now men, you have a work to do. It is a laborious work, and you have my sympathy. Keep your chin up, work hard at it for the LORD, and He will bless you. And remember this, I am praying for you." This is wonderful, isn't it? So, the prince walks away quite happy with himself, but the Merarites are saying to themselves, "How are we ever going to transport these heavy articles of the tabernacle?"

GOD USING THE UNGODLY

Let me say this. If God calls a man, He WILL provide for that man, even if He has to use the ungodly to do it! "Oh!" you exclaim, "is it right to let the ungodly help you?" Without hesitation I reply, "Absolutely yes!" Scripture will support my unhesitating answer. Look at John 4:7. "Jesus said unto her, 'give Me to drink.'" What would you call that? She was a sinful woman, and He was wearied, thirsty and hungry, and He asks her a favor.

I remember on one occasion being well over a hundred miles from any assembly. A storm came, and my tent blew down. Immediately, I notified a woman, who in turn, rounded up a group of ungodly and rough coal miners. In record time, they had my tent back up again, and I was able to preach in it that same night. They did me a favor that I never forgot. What would you have done? Would you have asked God to send some angels to re-pitch the tent? Or would you have made a long-distance call to an assembly to come when possible to put your tent back up again. Let us be realistic. The Lord asked a sinner for a drink of water.

Come again with me to an island called Melita. Paul had just suffered shipwreck. He was soaking wet, cold, and hungry. However, God had provision for him. Notice the divine report. *"And the barbarous people shewed us no little kindness: for they kin-*

dled a fire, and received us every one, because of the present rain, and because of the cold ... In the same quarters were possessions of the chief man of the island, whose name was Publius; who received us, and lodged us three days courteously"* (Acts 28:2, 7).

Now what are you going to do with these scriptural exposures as to the behavior of our Lord and the apostle Paul? What is an evangelist to do when he has been looking to God to meet his need, and at the same time receives no communication from a scriptural assembly, or from a child of God? Well, I suppose that he could seek to help a farmer make hay and get a little money to pay for his food. But what if he is too frail to do laborious work? What if there is no available work? Then what? Oh you say, "I will pray for him?' Ah, that's great, that's thoughtful, but what about his motel bill? Well, some have had these experiences and have never been brought to destitution and utter despair as a result. Some have actually experienced the motel owner refusing rent for the room after using it for a number of weeks. What do you think of that? What is a preacher to do when he enters a little store in the country to pay for his gas and the owner of the store hands him a bag of free groceries as help along the way? Again I repeat, what is he to do? Is he to say, "You are a Gentile sinner, and I am to take nothing of you Gentiles, for I am a servant of the Most High God!" Is that what he should say? Would he ever win a soul to Christ with that attitude? Hardly! No! He receives from their hand in circumstances of that nature. He doesn't take collections, and he tactfully refuses their money if at all possible, but he certainly would receive a meal at their table. What I am saying is this; if you are not exercised to help a servant of the Lord with your monetary substance, God will provide for him from other sources. Remember, it was unclean birds that God employed to sustain his servant Elijah.

PROVISION FOR THE PRIESTS

Not only did the princes provide for the laboring Levites, but they also provided an abundance for the ministering priests. Each priest had *"his day,"* to offer (Num. 7:11). They were not pressured, or intimidated to contribute. Ah no! This was done of their own accord, and what they offered was minutely recorded by the LORD. Yes, my friend, the LORD closely observes and carefully records every single sacrifice you present to Him. It may be transporting an aged saint to the assembly meeting in your vehicle. It may be in visiting a discouraged, shut-in saint with comforting words. God is not unrighteous to forget your work and labor of love.

These princes, in presenting their gifts, were in reality, enriching the house of God, and also encouraging those priests officiating in God's house. There would have already been a golden spoon to use in offering incense on the golden altar, but these men brought twelve more. What a blessing that was, for if a second or a third priest came on the scene to burn incense, he would have had to wait his turn if there was one before him already using the golden spoon. However, the offering of the princes eliminated any waiting of such sort. In other words, they provided a convenience for the priests. Let me ask you, do you make it easier for responsible men in your assembly? Have you enriched God's house? Are you a joy to them or a grief? Do you contribute to the weekly Bible reading? If you do not know much, then let me put it this way, do you contribute intelligent questions? When Christians gather together in assembly capacity, they all bring at least one thing – they bring themselves. However, are we not expected to bring more that just our bodies? Can we not also bring contributive thoughts for the Bible reading? Can we not bring some of our treasure for the offering? Can we not bring a cheery spirit for the hearts of others? Or are we like a drifting iceberg that chills everything that it passes? The princes offered valuable items, enriching the house, and encouraging the priests. In this respect, let us be princely.

Each prince brought the same as the other princes. The order of their coming was according to the order in which they were arranged around the tabernacle (chapter 2), commencing at the east, then moving to the south, then west, and ending at the north. That also was the order in which they journeyed, namely: Judah, Issachar, and Zebulun; then Reuben, Simeon, and Gad; then Ephraim, Manasseh, and Benjamin; finally, Dan, Asher, and Naphtali.

Another thing worthy of notice is that Nashon, of the tribe of Judah, was the first man to offer, but the word *"prince"* is not attached to his name. It has been suggested, the reason being, that the distinction of being the first one to offer involved in itself a kind of principality, inasmuch as the tribe of Judah, pictured in Nashon, represented the Lord and Saviour, Who descended from Him, and Who was *"in all things to have the pre-eminence."* An old Rabbinical writer remarked that "He is not called prince, that he might not be puffed up because he offered first; and all others are called princes, for that they submitted themselves and offered after him."[63] However, I find this Rabbi's thought hard to accept, for Moses' recording of this event would be perhaps years after they offered, thus Nashon would not even be aware of the omission of the word *"prince"* after his name.

EQUAL OFFERINGS

Every tribe offered the *same kind of offering*, and in the *same quantity*, to show, that as every tribe was equally indebted to God for its support, so each tribe should manifest an equal sense of obligation to the LORD. Applying this to ourselves, no matter to what nation we belong, we all have an equal obligation to the LORD. We can also all share in the altar and its blessings. The princes all thought alike. We too, should all be of one mind. Not one prince would be able to brag that he had brought more than other princes. They all worked alike, and we too, should all work alike for the good of the assembly, even though our abilities may differ.

Some people have more brains than others, but let us remember that God measures my attitude and the degree of my efforts more than my accomplishments. Years ago, I remember

---

63 Rabbi Chazkuni

a brother faulting another brother who was a bit on the "slow side." So I spoke to the faulting brother and said, "Now look, most folks have a V-8 motor, but some are only running on five cylinders, but the brother you are faulting only has a four cylinder motor, but at least he is running on all four." That's what God appreciates – wholeheartedness.

ONE SIN OFFERING

You will also notice that each prince presented three animals for a burnt offering, seventeen animals for peace offerings, but only one kid of the goats for a sin offering. This seems to point to a truth in the New Testament, that there is only *one* sacrifice for sin.

> *"When He had by Himself purged our sins, sat down on the right hand of the Majesty on high"* (Heb. 1:3).

> *"Once in the end of the world hath He appeared to put away sin by the sacrifice of Himself"* (Heb. 9:26).

> But this Man, *after He had offered one sacrifice for sins for ever, sat down on the right hand of God"* (Heb. 10:12).

> *"Now where remission of these is, there is no more offering for sin"* (Heb. 10:18).

The Roman Catholic Church, and the Eastern Orthodox Church teach that; *"the bread and wine of Communion, become in substance but not in appearance, the body and blood of Jesus Christ at consecration."* The mass is a celebration of the re-offering of the body and blood of Christ as a sacrifice for sin. This doctrine, called, *"transubstantiation"* is blasphemous to say the least. As you can plainly see, it is a direct contradiction of the Holy Scripture.

Christians rejoice in the fact that the sufferings of Christ for sin are forever past. The fact that He cried on the Cross, *"It is finished,"* (*"paid in full"*) proves that the whole debt, and question of sin, were forever done with. It would never have to be repeated. Paul relates to this in Romans 6. *"Knowing that Christ being raised from the dead dieth no more; death hath no more dominion over Him. For in that He died, He died unto sin once: but in that He liveth, he liveth unto God"* (verses 9–10). Thus we can sing like Horatius Bonar:

> "Done is the work that saves,
> Once and forever done;
> Finished the righteousness
> That clothes the unrighteous one.
> The love that blesses us below
> Is freely flowing to us now."

THE SHEKEL OF THE SANCTURY

It is interesting to notice that what the princes brought of gifts that were weighed, the weight of a shekel was not after the fluctuating standards of man, but after *"the shekel of the sanctuary."* The standard was set. It was a divinely appointed weight, preserved in the sanctuary as a measure, and never changing. The faith (the doctrine), once and for all delivered unto the saints, is of the sanctuary, and never changes. We have a fixed standard. Is everything in our life agreeable to God's standard? It should be! The peace offerings would prompt much joy and communion, not only with each other, but also with the LORD.

THE VOICE OF GOD

"And when Moses was gone into the tabernacle of the congregation to speak with Him, then he heard the voice of One speaking unto him from off the mercy seat that was upon the Ark of testimony, from between the two cherubims: and He spake unto him" (Num. 7:89).

Thus, we have a distinct statement that the LORD actually spoke to him in an audible human voice. This was the fulfillment of the promise made: *"And thou shalt put the mercy seat above upon the Ark; and in the Ark thou shalt put the testimony that*

I shall give thee. And there I will meet with thee, and I will commune with thee from above the mercy seat, from between the two cherubims which are upon the Ark of the testimony, of all things which I will give thee in commandment unto the children of Israel" (Ex. 25:21–22).

Moses alone was allowed to enter into the immediate presence of God. However, today every Christian has the liberty to enter the holiest by the blood of Jesus. We have all the rights that Moses had, all due to the work of Christ on our behalf. How precious are the words of the Spirit: *"Having therefore, brethren, boldness to enter into the holiest by the blood of Jesus, by a new and living way, which He hath consecrated for us, through the veil, that is to say, His flesh; And having an High Priest over the house of God; Let us draw near with a true heart in full assurance of faith, having our hearts sprinkled from an evil conscience, and our bodies washed with pure water"* (Heb. 10:19–22).

SUBSTANCE – SCRIPTURES

In closing this most interesting section, let me mention this. Not only did Moses speak to God, but God also spake to Moses. Let me apply it this way. Some expositors believe that this verse, Numbers 7:89, is not in chronological order with the previous verses. This may be, but let me apply a precept from the order in which it is mentioned. It was not until *after* God had been presented with valuable contributions for His sanctuary, that we read of Him speaking to Moses. Going to the New Testament, I find the Lord speaking these words. *"If therefore ye have not been faithful in the unrighteous mammon, who will commit to your trust the true riches?"* (Luke 16:11). In other words, if you have not made yourself friends (those won to Christ through the gospel) by means of the mammon of unrighteousness (as a result of your money having been used to bring the gospel to them); if you have not been faithful in the unrighteous mammon (your money), who will commit to your trust the true riches (the influences of the Spirit, and the voice of God speaking to you through His Word). God commits His Word to those who honor Him with their substance. If a man withholds what is due to God, God will, in return, withhold from him treasures from the Holy Scriptures. Christians are not to give grudgingly, or of necessity. They are to give cheerfully, *"for God loveth a cheerful giver"* (2 Cor. 9:7). For the cheerful giver these promises are given: they will always have sufficiency in all things; their seed sown will multiply, their fruits of righteousness will increase, and they will be enriched in everything (verses 10–11). Solomon understood this truth and wrote: *"There is that scattereth, and yet increaseth; and there is that withholdeth more than is meet, but it tendeth to poverty"* (Prov. 11:24).

Do you want to hear the voice of the Lord speaking to your soul when you read the Scriptures? Do you desire to have a greater knowledge of divine truths? Then take in the truth of these words, and act accordingly! *"Honour the LORD with thy substance, and with the firstfruits of all thine increase: So shall thy barns be filled with plenty, and thy presses shall burst out with new wine"* (Prov. 3:9–10).

The princes honored God with their substance, and Moses heard the voice of the LORD!

20

THE CONSECRATION OF THE LEVITES

NUMBERS 8

The consecration of the Levites to the service of the tabernacle is preceded by the mention of the lighting of the lamps in the holy place. Moses had already written of this in Exodus 25:37, and the question arises, why is it mentioned again? The simplest explanation would be that it shows the Divine concern on the subject. The Lampstand divinely illuminated the sacred vessels of the holy place, which in turn speaks to us of a number of things. First, the Lampstand with its burning lamps portray to us that One Who is the light of the world (John 8:12; 9:5). That One Who drew near to those two on the way to Emmaus, *"And beginning at Moses and all the prophets, He expounded unto them in all the Scriptures the things concerning Himself"* (Luke 24:27). So bright was the light of illumination, that they were made to exclaim; *"Did not our heart burn within us, while He talked with us by the way, and while He opened to us the Scriptures?"* (Luke 24:32).

Not only this, the lampstand prefigures God's redeemed people, who have been called out of darkness into His marvelous light to become children of light (1 Thess. 5:5). As such, we are to let our light shine as the Lord commanded: *"Ye are the light of the world. A city that is set on an hill cannot be hid. Let your light so shine before men, that they may see your good works, and glorify your Father which is in heaven"* (Matt. 5:16). The world lies in darkness. We are light, therefore our difference is very obvious! As light, Christians by their life expose the hidden things of darkness. They provide a contrast to others. Why is a godly saint so peaceful, so balanced, and so content? It is because he is bathing in the sunshine of God's immeasurable love.

The Lord tells us: *"Let your light so shine before men."* This means that the Christian's confession of Christ, causes men to connect what he does with his confession. They behold the Christian's good works and do not come to the conclusion that his good works come because of a mild disposition. No, no! That will never do, for there are many unconverted folk who have a mild disposition and do good unto others. Quite the contrary. They see the person's good works as the result of Him being a Christian. He confesses Christ to all. That way, God is glorified in the good works, not in the individual himself. He conducts himself in such a way, that when the ungodly behold his love, his mildness, his willingness to benefit others, and his complete change to what he was prior to his salvation, they will confess, "There must be something to this Christianity."

My dear believer, are you living up to this? Is your light brightly shining before men? The lamps were directly united with the central shaft, namely the lampstand. They were part of the branches. We too, are directly linked to Christ the Vine. We are the branches (John 15:5). Both He and His saints are light in a dark and dismal world.[64]

THE LEVITES

Moses now brings the consecration of the Levites before us. Who were these men, what was their designated work, and how do they apply to Christians today?

---

64 For a further exposition on the lampstand consult: *"Things Written Aforetime – The Tabernacle,"* by Robert E. Surgenor. Available from Gospel Folio Press, or the author.

Out of the tribe of Levi, God chose Moses to be the lawgiver and leader of His people. From this tribe, He also chose Aaron and his sons to be custodians of the sanctuary. They were consecrated as priests through a solemn ceremony (Lev. 8). Then lastly, the whole tribe was chosen in place of the firstborn of all the tribes, to assist the priests in their duties relative to the sanctuary. They also would be responsible to guard the court gate, as to who entered. When the tabernacle setteth forward, the Levites were to take it down, and when it was to be pitched, they were to set it up. They were to pitch their tents round about the tabernacle of testimony and to keep the charge of the tabernacle (Num. 1:51, 53).

CLEANSING BEFORE SERVING

The first thing noticed was the Levite's cleansing prior to being positioned to serve. This alone affords us a most solemn truth, namely, that a person must be clean to serve God. A sinner cannot serve God. He must first be washed in the blood of the Lamb. That is a well known principle. However, even though washed and judicially cleansed by the blood of Christ, there must be a moral cleanness in order for a saint to serve the Lord. Remember the advice Paul gave to the Corinthian assembly. *"Let us cleanse ourselves from all filthiness of the flesh and spirit, perfecting holiness in the fear of God"* (2 Cor. 7:1). Do you expect God to hear and answer your prayers? There is a requisite first – cleanliness! For, *"If I regard iniquity in my heart, the Lord will not hear me"* (Ps. 66:18). Coming back to Jerusalem from captivity, the Jews were carrying the vessels of the temple which Nebuchadnezzar had taken away, and the exhortation was this: *"Depart ye, depart ye, go ye out from thence, touch no unclean thing; go ye out of the midst of her; be ye clean, that bear the vessels of the LORD"* (Isa. 52:11). Christ proclaims: *"Blessed are the pure in heart: for they shall see God"* (Matt. 5:8).

THE WATER OF PURIFYING

The cleansing involves a number of things. First, Moses was told: *"Sprinkle water of purifying (mey chattath, water of sin, or water of the sin-offering) upon them."* More than likely this purifying water was made by the ashes of the red heifer, cedar-wood, hyssop, and scarlet; and the heifer herself was sacrificed, and her blood sprinkled seven times before the tabernacle, she may be considered as a proper *sacrifice for sin*, and consequently, the water thus prepared is termed the *water of the sin-offering*. (Num. 19:3–6). It seems probable that this ordinance (the red heifer) was instituted before this time, yet not recorded by Moses until chapter nineteen. It is readily seen how Scripture applies the red heifer to Christ and the cleansing of His people in this dispensation. Notice: *"For if the blood of bulls and of goats, and the ashes of an heifer sprinkling the unclean, sanctifieth to the purifying of the flesh: How much more shall the blood of Christ, who through the eternal Spirit offered Himself without spot to God, purge your conscience from dead works to serve the living God?"* (Heb. 9:13–14).

HAIR AND CLOTHING

Moses then instructed them to shave all their flesh, and to wash all their clothes, to make themselves clean. This external rite was for the purpose of impressing them that they were to mortify all carnal and worldly desires, and keep purity in their heart, and their life, which would be in character for ones designated as the servants of God.

Not only this, but we have a divine principle, applicable to our day. Before us is portrayed the application of death to the flesh, namely all the habits of a sinful, fleshly nature. This is brought about by the Word of God being brought to bear upon one's conscience. The razor (God's Word) was brought to eliminate all that was the mere growth of nature (the body hair). They were to wash their garments, symbolizing the cleansing of one's character and habits, according to the prohibitions, and commandments of the Word of God. The Levites were not naturally fit to approach the sacred vessels of the sanctuary, nor be a help to the priests prior to the sprinkling of the water of purifying, the shaving of their bodies, and the cleansing of their clothes. This was God's way of fitting these men for holy service.

Let me say this. God's ways do not change! In order for men to serve in God's assembly they must be clean, morally and spiritually. They must be saints that have crucified the flesh with the affections and lusts thereof (Gal. 5:24). Those who have cleansed their habits, and who have totally submitted to the Word of God, these, and these only, are fit for the service of God. When this vital issue is side-stepped, and there is an allowance of nature among those who serve the Lord, spiritual death will be the result. C. H. Mackintosh once remarked, *"There never was a more fatal mistake than to attempt to enlist nature in the service of God. It matters not how you may endeavor to improve or regulate it. It is not improvement, but death that will avail."*

THE CAUSE OF PROBLEMS

What is the cause of the many problems that beset the gathered-out companies of the Lord's people today? What has brought about our lack of power in the gospel? What has brought about such a state of self-complacency, and lack of discernment? Why are things being introduced that were unknown among us two decades ago? Why are we so different from the saints of three generations ago? Just what is the problem? Well, my dear brethren, I believe that this is the reason for the problem. We have partially set aside the complete control of the Holy Spirit, individually and collectively. Let me prove that blunt statement.

UNCONTROLLED SISTERS

Consider the complete control of the Holy Spirit in a sister's life. Allow me to mention just three areas where we observe the setting aside of the Spirit's plain teaching. We will term it the "Three H's."

(1) **The Home**. A wife is to be a keeper at home (a guard) (Titus 2:5). How many sisters do you know that impose their little children on to others, while they leave their God-appointed sphere, to enter the workforce of a godless society?

(2) **The Habit** (clothing). The Spirit demands that she is to dress modestly (1 Tim. 2:9). Uncovering most of one's legs in public could hardly be termed modest. Shorts display the shame of nakedness. There were those in Jeremiah's day walking contrary to the precepts of God, of whom it was said; *"Were they ashamed when they had committed abomination? nay, they were not at all ashamed, neither could they blush"* (Jer. 6:15; 8:12). The same lack of conscience is seen today. Most ungodly people today have no shame, and when they sin, they are not ashamed, neither can they blush. Consequently, what do I see in a smiling Christian sister parading about in shorts? Well, I see a soul that has a seared conscience. She doesn't blush over being seen in public with bare legs. I observe a saint that is not behaving saintly. I see a woman that is grieving the Holy Spirit, consequently introducing weakness into the assembly where she is in "fellowship."

Please bear with me in this most negative subject. Let us consider another item of clothing. How many Christian women wear *"that which pertaineth to a man"* in spite of the fact that the Spirit declares that: *"the woman shall not wear that which pertaineth unto a man, neither shall a man put on a woman's garment: for all that do so are abomination* ("disgusting") *unto the LORD thy God"* (Deut. 22:5).

EXCUSE V. LAVATORY DOORS

You can be sure, that there is an excuse for this unwarranted behavior. I have been informed that since woman's pants and slacks are expressly made for females, and are purchased in the lady's section of the store, that this verse does not apply at all to today's culture. Now that is very interesting, isn't it? However, the Spirit doesn't simply say that the woman is not to wear man's clothing. Not at all! He goes farther than this and very plainly states that the woman is not to wear that with PERTAINETH to a man. Do you realize what that big word means? It simply means this in our language: "Applies; relates; parallel (similar, likeness); refer; correspond; appertains." That is why when you enter a public facility and head for the lavatories, you will observe on one door the word "women," and on the other door the word "men." However, for those who do not understand English, the facility has made it easy for them to know which door to enter, for by the word "women" is the figure of a human being in a skirt, and on the door that says "men," you will see a figure dressed in pants.

MENNONITES AND AMISH

So then, men wear *"britches,* or *trousers"* which are normally called *"pants."* When a woman wears a pantsuit, she wears a garment that corresponds; that is like, and that is similar, to a man's britches. Am I right or wrong? Men wear "slacks." Women wear "slacks." Men wear "pants." Women wear "pants." Not only do the items correspond to each other, and are similar, they are even given the same names! How can you say then, that a woman's blue jeans, or her slacks do not pertain to a man's garment? If honest before God, you can't! It is amazing to me that in our society we have professing Christians that know very little of the truth that we in God's assemblies have been privileged to learn. We claim to understand the Scriptures above those in the denominations. Yet, in spite of our high privileges, as gathered out Christians, why do we find a higher standard of dress among some professing Christian women that are in certain denominations? Take the Mennonites for example. How many Mennonite women have you seen in slacks, or shorts? How many Amish women have you observed sporting around in blue jeans, or shorts? Even in certain Pentecostal groups, you won't find one woman in their congregation that would ever wear pants or shorts. Observe their children, and you will find the same strictness in observing the Spirit's command, *"the woman shall not wear that which pertaineth to a man."*

OLD WITNESSESS

Now then, let me relate to the last part of that verse, rarely quoted. *"Neither shall a man put on a woman's garment: for all that do so are abomination unto the LORD thy God"* (Deut. 22:5).

> "Reference was made to unbecoming levities practised in common life. They were properly forbidden; for the adoption of the habiliments (clothes, or, clothing) of the one sex by the other is an outrage on decency, obliterates the distinctions of nature by fostering softness and effeminacy in the man, impudence and boldness in the woman as well as levity and hypocrisy in both; and, in short, it opens the door to an influx of so many evils that all who wear the dress of another sex are pronounced "an abomination unto the Lord." (Jamieson, Fausset, Brown Commentary).

John Wesley has an interesting comment on this verse.

> "Shall not wear - namely, ordinarily or unnecessarily, for in some cases this may be lawful, as to make an escape for one's life. Now this is forbidden, both for decency sake, that men might not confound those sexes which God hath distinguished, that all appearance of evil might be avoided, such change of garments carrying a manifest sign of effeminacy in the man, of arrogance in the woman, of lightness and petulancy in both; and also to cut off all suspicions and occasions of evil, which this practice opens a wide door to."

Arno C. Gaebelein also has a very enlightening comment on

this abominable practice, written between 1912 and 1922.

> "The immediate design of this prohibition was not to prevent licentiousness, or to oppose idolatrous practices; but to maintain the sanctity of that distinction of the sexes, which was established by the creation of man and woman, and in relation to which Israel was not to sin. Every violation or wiping out of this distinction – such even as emancipation of women – was unnatural, and therefore 'an abomination in the sight of God.' Yet today we find a universal movement in the world for the complete emancipation of women, which ignores, and even defies, the place which the Creator has given to women."

Regarding this issue, C. A. Coates writes:

> "Divine order is ever to be observed, and it is most important to have regard to this in a day when every feature of that order is being so largely set aside. In Christianity, the man and the woman each have their distinctive clothing, and are only suitably adorned as they appear in it. The whole tendency of things today is to subvert divine order, but that order is to be maintained in God's assembly. Nature itself teaches a woman to be retiring and modest. He glory is her long hair which is given to her. Her distinctive glory according to nature suggests what is her true moral glory. Her 'clothing' would represent her whole deportment and appearance, not excluding her actual dress. It is to be suitable to the place which she has of expressing in her own person how the assembly is subjected to Christ."

Now I have resurrected these old writers for a purpose, and that is, to show you that my discourse on this unpleasant subject is not merely a "brainstorm" that has recently overcome me. Not at all! I hope that you believe that I am sane. What I am relating to you is something that was often preached in days past, but we very rarely hear it declared from our pulpits anymore. Yet, it is a vital truth, and as old as the Holy Scriptures themselves. The older preachers thundered it out, but today, we have a different breed of men and women. We are beset with people who have very few convictions, and a seared conscience. Carnality is on the rise, and godliness is taking a "back seat." Consequently, this saddening trend is weakening our assemblies to the point that feebleness is very evident.

MEN DRESSED LIKE WOMEN

Regarding a man wearing a woman's garment. Why would a man ever desire to dress like a woman? There could be a number of reasons. I will only give you one. History tells us that Clodius, a Greek politician, born about BC 92, dressed himself like a woman that he might mingle with the Roman ladies in the feast of the *Bona Dea*. The result was that he was universally declared accursed. Years ago the fashion world was going to introduce skirts and dresses for men. For some reason, their obnoxious idea never got off the ground. Thankfully, it sank like the Titanic, into the sea of oblivion.

I remember an amusing incident. A preaching friend of mine warned his wife, "If you ever put on a pair of slacks, I will buy a dress and when you walk downtown, I will be walking in my dress beside you!" Of course, the Irish preacher knew that he was perfectly safe, for his wife was the kind of Christian lady that would never even "dream" of wearing anything pertaining to a man.

The last "H" I want to consider is; **The Hair**. What does the Spirit teach relative to the sister's hair? Notice 1 Corinthians 11:15. *"But if a woman have long hair, it is a glory to her."* The word *"long"* indicates hair that has never been tampered with. It is untrimmed hair. Like the Nazarite, it has been allowed to grow long with no cutting instrument having been applied to it. God has given the woman her hair for her glory, thus, any godly woman would never cut, and let fall to the floor, that which God has graciously given to her. But look around. How many sisters in God's assemblies do you know that are tampering with their hair? Did you ever see an Amish woman, or a Mennonite woman, with cut hair? So much for the *individual* setting aside the complete control of the Holy Spirit.

THE SPIRIT SET ASIDE COLLECTIVELY

What about us *collectively?* Have we set aside the complete control of the Holy Spirit? Have we become programmed in certain areas? Most certainly we have! In some assemblies, the Holy Spirit has been, as one faithful preacher put it, "put into a box." He ceases to be the controlling element assembly-wise. Some conferences are manifesting this strange spirit, by not only selecting the speakers, but also dictating to them what to speak and how long to speak. This concept was totally foreign to our conferences three generations ago in the United States. What is the problem? We are seeking to improve a sad situation by human intervention. We are not godly enough to experience the Spirit's leading. He, in many areas, has become silent because of our lack of putting to death the flesh. Consequently, without His guidance, there is only one other recourse, and that is to jump in and seek to solve the barren situation with human engineering and expertise. Woe is me!

PROGRAMMED PREACHING

Three generations ago, a gospel series may have normally lasted five to nine weeks, and perhaps even longer. How often do we witness that today? Granted, sinners do not attend gospel series as in former days. Yet, how often do you hear of gospel meetings with a closing date, even before they commence? What is this? Well, to be very candid, it is that such are dictating to the Holy Spirit, instead of allowing the Holy Spirit to dictate to them. Can this be right when the Spirit says to the preacher, "Continue with the meetings," and the preacher replies, "It is time for me to cease." Of course, for every strange move, there is an excuse. So what do some say when sinners are attending, and wanting to be saved, yet the preacher, or the assembly, closes the meetings? Well the excuses are numerous, one being, that the preacher has booked ahead and is scheduled for another series the next week. Shame! Another excuse is that if they close, those who are troubled will be pressured to confess and receive Christ. Again I repeat – shame!

Perhaps you will accuse me of "harping." Yes, I must admit that I have been persistent, but God says that we *"should earnestly contend for the faith* (the truth of God) *which was once delivered unto the saints"* (Jude 1:3), and that is simply what I have been doing. If for any reason you can discredit from the Holy Scriptures what I have been "harping" about, notify me, and I will write you an apology. Otherwise, I stand firm on what I have written.

The inconsistencies just considered are the primary reasons, my friend, for our lack of power with God in the midst of a crooked and perverse generation. The Levite shaved his hair, and washed his clothes, and then God could use him, but not until then!

THE LEVITE'S AGE

God gave the Levites as a gift unto Aaron and his sons and they were valuable men. One might well term them "helpers." They would make the work of the priests much easier. Entering the work, it was required that they be at least twenty five years of age (Num. 8:24), and at fifty years of age, they were to *"cease waiting upon the service thereof."* Numbers 4:3 informs us: *"From thirty years old and upward even until fifty years old, all that enter into the host, to do the work in the tabernacle of the congregation."* The expression, *"from thirty years old and upward even until fifty years old,"* appears also in verses, 23, 30, 35, 39, 43, and 47. It would appear that for five years (25 years to 30 years) the Levites would be in training, and not expected to bear the heavy burden of transporting the tabernacle. When the age of 30 is mentioned, it is in connection with the moving of the tabernacle (Num. 4:1–33). That was hard, laborious work. But when the age of 25 is mentioned, it is in connection with going in *"to wait upon the service of the tabernacle of the congregation"* Notice: *"This is it that belongeth unto the Levites: from twenty and five years old and upward they shall go in to wait upon the service of the tabernacle of the congregation"* (Num. 8:24). The wording of this verse is very interesting. Observe the margin of your Bible. *"They shall go in to war the warfare of the service of the tabernacle."* This implies that they were to work vigorously. Doesn't this remind you of Paul's exhortation to Timothy? *"This charge I commit unto thee, son Timothy, according to the prophecies which went before on thee, that thou by them mightest war a good warfare"* (1 Tim. 1:18).

In other words, there was an earnestness to this work. The word means, *"to energize, to work vigorously."* In other words, God demanded wholeheartedness. Solomon declared; *"Whatsoever thy hand findeth to do, do it with thy might"* (Eccl. 9:10). Paul, at the end of his life for God, could truthfully say, *"I have fought a good fight."* He warns Timothy, *"No man that warreth entangleth himself with the affairs of this life; that he may please Him who hath chosen him to be a soldier"* (2 Tim. 2:4). The Levites were certainly not entangled with things outside the court of the tabernacle. No, no! Their undivided attention was with the service of God inside the court, before the door of the tabernacle. What about ourselves? Are we caught up (entangled) with the pursuits and pleasures of this world, or, are we engrossed in the things of God connected with His assembly? The Levites were good "soldiers."

APPRENTICESHIP

At the age of twenty-five years, a Levite would begin his training under a supervisor. He would learn by assisting the priests with the offerings, and any other work connected with the tabernacle court. Then at the age of thirty, the burdens would be heavier, as he would be expected to assist in the taking down, the moving, and the setting up of the tabernacle.

There would be the necessity of fitness for the heavy service of God. Any man seeking to be a craftsman, first needs to learn that craft from an experienced craftsman. This is called "an apprenticeship."

Working part-time in a factory at the age of fourteen, I decided to spend my wages on flying. Now then, do you think that the owner of the aircraft would allow me to take-off and try to fly the plane upon first sight? Hardly! If he had, and I had been fool enough to try it, the end would have been a wrecked aircraft and a dead fourteen-year-old. No, the program was that I sat in the plane and the instructor flew the plane. Each time we went up, he would show me things, and soon he was allowing me to fly the aircraft for short amounts of time. I was learning. Finally, at the age of fifteen he allowed me to fly the plane without him being in it. I was alone. They call that soloing. That was an experience. However, with only a student's license, I was not allowed to take any passenger on board, unless they were a pilot themselves. However, after accumulating a number of flying hours, and reaching the tender age of eighteen, I was allowed to take a test, and upon passing the test, I obtained what is called a "private license." The private license allowed me to take passengers in the aircraft. My days of basic training were over.

You have the same principle with the Levites from the age of 25 to 30. They had five years of training, possibly being instructed by a Levite who had passed the 50-year mark.

PRESENT-DAY HELPERS

Now then, let us apply these truths to ourselves. The Spirit has ordained various services regarding a local testimony. There are pastors, who shepherd the flock. There are also teachers who instruct the flock. Then, there are deacons and deaconesses, who are helpers to the truth. Phebe would fit the description of a true Levite. Notice the commendation that Paul gives this godly woman. *"I commend unto you Phebe our sister, which is a servant of the church which is at Cenchrea: That ye receive her in the Lord, as becometh saints, and that ye assist her in whatsoever business she hath need of you: for she hath been a succourer* (assistant) *of many, and of myself also"* (Rom. 16:1–2). Notice what Paul says of a godly couple. *"Greet Priscilla and Aquila my helpers* (companions in labor) *in Christ Jesus"* (Rom. 16:3). Consider his compliment of a godly, family man. *"The Lord give mercy unto the house of Onesiphorus; for he oft refreshed me, and was not ashamed of my chain"* (2 Tim. 1:16).

ANY HELPERS?

Paul was ever grateful for these godly individuals, for they proved to be a help unto him in his labors for God. Let me ask you, are you a Levite in God's assembly? Perhaps you have not been positioned in a place of responsibility, but nevertheless, you can be a great help to those who are in the place of responsibility. Do you contribute to the work of God in the assembly where you are in fellowship? Paul mentions the gift of *"helps"* (1 Cor. 12:28). What a broad sphere *"helps"* embraces.

Consider these things. The lawn at the hall needs to be cut. Any helpers? The windows need to be washed. Any helpers? The hall needs to be cleaned. Any helpers? The tablecloth used at the Lord's Supper needs to be washed and ironed. Any helpers? The wine has to be purchased and the bread baked. Any helpers? A light or two needs replaced. Any helpers? The snow needs to be removed. Any helpers? An aged saint needs to be transported to the meeting. Any helpers? The utility bills need to be paid. Any helpers? The hall needs repair. Any helpers? Evangelistic meetings are coming and invitations need to be distributed in the surrounding area. Any helpers? The evangelist needs sinners to be influenced and brought to the meetings. Any helpers? A mother is sick and her home and children need attention. Any helpers? Or do we say, "Oh, let John or Jane do it"? The Levites were hardworking helpers! It was like a warfare to them. Are you a Levite in that sense of the word?

THE FIFTIETH YEAR

When the Levites reached their fiftieth year, their laborious work was over. They would still be involved in directing the junior Levites, ministering with their brethren in the tabernacle, and keeping the charge, as guards, to see that no stranger or unclean person drew near to the holy things. They would not be put to any service that would be a fatigue to them. Their very presence would draw forth honor from the younger Levites. They had borne the burden and heat of the day in their younger years. They had earned deep respect from the younger brethren. Is this not as it should be? Honor to whom honor is due. Let us not look lightly upon older saints who have been helps, just because they have become feeble in their old age. God forbid that we should be so callous. May the Lord help us to deeply respect the hoary head that has lived a life for God. *"Thou shalt rise up before the hoary head, and honour the face of the old man, and fear thy God: I am the LORD"* (Lev. 19:32).

THE LEVITE'S SACRIFICE

On this solemn occasion, the Levites were to lay their hands on the heads of the bullocks, one being offered for a sin offering and the other for a burnt offering. This typified the fact that their sins were dealt with and that they were offered unto the LORD, and before the LORD. The Levites laid their hands upon the heads of the bullocks, thus identifying themselves with the sacrifices. In return, the people (probably the princes who represented the people of their tribe) laid their hands upon these men, thus identifying themselves with them, ere they entered the full-time service for God in the tabernacle. In the laying on of the Levite's hands upon the bullock of the burnt offering, he could of well said, "this bullock is going to be consumed upon the altar, all for God, and I too, am laying myself upon the altar as a sacrifice totally for God." Paul takes up this very thought when he exhorted the Roman saints. *"I beseech you therefore, brethren, by the mercies of God, that ye present your bodies a living sacrifice, holy, acceptable unto God, which is your reasonable service"* (Rom. 12:1).

Thus, the Levites were waved before the Lord for an offering of the children of Israel, that they might execute the service of the LORD. The closing verse of this interesting chapter states that the older Levites *"shall minister with their brethren in the tabernacle of the congregation, to keep the charge, and shall do no service. Thus shalt thou do unto the Levites touching their charge"* (Num. 8:26). Doing no service means that they would be exempt from the heavy work of transporting the tabernacle, but would still function about the altar, ministering with their brethren. Isn't it beautiful to see a saint, nearing the end of their sojourn down here, still useful for God, still in fellowship with his brethren, and keeping the charge, that is, guarding the sacred truths of God? May the good Lord help us all, and give us the needed grace to finish our course well.

21

THE PASSOVER & THE CLOUD

NUMBERS 9

Israel had been given the instructions concerning the Passover while they were still in Egypt. One year has passed by and we are introduced to this same ordinance again. The question arises, why? A careful reading of this chapter will reveal to us the answer, and that is what we wish, at this point, to expose to you. Notice that from verses nine to fourteen, we are given a supplement to this most important feast. Three questions arise that had never been considered before. We shall consider these later on in this chapter, but first, let us consider the Passover itself.

The design of God in instituting this unique ordinance was for various reasons. Perhaps the most important reason would be to show us that the method of salvation could only be accomplished through the blood of the Lamb. Remember Paul's exclamation: *"Even Christ our Passover is sacrificed for us"* (1 Cor. 5:7). It would also impress the Jewish nation that God required the death and the blood of a lamb for its redemption. To Israel, this was a most important event, and headed the list of the seven feasts of Jehovah that God expected His people to observe (Lev. 23).

It would seem from the injunction in Exodus 12:24–25, that Israel might have concluded that they were not to keep the Passover until they reached the land of Canaan. However, considering the fact that the anniversary of the Feast occurred while they were still in the desert of Sinai, a special command is given to them to keep it. Had it not been for their unbelief at Kadesh, they probably would have been in the promised land to celebrate their third Passover, but that was not the case. They were doomed on that occasion to wander in the wilderness for thirty-eight more years before claiming their inheritance.

PASSOVER – LORD'S SUPPER

How closely the Passover is connected with the sacrifice of our Lord, Who is the Lamb of God. In some aspects, it can also be associated with the Lord's Supper. Considering these two aspects, we have some very interesting things in this chapter that are so often read with no gleanings. Let us move slowly over these fourteen verses with our spiritual plow, and uncover a few gems that lie underneath the surface.

CHRIST THE LAMB

First, consider the fact that the Passover involved not a ram or a bullock, but a lamb. Why? Simply because this feast prefigures Christ Who was announced on Jordan's banks, as the Lamb of God. A lamb is meek and innocent. The Lord informs us of His Lamb-like character. *"I am meek and lowly in heart"* (Matt. 11:29). Isaiah writes of Him as a Lamb (Isa. 53:7). Peter has the same theme (1 Pet. 1:19). John wrote five books, and in the first and the last of these five he speaks of Christ as the Lamb (John 1:29; Rev. 5:6).

The lamb was to be chosen from the flock. Israel was God's flock, and out of that flock, Jesus, the Lamb of God was chosen. Peter gives thought to this, stating; *"A Prophet shall the Lord your God raise up unto you of your brethren, like unto me; Him shall ye hear in all things whatsoever He shall say unto you"* (Acts 3:22). Yes, He was even foreordained before the foundation of the world! (1 Pet. 1:20). What a tremendous statement!

The lamb was to be a male of the first year. It was in the prime of His days that He ministered, suffered at the hands of men, and then finally on the Cross, suffered at the hand of His God.

The Lamb was to be without blemish. Christ was the only Man Who ever walked on earth, Who never sinned, neither could He sin. John, Paul, and Peter all attest to this tremendous fact through the divine inspiration of the Holy Spirit. He was the true Lamb, without blemish and without spot (1 Pet. 1:19).

Next, we consider the fact that the lamb was to be slain. Compare this with Revelation 5:12, where our blessed Lord is heralded as the Lamb that was slain, worthy to *"receive power, and riches, and wisdom, and strength, and honour, and glory, and blessing."*

The slaying of the lamb took place before the whole assembly (Ex. 12:6). Regarding the slaying of Christ, Paul reminded Agrippa; *"This thing was not done in a corner"* (Acts 26:26). What busier time could there have been for the nation of Israel than at the Passover? Jews were present from numerous nations to celebrate their feast, and that is exactly when our Lord, the true Passover, was sacrificed for us. Amazing, isn't it?

Israel's Passover lamb was set aside four days before it was to be slain (Ex. 12:3, 6). It is apparent through a close examination of all four gospels that Christ entered the city of Jerusalem four days before His crucifixion. Also, His total ministry, proving His Messiahship, lasted three and one-half years, which according to Jewish reckoning would be termed four years.

The blood of Israel's Passover was sprinkled. The blood of Christ is spoken of as being sprinkled. *"To Jesus the Mediator of the new covenant, and to the blood of sprinkling, that speaketh better things than that of Abel"* (Heb. 12:24). *"Elect according to the foreknowledge of God the Father, through sanctification of the Spirit, unto obedience and sprinkling of the blood of Jesus Christ"* (1 Pet. 1:2).

The Passover Lamb's blood was to be applied to the lintel and the two side posts, but not on the doorstep. In like manner, the blood of Christ is not to be trodden under foot (Heb. 10:29).

The applied blood proved to be a refuge for the firstborn, and in like manner, the blood of Christ applied to the soul by faith, proves to be an everlasting shelter for the sinner, from the coming storm of God's eternal wrath.

The lamb was to be roast with fire, indicating the severe sufferings of our blessed Lord under the fires of God's unmitigated wrath.

No bone of the lamb was to be broken in their eating of the Passover. It is amazing that there are over twenty five bones in the foot and hand of a human being, yet when they nailed the Lamb of God to the tree, not one of them was broken. In fact, God would not allow the cruel Roman soldiers to break His legs to hasten His death on the Cross, for He was dead already, prior to them coming to perform this cruel deed. Scripture had previously stated; *"He keepeth all His bones: not one of them is broken"* (Ps. 34:20). John writes of this as being a fulfillment of the Scripture (John 19:36). Wondrous indeed!

The lamb was to be eaten in haste, with their staff in their hand, and a readiness to quickly leave Egypt, indicating the pilgrim character that would be theirs. We too, are to be pilgrims and strangers in a world that crucified our Lord, and we should be feasting on Christ the Lamb, ready for the glory at His call.

As Israel ate the Lamb accompanied with bitter herbs, even so, as we feast on our blessed Lord, the fire burns within and we realize more fully the bitterness of our sin which called for His sacrifice for us.

Their loins were to be girded and shoes on their feet as they partook of the roasted lamb. Ah brethren, are your loins girded? If not, then; *"let your loins be girded about, and your lights burning; And ye yourselves like unto men that wait for their Lord, when He will return from the wedding; that when He cometh and knocketh, they may open unto Him immediately"* (Luke 12:36). Let us also gird up the loins of our mind, be sober, and hope to the end for the grace that is to be brought unto us at the revelation of Jesus Christ. (1 Pet. 1:13). Our feet are shod with the freedom happiness that comes only by being associated with Christ.

Just as the Passover was eaten with unleavened bread, so we, the saints of God, should live a life of purity and unfeigned sincerity (1 Cor. 5:7–8).

In the light of all these parallel thoughts, who would dare to say that Israel's Passover gave no indication of Christ and His people today? To do so would be ludicrous. As an old saying goes: "The New is in the Old concealed. The Old is in the New revealed." Yes! *"Whatsoever things were written aforetime were written for our learning"* (Rom. 15:4).

A PASSOVER PROBLEM

We now come to a problem connected with keeping the Passover. We find certain men who had been defiled by the dead body of a man, consequently, they could not keep the Passover on the divinely appointed day. *"And those men said unto him (Moses), 'We are defiled by the dead body of a man: wherefore are we kept back, that we may not offer an offering of the LORD in His appointed season among the children of Israel?'"* (Num. 9:7). It was very evident that these men were sincere. They saw the importance of keeping the feast, yet realized that they would be prohibited because of their condition. So, humbly, they made inquiry unto Moses as to what to do. Did you ever wonder who these men might have been? I am not prepared to say for to do so would be pure conjecture. However, I do know that Mishael and Elizaphan, cousins of Nadab and Abihu were called upon to bury their cousins after the LORD slew them (Lev. 10:1–5). Consequently, at the time we are considering, they would have been defiled.

The question of these men to Moses, *"why are we kept back,"* infers, that prior to this, there had been no express command that such should not partake of the Passover. This injunction came upon them suddenly, and they were sincerely concerned. They didn't become hostile and insulting. Ah no, they were sincere and humble men, simply wanting to know what to do. They came to their leader seeing advice.

Let us relate to this regarding our day. Are we willing to take the humble place, and in all sincerity, seek the advice of leaders in the assembly? When you have a problem, are you humble enough to go to an elder seeking a solution? Would you believe that some Christians have been known to run to a secular psychiatrist for help? What possible help could you receive from a man who desperately needs help himself? The secular psychiatrist is in direct competition with the Bible. He claims the Bible to be just mere literature, and that he, not the Bible, has the right solution regarding emotions, feelings, attitudes, human relationships, outlooks, and values. The ungodly, atheistic, and immoral, Sigmund Freud, was the founder of psychoanalysis and modern psychiatry. Avoid such counselors, especially those who claim to be Christian psychologists.[65] *"Blessed is the man that walketh not in the counsel of the ungodly, nor standeth in the way of sinners, nor sitteth in the seat of the scornful. But his*

---

[65] The definition "Christian psychology" is a misnomer! "Psychology is, in fact, a rival religion with its own anti-Christian gospel which offers an unbiblical diagnosis and godless cure for the human condition. One of Freud's most powerful motives in life was to inflict vengeance on Christianity. Whether a psychiatrist or psychologist is a Christian or an atheist, he must have passed the same exams and met the same standards in order to be licensed by the state. The simple truth is that no such thing as Christian psychology exists. There are no such listings ("Christian Psychology") in the index of any psychology textbook. At a professional gathering of psychologists, two Christian psychologists stated, with the agreement of the listeners: 'there is no acceptable Christian psychology that is markedly different from non-Christian psychology.'" Quoted from Dave Hunt's book Occult Invasion. Harvest House Publishers, Eugene, Oregon. P. 457, 458. Jacob, Joseph, Job, Daniel, and Paul, had far more severe trials than any of us. What psychiatrist did they consult? Or, were God and His Word sufficient? Psychiatry promotes humanism, and is basically EVIL!

delight is in the law of the LORD; and in His law doth he meditate day and night" (Ps. 1:1–2). The soul that seeks the Holy Scriptures will find the solution to any problem that he may encounter in his whole lifetime. As the rest of the Psalm assures us, he will never wither, but instead, he will prosper.

Elders should be well acquainted with their Bibles, so that when a sheep has a problem, they will have the scriptural answer for them. Now let me say this, so that you will not misunderstand me. There are Christian counselors that can be a tremendous help to Christians with a mental problem. Are they are employed in Sigmund Freud's theology? No! No! They are Christians who do not use secular psychology as their way of operating. They do not take the approach that man is basically good and the answer to his problems lies within himself. They do not believe in humanism which teaching rejects the authority of the Bible. "Biblical counselors are opposed to psychotherapists, and see the Bible alone as the source of a comprehensive and detailed approach to understanding and counseling people." Any Christian counselor that promotes the need for self-esteem, for love and acceptance, and teaches that if these needs be met, that the afflicted person will be happy, has missed the mark. That is a humanistic approach employed by secular psychologists. The Scripture is very plain on that subject. It teaches that it is God, not ourselves, who changes our desires and that true happiness can only be found in the desire for God and godliness.

Today I read a rather noteworthy phrase coined for Christians.

"Give God your HEART
and He'll comb the kinks out of your HEAD.
(THE HOLY BIBLE)
When all else fails, read the instructions!"

"Be careful for nothing; but in every thing by prayer and supplication with thanksgiving let your requests be made known unto God. And the peace of God, which passeth all understanding, shall keep your hearts and minds through Christ Jesus" (Phil. 4:7).

Let me ask you. Is this true or not? Now the Bible tells us to *"be careful for nothing,"* that is, *over anxious.* Is the way to accomplish this, to run to a psychiatrist? Is that what God says? Most certainly not! So what is the Christian to do in order to live a life with no undue anxiety? Well now, the answer is right next-door. *"But in everything by prayer and supplication, with thanksgiving, let your requests be made known unto God."* There's your answer. There's the divine solution to mental problems. What happens then, when the soul does what God instructs? Why again we have the answer right next-door. *"And the peace of God, which passeth all understanding, shall keep your hearts and minds through Christ Jesus."* What is so complicated about that? *"The peace of God."* What is that? Albert Barnes says: "The peace here particularly referred to is that which is felt when we have no anxious care about the supply of our wants, and when we go confidently and commit everything into the hands of God." *"Thou wilt keep him in perfect peace whose mind is stayed on Thee"* (Isa. 26:3). The Lord Jesus said: *"Peace I leave with you, My peace I give unto you: not as the world giveth, give I unto you. Let not your heart be troubled, neither let it be afraid"* (John 14:27). Matthew Henry states that "the peace of God will keep us from sinning under our troubles, and from sinking under them; keep us calm and sedate, without discomposure of passion, and with inward satisfaction."

Now then, just how does a Christian get his mind stayed (*"to lean upon or take hold"*) upon Jehovah? How does a troubled soul accomplish this? The answer is simple, he gets on his knees, and lifts his troubled heart in prayer and supplication, and the result will be that the peace of God will flood his soul. You may say, "Oh yes, that's very easy for you to say, but there must be more to it than that!" Yes, perhaps there is more than that. If there has been sin, or inconsistencies in the life, they must be confessed. If there has been a failure to face one's responsibilities, that must be confessed. There must be the attitude that the psalmist manifested when he wrote: *"Search me, O God, and know my heart: try me, and know my thoughts: And see if there be any wicked way in me, and lead me in the way everlasting"* (Ps. 139:23–24).

There is one more guarantee that is good to grasp, namely: *"For God hath not given us the spirit of fear; but of power, and of love, and of a sound* (disciplined) *mind"* (2 Tim. 1:7). Let us thank God daily for the tremendous privileges and faculties that God has imparted to us. Let us keep short accounts with Him by prayer and supplication, lest, by neglect, we fall into the slough of discouragement and despair.

We admittingly have somewhat deviated from our subject, nevertheless, I felt it a burden to warn my fellow believers of mere man's solution to our problems, and how they are in contrast to God's solution.

I also want you to know, that I do believe that there are some people possessed mental problems, due to a chemical imbalance in their body. If that is the case, then medical assistance should certainly be sought.

MOSES SEEKS GOD

Notice the attitude of Moses when he was confronted with this problem. *"And Moses said unto them, 'Stand still, and I will hear what the LORD will command concerning you'"* (Num. 9:8). Isn't that beautiful? He didn't get all flustered and make out like he knew more than he did. Ah no, that's the behavior of a godly man. He just admitted that he didn't have the answer. He wasn't ashamed to expose his ignorance. Beware of the man who manifests flippant, self-confidence, and pretends to have knowledge that he does not possess.

However, he knew that God had the answer, and he was humble enough to take time out to seek the face of God about it. It is hard for the flesh to stand still, but God's people are called upon to stand still on various occasions and for various reasons. On this occasion, it was to find out the mind of God. How often unforeseen problems arise in an assembly! The elders have no definite, *"thus saith the Lord."* What are they to do? The answer is found in a number of Scriptures, of which we quote only three. *"If any of you lack wisdom, let him ask of God, that giveth to all men liberally, and upbraideth not; and it shall be given him"* (Jas. 1:5). *"Let us therefore come boldly unto the throne of grace, that we may obtain mercy, and find grace to help in time of need"* (Heb. 4:16). *"And I say unto you, ask, and it shall be given you; seek, and ye shall find; knock, and it shall be opened unto you"* (Luke 11:9). Are we willing to stand still? Are we willing to wait on the Lord? Are we willing to make the matter one of earnest and constant prayer? Those who submit to these conditions, invariably find from God, the solution to the problem.

Moses waited upon God, and received an answer. That expression, *"and the LORD spake unto Moses,"* is found 99 times in your Bible! Thus, the Lord made provision for the defiled men by stating that they could keep the Passover the same day on the following month. The men in question had no way that they could avoid their ceremonial defilement. In fact, it was only right that they bury their dead, yet in doing so, they were automatically shut out from participating in that which God commanded, even the Passover. Theirs was an unavoidable situation, yet how gracious was the LORD in providing a way for such persons to partake of the Passover. Even those, due to unforeseen and unavoidable circumstances, who would be on a journey afar off (no less than fifteen miles), were given the same provision by God.

It is interesting to note that in Hezekiah's day, the king availed himself of this gracious provision. On the due date, the priests had not sanctified themselves sufficiently, nor had the people gathered themselves together to Jerusalem. Consequently, God allowed them to hold the Passover one month later (2 Chron. 30:2–3).

INTRICATE DIRECTIONS

Have you noticed that when it comes to the Passover being kept one month later due to human problems, that the directions for its keeping are far more intricate than the directions for the keeping of the Passover on its regular appointed time? A comparison of Numbers 9:3, and 9:11–12, will confirm this. What is the lesson in this for us? Simply this, that just because of the failure and weakness of the Lord's people, we are never to lower the divine standard originally set by God. In fact, even though we may be living in days of failure and even departure, we are called upon to maintain the divine standard. The faith (the pattern) has once for all been delivered unto us, and we are enjoined to earnestly contend for it (Jude 1:3).

THOSE WHO FORBEARED

However, there was a third class of men that God would not tolerate. *"But the man that is clean, and is not in a journey, and forbeareth to keep the Passover, even the same soul shall be cut off from among his people: because he brought not the offering of the LORD in his appointed season, that man shall bear his sin"* (Num. 9:13). One can readily see the extreme importance of keeping the Passover simply by noticing the threat imposed for not keeping it if at all possible. A flagrant disobedience to God's command drew forth the punishment of Jehovah.

KEEPING THE LORD'S SUPPER

Let me impose this thought before going further. I believe that there is a definite connection with the observation of the Passover in Old Testament times, and the keeping of the Lord's Supper in New Testament days. In fact, the connection is very obvious indeed! The Passover was a *type* of the death of Christ, while the Lord's Supper is a *memorial* of the death of Christ. The one pointed to a future event at Calvary, the second pointed back to a past event at Calvary. The Passover was a memorial of Israel's tremendous deliverance from the bondage of Egypt. The Lord's supper is a memorial of our deliverance from the tremendous bondage of sin and Satan. You would hardly find a godly Israelite that would not be very conscious to observe the Passover, without fail. In like manner, every godly Christian will be very exercised to faithfully keep the Lord's Supper on the first day of every week (Acts 20:7). He will be very careful to keep it according to the divine pattern given so plainly in 1 Corinthians chapters 10 and 11. As the Scripture teaches, all will partake of one cup of the fruit of the vine. In like manner, one loaf of bread shall be broken and partaken of by all those who are present in the fellowship. The sister's long hair will be a veil, which will be covered with her self-provided veil. This holy activity will declare His death to the Father, and will be done in remembrance of their blessed Lord, Who died for their sins.

It has been stated, without much thought, that all the assembly meetings are equally important. If you are thinking that way, let me ask you just one question. If the doctor restricted your activity to the extent that you were only allowed to leave your home for an assembly meeting once a week, which meeting would you choose to attend, the gospel meeting; the prayer meeting; the Bible reading; or the Lord's Supper? If you answer the question truthfully, you will agree with me, that no meeting surpasses the Lord's Supper in importance. It is the greatest of all assembly gatherings. May we ever treasure it. May the Lord preserve us from ever degrading to the state that we would willfully absent ourselves from such a paramount meeting.

DEFILED BY THE DEAD

As for people defiled by the dead, and those on a journey, I look at it simply this way. Sometimes there are unforeseen things that come into our lives that may hinder us from partaking of the supper at the appointed time. Some men on shift-work are required to work on some Lord's Day mornings. Others may find themselves unable to drive to the gathering because of severe weather conditions. Others may be hindered because of sickness. However, having missed the supper for any legitimate reason, God gladly receives them on the next appointed day, and that day is the first day of the week. However, one who willfully stays away, without any legitimate excuse, should be questioned by the elders as to his wayward activity.

Such people are wandering sheep, or sick sheep, in need of spiritual counsel.

Finally, the stranger is considered. *"And if a stranger shall sojourn among you, and will keep the Passover unto the LORD; according to the ordinance of the Passover, and according to the manner thereof, so shall he do: ye shall have one ordinance, both for the stranger, and for him"* (Num. 9:14). Let us relate this to New Testament times. Remember how the Hebrews were exhorted? *"Be not forgetful to entertain strangers"* (Heb. 13:2). The context is that in those days of persecution, many Jewish brethren had to flee their homes, leaving their villages to seek refuge elsewhere. When such came to the door of another Christian, that person was enjoined to take them in and help them. Christian love and hospitality was to be manifested. Now then, let us establish the fact that the word strangers regarding the Passover, could apply, in our day, to traveling saints stopping for a visit. So, on Lord's Day morning they appear at the door of the hall. Are they fit to partake of the Lord's Supper? Perhaps so, perhaps not. In Israel's day, the stranger was allowed to keep the Passover, but only under certain conditions. He was allowed only according to the ordinance of the Passover and according to the manner thereof. What was the ordinance, and what was the manner? The ordinance was the custom, and the decree was the judicial verdict. Those who partook of the Passover must conform to the divine standard laid down at its institution in Exodus 12. In other words, that stranger would have to meet certain requirements before he could ever partake of the Passover, and he would be expected to keep it in the appointed way. No deviation was allowed. The ordinance was the same, whether the person was born in the land, or whether he was born elsewhere. The standard was inflexible. No allowances were made.

SAVED VISITOR'S

So, lo and behold, one Lord's Day morning a family presents themselves at the entrance of the meeting hall. The assembly saints are seated in a circle. Can they partake of the Lord's

Supper? That depends. They say that they are born-again believers, but no one knows them. They are unlearned in divine truths relative to a local assembly. Consequently, they are given the *"room of the unlearned,"* a place scripturally provided outside of the circle of believers in fellowship (1 Cor. 14:16). Usually, this is a group of seats in back of the circle. This is so they can observe the assembly carrying out the Lord's Supper. In other words, they don't measure up to the criteria of believers who have taken their position with the Lord, outside the camp of Christendom. On the other hand, another company of strangers appear at the meeting on Lord's Day morning, and they have a letter of commendation from another scriptural assembly, commending them to the care of the assembly that they have come to visit. Their letter is signed by responsible elders from the assembly in which they are in fellowship. Immediately, the receiving brethren have confidence in those strangers and they are received into the fellowship and the privileges of that assembly as long as they visit. They possessed a "letter of commendation," which declared their acceptable status (2 Cor. 3:1).

UNSAVED VISITORS

Then, another party arrives at the gathering. They know nothing of salvation. They are still in their sins. Consequently, they are graciously informed that they can sit in the back and observe the assembly function in the breaking of the bread. If they agree, then they are led to the room of the unbeliever, which is seats provided in the back of the circle. Consequently, we have four classifications of people in the gathering: (1) Those born again, living in the locality, that have taken their place outside the camp unto Himself. (2) Visiting saints, who having presented a letter of commendation, are welcomed into the fellowship of the assembly they are visiting. (3) Believers who do not recognize divine requirements and truths because of ignorance. They consider God's assembly just "another church." (4) Those who are still in sins darkness, but out of curiosity, have come to see what was going on. The first two groups partake of the Supper, and the last two groups simply observe. Like the Passover, the Supper is kept according to the manner and the ordinance thereof.

What happens after the Lord's Supper is over? If there is a Bible reading, or a ministry meeting, all are given a hearty welcome to stay. Finally, when the meetings are over, whether a visitor with a letter, or an unlearned saint, or an unbeliever, all should be shown hospitality and given an invitation to the homes of the local believers in that particular assembly to enjoy a meal. Christians are to do good unto all men, especially to those who are of the household of faith (Gal. 6:10). In doing so, we are letting our light shine.

ACTIVITY OF THE CLOUD

Having considered the Passover and its possible problems, the Spirit then directed Moses to record the activity of the cloud. This cloud was not a mere atmospheric cloud, but rather a supernatural one created by the LORD for a specific purpose. This cloud, as we have already observed, was not only a protection to the nation day and night, but it was also the visible sign and symbol of God's presence with Israel. Not only this, it was their guide through the wilderness as they journeyed (and wandered) on to the promised land. There is no doubt in my mind that other nations recognized the cloudy pillar as something supernatural, and this alone would put the nations in fear of God's journeying people. It was a phenomena that was far from being a secret, for it hovered over a nation of over two million people for forty years.

Matthew Henry points out, "that which appeared as a cloud by day appeared as a fire all night. Had it been a cloud only, it would not have been visible by night; and, had it been a fire only, it would have been scarcely discernible by day; but God would give them sensible demonstrations of the constancy of His presence with them, and His care of them, and that He *kept them night and day."*[66] One naturally is reminded of the LORD'S promise to Israel in Psalm 121.

> *"He will not suffer thy foot to be moved: He that keepeth thee will not slumber. Behold, He that keepeth Israel shall neither slumber nor sleep. The LORD is thy keeper: the LORD is thy shade upon thy right hand. The sun shall not smite thee by day, nor the moon by night. The LORD shall preserve thee from all evil: He shall preserve thy soul. The LORD shall preserve thy going out and thy coming in from this time forth, and even for evermore."*

It is wonderful to see the consideration and grace of Jehovah, assuring His people of His constant guidance and protection for them before they began their journey into the vast wilderness from Sinai. However, obedience was required in order to be thus guided and protected by the LORD, for no matter how comfortably they were encamped at any given place, whether the cloud moved by day or by night, they were required to immediately break up camp and follow it. Those keeping the charge (guarding) at the tabernacle door, would be appointed to stand as sentinels day and night to sound the alarm to move. Of course, for the nation, there would be a constant uncertainty as to their lodging. They would be in constant readiness to march with very short warning – always ready to move at the commandment of the LORD.

> *"At the commandment of the LORD the children of Israel journeyed, and at the commandment of the LORD they pitched* ("abode, rested"): *as long as the cloud abode upon the tabernacle they rested in their tents"* (Num. 9:18).

So great was this miracle, that it remained in the minds of God's people. The Psalmist relates to it with these inspired words:

---

[66] Matthew Henry's Commentary on the whole Bible, World Bible Publishers, Iowa Falls, Iowa. P. 600

"He spread a cloud for a covering; and fire to give light in the night" (Ps. 105:39). Moving on to the days when those of the captivity had returned to their land, the cloud was brought to their remembrance, through the voice of the Levites, saying: *"Yet Thou in thy manifold mercies forsookest them not in the wilderness: the pillar of the cloud departed not from them by day, to lead them in the way; neither the pillar of fire by night, to shew them light, and the way wherein they should go"* (Neh. 9:19). The prophet Isaiah wrote of it, linking the cloud to the Spirit. *"As a beast goeth down into the valley, the Spirit of the LORD caused him to rest: so didst Thou lead Thy people, to make Thyself a glorious name"* (Isa. 63:14).

God's redeemed people are a guided people. The psalmists had this assurance, declaring; *"Thou shalt guide me with Thy counsel, and afterward receive me to glory"* (Ps. 73:24). *"For this God is our God for ever and ever: He will be our guide even unto death"* (Ps. 48:14).

THE HOLY SPIRIT

Now then, I believe that we have successfully established the fact that Israel's cloudy pillar is a symbol of the Holy Spirit of God and His impressions upon God's people in the Church age. Paul is quick to relate, *"If any man have not the Spirit of Christ, he is none of His"* (Rom. 8:9). Now that is a very plain fact. Every child of God is indwelt by the Holy Spirit. You will remember his words to the Ephesian believers. *"In Whom ye also trusted, after that ye heard the word of truth, the gospel of your salvation: in Whom also after that ye believed, ye were sealed with that Holy Spirit of promise"* (Eph. 1:13). The words, *"after that ye believed,"* could be more correctly translated, *"upon believing,"* as they are in the aorist participle. Mr. Newberry translates it, *"having believed."* Thus we see that there is no "waiting period" for the Spirit to enter the person that has trusted Christ. When Israel commenced their journey, the pillar of the cloud was there to direct and protect them. The moment we trusted Christ, the Holy Spirit took up residence within us to protect and to guide us on our journey as pilgrims and strangers. Isn't this wonderful? Isn't this tremendous? Just to think, that you are indwelt with divine power that no power of darkness can withstand! Do you understand this? Do you really appreciate it? Are you reveling in the fact that you have a guiding light on your journey home to heaven that no unconverted mortal has ever experienced? Christ is *"unto us wisdom"* (1 Cor. 1:30). We have an inherent wisdom that the world does not possess. Are you aware of this? "Well," you may say, "I have made some awful blunders in my life, how can this be?" The answer is very simple my erring one. You have neglected to totally submit yourself to the promptings of the Holy Spirit. You have acted on your own impulses, or perhaps your own so-called wisdom. You have failed to stand still and wait on God. That is your problem, consequently, you have made large blunders in your life. What else could you expect?

DIVINE GUIDANCE

Now then, Paul speaks of being led by the Spirit of God, just as Israel was led by the cloud. *"For as many as are led by the Spirit of God, they are the sons of God"* (Rom. 8:14). Solomon acknowledged the sanity of such behavior, stating; *"In all thy ways acknowledge Him, and He shall direct thy paths"* (Prov. 3:6). Notice! God must be acknowledged! That is, as we read His Word and He speaks to us, we must obey what He says. We cannot afford to turn to our own way, for if we do, we certainly cannot expect to receive the wisdom that is from above, neither can we expect to be divinely guided by Him. It is in this very area where some saints go astray, and end up with severe problems that could have been avoided if they had only waited on the guidance of the Holy Spirit.

Let me illustrate divine guidance in Paul's labors. Do you think that he marched into any area of his own volition? If you think that, you are seriously wrong. Consider this mighty servant of God on his second, and most extensive, missionary journey. Having completed their mission in Phrygia and the region of Galatia, they were forbidden of the Holy Ghost to preach in Asia. So on they went and coming to Mysia they assayed to go into Bithynia, but the Spirit suffered them not. From Mysia, they landed at Troas, 400 miles to the west. As this mighty man of God stands on the shores of the Aegean Sea at Troas, he waits on God to know where and when the Lord would have him go.

Now such a situation can be very vexing to an impatient man, especially if he is not in close fellowship with God. So, I have the right to say that Paul was not vexed at all. He was quite willing to "stand still" to obtain divine directions. One night while in Troas, God revealed His mind to Paul, telling him where to preach the gospel. *"Assuredly gathering,"* means that Paul wove the threads together. He weighed everything in the light of the divine sanctuary, and received the assurance that he was to enter Europe, a continent that had never yet heard the gospel. Remember this, that just a few days prior to this, he did not have a clue where he was going to be in a couple of weeks, but the Spirit knew, and Paul, being very conscious of the Spirit's leading, was guided to the right place at the right time. The "cloud" moved, and he journeyed. The "cloud" rested, and he stopped.

EVANGELISTIC WORK

In evangelistic work, it is very hard at times to know the mind of the Spirit relative to movement. Evangelists, led by the Spirit, arrive at a location to preach the word. This is all well and good. However, when do they quit? That is the paramount question, and a cause of great exercise in prayer by the men that seek to be guided by the Holy Spirit. *"The steps of a good man are ordered (prepared or established) by the LORD: and He delighteth in His way"* (Ps. 37:23). God takes delight in His servants whose steps follow the ordering of the Lord.

TEACHERS GUIDED

How delightful to see the guidance and promptings of the Spirit at a conference. Gifted men with different personalities and also different messages from God, rising one by one, under the supervision of the Holy Spirit, to deliver their message, whether it takes them fifteen minutes or fifty minutes to project that which they have received of the Lord for that particular occasion. Christendom, on the other hand, has become a mechanical organization. When the cloudy pillar moved, Israel moved. When the cloudy pillar rested, Israel rested. What a lesson for us today!

22

THE TWO TRUMPETS OF SILVER

NUMBERS 10

"And the LORD spake unto Moses, saying, make thee two trumpets of silver; of a whole piece shalt thou make them: that thou mayest use them for the calling of the assembly, and for the journeying of the camps. And when they shall blow with them, all the assembly shall assemble themselves to thee at the door of the tabernacle of the congregation. And if they blow but with one trumpet, then the princes, which are heads of the thousands of Israel, shall gather themselves unto thee. When ye blow an alarm, then the camps that lie on the east parts shall go forward. When ye blow an alarm the second time, then the camps that lie on the south side shall take their journey: they shall blow an alarm for their journeys. But when the congregation is to be gathered together, ye shall blow, but ye shall not sound an alarm. And the sons of Aaron, the priests, shall blow with the trumpets; and they shall be to you for an ordinance for ever throughout your generations. And if ye go to war in your land against the enemy that oppresseth you, then ye shall blow an alarm with the trumpets; and ye shall be remembered before the LORD your God, and ye shall be saved from your enemies. Also in the day of your gladness, and in your

solemn days, and in the beginnings of your months, ye shall blow with the trumpets over your burnt offerings, and over the sacrifices of your peace offerings; that they may be to you for a memorial before your God: I am the LORD your God" (Num. 10:10).

Before their march from Sinai, one more thing was needed, namely instructions regarding the signals to be given to commence various operations. To produce the various signals, two silver trumpets were ordained of the LORD. A careful reading of Numbers 10 will reveal the various occasions when the nation would hear the sound. The blowing of the trumpets was a priestly work. They were to make known to the children of Israel what the LORD was calling upon them to do. God would not have the nation in ignorance as to His mind. He would guide them through their eyes in the moving of the cloud, and He would guide them through their ears with the blowing of the trumpets. There would be no excuse for not knowing the mind of the LORD. We may say the same today regarding the knowledge of God's mind. There is no excuse for ignorance, for we have a complete, divine revelation from the LORD, given to us in the Holy Scriptures. Besides this, if you are in a scriptural and healthy assembly, there are men called of God in that assembly to declare to you the mind of the LORD. This is conveyed through the public ministry of the word, or through Bible readings.

The blowing of the trumpets shows us the all-sufficiency of God for guidance. There was the blowing of both trumpets for the calling of the whole assembly to assemble at the door of the tabernacle of the congregation. Then, there was the blowing of only one trumpet for the gathering of the princes. Following this, there was the dual blowing of an alarm for the marching of the people. This alarm would be sounded as soon as the priests saw the pillar of the cloud begin to move from its resting place over the tabernacle. Following this, there was an alarm to be blown when they were to go to war against their enemies. Finally, instructions were given to blow with the trumpets over their burnt offerings on the days of their gladness and solemn feasts, that they may be for a memorial before their God.

THE FIRST TRUMPET

Consider the first trumpets blown to gather God's people to God's dwelling place. Could we not apply this to the announcing of the meetings of the assembly to the saints gathered together on Lord's Day? After the breaking of the bread, the announcement is made concerning the remainder of the meetings for that day and for the meetings following on various nights of that week. Thus, the Lord's people, or any strangers present, are reminded and made aware of the various gatherings of that assembly.

THE SECOND TRUMPET

The next sound was different. Only one trumpet was to sound. Upon hearing that sound, the princes of Israel would make their way to the tabernacle. Today, announcements are made regarding the meeting of the elders of the assembly. Those meetings would be to discus various problems related to the assembly, or perhaps to discuss the handling of coming events connected with the testimony. The meeting of the elders should not be a spontaneous, or haphazard sort of thing. No, that will never do! The meeting of elders is a pre-planned event, not just something tagged on to a prayer meeting, or after a gospel meeting. An orderly way is for the elders to set aside a designated time on a regular basis to meet together to discuss assembly affairs and problems. Such gatherings should be opened with earnest prayer, seeking the mind and the help of God for the solemn occasion.

Such meetings need not necessarily be in the confines of a hall. It could be in a home. Remember how Paul called for the elders of the Ephesian assembly, who upon hearing "the trumpet," came from Ephesus to Miletus to confer with him (Acts 20:17). Going back in time, we see the apostles and elders coming together to consider a matter in Jerusalem (Acts 15:6). That meeting would more than likely be in a building where the church met.

THE THIRD TRUMPET

The next trumpets blown were an alarm for the commencement of the march to the next resting place. It could take place at the break of day, at noon, afternoon, supper time, perhaps at midnight, or later on toward the rising of the morning star. They just did not know when the trumpets would sound. But when they did, they must go immediately!

Allow me to introduce a good analogy. Are you waiting for the last trump? Are you living in expectation of the home-call? The marching orders are nearing. *"For the Lord Himself shall descend from heaven with a shout, with the voice of the archangel, and with the trump of God: and the dead in Christ shall rise first: Then we which are alive and remain shall be caught up together with them in the clouds, to meet the Lord in the air: and so shall we ever be with the Lord"* (1 Thess. 4:16–17). *"Behold, I shew you a mystery; We shall not all sleep, but we shall all be changed, in a moment, in the twinkling of an eye, at the last trump: for the trumpet shall sound, and the dead shall be raised incorruptible, and we shall be changed"* (1 Cor. 15:51–52).

The last trump? Yes, but not the last trump in the Bible, for there are some trumpets regarding Israel in the Book of the Revelation. However, as far as we of the Church age are concerned, it will be our final move. That is why it is termed *"the last trump,"* for we on earth will never be moving from here to there again. His coming will climax our earthly sojourn, and we will never wander about again. In a moment, we shall be transported from the dark scenes of this earth into bright glory of the celestial home in heaven. Are you waiting? Are you ready?

After the rapture of the Church, there will be a trumpet sounding for the nation of Israel. The Lord Jesus speaks of this even with these words: *"And He shall send His angels with a great sound of a trumpet, and they shall gather together His elect from the four winds, from one end of heaven to the other"* (Matt. 24:31). That certainly will be a day of ingathering for His earthly people. From the four corners of the earth they will flock back to their homeland, the land given by their God to Abraham. Isaiah relates to this great event with these words: *"And it shall come to pass in that day, that the great trumpet shall be blown, and they shall come which were ready to perish in the land of Assyria, and the outcasts in the land of Egypt, and shall worship the LORD in the holy mount at Jerusalem"* (Isa. 27:13). A small number of Jews are back in the land, but this is very minor compared to what it will be when the trumpet for Israel to move back is blown.

THE FOURTH TRUMPET

The next trumpet was for military purposes. Many reasons have been suggested why the trumpets were blown at this particular time. One is, that such activity would give the Israelites assurance that God Himself was with them, and that this would animate and encourage them as they went out to fight. Another thought is, that the blowing of the trumpets was an appeal to heaven for wisdom in the battle and a prayer for victory, and that God would take notice and engage Himself to fight their battles.

It has been remarked, "Great force is in the sound of instruments of any sort, to stir up both courage and cheerfulness in the hearers of them. But these trumpets were blown to express their dependence upon God, and to inspire their faith in Him. Like the priests with the silver trumpets, the minister of the gospel should encourage Christians to battle against evil, by inciting them to trust in God. He gives the victory. We conquer through Him. 'The God of peace shall bruise Satan under your feet shortly.' 'We are more than conquerors through Him that loved us.' 'Above all taking the shield of faith – fight the good fight of faith.'"[67]

---

67 The Preacher's Homiletic Commentary on Numbers. Baker Books. P.159

I hope that you are aware, that the moment you were saved, you entered a battle, an actual battle against your old nature, the flesh, and the powers of darkness, the devil. Peter was concerned about this and the Spirit has him write: *"Dearly beloved, I beseech you as strangers and pilgrims, abstain from fleshly lusts, which war against the soul"* (1 Pet. 2:11). There's the trumpet! He is warning us against our fleshly lusts. What have they done? Why, they have put on their armor and declared war against us. Upon being "born again" we inherited a new nature. The Spirit of God took up residence within us. The old nature deeply resented being displaced by the new nature, thus he declared war on us. Paul refers to this very thing, using Ishmael and Isaac as an analogy. Ishmael dwelt in Abraham's house for thirteen years as an only son. He received all the attention. However, another child entered that home named Isaac. Ishmael then had to take second place, and this produced a deep resentment in his heart. He hated Isaac. Thus Paul writes: *"But as then he* (Ishmael) *that was born after the flesh persecuted him* (Isaac) *that was born after the Spirit, even so it is now"* (Gal. 4:29). *"For the flesh lusteth against the Spirit, and the Spirit against the flesh: and these are contrary the one to the other: so that ye cannot do the things that ye would"* (Gal. 5:17). This whole subject was dealt with in chapter ten under the subtitle of Amalek. There is no need to expound it more here, except to say, that we have heard the silver trumpet, and have gone forth to war with the flesh. Let us always remember the secret of our victory expressed in few words: *"Walk in the Spirit, and ye shall not fulfil the lust of the flesh"* (Gal. 5:16).

Not only has the Christian gone to war with the flesh, but he has also declared war on the powers of darkness. Putting on the whole armor of God, the saint has invaded the enemy's camp with the sword of the Spirit. Do not think that the devil looks lightly upon this. In the Church's beginning, we see two preeminent traits of the evil one (lying and murder, John 8:44) surfacing very prominently. For one example, *consider "Stephen, a man full of faith and of the Holy Ghost"* (Acts 7:5). There arose certain men of the synagogue who were not able to resist the wisdom and the spirit by which he spake. So what did these men do? Well, the devil was controlling them, so he energized them to induce men (possibly with a bribe) to falsely testify against godly Stephen, saying, *"'We have heard him speak blasphemous words against Moses, and against God.' And they stirred up the people, and the elders, and the scribes, and came upon him, and caught him, and brought him to the council, and set up false witnesses, which said, 'This man ceaseth not to speak blasphemous words against this holy place, and the law'"* (Acts 7:11–13). What was the result of the false charges? They murdered him by stoning (Acts 7:57–60). There you have it! And this perverse activity has been going on ever since, even up to our day. Numberless Christians have been hailed to "kangaroo courts," in numerous nations, falsely accused, then murdered. China, Muslim countries, and certain parts of Africa, abound in these atrocities masterminded by Satan. Many Christians never even see a "kangaroo court," but are just apprehended at random and murdered on the spot.

Our enemy is real. He is full of wisdom, and he is very cunning. The silver trumpet of redemption through Jesus' blood has been sounded. Are you fighting the battle? Have you put on the whole armor of God (Eph. 6:11)? Are you prepared for this great onslaught of wickedness that is pervading the very atmosphere in which you live? In this same epistle, Paul speaks of *"the prince of the power of the air, the spirit that now worketh in the children of disobedience"* (Eph. 2:2). He writes about *"the unfruitful works of darkness,"* that we are to reprove (Eph. 5:11).

Many Christians are living in a "dream world," a world of fantasy. They fail to understand the true nature of *every* unbeliever. True, there are many "fine and moral" people in this world that are not saved, but let us remember, that essentially, every unbeliever is a hater of Christ. He may have a lovely veneer, but deep down inside, he is programmed by a nature that is fallen, a nature that has no true regard for God, His Son, and for the principles of God. If unbelievers were truthful, they would have to confess; *"All we like sheep have gone astray; we have turned every one to his own way"* (Isa. 53:6).

How then is it possible to have fellowship with this class of people? We love them, and we should seek to see them saved, but how can we ever fraternize with them? They are in darkness, and we that are saved are in light. What fellowship hath light with darkness? It cannot be! Yet, I have found professing Christians quite at home in the company of the unsaved. I have beheld Christian men keeping company with an unsaved woman, and vice versa. I have observed Christians joining ungodly organizations, linking themselves with unbelievers for some cause. What is the matter? The problem is, that such Christians are living in a fantasy world, their mind has been alienated from divine principles laid down so plainly in the Holy Scriptures. They have not heeded the silver trumpet. Their hands are active in some "club," or organization, instead of holding the sword of the Spirit. Alas for such, for the Judgment Seat of Christ will reveal a tremendous loss for them. Ah brethren, let us be alert as to our responsibilities. Let us be fully aware of the devil. Let us not be ignorant of his devices. Let us fight the good fight of faith! Let us go forth for His name's sake, into the enemy's camp, in the fear of God, with our gospel witnessing. We are responsible to make men understand their plight. We are held accountable to make known our blessed Lord's name.

> "Cry aloud, spare not, lift up thy voice like a trumpet, and shew My people their transgression, and the house of Jacob their sins" (Isa. 58:1).

May our ears ever be tuned to the battle sound of the silver trumpets! Amen!

THE FIFTH TRUMPET

We have considered the blowing of the trumpets for various occasions, namely: (1) For the calling of the assembly; (2) For the gathering of the princes; (3) For the march to the next resting place; (4) For Israel's military activity; and now finally (5) for a memorial.

> *"Also in the day of your gladness, and in your solemn days, and in the beginnings of your months, ye shall blow with the trumpets over your burnt offerings, and over the sacrifices of your peace offerings; that they may be to you for a memorial before your God: I am the LORD your God"* (Num. 10:10).

Their burnt offerings would indicate their total devotion to God, and their peace offerings would declare their fellowship and joy in the Lord. This was to be publicly declared in the blowing of the trumpets. They were engaging in the service of God with great delight and the sound of the trumpets magnified that wonderful condition of soul, for all to hear.

The trumpet sound was also for a memorial that the LORD would remember them for good, and would accept and bless them. Always remember, that when we take pleasure in our spiritual exercises, God, in return, takes pleasure in us. Charles Wesley said, "Holy work should be done with holy joy."

Let me ask you, when you sit at the Lord's Supper, are you there out of duty, or out of extreme pleasure and joy? Those who sit at the Supper just because they are supposed to be there, bring no joy to the heart of God. This business of serving God because He demands it will never do. What a dry affair that could be! God hates formalism, and "dutyism."

CHRIST'S PLAINNESS

I wonder if we have people in God's assemblies just because their mother and father are there? They have made their wee profession, and from the first day of supposed conversion, they have simply been going through the motions. What a sad affair indeed. There were people like that in Jerusalem called scribes and Pharisees. Christ saw through their hypocrisy and cried out against them saying; *"Well hath Esaias prophesied of you hypocrites, as it is written, This people honoureth Me with their lips, but their heart is far from me"* (Mark 7:6).

There you have it. Wasn't our Lord plain? He never sought to please His audience by watering down the blunt statements of Scripture. I hear so much today, that we need "Christ exalting ministry." That may be true, for such ministry warms the heart. However, we also need down-to-earth exposing, and corrective ministry, for those whose hearts are not in tune with God. The Lord never minced His words. He was the Faithful Witness, telling it as it was! *"Hypocrites!"* What an accusation to hurl at an audience! Was that proper? Why certainly, for they *were* hypocrites! He was only declaring to them what they really were. There is nothing wrong with that, is there? Ah, there was no blowing of trumpets with those hypocrites. All they were doing was their legal duty.

ISRAEL'S DECLINE

As Israel's history progressed, things got worse. Notice the closing comments of their history relative to their so-called worship. It is a sad commentary indeed. *"Ye said also, Behold, what a weariness is it ! and ye have snuffed at it, saith the LORD of hosts; and ye brought that which was torn, and the lame, and the sick; thus ye brought an offering: should I accept this of your hand? saith the LORD"* (Mal. 1:13). What a disgusting, sad, sick, and sobering résumé of the nation in the closing of its historical days.

We can relate this to our day, which is portrayed in the church of the Laodiceans. We are neither cold nor hot. We are rich and increased with goods and have need of nothing (Rev. 3:14–17). Like those in Israel's declining days, we have people offering *"the blind for sacrifice"* (unscriptural expressions); *"the lame"* (worn out expressions); *"and the sick"* (no benefit to others); and *"that which was torn,"* (stolen, at no cost to them) (Mal. 3:8, 13). Formality and ritual reigns in the hearts of some. How grevious this must be to the Lord Who dwells in the midst.

SAINTS BLOWING TRUMPETS

Thank God for saints that possess great joy, blowing the silver trumpets. They are the nearest to heaven on earth when they are gathered with His own, with Him in their midst. With awe and reverence they realize His most holy presence. There is no spiritual apathy with them. There is no irreverence displayed. There is no casualness in their attitude, their prayers, their preaching, or even in their attire. They can say like the psalmist, *"With my whole heart have I sought Thee"* (Ps. 119:10). *"Praise ye the LORD. I will praise the LORD with my whole heart, in the assembly of the upright, and in the congregation"* (Ps. 111:1). They are never so happy as when going to the assembly of God, to meet with Him. They can say like David: *"I was glad when they said unto me, Let us go into the house of the LORD"* (Ps. 122:1).

Recently, I sat in the circle of an assembly gathering on a Lord's Day morning, and watched one young couple after another enter. Some had little toddlers at their side, while others had infants in bassinets. The parents were all smiles. The two-year-olds and older children sat quietly in the back seats. They had been trained to show reverence. The infants in bassinets were placed at the parent's side. There was happiness, yet reverential quietness. As the meeting commenced, one hymn was given out and sung heartily. Then, one by one, all the brethren worshipped audibly. When all twelve brethren had prayed, two brethren rose for the second time to give brief thanks for the emblems. Then a word was ministered, and the meeting was closed in thankful prayer. There was no disturbance from any of the children. They had been trained to be quiet. It was a wondrous sight to see! It was like a miracle to behold. There were no programs. There was no schedule. There was no confusion. The Holy Spirit was in full control.

People spend good money to go see the "Holy Land," but on that Lord's Day morning, all of us drew near and sat under the shadow of Calvary to behold, by faith, our Lord suffering for our sins on the tree. What a blessed occupation. It was far more valuable and blessed, than seeing the "Holy Land." A meeting with the highest dignitary on earth, whether president, king, or queen, would certainly take second place to a meeting with the Lord at His table freshly spread. Ah yes, on that blessed occasion, the silver trumpets were blowing loud and clear! Praise God, from Whom all blessings flow! Do you blow the silver trumpet? Is your whole life centered around God's assembly? If truly saved, it should be!

C. H. MACINTOSH'S THOUGHTS

Now then, perhaps I have been a little hard on some of my readers in seeking to expound the truths gleaned from the silver trumpets. I must admit that many words have been very challenging. However, after writing all those terse words, I read what C. H. MacIntosh had to say about the silver trumpets, and found out that his train of thought 155 years ago, was no different than mine. Is that not interesting, that a school teacher and a steel worker, living so many years apart and from vastly different occupations, and cultures, should be thinking the same way? How else could this be unless the same Spirit was directing both to write from truths gleaned from the same Book – the Holy Bible? So below, I have interjected this godly man's thoughts on the subject.

> "Moreover, it pertained to the sons of Aaron, the priests, to blow with the trumpets, for the mind of God can only be known and communicated in priestly nearness and communion. It was the high and holy privilege of the priestly family to cluster round the sanctuary of God, there to catch the first movement of the cloud, and communicate the same to the most distant parts of the camp.
>
> To move without the testimony would be to move in the dark; to refuse to move, when the testimony was given, would be *to remain in the dark.*
>
> This is most simple and deeply practical. We can

have no difficulty in seeing its force and application, in the case of the congregation in the wilderness. But let us remember that all this was a type; and, further, that it is written for our learning. ... It teaches a lesson to which the Christian reader should give his most profound attention. It sets forth, in the most distinct manner possible, that God's people are to be absolutely dependent upon, and wholly subject to, divine testimony, in all their movements. ... It was not, by any means, a question of their likings or dislikings, their thoughts, their opinions, or their judgement. It was simply and entirely a question of implicit obedience.

If there is one feature more characteristic than another of the present hour, it is insubjection to divine authority-positive resistance of the truth when it demands unqualified obedience and self-surrender. It is all well enough so long as it is truth setting forth, with divine fullness and clearness, *our* pardon, *our* acceptance, *our* life, *our* righteousness, *our* eternal security in Christ. This will be listened to, and delighted in. But the very moment it becomes a question of the claims and authority of that blessed One who gave His life to save us from the flames of hell, and introduce us to the everlasting joys of heaven, all manner of difficulties are started; all sorts of reasonings and questions are raised; clouds of prejudice gather round the soul, and darken the understanding, the sharp edge of truth is blunted or turned aside, in a thousand ways. There is no *waiting* for the sound of the trumpet; and when it sounds, with a blast as clear as God himself can give, there is no response to the summons. We move when we ought to be still; and we halt when we ought to be moving. Reader, what must be the result of this? Either no progress at all, or progress in a wrong direction, which is worse than none. It is utterly impossible that we can advance in the divine life, unless we yield ourselves, without reserve, to the word of the Lord.

How would it have been with Israel in the wilderness, had they refused attention to the sound of the trumpet? The answer is as plain as a sunbeam. Let us ponder it. It has a lesson for us. Let us apply our hearts to it. The silver trumpet settled and ordered every movement for Israel of old. The testimony of God ought to settle and order everything for the Church now. That silver trumpet was blown by the priests of old. That testimony of God is known in priestly communion now. A Christian has no right to move or act apart from divine testimony. He must wait upon the word of his Lord. Till he gets that, he must stand still. When he has gotten it, he must *go forward*. God can and does communicate His mind to His militant people now, just as distinctly as He did to His people of old. True, it is not now by the sound of a trumpet, or the movement of a cloud; but by His word and Spirit. It is not by anything that strikes the senses that our Father guides us, but by that which acts on the heart, the conscience, and the understanding. It is not by that which is natural, but by that which is spiritual, that He communicates His mind.

But let us be well assured of this, that our God can and does give our hearts full certainty, both as to what we should do, and what we should not do; as to where we should go, and where we should not go. It seems strange to be obliged to insist upon this—passing strange that any Christian should doubt, much less deny it. And yet so it is. We are often in doubt and perplexity; and some there are who are ready to deny that there can be any such thing as certainty as to the details of daily life and action. This surely is wrong.

Are we to suppose, for a moment, that the Church of God is worse off, in the matter of guidance, than the camp in the desert? Impossible. How is it, then, that one often finds Christians at a loss as to their movements? It must be owing to the lack of a circumcised ear to hear the sound of the silver trumpet, and of a subject will to yield a response to the sound. It may, however, be said that we are not to expect to hear a voice from heaven telling us to do this or that, or to go hither or thither; nor yet to find a literal text of scripture to guide us in the minor matters of our every day history. How, for example, is one to know whether he ought to visit a certain town, and remain there a certain time? We reply, if the ear is circumcised, you will assuredly hear the silver trumpet. Till that sounds, never stir: when it sounds, never tarry. This will make all so clear, so simple, so safe, so certain. It is the grand cure for doubt, hesitancy, and vacillation. It will save us from the necessity of running for advice to this one and that one, as to how we should act, or where we should go, and, furthermore, it will teach us that it is none of our business to attempt to control the actions or movements of others. Let each one have his ear open, and his heart subject, and then, assuredly, he will possess all the certainty that God can give him, as to his every act and movement, from day to day. Our ever gracious God can give clearness and decision as to everything. If he does not give it, no one can. If He does, no one need. May the Holy Spirit impress upon our hearts the needed lesson of 'the silver trumpets!'"

THE TABERNACLE DISSEMBLED

Having given instructions regarding the blowing of the silver trumpets, Moses proceeds to record the activities on the twentieth day of the second month, in the second year. It was on this day that the cloud was taken up from off the tabernacle of the testimony. If you are a careful reader, you will have noticed that the tabernacle was reared up *"in the first month in the second year, on the first day of the month"* (Ex. 40:17). Linking this with Exodus 12:2, and 19:1, we see that Israel had been at Sinai nine months prior to the rearing up of the tabernacle, and that it was reared up exactly one year to the day that the Lord instituted the Passover for the nation. The applied truth is simply this; that the beginning of spiritual life and becoming a temple of the Holy Spirit coincide. The tabernacle, after being pitched in Sinai for one month and twenty days, was to experience its first dissembling, for the cloud had been taken up, and soon would begin to move, taking them to another resting place (Num. 10:11). There would, no doubt, be much activity in the camp.

THE GERSHONITES

The Gershonites would be carefully removing the tabernacle badger skin covering and the goat's hair curtain underneath, with the ram's skins dyed red, and the fine linen curtain. Others would be removing the long linen court curtain, folding it carefully, along with the linen hangings for the gate, and the tabernacle door. How thankful they would be for the contribution of wagons furnished by the princes to help transport all these heavy, and very valuable articles.

THE MERARITES

The sons of Merari would be taxed even greater, as their responsibility was to take down and transport the 56 court pillars, and the four gate pillars, all of them about eight feet high. Perhaps their most laborious work would be taking down and loading the tabernacle boards. Shittim wood is dense and consequently very heavy. Those boards were about fifteen feet long, two and a quarter wide, and ten inches thick! What a tremendous weight, and there were 48 of them! Besides that, the Merarites were also responsible for the removal and transporting of the 96 silver sockets that supported the boards. Friend, we are looking at almost five tons of silver! Not only this, but these men were also responsible for the five pillars in front of the tabernacle, and their sockets, along with the four pillars and their sockets that held the vail. These men had heavy burdens, yet never do we read of them complaining about the work that God had entrusted to their hand. The sacred trust was theirs, and they performed their labor for God quite willingly.

THE KOHATHITES

The third group of men were the Kohathites. They worked nearer to the priests than the Gershonites and the Merarites, for they had charge of transporting the holy vessels of the sanctuary. Theirs was a most solemn service. It was Aaron and his sons that carefully removed the vail, covering the Ark with it, then spreading over it a cloth wholly of blue (Num. 4:4–6). All the vessels used by the priests were personally covered by those priests. No one else would dare draw near. When all was covered, then the Kohathites stepped in to do their service. Thus we read:

> *"And when Aaron and his sons have made an end of covering the sanctuary, and all the vessels of the sanctuary, as the camp is to set forward; after that, the sons of Kohath shall come to bear it: but they shall not touch any holy thing, lest they die. These things are the burden of the sons of Kohath in the tabernacle of the congregation"* (Num. 4:15).

Everything that the Kohathites transported had to be borne on their shoulders. Unlike the Gershonites and Merarites, they were not allowed to use a wagon of any sort. Everybody had their own particular work to do. Women preparing a meal would suddenly have to dismiss their work and start packing their belongings, as their men folk would be busy taking down their tents. Activity would abound as the cloud began to rise and the silver trumpets began to blow. On the other hand, the cloud might rise in the middle of the night, when deep sleep would have fallen upon most. The watching priests would blow the trumpets with no uncertain sound, and the "packing up" procedure would commence immediately. There would be no dilly-dallying. When God moves – they *must* move!

HOLY SPIRIT GUIDANCE

Now then my dear Christian, are you that sensitive to the Holy Spirit's guidance? Are you ready to move when He moves? Also, are you ready to sit still when He sits still? In other words, does the Spirit have complete control of your life, your activities and pursuits? If not, it is time for you to seek the Lord, and call upon His name while He is near? What folly to do things "on your own." No, no, that will never do. We do not necessarily need human guidance, less yet, fleshly guidance. What we need is the total guidance of the Holy Spirit of God. As a preacher, where I preach, what I preach, and how long I preach, should be entirely up to one Person – the Holy Spirit of God. As a "member" of an assembly, where I live, where I work, where I travel, how I walk, how I worship, how I witness, and how I treat my family, and my employer, should all be entirely under the guidance of the Holy Spirit. We do not audaciously say, "I am going to do this, and I expect the Spirit to bless." Ah no, poor soul, that will never work! What we need to say is, "The Spirit will tell me what to do, that He may bless." That's the formula we need to follow. Israel was compelled to do it or be left behind. We are expected to do it, or be left in the dark.

THE BLIND SISTER'S SONG

In 1820, there was a child born in Southeast New York. Due to improper medical treatment she was blinded at the age of six weeks. However, with her eyes of faith she saw that Jesus died for her sins, and through trusting Him, she was saved. During her ninety five years on earth, she wrote an estimated 8,000 gospel song texts, using over 200 pen names besides her own. On one occasion she was in need of five dollars. Turning to God in prayer she told Him of her desperate need. Within a few moments a stranger came to her home with the five dollars she had requested from God. Evidently, God had put it into the heart of this benevolent fellow to give her the money. Her first thought was of the wonderful way in which God had led her, and immediately she sat down and composed the hymn you are about to read. Can you, like the author, Fanny J. Crosby, sing it truthfully?

> "All the way my Saviour leads me;
> What have I to ask beside?
> Can I doubt His tender mercy
> Who thru life has been my Guide?
> Heavenly peace, divinest comfort,
> Here by faith in Him to dwell!
> For I know, whate'er befall me,
> Jesus doeth all things well."

THE ORDER OF THE MARCH

The march begins! *"In the first place went the standard of the camp of the children of Judah according to their armies: ... "The sons of Gershon and the sons of Merari set forward, bearing the tabernacle. And the standard of the camp of Reuben set forward according to their armies: ... And the Kohathites set forward, bearing the sanctuary: ... And the standard of the camp of the children of Ephraim set forward according to their armies: ... And the standard of the camp of the children of Dan set forward, which was the rereward of all the camps throughout their hosts: ... Thus were the journeyings of the children of Israel according to their armies when they set forward"* (Num. 10:14–28).

God had reasons for the order of the march. Notice who was first. Why, it was Judah. Why Judah? God saw that in all things, Judah, as the progenitor of Christ the Lord, might have the pre-eminence. Following Judah were the Gershonites and the Merarites bearing the tabernacle. They would be the first ones on the scene at the next resting place, so that they would be able to immediately set up the tabernacle and have it ready at the arrival of the Kohathites bearing the sacred vessels with which the tabernacle was to be furnished. That is probably what is meant by the words; *"The other* (the Gershonites and the Merarites) *did set up the tabernacle against they* (the Kohathites) *came"* (Num. 10:21 in margin).

Following the standard of the camp of the children of Judah was the standard of the camp of Reuben, followed by the Ark and all other vessels connected with the tabernacle. Following that we have two other standards following, namely Ephraim and Dan. So, where does this divine order place the Ark? Why, God placed the Ark in the very midst of the whole camp of Israel! That Ark speaks of Christ in greater magnitude than all the other vessels. Thus, we see that the Lord was always in the midst, whether they were settled and camped, or whether they were marching and on the move. How wonderful! How instructive! How important to see, that in all things, He, and He alone, is to be the very center of our attraction and attention.

What a sight that must have been. Over two million people marching in divine order to the guidance of the LORD Himself, through the instrument of a cloudy pillar. If there ever was a miracle worth noting, it was this! No nation on earth had ever been so privileged as to be guided thus. I am sure that the news spread over the whole known world about these people in the wilderness. How that the whole land of Egypt lay in desolation over their deliverance; how that the mighty Red Sea, violating all the laws of nature, parted in the middle to afford these unique people a path of escape from the pursuing enemy, and also how at the mere raising of a rod, the Almighty brought the mighty water crashing back together to close the bridge and drown all their foes. Tremendous! Absolutely fantastic, if I may so use that word! And now, another phenomena! We observe a huge pillar of a cloud turning into fire every night, and turning back into a protective cloud every day, hovering over this most unique nation! What a report for the other nations to publish! There was nothing like it! But wait! That is not all. By no means is that all! The pillar actually moves! It is not only their protector, but it is their guide! The mighty God of heaven and earth; The Lord of hosts; The mighty God of Abraham, Isaac, and Jacob; the Creator and Sustainer of all things is actually, and personally, carefully guiding His people through a waste-howling wilderness, on to their inheritance! It is so beautiful to behold! I really am at a loss to fully express my amazement and delight over this whole thing! Little wonder Samuel Davies exclaimed:

> "Great God of wonders! all Thy ways
> Display Thine attributes divine;
> But the bright glories of Thy grace
> Above Thine other wonders shine."

Ah, but another thing is equally wonderful. Look at us! Israel was His earthly people, but we are His heavenly people. Do you think that the God of Abraham, Isaac, and Jacob is doing anything less for us? Shame on you if you think so. We are inseparably baptized into Christ, and the God of Israel is also the God and Father of our Lord Jesus Christ. In fact, our relationship to God as His heavenly people is far greater than Israel's relationship to Him. Do you think then, that we are less privileged? How can we be? Such a thought is a contradiction of the truth my dear friend. Listen to our Lord's words. *"If a man love Me, he will keep My words: and My Father will love him, and We will come unto him, and make Our abode with him"* (John 14:23). Now, what more could you want than that? What a tremendous statement. What a blessed unfolding of a wonderful truth. What need we more? Nothing, absolutely nothing! Rejoice my fellow believer, for you are fully blessed!

THE ARK GOING BEFORE

For the first and only time in the wilderness, the Ark went before them to search them out a resting place. We have already considered the reason for this in the chapter dealing with Moses' father in law. The Ark is defined in various ways in the Scriptures and it is interesting to notice how it is spoken of here. It is called, *"the Ark of the covenant of the LORD."* When the wilderness journey was behind them, once again we read of *the Ark of the covenant of the LORD* passing over before the people (Josh. 3:11). During the wilderness journey it is called *"the Ark of the testimony,"* as that was its character relative to the wilderness. It is never called this after they entered into the land of promise. It is termed *"the Ark of the covenant"* forty times in the Old Testament and once in Hebrews 9:4, pointing us to Christ, the Mediator of the New Covenant. The description would also remind Israel of the covenant God made with their father, Abraham, concerning their inheritance. The term, *"the Ark of the LORD,"* would remind us of Christ, in Whom all the rights of Jehovah are maintained. We find it described thus 35 times, all of them after the crossing of Jordan. However, both in the wilderness, and in the land, we find the Ark termed, *"the Ark of the covenant of the LORD."*

23

THE MIXT MULTITUDE

NUMBERS 11

After Israel's three day journey, we find them at a place that was named Taberah, because of what took place there. It is a sad story indeed, but things written aforetime were written for our learning, so perhaps we will profit through our consideration of Taberah.

> *And when the people complained, it displeased the LORD: and the LORD heard it; and His anger was kindled; and the fire of the LORD burnt among them, and consumed them that were in the uttermost parts of the camp. And the people cried unto Moses; and when Moses prayed unto the LORD, the fire was quenched. And he called the name of the place Taberah: because the fire of the LORD burnt among them* (Num. 11:1–3).

Dwelling at Sinai for almost a year must have been a pleasant experience. Life for them was probably fairly well settled after a few weeks. But then, the cloudy pillar moved, so packing up, they commenced their first journey into the wilderness, which lasted three days. During those three days, something was happening in the hearts of many, but was unknown to Moses. They were secretly fretting and murmuring in the recesses of their souls, and the question arises – why? The Scripture doesn't tell us, but the reasons may have been manifold. Some perhaps were complaining to themselves over being forced to leave their pleasant surroundings to journey into "nowhere." Perhaps the burden of the journey involving privation and difficulties caused some to be discontent. Others were perhaps fretting inwardly over inconveniences that had been imposed upon them. These people were complainers. Nothing seemed to satisfy them. I'm sure that you have met such characters in your life.

> Some people grumble – the weather's too hot.
> Others complain – it's too cold, is it not?
> Some say the sun is baking my crops.
> While others complain, there's too many drops.
> There are those who complain, the preacher's too loud.
> And other's remark – I think he's too proud.
> Others may say – I think he's too meek,
> Why can't he shout more, I can't hear him speak.
> The brethren just can't do anything right.
> The hall's far too hot, or it's too cold at night.
> And nobody's right, and all folks are wrong,
> This my friend, is the complainer's old song.

However, even though Moses did not perceive this condition, yet it was fully known by God. Isn't it sad that the very first incident recorded on Israel's journey between Sinai and the land of promise was the sin of murmuring? How quickly these people had forgotten the mighty hand of God on their behalf, delivering them from their cruel taskmasters in Egypt. How soon the glorious deliverance from the Egyptian army at the Red Sea had evaporated from their memory. How rapidly the giving of the manna and the abundant provision of water from the smitten rock had faded in their mind. They had forgotten to count their blessings, one by one.

Let me ask you, how do you react to little difficulties that arise in your circumstances? How do you respond when weak in health, or when "friends" do not treat you as expected? When the weather is inclement you may rightly become concerned, but do you complain? Do you complain over your lot at work, that your fellow-workers are inconsiderate, and that your boss is a "Mr. Toil?" Now "concern" and "complain" start with the same letter ("C"), but they are vastly different attitudes. I might rightfully be concerned over a number of issues, but the place that God has put me should never draw forth complaints. Israel complained in their hearts, and the LORD was displeased.

SEVERITY OF PUNISHMENT

So great was the anger of the LORD, that *"the fire of the LORD burnt among them."* The question has been raised, that when they sinned on other occasions, why was there no severity in the punishment of God as seen here? It is a sobering thought, but the truth is, that on this occasion they knew far more about the LORD than on previous occasions. At Sinai, they had become acquainted with the power and goodness of God, and had solemnly entered into a covenant with Him. With the tabernacle being set up there, God had taken up His dwelling with them, so their responsibilities became greater with their privileges. Let me say this, the more intelligent you become in the things of God, the greater your responsibilities to obey become. We certainly do not condone sins of ignorance, but on the other hand, there are ignorant Christians that can carry out God's work unscripturally, and their chastisement will be far less than it would be if you acted as they have. The greater the position before God, the greater the punishment called for. Let me put it this way. Paul, in writing to Timothy regarding sinning elders, told him that they were to be *"rebuked before all, that others also may fear"* (1 Tim. 5:20). Two men may commit the same sin, but the man that has the higher status before God, has greater guilt. The sinning elder was to bear the shame of a public announcement being made to the assembly concerning his sin. You do not find that rule with the "rank and file believer." Go back to the Aaronic priesthood and what do you find? You discover different classes of people regarding sin. Tell me, if all men are equal, why then were the prominent men required to bring a more valuable sin offering than the ordinary believer? The priest was required to bring a bullock. A ruler was to bring a kid of the goats, a male without blemish. If any one of the common people sinned, they were to bring a kid of the goats, a female without blemish (Lev. 4:3, 22-23, 27-28). Our Lord indicated this when He said: *"And that servant, which knew his lord's will, and prepared not himself, neither did according to his will, shall be beaten with many stripes. But he that knew not, and did commit things worthy of stripes, shall be beaten with few stripes. For unto whomsoever much is given, of him shall be much required: and to whom men have committed much, of him they will ask the more"* (Luke 12:47–48).

The question has arisen, what was the character of the fire? Was it a vehement hot wind of the desert called a simoom, or was it a flash of lightning, or was it a bursting forth of fire from the cloudy pillar, or was it an internal burning within their mortal bodies? The Scripture is totally silent as to its qualities. However, it was fire, a destructive fire that consumed and reached to the uttermost parts of the camp. Some have thought that this section of the camp was where the mixed multitude dwelt, and that they were the ones, that more than likely, were the complainers. However, Samuel Bochart (1599-1667), shows that there is considerable evidence that the original word rendered *"the uttermost parts,"* does not always signify an extremity, but *"any part, every part, in all, throughout."* Possibly then, the thought is that the fire *consumed some in every part of the camp*. Thus, it was not only the fringe of the camp where it fell, but the whole camp, even to the very outskirts. The psalmist alludes to this, writing: *"Therefore the LORD heard this , and was wroth: so a fire was kindled against Jacob, and anger also came up against Israel"* (Ps. 78:21). *"For our God is a consuming fire"* (Heb. 12:29). Someone has rightly said, "When we complain without a cause – God can give us cause to complain."

> *"And the people cried unto Moses; and when Moses prayed unto the LORD, the fire was quenched"* (Num. 11:2).

Israel, immediately recognizing their sin and the source of the judgmental fire, did not cry to Aaron, Joshua, or Miriam. No, they were intelligent enough to beseech their mediator –

Moses. Moses was the God-ordained man to come between Himself and the people. It would have been fruitless for them to cry to Aaron, as great a man as he was. Joshua was a mighty man too, but he certainly was not called upon to fill the office of mediator. Ah no, this office was unique, and committed to one man, and one man alone, even Moses!

You might wonder why I am emphasizing this to such an extent. The reason is, we have a severe problem today in religious circles. The problem is simply this. There are "religious" people that pray to Mary, the mother of our Lord. They have been erroneously taught that she is the mediatrix between God and man. What do the Scriptures plainly declare? Why a five-year old could understand them. Let me quote them to you. *"For there is one God, and one Mediator between God and men, the Man Christ Jesus"* (1 Tim. 2:5). The theology of Rome teaches otherwise, but what does the Holy Spirit teach? Why He teaches the opposite to the Pope. So, who am I to believe? The Pope of Rome, or the Holy Spirit of God? There is "ONE Mediator." Not two mediators. Not three mediators. No, no! ONE! Living saints do not pray to dead saints, nor to angels, nor to Mary! Perish the thought! It is blasphemy to thus displace our glorious Lord Whom the Father hath made the One and only Mediator between Himself and man. Do you appreciate this? Do you revel in it? Is your innermost being thrilled by it? Moses wrote; *"Hear, O Israel: The LORD our God is one LORD"* (Deut. 6:4). *"The Jehovah our Elohim is one* Jehovah (the Ever-existing One)" (Newberry Bible). Elohim, the triune God. Father, Son, and Holy Spirit – ONE in unity and in purpose! Thus, we have a Father to *supplicate,* a Son to *mediate,* and the Spirit to help us *supplicate.* Also, in the Son we have an *advocate,* His present position for us as a legal assistant Who pleads our cause if we sin. We are a most blessed people indeed! *"The people cried unto Moses."* What an earnest cry that must have been. What a powerful man Moses was, for he had an unwavering hold on God. *"And when Moses prayed unto the LORD, the fire was quenched."*

THE MIXT MULTITUDE

> *"And the mixt multitude that was among them fell a lusting: and the children of Israel also wept again, and said, Who shall give us flesh to eat? We remember the fish, which we did eat in Egypt freely; the cucumbers, and the melons, and the leeks, and the onions, and the garlick: But now our soul is dried away: there is nothing at all, beside this manna, before our eyes. And the manna was as coriander seed, and the colour thereof as the colour of bdellium"* (Num. 11:4–7).

The question arises, who were these people termed "the mixt multitude?" The Hebrew word is, *"hasaphsuph,"* meaning *"the gathered, the riff-raff, ruff-scuff, or rabble."* The doubling of word forms in the Hebrew intensifies the meaning and makes them equivalent to superlatives. Bochart terms the meaning as *"the dregs, or scum of the people from every quarter."* An old English version terms them *"the rascal people."* While in Egypt, they could be called, "opportunists." They had never experienced the Passover, but they saw a good thing coming for Israel, and they wanted the benefit of Israel's coming fortune by joining them. Perhaps most of these characters had wandered into Egypt from other parts, and had been made slaves. They saw a good chance to escape their bondage, by mingling with God's people and leaving Egypt with them. They probably thought that in a matter of a few weeks, they would be living a life of ease in Canaan, by "joining the crowd." They certainly were not prepared for the hardships of the way, and it wasn't very long until they hankered after the luxury food that Egypt's slaves enjoyed. Worse yet, they seemed to have a tremendous influence on God's people, causing them to sin against God. It is conjecture, but we suggest that perhaps many of them may have been offspring of mixed marriages in Egypt. We read in Leviticus 24:10, of the son of an Israelitish woman, by an Egyptian father. Half-breeds in such cases would follow their mothers, marching with Israel of the various tribes with which they were connected, for the purpose of gaining some personal advantage. They were like leaven, leavening the whole lump. God never included them with His people, yet Israel, forgetting their high calling, associated themselves with these criminals.

What a sobering lesson for us today. Do we associate with the ungodly who try to link themselves with us? Would it surprise you to know that perhaps we have them in God's assemblies? The late William Warke once remarked to me, that when some assemblies become small, the brethren get desperate, and allow folks to enter the fellowship that certainly do not qualify. Then there are those who seem to be a plausible candidate for fellowship, but the hidden fact is that they have never been born again. They have a convincing story, perhaps even being deceived themselves, and are received into the fellowship. All seems to go well, and their behavior appears to be commendable, but as time wears on, they wear down. Their supposed joy, like the morning dew, evaporates, and they begin to thirst after the former things. The world has always been in their heart, but temporarily placed into a corner, over their "exciting" profession. However, as spiritual things become duller by the day, the world, like the morning sun, arises within their hearts, and they begin to lust after the former pleasures of the world. A discontentment arises as they remember, with desire, the former life. They lose interest in the Scriptures, that is, if they had any to begin with. Attending meetings becomes a mechanical procedure, or there may be enough social activities to keep them interested to a small degree. The attending of conferences is not particularly with the purpose of being searched by the Word of God, but rather to socialize with others of like mind.

These people correspond to the mixed multitude in Israel, and their influence over weak believers can be devastating. The Church, in its early days, became greatly corrupted after the departure of the apostles. The apostle Paul speaks of, *"false brethren unawares brought in"* (Gal. 2:4), and Jude warns of the same, writing, *"for there are certain men crept in unawares … ungodly men"* (Jude 1:4).

THE STRANGE CHILDREN
INTRODUCING DEPARTURE

The assemblies began to be infiltrated with *"strange children."* When some of these *"strange children"* rose to positions of authority in assemblies, things were introduced that were contrary to the Word of God. By the end of the second century, the importance of a personal conversion became less important. Christian's children were considered worthy of assembly fellowship. The baptism of infants and baptismal regeneration was acknowledged. A hierarchical government was acknowledged, with a clergy and a laity. There was the development of the Episcopal office beyond the limits of the local company, and a bishop was distinct from an elder. By the year 245, the clergy received a salary and was forbidden to work. Five distinct heads were formed over all the bishops. They were called patriarchs, and they ruled from Alexandria, Antioch, Jerusalem, Constantinople, and Rome. By 310, prayers were being said for the dead, and the sign of the cross was employed. In 431, the assembly at Ephesus held a council, declaring that Mary was to be worshipped, as the "Mother of God." In 324, Emperor Constantine forced Christianity on the heathen, thus flooding the assemblies with more "strange children." It was then that the pilgrim Church became married to the world, thus we have what is called "Christendom" today.

THE GREAT REVIVAL

In 1827, godly men met in Dublin, Ireland, and through much prayer and study of the Scriptures, they came out from Christendom, and formed scriptural assemblies that simply gathered unto the name of our Lord Jesus Christ. In 1859 there was a great revival in Scotland, resulting in the formation of scriptural assemblies. In 1872, the work spread to Canada and the United States.

However, in recent years, we have observed subtle changes. Perhaps this is due to the influence of "strange children" occupying responsible positions in the assemblies. As I carefully observe the whole history of the Church from its commencement, I see early history repeating itself in our day. Brethren, this is something to be very concerned about. David cried, *"Rid me, and deliver me from the hand of strange children, whose mouth speaketh vanity, and their right hand is a right hand of falsehood"* (Ps. 144:11). May we not cry the same?

"The children of Israel also wept again." The Hebrew equivalent to this expression is found in the marginal rendering of most Bibles; *"they returned and wept."* It simply means *"they changed their mind."* The contagious example of the mixed multitude caused them *to fall away from a previous state of mind,* thus involving themselves in the rebellious conduct referred to here. Prior to this, nothing is said of their weeping. This seemed to be the first occasion. They had a change of mind, from better to worse. A careful consideration of the references in the footnote will confirm this interpretation of those words "wept again."[68] It has been well put, that instead of weeping compassionately over the disaffected multitude, they wept perversely *with* them, and thus contributed to provoking of the divine displeasure.

How distasteful! They *"lusted a lust."* Where animal appetites reign, satisfaction is impossible. If a man's appetite is not controlled by spiritual principles, he will ever remain restless and unsatisfied. *"The eye is not satisfied with seeing, nor the ear filled with hearing"* (Eccl. 1:8).

"THE GOOD OLD DAYS "

Ah yes, they had good memories in certain areas. They vividly remembered their Egyptian food, and longed for it. However, they also had failing memories, for they soon forgot their bondage, the brick-kilns, the taskmasters, and the cruel whip. It

---

68   Ps. 78:34; Eccl. 4:1,7; 9:11; Isa. 19:22; Isa. 55:7; Mal. 3:18; Judg. 11:35 (go back – return). Eze. 14:6; 18:30 (repent Heb. Return). All these cases refer to a mental act, a change of views, thus a change in one's mental state.

reminds me of some old folks today as they reminisce and speak about "the good old days." Ah yes, they were good alright! Men worked like slaves, many of them twelve hours a day. There was no air conditioning for those desperately hot days, and there was no central heating in the homes on those bitter, winter nights. Light came from an oil lamp, and it was dim at its best. There were no washing machines, but rather scrub-boards. One couldn't go very far in an automobile without experiencing a flat tire, and the flivver had to be hand-cranked to start. Many motorists found their cars up to the hubcaps in mud on wet days. There were no paved roads. Some had no heaters, and the motor was worn out before 10,000 miles. Did I hear that old man say, "The GOOD old days?" This all sounds like the complainers at Taberah, doesn't it? I have never met a Christian who mourned over his salvation, complaining that he was better off before he was saved. What nonsense! Such an attitude is totally incompatible with true, Christian testimonials. God has blessed us with all spiritual blessings in Christ, and He has promised to meet all of our need.

THE BLESSED MAN

"Our soul is dried away." They were acting as if God was depriving them. In other words, they were disappointed, and they were withered. *"There is nothing at all, beside this manna, before our eyes."* Yes! And that is the way God wanted it! Are you satisfied with just Christ? Some time ago, a good Christian friend of mine told me that a person might go "crazy" if they did nothing but read the Bible, and that the human mind needed diversions in reading material. To support his thought, he quoted Mark 6:31, where the Lord said, *"Come ye yourselves apart into a desert place, and rest a while: for there were many coming and going, and they had no leisure so much as to eat"* (Mark 6:31). In other words, we need a rest from just being occupied with the Bible. What my friend failed to see was, that when the Lord advised them to come apart to a desert place for rest, that He would still be with them. They would still be occupied with Him, and none other. Frivolous and light amusements were not on their agenda.

Do not worry, you will never go crazy being totally occupied with the Scriptures. If that were the case, then the apostle Paul was insane, for he certainly filled the criteria of being a Scripture-absorbed man. Notice what he advised Timothy. *"Meditate upon these things; give thyself wholly to them; that thy profiting may appear to all"* (1 Tim. 4:15). The psalmist confessed, *"O how love I Thy law! it is my meditation all the day"* (Ps. 119:97). *"Blessed is the man that walketh not in the counsel of the ungodly, nor standeth in the way of sinners, nor sitteth in the seat of the scornful. But his delight is in the law of the LORD; and in his law doth he meditate day and night"* (Ps. 1:1–2).

Is God, or the inspired writers, encouraging us to go beserk? Hardly! Remember the instructions given to Joshua. *"This book of the law shall not depart out of thy mouth; but thou shalt meditate therein day and night, that thou mayest observe to do according to all that is written therein: for then thou shalt make thy way prosperous, and then thou shalt have good success"* (Josh. 1:8).

He certainly didn't say, "Now be careful Joshua, you need a change of literature. You need to enter a dream world to loose you from all this strain." Most certainly not! The man was encouraged to give 100% of his reading and meditation to the books of Moses. The Scriptures support the fact that the person who constantly reads and meditates on the Holy Scriptures, is a very happy Christian.

AN APPEAL FROM C. H. M.

"And the manna was as coriander seed, and the colour thereof as the colour of bdellium" (Num. 11:7).

It is enlightening to notice, that immediately after the people said *"there is nothing at all, beside this manna, before our eyes,"* that God gives a description of their heavenly food. In Exodus 16:31 where we find the first description of the manna, *"the taste of it was like wafers made with honey."* However, at their first encampment, after leaving Sinai, the manna is described as having *"the taste of fresh oil."* It would seem that the provision of God for them had lost its sweetness. That which they formerly delighted in, had lost its attractiveness to them. How often is this the case with us! Let me quote C. H. MacIntosh again. His thoughts are right on the line for today, even though written over 100 years ago.

> "When once the heart loses its freshness in the divine life — when heavenly things begin to lose their savour — when first love declines — when Christ ceases to be a satisfying and altogether precious portion for the soul — when the word of God and prayer lose their charm and become heavy, dull, and mechanical; then the eye wanders back toward the world, the heart follows the eye, and the feet follow the heart. We forget, at such moments, what the world was to us when we were in it and of it. We forget what toil and slavery, what misery and degradation, we found in the service of sin and of Satan, and think only of the gratification and ease, the freedom from those painful exercises, conflicts, and anxieties which attend upon the wilderness path of God's people.
>
> All this is most sad, and should lead the soul into the most profound self-judgment. It is terrible when those who have set out to follow the Lord begin to grow weary of the way and of God's provision. How dreadful must those words have sounded in the ear of Jehovah, *'But now our soul is dried away: there is nothing at all, beside this manna, before our eyes.'*
>
> Ah! Israel, what more didst thou need? Was not that heavenly food enough for thee! Couldst thou not live upon that which the hand of thy God had provided for thee? Do we count ourselves free to ask such questions? Do we always

find *our* heavenly manna sufficient for us? What means the inquiry raised by professing Christians as to the right or wrong of such and such worldly pursuits and pleasures? Have we not even heard from the lips of persons making the very highest profession such words as these: 'How are we to fill up the day! We cannot be always thinking about Christ and heavenly things. We must have some little recreation.' Is not this somewhat akin to Israel's language in Numbers 11? Yes truly; and as is the language, so is the acting. We prove, alas! that Christ is not enough for the heart, by the palpable fact of our betaking ourselves to other things. How often, for example, does the Bible lie neglected for hours, while the light and worthless literature of the world is greedily devoured. What mean the well-thumbed newspaper and the almost dust-covered Bible? Do not these things tell a tale? Is not this despising the manna, and sighing after, nay, devouring, the leeks and onions?

We specially call the attention of young Christians to that which is now before us. We are deeply impressed with a sense of their danger of falling into the very sin of Israel as recorded in our chapter. No doubt we are all in danger; but the young amongst us are peculiarly so. Those of us who are advanced in life are not so likely to be drawn away by the frivolous pursuits of the world — by its concerts, its flower shows, its pleasure parties, its vain songs and light literature. But the young *will* have a dash of the world. They long to taste it for themselves. They do not find Christ an all-sufficient portion for the heart. They want recreation.

Alas! alas! what a thought! How sad to hear a Christian say, 'I want some recreation. How can I fill up the day? I cannot be always thinking of Jesus. We should like to ask all who speak thus, How will you fill up eternity? Shall not Christ be sufficient to fill up its countless ages? Shall you want recreation there? Will you sigh for light literature, vain songs, and frivolous pursuits there?"[69]

CHANGING THE MANNA

Not satisfied with the manna as God gave it, they proceeded to change it. They *"ground it in mills, or beat it in a mortar, and baked it in pans, and made cakes out of it."* This was a vain effort to suit their natural taste. The Scripture declares, *"Jesus Christ the same yesterday, and to day, and for ever"* (Heb. 13:8). In other words, His character never changes, and truths concerning His Person remain indelibly the same. Yet what do we find today in Christendom? Alas, we find the manna "ground, beaten, and baked!" Paul lamented to the Corinthians, *"For if he that cometh preacheth another Jesus, whom we have not preached, or if ye receive another spirit, which ye have not received, or another gospel, which ye have not accepted, ye might well bear with him"* (2 Cor. 11:4).

Those who build "Mega-Churches," preach *"another Jesus."* Loose living individuals that claim to be Christians, have a Jesus of their own imagination. The biblical truths taught by our Lord are either perverted, or tossed to the ground, and behavior in the name of Jesus is introduced which is contrary to the plain teachings of Scripture. The question asked by our Lord could be properly addressed to them. *"And why call ye Me, Lord, Lord, and do not the things which I say?"* (Luke 6:46). There are groups that erroneously teach that Jesus was no more than a mere man, and that He never physically rose from the dead. Others teach that He is not able to keep His sheep, but that they must "hold on, and endure to the end in order to be saved." Other religious cults deny His Deity, and others place Him in second place to Mary. The list could go on and on, but we forbear,

---

69   End of quote from C. H. MacIntosh on Numbers 11.

lest we weary you with pages of distressing reports. Like Israel, who changed the manna as God originally gave it, so men today have "changed" Christ.

The manna was like coriander seed, a very small brownish, and beautifully fine-textured, aromatic seed. It speaks of Christ, Who was meek and lowly in heart, Whose finely textured ways brought fragrance and pleasure to the heart of God. The manna was also described *as "the colour of bdellium,"* an unidentified substance mentioned in the Bible (Gen. 2:12, and Numbers 11:7), variously taken to be a gum, a precious stone, or pearls, or perhaps a kind of amber found in Arabia. It is spoken of as unique in its taste, and fragrant to the smell. Relating to this, Christians can exclaim that not only is there a fragrance to Christ, but also, as we feast upon Him, tasting and seeing that the Lord is good, there is a unique sweetness incomparable to any mere mortal man.

> *"Then Moses heard the people weep throughout their families, every man in the door of his tent: and the anger of the LORD was kindled greatly; Moses also was displeased"* (Num. 11:10).

The dissatisfaction had spread, becoming more and more open, and Moses was displeased. It would seem that this whole incident was too much for his endurance. He hastily said, *"Wherefore hast thou afflicted Thy servant? and wherefore have I not found favour in Thy sight, that Thou layest the burden of all this people upon me"* (Num. 11:11). It was an exaggeration to accuse God that He had laid all the burden of Israel upon him. The Lord had constantly assisted him in direction and help. God had, time and time again, exposed Himself as the All-sufficient One to Moses, yet we get this unwarranted complaint. It seems as if he had overlooked the history of God's dealings with them, the high hand and the outstretched arm on their behalf. It would seem that he had forgotten God's promise, *"My Presence shall go with thee, and I will give thee rest"* (Ex. 33:14). Ah, but wait! Are we not the same? When burdens press us severely, and our grief becomes overbearing, do we not also, on occasions, speak unadvisedly with our lips? Poor, mortal, and frail humans we still are! No, Moses can't be accused of the murmuring of unbelief. His was the language of the discontent of despair. Moses was at the point of breaking down under the tremendous burden laid upon him. Did he not admit this to Jehovah? Notice his cry. *"I am not able to bear all this people alone, because it is too heavy for me"* (Num. 11:14). Some have faulted Moses for this attitude. However, do notice that God never rebuked him for his confession. Why no, God graciously stepped in and provided tremendous relief for His burdened servant. I cannot help but think of Paul's comforting words. *"There hath no temptation* (trial) *taken you but such as is common to man: but God is faithful, Who will not suffer you to be tempted above that ye are able; but will with the temptation also make a way to escape, that ye may be able to bear it"* (1 Cor. 10:13). The solution to Moses' problem is God-given. Seventy, able and mature men, are chosen in the presence of God, to assist Moses in any further problems that might arise. Consider a scriptural church today. There is no such thng as a one man rule. No, no! There is always a plurality of elders, appointed by God to rule the local assembly.

QUAILS

The last part of this interesting chapter provides another lesson for us. God as much as said, "Alright, you are not satisfied with My provision, I will give you over to your own fleshly lusts, and provide for your greed." I say that this is most strange, but at the same time, it provided a warning and a cure. They lusted after flesh to eat, so God gave them flesh. Not just a little taste to excite their palates, but a total month of it, until the flesh came out their nostrils, and became loathsome to them (Num. 11:20). Using nature, the divine Controller of the universe brought quails from the sea by means of a wind.

> *"And there went forth a wind from the LORD, and brought quails from the sea, and let them fall by the camp, as it were a day's journey on this side, and as it were a day's journey on the other side, round about the camp, and as it were two cubits high. And the*

people stood up all that day, and all that night, and all the next day, and they gathered the quails: he that gathered least gathered ten homers: and they spread them all abroad for themselves round about the camp" (Num. 11:31–32).

The general notion is, that the quails were so plentiful, that they fell in such abundance, as to lie two feet thick upon the ground; but the Hebrew will not bear this thought. The Vulgate has expressed the sense: *Volabantque in aere duobus cubitis altitudine super terram.* "And they flew in the air, two cubits high above the ground." Jarchi, a Jewish commentator, says, "They flew so high as against a man's heart, that he was not fatigued in getting them, either by reaching high, or stooping low." Common sense would tell you that the quail were not lying on the ground two cubits deep, for if that were the case, the greater part of them on the bottom of the pile would have been dead, before they could have been collected. Therefore they would have been unfit to eat since the Israelites could eat nothing that had died of suffocation.

Other commentators have suggested that the food the wind brought them from the African side of the Sea was locusts, and that the original term denotes *locusts*, instead of *quails*. However, Psalm 78:27 discounts this interpretation, where their food is described as, *"feathered fowls"* (Hebrew - *"winged fowl"*).

Fatigued with the strong wind, and the distance they had come, they were easy prey for the lusting people, who, standing, caught them with their hands, or by hitting them with clubs. Having caught the quails, they would have plucked them, and then laid them out in the sun to dry, as the Egyptians did to their fish. This is what Moses meant when he wrote *"they spread them all abroad for themselves round about the camp."*

It may be added that the Israelites, in feeding on the quail, showed a similarity to the quails themselves. Ephraim is compared to *"a silly dove without heart"* (Hos. 7:11), that is, they lacked understanding.

The psalmist describes this incident with these words. *"They soon forgat His works; they waited not for His counsel: But lusted exceedingly in the wilderness, and tempted God in the desert. And He gave them their request; but sent leanness into their soul"* (Ps. 106:13–15). They were so lustful, that they stood up all that day and all that night, and each gathered ten *homers*. It has been suggested that an Israelite received for his daily food one *omer* of manna (almost two quarts), which is a tenth part of an *ephah* (almost twenty quarts). However, an *ephah* is a tenth part of a *cor*, and a *cor* (six bushels), contains an hundred *omers*. Consequently, if one *omer* is sufficient for one day, then one *cor* is sufficient for one hundred days. That amounts to enough food for over three months. But notice, they gathered ten *cors* of quails (sixty bushels). That amounted to thirty times more than God had promised!

However, not satisfied with this way of reckoning, Bochart has proposed another solution, that *ten homers* are *not ten cors*, but *ten heaps*. In this sense, the word is used in Exodus 8:14, and Habakkuk 3:15. Other interpreters also render *it "ten heaps."* If this is the right interpretation, then we must assume that Moses is not determining the quantity of these birds which everyone gathered, but only that everyone gathered at least ten heaps. At any rate, the amount collected was immense. The psalmist indicated this. *"He rained flesh also upon them as dust, and feathered fowls like as the sand of the sea"* (Ps. 78:27).

How zealous they were! Indulgently, they feasted themselves on their new luxury. Their appetites were tremendous! Their hunger was voracious. They were so afraid of losing any of their prey, that they actually stood up throughout the whole night in order to catch, and hoard the food they lusted after.

What a picture this is of a lustful and covetous world. Men are seeking, thirsting, craving, after what? Righteousness? Hardly! As I write this portion, today is "Black Friday," the day after Thanksgiving Day. It is a day when merchants bait the masses. Most of the stores opened between 3 and 5 a.m. this morning. Can you picture this? Our mall nearby is over one mile long. As the sun arose in the eastern sky, the parking lot was jammed full. When home, occasionally I go to that mall to walk. But today was different. It was packed to capacity. Prices had been slashed until noon, and crazed people were buying, buying, buying. They already had sufficient in their homes, but that made no difference, they were buying, much to the delight of the merchants.

TOBIN'S STORE

I remember an incident 72 years ago. I had a friend named Daniel Tobin, whose Jewish father had a little clothing store on Kinsman Avenue. He was overstocked on a certain item, and couldn't seem to sell it very well. So, what did he do? He must have known human nature, for he removed the items to the storeroom of his little store, and set up a table in the middle of the display section. On that table he put just a few of his "hard-to-sell" items, and marked them 75% above their selling price. Then he slashed a red line through the inflated price and marked it down to the normal selling price. The sign read, "Reduced! Few left! Buy while they last!"

Customers observing the sign thought that since the merchandise was marked down and that not many items were left, should scoop them up before someone else got them. As the stock on the table was "grabbed up," Mr. Tobin would go to the back room and bring out a few more to be placed on his "bargain table." Within a week, his items that were not selling, were completely "sold out!"

Now let us just suppose that a gospel preacher could obtain permission from the mall owners to preach the gospel in their mall on a Lord's Day morning, two hours before the stores opened. The time would be set for 8 a.m. On the same day, at the downtown, outdoor stadium, there would be a professional football game sceduled. Let us say that on that day it was sleeting, cold, and "miserable" outside. Tell me, what occasion would draw the crowd, a warm, comfortable mall, or a cold, wet, "miserable" stadium? Where would the crowd be? Listening to the good news of the gospel, or shouting in the sleet for their team? Why the answer is simple. They would be at the sports event, not the scriptural event. Why is that? Why would people rather go to hell than hear the gospel? Why would they rather sit in the sleet and cold, to see a game, rather than be seated in a warm mall to hear how they could be saved, and have a glorious home in heaven for eternity? There are definite reasons for this perverted behavior. First of all, many are deceived into believing that they are not going to hell, or some even believe that there is no hell. Also, there is nothing in the gospel that appeals to their sinful nature. They do not want preaching, they want pleasure. And today, they go in for it with their whole heart, "hook, line, and sinker." *"There is no fear of God before their eyes"* (Rom. 3:18). This, my friend, is society in our day. Israel stayed up all night. They were extremely diligent. They were very much awake – all to satisfy their wicked lusts.

We live in a greedy, grasping society, where *"all seek their own, not the things which are Jesus Christ's"* (Phil. 2:21). Just as the Israelites stood up all that day and night, with diligence, gathering and preserving the quails, so the earth-dwellers today pursue pleasure, and scheme and sweat for money. One cannot help but notice the contrast between the eagerness with which men pursue vain, earthly things, and their luke-warmness and slothfulness as to the things which are spiritual and eternal. They diligently pursue the perishable things of earth, accumulating what they will never live to fully enjoy. Just as they are about to enter their retirement with the hope of taking their ease, eating, drinking, and being merry, death cuts them down in the midst of their possessions, and they leave this world as they entered – empty-handed.

> *"Lay not up for yourselves treasures upon earth, where moth and rust doth corrupt, and where thieves break through and steal"* (Matt. 6:19). *"Labour not for the meat which perisheth"* (John 6:27).

LEANNESS

It is sobering to read, *"He gave them their request; but sent leanness into their soul."* Yes, they paid a costly price indeed! Does God do the same today? Absolutely! When men pursue their sin in spite of the warnings and call of God, there comes a time when God gives them up. Consider Israel in Jeremiah's day. God spake unto them in earnest, but they heard not. He called unto them, but they answered not. Finally, God said to Jeremiah, *"Pray not thou for this people"* (Jer. 7:13; 11:14; 14:11). With their attitude, they unknowingly had pronounced judgment upon themselves, and it was not long before it fell.

We have a class of people mentioned by Paul in Romans 1. *"Because they did not like to retain God in their knowledge, God gave them over to a reprobate mind, to do those things which are not convenient"* (Rom. 1:28). So there is the homosexual, more commonly termed, "gay." Under the Law of Moses, *"If a man also lie with mankind, as he lieth with a woman, both of them have committed an abomination: they shall surely be put to death; their blood shall be upon them"* (Lev. 20:13).

The numbers today that believe in an "alternate lifestyle" are increasing. They hate the Word of God, because it condemns their wicked and abominable activities. They do not like to retain God in their knowledge, consequently, God has given them over to a reprobate (worthless) mind. Because of their determination to sin against God, He in return has given *"them up unto vile affections"* (Rom. 1:26).

They are so wicked, that in some states they are moving to get legislation passed that will make it a felony for anyone to publicly quote the Word of God condemning their perverted ways. In other words, a preacher could be arrested and thrown into jail for quoting any Scripture that condemns homosexuality. What are we coming to?

> *"And while the flesh was yet between their teeth, ere it was chewed, the wrath of the LORD was kindled*

against the people, and the LORD smote the people with a very great plague. And he called the name of that place Kibrothhattaavah: because there they buried the people that lusted. And the people journeyed from Kibrothhattaavah unto Hazeroth; and abode at Hazeroth" (Num. 11:33–35).

"While the flesh was yet between their teeth," means that before the quail ceased at the end of the month the wrath of God fell upon them. Little did they realize that while they were enjoying their lusted food, the wrath of God was hovering over them like a dark, ominous cloud, until it finally burst with unmitigated fury upon their heads. The *"very great plague,"* is equivalent to *stroke*, or *judgment*. It was probably some kind of bodily disease, or pestilence. An old writer remarked, "Their sweet meat had sour sauce." So it is today. The ungodly continue on, fulfilling the desires of the flesh and of the mind, heeding not the call of God, and because the sentence against their evil work is not executed speedily, their hearts are fully set in them to do evil. They consider not their latter end, and in a moment they are cut down and taken away.

24

AARON and MIRIAM'S SLANDER

NUMBERS 12

"And Miriam and Aaron spake against Moses because of the Ethiopian woman whom he had married: for he had married an Ethiopian woman. And they said, Hath the LORD indeed spoken only by Moses? hath He not spoken also by us? And the LORD heard it" (Num. 12:1–2).

Solomon observed envy and wrote; *"A sound heart is the life of the flesh: but envy the rottenness of the bones"* (Prov. 14:30). *"Wrath is cruel, and anger is outrageous; but who is able to stand before envy?"* (Prov. 27:4). We see this very thing springing into action in the opening of our chapter. The LORD had distinguished Miriam as a prophetess above all the women of Israel, while Aaron had been invested with the high priesthood of the nation, but the pride of their natural heart was not satisfied with this. They envied Moses! That cruel envy manifested itself in the form of a complaint against Moses. They faulted Moses for the pre-eminence of his high calling, and his exclusive position over the nation.

ZIPPHORAH, OR SOMEONE ELSE?

Some, such as Josephus, Philo, and others, have surmised that the woman spoken of here was another woman beside

Zipporah. Their reason being that if the wife had been Zipporah, why did it take so long for their complaint to be made known, for Zipporah had been married to Moses ever since he fled to the desert which was forty years prior to him leading Israel out of that land of bondage into a waste-howling wilderness. Now this seems most plausible, however, do we really understand envy? People can harbor complaints in the recesses of their hearts for many years, yet never make their complaint known –until – something arises that greatly irks them, and then the heart's door swings widely open and out comes those hidden thoughts, in the form of a complaint. Miriam could have smiled in Zipporah's face all those years, yet despised her in her heart. Moses had consulted his father-in-law, and received his advice regarding the choosing of seventy elders to help in the governing of the nation. Aaron and Miriam had never been so much as approached about the vital matter. It must have hurt their pride to think of Moses going to an "outsider," his wife's father, and they were not even considered. Miriam's thoughts could well have been like this: "Who does Moses think that he is. Are we not important? Hasn't the LORD also spoken by us? And that wife of his, an outsider, a Cushite, and her own father advising us what to do, who do they think that they are?" Ah yes, it is just as the Lord Jesus said; *"For from within, out of the heart of men, proceed evil thoughts"* (Mark 7:21).

Matthew Henry's comment is worthy of note. "About his marriage: some think a late marriage with a Cushite or Arabian; others because of Zipporah, whom on this occasion they called, in scorn, an Ethiopian woman, and who, they insinuated, had too great an influence upon Moses in the choice of these seventy elders. Perhaps there was some private falling out between Zipporah and Miriam, which occasioned some hot words, and one peevish reflection introduced another, till Moses and Aaron came to be interested."

John Wesley has this to say: "Zipporah, who is here called an Ethiopian, in the Hebrew a Cushite, because she was a Midianite: the word Cush being generally used in Scripture, not for

Ethiopia properly so called below Egypt, but for Arabia. If she be meant, probably they did not quarrel with him for marrying her, because that was done long since, but for being swayed by her and her relations, by whom they might think he was persuaded to chose seventy rulers, by which co-partnership in government they thought their authority and reputation diminished. And because they durst not accuse God, they charge Moses, his instrument, as the manner of men is."

MIRIAM

You will notice, that Miriam is mentioned before Aaron as being the chief instigator and leader of the sedition. This is confirmed by the fact that it was she, not Aaron, that the LORD smote with leprosy. Also, the fact that the feminine verb employed in verse one, points to Miriam as the primary troublemaker.

This aged woman presents a sad history. When at the age of about fifteen, we observe her *sisterhood*, carefully watching over her baby brother, Moses, as he lay in a little ark, floating among the bulrushes in the River Nile (Ex. 2). From there, we observe her *song*, a woman perhaps ninety five years of age, with a timbrel in her hand, dancing with the women of Israel and singing praises of triumph to the LORD. One year passes by, and what do we see? Miriam's *slander!*

May the Lord help us, who are His own, not to imitate this aged woman. She started her course well, but finished badly. How often this same pathway is seen in believers. When first saved, they are jubilant and in love with all of God's people. However, as time marches on, they become fault-finders, and very little seems to please them. The source of their complaining can be varied. Perhaps they have been wronged, so for the rest of their life they have nothing good to say about the ones that wronged them. Or, perhaps the spirit of jealously has taken possession of their heart. They have nothing good to say about anybody that has more than they, whether it be a spiritual gift, or material possessions. It even might involve a person being appointed to a position, or work, that they themselves felt should have been chosen.

Solomon wrote, this thing called envy is *"rottenness of the bones."* It is a spiritual leukemia that weakens and affects the whole body. This spiritual disease causes one to lose his vibrancy, his joy, and his song. It hinders true fellowship, and it even affects the muscles of the face, causing a "sour look," which is certainly a poor advertisement to Christianity. Some people are so affected by envy and jealously, that like a hermit crab, they crawl into their little shell and live a somber and secluded life. What a loss this will involve at the *"Judgment Seat of Christ"*! Poor things, they are to be most pitied!

ELDERS

Let me ask you elders, when you observe these traits in a sheep of yours, are you prepared, are you qualified, to remedy that awful condition? Remember, it is your responsibility to rescue such. Do you know how to deal with such a situation? When you observe one of your sheep in a sickly state, are you prepared to move in with the spiritual remedy? Remember this, you will give an account at the Judgment Seat of Christ how you have tended the sheep that the Chief Shepherd has entrusted to your care.

> *"Brethren, if a man be overtaken in a fault, ye which are spiritual, restore such an one in the spirit of meekness; considering thyself, lest thou also be tempted"* (Gal. 6:1).

I understand that the word *"restore"* means to fix and reset a broken bone, thus enabling the sheep to walk properly again. Perhaps the reason for a lack of this ability, or exercise in some so-called shepherds, is because they lack the two essentials mentioned in Galatians 6:1, namely, *spiritual and meekness*.

A SAD STORY

While on the subject of shepherding, let me relate a sad incident to you. I know of a man who was a little simple, but he was a lovely and faithful brother. He never missed an assembly meeting. He always worshipped audibly at the breaking of bread, and gave his portion to the Lord faithfully. The day came when he was sent to a nursing home. One year and six months passed by – but none of the "elders" from his assembly visited him. In fact, not one even phoned him. Is this shepherding? Finally, after nineteen months, one of the "elders" stopped in for a brief visit. How do you assess this my friend? How does this correspond to Isaiah's appraisal of the True Shepherd? *"He shall feed His flock like a shepherd: He shall gather the lambs with His arm, and carry them in His bosom, and shall gently lead those that are with young"* (Isa. 40:11). Or how does this measure up to Ezekiel's description of the Lord as a Shepherd? *"I will feed My flock, and I will cause them to lie down, saith the Lord GOD. I will seek that which was lost, and bring again that which was driven away, and will bind up that which was broken, and will strengthen that which was sick"* (Ezek. 34:15–16). I am afraid that in this case there is no comparison.

Let me ask a pertinent question. When a person assuming the place of a shepherd can take his family on a cruise ship for two weeks, but cannot find the time to visit a shut-in sheep – is that person a true shepherd? I would say such a man would more fittingly fill the description given by the prophet Jeremiah. *"Therefore thus saith the LORD God of Israel against the pastors that feed my people; ye have scattered my flock ... and have not visited them"* (Jer. 23:2). Although not guilty of scattering the flock, yet the description, *"not visited them,"* places the LORD *"against"* them.

Now then, do forgive me for being so blunt, and for not employing "political correctness (which thing I hate). I am only relating to you cold, bare facts, that should make us, as the gathered out people of God, ashamed. There seems to be a "downhill trend" in many assemblies today. We are drifting toward sectarianism. Our brethren of 1827 came out of Christendom.

They saw the error in a one-man ministry, programs governing "church" meetings, a paid ministry, and a host of other irregularities seen in the religious world of supposed Christianity.

What is happening today? Well folks, it seems very apparent that we are drifting back into the very thing from which these godly brethren came out. I feel that one of the problems is that we are not reading our Bibles as we ought. Another reason is, that we have received into our assemblies people that are not truly born again. As these unconverted professors continue in any local testimony, eventually they reach the place of power and authority, and true to their fallen nature, they seek to introduce unscriptural ideas that eventually lead to the downfall of a scriptural testimony.

The reason that I have called your attention to this threatening situation is that many godly brethren have approached me about it. They are deeply concerned. Not just older brethren, but some younger ones as well. It is a perplexing problem and worthy of fervent prayer, that God will intervene and preserve the things that remain, lest we just melt into the mainstream of Christendom.

Now, after this diversion, we must get back to Miriam. We have considered her *sisterhood*, her *song*, and her *slander*. Following her ill speaking, we now come to her *"shutting out."*

> *"And the LORD spake suddenly unto Moses, and unto Aaron, and unto Miriam, Come out ye three unto the tabernacle of the congregation. And they three came out. And the LORD came down in the pillar of the cloud, and stood in the door of the tabernacle, and called Aaron and Miriam: and they both came forth. And he said, Hear now my words: If there be a prophet among you, I the LORD will make myself known unto him in a vision, and will speak unto him in a dream. My servant Moses is not so, who is faithful in all mine house. With him will I speak mouth to mouth, even ap-*

parently, and not in dark speeches; and the similitude of the LORD shall he behold: wherefore then were ye not afraid to speak against my servant Moses? And the anger of the LORD was kindled against them; and he departed. And the cloud departed from off the tabernacle; and, behold, Miriam became leprous, white as snow: and Aaron looked upon Miriam, and, behold, she was leprous. And Aaron said unto Moses, Alas, my lord, I beseech thee, lay not the sin upon us, wherein we have done foolishly, and wherein we have sinned. Let her not be as one dead, of whom the flesh is half consumed when he cometh out of his mother's womb. And Moses cried unto the LORD, saying, Heal her now, O God, I beseech thee. And the LORD said unto Moses, If her father had but spit in her face, should she not be ashamed seven days? let her be shut out from the camp seven days, and after that let her be received in again. And Miriam was shut out from the camp seven days: and the people journeyed not till Miriam was brought in again"* (Num. 12:4–15).

SUDDEN AND SEVERE JUDGMENT

At the beginning of any dispensation, God seems to act more severely toward sin. As that particular dispensation moves on, the immediate and severe hand of God punishing sin is not so prevalent. Take for example the dispensation of grace, commencing on the day of Pentecost at the birth of the Church. Notice Ananias and Sapphira. They lied to the Holy Ghost. Immediately, they were smitten by God, and buried by their brethren the same day that the sin was committed. Look at the assembly at Corinth. Some were not discerning in the emblems the body of the Lord. They were partaking of them in an unworthy manner. What was the result? Paul tells the assembly, *"For this cause many are weak and sickly among you, and many sleep"* (1 Cor. 11:30). Come to our day. Do we find the same immediate and severe judgment? Not at all! You see, the longer the dispensation runs, the less severe the judgment is. The late William Warke thought that it was due to a lesser manifestation of the divine presence among us. He said that in a way it was a mercy, for if the presence of God was as manifest now as it was in apostolic days, many of us would be dead from the judging hand of God.

Establishing this principle in our minds, we can readily see why Miriam was dealt with so severely. The dispensation of Law had just commenced, thus, the hand of God acted immediately and with severity.

At the commencement of the Scripture you have just read we have an inserted statement. *"(Now the man Moses was very meek, above all the men which were upon the face of the earth)"* (Num. 12:3). If Moses was meek, why then did he write this about himself, especially when God's mind is, *"Let another man praise thee, and not thine own mouth; a stranger, and not thine own lips"* (Prov. 27:2)? Some have even gone so far as to say that this statement was inserted by another at a later date. However, we do want to consider that this statement seems to be a necessary vindication of himself from their unjust reproach, rather than a statement made from self-conceit. You will find the same principle in the apostle Paul when injurious attacks were made on his integrity. Notice his rebuttal. *"As the truth of Christ is in me, no man shall stop me of this boasting in the regions of Achaia ... Are they ministers of Christ (I speak as a fool) I am more ... for in nothing am I behind the very chiefest apostles"* (2 Cor. 11:10, 23; 12:11).

Moses was stirred up to holy indignation because God was offended and dishonored, and like Paul, would have been perfectly in order writing about himself thus. But there is far more to this than that. Please consider the fact that the penmen of Holy Writ were not tied to the same rules as are prescribed to other writers, for a divine influence was guiding them to write exactly what they were told by the Spirit. Thus we conclude that the statement of Moses' meekness was rather the testimony of the Holy Spirit respecting Moses, so Moses, the mere penman, was compelled to record those very words.

AARON AND MIRIAM'S SLANDER

There was no delay in the action of God. He spake suddenly! The more we are silent in our own cause, the more God is engaged to plead it. This was the case here. The judicial summons was given to Moses, Aaron, and Miriam, to come out to the door of the tabernacle of the congregation. Whether they came out of their tents, or came out from a supposed crowd of people assembled nearby is not known. The pillar of the cloud moved from over the most holy place to the front of the tabernacle where the three stood. Aaron and Miriam were called to step forward. I wonder what their feelings were at that moment with the very presence of Jehovah before their faces. What a solemn moment, one to be greatly feared. In our translation, eighty words complete the LORD'S message to them. He mentions the uniqueness of Moses as His servant above all prophets. They were reminded that His means of communicating to Moses was of a far superior nature than to any other mortal. Having vindicated Moses, the LORD asks them a most searching question. *"Wherefore then were ye not afraid to speak against my servant Moses?"* (Num. 12:8). The LORD did not wait for any answer, but in kindled anger, He immediately departed from them. There the two of them silently stood, rebuked and condemned. *"Be sure your sin will find you out"* (Num. 32:23). Removing His presence, the cloud departed from off the tabernacle, rising to an greater height than usual above the sanctuary of God. All Israel would know that something serious had taken place.

The withdrawal of the LORD'S presence and the invasion of Miriam's leprosy were simultaneous. It was leprosy of the worst kind. This leprosy came on in stages and progressed through time, but in Miriam's case, there was no progression, for she felt the mature effects of this dreaded disease immediately. Someone has quaintly said, "her foul tongue was justly punished with a foul face." As a result of her disease, she was shut out of the camp for seven days – a disgraced leper! What a tragedy! What a blight on her testimony! The sequel ends with a very interesting note. *"And the people journeyed not till Miriam was brought in again."* Her sin had stopped the progress of the whole nation! Solomon said; *"One sinner destroyeth much good"* (Eccl. 9:18).

The question arises, even though Aaron did not seem to be the leader in the sin of railing, yet he was guilty. Why then was he spared from the same plague that came so suddenly upon his sister Miriam? Did his high priestly office exempt him from the punishment? Not at all! It would seem that this weak, easily swayed individual, was spared simply because he immediately repented of his sin. Moses' recording his confession betrays this fact. *"Alas, my lord, I beseech thee, lay not the sin upon us, wherein we have done foolishly, and wherein we have sinned."* Look for Miriam's confession, and you won't find it. She is silent. Aaron is a broken man, but Miriam seems yet to be a belligerent woman.

Is there not a sobering lesson in this for all of us? Excommunication from an assembly is the most drastic action that an assembly is called upon by the Lord to execute. For the sin of rebellion against the oversight (Matt. 18:15–18); fornication; covetousness; extortion; idolatry; railing; and drunkenness (1 Cor. 5:9–13); excommunication is required until full repentance is manifested in the "wicked person." Not until then, can the sinning one be brought back into the fellowship of the assembly. The purpose of the discipline is fourfold. (1) To maintain the purity of the assembly. (2) For the restoration of the offender. (3) To furnish a warning to all the saints. (4) To vindicate the name of God.

Peter indicates that as far as a Christian is concerned, such behavior as Aaron and Miriam's should be a thing of the past, something taken off and discarded as an undesirable garment. *"Wherefore laying aside all malice, and all guile, and hypocrisies, and envies, and all evil speakings ..."* (1 Pet. 2:1). *"Laying aside"* is an aorist participle indicating something having been done. The creation is new, the individual just saved is changed, and the old behavior of harboring *malice* (evil thoughts and grudges), *guile* (craft and dishonesty), *hypocrisies* (play-acting), *envies* (jealousy, tormented by another's good), and all evil speaking, is a thing of the past. Sad to say, that in some cases, we are forced to reword that and say, *it should be a thing of the past!*

25

FAILURE TO ENTER IN

NUMBERS 13 – 14

"And the LORD spake unto Moses, saying, Send thou men, that they may search the land of Canaan, which I give unto the children of Israel: of every tribe of their fathers shall ye send a man, every one a ruler among them. And Moses by the commandment of the LORD sent them from the wilderness of Paran: all those men were heads of the children of Israel. And these were their names ..." (Num. 13:1–4).

It has been slightly over one year since Israel left the land of bondage. They have learned much. The crossing of the Red Sea manifested to them the tremendous delivering power of God on their behalf. They had experienced the bitter waters of Marah made miraculously sweet, and they had witnessed the protective and delivering power of Jehovah when Amalek made his sneak attack. At Sinai, they had witnessed the august majesty, holiness, and awesomeness of the Almighty, enough to make their leader Moses fear and quake (Heb. 12:21). Various laws and restrictions had been delivered to their hand through their lawgiver Moses. They were now an organized and established nation under the banner of Jehovah. You might say, that as long as they were obedient and trusting their God that they were invincible! There was no nation on earth like them. They were not really experienced and trained in warfare, yet there was no army that could withstand them, for Jehovah would fight for them. I tell you that there was never a nation like it on the face of this earth! Is it any wonder that the inhabitants of Canaan trembled when they heard of this mighty people crossing the Red Sea. To them, it would only be a matter of time for their downfall. God would be using His people for two purposes. The first reason being to fulfill His promise to Abraham in giving his posterity the land. Second, using Israel as His weapon to bring judgment upon the inhabitants of the land for their wickedness.

THE SENDING OF SPIES

If you would only read this chapter regarding the spies, you would think that this was the plan of God. Nothing could be farther from the truth! It was not God's intention at all for spies to search out the land prior to their invasion of it. I know the chapter standing alone would give that impression, but when you turn to Deuteronomy 1:19–24, you gain a deeper insight to the whole affair. Notice:

> *"And when we departed from Horeb, we went through all that great and terrible wilderness, which ye saw by the way of the mountain of the Amorites, as the LORD our God commanded us; and we came to Kadeshbarnea. And I said unto you, Ye are come unto the mountain of the Amorites, which the LORD our God doth give unto us. Behold, the LORD thy God hath set the land before thee: go up and possess it, as the LORD God of thy fathers hath said unto thee; fear not, neither be discouraged. And ye came near unto me every one of you, and said, We will send men before us, and they shall search us out the land, and bring us word again by what way we must go up, and into what cities we shall come. And the saying pleased me well: and I took twelve men of you, one of a tribe: And they turned and went up into the mountain, and came unto the valley of Eshcol, and searched it out."*

FAILURE TO ENTER IN

It seems evident, that this whole plan of sending spies, did not originate with the LORD, nor yet with Moses, but with the people as a whole. Moses has total confidence in the LORD, and encourages God's people to go forward and take the land God had promised them. However, lurking in their ears was that insidious virus of unbelief. Paul, in writing to the Hebrews, reminds them that Israel had an evil heart of unbelief (Heb. 3:12). Bishop Hall wrote;

> "What needed they doubt of the goodness of that land, which God told them did flow with milk and honey? What needed they doubt of obtaining that which God promised to give? When we will send forth our senses to be our scouts in matters of faith, and rather dare trust men than God, we are worthy to be deceived."

God chose their delusions in permitting them to have their own way. Seeing that the people were intent on sending spies, He did not prevent it, but left them up to their own devising. He yielded to the importunity of their hearts just as we will see later in His dealings with Balaam. God could have said, *"Since you do not trust My ability to give you the land, and cannot accept My promise to you, go ahead with your plans, and send your men to spy out the land and satisfy yourselves in your own way."*

Have you ever considered the fact that God had already gone before them and spied out the land Himself? *"In the day that I lifted up Mine hand unto them, to bring them forth of the land of Egypt into a land that **I had espied** for them, flowing with milk and honey, which is the glory of all lands"* (Ezek. 20:6). So, if God had already spied out the land for them, would it not be uncalled for, and unnecessary for them to spy it out? Absolutely! However, they had their mind made up, so the LORD just as much as said, "Go right ahead."

What a total waste of energy and time! Besides all of this, the whole affair ended in a total disaster, and those of that generation never did enter into the land. They all died in that waste howling-wilderness. They were given the promise, but never experienced it. A sad story indeed!

Paul takes this incident up in Hebrews 3 and 4, warning his brethren in the flesh that they too, in their unconverted state, were manifesting the same spirit as Israel on this sobering occasion. He likens Israel to an unbeliever, and the promised land as a picture of God's salvation. He terms it a *"rest."* Notice how he employs that little word, *"lest." "Take heed, brethren,* **lest** *there be in any of you an evil heart of unbelief, in departing from the living God. But exhort one another daily, while it is called To day;* **lest** *any of you be hardened through the deceitfulness of sin ... Let us therefore fear,* **lest***, a promise being left us of entering into His rest, any of you should seem to come short of it"* (Heb. 3:12–13; 4:1). Just as Israel came short of entering into their rest (the land of Canaan), so the Jew in Paul's day was in danger of failing to obtain God's salvation. In both cases, Israel in Moses' day, and the Jews in Paul's day, their failure to receive what God had provided for them was the result of their unbelief.

CHOOSING GOOD MEN

The men chosen for this endeavor were *"rulers,"* one from each tribe (Levi excepted). It was only fit that men of authority, prudence, character, and position were chosen. Let me interject this while passing. You don't assign men to responsible activity in an assembly to encourage them. You assign them because of their qualifications. So we have a case in an assembly where we want to encourage a lax brother, so we assign him the position of opening the Sunday School. Or we take a novice in the faith and assign him the responsibility of opening an assembly Bible reading. We want to make him feel that he is needed, that he is somewhat important. This is not only unscriptural, but it is also utter nonsense! Trying to make unimportant fellows feel important, is a good way to ruin them. Where does worthiness come in?

When Ezra returned to Jerusalem from Babylon, on their journey they camped out in tents by a river, and having viewed the people, they discovered that none of the sons of Levi were with them. So what did Ezra do? Notice. *"Then sent I for Eliezer, for Ariel, for Shemaiah, and for Elnathan, and for Jarib, and for Elnathan, and for Nathan, and for Zechariah, and for Meshullam, chief men; also for Joiarib, and for Elnathan,* **men of understanding**" (Ezra 8:16). He sent for men that had proved themselves. Godly men of maturity. He had them perform an errand and did they bring him a youth, an ignoramus, and an unproven fellow? Why no! That is not what they brought! They brought *"a man of understanding"* (Ezra 8:16, 18). Why did they bring a man of understanding? Simply, because they were men of understanding. They had common, and spiritual sense.

To push novices into responsible positions proves that those who do so have no understanding. They are lacking in divine wisdom and knowledge. The word *"understanding,"* means, *"to discern, to have intelligence."* Now do not misunderstand me, we seek to encourage all of God's people, but there certainly is a divine way to do it.

For men of understanding, who have borne the heat and burden of the day for God, who are mature, grayheaded, and knowledgeable in the Word, to be subject to sit and listen to a "youngster" try to open and lead a week-night Bible reading is the height of folly. Consider what the Holy Spirit says: *"For every one that useth milk is unskilful in the word of righteousness: for he is a babe"* (Heb. 5:13). *"Likewise, ye younger, submit yourselves unto the elder"* (1 Pet. 5:5). Solomon was a very observing man. Please notice what he said: *"Delight is not seemly for a fool; much less for a servant to have rule over princes"* (Prov. 19:10). *"For three things the earth is disquieted, and for four which it cannot bear: For a servant when he reigneth; and a fool when he is filled with meat ..."* (Prov. 30:21–22). *"I have seen servants upon horses, and princes walking as servants upon the earth"* (Eccl. 10:7). The men chosen to spy out the land were men of stamina, character, and authority.

Before leaving, these men were instructed as to what to look for. They were to observe whether the inhabitants were strong, weak, few, or many (v. 18). They were to determine whether the land was good or bad. Was it healthy, or run down? Also, what were the cities like? Were they living in tents, or in strongholds? In other words, were the cities walled, or unwalled? The Chaldean, Greek, and Vulgate render it this way, which seems to be the correct interpretation. They were to determine, by observation, whether the land was fat (fertile) or lean (barren), and whether there were forests or not. This might have even included fruit trees. Thus, the quality of the soil was to be investigated. Ah yes, they just had to satisfy their carnal curiosity. Even before they left Egypt God had proclaimed that it was a good land and large, a land flowing with milk and honey (Ex. 3:8). So what did it matter what they discovered?

THE SPIRIT'S OMNISCIENCE

All of this reminds me of the practice of some that preach the gospel. They have an audience, and in many Gospel Halls, hanging on the back wall, facing the preacher is this text in bold letters; *"Preach the Word"* (2 Tim. 4:2). But that is not sufficient in the eyes of some preachers. In order to preach more intelligently to sinners (so they think) they make it their business, during a gospel series, to hold interviews with particular sinners, one by one, to find out their problems and their background. Now why this? Well, they want to know all about the individual, to determine how they are going to preach to them. What do you term this? I call it the height of nonsense!

One would think that the Holy Spirit was totally ignorant of the people brought under the preaching. No, He is not ignorant. He knows more about that individual than they even know about themselves! All the evangelist has to do is be obedient to the leading and guiding of the Holy Spirit, and He will supply the preacher with all the material that he needs for the Holy Spirit to bring conviction of sin to the souls of those listening. "Preach the Word." "Preach the Word." "Preach the Word." I cannot emphasize this too strongly! "Preach the Word."

The Spirit-guided preacher reminds me of a warrior in a chariot in the days of Ahab and Jehoshaphat. Micaiah the prophet had told Ahab that he would be slain in the battle in which he was to be engaged. So what did wicked Ahab do? He disguised himself before entering the battle, but he encouraged Jehoshaphat to wear his own kingly robes. Ahab figured that if they were going to kill him, the king of Israel, they would think that Jehosaphat would be that king and kill him by mistake, allowing him to flee. So what happened? Well now, this is most interesting. God had Ahab singled out no matter how cunning his disguise. As the battle raged, *"a certain man drew a bow at a venture, and smote the king of Israel between the joints of the harness"* (1 Kgs. 22:34). Now that fellow with the bow knew nothing, but in his simplicity, he shot and killed the very man that God had singled out for death.

Here is the lesson. A preacher does not have to discover the history of a sinner to effectively preach to that particular person. All he has to do is, "Preach the Word." When Paul entered Europe and won souls at Philippi, did he hold an investigation and spy out the background of those women gathered by the riverside? When he was thrown into prison, with his feet fast in stocks, did he hold a consultation with the jailor first? Why no, how could he, even if he wanted to do so? Such foolish thoughts never entered his mind. Well then what did he do? How did he win them to Christ. The answer is simple. He simply preached the Word! *"So then faith cometh by hearing, and hearing by the word of God"* (Rom. 10:17). Again I say, "Preach the Word."

GRAPES, POMEGRANATES, AND FIGS

If one can rely on the maps provided at the back of many Bibles, the spies would have traveled approximately 350 miles north, and 350 miles back, making an average of seventeen and one half miles a day. However, they may have separated at certain points and then met together at another point, which would lower the average miles per person for the day.

Verse 22 states, *"And they ascended by the south, and came unto Hebron,"* where was a nearby cave containing the bones of Abraham, Sarah, Isaac, Rebekah, Jacob, and Leah, receivers of the promise. Certainly their testimony would put unbelief to shame, would it not? There is not much doubt in my mind that these spies would stand and gaze with reverence at that tomb which presented such a memorial to faith.

It was *"the time of the firstripe grapes,"* being August to mid-September, so that the owners would be keeping watch at this time of the year. The spies would have to be very skilful in moving about. In verse 22 we read, *"(Now Hebron was built seven years before Zoan in Egypt.)"* Ask yourself, why is this mentioned? What is the purpose in it? There must be a reason for it. There is, and there is even more than one reason. First of all, our attention is drawn to the fact that what is being stated proves that Egypt (as she boasted) was not the most ancient nation in the world. Second, we consider a spiritual truth. Egypt is a picture of the world, and Canaan a picture of our heavenly inheritance. The country to which we are going is older than this world, having been prepared before the foundation of the world (Eph. 1:4; Heb. 11:16).

> *"And they came unto the brook of Eshcol, and cut down from thence a branch with one cluster of grapes, and they bare it between two upon a staff; and they brought of the pomegranates, and of the figs. The place was called the brook Eshcol, because of the cluster of grapes which the children of Israel cut down from thence. And they returned from searching of the land after forty days"* (Num. 13:23–25).

"And they came unto the brook of Eshcol." The word is, *"Nahal,"* signifying both a stream of water, and the valley through which it runs. *"Eschol"* signifies *"a cluster, a bunch,"* and this name was given to the place as a memorial of what took place. History relates that such a cluster weighed twelve pounds and was three feet long. The word *cluster* could also be translated *bunch*, and if that be the case, then there is the possibility that what the men

carried were several bunches of grapes that were so heavy on the branch that they appeared as one huge cluster. The grapes of that part of the country are still very large in size, and noted for their superiority. Two men were assigned to carry this large cluster to prevent the grapes from being bruised in being transported for such a considerable distance.

Thus, grapes, pomegranates, and figs were transported back to the nation of Israel, revealing the wealth of the land. There is a spiritual application to these three items that prove most interesting. **(1) Grapes.** The fruit of the vine. First, we see the planting of the vine. Israel was planted by Jehovah, through which Messiah would come. Then the cluster on the vine, which conveys the shadows of that great coming event – the Old Testament prophecies foretelling of the Cross. Then, we see the cluster in a basket, a picture of our Lord in a manger, followed by His ministry unto men. Following this, we view the winepress, the crushing of the grapes, having been brought in a basket. This is a picture of Calvary, where He was crushed under the wrathful hand of God on our behalf. From the crushing flows the juice of the grape, which when fermented *"maketh glad the heart of man"* (Ps. 104:15). God's salvation has brought to men *"joy unspeakable and full of glory"* (1 Pet. 1:8).

(2) Pomegranates. Weavings of this fruit were on the robe of the Ephod (Ex. 28:33). The colors of the pomegranates were to be of *blue, purple,* and *scarlet. Blue* indicates that we are a *holy priesthood*, entering the sanctuary to worship and minister unto God. *Purple* indicates that we are a *royal priesthood*, entering the street, to minister unto men with the gospel (1 Pet. 2:5, 9). *Scarlet* points to the fact that the blood affords us liberty to enter the holiest as holy priests, and the blood of Christ being the theme of the royal priests in the presentation the gospel.

Upon the hem of the ephod these pomegranates were made, *"and bells of gold between them round about."* Thus, as the high priest entered the holy place to minister, people on the outside would be made aware that their high priest was in the sanctuary, ministering unto God on their behalf, thus bringing comfort and assurance to their souls. We claim the same, do we not? The golden bells are ringing. To me the golden bells are the many verses in the Bible that give me the absolute assurance that I have a living and functioning Great High Priest, ministering in the presence of God on my behalf.

(3) Figs. They represent the sweet fruits of righteousness. In this, Israel failed. That is the meaning of our Lord's parable in Luke 13:6-9. The fig tree failed to produce fruit that was sought for three years. The verdict was to *"cut it down."* Our Lord moved among the nation for three years, but there was no fruit of repentance on their part, neither was there any fruits of righteousness. Finally, it was cut down. Israel lost its position and was set aside that the blessing of the Gentiles might come in. Now the fruits of righteousness are seen in born again believers, as Paul relates to the Philippian assembly. *"Being filled with the fruits of righteousness, which are by Jesus Christ, unto the glory and praise of God"* (Phil. 1:11).

FORTY – THE NUMBER OF TESTING

They returned after spying out the land for forty days. How prevalent the number forty is in Scripture. It usually speaks of a time of testing. In Noah's day *"the rain was upon the earth forty days and forty nights"* (Gen. 7:12). After the tops of the mountains were seen, at the end of forty days he opened the window of the ark, and sent forth a raven (Gen. 8:6–7). *"And Isaac was forty years old when he took Rebekah to wife"* (Gen. 25:20). *"And Esau was forty years old when he took to wife Judith the daughter of Beeri the Hittite, and Bashemath the daughter of Elon the Hittite"* (Gen. 26:34). Concerning the death of Jacob it is said: *"And forty days were fulfilled for him; for so are fulfilled the days of those which are embalmed"* (Gen. 50:3). *"And the children of Israel did eat manna forty years, until they came to a land inhabited"* (Ex. 16:35). *"And Moses went into the midst of the cloud, and gat him up into the mount: and Moses was in the mount forty days and forty nights"* (Ex. 24:18). On each side of the tabernacle there were forty sockets of silver for the boards (Ex. 36). Goliath challenged Israel for forty days (1 Sam. 17). Elijah *"arose, and did eat and drink, and went in the strength of that meat forty days and forty nights unto Horeb the mount of God"* (1 Kgs. 19:8). Eli judged Israel forty years. Saul, David, and Solomon all reigned exactly forty years. *"Joash was seven years old when he began to reign, and he reigned forty years in Jerusalem"* (2 Chron. 24:1). Ezekiel was told, *"Lie again on thy right side, and thou shalt bear the iniquity of the house of Judah forty days"* (Ezek. 4:6). Jonah's alarming message was, *"Yet forty days, and Nineveh shall be overthrown"* (Jon. 3:4). Ezekiel's prophecy concerning Egypt has been fulfilled. *"Behold, therefore I am against thee, and against thy rivers, and I will make the land of Egypt utterly waste and desolate, from the tower of Syene even unto the border of Ethiopia. No foot of man shall pass through it, nor foot of beast shall pass through it, neither shall it be inhabited forty years"* (Ezek. 29: 10–11). Christ *"was there in the wilderness forty days, tempted of Satan"* (Mark 1:13). The Lord ascended to heaven forty days after His resurrection (Acts 1:3).

THE LACK OF FAITH

The spies were tested for forty days, and out of the twelve, only two manifested faith in Jehovah. They admitted that it was a land that flowed with milk and honey, and they produced the luscious fruit of that land that they had gathered, but verse twenty eight commences with a most distressing word, "NEVERTHELESS." The facts were positive, but their attitude was very negative! They were greatly impressed with the quality of the land, but they were fearful to trust the ability of their God. They had no faith in His word to simply march in under the power and direction of Jehovah, to witness their enemies literally melt away before them as they advanced into their inheritance. So, they decided to walk by sight, thus they searched out the land for their own satisfaction. Nevertheless, they were still fainthearted. Unbelief permeated their heart, and they fainted at the very thought of marching in under the banner of Jehovah. You would think that they thought that God was asleep to their position. That God was not really the Almighty. That perhaps He would not fight for them and consequently, they would be sadly defeated.

This business of not trusting God is quite common, isn't it? We see it all around us in Christian circles. Much money is doled out to insurance companies that could be used for the furtherance of the gospel, or for the benefit of needy saints. There was an "old-timer" in the hills of West Virginia who was wise, yet quaint. One day he said, "You know, it's like this. When an insurance company tries to convince you that you need insurance, they don't believe that you need it, or they would never insure you, for fear of losing money. But they try to convince you that you do need it, for they want your money." In other words, they seek to convince people that all kinds of misfortunes could happen to their property, yet they themselves don't believe it, for if they did, they wouldn't insure them. We are quite willing to trust the Lord with our soul's eternal destiny, but it seems that we have a problem trusting God to supply us in life's journey.

Now let me clarify some things. There are laws of the land that the Christian is required to keep. Let us take the automobile for an example. The law stipulates that the owner must carry liability insurance. That is, he must have insurance covering the other fellow involved in an accident. That is a moral law. But when a Christian covers himself with comprehensive insurance, what in essence is he doing? Well, he is afraid that if he damages his car, that the Lord won't provide him enough means to repair it, so he goes to the "Egyptian Insurance Company" to foot the bill. "Ah!" you say, "But the law requires you to have comprehensive insurance." Really? Think again! The only way that a Christian can be forced to pay comprehensive insurance is because the vehicle that he is operating is *not* really his! It is the lending institution's automobile. Consequently, they require their debtor to pay the insurance, for in reality, they own the car.

A SENSIBLE FAMILY

However, what would possess a Christian to drive a car that they cannot afford? Is this right? The late Archie Stewart told such debtors, *"'Owe no man anything'* (Rom. 13:8). Pay up like a man!" I know of a couple that never paid over $1,000 for a car. They raised twelve children, owned a dairy, and never had health insurance, property insurance, or automobile insurance. They paid cash for everything they owned. How are they fairing today, now that all the children are raised, and most of them married? Well my friend, they are doing simply wonderful! Some time ago, his wife was given a fourteen year old Buick, and he drives three rusted Oldsmobiles made in the early eighties. Most of their food is raised on their farm, and occasionally, a cow is sold, enabling them to buy used clothing at the Goodwill store in a nearby town. They are among the richest people on earth, for *"godliness with contentment is great gain"* (1 Tim. 6:6). Are they happy? My oh my, they are far happier than the richest billionaire on earth, for they have the Lord as their Shepherd, godly saints as their companions, and heaven as their home. They can truthfully exclaim like the Psalmist, *"The lines are fallen unto me in pleasant places; yea, I have a goodly heritage"* (Ps. 16:6). They are extremely happy with the simple things of life, and best of all, they owe no man anything!

The person that buys a $30,000 car and obtains a five-year loan at 5%, paying $500 each month ends up not only paying $30,000 for his vehicle but also $4516 in interest! Beside all this, he is forced to take out full coverage insurance, that adds a few more thousand dollars to be paid out. It is far better to drive an affordable old car, and be clear of debt, saving one's money in the meantime to move up to a newer, and perhaps more dependable car.

Of course, when people that waver in trusting God for everything are confronted, they are very alert in producing all kinds of excuses. Such as, "medical bills today could bankrupt one for life." Or, "If my house burned to the ground, I don't have the means to build another one." Or, "If I wrecked my car,

I couldn't afford to replace it." However, how does God expect us to respond to our Lord's words in Luke 12:22–30? He warns us against being over-anxious and troubled with cares. He tells us to look at nature, and by the way, that's the only way I could be termed a "naturalist." He proceeds to explain to us how he cares for the ravens and the lilies, and if that is the case, can He not also care for us who are of far more value to Him than they? He tells us to not seek what we shall eat or drink, neither to be of a doubtful mind. In other words, we are not to live in a state of suspense, *"for all these things the nations of the world seek after,"* and rightly so, for they do not have a Father in heaven watching for their welfare, as we do.

THE LANGUAGE OF UNBELIEF

You will notice how these faint-hearted spies (Josh. and Caleb not among them) used exaggeration to discourage the people from going into their land. Ah yes, it is a good land, but *"NEVERTHELESS"* the people are strong, the cities are walled, and very great. They are stronger than we. *"It is a land that eateth up the inhabitants thereof,"* meaning that all those inhabitants were constantly at war with each other, consequently, all of them were skilled in warfare. *"All the people that we saw in it are men of great stature. And there we saw the sons of Anak, which come of the giants; and we were in our own sight as grasshoppers, and so were we in their sight"* (v. 32–33). In other words, *"we don't stand a chance! Go to that place? No way! It will eat us up!"* I wonder where they thought Jehovah was when they were spewing out such words of unbelief? By the same token, I wonder what God thinks when His people today cannot trust Him? Perhaps we desire a higher lifestyle than God the Lord deems good for us, so we resort to our own means to elevate our standard of living, even if it means being indebted to the ungodly. Shame on us if that is so.

So effective was the negative report that *"all the congregation lifted up their voice, and cried; and the people wept that night"* (Num. 14:1). During World War II, the recruits that rated "4-F" on their physical were deemed unfit to be drafted into the army. This multitude could be rated as "4-F." Failing Memories. Flowing Tears. Faulting Mouths. Fainting Hearts. Such a people were totally unfit to march into Canaan and possess the land.

CALEB – THE MAN OF FAITH

Thank God for a man like Caleb who stilled the people, and said, *"Let us go up at once, and possess it; for we are well able to overcome it. But the men that went up with him said, We be not able to go up against the people; for they are stronger than we"* (verses 30–31). Perhaps we can see in this episode, that it is easier to weaken the hands of our brethren than it is to strengthen their hands. It does not take any skill to break things down, but it does take skill to build a house. In this case, the majority were out of touch with God and the minority were in touch with God. The multitude chose to believe ten faint-hearted men, rather than two faithful men.

THE CONGREGATION OF COWARDS

So faint did their hearts become, that they proposed to make a captain to assist them in returning to Egypt. I call this the extremity of their despair, unbelief, and ungratitude. Forty five years later, Caleb relates this incident with these words. *"Forty years old was I when Moses the servant of the LORD sent me from Kadeshbarnea to espy out the land; and I brought him word again as it was in mine heart. Nevertheless my brethren that went up with me made the heart of the people melt: but I wholly followed the LORD my God"* (Josh. 14:7–8).

The congregation *"**lifted up** their voice, and cried"* (v. 1). In Psalm 106:26, we find that when Israel despised the pleasant land, and believed not His word, but murmured in their tents, and hearkened not unto the voice of the LORD, that *"He **lifted up** His hand against them, to overthrow them in the wilderness"* (Ps. 106:24–26). In both cases, the same Hebrew word "yissa" (*"lifted up"*) is used. Thus we see, that just as Israel lifted up their voice in a rebellious complaint against the LORD, in like manner, the LORD lifted up His hand against them. With a righteous decree, He banned them from the Promised Land!

How frightfully sad! Instead of raising up their flags with a brave determination to march into the land, defying all their enemies in the name of the Lord, we see them sitting down as cowards in despair, giving way to crying and tears. They are weeping, afraid of enemies that they had never even seen. What cowardness! What wretchedness! What imbecility! What shame! Their minds were so negatively affected that they are begging to return to slavery in Egypt! How soon they had forgotten the hardships of their bondage. How soon that had forgotten the gracious and delivering power of their God on their behalf! How soon they had forgotten the miraculous provision of Jehovah, the opening of the Red Sea, the bitter waters made sweet, the angel's food from heaven, and the water from the rock. A dreadful picture painted and displayed by unbelief is all that stands before them! They are now choosing their future. Instead of marching into the land as triumphant soldiers with swords in their hands, they are making a choice that will make them die as rotten sheep in a waste-howling wilderness. Bishop Hall has saliently remarked:

> "The rods of their Egyptian task-masters had never been so fit for them as now for crying. They had cause indeed to weep for their infidelity; but now they weep for fear of those enemies they saw not. I fear, if there had been ten Calebs to persuade, and but two faint spies to discourage them, those two cowards would have prevailed against those two solicitors: how much more, now ten oppose and but two encourage!"

Upon hearing the words of the multitude, Moses and Aaron fell on their faces before all the assembly of the congregation of the children of Israel. The people's ungrateful attitude caused these leaders to prostrate themselves in the presence of the Almighty that they might pray more devotedly. You would think that the transgressors would have been falling down, begging for pardon in the presence of the Mighty God Who had acted so benevolently on their behalf, but this is not the case. Transgressors seem to be less impressed with the greatness of their guilt than those they transgress against. The Lord enjoins the transgressed ones; *"Bless them that curse you, and pray for them which despitefully use you"* (Luke 6:28), and this is the attitude we see in Moses and Aaron in this vexing situation. They provide a good example for the godly Christian today.

They *"fell on their faces."* The usual posture of prayer with the Jewish people was standing. In times of deep distress, or when anxious for a favorable response, they would resort to kneeling. However, in the most desperate cases, and deepest desire to be heard, they would fall on their face. When our Lord's soul was heavy, even unto death, He fell on His face in holy prayer. Compare Luke 22:41 with Matthew 26:39, and notice the difference. A Man kneeling, but also a King on His face – in prayer.

THE RENDING OF CLOTHES

The testimony of Caleb is remarkable and well worth noting. In this most vexing situation, both he and Joshua rent their clothes. Many men have been recorded in Holy Writ of rending their clothes. Reuben, in distress as to the whereabouts of his brother Joseph, rent his clothes (Gen. 37:29). When Joseph's brethren found his cup in Benjamin's sack, in distress, they all rent their clothes. When the men of Ai overpowered Joshua's men, he rent his clothes, and fell to the earth upon his face (Josh. 7:6). On a solemn occasion which would affect his only daughter, in dismay, Jephthah rent his clothes (Judg. 11:35). When David heard the sad news of the death of Saul and Jonathan, he took hold of his clothes and rent them (2 Sam. 1:11). When Rabshakea blasphemed the God of Israel Hilkiah, Shebna, and Joah, came to Hezekiah with their clothes rent. When these men presented the news to the king, he also rent his clothes, and covered himself with sackcloth. When Job received the devastating news of his tremendous loss, he rent his mantle. When Mordecai perceived the plot to kill all the Jews, he rent his clothes and put on sackcloth with ashes (Est. 4:1). At the trial of Christ, the high priest rent his clothes. When Paul and Barnabas preached at Lystra, the people would have elevated them to the place of being gods. Upon hearing this, in horror, both Barnaba and Paul rent their clothes.

It is easy to surmise from these Scriptures what the rending of the clothes involved. They were times of shock, distress, perplexity, indignation, sorrow, or excessive grief. Having outwardly expressed their dismay, Joshua and Caleb stood up and witnessed to the nation. What courage! What fidelity! These men were fearless, faithful, accurate, and sincere! These are just the qualifications needed for every preacher and teacher today! I cannot help but love these men. They remained undaunted in spite of the attitude of their unbelieving audience. They did not care what the other spies said, they were quick to contradict them. Rather than offend their God, they immediately contradicted their comrades. They were far more concerned about what God thought than what the people thought. I remember sitting with a respected teacher at a conference in Northern Ireland. There was a "sing song" sort of a man ministering. I wondered about him, and asked my companion, "What type of a man is he?" He replied, "If sisters were in this audience with hair as short as scrub brushes, that man would never raise his voice against it." Ah, we must be politically correct. We dare not offend any, even though we offend God. We would rather offend God than man. We would rather try to "build up" the disobedient saint, rather than rebuke and exhort them. We cannot afford to be "politically correct." This, it seems to me, is the thought of some preachers. May God help us to be men like Caleb and Joshua.

CALEB AND JOSHUA'S FAITHFUL TESTIMONY

Isn't it refreshing to see how these noble men conducted themselves in spite of the fact that the whole nation was against them? What fortitude! What courage! What reverence to God!

FAILURE TO ENTER IN

They faithfully bore testimony to how great and how good the land of promise was. They spoke of it as *"a land which floweth with milk and honey."* What is the import of that statement? It occurs twenty times in Scripture: Four times in Exodus; once in Leviticus; four times in Numbers; six times in Deuteronomy; once in Joshua; twice in Jeremiah and twice in Ezekiel. *"Flowing with milk and honey,"* is a general expression showing the richness and fertility of the farmland in Canaan, most excellent for crops and pasturage; milk and honey being among the principle products of that land.

Joshua and Caleb recognized the fact that the people were rebelling against the Lord, and were fearful of the nations dwelling in Canaan. However, these two faithful spies had the fear of God, and total confidence in Jehovah's ability to give them the land. *"They are bread for us,"* they exclaimed. In other words, we shall consume them as a hungry man does bread. Then they added, *"Their defence is departed from them, and the LORD is with us: fear them not"* (14:9). What they said was in direct opposition to the testimony of the other ten spies. One is reminded of Elisha and Paul. In spite of a host compassing the city with both horses and chariots, and Elisha's servant crying out; *"Alas, my master! How shall we do?"* Elisha answered, *"Fear not: for they that be with us are more than they that be with them"* (2 Kgs. 6:15–16). Consider Paul in dire straits. What are his convictions? Notice! *"I can do all things through Christ which strengtheneth me"* (Phil. 4:13). That is always the way it is with men that totally trust God. They are not fatalists. Oh no! They consider the circumstances they are in, and are not rash or foolish in making decisions. But one thing characterizes godly men, and it is the fact that they have total confidence in their God to empower them for the circumstances to which the Lord had brought them. *"We are well able to overcome it."* What words of courage! What an expression of confidence in God!

In the original Hebrew the verse reads, "Their defence is departed from them" *(tzillam)*. There is more that meets the eye in this than in the KJV translation. It carries this meaning; "Their

521

shadow, or shade (their defence, protection), has departed from them." The Vulgate renders it, "All aid or protection is gone from them." The Greek rendering furnishes another thought. "For their time (the season of their prosperity) has withdrawn from them." This implies that their iniquities had come to the full, and that any Divine favor was now withdrawn. Israel was to be God's weapon to destroy those nations for their iniquity. The time had come! So, why should Israel fear and draw back, when the LORD was going to go before them and use them as His instrument to accomplish His punitive actions against the idolaters of that land?

THE SAD RESULT OF A FAITHFUL TESTAMONY

What was the result of all their persuasive words? Oh, it was so sad! It was almost unbelievable! But here is Moses' account: *"But all the congregation bade stone them with stones"* (14:10). What a way to be treated for preaching the truth.

> "Though Moses and Aaron entreat upon their faces, and Joshua and Caleb persuade, yet they move nothing. The obstinate multitude, grown more violent with opposing, is ready to return them stones for their prayers. Such have been ever the thanks of fidelity and truth. Crossed wickedness proves desperate; and, instead of yielding, seeks for revenge. Nothing is so hateful to a resolute sinner, as good counsel" (Bishop Hall, 1574 – 1656).

Through the ages, mankind has not changed regarding the truth. In the dark ages, martyrs were burned alive for preaching the truth. Today in Christendom, humanity is too civilized and sophisticated for such rash treatment of truth-bearers. However, men have devised another way to silence the truth. They just tell the visiting preacher not to come back, that his ministry is not acceptable. In many heathen lands, truth-bearers are imprisoned. One old Puritan remarked, "There are some professing Christians that cannot stand the glare of an open Bible." I am afraid that in some areas of professing scriptural assemblies, we have developed a culture that speaks like those in Isaiah's day. *"Which say to the seers, See not; and to the prophets, Prophesy not unto us right things, speak unto us smooth things, prophesy deceits"* (Isa. 30:10).

"And the glory of the LORD appeared in (on) *the tabernacle of the congregation before all the children of Israel"* (Num. 14:10). Had it not been for the sudden manifesttion of the Divine glory, the murderous congregation would probably have ended the life of those faithful witnesses. God intervened! Unknown to the murderous cowards, the Divine eye had been looking down on the whole scenario, and now His glory was revealed. The LORD became visibly manifest! How awesome that sight must have been!

GOD'S PROPOSAL TO MOSES

God speaks, and a proposal is offered to Moses. *"I will smite them with the pestilence, and disinherit them, and I will make of thee a greater nation and mightier than they"* (Num. 14:12). What a golden opportunity! What dictator would not jump at a promotion such as this? It was a "once-in-a-lifetime" offer! The world would consider anybody a madman who would ever refuse such a tremendous offer. Look at the elevation connected with it? Consider the greatness of it. However, Moses was not a man that coveted position, fame, and power. Not at all! Even though personal fame and fortune lay at his doorstep, he humbly besought God to have mercy on His people. He mentioned to the LORD, that if the annihilation of Israel took place, slander to the name of Jehovah would rise from all the nations round about. Moses had two great things before him in his refusal; first, the glory of God, and second, the good of Israel. He thought nothing of himself. Oh for men of this caliber among us! If we had more of them, you would never hear that terrible word "power struggle" connected with any assembly. But alas, that is not the case. It is obnoxious, to say the least, to see someone rise up in God's assembly with the purpose of being "somebody." People with that attitude are really "nobodies." God hates pride, self-elevation, and self-importance, which are so readily seen in humanism, but should never be seen in Christianity.

GOD'S VERDICT ON ISRAEL

"Because all those men which have seen My glory, and My miracles, which I did in Egypt and in the wilderness, and have tempted Me now these ten times, and have not hearkened to My voice; Surely they shall not see the land ..." (Num. 14:22).

God rehearses the failures of the nation before Moses. Imagine! They had tempted the LORD ten times up to this point. Let me enumerate them for your consideration.

(1) Exodus 14:11. Before crossing the Red Sea. They wish to die in the wilderness. ***They doubted God's ability to preserve.***

(2) Exodus 15:24. At Marah. "What shall we drink?" ***They doubted God's goodness.***

(3) Exodus 16:2. In the Wilderness of Sin. Accused Moses and Aaron of killing them with hunger. ***They doubted God's provision.***

(4) Exodus 16:20. They kept the manna over and hearkened not unto Moses. ***They doubted God's instructions.***

(5) Exodus 16:27. They gathered manna on the Sabbath. ***They doubted God's commandments.***

(6) Exodus 17:3. At Rephidim, they accused Moses of killing them and their children with thirst. ***They doubted God's presence.***

(7) Exodus 32:1. They worshipped a golden calf. ***They doubted God's existence*** (32:4).

(8) Numbers 11:1. At Taberah, they were sighing and complaining habitually. **They doubted God's guidance.**

(9) Numbers 11:4. They desired Egypt's food. **They doubted God's ability to satisfy.**

(10) Numbers 14:2. They cried and wept all night. **They doubted God's omnipotence.**

Consequently, because of their unbelief, God made a most solemn announcement: *"Surely they shall not see the land which I sware unto their fathers, neither shall any of them that provoked Me see it: But My servant Caleb, because he had another spirit with him, and hath followed Me fully, him will I bring into the land whereinto he went; and his seed shall possess it"* (Nimbers 14:23–24).

The question arises, what about Joshua, was he not included in the promise, and if so, why is he not mentioned on this occasion? Perhaps the reason would be that Joshua was not classed with the mass of the people as Caleb, being the personal attendant of Moses. What a commentary about these men. *"They have wholly followed the LORD!"* (32:12). That expression about those men is also found in Deuteronomy 1:36; Joshua 14:8–9, 14. Is not this the great commandment of all? *"Thou shalt love the Lord thy God with all thy heart, and with all thy soul, and with all thy mind, and with all thy strength: this is the first commandment"* (Mark 12:30). This my brethren, is the divine standard. Are we living up to it? You say, "It is impossible!" Really? Then how do you reconcile your thoughts with the testimony of King Josiah? *"And like unto him was there no king before him, that turned to the LORD with all his heart, and with all his soul, and with all his might, according to all the law of Moses"* (2 Kgs. 23:25). Are you a Joshua? Are you a Caleb? Are you a Josiah? Are you wholly following the LORD?

Thus, the verdict was passed, Israel was now doomed to wander and eventually die in the wilderness. They had *"despised"* (14:31) the Promised Land, and thus forfeited their right to enter it. Only those under twenty years of age, the Levites, and Joshua and Caleb were exempt. Their language had been, *"Would to God we had died in this wilderness,"* so God was going to make them "eat their own words." One is reminded of the verdict spoken by Paul in Antioch of Pisidia: *"Behold, ye despisers, and wonder, and perish: for I work a work in your days, a work which ye shall in no wise believe, though a man declare it unto you"* (Acts 13:41).

LEVI EXEMPT

Why was the tribe of Levi exempt? You will remember in Numbers chapter one that we find twelve tribes numbered. Levi is not among the number, being the priestly tribe. The LORD was their inheritance, thus they stood apart from their brethren in a unique way. No spy was chosen to represent them. Those that were numbered of the twelve tribes were all twenty years of age and upward, all that were able to go forth to war (Num. 1:45). The spies had searched out the land for forty days, and now, for a total of forty years (one year for each day), Israel was to experience a waste-howling wilderness, with no prospect of entering the land that Jehovah had promised them. Thus, there must be a perfect correspondence between sin and its punishment. Only those under twenty years of age had any hope of entering. By that time the oldest would be sixty years of age.

After the verdict came, the plague from God fell upon the unfaithful spies. They died before the LORD. Accompanying this, *"Moses told these sayings unto all the children of Israel: and the people mourned greatly"* (Num. 14:39). *"They sat down in excessive grief"* (Syrian). The word *"mourned"* is found fifty six-times in the Old Testament, yet only here is the word *"greatly,"* connected with it. It was a tremendous occasion indeed! Israel had mourned after worshipping a golden calf at Sinai, and now they are mourning after searching out the land. They confessed, *"we have sinned"* (v. 40), but it was too late. They had crossed the line and were doomed to die in the wilderness. This whole scenario reminds me of a song often sung in gospel meetings.

> "There's a line that is drawn,
> by rejecting our Lord.

Where the call of His Spirit is lost.
And you hurry along,
with the pleasure-mad throng.
Have you counted,
have you counted, the cost?"

ISRAEL'S RASHNESS

Rising up early in the morning, having repented of their sin of unbelief, Israel now proposed to go forward and enter the land, with full confidence in Jehovah. They were acting rather rashly, for the decree had gone out and nothing would change it – *"Your carcases shall fall in this wilderness"* (14:29). Nevertheless, they purposed to go, and nothing would stop them! They thought that they could make up for past failure by implicit obedience, thus expecting the divine favor of the LORD. *"They presumed to go up."* The verb implies "to be elevated, or elated mentally; to be proud, arrogant, or presumptuous." The verb is rendered by Henry Ainsworth (1569–1622), "loftily presumed." The Chaldean reads, "They dealt wickedly or turbulently." This promotes the idea of an *audacious adventuring* upon what is forbidden. Jewish writers employ the thought of *darkness*, or *obscurity* with this verb, thus rendering it, "They went dark, or obscure." That is, they went without permission, or leave, from God. Thus the Vulgate renders it, *"They being blinded went up."* The cloud never went before them. This should have spoken volumes to their souls, but evidently they were in such a fervor, and so excited about their mission, that God was left entirely out of their plans. Thus, by moving without the cloud before them, they were advancing on their own responsibility, and in direct opposition to the tokens of the Divine will.

UNSCRIPTURAL ZEAL

The lesson for us is this. Let us be careful when we are zealously affected to do something for God. Let us make sure that we have the Divine will for doing what we are seeking to accomplish. Do we have a "thus saith the Lord" for what we purpose in our heart to accomplish for God? The plan may seem plausible, but is it scriptural?

I have witnessed denominational places using various tactics, in their zeal, to increase the number of their audiences. One place hired a "gospel puppet" evangelist to build up their Sunday School. And what did he do? Why he entertained the children with Bible stories, using puppets! Then another place, in a zealous effort to build up their numbers, devised a program involving "community dinners," where, at a fair amount of effort and expense, meals were prepared for the neighborhood, and all were invited to come and get acquainted. Another place devised a sports program in their zeal, and the young folks were taken to pool rooms, bowling alleys, golf courses, health clubs, and various other places of entertainment, in an effort to make them comfortable enough to want to keep coming to the Sunday School.

Now then, let us sit down quietly in the presence of God and evaluate all this "nonsense." What is it? Well, it is a deviation from the divine pattern. It is a lack of faith in the power of God to save souls only through the conviction of sin. It is an absolute denial of the divine pattern. It reminds me of the Assyrian altar that attracted King Ahaz, so much so, that he had one made after its likeness, to replace the scripturally made brazen altar in front of God's house. Ah yes, his altar was much bigger. It was fancier! It was more attractive to the flesh, and this is just what all these innovations by man are when it comes to trying to attract people to God's assembly. It won't work. That is, it won't work for good, but rather to the tearing down and total destruction of the testimony. I leave this subject, having, I believe, made my warning unmistakingly clear. May God help us in our zeal, to be scriptural in our plans and movements!

SCRIPTURAL METHODS FOR SUCCESS

However, before leaving this subject, lest you think that I have been too hard, or too overbearing, let me clear myself of any such charges. Consider this. When I sit down to write, what am

I expected to do? Well you say, "I expect, that as the author, you will stick close to the Holy Scriptures, and not go far out in 'left field' ranting and raving about things that you can't back up with the Bible." Good for you, if you are thinking in these avenues, for that is exactly how I feel about this whole situation of writing.

As an author, I want to be righteous, not radical; scriptural, not silly; faithful, not feigning; loving, not lashing; and most of all, pleasing to God, not simply pleasing to men. With this in mind, allow me to take you to the source of my convictions. What I have written has not been something just conjured up in my little head. No, no! Not at all! That would never do! Regarding what I have said about methods, let us look into the book of the Acts and discover just how the early Church behaved itself. Let us see just what programs they initiated to attract people. That's fair enough, isn't it? Why has God recorded their history? The answer is very simple. He has given us their record that we may imitate them! We don't read the book of Acts just to fill our brains with historical facts. Not at all! We read the book of the Acts so that we will learn how to evangelize, and how to conduct ourselves as a scriptural testimony.

THE FIRST ASSEMBLY FORMED

> "Then they that gladly received His word were baptized: and the same day there were added unto them about three thousand souls. And they continued stedfastly in the apostles' doctrine and fellowship, and in breaking of bread, and in prayers ... And they, continuing daily with one accord in the temple, and breaking bread from house to house, did eat their meat with gladness and singleness of heart, Praising God, and having favour with all the people. And the Lord added to the church daily such as should be saved" (Acts 2:41–42, 46–47).

Thus, we have the first assembly formed. Notice the preaching that convicted them. Peter assured them that it was they who crucified Christ, and that they needed to repent for the forgiveness of sins. He assured them not only of the crucifixion, but also of the resurrection of the Lord, and His exaltation to the right hand of God. In other words, he made much of the graces of Christ, and much of the guilt of his audience. His words were not flowery and sensuous, but factual, and scriptural. These people heard sound, sincere, and scriptural preaching, consequently, God was honored and saw fit to work. There were no gimmicks, plays, entertainment, or any such thing. Just the plain, unadulterated Word of God, delivered in the power of the Holy Spirit. The results were positive. They gladly received the word, were baptized, and added to the testimony in Jerusalem. Then, how did they conduct themselves. Did they say, "This is great! We want to share this with anybody we can attract. Let's take all the children we can to the games of the world. Let's bribe them with lavish gifts for attending our Sunday School"? Tell me, my dear reader, is this what they did? If so, then let's all imitate them, and get going on some fancy programs.

"Ah," but you say, "I don't see them doing that." You are right! And why are they not doing that? Simply because the Lord never ordained them to act after that manner. There were no programs. There was no "polish." Yet, the positive results were absolutely tremendous! It was the Lord Who added to the church, and not a result of their own efforts.

ORDAINED TO ETERNAL LIFE

Do you believe that people are ordained unto eternal life? If not, then how do you reconcile your thoughts with this divine statement? *"And when the Gentiles heard this, they were glad, and glorified the word of the Lord: and as many as were ordained to eternal life believed"* (Acts 13:48). These saints were all in one accord. They gathered, it seems, on a daily basis. They were saintly, God-fearing individuals, totally separated from the world, with its attractions and amusements. Yes, they certainly witnessed, but it was backed by a godly life, thus God honored them with souls being added to their company. No fancy programs and gimmicks were needed. There's the divine pattern, my inquiring friend.

UNCEASING LABOR

Let's take another look down the road of the early Christians. Look at the apostles and others. *"And daily in the temple, and in every house, they ceased not to teach and preach Jesus Christ"* (Acts 5:42). *"They ceased not!"* There was no stopping them. They were not sitting back saying, "Ho hum, if God is going to save folks we are not needed." Nothing of the sort. They believed in election, but they also acknowledged the truth of man's individual responsibility. *"They ceased not"*! It was almost as if they were desperate about it. What were their programs to induce people to listen? Did they have an orchestra? Were they thinking that lovely instrumental music would attract a crowd to hear the preaching? Nothing of the sort! Well, what about amusements of another nature, such as games, acting, banquets, and the sort? Did they employ such attractive devices? If so, please show me where in the divine record we find such carry-ons. No my friends, they simply *"ceased not to preach and teach Jesus Christ."*

LABOR IN ANTIOCH

Move on to Acts 11, and what do you find? You find a group of persecuted people fleeing Jerusalem and going about 240 miles to the north to a place called Antioch. Now, just what did they do? Go into hiding? Why no, they preached the Word! Some *"spake unto the Grecians, preaching the Lord Jesus"* (11:20). We read that a great number believed. So what was the secret of their success? Was it because these Christians entertained them with a lot of worldly amusements? Was it the result of community dinners? Nothing of the sort my friend. "Well then," you may say, "it was that perhaps they were eloquent speakers using drama, theatrics and the like." No, no, it certainly wasn't that! Well then, what caused this great success in their preaching? What brought this *"great number"* to the faith? Ah my friend, the answer is beautiful! It is simply lovely. Listen to it. *"The hand of the Lord was with them"* (11:21). There's the secret – the hand of the Lord with us! Without that, it is useless to try to influence people by any other means.

A ROMAN CATHOLIC BLIND MAN

I wonder if your mind-set is this; "Well, we have gotten crowds by providing entertainment, and souls have been saved as a result of our programs." Is that so? Well, there are different ways of looking at such situations. First of all, God *is* sovereign. I knew a blind man saved in a Roman Catholic Church while the priest was conducting a mass. He heard the priest read John 3:16, and he drank in the truth, and was saved. This resulted in him being excommunicated from the church as a heretic, but the dear man finally found his way into God's assembly and was quite active as a born again Christian. But nevertheless, the end does not justify the means.

The second thought is that some have professed under such man-devised programs, and have been incorporated into a scriptural assembly, but they are false. They have never been "plowed up," and brought under the conviction of sin. They have never been lowered by the working of the Holy Spirit to the place of true repentance. They simply have a profession, without a true possession of Christ or salvation. Later down the line, they begin to present problems, favoring carnal agendas in the assembly, until finally, that once scriptural assembly, has been lowered to the same standard as those religious organizations called "churches" in Christendom.

W. J. MCCLURE'S THOUGHTS

Last night, at random, I pulled a bound volume of the Words in Season Magazine – 1979, off the shelf, and while browsing through it, I came unexpectedly on an article written many years before 1979, by a well-known preacher at the time, named

W. J. McClure. I was amazed how it seemed to fit with my current of thoughts at that particular time. So please allow me to insert some statements from his pithy article.

> "SOME THOUGHTS SUGGESTED BY THE HOME-GOING OF OLDER BRETHREN. The Home-going of older men of God should deepen in us who remain the desire to end well, to cleave to the Lord and His Word in these days when it is so easy to drift away from that which has reproach connected with it, and to seek a path more congenial to our flesh.
>
> During about fifty four years connected with the assemblies gathered to the Name of the Lord Jesus, I have observed a considerable change, both in meetings and preachers. (He then mentions Donald Ross, Donald Monroe, James Campbell, W. McLean, J. R. Caldwell, and John Ritchie).
>
> Of the class to which these men belong, very, very few now remain, and the going of each one leaves us weaker and poorer. The saddest part of it is that they are not being replaced by men of the same spiritual power and energy.
>
> What gives us much concern is the coming crop of preachers. Again and again it has presented itself to us like this. What is to become of the testimony of assemblies if we are not to have men of spiritual power and energy to stand in the gap and make up the hedge? We dread to think what assemblies will be like in twenty or thirty years, should the Lord not come before then.
>
> One thing we judge that all must admit who have eyes to see, and that is, that each successive generation of preachers is weaker than the preceding one. Is the Lord thus letting the glory depart?

Shall things be at a low, or at the lowest ebb when He comes? Who that remember can help but comparing the dear men we have just mentioned with so many recent preachers. These dear men had such a grip on God that they could push into new fields and plant assemblies. The usual thing now is making a round of the assemblies, and rarely ever touching a new place. Hundreds of towns and cities are passed by, in which there are no meetings, and the place which has a meeting, with local brethren capable of preaching the gospel, gets all their time. These dear men of days gone by kept themselves in form by getting a bag of tracts and scattering them from door to door.

To go into the gospel meetings conducted by some of the newer preachers, one would think that it was some sectarian mission in which one had come, the methods and ways are so identical with these of the sects. Now, if the rule holds which we have observed, namely deterioration, then what shall we expect of the generation which will succeed the present?"

W. J. McClure was preaching in tent work over 110 years ago. I wonder what he would say if he were living today, considering the fact that he observed such a drift so many years ago?

THE CHRISTIAN'S BEHAVIOR TOWARD THE UNSAVED

In regards to our behavior before the dear unsaved, let us be careful to be kind to them. There is certainly nothing wrong with inviting a lost couple into your home for a meal, with the purpose of influencing them to attend a gospel meeting. Let us be quite willing to go out of our way to encourage them to get under the sound of the gospel, even if it means using our vehicles to transport them to hear the Word of God. The Scripture advocates, *"as we have therefore opportunity, let us do good unto all men, especially unto them who are of the household of faith"* (Gal. 6:10). Do you know of an unsaved couple in need of help financially? Then help them! Influence them all that you can. Win them to yourself, that you may see them won to Christ. That is the manward side of things. Pray for them, that the Holy Spirit will convict them of their sins and reveal Christ to their souls. Let us leave the fleshly entertainment out of the picture, and look to the Spirit alone to work. Seek souls, and at the same time, seek to maintain the Scriptural standard that God has given unto us. Then we can expect true blessing from above.

Coming back to Israel, we observe that in their thoughtless zeal, they went up the mountain, which was no small journey. They were, as it were, on fire for God. Alas, but it was too late! Their destiny was sealed, they would never dwell in the Promised Land. Moses sought to discourage them in their vain desire, but no, they would not hearken. Presumptuously they went, only to experience a smarting defeat. God blew upon their whole plan! Brethren, let us be careful that God is in all of our plans as we seek to serve Him, lest all of our efforts come to naught.

26

THE SABBATH BREAKER THE RIBBAND OF BLUE

NUMBERS 15

"And while the children of Israel were in the wilderness, they found a man that gathered sticks upon the Sabbath day. And they that found him gathering sticks brought him unto Moses and Aaron, and unto all the congregation. And they put him in ward, because it was not declared what should be done to him. And the LORD said unto Moses, The man shall be surely put to death: all the congregation shall stone him with stones without the camp. And all the congregation brought him without the camp, and stoned him with stones, and he died; as the LORD commanded Moses" (Num. 15:32–36).

There were ordinances delivered to Israel that were to be carried out after they occupied the land of Canaan, but we are going to look at an ordinance delivered to the nation that was to be kept continually from the day they received it. That ordinance was that they were to keep the Sabbath holy. No work was permitted on that sacred day. Its first institution was given in connection with the giving of the manna, and soon afterwards it was re-enacted in the fourth commandment, at the giving of the Law at Sinai. It was one of the signs of the Covenant. It was extremely important to the nation that they keep the Sabbath, as we observe by reading Isaiah 58:13–14; Jeremiah 17:21–27; Ezekiel 20:21; and Nehemiah 10:31; 13:15–22.

Moses, and all Israel were aware that a violation of the Sabbath called for the death penalty, for it had been previously decreed (Ex. 31:14–15; 35:2). Why then was this violator put in ward to see what should be done unto him? The answer lies in the fact that perhaps Moses hesitated to carry out such an extreme penalty for such a minor violation, without a further appeal. They were not fully resolved in their own minds as to what precise manner this case was to be dealt with, thus they were willing to wait for a specific direction from the Lord Himself. I would term this "working with a cool and collected mind." A hot-tempered man would be unfit in a situation of this nature. So would a cruel, callous, and legal man. Men that have a grudge, or an axe to grind, or are impetuous, or over-zealous in their cause, are totally unfit to judge any case for the assembly, or for God. Oh for careful men in the assemblies to judge severe cases. How valuable they are!

THE SABBATH-BREAKER

Consider the character of the man that they were called upon to deal with righteously. He had flagrantly broken an established law. His was not the sin of ignorance. Oh no, not this vain fellow! He could have cared less what God said. He was presumptuous in his sin against the Almighty. He was an obnoxious, willful, high-handed violator. He certainly couldn't plead ignorance in what he had done. He despised the requirements of the law. He was a selfish man, living in total disregard for God, concerned only about himself and his own comfort. He had a Pharaoh-heart that silently muttered, *"Who is the LORD, that I should obey His voice?"* Is it not true, that man's independence invariably leads to disobedience? And just as Pharaoh died under the waters of the sea, this man was to die under a hail of stones. In order to maintain purity in the camp he was led by *"all the congregation,"* probably referring to the responsible leaders, without the camp, and stoned to death.

"We would remind the young Christian reader, especially, that the true safeguard against sins of ignorance is the **study of the word;** and the true safeguard against presumptuous sins, is **subjection to the word.** We all need to bear these things in mind; but our younger brethren particularly. There is a strong tendency amongst young Christians to get into the current of this present age, and to drink in its spirit. Hence the independence, the strong will, the impatience of control, the disobedience to parents, the headiness, highmindedness, and self-confidence, the pretentious style, the assumption, the setting up to be wiser than their elders — all these things so hateful in the sight of God, and so entirely opposed to the spirit of Christianity. We would most earnestly and lovingly entreat all our young friends to guard against these things, and to cultivate a lowly mind. Let them remember that 'God resisteth the proud, but giveth grace to the lowly.'" [70]

A RIBBAND OF BLUE

"And the LORD spake unto Moses, saying, Speak unto the children of Israel, and bid them that they make them fringes in the borders of their garments throughout their generations, and that they put upon the fringe of the borders a ribband of blue: And it shall be unto you for a fringe, that ye may look upon it, and remember all the commandments of the LORD, and do them; and that ye seek not after your own heart and your own eyes, after which ye use to go a whoring: That ye may remember, and do all my commandments, and be holy unto your God. I am the LORD your God, which brought you out of the land of Egypt, to be your God: I am the LORD your God" (Num. 15:37–41).

---

[70] C. H. MacIntosh Notes on Numbers, Loizeaux Brothers P. 89.

The Jews are distinguished from other people in various ways, by circumcision, the fashion of their beards, their peculiar diet, and also by their dress. God would have His people different than the heathen of the nations round about them. We have just considered the willful sinner, but now we want, for a few moments, to briefly consider the ribband of blue, which God ordained as a help to keep His people from sinning.

I am not prepared to give an absolutely exact definition of this addition to their dress, due to the many different ways certain words in the text have been translated. For example, the word *"fringes"* is also translated *"tassel,"* since it is derived from the Hebrew word. The word *"border"* could also mean *"hem, corner, wing,"* or *"skirt."* The word translated in our KJV Bible, *"rit band,"* is also translated, *"cord, thread, string, lace,"* and *"rope."* It could be that there were tassels inserted in the fringe, hanging down from the edge of the garment somewhat like locks of hair. The word *"fringes"* is translated *"borders"* in the KJV *"But all their works they do for to be seen of men: they make broad their phylacteries, and enlarge the borders of their garments"* (Matt. 23:5). This border distinguished the Israelite from other people. He stood out as different. The Pharisees, in their hypocrisy, enlarged the borders of their garments to attract attention to themselves. The Lord condemned them for their pretentious display.

You will notice that the Lord also wore a garment that displayed *a "fringe,"* commonly called a *"hem."* It was the woman with the issue of blood that came behind our Lord and touched the hem of His garment (Luke 8:43). The word *"hem,"* also being, *"a border, fringe or tassel."* From this we see that not only was the hem in the front of the garment, as the law required it to be under the wearer's eye, but it was also in the back, for that is where the diseased woman came to touch His hem.

Coming back to Moses' day, we see this particular dress imposed upon the Lord's people, not only to distinguish them from the heathen, but also to be a reminder to them of their duty to God as a holy and consecrated nation. Their eye would observe the blue, indicative of things heavenly, and of the dwelling place of the Most High. Blue was also the color of the priest's robe, reminding Israel of the original plan of God that they be a kingdom of priests, thus bound to act accordingly, as a holy and royal nation. The ribband of blue! A forceful reminder of what kind of people they should be. Furthermore, let me add this. When the person wearing the tassels dies, the *ribband of blue* is removed from the *tzitzits* when the *talit* is folded and placed over the face of the departed one.

Taken in this sense, one could term the Holy Scriptures a "ribband of blue." For gazing upon its sacred page on a daily basis, we will be ever reminded that we have been called out of darkness into His marvelous light to be a chosen generation, a royal priesthood, an holy nation, a purchased people. And as such, we are to show forth the virtues of Him Who hath called us to this tremendous, and exalted position (1 Pet. 2:9). God would have us, His people, ever remember what we were, what we presently are, and what we are going to be forever.

Before closing this exposition on the ribband of blue, allow me to draw your attention to the color blue. As noticed, the *"fringes"* were actually *"tzitzits,"* or *"tassels."* These were worn to remind them of the commandments of the Lord, and to do them. These tassels have a message for us, they have something to say. Each letter in the Hebrew language has a numerical value. Scholars speak of this as "gematria." I met, and had quite a lengthy conversation, with an ultra-orthodox Jew one night in the Chicago airport. Hanging on his side were a number of tassels. I enquired, and he gladly informed me. On each tassel (*tzitzit*) there were 39 windings (7+8+11+13) separated by double knots. These numbers add up to 39. The numerical value of YHVA (*Jehovah*) is 26, and the numerical value of ONE (*Echad*) is 13. Adding the two numbers, one arrives at the number 39, the very same number as the windings on the tassel. Thus, these windings on each tassel proclaim this vital truth that *"YHVH is One."* This is the fundamental accepted truth of the Jewish faith, known as "HaShem." *"Hear, O Israel: The LORD our God is one LORD"* (Deut. 6:4).

According to the passage we are considering, the fringes (*"tzitzits"*) were to contain a strand of blue, called the "Shamash," or servant. Each "tzitzit" had seven white strands, the number that indicates *perfection*. This was combined with *the ribband of blue* (servant), and speaks of *royalty*. With the blue strand incorporated with the *seven* white strands the total number of strands in each *"tzitzit"* came to *eight*, indicating a *new beginning*. Another interesting thing is that the numerical value of the word *tzitzit* is 600. Add this to the 5 knots and the 8 strands, and you arrive at the number 613. Would you believe that the number of *mitzvahs* (Jewish instructions) that are found in the Old Testament is 613. This represents the Torah.

In talking to my Jewish acquaintance, I noticed a lack of blue in the tassels he was wearing. Lately, I found out the reason. It all has to do with tradition. The only ancient source of permanent blue dye originally used in the making of *"the ribband of blue,"* was found in the *chillazon snail,* from the Mediterranean Sea. The dye was extracted from the snail by a process only known by a few from the days of the Exodus until the destruction of the Temple in 70 AD. More amazing is the fact, that ever since the temple was destroyed, and Israel lost its national identity, this particular snail disappeared from the Mediterranean Sea. It was believed to be extinct. However, even though this snail disappeared after the crucifixion of our Lord, just of late it is making a comeback! Following tradition, soon the Jews will be able, once again, to incorporate the true blue ribband into their tassels. Is this not a reminder to intelligent Christians that the return of the King to Israel is eminent? Bless His name, seven years before that takes place, the saints of the Church, shall be snatched away at the last trump! *"Amen! Even so come Lord Jesus!"*

27

THE REBELLION OF KORAH

NUMBERS 16

"Now Korah, the son of Izhar, the son of Kohath, the son of Levi, and Dathan and Abiram, the sons of Eliab, and On, the son of Peleth, sons of Reuben, took men: And they rose up before Moses, with certain of the children of Israel, two hundred and fifty princes of the assembly, famous in the congregation, men of renown: And they gathered themselves together against Moses and against Aaron, and said unto them, Ye take too much upon you, seeing all the congregation are holy, every one of them, and the LORD is among them: wherefore then lift ye up yourselves above the congregation of the LORD? And when Moses heard it, he fell upon his face" (Num. 16:1–4).

Perhaps in all the previous problems due to pride, unfaithfulness, and discontent, the one now before us was the most serious of all. When men of position become dissatisfied with that which God has allotted them, and consequently, seek to rise higher than God intended, we have serious trouble. When men of high standing sway all of the common folk to their impetuous way of thinking, a most vexing situation can arise, and that is just what the case of rebellious Korah and his followers present.

Who were these rebellious men? To understand the situation more correctly we must discover just who they were, and that is what we will now proceed to do. First of all, who is Korah? He was a Kohathite of the tribe of Levi. Being thus, he was related to Aaron and Moses, that relationship being termed a cousinship. As you know, the Kohathites were appointed to attend to the sacred vessels in transporting the tabernacle. Not only this, they were attendants to the priests, the sons of Aaron, who also came from the tribe of Levi. These men, apart from the Aaronic priesthood, occupied the highest position in all of Israel. They were attendants to the brazen altar and assisted the priests in their functions of offering sacrifices. In other words, they were ministers of no mean standing. Their tents were pitched as close as possible to the tabernacle, on the south side. Just south of their tents were the Reubenites. Just keep that in mind, the Koahathites and the Reubenites were "next-door" neighbors. The Koathites were very important men, and this is where the real danger lay.

REUBENITES

What about the next mentioned men, Dathan, Abiram, and On? Well, they were Reubenites, the men that lived nearest to the Koathites. In the hearts of these men lurked that vicious germ called envy. The reason I know that is because the Psalmist relates to these men with these terse words. *"They envied Moses also in the camp, and Aaron the saint of the LORD"* (Ps. 106:16). Now envy is a terrible "disease." *"Wrath is cruel, and anger is outrageous; but who is able to stand before envy?"* (Prov. 27:4). *"A sound heart is the life of the flesh: but envy the rottenness of the bones"* (Prov. 14:30). Envy shows no mercy. It is incompatible with grace. Like rottenness of the bones, when it infests a person, it permeates his whole way of thinking. It makes him like a madman, and nothing but direct intervention from God can stop him. Such was the case here. Beneath the surface this awful infection of envy had been seething.

ENVY IN THE ASSEMBLY

Bring this vicious germ into God's assembly and what will be the ultimate result? Disaster! I have seen it, enough at times to make me weep. It can happen very easily in God-gifted men. Those who have been elevated to a responsible position, or a place of prominence in the assembly seem to be more susceptible to this virus than one that is just a common, humble, not greatly gifted person. Once the virus of envy invades the spiritual bloodstream of an individual, he will brood over the situation that he dislikes perhaps for months, and then he will begin to move. Most problems arise from men, or even women, that are intelligent and capable of swaying the minds of those that are less intelligent than themselves. They know how to stir up the passions of fellow-believers and how to control them after they are stirred.

"Their most potent agency – the lever with which they can most effectively raise the masses – is some question as to their liberty and their rights. If they can only succeed in persuading people that their liberty is curtailed, and their rights infringed, they are sure to gather a number of restless spirits around them, and do a great deal of serious mischief." [71]

Notice how these "brainy" fellows work. Remember, these men are smart! Very smart! Of course, these are the kind of tools that the devil can use most effectively. He uses clever and shrewd men that are energetic. Men that have charisma, that can charm, as well as influence people. I have seen men of this caliber performing all kinds of favors for people with a view to effectively influence them later to their way of thinking. Don't forget, it is Satan that seeks to destroy God's assemblies, and he can even influence and arm noted men in assemblies to achieve his hellish purposes. This is a most solemn thing indeed!

KORAH'S CAMPAIGN

In the rebellion, notice first of all that these prominent fellows "*took men*" (v. 1). In your Bible, the word "*men*" is in italics, indicating that the word is not in the original text, and should

---

71 C. H. MacIntosh Notes on Numbers, Loizeaux Brothers P. 295.

simply read that these men *"took."* The question now arises, what did they take? Various manuscripts (ancient versions) only add to the confusion as to what they actually took. However, the Arabic says, *"aggressus est,"* which means, *"he made an attempt."* So one could translate it this way, *"He undertook."* This conveys the thought that *"he took counsel."* In other words, Korah became engaged in a campaign, he devised a scheme. Persuading his fellows, they undertook a project and rose up in defiance against God's appointed authority – Moses!

"And they rose up before Moses" (v. 2). What makes this uprising so serious is the quality of the men. The scriptural definition is: *"princes, famous, men of renown."* These men carried a lot of weight among the congregation. *"They gathered themselves together against Moses and Aaron."* Let me say this; no matter how influential men may be, when they conspire against what God has ordained, they are placing themselves in great danger. These men were on dangerous ground, but they never perceived it in their proud and envious hearts. Excitement was high, and common sense was at an all-time low, as it usually is in times of high emotion. One wonders just what sparked this outburst of rebellion. It seems to me that the pot had been seething for quite some time, and now that they had been denied entrance into the promised land, things suddenly came to a boiling head.

KORAH'S TWO-FOLD PLOT

Their plot was two-fold. First: to depose Moses from his position as head of the civil life of the nation. Second: to remove Aaron from his position as head of their religious life. Before the plot fully formed, there may have been discontentment. Take Korah for instance. In that family of Kohath there were the Amramites, the Izeharites, the Hebronites, and the Uzzielites. These were all termed Kohathites. Out of those four sons, Elizaphan, the son of Uzziel was selected to be the chief of the house of their father. Korah was the son of Izhar, whose house is termed *"the Iseharites."* Do you see the picture? It was Elizaphan who was chosen for this exalted position, not Korah's father Izhar. Thus, Korah may have been aggravated because the Uzzielities had been preferred in the person of Elizaphan to the Izharites. Perhaps it was then that jealously and envy began to work in his heart.

The whole scenario boils down to this. These men thought that they were more worthy than the position in which they had been placed. In other words, they thought a lot of themselves. They were proud men, with no fear of God before their eyes. Their thoughts could well have run like this. "We deserved better than what we have gotten. Who do Moses and Aaron think they are? Are we not just as capable, and perhaps even more so than they?" Pride has no limit to lofty thoughts about self. Not only this, but their pride, jealously, and envy have so warped their minds that they had convinced themselves that Moses had elevated himself to his position. They refused to recognize that God had placed him in the position that he occupied. Of course, we that are still sane know better, don't we?

MOSES ACCUSED

Notice their ignorant statement. *"Ye take too much upon you"* (v. 3). The truth of the matter is, they never took anything upon themselves. It was God that placed this tremendous responsibility upon them. In fact, Moses was even guilty of shirking the taking on of such responsibility. Remember his "interview" with Jehovah in Exodus chapters 3, 4, 5, and 6. He pleads no fitness, no message, no authority, no gift of speech, until finally in Exodus 5:22, he cries out, *"why is it that Thou hast sent me."* Finally, he pleads before God with these words, *"Behold, I am of uncircumcised lips, and how shall Pharaoh hearken unto me?* (Ex. 6:30).

Now folks, does this sound like a proud egotist? Does this appear to be like a man pushing himself, overzealous of vain glory? Hardly so, yet this is the accusation hurled into his face by these impudent men! How would you like to be treated like this? Here is a saintly man that forsook all the riches of Egypt, to live like a nomad in a waste-howling wilderness, for the glory of God and for the good of God's people. He had sacrificed a life of luxury in a palace, in exchange for a tent in the desert. He is listed in the great Hall of Faith, and this inscription is indelibly written on the eternal record:

> *"By faith Moses, when he was come to years, refused to be called the son of Pharaoh's daughter; Choosing rather to suffer affliction with the people of God, than to enjoy the pleasures of sin for a season; Esteeming the reproach of Christ greater riches than the treasures in Egypt: for he had respect unto the recompence of the reward. By faith he forsook Egypt, not fearing the wrath of the king: for he endured, as seeing Him who is invisible"* (Heb. 11:24–27).

MOSES' SPIRITUALITY

What greater commendation could any mortal receive? Yet these men are not one bit slow to accuse this saintly man of self-assertion, pride, and dictatorship. Once again, the meekest man in all the earth is tested. What does he do? What would you do? Well now, would it not be natural to give these vain fellows a piece of your mind? Would it not be natural to tell them of all your victories and exploits for God, and at the same time remind them of all their failures? Yes, it would be absolutely natural. But Moses was not a natural man, but rather a spiritual being. He passes the test of being the meekest man by falling on his face. Then addressing these gainsayers, he brings the LORD before them. Have you noticed, that he never leaves God out of any situation. He never defends himself, but quietly tells them that tomorrow the LORD will fully reveal to them Who He has chosen for leadership among His people.

That is characteristic of a saintly man. When he is accused, he never flares up, and he never defends himself. No, no, he just commits his cause to his Lord, and lets the Lord take care of the situation. *"Commit thy way unto the LORD; trust also in Him; and He shall bring it to pass"* (Ps. 37:5).

ANOTHER ACCUSATION

They also accused Moses and Aaron; *"Wherefore then lift ye up yourselves above the congregation of the LORD?"* This statement is very interesting. "Why such lofty superiority over your brethren." The original word *"above"* in this verse is also translated *"against"* in the same verse. This carries the thought that they were accusing Moses and Aaron of taking a stand *against* the congregation in such a way as to be oppressive to them. Nothing could be farther from the truth, but you will have to consider that we are looking at excited, irrational people, and in that state, wild things are usually uttered, as noticed on this occasion.

How true of men that seek to exalt themselves. They seek to undermine the character of those greater than them, so that they will be lifted up in the eyes of the people. Absalom was of this nature as he sought to steal the throne from his father David. How smooth and deceitful are his words to the people. *"Oh that I were made judge in the land, that every man which hath any suit or cause might come unto me, and I would do him justice!"* (2 Sam. 15:4).

MOSES PROPOSES A PLAN

The man in touch with God proposes a plan that will settle the question forever. Moses is not about to defend himself, but tells the usurpers that there can be no doubt about leadership if it is the Lord Himself that will judge the case. They are called upon to return on the morrow for the verdict from the Judge of all the earth. He then rebukes them for their activity, reminding Korah, the sons of Levi, of the high position God had entrusted to them above most in Israel, *"to do the service of the tabernacle of the Lord, and to stand before the congregation to minister unto them"* (Num. 16:9). He reminds them that they had essentially gathered themselves together against, not him, but against the Lord Himself. What a serious charge. Let us also be very careful at leveling charges against those that the Lord has placed over us. Be slow to speak and slow to wrath.

EGYPT TO CANAAN

MEN LIKE DIOTREPHES

Behind a cloak of hypocrisy, Korah was really seeking the high priest position that was Aaron's. Not content with the ministry that God had entrusted to his hand, this usurper was attempting to exalt himself in Israel. One is reminded of a man in a New Testament assembly named Diotrephes, who loved to have the preeminence among the brethren (3 Jn. 1:9). It is amazing how such people work, and seem to so easily achieve their self-important purpose. They rise up in the midst of an assembly and no one dares to oppose them. These people have an overpowering influence. Pride motivates them. Their energy is ceaseless when it comes to achieving their purpose of climbing to the top, in order to be the master-controller of the assembly. Meek and lowly brethren are pushed aside. Nobody seems to have the spiritual grit to rise up against them. Some elders have even removed themselves from the oversight to avoid a conflict. I cannot see in the Scriptures where we find overseers quitting their Spirit-appointed position. It is just not there. Assembly elders are in one respect similar to U. S. Supreme Court judges, they are appointed for life. Only a serious sin, calling for excommunication can remove an elder from his Spirit-given responsibilities. An elder is wrong in removing himself.

However, in spite of God's order, I have seen godly men give up in despair, and leave the oversight. Ambitious and determined men rise up with an agenda to introduce unscriptural ideas into the assembly, and instead of having their mouths stopped (by using the Scriptures – Titus 1:1), meek and godly men simply withdraw from the oversight. Thus, they "lose their authoritative voice," and things begin to gradually grow worse. Now brethren, I am not just throwing out words from the top of my head. I have been in God's assemblies for over 57 years, and have personally witnessed such tragedies. It is no small thing. Such behavior is so serious, that God gives a warning against it, saying, *"if any man defile the temple of God, him shall God destroy; for the temple of God is holy, which temple ye are"* (1 Cor. 3:17).

A Diotrephes is a man that will seek to intimidate you if you oppose him to his face. He will work behind your back to eventually destroy you. If you pose a threat, or a problem to him, he will work insidiously to have you so frustrated, or beaten down, that you will even possibly leave the assembly. He cares not for the good of the assembly. There is no true love for the sheep. He is not meek and lowly. He is a self-appointed, self-important, and self-seeking individual, in control! Oh brethren, do beware of a Diotrephes spirit developing in any saint, and immediately squelch it, lest it grow into a monster, and overcome the testimony, to the dishonor of His worthy Name, unto which we have been called.

TIME GIVEN TO REPENT

> *"And he (Moses) spake unto Korah and unto all his company, saying, Even to morrow the LORD will shew who are His, and who is holy; and will cause him to come near unto Him: even him whom He hath chosen will He cause to come near unto Him. This do; Take you censers, Korah, and all his company; And put fire therein, and put incense in them before the LORD to morrow: and it shall be that the man whom the LORD doth choose, he shall be holy: ye take too much upon you, ye sons of Levi. And Moses said unto Korah, Hear, I pray you, ye sons of Levi: Seemeth it but a small thing unto you, that the God of Israel hath separated you from the congregation of Israel, to bring you near to himself to do the service of the tabernacle of the LORD, and to stand before the congregation to minister unto them? And He hath brought thee near to Him, and all thy brethren the sons of Levi with thee: and seek ye the priesthood also? For which cause both thou and all thy company are gathered together against the LORD: and what is Aaron, that ye murmur against him?"* (Num. 16:5-11).

The rebels were given one day to reflect upon their misbehavior, and perhaps repent of their waywardness and retrace their steps. However, this was not the case. Their minds were fully made up, and nothing would stop them from their purpose to overthrow God's government. The instructions were for them to bring their censers (fire-pans) and put fire therein with incense upon them before the LORD. Where they acquired the fire-pans we are not told. They may have been household utensils for carrying fire, or they may have been hastily made for the occasion. Or, as Mathew Henry suggests, they were probably the small platters, common in Egyptian families, where incense was offered to household deities and which had been among the precious things borrowed at their departure.

By coming before the LORD in this fashion they would be saying in so many words, "we are performing the office of priests, and have a right to do so!" It would be a blatant display on their part of pride, rebellion, and total disregard for God's order. These men are setting forth to Christians, just what we should NOT be! We find quite the opposite in Colossians 3, don't we? *"Put on therefore, as the elect of God, holy and beloved, bowels of mercies, kindness, humbleness of mind, meekness, longsuffering; Forbearing one another, and forgiving one another, if any man have a quarrel against any: even as Christ forgave you, so also do ye. And above all these things put on charity, which is the bond of perfectness. And let the peace of God rule in your hearts, to the which also ye are called in one body; and be ye thankful."* That little word *"rule"* carries the thought of *"being an umpire, to decide."* How lovely to see such a disposition in beloved brethren. With Korah and his congregation, this was not the case!

REFUSAL BY DATHAN AND ABIRAM

When Moses sent for Dathan and Abiram, they flatly refused. Imagine these men speaking of Egypt the same way in which God described the Promised Land? What blindness! What impudence! It is almost unbelievable, the blindness f their perverted heart!

> *"Is it a small thing that thou hast brought us up out of a land that floweth with milk and honey, to kill us*

in the wilderness, except thou make thyself altogether a prince over us? Moreover thou hast not brought us into a land that floweth with milk and honey, or given us inheritance of fields and vineyards: wilt thou put out the eyes of these men? we will not come up"* (Num. 16:13–14).

Not only this, these wicked men accused Moses of self-elevation, the very thing they were doing themselves! That is often the way with usurpers. They hurl accusations at their victims, which in reality, fit their own case. Here is one example. I have seen brethren introduce some new thing into an assembly, thus causing division. However, if anybody objects to their agenda, and stands for the truth, it is the objectors that are accused of causing a division. In other words, saints that object to an unscriptural change are accused of causing a division. School systems today endorse and teach "self-esteem." They have produced a generation of youth that think very highly of themselves. *"Numerous studies by secular psychologists and psychiatrists have demonstrated that the higher one's self-esteem, the more likely one is to be immoral, violent, and prone to trample on the rights of others."*[72]

SELF-ESTEEM

Many famous religious authors, such as Billy Graham, James Dobson, the late Jerry Faldwell, the late Norman Vincent Peale, and Robert Schuller, have unwittingly endorsed that which God hates, namely, self-esteem. Proof of God's hatred of self-esteem lies in the following verses. *"The heart is deceitful above all things, and desperately wicked"* (Jer. 17:9). *"And He said to them all, if any man will come after Me, let him deny himself, and take up his cross daily, and follow Me"* (Luke 9:23). *"Let nothing be done through strife or vainglory; but in lowliness of mind let each esteem other better than themselves"* (Phil. 2:3). *"For I say, through the grace given unto me, to every man that is among you, not to think of himself more highly than*

---

[72] Occult Invasion, Dave Hunt, Harvest House Publishers, Eugene Oregon. P 472.

he ought to think; but to think soberly" (Rom. 12:3). Jacob confessed, *"I am not worthy of the least of all the mercies, and of all the truth, which thou hast shewed unto thy servant"* (Gen. 32:10). Job cried, *"I abhor myself"* (Job 42:6). Mephibosheth *"bowed himself, and said, What is thy servant, that thou shouldest look upon such a dead dog as I am?"* (2 Sam. 9:8). Paul confessed, *"I [be] nothing"* (2 Cor. 12:11).

Now tell me, where do you find self-esteem in these godly men? You don't! The truth of the matter is, that the more we realize our guilt and wretchedness, the greater will be our gratitude and love to the One Who stooped so low to rescue us.

Dathan and Abiram continued their ranting, accusing Moses of failing to bring them into Canaan, when indeed, it was their own unbelief that shut them out from occupying the good land. They were the cause of not being allowed to enter in, but true to form, they accused Moses. Then they hurled an accusation in the form of a question; *"wilt thou put out the eyes of these men?"* What they were saying was this. "Do you think that you can so blind us, that none of us will discern your craftiness, and your ambition for self? Do you think that you are able to so fool us, and push us around at your pleasure, as if we were blind, under the pretense of bringing us into the Promised Land?" Thus, Moses was accused of being a master deceiver. This whole thing, to me, is outrageous! Twice they dared to refuse the summons of Moses. Instead, they hurled impudent charges against him. They denied his power, and despised his authority. Little did they know, that they were ripe for destruction.

Much later in Israel's history God laments in the writing of Jeremiah saying, *"Therefore thus saith the LORD God of hosts, the God of Israel; Behold, I will bring upon Judah and upon all the inhabitants of Jerusalem all the evil that I have pronounced against them: because I have spoken unto them, but they have not heard; and I have called unto them, but they have not answered"* (Jer. 35:17). We find the same attitude today. Gospel meetings can be held on a nightly basis and thousands of invitations delivered personally to the neighboring homes, yet, hardly a soul responds by attending. Wisdom cries out, *"Because I have called, and ye refused; I have stretched out my hand, and no man regarded; But ye have set at nought all my counsel, and would none of my reproof: I also will laugh at your calamity; I will mock when your fear cometh; When your fear cometh as desolation, and your destruction cometh as a whirlwind; when distress and anguish cometh upon you. Then shall they call upon me, but I will not answer; they shall seek me early, but they shall not find me: For that they hated knowledge, and did not choose the fear of the LORD"* (Prov. 1:24–29). It would seem to me, that the same thing could be said of God. Man will heed the call of every conceivable worldly entertainment, but he has no ear for the call of God. Like Dathan and Abiram, little does mankind know its precarious position. The wrath of God abides upon them, soon to break with divine fury upon their Christless souls, thus hurling them down to eternal perdition.

A holy indignation in Moses did not come from any personal insult, but from the indignity and insult cast upon the Lord by Dathan and Abiram. He was very wroth. Is it wrong to be angry? Sometimes it is, but sometimes it is not. Sometimes it is a sin not to be angry! You will remember that Christ never sinned, yet He was angry with the Pharisees (Mark 3:5). Moses was angry in a righteous way, and prayed that God would not respect the offering of these men.

KORAH STANDING BEFORE THE LORD

The next day, Korah with all his company, stood before the Lord, Moses, and Aaron. What a sight that must have been! This trial seems to have been set in the court of the tabernacle. As they gathered, suddenly the glory of the LORD appeared. That same glory was manifested when Aaron was initiated into the priesthood, and now it reappeared to confirm his position as high priest (Lev. 9:23). This was designed to confound the usurpers, and to divinely verify Aaron as God's chosen priest before their eyes. The *Shekinah*, or divine Majesty, which ordinarily dwelt between the cherubim over the Ark, now was publicly seen over the door of the tabernacle, to the terror of the whole congregation, though they saw no manner of similitude. There is little doubt that the appearances of the light and fire were visibly seen, thus showing that God was angry with them; as when He appeared when the congregation bade stone Joshua and Caleb (Num. 14:10).

Being a Kohathite, Korah's tent could not have been in the Reubenite camp, and it does not appear that he himself was on the spot where Dathan and Abiram stood with their families. Their attitude of defiance indicated their daring and impenitent character, regardless of God and man.

MOSES GOES TO DATHAN AND ABRIAM

While Korah and 250 rebellious men burned incense before the door of the tabernacle, God instructed Moses to go to the tents of Dathan and Abriam, since they refused to come at Moses' bidding to meet with him in the tabernacle courtyard. Moses was a wise man, so for safety sake, he took seventy of the elders of Israel with him. They also would provide a faithful witness as to Moses' dealing with the rebels. This is another reason that I believe that the choosing of these seventy men at the advice of Moses' father-in-law was of God. Some say that choosing these men was a failure of faith on Moses' part, but I believe their accusation to be unfounded. *"In multitude of counselors there is safety"* (Prov. 24:6).

As they approached these tents in the encampment of Reuben, they observed a gathered crowd. Whether they gathered out of curiosity, or out of support for Dathan and Abriam, we are not told. However, in love to them, Moses *"spake unto the congregation, saying, 'Depart, I pray you, from the tents of these wicked men, and touch nothing of theirs, lest ye be consumed in all their sins'"* (Num. 16:26). It reminds me of Peter on the day of Pentecost preaching the gospel to his countrymen. In his preaching, he testified and exhorted them saying: *"Save yourselves from this untoward generation"* (Acts 2:40).

THE REBELLION OF KORAH

Moses saw the judgment of God coming. He realized the dangerous ground the bystanders were on, and he earnestly pleaded with them to depart to safer ground. I wonder, as we see the coming wrath of God hovering over the heads of poor sinners, if we, in the preaching of the gospel are as earnest as Moses was on that occasion? How is it that many Christians can "sit back" and enjoy life, while all around them are poor souls with a burning hell beneath their feet, and only the thin, brittle thread of life, keeping them from falling therein?

The crowd stood with men that harkened not to the call of Moses. They would not come to him when he sent for them. However, notice, that he went to them. Leaving the court of the tabernacle, he walked over to the encampment of Reuben where these rebels lived. That is interesting, isn't it? He went to them! This great leader actually walked the path to where they stood. I am reminded of the words concerning our Lord; *"And he must needs go through Samaria"* (John 4:4). Why? Simply because there would be a sinner at Jacob's well that He desired to reach. Our blessed Lord inconvenienced Himself for her sake. The call goes out today, are there any men willing to inconvenience themselves in order to reach the lost? The word still stands, *"Go out into the highways and hedges, and compel them to come in, that My house may be filled"* (Luke 14:23). Thank God, there are men today that have made tremendous sacrifices to reach the lost. They have forfeited a normal way of life, going to the regions beyond, in love to poor souls. They are not well known. They are not constantly before the Christian's eye. Popularity with men has never been their aim. Some, enduring hardship for Christ, have quietly plodded on for years, seeking the lost in places where there is no scriptural testimony. In this respect, they are like Moses. He rose up, and went to them (Num. 16:25).

What a mercy for those who heeded the advice of Moses. As the crowd left, *"Dathan and Abiram came out, and stood in the door of their tents, and their wives and their sons, and their little children."* As they stood there, defiantly facing God's mediator, Moses, they were informed that they were about to realize their error. Moses said, *"Hereby shall ye know that the LORD hath sent me to do all these works; for I have not done them of mine own hand"* (Num. 16:28).

It is very sad when people come to the realization of the truth, but only when it is too late. In Luke 16, for the first time, the rich man realized his lost condition, but it wasn't until he was in hell. Then it was too late for him to escape his awful fate. Men may mock Christ, men may believe in a heathen god, and men may be atheists, but as soon as they descend into the pit, they are believers. Being rudely awakened they will realize that the Lord Jesus Christ is the only Saviour for mankind – but it will be too late! God is very clear on this truth as stated in Philippians 2:9–11: *"Wherefore God also hath highly exalted Him, and given Him a Name which is above every name: That at the name of Jesus every knee should bow, of things in heaven, and things in earth, and things under the earth; And that every tongue should confess that Jesus Christ is Lord, to the glory of God the Father."*

Notice! *"Things under the earth."* Who are they? They are those who have gone down to the pit. They are the prisoners of hell!

It is appalling, it is grievous, and it is depressing, to think that millions, if not billions, that were deceived, are going to be in hell. On earth, at the time of this writing, there are over one and one half billion people bowing down to a moon god named Allah. Millions have embraced Buddhism, Taoism, Confucianism, and a host of other gods. What is the end result? Many of these people are devout and sincere. Where are they going to be in eternity? Only the Holy Scriptures hold the answer. Acts 4:12 says, concerning Jesus Christ of Nazareth: *"Neither is there salvation in any other."* Consequently, these people do not possess salvation, and if they continue through life and die in their sins without the Lord Jesus Christ as their only Saviour, they will go down into the pit. They will perish eternally in hell and in the lake of fire. What a sad commentary on the human race, especially since God loved the world and made full provision for all mankind through the death and resurrection of His beloved Son, the Lord Jesus Christ.

THE EARTH SWALLOWED THEM UP

The LORD that parted the sea, now parted the soil. *"The ground clave asunder that was under them: And the earth opened her mouth, and swallowed them up, and their houses, and all the men that appertained unto Korah, and all their goods. They, and all that appertained to them, went down alive into the pit, and the earth closed upon them: and they perished from among the congregation. And all Israel that were round about them fled at the cry of them: for they said, 'Lest the earth swallow us up also.' And there came out a fire from the LORD, and consumed the two hundred and fifty men that offered incense"* (Num. 16:31-35). As the earth swallowed them up, their mortal bodies died, thus releasing their doomed souls to hell (*"Sheol"*). Sheol, at that time, had two compartments, the place of comfort, and the place of torment. The rich man in Luke 16 went to the place of torment. The beggar, Lazarus, went to the place of comfort. When our Lord died, He descended to the lower parts of the earth, into Sheol (*"Hades"*), the place of comfort. Upon His entering into Sheol where all the Old Testament saints were, His blessed presence made it a virtual paradise. Thus He could say to the saved thief on the cross, *"To day shalt thou be with Me in paradise"* (Luke 23:43).

The little ones of these wicked men also perished physically, but I believe that the Scriptures would teach that the souls of these little ones entered the place of comfort, to await the resurrection in a coming day.

FIRE FROM THE LORD

Presumably, at the same time, as Aaron stood at the door of the tabernacle with 250 rebels burning incense, a fire came out from the LORD, and consumed Korah and his men. Imagine,

250 burned corpses lying on the sand inside the court of the tabernacle. What a horrifying sight that must have been! What a voice from God! The judgment was swift, and without mercy.

Moses records later that *"they became a sign, notwithstanding the children of Korah died not"* (Num. 26:10–11). The little children of Dathan and Abiram died, but the children of Korah lived. *"How unsearchable are His judgments, and His ways past finding out"* (Rom. 11:33).

ELEAZAR ACTS

Eleazar is ordered to gather up the censers out of the burning and scatter the fire, with the incense that was kindled with it, in some unclean place without the camp. This action on his part would convey God's abhorrence of the rebels' offering as a polluted thing: *"The sacrifice of the wicked is an abomination to the Lord"* (Prov. 15:8).

More than likely, Eleazar was chosen instead of Aaron, for the activity of moving among the dead, would defile him ceremonially. Thus, by Eleazar performing this service, it would leave Aaron free to continue functioning as high priest.

You will also notice, that once these censers had been employed by divine command in the holy service of the sanctuary, they were henceforth forbidden to be put to any other use. Since things written aforetime were written for our learning, I discover a lesson here. After the breaking of bread, what do we do with the emblems? True, they are only bread and wine. They have not been changed mysteriously into the body and blood of our Lord, as Rome claims. No, no! They are just ordinary substances. Considering this then, is it right to take them home and feast on them with our meal? Is it right to let children "play church" with them? I don't believe so. If the brazen censers were constituted holy because of how they had been employed, could we not take the same attitude to the emblems that have been employed in a sacred way? I believe so. I personally think it only proper to dispose of the remains in a quiet and reverent way. True, if the saints were starving and there was no other food in the area to sustain life, the same rule would apply to us as to David, when he ate the shewbread. However, I do not believe any of us have ever come to that point of destitution. Let us be reverent in our disposal of the emblems.

CENSERS VENEERING THE ALTAR

In order to visibly remind the ministering priests, Levites, and the nation, of God's hatred of rebellion, and to constantly warn them not to rebel against His divine order, the censers were beaten into thin plates and veneered over the brazen altar as a sign. I would say that when we, as worshipping believers, sit on Lord's Day morning to function as priests offering up spiritual sacrifices, the emblems before our eyes would be like a sign. They would draw us to remember the enormity of our sin, which required such a unique offering to put them away. The emblems would speak loudly to our redeemed souls of His body that was offered as the required payment to bring us back to God. It also reminds us of His precious blood freely shed to cleanse us and to afford us, as priests, to enter into the immediate presence of God.

With the plates as a sign, the altar now showed that there was a distinct, priestly family, connected with its service. King Uzziah lost sight of this, and foolishly went into the temple to burn incense, but God intervened, and in disgrace and shame, he quickly left the temple, having been smitten by the LORD with leprosy (2 Chron. 26:16–21). It is a most serious thing to function as a holy priest. Do you realize that? Any man who is not indwelt with the Holy Spirit can ever be a priest. He might be an icon in the religious world. He might be a leader of a nation. He might be a star in the eyes of the world. However, if he is not born again, he is not a priest. He cannot function.

EGYPT TO CANAAN

POSITIONED AS PRIESTS

This positioning of a person as a holy priest is a most serious thing. Does it humble you to think that upon receiving Christ as your Saviour, you immediately became a priest unto God? Does it make you tremble in reverence and awe? It should! And when you enter into His presence in a collective way, does it fill your heart with gratitude that you have been thus chosen out of so many? How could any soul manifest lightness on such occasions? It amazes me that some do act rather lightly, but if only they knew the dangerous ground they are standing on through such behavior! God enjoins upon us: *"Be ye holy; for I am holy"* (1 Pet. 1:16).

A MURMURING CONGREGATION

"But on the morrow all the congregation of the children of Israel murmured against Moses and against Aaron, saying, Ye have killed the people of the LORD" (Num. 16:41).

One can hardly believe this! You would think that with all that transpired the day before, these people would be walking very softly, that they would be humble and grateful that God spared them. But sadly, this was not the case! Imagine, not just a few, but all the congregation gave way to groundless complaints. I wonder how many brethren among us could react as Moses did from such onslaughts? Not very many I am afraid. Consider *"brother Touchy."* He imagines a lot, and any little thing that one may say that he does not like, throws him into a pout. Then there is *"brother Flare-up."* He is like a stick of dynamite with a very short fuse. He has never learned to control his temper. If things do not go his way, he "blows up." We also have *"brother Grudge."* He is a sinister sort of fellow in the fact that you never suspect the venom he is accumulating against anyone that rubs him the wrong way. He speaks ill of those he does not like, and cannot tolerate any that do not agree with him. Not so with Moses, the meekest man in all the earth! Imagine being accused of causing the death of the rebels! What did Moses and Aaron do? Well, the answer is simple and sweet. Notice!

> "And Moses and Aaron came before the tabernacle of the congregation" (Num. 16:43).

They looked to God alone. He was their only source. Can we say like David: "*I will lift up mine eyes unto the hills, from whence cometh my help?* [73]*My help cometh from the LORD, which made heaven and earth* (Ps. 121:2). God was looking on, and His glory appeared. The anger of God against the accusers is made known to Moses, and what does he do? Does he say, "Good, they are going to get what they deserve"? Not a bit of it! He is not a revengeful man. Oh how often he manifests his meekness and love for God's wayward people. What vital lessons he affords us, brethren. Do you consider this great and noble man? If anyone is an example to the believers, even in our dispensation, it would be Moses. What character, what patience, what fortitude, what love, and what grace are seen in this exemplary man.

AARON'S INTERCESSION

"*Aaron ran into the midst of the congregation.*" He was earnest, and fearless. He didn't say, "Oh my, these people are infected with a plague, and if I get into their company, I too might become diseased." Not a bit of it! He wasn't thinking that way at all! Do you think that he said to himself, "These people are insane. They are viciously angry. They may tear me apart if I get too close to them." Is that what he thought? Not at all! He ran! Yes, he literally ran! This man was in dead earnest. He could not afford to waste time, because souls were dying like flies! God was sending him into their midst! What a responsibility. What a privilege! What a mission! There was nothing like it! He was God's representative. The incense that caused death when it *was not* in the hand of a priest, gave, or preserved life, when it *was* in the hand of a priest. God chose to end the plague through

---

73 The Newberry Bible rightly inserts a question mark here, not found in the KJV.

Aaron's intercession. This plan was enacted so that Aaron's activity afforded another convincing testimony that God's high priest was acting in his hallowed office, solely by the LORD'S appointment, and under His control. He stood between the dead and the living, and the plague was stayed. What a mercy! However 14,700 paid for their murmuring with their lives.

WHAT IS YOUR CONCERN?

Have you ever considered those around you? Over 153,000 people are dying every day! What is your concern? They are dying from the plague of sin. Are you earnest about it? Do you approach them about it? Do you educate them about it, with a gospel tract? Are you not an ambassador for Christ? Do you have the same attitude as Paul? *"Now then we are ambassadors for Christ, as though God did beseech you by us: we pray you in Christ's stead, be ye reconciled to God"* (2 Cor. 5:20). Philip ran to bring a message to the Ethiopian Eunuch (Acts 8). A true ambassador, and a true evangelist, are earnest. You may not be an evangelist, but if saved, you are an ambassador. Are you earnest! Aaron had the censer, the coals, and the incense. We have the greatest message in all the world brethren – the story of the Cross! Look at your fellow men dying all around you, and ask yourself the question, am I earnest?

We have shown Aaron to be a picture of God's people as royal priests, running to sinners with the gospel, but basically, he is a picture to us of our great High Priest, the Lord Jesus Christ. As our Sin Offering, He died for our sins on the Cross. He was *"once offered to bear the sins of many"* (Heb. 9:28). But now He has ascended into heaven to appear in the presence of God for us (Heb. 9:24). In God's holy heaven, He intercedes for us. He pleads on our behalf. As we travel through this waste-howling wilderness, called *the world*, we are beset with many trials. Some are more severe than others. There are trials that would drag us down to the dust. However, thank God, we have a great High Priest, Who was made a Surety of a better testament. He is a Priest Who continueth ever, Who has an unchangeable priesthood. *"Wherefore He is able also to save them to the uttermost that come unto God by Him, seeing He ever liveth to make intercession for them"* (Heb. 7:22–25). That is, He is able to save, and keep us from falling, through His intercession for us, until we reach the end of our journey down here. Thus, in Aaron, we see a twofold picture of Christ in heaven interceding for us, and God's people on earth as ambassadors for Christ.

28

AARON'S ROD THAT BUDDED

NUMBERS 17

"And the LORD spake unto Moses, saying, 'Speak unto the children of Israel, and take of every one of them a rod according to the house of their fathers, of all their princes according to the house of their fathers twelve rods: write thou every man's name upon his rod. And thou shalt write Aaron's name upon the rod of Levi: for one rod shall be for the head of the house of their fathers. And thou shalt lay them up in the tabernacle of the congregation before the testimony, where I will meet with you. And it shall come to pass, that the man's rod, whom I shall choose, shall blossom: and I will make to cease from me the murmurings of the children of Israel, whereby they murmur against you" (Num. 17:1–5).

This question may have been lurking in the minds of the people; who really was God's high priest? Was Aaron positioned as such by Moses, just because he was his brother? God is now going to dispel such vain thoughts from the minds of the people. The proof of the validity of Aaron's priesthood is now going to be divinely made known. There will be no reasoning or questions about it. God will make it clearly manifest what person was His choice.

OVERSEERS

The opening of our chapter, which you have just read, gives us the divine plan. What profound wisdom we observe in this arrangement. The matter is completely taken out of the hands of man, and placed into the hands of God. It was not a question of a man appointing himself, or some other fellow. No, no, that would never do! The selection of who was priest was entirely God's. Man had nothing to do with it. Is that not what Paul states when writing to the Hebrews?[74] *"And no man taketh this honour unto himself, but he that is called of God, as was Aaron"* (Heb. 5:4). Before we go further, let me ask, who makes overseers? Can a father appoint his son as an overseer? Does a man's success in secular business constitute him an overseer? Does a man's personality, or perhaps his wealth, make him an elder? Why no! None of these features place a man into the oversight. Then who does position men to function as an elders in God's assembly? Why, the answer is very simple, and is proclaimed in one verse. *"Take heed therefore unto yourselves, and to all the flock, over the which the Holy Ghost hath made you overseers, to feed the church of God, which He hath purchased with His own blood"* (Acts 20:28).

What an impressive sight that must have been; twelve princes, the leading men of each tribe, walking to the tabernacle door with a rod in his hand. There they stood before Moses, each one with great expectation that perhaps their tribe would be selected by God for the priesthood. It would seem that the plague had just recently passed, and I suppose that these people were yet in an excited state of mind. The scene was volatile, but God was going to settle their imaginations regarding priesthood, once and for all. Standing at the door of the tabernacle, they placed into the hand of Moses their rods. Each rod was identified with every man's name upon his rod. Aaron's rod was included with theirs. Moses walked into the sanctuary, and with utmost reverence drew aside the vail, and

---

74 For proof on who wrote the Hebrews read, Jesus in Hebrews, by R. E. Surgenor. Pages 9–19. Gospel Folio Press, 304 Killaly St. W. Port Colborn, ON. Canada.

entered into the immediate presence of God with the rods, and laid them before the LORD.

Every rod was lifeless. How could a piece of dead wood bring forth buds, bloom blossoms, and yield almonds? The natural man would sneer at the whole thing, and cry out, "impossible!" The infidel, who shuts out God, would cry out, "trickery!" However, on the morrow, all doubts were abolished!

> *"And it came to pass, that on the morrow Moses went into the tabernacle of witness; and, behold, the rod of Aaron for the house of Levi was budded, and brought forth buds, and bloomed blossoms, and yielded almonds"* (Num. 17:8).

The original word for *"rod"* (*matteh*), is usually used to denote a *staff, stick, walking-stick,* or *wand,* rather than a branch, or bough. The princes of the tribes carried staves in their hands, as a kind of *baton,* that served as a badge of authority. Compare Numbers 21:18, which reinforces my statement.

AARON'S ROD THAT BUDDED

What a revelation on the morrow! Not only did Aaron's lifeless rod blossom, it also manifested all the stages of nature employed in fruit-bearing! The miracle manifested sudden vegetation on Aaron's rod. It was in different stages, and that alone was contrary to nature, for in nature you would discover first the buds, then later on, the blossoms which later would bring forth fruit. However, on this miraculous occasion, all three stages are manifested at the same time. How could this be? Man cannot make a dead stick live, and nature cannot make a live stick immediately bear fruit, apart from the first two stages. Ah my friend, God can do what man cannot do, and God can accomplish what nature finds impossible. *"With God all things are possible"* (Matt. 19:26). Do you believe that intellectually, or do you believe that with all of your heart? Does that blessed truth govern your life?

"Thus, in reference to Aaron's budding rod, if any inquire, 'How can such a thing be? It is contrary to the laws of nature; and how could God reverse the established principles of natural philosophy?' Faith's reply is sublimely simple. God can do as He pleases. The One who called worlds into existence, could make a rod to bud, blossom, and bear fruit in a moment. Bring God in, and all is simple and plain as possible. Leave God out, and all is plunged in hopeless confusion. The attempt to tie up — we speak with reverence — the Almighty Creator of the vast universe, by certain laws of nature, or certain principles of natural philosophy, is nothing short of impious blasphemy. It is almost worse than denying His existence altogether. It is hard to say which is the worse, the atheist who says there is no God, or the rationalist who maintains that He cannot do as He pleases.

We feel the immense importance of being able to see the real roots of all the plausible theories which are afloat at the present moment. The mind of man is busy forming systems, drawing conclusions, and reasoning in such a manner as virtually to exclude the testimony of Holy Scripture altogether, and to shut out God from His own creation. Our young people must be solemnly warned as to this. They must be taught the immense difference between the facts of science, and the conclusions of scientific men. A fact is a fact wherever you meet it, whether in geology, astronomy, or any other department of science; but men's reasonings, conclusions, and systems are another thing altogether. Now, Scripture will never touch the facts of science; but the reasonings of scientific man are constantly found in collision with Scripture. Alas! alas! for such men!

And when such is the case, we must, with plain decision, denounce such reasonings altogether, and exclaim with the apostle, *'Let God be true, and every man a liar.'"*[75]

When Moses came out from the presence of God with the rods in his hands, what an assurance it must have been to Aaron, and what an amazement to the rest. I can just picture those princes, humbly, and quietly walking back to their respective tribes with their "dry sticks" in their hands. They went back the same as they came forth. Nothing had changed except perhaps their way of thinking. What a testimony to Aaron! Who could deny it? What an incontestable evidence of the LORD'S designation!

MOSES WITH AARON'S ROD

Once again, Moses enters through the vail. This time there is only one rod in his hand, a rod with buds, blossoms, and almonds – Aaron's rod. The matter is now settled, and Aaron's rod before the testimony of the LORD was to be kept for a token against the rebels. Never again would the unique priesthood of Aaron be brought into question. Thus, in the Ark were three things. The tables of stone, the golden pot that had the manna, and Aaron's rod that budded. All through their forty years of wandering through the wilderness, the witness of God's precepts, His provision, and Priesthood, were contained in the Ark of the testimony, in the holy of holies. When Israel's wilderness wanderings were over, the manna and Aaron's rod, symbols of the provisions of God's grace for the wilderness, were no longer in the Ark. Nothing remained except the commandments of God, which was the foundation of His righteous government in the midst of His gathered out, and redeemed people.

The tabernacle in the wilderness is a beautiful picture of the Church in this world, awating her consummation. During our journey, we feast on Christ, the true Manna, and we experience His priestly ministry for us on a daily basis. However, when

---

75   <u>Notes on Numbers.</u> C.H.M. Loizeaux Brothers. Ch. 17.

the Church is raptured home to heaven we have another state. That state is pictured in Solomon's temple. Just as that temple had a floor of gold, in like manner we shall walk the street of gold. Just as the Ark still contained the testimony of stone, so the testimony of God will be there. *"For ever, O LORD, Thy word is settled in heaven"* (Ps. 119:89). However, you will notice that in Solomon's temple, Aaron's rod is not mentioned. Let me ask this, do you think that our Lord will be officiating as a priest for us up there? I believe that when the Church is glorified, that it will no longer need a priest. What about the golden pot with the hidden manna? It too is not mentioned, and the lesson is that in heaven we shall be eating the hidden manna. It will be no longer hidden. That hidden manna speaks of all the things our Lord did in His humanity that is not recorded in the Word. In that coming day, it will please Him to unfold to us all those hidden truths about Himself. What a blessed eternity awaits us brethren.

29

THE RED HEIFER

NUMBERS 19

We want to consider with you now, a most unique sacrifice – a red heifer. This most unusual sacrifice is mentioned in Hebrews 9. *"For if the blood of bulls and of goats, and the ashes of an heifer sprinkling the unclean, sanctifieth to the purifying of the flesh: How much more shall the blood of Christ, who through the eternal Spirit offered Himself without spot to God, purge your conscience from dead works to serve the living God?"* (v.v. 13–14). With this inspired statement before us, it is no stretch of the imagination to apply the red heifer of Numbers 19, to the Lord Jesus Christ. The red heifer was a type of Christ in many unique ways, and this uniqueness is what we wish to consider with you for a few moments.

Writers have various thoughts and applications on this subject, but we will give you our simple meditations, hoping that they will warm your heart as they did mine. It is wonderful to me, to see the Holy Spirit delighting to unfold the virtues of our blessed Lord in types and shadows of the Old Testament. It is equally wonderful to have the Spirit expose His thoughts to us in our quiet meditation of Him Whom we love. How immensely profound the sacrifice of Christ was. Let me say, that you will never appreciate the offering of Christ, in a profound way, if you are not familiar with the Spirit's writing through His servant Moses. One "sister" lamented to me one day that she never got much when she read the Bible. I asked her how she read the Scriptures. She confessed that she read a couple of verses before going to work and that was it for the day. I asked her if she ever heard of anorexia, and went on to explain to her that she was starving herself spiritually. Due to the lack of spiritual food, she was fainting by the way. Her course never changed, until finally, she quietly left God's assembly, never to return. Then I began to wonder, was this woman really saved or not? Possibly, her lack of hunger for the Word was due to the sad fact that she possessed no new nature within, to crave the Scriptures.

Paul stated that *"whatsoever things were written aforetime were written for our learning"* (Rom. 15:4), so let us consider this red heifer of aforetime, for our learning.

AN ORDINANCE OF THE LAW

The first thing that you will notice is that the Lord commanded this as an ordinance of the law. The whole plan was God's, not man's. Who devised the plan of redemption? Why, it was God! He foreordained His Son before the foundation of the world to be the sacrifice for our sins, that we might be brought back to Himself. The heifer was to be without spot, wherein there was no blemish. Is not this the very language that the Spirit employs concerning our Saviour, when speaking of redemption? *"Forasmuch as ye know that ye were not redeemed with corruptible things, as silver and gold, from your vain conversation received by tradition from your fathers; But with the precious blood of Christ, as of a lamb without blemish and without spot"* (1 Pet. 1:18–19).

NO YOKE

The next statement about this heifer was: *"Upon which never came yoke."* What is the implication here? Well, first of all, ask yourself the question, what is a yoke for? In the Scriptures it is used different ways. Sometimes it refers to bondage, being unwillingly under the dominion and power of another. The first time the word is employed is in Genesis 27:40, relating to Esau and Jacob. Thou *"shalt serve thy brother; and it shall come to pass when thou shalt have the dominion, that thou shalt break his yoke from off thy neck."* You have the same thought in 1 Kings 12:4, when Jereboam came to Rehoboam, complaining about the grevious yoke laid upon them by Solomon. That's the first thing that we notice about a yoke, namely *servitude*. The Scriptures also speak of oxen being yoked together, thus we see not only the linking of the two together, but also control, having been brought under constraint.

Let's consider these facts now relative to our Lord. The heifer was never under a yoke. This beautifully portrays to us the fact that Christ was never under the yoke of man's dominion. Remember what He said to Pilate? *"Thou couldest have no power at all against Me, except it were given thee from above"* (John 19:11). Not only this, He never needed to be restrained. He always did those things that pleased the Father. How could He ever need to be restrained, for He was without sin. One more thing; He was never yoked with any mortal. Yes, He ate with publicans and sinners, but He was distinctly separated from them in all His ways. Thus, like the red heifer, He was never brought under a yoke.[76] Arno C. Gaebelein states: "A yoke is put on an animal to restrain the wild nature, to bring it to subjection. Our blessed Lord needed no yoke, for He came willingly. 'Lo, I come to do Thy will.'"

COLOR MENTIONED

Another thing worthy of our notice is that this is the only sacrifice where the color of the animal was mentioned, and required. The Jews claim that two white hairs, or two black hairs on a red heifer would disqualify it from being accepted. Thus,

---

[76] As much as we respect William Kelly, we are a little slow in agreeing with him on the meaning of a yoke. He states that it means the "the pressure of sin." Considering the fact that the Lord has a yoke for us to bear (Matt. 11:29), we believe the yoke to suggest one being under the power of another, and also being linked with another. Thus, we are called upon to labor under His authority in our service, and to walk with Him in sweet fellowship. In that sense, we are not the servants of men, but the servants of God.

we see the absolute uniqueness of our Lord. He was vastly different than the normal human being. His thoughts were sinless, His words were always with power and divine authority. His walk was faultless, and His power was limitless. He was fairer than all the sons of men. He is called the "begotten Son," which, in other languages, is translated "unique Son," and unique He was! Red is also the color of blood, and our blessed Lord was obedient unto death, even the death of the Cross.

It was slain without the camp. This immediately draws us to Hebrews 13:12: *"Wherefore Jesus also, that He might sanctify the people with His own blood, suffered without the gate."*

ELEAZAR, NOT AARON

Now a question arises. With such an important offering, why was Eleazar, Aaron's son, chosen to officiate in the slaying of the red heifer? The answer is simple. By officiating, he became ceremonially unclean until the evening. Aaron, the high priest of Israel, was to maintain his dignified position, and not have his functions cease because of uncleanness. Thus, he took no part in this particular offering. Ah brethren, we have a great High Priest that will never know defilement. People talk today of "twenty-four, seven," meaning that the store's service is provided 24 hours a day, 7 days a week. I certainly do not want to be disrespectful, but in today's language we can exclaim that we have a twenty-four, seven, great High Priest. "He tends with sweet unwearied care, the flock for which He bled."

An unnamed man was to slay the heifer before the face of Eleazar (v. 3). Is it not true, that the chief priests had a principle hand in the death of our Lord? Absolutely! The Romans crucified Him, but Israel's priests looked on.

SPRINKLING OF BLOOD

In the next step, we find Eleazar taking a container of blood from the victim and approaching the tabernacle. With his finger, he sprinkles the blood of the heifer *"directly before the tabernacle of the congregation seven times"* (v. 4). Seven is the number of that which is complete, or, perfect. Thus, we have a picture of the blood of atonement. Before the very face of God our Lord made atonement. It was a complete work, and it was a perfect work.

> "Done is the work that saves,
> Once and forever done;
> Finished the righteousness
> That clothes the unrighteous one.
> The love that blesses us below
> Is flowing freely to us now." [77]

BURNING THE RED HEIFER

Regarding the burning, nothing of the red heifer was to be spared. Every single part of that animal was to experience the fire, outside the camp. Come with me, my brother, my sister, and let us walk out through Jerusalem's gate to Calvary, and what do we see? We see a "Victim" bound to the accursed tree. We view the plowed back, with ribbons of flesh hanging, red with blood. We see spikes through His hands, and a spike through His feet. We observe His blessed face, pummeled and displaying raw flesh. We gaze closer and notice chunks of flesh missing where the hairs were plucked off of His face. Mixed with gore, we see human spittle covering the open wounds on His face. Our gaze moves upward to His brow. Was the crown of thorns still there? We cannot say, for Holy Writ is silent regarding it. As we stand at Calvary, with reverent and contrite hearts, we weep and sing the words of Isaac Watts:

> "When I survey the wondrous Cross
> On which the Prince of glory died,
> My richest gain I count but loss,
> And pour contempt on all my pride."

---

[77] Horatius Bonar. The Believer's Hymn Book. John Ritchie Ltd. P. 38

How humbling it is to stand at the foot of the Cross! To see Him on the tree, atoning for our sins is enough to melt the hardest heart. I would say that there would be far less of the world about us, and there would be far more of the love of God toward our fellow brethren, if we only stood more often at the foot of the Cross.

"When I gaze upon His blessed brow
His wounded feet and side
And think upon His sacrifice
That just for me He died.

It moves, my heart, and melts my eyes
Earth's vain delights are gone.
And as I walk the narrow way,
This now becomes my song.

I love the Lord, I love the Book,
I love those for whom He died.
I cannot help but speak of Him,
For my sins He was crucified." RES

CEDAR WOOD, HYSSOP, AND SCARLET

"And the priest shall take cedar wood, and hyssop, and scarlet, and cast it into the midst of the burning of the heifer" (Num. 19:6). The question arises, what do these materials typify? I believe that they typify the world. The world with all its glory, was righteously dealt with and judged at Calvary. The scarlet is a bright color and typifies the glory of the world. Belshazzar decreed that anyone that could read the writing and show the interpretation, would be honored by being clothed in scarlet (Dan. 5:7). It was said of the army of Israel: *"The valiant men are in scarlet"* (Nah. 2:3). The beast of Revelation and the woman that rides the beast (Rome), are both arrayed in scarlet. Thus we see, that the world's pomp, glory, and power, are connected with the color scarlet.

With the scarlet, we also find cedar wood and hyssop. These certainly are two extremes, the lofty cedar and the lowly hyssop.

Nature, from its highest to its lowest, which includes every section, or organization of this world, was brought under the power of the Cross. "The believer sees in the death of Christ the end of all his guilt, the end of all earth's glory, the end of the whole system of nature – the entire old creation."[78]

The words of our Lord come to our mind: *"Now is the judgment of this world: now shall the prince of this world be cast out"* (John 12:31). Paul writes: *"And having spoiled principalities and powers, He made a shew of them openly, triumphing over them in it"* (Col. 2:15). As we consider a judged world at the Cross, we can confess, like Paul, regarding our own personal relationship with a godless world: *"But God forbid that I should glory, save in the cross of our Lord Jesus Christ, by whom the world is crucified unto me, and I unto the world"* (Gal. 6:14). Thus, we sing like William Cowper:

> "I thirst, but not as once I did,
> The vain delights of earth to share;
> Thy wounds, Emmanuel, all forbid
> That I should seek my pleasure there.
>
> It was the sight of Thy dear Cross
> First weaned my soul from earthly things,
> And taught me to esteem as dross
> The mirth of fools and pomp of kings."

CEREMONIALLY UNCLEAN

Have you noticed that all those involved in the preparation of the red Heifer and its ashes became ceremonially unclean until that evening? Strange, isn't it, that the offering that was to provide cleanness, made those that prepared it unclean. It points to the fact that all that had a hand in putting our Lord to death, contracted guilt by it. Yet in spite of this, the offering of our Lord's body was a payment due for sin, and the centurions that contracted even more guilt upon their souls by crucifying

---

[78] Arno C. Gaebelein. The Annotated Bible, Vol.1. Loizeaus Brothers. P. 245.

Him, at the same time, came under the good of His offering, and their guilt was washed away in His precious blood before the Lord's body was taken down. Their confession of Him would seem to indicate that the Lord's prayer had been answered, *"Father, forgive them; for they know not what they do"* (Luke 32:34).

ASHES

After the fire did all that it could possibly do, the ashes remained. Our Lord remained on the tree until all the fires of God's wrath for our sins had been spent. There was no more payment to be made. The Roman Catholic mass is a tragedy, for it projects the blasphemous thought that the Lord's work on the Cross was not sufficient. In every mass, the wafer is supposedly turned into His body and re-offered for sin. The cup of wine is supposedly transformed into the actual blood of Christ, and re-shed. What travesty! What total wickedness! What a flagrant perversion of Biblical truth! How it must grieve the heart of God to see pompous, Babylonish priests dressed in scarlet robes, supposedly re-offering our blessed Lord as a sacrifice for sins. Away with the whole affair!

Ashes! There is nothing so incorruptible as ashes! You cannot burn ashes, for it is a witness that the fire has previously done all that it could. What a striking symbol of the everlasting efficacy of the sacrifice of our Lord. These ashes were laid up as a reservoir for the continual purification of those who would become unclean. This is another factor that made the offering of the red heifer so unique. All the other offerings were made for a special occasion. However, this offering provided cleansing throughout the Israelite's sojourn.

CHRIST, OUR SIN OFFERING

Now then, my beloved brethren, in the sin offering aspect of Christ's death, we see a once-for-all offering for our sins. At

Calvary, they were righteously dealt with, and forever put away. But as the days go by, and we rub shoulders with the world, there are times when we become defiled. *Judicially*, we are cleansed once and for all, but *positionally*, there are times when our *state* does not measure up to our *standing* in Christ, simply because we have sinned. Our sin may have been committed ignorantly or even presumptuously, causing us to become defiled. Sinning thus does not sever one's union with the Lord, but it does break communion with Him. Thus, cleansing is needed. Where can this cleansing be found? It is found in the precious blood of Christ, and the realization of His cleansing power. The Holy Spirit convicts us. Then, having repented of our sin, He gives us that divine assurance that we are cleansed, and back into fellowship with God. I believe that is what we have pictured in the ashes mixed in water. The water is an emblem of the Holy Spirit. It is good to realize the importance and necessity of the Holy Spirit's engagement when it comes to the cleansing from sin. Consider the following verses: *"Ye are sanctified, but ye are justified in the name of the Lord Jesus, and by the Spirit of our God"* (1 Cor. 6:11). *"Elect according to the foreknowledge of God the Father, through sanctification of the Spirit, unto obedience and sprinkling of the blood of Jesus Christ"* (1 Pet. 1:2). The defiled Israelite could not be cleansed by only applying the ashes. Oh no, that would never do! The ashes must be in running water, and applied, to effect cleansing.

INTELLECTUAL, EMOTIONAL, THEATRICAL, PREACHING

I am afraid that with the low quality of preaching in some quarters, we have professors who think that they have been saved, but in reality, they have never been effectively cleansed. Perhaps they have listened to intellectual preaching, consequently making a profession of faith in Christ by acknowledging Biblical facts. However, the Holy Spirit has never convicted them of their sin and the need of repentance. Their profession just amounts to "a matter of fact" sort of thing, a mere mental consent.

Then, there is a form of preaching that involves a bit of acting, and emotionalism. Thus, the hearer is disturbed emotionally, but the Holy Spirit is not producing this. Thus, with great excitement and clamor they make their profession. The Spirit has never convicted them of their sin, consequently, there can be no real repentance. The Lord plainly stated, *"except ye repent, ye shall all likewise perish"* (Luke 13:5). You cannot separate the ashes from the water, neither can you separate the work of Christ and the work of the Spirit, when it comes to the imparting of salvation.

However, we are not basically considering a sinner in need of salvation, but rather a saint becoming defiled. Thus, as already stated, it is the Holy Spirit that works on the soul, bringing the defiled saint to an awakening of his need of cleansing. What a comforting assurance we find in 1 John 2:1: *"If any man sin, we have an advocate with the Father, Jesus Christ the righteous."* That is, we have One Who is our legal assistant, Who pleads our cause. Prior to this, John mentions the fact that confession is needed before cleansing. This confession, in a private manner before God, is wrought through the operation of the Holy Spirit upon the defiled one's soul. *"If we confess our sins, He is faithful and just to forgive us our sins, and to cleanse us from all unrighteousness"* (1 Jn. 1:9). Thus we see, that the offering of the red heifer, and the continual application of its ashes mixed into living water, is a beautiful picture of the efficacy of the offering of Christ on our behalf.

DEFILEMENT LIKE A VIRUS

Now let me burden you a little more with some thoughts on defilement. Defilement is a most easy thing to contract. Like a virus lurking in the atmosphere all around us, the traps of defilement lay all around us. Picture the Israelite. He is in his tent with others. All of a sudden one in the tent dies. Immediately, the living in that tent are ceremonially defiled. Help is called for, so certain men come and carry the dead body out of the tent to give it a decent burial. They are doing a noble service, however, through touching a dead body, they too become defiled.

Then we are presented with another situation. A man is slain by the sword, and his son lies dead in a field. Out of respect, his corpse is taken back to the camp to be given a decent burial. However, those responsible for transporting the body are immediately defiled. In Israel's day, taking care of the dead, stripping, washing, placing the corpse in a shroud, then carrying it out for a decent burial, was a most pious and loving duty. Yet, under the Law, it brought defilement. So you can readily see, that it was exceedingly easy to become defiled!

So here comes a man from the burial. He is defiled, and is seeking cleansing. The water of purification, containing the ashes of the red heifer was brought forth, and a bunch of hyssop was dipped in the water, then sprinkled on the individual. This ceremony took place on the third day. It was repeated on the seventh day, and then that person was to purify himself, wash his clothes, bathe himself in water, and wash his garments. Having accomplished these ordinances, he would then be clean that evening. However, failure to observe this ordinance would then constitute that person, not only ceremonially defiled, but also morally defiled. He would then be cut off from the congregation, because he had defiled the sanctuary of the LORD. The lesson is this. It is a most solemn thing to think lightly of divine observances, though they may seem trivial. Let us be very careful to not set aside even the most minute ordinance of God. We may excuse ourselves regarding what we have done, terming it "something little." However, no matter how "little" the sin or shortcoming may have been, if not repented of, it will bring us down, perhaps even to our ruin.

Is it easy to become defiled, and lose communion with God? Absolutely! A mere glance at something immoral defiles. A wayward thought defiles. Neglecting to pray can bring defilement. A wrong motive in ministering the Word, or preaching the gospel can contract defilement. Mistreatment of others will defile us. Even disobedience to any righteous laws imposed by the powers that be, will defile us. The pollution of sin cleaves to our best service. You will remember our Lord's statement regarding defilement. *"For from within, out of the heart of men, proceed evil thoughts, adulteries, fornications, murders, thefts, covetousness, wickedness, deceit, lasciviousness, an evil eye, blasphemy, pride, foolishness: All these evil things come from within, and defile the man"* (Mark 7:21–23). Solomon, through the Spirit, endorses the fact that sin lurks at every corner, waiting to cleave unto us. *"For there is not a just man upon earth, that doeth good, and sinneth not"* (Eccl. 7:20). John speaks out exclaiming, *"If we say that we have no sin, we deceive ourselves, and the truth is not in us"* (1 Jn. 1:8). Let us freely admit that we sin daily. But let us also rejoice, that we have One Who comes to our defense, even our Advocate, our Redeemer, Saviour and Lord, Jesus the Son of God! Halleluiah, what a Saviour!

In closing this subject, let me also add this; let us keep a very tender conscience toward defilement, and let us daily approach our Advocate, that our communion with the Lord might remain sweet during our sojourn down here, in a world that is steeped with defilement. Regarding the ordinance of the red heifer, David cried out: *"Purge me with hyssop, and I shall be clean: wash me, and I shall be whiter than snow"* (Ps. 51:7). May our concern be the same.

> "Break every barrier down,
> Thou Lamb of Calvary;
> Show me the awfulness of sin,
> The thing which grieveth Thee:
> Purge Thou my soul from dross,
> Cleanse me from every sin,
> Wash me in Thine atoning blood,
> And make me pure within."[79]

---

79 Bertha Mullen. <u>The Believer's Hymnbook.</u> John Ritche Ltd. P. 314

30

MIRIAM AND AARON'S DEATH

THE SMITING OF THE ROCK

NUMBERS 20

All of a sudden, we are brought to the end of 38 years of wandering for the children of Israel. Chapter 20 brings us to the last year before Israel was to enter the land of Canaan. One may wonder, why 38 years of total silence? The truth of the matter is, that Moses was not a historian, but a legislator. However, other portions of Scripture reveal to us some of the events that took place in those 38 silent years, and the reports are not too favorable. We shall consider them in this chapter, as the Lord directs.

This chapter is a "famous funeral chapter." It commences with the death of Miriam and concludes with the death of Aaron. Sandwiched between these two memorable events we have recorded the failure of Moses, that cost him the privilege of entering into the Promised Land. It is a chapter of sad events indeed, and there are many lessons in it for us of this modern day. The history of Miriam has a sad note. She started her journey singing on the shores of the Red Sea, but ended her journey on a sour note. It was during Israel's four-month stay in Kadesh that she died and was buried. Thirty-eight years prior to this, it was at Kadesh that the spies brought back an evil report, thus discouraging Israel from entering into their inheritance.

Consequently, the whole congregation of Israel, from **twenty** years old and upward, saving the Levites, Caleb, and **Joshua**, were doomed to die in the wilderness. Now it was **Miriam's** turn to die. She died four months before Aaron and eleven **years** before Moses, at the age of about 130 years.

AARON'S FUNERAL

> *"And the children of Israel, even the whole congregation, journeyed from Kadesh, and came unto mount Hor. And the LORD spake unto Moses and Aaron in mount Hor, by the coast of the land of Edom, saying, Aaron shall be gathered unto his people: for he shall not enter into the land which I have given unto the children of Israel, because ye rebelled against my word at the water of Meribah. Take Aaron and Eleazar his son, and bring them up unto mount Hor: And strip Aaron of his garments, and put them upon Eleazar his son: and Aaron shall be gathered unto his people , and shall die there. And Moses did as the LORD commanded: and they went up into mount Hor in the sight of all the congregation. And Moses stripped Aaron of his garments, and put them upon Eleazar his son; and Aaron died there in the top of the mount: and Moses and Eleazar came down from the mount. And when all the congregation saw that Aaron was dead, they mourned for Aaron thirty days, even all the house of Israel"* (Num. 20:22–29).

God designates the time and the place where His servants lay down in death. Aaron's time had arrived. There is no **manifested** terror. There are no cries to live longer. All is resolved, and Aaron is at peace. While still living, Aaron attends his own funeral procession. He was to die on a mountain top, as Moses also would eleven months later. There is no indication that Aaron was in poor health; quite the contrary. He was 123 years old and still able to function in his God-appointed office. However, the time had come when he had performed his last priestly function, he had offered his last offering, and he had stepped out of the sanctuary, never to return to it again. There was a finality about the whole procedure. He would never again minister before the Lord on earth. It was a very solemn scene: A brother and a son accompanying him on his upward ascent to his burial ground. Do you think that as these three man made their way up Mount Hor there was lightness and frivolity? Do you think that they were joking along the way? Hardly! I am sure that the conversation was about the LORD, and about heaven.

I have spoken to saints on their death beds, and the things of this earth had become very dim to them. There was no lightness, and no silliness. Nothing of this earth mattered. Material possessions were not held in value, as they neared the doors of the shadow of death. God had graciously fixed their minds upon Himself, and they were at perfect peace. They experience the promise: *"Thou wilt keep him in perfect peace, whose mind is stayed on Thee: because he trusteth in Thee"* (Isa. 26:3).

This I believe to be true of Aaron. I can picture a heavenly calmness enshrouding that unique scene. It was public up to a point. All Israel stood looking up, as these three men of God ascended the mount, out of their gaze. Finally coming to Aaron's final resting place, the hands that clothed him with priestly garments, are now employed in stripping him of his robes. As Aaron watches his brother, Moses, placing those high priest's garments upon his son Eleazar, he lays down, with heavenly assurance that the functions of a high priest in Israel will continue. Perhaps a farewell is given to his brother and son, and then, the Lord terminates his sojourn, and Aaron was gathered to his people. He died.

Just as Aaron had finished his work, we too shall be called upon to depart when our work is finished. Departure will come, either by way of death, or by way of the last trump. Some saints die in seclusion, far from the sight of men. Others leave earth with loved ones surrounding them. If called upon to go the way of all the earth, may God give us the grace to die, as it were, on the mountain top – nearer to heaven than ever before. Stephen got a glimpse of heaven before leaving earth. Paul had a desire to depart and be with Christ, which he said was *far better*. The psalmist placed a true value on such deaths, exclaiming: *"Precious in the sight of the LORD is the death of his saints"* (Ps. 116:15).

MOSES' MISTAKE

Coming back in this chapter, we would consider Moses' traumatic mistake. Upon camping at Kadesh they found no water, and usual to their past conduct, the people gathered themselves together and chode with Moses, expressing that they wished they had died when their brethren had died before the Lord. Their departed brethren were rebels, but these complainers elevated them. Moses had just been bereaved of his sister, and instead of mourning with him, they are murmuring against him. They expressed no consideration for Moses, and even went so far as to blame him for their distress.

> *"And Moses and Aaron went from the presence of the assembly unto the door of the tabernacle of the congregation, and they fell upon their faces: and the glory of the LORD appeared unto them. And the LORD spake unto Moses, saying, Take the rod, and gather thou the assembly together, thou, and Aaron thy brother, and speak ye unto the rock before their eyes; and it shall give forth his water, and thou shalt bring forth to them water out of the rock: so thou shalt give the congregation and their beasts drink. And Moses took the rod from before the LORD, as he commanded him. And Moses and Aaron gathered the congregation together before the rock, and he said unto them, Hear now, ye rebels; must we fetch you water out of this rock? And Moses lifted up his hand, and with his rod he smote the rock twice: and the water came out abundantly, and the congregation drank, and their beasts also"* (Num. 20:6–11).

Then came the fatal mistake, and Moses paid dearly for it. God denied him the privilege of entering into the Promised Land. Men often fail in their strongest points. Moses' strong point was his meekness, and this is exactly where he failed. *"They angered him also at the waters of strife, so that it went ill with Moses for their sakes: Because they provoked his spirit, so that he spake unadvisedly with his lips"* (Ps. 106:32–33).

The first time that Moses smote the rock (Ex. 17) it was with his own rod, the rod of judgment. Thus setting forth the type of Christ being smitten under the judgment of God for sin. However, this scene was different. Moses was to take the rod of Aaron and speak to the rock in the midst of all the congregation. In doing this, God assured Moses that the waters would flow out to meet the need of His people. The first smiting of the rock was not to be repeated, expressing the truth that Christ was to be smitten only once. As the hymn writer has put it:

> "Never more shall God Jehovah,
> Smite the Shepherd with the sword;
> Ne'er again shall cruel sinners
> Set at naught our glorious Lord."[80]

Aaron's rod typified the resurrection of our Lord and His priestly work on behalf of His redeemed people. All that was needed was a word, not a smiting in judgment, to bring forth blessing to His people. Moses failed in presenting that type, for instead of holding Aaron's rod and speaking to the rock, in anger, he smote the rock twice with his own rod, the rod that spoke of judgment. In the Old Testament, I have noticed that there was always severe judgment from God on any person that destroyed a type of Christ. This was the case with Moses.

It is evident that Moses was excited, irritated, and indignant, and he calls the people *"ye rebels."* Then, he assumes that if any water would come out of the rock, it would have to be

---

80 Robert C. Chapman. <u>The Believer's Hymn Book.</u> John Ritchie Ltd. P. 99

him that would do it. *"Must we fetch you water out of this rock?"* Instead of speaking to the rock, he speaks to the people, and then smites the rock with his rod of power and judgment, not once, but twice! He was an old man of 120 years, who had constantly been abused by the people's grumbling and accusations for forty long years. The old generation was gone and a new generation had arisen, and lo and behold, they were of the same makeup as the murmurers that had died in the wilderness. It must have depressed him greatly.

Even though Moses believed not the LORD to sanctify Him in the eyes of the children of Israel, yet God in His grace caused the water to come out of the rock abundantly, and the congregation drank and their beasts also.

Now, there is a little lesson here for us. Just because we see blessing from our work, it does not necessarily imply that we have done that work properly. What should be the main objective in working for God? A Christian's main objective should be doing God's work in God's prescribed way. Success is secondary, obedience is first. *"Behold, to obey is better than sacrifice, and to hearken than the fat of rams"* (1 Sam. 15:22). The end does not justify the means. Let me put it this way. Take, for instance, the preaching of the gospel. Certain unscriptural methods may be employed, and success seen in the salvation of souls. Now then, does that say that it is right to do God's work the wrong way, simply because God blessed? Hardly! I know that many brethren have said that God cannot bless unless His work is done properly? If that is so, then tell me why souls have been saved in unscriptural gatherings for the preaching of the gospel? Musical entertainment, altar calls, and other unscriptural methods have been employed, and souls have been saved. What is the answer to all of this? It is the fact that God is sovereign, and He often overrules the mistakes of men to further His design. God had many souls ordained unto eternal life in Corinth. When they heard the gospel, they were going to be saved, and God gave Paul that assurance as he labored in that city. Regardless of the methods used, these souls were chosen by God unto eternal life, yet Paul was very careful to employ proper methods in the presentation of salvation truths. His words in 1 Corinthians 2, would attest to that. In spite of Moses' error, the people were blest.

However, the results for Moses were traumatic. *"And the LORD spake unto Moses and Aaron, 'Because ye believed Me not, to sanctify Me in the eyes of the children of Israel, therefore ye shall not bring this congregation into the land which I have given them'"* (Num. 20:12). Moses' high position, his former faithfulness to God, his meekness, his many intercessions for God's people, and his faithfulness in all of God's house, were not enough to compensate for this sin, and relieve the punishment inflicted through his disobedience. This is a very sad commentary indeed, but it affords us a vital lesson. Our past laurels are not enough, and any disobedience on our part will cause us to suffer loss at the Bema of Christ. Consider the Lord's warning to the church at Philadelphia: *"Behold, I come quickly: hold that fast which thou hast, that no man take thy crown"* (Rev. 3:11).

31

THE SERPENT OF BRASS

NUMBERS 21

"And when king Arad the Canaanite, which dwelt in the south, heard tell that Israel came by the way of the spies; then he fought against Israel, and took some of them prisoners. And Israel vowed a vow unto the LORD, and said, If thou wilt indeed deliver this people into my hand, then I will utterly destroy their cities. And the LORD hearkened to the voice of Israel, and delivered up the Canaanites; and they utterly destroyed them and their cities: and He called the name of the place Hormah" (Num. 21:1–3).

As Israel neared their entrance into the land of Canaan, the people of that land were distressed. Rahab admitted; *"Your terror is fallen upon us, and that all the inhabitants of the land faint because of you. ... Our hearts did melt, neither did there remain any more courage in any man, because of you"* (Josh. 2:9, 11). According to Judges 1:16, Arad was the name of a city on the southernmost borders of Canaan, about twenty miles from Hebron. The Israelites were advancing northward, though still lingering about the south-eastern border of Edom, when this king heard of their movements. To keep any war at a distance, he marched out of his own land and invaded Israel. This was an attempt to discourage Israel's further progress. Catching some of the Israelites off guard, he took them prisoners. He experienced a seeming victory, but it was not for long, for Israel immediately responded by calling upon their God. Isn't that wonderful to see? Their confidence in their God during this trying circumstance is to their credit.

"He heard that Israel came by way of the spies." This could mean that this Canaanite king was well aware of Israel's history. He knew the stealthy manner in which Israel's spies had entered Canaan 38 years prior to his invasion. Or, it could mean that spies were sent by himself to ascertain the plans and movements of the Israelites. Seeing Israel moving near had greatly alarmed him, and he was determined to put a stop to their advance. However, it was to his complete ruin, for after Israel implored the face of their God, the LORD went before them. After crossing Jordan, they utterly destroyed this impetuous king's people, their land, and their cities.

The vow of Israel was that they would devote these enemies and their cities to the Lord. That simply means that they would utterly destroy those cities, as devoted to God, and not take the spoil of them for their own use. The inhabitants were to die, the beasts to be killed, the cities burnt, and the goods given over to the Lord's treasury. They promised not to reserve any of the captured possessions of the king to their own use, but would devote it all to destruction, which was the nature of the vow called, *"Herem."* It was praiseworthy indeed that Israel was not willing to avail themselves of a comfortable home, by destroying those cities of Arad, acquired by the right of war.

To a hasty reader, it would seem that the overthrow of this Canaanitish king and his cities occurred immediately upon the assault mentioned in verse one. However, this is not the case. Israel's position at this time was in the vicinity of Mount Hor, far to the southeast, Between Israel and the cities of Arad there was a mountain range of Edom, populated with hostile tribes. For Israel to destroy Arad, it would have been necessary for them to push through this mountain range into the land of Canaan. Then, after achieving their conquests, they would have to fall back to the area of Mount Hor, where the tabernacle was pitched, and from there, continue their journey round the head of the Dead Sea, and the country of Moab.

All of this appears improbable. If this movement had been the case, it would seem reasonable that we should find some intimation of it elsewhere. However, there is no mention of it in any other Scripture. Thus, we come to the sensible conclusion that the events mentioned regarding the total destruction of Arad, did not take place until *after* Israel's arrival in Canaan, under the leadership of Joshua. It was at that time that Israel's vow was executed. In Joshua 12:14, *the "king of Arad"* is mentioned among the kings *"which Joshua and the children of Israel smote."* Which, of course, took place after taking possession of the land of Canaan.

It is also important to note what is recorded in Judges 1:17. *"And Judah went with Simeon his brother, and they slew the Canaanites that inhabited Zephath, and utterly destroyed it. And the name of the city was called Hormah"* (Judg. 1:17). Arad and Zephath were identical. This then was the time when the vow mentioned in Numbers 21:2 was fulfilled.

GREATER TRIALS AHEAD

The lesson is this. Do not think that as we near the end of our wilderness journey that our trials will lesson. Ah no, in many cases the trials increase. There are many "King Arads" to come out against us. Paul experienced trials, right to the end of his pilgrimage. *"For, when we were come into Macedonia, our flesh had no rest, but we were troubled on every side; without were fightings, within were fears"* (2 Cor. 7:5). We are not yet released from combat. Our faith, and our endurance, are constantly being tested by new forms of trial, new enemies to fight, so that there is no discharge in this war. We wrestle against principalities and powers. All the forces of hell are against us. The world is against us, and we need, on a daily basis, to implore our God for help in time of need. Thank God for a great High Priest, to Whom we can flee, to obtain mercy and find grace to help in time of need. Remember brethren, that God is stronger than our foes!

After vowing to destroy Arad (Zephath), did they exclaim, "Victory! Our enemies will be completely destroyed! God is with us, and God is for us! When we enter the land, our God shall give these enemies into our hand, and we will utterly destroy their cities for our God! Let us rejoice in our God-given power and future success!" Was that the case with Israel here? Surprisingly – NO! We read these sad words: *"And they journeyed from mount Hor by the way of the Red sea, to compass the land of Edom: and the soul of the people was much discouraged because of the way"* (Num. 21:4). "Disappointment on finding themselves so near the confines of the promised land without entering it; vexation at the refusal of a passage through Edom and the absence of any divine interposition in their favor; and above all, the necessity of a retrograde journey by a long and circuitous route through the worst parts of a sandy desert and the dread of being plunged into new and unknown difficulties—all this produced a deep depression of spirits. But it was followed, as usually, by a gross outburst of murmuring at the scarcity of water, and of expressions of disgust at the manna."[81]

What a distressing testimony! What a sad situation! How can this be? These people have experienced God with them throughout their forty years in the wilderness, and His promise of victory after invading Canaan, yet we read that they were discouraged. Why? Well, read carefully the rest of the verse. It says, *"because of the way."* Moses does not record what that particular way involved. However, we have considered in the previous paragraph what some of their problems might have been. Moses just tells us the sad result – they were discouraged. After their victory over the enemy, things must have transpired that were very trying, so much so, that Satan used the trials, whatever they may have been, to drag them down into the slough of despond.

---

81 J. F. B. MacSword for Mac OS X

A discouraged soldier is a defeated soldier. Satan recognizes this, and would seek to bring circumstances into our life to discourage us. Are you discouraged? If so, why? Are we to become discouraged when things go wrong? Presently, the economic situation is very depressed, and folks are losing their incomes, and some their homes. Men with little families, through losing their employment, hardly know which way to turn. Others are standing by the bedside of loved ones, watching them slowly die. Others have contracted a severe sickness, leaving them in pain and weakness. Some are experiencing distressing situations in their assembly. Others are longing to see their indifferent loved ones saved. We are walking through a vale of sorrow and tears. An old American Indian proverb says: "Never judge a man until you walk in his moccasins." So let us be slow to fault saints for being discouraged.

However, is it right to fall into a depressed state of mind? Is it the mind of God for us to become discouraged? Does it glorify Him? Does it cause heaven to rejoice? Does it honor our Lord Jesus Christ? Does it encourage fellow believers? Does it help us to enjoy our great salvation? Does it impress the unsaved to believe that we have a God that loves us? To all of these questions we answer – most certainly not! What is the preventative medicine for the disease of discouragement? There is an answer!

PREVENTATIVE MEDICINE FOR DISCOURAGEMENT

Years ago, there was a man from Ireland, living in Ontario, Canada, who came into severe trials. His mother in Ireland was not well, so he wrote a poem to encourage her, and in that poem he wrote: "We should never be discouraged: Take it to the Lord in prayer." His name? – Joseph Scriven. His poem is well known. And perhaps you have often sung it. It begins like this:

> "What a Friend we have in Jesus,
> All our sins and griefs to bear!

What a privilege to carry
Everything to God in prayer!"

Prayer will drive discouragement away. Another preventative to discouragement is meditation in the Book. The psalmist hid it in his heart that he might not sin against God (Ps. 119:11). Discouragement is sin. Another way to keep from discouragement is to be in close fellowship with those of like mind. We need one another. Solomon endorses this thought, saying: *"Two are better than one; because they have a good reward for their labour. For if they fall, the one will lift up his fellow: but woe to him that is alone when he falleth; for he hath not another to help him up"* (Eccl. 4:9–10). *"Then they that feared the LORD spake often one to another: and the LORD hearkened, and heard it, and a book of remembrance was written before Him for them that feared the LORD, and that thought upon His name"* (Mal. 3:16). We cannot stress too much the importance of holy fellowship.

Notice one more thing. When David and his men returned from their battles to Ziklag, to their dismay, they found that the Amalekites had invaded the south, and Ziklag, and burned it with fire; and had taken their wives and children captive. Upon this discovery, David and his men lifted up their voice and wept, until they had no more power to weep. Then we read; *"And David was greatly distressed; for the people spake of stoning him, because the soul of all the people was grieved, every man for his sons and for his daughters"* (1 Sam. 30:6). This perhaps was one of the most grievous situations that ever came into David's life. So what did this mighty man do? Did he slide into the slough of discouragement? Not at all! How refreshing is the remainder of that verse, which reads; *"but David encouraged himself in the LORD his God."* May the Lord give us the same quality of grace that was seen in David on that memorable occasion.

Israel's discouragement led to something of a more serious nature. They commenced to speak against God, and against Moses! It is almost unbelievable! Not only this, they publicly stated that they loathed God's heavenly provision, the manna, and spoke of it as *"this light bread."* In other words, "this vile, this *worthless*, this *contemptible* bread." Can you now see where discouragement leads? It leads to faultfinding, and disrespect, or lack of appreciation for divine things. It leads to a very low appreciation of Christ, for the manna was a type of our Lord. Remember how we considered the fact that any type of Christ abused in the Old Testament was visited with severe judgment? Well, so it was here! Their complaint, and refusal to be satisfied with God's unique provision, wrought for them severe, and immediate punishment.

> *"And the LORD sent fiery serpents among the people, and they bit the people; and much people of Israel died"* (Num. 21:6).

GUARDIAN ANGELS

For forty years, God had led them through *"that great and terrible wilderness, wherein were fiery serpents, and scorpions, and drought, where there was no water"* (Deut. 8:15). However, upon this last complaint of Israel, the Lord withdrew His protective hand against fiery serpents, and allowed these snakes to invade their camp and bite them. Have you ever considered the fact that there are evil forces surrounding us that would like to invade our lives and destroy us. The atmosphere is full of wicked demons. Be thankful for this my fellow-believer, that in the midst of evil spirits, and in the midst of a crooked and perverse society, we have guardians that preserve us. Angels are *"ministering spirits, sent forth to minister for them who shall be heirs of salvation"* (Heb. 1:14). They are our attendants, and they surround us and protect us from evil forces. *"The angel of the LORD encampeth round about them that fear Him, and delivereth them"* (Ps. 34:7).

Remember when Paul was on a ship in the midst of a tempestuous sea, and everyone thought they were doomed to drown, Paul had a word for them, announcing: *"And now I exhort you to be of good cheer: for there shall be no loss of any man's life among you, but of the ship. For there stood by me this night the angel of God,* whose I am, and whom I serve, saying, Fear not, Paul; thou must be brought before Caesar: and, lo, God hath given thee all them that sail with thee" (Acts 27:22–24). There it is! An angel on board the ship with Paul! Isn't that wonderful? How gracious of our God to provide us ministers to protect us along life's pathway to the celestial city. Let me ask you this. I am certain that you thank the Father repeatedly for His Son. Do you ever thank Him for the Holy Spirit that brought you to Christ for salvation? As the Spirit opens the Word of God to your understanding, do you ever thank the Father for the guidance and help of the Holy Spirit? One more question. How often have you thanked the Father in the past month for the angels? Remember, they are very busy attending to you. They are ministering spirits sent by God on your behalf. Do you thank God for them? Ah, can't you see by these pertinent questions perhaps how incomplete our prayers are? May the Lord exercise us about these things.

FIERY SERPENTS

The serpents were fiery. That description can mean several things. Perhaps they were red in color. Or, perhaps they were fiery in their nature, that is, quick to strike. Or, it might even mean the effects of their bite, such as an intense burning, the enflaming of the body, and scorching the person with an insatiable thirst. Perhaps all three could be included together. The region in which this punishment took place, still abounds with serpents. When the Lord sent fiery serpents among them, He did not have to create them just for that occasion, for they were already there. The fact is, that even though parts of the wilderness abounded with serpents and scorpions, the people were exempt from attack, through the providential care of God. At the point of our chapter, that protective care in restraining these little beasts from attacking, was withdrawn. They were bitten – and many died!

"We have sinned," comes the cry from the congregation. That particular expression is first heard from Aaron regarding his speaking against Moses and his wife in Numbers 12:11, and it is last recorded in Daniel's confession in Daniel 9:15. The expression occurs about 19 times, and all of them are in the Old Testament. The invasion of fiery serpents had brought them down to the place of repentance. Notice the change of mind. Observe how they stopped to think. Prior to their affliction, they were haughty, proud, unthankful, belligerent, impudent, and hateful of Moses. What a dramatic change! They have been lowered to a place of desperate need – they are dying! There seems to be no hope. Death is staring them in the face. Multitudes were writhing in their death throes. Some were violently twisting, as the venom coursed through their veins, into their brains and vital organs. There would be the groans and cries, as death would be taking its final hold on their stricken bodies. Death gurgles would be sounding throughout the camp as souls left their fire-plagued bodies for the great eternity. It must have been a gruesome sight.

LOOKING TO MOSES

Moses was now a different person to them. They suddenly recognized his power and authority. They no longer looked upon him as one who had led them out of Egypt to slay them in the wilderness. Ah no, they were now looking to him to plead to the LORD that they might be saved. What a vivid manifestation of repentance! As stated before, there can be no deliverance without it. It is an absolute, divine requirement, that a soul repents before it can be saved.

"Pray unto the LORD, that He take away the serpents from us," was their plea to Moses. They freely admitted that they had spoken against the LORD, and His servant Moses, and now, the man that they had spoken against, is implored to pray for them, his former persecutors. Once again, we observe the meekness of Moses. He could have said, "Pray for you? Don't you see that God sent this plague because of your wickedness, and you are just getting what you deserve? And besides, you constantly gave me a hard time, and now you are justly reaping what you have sowed. You made your own bed, so go lie in it you rebels!" However, we

see exactly the opposite. Why? Well, first of all, he dearly loved the people that had previously hated him. Is not this Christ-likeness? Remember the Lord's exhortation to us: *"But I say unto you, Love your enemies, bless them that curse you, do good to them that hate you, and pray for them which despitefully use you, and persecute you"* (Matt. 5:44). This is almost a total impossibility apart from the indwelling and power of the Holy Spirit in an individual. It is through the power of the Holy Spirit that Christians can bless their enemies, and pray for them that abuse them.

This whole episode reminds me of Paul and Silas at Philippi. The jailor, a rough man indeed, gladly thrust God's servants into the inner prison, making their feet secure in stocks. Then, in the hardness of his heart, he retired for the night, but long before the sun arose, he was awakened by an earthquake, and we find the hard-hearted jailor at the apostle's feet crying out; "Sirs, what must I do to be saved?" What a tremendous change took place in a matter of hours. Just like Moses, Paul had been praying for those who had mistreated them, and just as Israel changed, so also the Philippian jailor changed.

Moses humbly prayed for them, and as soon as he did, the LORD spake unto him.

> *"Make thee a fiery serpent, and set it upon a pole: and it shall come to pass, that every one that is bitten, when he looketh upon it, shall live. And Moses made a serpent of brass, and put it upon a pole, and it came to pass, that if a serpent had bitten any man, when he beheld the serpent of brass, he lived"* (Num. 21:8–9).

Had the serpents simply been removed, as the people desired, that would not have healed the wounded. God was going to provide a full remedy, one that would not only save the living, but also recover the dying. We all recognize the fact that this is one of two events in the Old Testament where the Lord applies the incident to Himself and the way of salvation.

"And as Moses lifted up the serpent in the wilder-

ness, even so must the Son of man be lifted up: That whosoever believeth in Him should not perish, but have eternal life" (John 3:14-15).

SIMILARITIES

Linking Numbers 21 with John 3, we see some startling parallels. The first thing that we notice is that the disease in both cases is similar. Israel was bitten by natural serpents, humanity was bitten by the Old Serpent, the Devil (Rev. 12:9). Sin is the biting of Satan, and it was deadly. He also has *"fiery darts."* These fiery darts inflame all the evil passions and lusts, helping to drag the victim into eternal perdition. Like poison, sin dwells within us, affecting not only the body, but also the soul. It ages the human frame, blinds the human mind, dulls the conscience, warps the affections, then with one last, mighty thrust, casts the soul down to the eternal burnings.

The second similarity we want to consider is this; the thing which cured was in the shape of that which wounded. They were bitten by a serpent, and thus wounded. They were to look to a serpent to be healed. Even though our Saviour was without sin, yet He was made in *"the likeness of sinful flesh."*

The third comparison is, that in both cases, the remedy was divine. Man had nothing to do with it. The infected Israelite was not told to fight the serpents. Ah, my friend, you cannot fight sin, your strength is far too small. If not saved, you are under its dominion, power, control, and authority. You are, what the Bible says, *"without strength"* (Rom. 5). They were not told to manufacture some kind of ointment for a cure. Nonsense! Many deceived souls have anointed themselves with the salve of religion. Ah, it has a fragrant and pleasant smell, and makes one feel so satisfied with self. But the problem of the poison of sin lies within, not on the skin. Ointment miserably fails to affect a cure.

God did not tell them to pray to the serpent. Ah no, what

are your vain prayers my friend? As the old Puritans once said, "You may pray until your knees become as hard as horns, but they will, in no way, move you one inch nearer to heaven. *'Ye must be born again!'*"

How about making an offering. Will that help? Not at all. Toplady, who wrote that hymn, *"Rock of Ages, cleft for me"* said, "Nothing in my hands I bring. Simply to Thy Cross I cling." That is good theology! Maybe if they had looked to Moses, that would have helped. Do you really think so? Well my friend, think again! No! No! No! Not one of these ideas could cure the soul. What then were they to do? Why, the answer is simple: *"When he looketh upon it, [he] shall live."* Imagine that! Just a look, by faith, on that lifted-up serpent of brass, and immediately the stricken one would be completely cured! Who could ever believe a thing like that? Only one who was willing to believe God! The cure was simple, immediate, lasting, and absolutely free! Oh my, what a glorious picture of God's salvation for poor, dying, sin-bitten sinners today! What a tremendous message God's people have to tell! Shout it out brethren! Let all sinners hear it in no uncertain terms! We have the most glorious, most grand, most blessed message, in the whole wide world. How can we keep silent with such a treasury within us?

Just a look! Nothing less and nothing more. LOOK! LOOK! LOOK! Many years ago in England, a humble shoe cobbler mounted the pulpit. Not many were there in that little church building because of a snowstorm. The preacher didn't even make it that Lord's Day morning, so the cobbler tried to preach. He had very little ability, but he read these words: *"Look unto Me, and be ye saved, all the ends of the earth: for I am God, and there is none else"* (Isa. 45:22). There was a little boy in the balcony at the back of the building who drank in the cobbler's words, for he kept repeating them over and over again. That little boy was Charles H. Spurgeon, who later, when still a youth, preached and saw thousands saved. That mighty man of God, as a little boy, was saved simply by a look of faith to Christ on the Cross, Who died for his sins. Is not that wonderful? Away with all the ritual and pageantry of Christendom! Away with the vestments of scarlet, the gold crosses, the "holy water," the rosary, the scepters, the incense, the tailor made robes, and the many rituals of a paganistic Christendom! God says: *"LOOK unto Me!"* There is nothing more vital to your eternal welfare, if you are not saved. One look by faith to the crucified Christ, trusting Him as the One Who died for your sins upon the tree, and fully believing that His blood can cleanse you from all of your sins – that, my friend, is salvation!

> "There is life in a look at the Crucified One,
> There is life at this moment for thee;
> Then look, sinner. look unto Him and be saved,
> Unto Him Who was nailed to the tree."

32

WATER AND WAR

NUMBERS 21

We now have arrived at the route of the children of Israel along the borders of Moab, in their progress toward the Land of Canaan. Cured of the poison of serpents, they broke up camp and journeyed to Zalmonah, pitching there for an undisclosed time. Departing from Zalmonah, they arrived at Punon, and pitched there. Then, departing from Punon, they arrived at Oboth, and set up camp.[82] The word *"Oboth"* means *"water skins."* Names were sometimes given to places because of some feature of that place, or because of some incident occurring there. If that be the case here, then we can rightly suppose that at this station along their final leg into Canaan, they were supplied with water.

Thus, we have a nation with all their water bottles filled. Can you see the beautiful picture? Man bitten by the venom of sin, finds his cure in a look at the crucified One, and then what happens? Why the very next thing that takes place is that he is indwelt with the Spirit of God, of which water is an emblem! Here is one incidence where Israel never murmured for water. In fact, after being cured of the invasion of serpents and their bites, they are never seen murmuring again. Isn't that how God would have His journeying people? As we march on to Zion, the beautiful city of God, with its street of pure gold before us, let us not walk down here on "Grumbling Street." Happy are those who carry a good supply of water with them. The first martyr of

---

82 See Numbers 33:41–43.

the church, Stephen was a man *"full of the Holy Ghost."* So also were the men chosen to be deacons in Acts 6. We take to ourselves the exhortation to the Ephesians: *"And be not drunk with wine, wherein is excess; but be filled with the Spirit"* (Eph. 5:18).

ARRIVING AT BEER

After a few other encampments, Israel arrives at Beer. Again, they are in need of water. The word "Beer," signifies *"well, or fountain."* You will notice that there is no more murmuring. Isn't that beautiful? Their whole attitude changed after their encounter with the fiery serpents. As they pitch in Beer, there seems to be a godliness to the scene. They are waiting on God to supply their need. The LORD then spoke to Moses, saying: *"Gather the people together, and I will give them water"* (Num. 21:16).

PRINCES WITH STAVES

In obedience to the divine command, Israel convened at the location where the water was to gush forth. They trusted God to fulfill His word, and in humble obedience they gathered together to wait. There is no clamoring, no impatience, just a quiet waiting on God. It must have been a beautiful scene. The princes are surrounding a certain spot with their staves, yet no evidence of water is seen. The dry and barren surface of the land indicates no water beneath. I see faith in the promise of God in action here. What a change had taken place in these people, who soon would be crossing Jordan and claiming their inheritance. Moses instructed them to dig. The princes' staves are put into action, the waters burst forth, and Israel sings; *"Spring up O well."* Waiting on God, and experiencing a manifestation of His exceeding love, grace, and care, ignites a song of celebration, making memorable this occasion on their behalf. One is reminded of the remnant of Israel in a coming day. Upon returning to their land they will exclaim:

> *"'O LORD, I will praise Thee: though Thou wast angry with me, Thine anger is turned away, and Thou*

comfortedst me. Behold, God is my salvation; I will trust, and not be afraid: for the LORD JEHOVAH is my strength and my song; he also is become my salvation.' Therefore with joy shall ye draw water out of the wells of salvation" (Isa. 12:1-3).

Certainly staves are not the proper implements for digging, and because of this, we think that the expression is poetical, meaning that the striking of their staves into the sandy soil would be the same as if they had dug a well with spades.

How lovely it is today, upon the command of Jehovah, to see His thirsty people gather together. In the gathering are the shepherds, men that can feed the flock. They would correspond to the princes in Israel. They have used their staves. In other words, in the quietness of their homes they have been into the Book, digging, searching, meditating, and putting truths together in an orderly fashion. Now that the assembly is gathered together for a Bible reading, they use their staves. They open the Scriptures and give the sense thereof, and God causes the waters of divine truth to gush forth for the cleansing, refreshment, and encouragement of God's people gathered together on that occasion. Is this the case in your assembly? Do you come to the assembly Bible reading thirsty for truth and then go home refreshed and encouraged? You should! And if this is not the case, you would do well to spend time in prayer, asking God to raise up men in the midst that will have the ability to feed the flock.

What will happen to God's assemblies if there are no men in the future to feed the Lord's people? The assemblies will lose their character, their identity, and progressively slip back into Christendom. The lament of Hosea: *"My people are destroyed for lack of knowledge"* (Hos. 4:6), may soon be the lament of the godly among us today.

When a testimony lacks "princes with staves," having no men with a knowledge of divine principles, the flesh will be allowed to raise its ugly head and dictate various avenues to pursue. In other words, any assembly lacking a teaching oversight, stands in grave danger of losing its identity as a scriptural assembly of God.

> *"To Him which smote great kings: for His mercy endureth for ever: And slew famous kings: for His mercy endureth for ever: Sihon king of the Amorites: for His mercy endureth for ever: And Og the king of Bashan: for His mercy endureth for ever: And gave their land for an heritage: for His mercy endureth for ever: Even an heritage unto Israel his servant: for His mercy endureth for ever"* (Ps. 136:17–22).

As you can readily see by the above Psalm, the events we are now about to consider, were long afterwards remembered and distinctly celebrated. They were raised as a memorial of the everlasting mercy of God.

THE AMORITIES

Approaching the borders of the Amorites, the nation of Israel sent messengers of peace to Sihon their king, desiring permission to pass peaceably through their land by way of the king's highway. They notified this king that they would not disturb anything in his country in their passing. However, it was not the mind of the king to let Israel pass through. Instead, he gathered all his people together and went out from his own borders to fight against Israel in the wilderness. Much to his surprise and dismay, Israel smote him with the edge of the sword and possessed his land from Arnon unto Jabbok. Having taken all their cities in Heshbon, they then dwelt in them. While dwelling in the land of the Amorites, Israel sent spies to Jaazer, and took their villages, driving out the inhabitants.

One may wonder why there was such an obstinate attitude on the part of this king? He not only denied a peaceable passage of Israel through his land, but also gathered all his people together and went out of his way to war with God's people. His country was not endangered in any way, so why this seemingly senseless attitude? The answer lies in Deuteronomy 2:30–33. *"But Sihon king of Heshbon would not let us pass by him: for the LORD thy God hardened his spirit, and made his heart obstinate, that he might deliver him into thy hand, as appeareth this day. And the LORD said unto me, Behold, I have begun to give Sihon and his land before thee: begin to possess, that thou mayest inherit his land. Then Sihon came out against us, he and all his people, to fight at Jahaz. And the LORD our God delivered him before us; and we smote him, and his sons, and all his people."*

Behind the scenes, God was programming the mind of this king to destroy himself so that Israel would inherit his land and his cities. *"The king' heart is in the hand of the LORD, as the rivers of water: He turneth it whithersoever he will"* (Prov. 21:1). The Amorites were among the nations that God had promised to Abraham and his seed, when the iniquity of the Amorites would be full (Gen. 15:16), and that time had now arrived. Let us remember, that no matter how adverse circumstances may seem, God is in complete control!

OG KING OF BASHAN

Coming next on the stage for utter destruction is Og, king of Bashan. You would have thought that this king would have manifested common sense by leaving Israel alone, but no, he came out against them. The battle was to take place at Edrei. *"And the LORD said unto Moses, 'Fear him not: for I have delivered him into thy hand, and all his people, and his land; and thou shalt do to him as thou didst unto Sihon king of the Amorites, which dwelt at Heshbon.' So they smote him, and his sons, and all his people, until there was none left him alive: and they possessed his land"* (Num. 21:34–35).

King Og was also an Amorite. More than likely, being filled with pride; he thought himself more capable in dealing with Israel than his neighbor, King Sihon. His problem was that he was unaware that he was fighting against God. He was a big man, and a rich man. The Bible witnesses to the *"oaks of Bashan."* They were the best. The Scriptures witness to the excellence of their cattle (Deut. 32:14). The Amorites had taken this beautiful and fruitful land from the Moabites, and were living quite smug and self-sufficient. Yes, God had "loaned" them this rich possession, but it was only for an allotted time. The time of giving it up had come, and Israel was to claim that land as their legal possession.

The whole affair reminds me of men today. They are quite satisfied with themselves. They have heaped to themselves pleasures and treasures, but little do they realize that it is only for a little time. The day is coming, when their comforts, pleasures, riches, and security, will be all whisked away, and they shall launch out into the vast and the dark eternity, to suffer their loss eternally.

With Israel's victory over these impudent foes, God was graciously affording Moses a little foretaste of what would be taking place when His people would enter into Canaan. Their victory was like an earnest of better things to come. Their victory over these two kings was but a small thing in comparison to the mighty victories that they would experience under the leadership of Joshua in the Promised Land.

33

BALAK AND BALAAM

NUMBERS 22–24

"Which have forsaken the right way, and are gone astray, following the way of Balaam the son of Bosor, who loved the wages of unrighteousness" (2 Pet. 2:15).

"Woe unto them! for they have gone in the way of Cain, and ran greedily after the error of Balaam for reward, and perished in the gainsaying of Core" (Jude 1:11).

"But I have a few things against thee, because thou hast there them that hold the doctrine of Balaam, who taught Balac to cast a stumblingblock before the children of Israel, to eat things sacrificed unto idols, and to commit fornication" (Rev. 2:14).

It would seem that as the Israelites moved along Moab's north-eastern border, that they had supplied Israel with provisions, perhaps in hopes of getting rid of them (Deut. 2:29). However, upon the total defeat of the Amorites (who had years before defeated Moab), they were terrified into action against Israel. They recognized the fact that they were not able to successfully engage in open hostilities, so they designed a subtle plan to achieve their purpose. That is where Balaam comes into the picture. Balak had a plan that since he couldn't ruin Israel by military force, he would have Balaam come and curse Israel. Balak was willing to pay for Balaam's assistance, and as Peter says, this ungodly prophet *"loved the wages of unrighteousness,"* consequently, Balaam came on the scene. He would correspond to the apostates in Christendom, who function through a religious office for personal gain as Jude describes them. They *"ran greedily after the error of Balaam for reward."* (Jude 1:11).

BALAAM'S PREPARATIONS

The preparations made for Balaam to utter his parables were quite extensive. A total of 21 bullocks, and 21 rams were offered on a total of 21 altars, prior to Balaam prophesying. Three locations were employed; the high places of Baal; the top of Pisgah; and the top of Peor. From these locations the parables of Balaam were spoken, which compose the first great prophetic utterances of the Bible. Balaam, against his will, is forced by God to say what He put into his mouth. Peter testified that; *"the prophecy came not in old time by the will of man: but holy men of God spake as they were moved by the Holy Ghost"* (2 Pet. 1:21). But this incident is unique, for Balaam was not a holy man, but rather an ungodly man, yet we see him being forced by the Holy Ghost to utter sublime revelations. God used a dumb ass to rebuke the madness of Balaam, and now the Spirit is using Balaam to bless the children of Israel.

Of course we recognize the fact that Moses was not on the scene to hear the false prophet speak. Israel, at that precise time, was totally unaware of what was going on behind the scenes. However, the Holy Spirit reported to Moses all that took place, and all that was said, thus, we have a record of it today.

The practice of Balaam, in the eyes of Balak, was to combine heathenish magic with the work of Jehovah. He purposed to perform his enchantments in the name of Jehovah, but such a combination was not permitted by the LORD. Consequently, when he was called upon to place a curse upon Israel, God forbade his madness, and compelled him to bless the nation, much to the utter dismay of King Balak. There are lessons for us in his utterances, for they not only concern God's earthly people, Israel, but they also form pictures to us of the Church.

BALAK AND BALAAM

When Balak took Balaam to view Israel, *"he brought him up to the high places of Baal"* (Num. 22:41). From this vantage point, Balaam only saw one fourth of the encampment of God's people. The next place that he was taken was to the top of Pisgah where he was afforded a more comprehensive view of this great nation. Then finally, when taken to the top of Peor, Balaam viewed the nation in its entirety. It was a tremendous thing for him to behold. The craftiness of Balak can be seen in this, for it seems that he tried to diminish the number, and the strength of Israel, in Balaam's eyes. However, if God was going to use this man to prophecy great things concerning Israel, He would also afford this heathen magician the most wondrous sight ever to fall upon his gaze, namely Israel encamped as gardens beside the riverside, and cedars beside the waters. There, nestled in the wilderness, far below his gaze, lay a nation in their tents with their banners flying overhead. He would view the tabernacle in their midst, and the pillar of the cloud resting protectively over the whole nation. It must have struck awe, and fear, into the heart of this strange prophet.

BALAAM'S FIRST PARABLE

It is very interesting to me, that just prior to Israel entering into the land, the LORD allows this man on the scene to present to our eyes some of the most sublime prophecies in all the Scriptures relating to Israel in a coming day. Considering this, I think it would be to our advantage to consider briefly the substance of what this heathen magician said, under the direction of the Holy Spirit. The first utterance comes from the high places of Baal, which, in Balak's eyes, would give additional efficacy to the cure uttered.

> *"And the LORD put a word in Balaam's mouth, and said, 'Return unto Balak, and thus thou shalt speak.' And he returned unto him, and, lo, he stood by his burnt sacrifice, he, and all the princes of Moab. And he took up his parable, and said, 'Balak the king of Moab hath brought me from Aram, out of the mountains*

of the east, saying, Come, curse me Jacob, and come, defy Israel. How shall I curse, whom God hath not cursed? or how shall I defy, whom the LORD hath not defied? For from the top of the rocks I see him, and from the hills I behold him: lo, the people shall dwell alone, and shall not be reckoned among the nations. Who can count the dust of Jacob, and the number of the fourth part of Israel? Let me die the death of the righteous, and let my last end be like his!" (Num. 23:5–10).

BALAAM'S IMPOSSIBILITY

The first thing we notice is, the impossibility of Balaam being able to place a curse on Israel. *"How shall I curse, whom God hath not cursed? or how shall I defy, whom the LORD hath not defied?"* When Balaam was first contacted by Balak, *"God said unto Balaam, Thou shalt not go with them; thou shalt not curse the people: for they are blessed"* (Num. 22:12). Consequently, what Balaam heard in secret from God, he was obligated to pronounce in public for God. Many have sought to curse the people that God has blessed, but it is to no avail. Isaiah, in his divine utterances, plainly said about Israel; *"No weapon that is formed against thee shall prosper; and every tongue that shall rise against thee in judgment thou shalt condemn"* (Isa. 54:17). Hitler tried it. The Arab nations are presently trying it. However, it will not prosper!

ISRAEL'S UNIQUENESS

The next thing Balaam uttered was: *"Lo, the people shall dwell alone, and shall not be reckoned among the nations."* It is true, that for centuries Israel has been scattered throughout the nations. Even so, the sons of Jacob have not lost their identity. The characteristics of the Jewish people are unique. Israel remains a stranger in a strange land. Through the ages, many nations have been conquered, and the inhabitants have melted into the customs and identity of their victors, thus losing their original identity. Not so with the Jewish people. Even though scattered throughout the face of earth, and living in many nations, they still remain a very distinct people. Their customs, laws, and their knowledge of the true God have kept them distinct from all Gentiles. Not until 1948 were they recognized as a nation, but even as such, the Arab world has an agenda to wipe them off the face of this earth, which of course, will not succeed.

THE CHURCH

The purpose of God for the Church is that it dwell alone, not being reckoned among the nations. Nations have tried to curse her, and put her out of existence, but to no avail. In fact, the Church prospered more when going through the fires of persecution. Christ announced: *"Upon this Rock I will build My church; and the gates of hell shall not prevail against it"* (Matt. 16:18).

The Church is a separate identity, not reckoned among the nations. The Lord said; *"I have given them Thy word; and the world hath hated them, because they are not of the world, even as I am not of the world"* (John 17:14). Even local assemblies are exhorted: *"Come out from among them, and be ye separate, saith the Lord, and touch not the unclean thing"* (2 Cor. 6:17). The warning was in regards to being unequally yoked with unbelievers.

THE DUST OF JACOB

The final statement of Balaam's first parable was: *"Who can count the dust of Jacob, and the number of the fourth part of Israel?"* When Jacob went out from Beersheba, he received this promise. *"Thy seed shall be as the dust of the earth."* It is very doubtful that Balaam was aware of God's promise to Jacob. We are convinced that his utterance, concerning the *"dust of Jacob,"* was put into his mouth by the Spirit, and was wholly independent of his own intelligence and will. In spite of all Israel's trials and shortcomings, the nation was impressively great. Consider Israel from the crucifixion of their Messiah until today. Even now, who can count the dust of Jacob?

However, we feel that this utterance goes beyond physical Israel, and that the theme of this prediction encompasses the spiritual seed, those who are the true people of God, through faith in Christ. Those numbers are continually swelling. Some of those members are mentioned in Revelation 7:9. *"I beheld, and, lo, a great multitude, which no man could number, of all nations, and kindreds, and people, and tongues, stood before the throne, and before the Lamb, clothed with white robes, and palms in their hands."*

In the conclusion of Balaam's first parable, he says: *Let me die the death of the righteous, and let my last end be like his!"* "Of the righteous - Of this righteous and holy people. The sense is, they are not only happy above other nations in this life, and therefore in vain should I curse them, but they have this peculiar privilege, that they are happy after death: their happiness begins where the happiness of other people ends; and therefore I heartily wish that my soul may have its portion with theirs when I die. Was not God now again striving with him, not only for the sake of Israel, but of his own soul?"[83] The first three letters of the word *"righteous,"* correspond to the first three letters of the word *"Israel."* It is also equivalent to *"Jeshurun,"* signifying *"upright"* or, *"righteous."* Thus Balaam, by using this word (*upright*), was implying the superiority of the nation in distinction and privilege, from that of other nations, wishing his own to be identical with it. However, in his case, refusing to live the life of the righteous, and intent on the wages of unrighteousness, he perished under Israel's hand by the sword (Num. 31:8; Josh. 13:22).

Oh what a voice to us today. I have seen individuals very conversant with God's people. They recognize the truth and realize the blessed end of the Lord's people. They envy them, yet they go their own way, never submitting to the claims of Christ, never repenting of their sins, and never trusting the Lord as their own Saviour. How sad to see souls, some even related to God's people, attending assembly meetings, even defending the Christians before scoffers, yet in the end, even though they

---

[83] John Wesley MacSword for Mac OS X.

would like to die as a righteous person, they slip from earth into hell, in their sins! Yes, in this respect, there are Balaam's among us today. A sad affair indeed!

BALAAM'S SECOND PARABLE

"And the LORD met Balaam, and put a word in his mouth, and said, Go again unto Balak, and say thus. And when he came to him, behold, he stood by his burnt offering, and the princes of Moab with him. And Balak said unto him, What hath the LORD spoken? And he took up his parable, and said, Rise up, Balak, and hear; hearken unto me, thou son of Zippor: God is not a man, that He should lie; neither the son of man, that He should repent: hath He said, and shall He not do it? or hath He spoken, and shall He not make it good? Behold, I have received commandment to bless: and He hath blessed; and I cannot reverse it. He hath not beheld iniquity in Jacob, neither hath He seen perverseness in Israel: the LORD his God is with him, and the shout of a king is among them. God brought them out of Egypt; he hath as it were the strength of an unicorn. Surely there is no enchantment against Jacob, neither is there any divination against Israel: according to this time it shall be said of Jacob and of Israel, What hath God wrought! Behold, the people shall rise up as a great lion, and lift up himself as a young lion: he shall not lie down until he eat of the prey, and drink the blood of the slain" (Num. 23:16–24).

On the second occasion, Balak is given a loud rebuke. He is told to rise up and hear! This is not a physical command, for they were already standing, but rather a call to mental alertness. Applying this, let me ask you. When the Word of God is proclaimed in a public gathering, do you *"stand up and hear,"* not physically, but mentally? Are you alert to what the speaker is going to proclaim, or are you slothful and uninterested in his words? Public speakers will attest to the fact that an interested audience makes it easy to speak. Boring looks from an audience can sometimes quench the Spirit in a speaker. Of course, we recognize the fact that the speaker should have good material for the people of God, so that their interest will be held. It is also sad to see a speaker with not much solid material, resort to entertainment, or even theatrics, in an effort to hold his audience. This procedure should be avoided at all cost.

Balak hears the solemn fact that God's promises to Israel are unchangeable, and can never be reversed. How true that every word, by every prophet of God, will come to pass. There are many prophecies regarding God's earthly people concerning their glorious future, that are yet to be fulfilled No power on earth, no matter how mighty it may be, will ever hinder, or void them.

> "Thus saith the LORD, which giveth the sun for a light by day, and the ordinances of the moon and of the stars for a light by night, which divideth the sea when the waves thereof roar; The LORD of hosts is His name: If those ordinances depart from before Me, saith the LORD, then the seed of Israel also shall cease from being a nation before Me for ever. Thus saith the LORD; If heaven above can be measured, and the foundations of the earth searched out beneath, I will also cast off all the seed of Israel for all that they have done, saith the LORD" (Jer. 31:35–37).

In other words, this prophecy means that Israel will never cease to be His people. How blessed to know that *"all the promises of God in Him (Christ) are yea, and in Him Amen, unto the glory of God by us"* (2 Cor. 1:20). The word *"yea"* means the faithfulness of His Word. *"Amen,"* is His *oath*, which makes our assurance of the fulfillment doubly sure. The whole array of Old Testament and New Testament promises are secure in their fulfillment for us in Christ. Regarding His word and His oath, it is impossible for God to lie (Heb. 6:18).

Brethren, let us take courage. He has promised that we have been given eternal life, and are held in His hand. We shall never (in no wise) perish (John 10:28). He has promised to never leave us nor forsake us (Heb. 13:5). He has also promised to come again, and receive us unto Himself in glory (John 14:3). What then have we to fear? His promises in Him are yea and amen. Let us then look up and rejoice, for if God be for us, who can be against us? (Rom. 8:31). We can exclaim like Paul: *"For I am persuaded, that neither death, nor life, nor angels, nor principalities, nor powers, nor things present, nor things to come, Nor height, nor depth, nor any other creature, shall be able to separate us from the love of God, which is in Christ Jesus our Lord"* (Rom. 8:38–39).

Balaam continues; *"He hath not beheld iniquity in Jacob, neither hath He seen perverseness in Israel."* The question arises, how do we reconcile this divine utterance with the following verses? *"And the LORD said unto Moses, I have seen this people, and, behold, it is a stiffnecked people"* (Ex. 32:9). *"You only have I known of all the families of the earth: therefore I will punish you for all your iniquities"* (Amos 3:2).

This is where the skeptic steps in and announces that the Bible contradicts itself. Such that do so are fools, for it is out of their ignorance and blindness regarding spiritual things that such statements are made. In this case, what is the answer to God's words through Balaam? The fact is, that God did not view their sins in such a way as to be provoked enough to curse them, forsake them, and ultimately destroy them. God not *seeing* their sins on this occasion, runs parallel to the thought of Him *"choosing not to remember them,"* as He declares in Isaiah 43:25; and Jeremiah 31:34. *"I, even I, am He that blotteth out thy transgressions for mine own sake, and will not remember thy sins." "I will forgive their iniquity, and I will remember their sin no more."* David speaks of the blessedness of the man whose sins are *covered* (Ps. 32:1). Hezekiah exclaimed; *"Thou hast cast all my sins behind Thy back"* (Isa. 38:17). Regarding the nation; Micah confesses *"Thou wilt cast all their sins into the depths of the sea"* (7:19).

The apostle takes up this very strain in his letter to the Hebrews concerning the one offering of Christ, stating God's promise: *"Their sins and iniquities will I remember no more"* (10:14,17).

Balaam continues his parable with these words: *"The LORD his God is with him, and the shout of a king is among them."* Jehovah with these people was the very source of their blessedness. The divine presence was in their midst, protecting and sustaining them. During the millennium, it will be manifested to a fuller degree. Today, in this dispensation of grace, we claim His presence in our midst (Matt. 18:20). In Revelation 2, He is seen in the midst of seven churches in Asia, but in Matthew 18, He is seen in the midst of the local testimony. We who gather together unto His name, claim the promise; *"there am I in the midst of them."* That promise holds good at all assembly gatherings, whether it be a meeting for discipline, for the breaking of bread, for prayer, for the preaching of the gospel, or for the public ministry of the Word – He is in the midst!

We also read; *"the shout of a king is among them."* The original word for *"shout,"* is *(teruath)*, which was used to indicate the alarm-sound produced by the silver trumpets. [84] This particular word was also used to denote a shouting of joy when a king returned in triumph of war. At the last trump, when death as the last enemy is destroyed, and we rise to meet Him in the air, truly the shout of a king will be ours! Hallelujah!

"God brought them out of Egypt; he hath as it were the strength of an unicorn." Balaam proceeds, and now we see something hidden to the careless reader. The word *"brought,"* is not something that God had simply done in the past. That is how it would appear to the superficial reader. No, no, it does not mean that at all! The word is in the *long tense*, not the *short tense*, and implies something continuous. It is something that is presently taking place. Also, the word *"God"* is *"El,"* God in the singular, the Mighty One. [85]

---

84 Referred to in Chapter 21 of this book.
85 The Newberry Bible

BALAK AND BALAAM

They left the land of Egypt by the mighty hand of God, but forty years later, God was still bringing them out. That is, He had not relinquished His guiding hand and His guardian care toward His redeemed people. Thus, to oppose them, would be, in reality, fighting against God, the Mighty One. It would be frail, mortal man, fighting against Omnipotence! The world with all its power can do nothing against those who have God as their Leader, as far as God's purposes for them is concerned!

What does the unicorn symbolize? The only way to answer that question is to go to the Scriptures to see how it is used. Compare the following verses, and then we will apply them to certain truths.

> *"God brought him forth out of Egypt; he hath as it were the strength of an unicorn: he shall eat up the nations his enemies, and shall break their bones, and pierce them through with his arrows"* (Num. 24:8).

> *"But my horn shalt Thou exalt like the horn of an unicorn: I shall be anointed with fresh oil"* (Ps. 92:10).

> *"His glory is like the firstling of his bullock, and his horns are like the horns of unicorns: with them he shall push the people together to the ends of the earth: and they are the ten thousands of Ephraim, and they are the thousands of Manasseh"* (Deut. 33:17).

> *"Will the unicorn be willing to serve thee, or abide by thy crib? Canst thou bind the unicorn with his band in the furrow? or will he harrow the valleys after thee? Wilt thou trust him, because his strength is great? or wilt thou leave thy labour to him? Wilt thou believe him, that he will bring home thy seed, and gather it into thy barn?"* (Job 39:9–12).

This animal was noted for its horn, and was a symbol of strength, and power. Whan applied to people it speaks of their ability, and skill against their enemies. The reference in Job reveals that the unicorn rejects the dominion of man, and refuses to be tamed. It refuses to serve others in any way. Thus, we see Israel with the ability to vanquish all their enemies, while they are conquered by none, and subject to none. In the spiritual realm, we, as the elect, confess like Paul: *"We are more than conquerors through Him that loved us"* (Rom. 8:37).

"Surely there is no enchantment against Jacob, neither is there any divination against Israel." I want you to consider the word *"against,"* for in other portions that same Hebrew word is translated *"in."* The Septuagint, the Targums, the Chaldee, and the Vulgate versions all favor the word *"in."* The Chaldean Version renders it; *"For auguries are not acceptable in the house of Jacob, nor does the house of Israel will that there should be divinations."*

Employing the word, *"in Jacob"* and *"in Israel,"* we would conclude that since God led Israel out of Egypt with an high hand, they were armed with a power that was invincible. Thus, they had no need to resort to the art of soothsaying and augury in order to acquire their knowledge of the divine will. God clearly revealed to them, at all times, what He would do, and what He expected them to do. They were constantly under the protection of heaven, which certainly rendered the plots and schemes of their enemies completely abortive.

On the other hand, the Arab version retains the word *"against,"* thus indicating that there was no augury used by the enemy that would harm the progeny of Jacob, nor was there any Pythonic art which would avail against the stock of Israel. Thus, we have two modes of rendering, however, we prefer the first mode which employs the word *"in."*

To apply this in a practical way, we say that there is no need to go to the world, with its psychology, psychiatry, fortune-telling, and curious arts, for help in our spiritual warfare. Our source of information and help is solely found in the Holy Scriptures. Israel had the presence of Jehovah in the midst, and Moses as their mediator, to convey to them God's mind relative to all of their activities. We have the Lord Jesus Christ in our midst, and the Holy Spirit of God in our bodies. What more do we want? What more is needed? [86]

Finishing his second parable, Balaam uttered: *"What hath God wrought! Behold, the people shall rise up as a great lion, and lift up himself as a young lion: he shall not lie down until he eat of the prey, and drink the blood of the slain."* The word *"hath"* is in the short tense, which indicates a definite action in the expanse of time, whether past, present, or future. Consequently, there is a difference in interpretation with expositors. Some state that this refers to His mighty working in bringing them out of Egypt (the past). Others believe it refers to them at the time Balaam was speaking (the present), while some project it to the day when Israel would enter into the land of Canaan, to experience the mighty works of God on their behalf, in giving them victory over their foes (the future). The word *"God,"* is *"El,"* meaning *"the Mighty One, the First Great Cause of all."* [87]

Israel has been pictured as invulnerable to all enemies, but suddenly, the defensive is turned to the offensive when the lion is mentioned. One never thinks of a lion as trying to defend itself. Ah no, the lion is the attacker – a crouching lion watching its prey. Then, the paralyzing roar, the sudden spring and the resistless attack, followed by the complete collapse of the victim. Thus, Israel is pictured as an attacker, totally destroying its prey. Enter the book of Joshua and notice Israel's movements, as nation after nation is attacked, overcome, and totally destroyed.

Is the Church to be characterized by a lion? The following thoughts by D. Young prove interesting.

> "The Church of Christ is a destroying institution, and this part of its work must not be concealed and softened down to suit the prejudices of the world. The claws of the lion must not be clipped when it is dealing with vested interests and estab-

---

86 See Chapter 20, footnote # 65, on psychiatry
87 The Newberry Bible

lished iniquities. As it is not the way of the lion to make compromises with its prey, so neither must we make compromises with any evil. We have nothing to do with evil, save, in the name of the God of righteousness to destroy it as soon as we can. Nor need there be any fear of carrying the comparison too far. He who has taken in the meaning of those words, 'Be wise as serpents, and harmless as doves,' will well understand how to be ardent, enthusiastic, uncompromising, almost fierce and lion-like, against monster evils, yet at the same time gentle as a lamb, pitiful as God Himself, towards the men whose hearts have been hardened and their conscience blinded by the way in which their temporal interests have become intimately mixed with wrong." [88]

Thus, we see the triumphs of the Church over their various enemies, Satan, sin, and the world, which in a coming day, will be totally overcome.

To me, it would have been somewhat amusing to see Balak at this time. He has been ordered to attention to hear this second parable from Balaam, and after hearing it, he blurts out: *"Neither curse them at all, nor bless them at all."* He is vexed, and impatient. However, his words had no import on Balaam. who was forced by God to pronounce nothing but good upon Israel. Time and expense had been put into Balak's efforts to have Israel cursed, and the result was that Israel was divinely blessed. This heathen king must have been beside himself, to say the least. However, he had not yet given up all hope, so he suggests to Balaam that perhaps at another place it would please God that Balaam would be able to curse Israel for him. So bringing Balaam to the top of Peor, he built seven more altars, and prepared seven more bullocks and seven more rams. It was at this point that Balaam was afforded the full view of the mighty nation of Israel. He was above the whole nation looking down.

---

88 D. Young. The Pulpit Commentary, Vol.2. P. 333

They were in the valley, quite unaware of what was transpiring at that moment. However, above Balak and Balaam was an all-seeing eye in heaven looking down on these two wicked men, knowing not only all that was transpiring, but even fully knowing the hidden thoughts of their hearts.

Consider for a moment the effort involved to obtain seven bullocks, and seven rams, and then to trudge up the mountain to the highest point. Not only this, perhaps material had to be lugged up the mountain as well, to facilitate the erection of seven altars. Finally, the summit is reached and with great expectation, Balak waits to hear words from Balaam that will place a curse upon God's people. Between the two men, Balaam was by far the wiser of the two for he saw that it pleased the LORD to bless Israel (Num. 24:1). Consequently *"he went not, as at other times to seek for enchantments, but set his face toward the wilderness."*

ENCHANTMENTS

The Hebrew word for *"enchantments,"* (*nehashim*), is closely related to the Hebrew term for *"serpent,"* (*nahash*), showing a distinct relation between the serpent and divination, or augury, (*i.e.* omens and signs in the natural world observed and interpreted according the artificial system as manifesting the purposes of God). It was one of the most common and worst of heathen practices.

Balaam, seeing that these magical arts were not helping him, sought them no longer, but set his face to behold the entire congregation of Israel. Upon looking upon Israel, the Spirit of God came upon him. On the two other occasions we read that the LORD put a word in his mouth. But here, the Spirit of God coming upon him seems to intimate a higher state of inspiration. Balaam was now fully persuaded that Israel was destined to be fully blest, and that nothing could thwart the purposes of God. He now yields himself to the full control of God.

BALAAM'S THIRD PARABLE

"And he took up his parable, and said, Balaam the son of Beor hath said, and the man whose eyes are open hath said: He hath said, which heard the words of God, which saw the vision of the Almighty, falling into a trance, but having his eyes open: How goodly are thy tents, O Jacob, and thy tabernacles, O Israel! As the valleys are they spread forth, as gardens by the river's side, as the trees of lign aloes which the LORD hath planted, and as cedar trees beside the waters. He shall pour the water out of his buckets, and his seed shall be in many waters, and his king shall be higher than Agag, and his kingdom shall be exalted. God brought him forth out of Egypt; he hath as it were the strength of an unicorn: he shall eat up the nations his enemies, and shall break their bones, and pierce them through with his arrows. He couched, he lay down as a lion, and as a great lion: who shall stir him up? Blessed is he that blesseth thee, and cursed is he that curseth thee" (Num. 24:3–9).

Israel is likened to gardens by the river side, as the trees of lign aloes, and as cedar trees beside the waters. Water will pour from his buckets, and his seed will be in many waters. This description of the nation's blessing and happiness is chanted every Sabbath day, and at every feast commanded by God, by orthodox Jews upon entering the synagogue. The fullness of it has not yet been realized. Balaam's vision had leaped over the centuries to the time when Israel's unbelief will be a thing of the past, and they, under Messiah's rule, shall be greatly blessed. Fertility and beauty shall characterize the nation in that day. Water will flow out of his buckets, meaning that Israel shall be an instrument and a medium of imparting an overflowing of spiritual blessing to the nations.

BUCKETS OF LIVING WATER

Coming to our day, are you a dispenser of the waters of life to thirsty souls? Living water is a picture of salvation! Are we free with it? Do we water the parched soil of a sin-cursed earth with it? There are people seeking. Are we searching them out so that we can dispense the truth of the living water to their thirsty souls? Paul speaks of ministering the gospel of God (Rom. 15:16). The word *"ministering,"* conveys the thought of priestly activity. As a royal priesthood, we show forth the virtues of Him Who hath called us out of darkness, into His marvelous light (1 Pet. 2:9). The Lord has made us a kingdom of priests (Rev. 1:6), and this is one of our priestly activities. Are you active my dear brother, my sister? Paul was not ashamed of the gospel of Christ. Are you ashamed of it, or do you pour out the living water to sin-deadened souls? *"Go ye into all the world and preach the gospel to every creature,"* was the divine commission. We all can't be preachers, and we all can't go to the uttermost parts of the earth, but we all can "gossip" the gospel in our community. The clerks at the store, when did you last give them a gospel tract? The soul at the toll booth, did they receive the good news in printed form? Your neighbor, have they ever received a little folded piece of paper telling them of their need and the way of salvation? The gas station attendant, the post office clerk, the pharmacist, the customers in the shopping mall, the person on the sidewalk, the shoe-repair man, and the list could go on and on. This is the world. Have you entered it with buckets of living water? Ah my friend, they are all around you. They are rubbing shoulders with you, and most of them are on the broad way, soon to drop into an agonizing hell! Don't you care? Is there no compassion in your soul for them?

WILLIAM BOOTH – THE SALVATION ARMY

William Booth started *The Christian Mission* which developed into the *Salvation Army*. How he became an enthusiast for salvation was through an infidel lecturer who said, "If I believed what some of you Christians believe, I would never rest day nor night telling men about it!" Booth heard, believed, and acted!

Slowly, the mission began to grow but the work was hard, and Booth would trudge home night after night haggard with fatigue. His clothes were often torn and often bloody bandages were on his head from being struck with stones. Nothing daunted his purpose to preach the Word. Evening meetings were held in an old warehouse where urchins threw stones and fireworks through the window. Outposts were eventually established and in time, attracted converts, yet the results remained discouraging. It was not until 1878 when *The Christian Mission* changed its name to *The Salvation Army* that things began to happen. The impetus changed. Heading, as he termed it, "An army fighting sin," his converts began to grow. By the time Booth died in 1912, the Army was at work in 58 countries.

The record of this man makes me ashamed. He was not a theologian. Yes, he may have held doctrines that were not scriptural, such as women public speakers, but what I am trying to emphasize is that this man possessed a tremendous zeal, and a willingness to put himself out for the spread of the message of salvation. At the age of 13, he was sent to work as an apprentice in a pawnbroker's shop to help support his mother and sisters. He then became a Methodist minister, but he certainly didn't sit behind a desk singing, "Rescue the perishing, care for the dying." Ah no, there was more to him than that. He went out to the slums, he contacted the poverty-stricken, and poured out buckets of living water for them. He toiled, he worked, he prayed, and he deprived himself of the comforts of life, all for the gospel's sake. As you sit complacent, and in comfort, how do you measure up to this man my friend? I feel like a pigmy beside him! Oh that God the Spirit would stir all of us up to empty the buckets of living water on poor hell-bound souls, even at the cost of self-comfort!

"*And his seed shall be in many waters.*" What is this? It reminds me of Isaiah's prophecy. "*Blessed are ye that sow beside all waters, that send forth thither the feet of the ox and the ass"* (Isa. 32:20). Rice is sown upon the water, and prior to its sowing, the ground is trodden by oxen and asses, who go mid-leg deep, preparing the ground for sowing. However, in a spiritual sense, we consider this to mean, that the effusion of water denotes the impartation of spiritual truths which goes to prepare the mind for a productive process, just as water which soaks the earth prepares it for the bringing forth of an abundant crop, from the seed sown. Let me ask you, if you have been subject to doctrinal truths, thus preparing your mind, has there been the abundant fruit of a holy life manifested? Remember, fruits are from watered seeds.

"And his king shall be higher than Agag, and his kingdom shall be exalted." Do Balaam's words refer to the king as being our Lord Jesus Christ? Possibly so! *"I will make Him my Firstborn, higher than the kings of the earth"* (Ps. 89:27). At the time of this prophecy, no greater king than Agag, the king of the Amalekites, was known. The Amalekites were the first of the nations (Num. 24:20). Balaam announces that the King of Israel would be the greatest of all kings. At that day, to be higher than Agag, was to be higher than the highest.

What a day of glory that will be for our presently rejected Lord. *"He shall have dominion also from sea to sea, and from the river unto the ends of the earth"* (Ps. 72:8). *"He shall speak peace unto the heathen: and His dominion shall be from sea even to sea, and from the river even to the ends of the earth"* (Zech. 9:10). The doxology of Revelation 5:12 fits here.

> **"Worthy is the Lamb that was slain to receive:"**
> **"Power."** Power to put down all opposing authority.
> **"And riches."** Ruling as Possessor of heaven and earth.
> **"And wisdom."** Divinely applying truth to all situations.
> **"And strength."** The ability to execute His will.
> **"And honour."** Worldwide recognition of His position.
> **"And glory."** Recognition of His Person.

"And blessing." Every form of happiness ascribed to Him.

Balaam finally closes his third utterance emphasizing once again the mighty hand of God in delivering His people out of Egypt, and the strength of Israel over her foes.

Poor Balak! He was devastated and angry! Smiting his hands together in total dismay, he rebuked the false prophet that had prophesied truthfully. The clapping of his hands indicated also indignation and contempt. *"Men shall clap their hands at him, and shall hiss him out of his place"* (Job 27:23). *"All that pass by clap their hands at thee; they hiss and wag their head"* (Lam. 2:15). I can picture this king considering that all his effort and expense had gone "down the drain." Trudging up three mountains, building 21 altars, and offering 21 bullocks, and 21 rams, all to no avail. It almost strikes me as amusing to see the puny efforts of man to have cursed what God had eternally blessed!

One is reminded of that coming day when man, with all his sophistication, intellect, power and experience, will seek to overthrow the government of God saying; *"Let us break their bands asunder, and cast away their cords from us. He that sitteth in the heavens shall laugh: the Lord shall have them in derision"* (Ps. 2:3–4).

It is interesting to notice that Balak made sure to inform Balaam that if he had only done what he had expected of him, that he would have promoted him to great honor. This coincides with what we have in our society today. Those who appear to be losers by obeying God rather than obeying man, are apt to be rebuked by worldlings as being fools for throwing away the advantages that could have been theirs. I have known conscientious Christians throw away the prospects of advancing with their company simply because they declined to join the Masons, or some other secret association. Some employees are promoted because they are willing to be dishonest for the corporation that employs them. Then the honest Christian is told of the "wonderful advancement" that he has missed, simply because he would not comply with his employer's dishonest principles.

Balaam was quick to vindicate himself from the charges laid against him. He admits to the fact that the constraining power of the Most High God had irresistibly controlled all his utterances. He had been bound by the power of the Spirit, against his own will, to utter his revelations as God would have it. Then, before leaving, he informed Balak that he would advise (advertise) him what Israel would do. It was on this occasion that Balaam gave counsel to Balak how to get Israel to commit trespass against the LORD (Num. 31:16).

BALAAM'S FOURTH PARABLE

Before departing from Balak and going back to his own country, Balaam utters his fourth and last parable. It contains the very breath of God. In the first parable, he mentions seeing the nation of Israel, but now, he mentions that he sees, not just the nation, but the God of that mighty nation. His description of the coming King is remarkable. *"There shall come a Star out of Jacob, and a Sceptre shall rise out of Israel"* (Num. 24:17). What a tremendous revelation! Christ is *"the bright and morning star"* (Rev. 22:16). A star has always been regarded in the East as a symbol of distinction, as the herald of any glorious birth among men, thus, we behold a star when the King of the Jews was born. Balaam uses the word star metaphorically, to designate an illustrious Ruler, even our blessed Lord. The Jew understood this prophecy as referring to their Messiah, the Christ of God.

Speaking of the Messiah as a Sceptre implies, that with regal authority and supremacy, He shall rule. Thus, Christ is seen in Balaam's closing parable, subduing the nations, which the day of the Lord will usher in, *"when the Lord Jesus shall be revealed from heaven with His mighty angels, in flaming fire taking vengeance on them that know not God, and that obey not the gospel of our Lord Jesus Christ: Who shall be punished with everlasting destruction from the presence of the Lord, and from the glory of His power"* (2 Thess. 1:7–9).

"And Balaam rose up, and went and returned to his place: and Balak also went his way" (Num. 24:25).

34

THE DAUGHTERS OF MOAB

NUMBERS 25

When all the attempts of Balak and Balaam to curse Israel proved fruitless, the cunning and diabolical prophet counseled Balak of another possible way to bring God's people down. God's presence and His power was resident with the nation as long as they remained a separated people unto Himself. If that wall of separation could be broken down, Israel would fall. Thus advised, Balak acted.

"*And Israel abode in Shittim*" (Num. 25:1). This was some part of the tract called, "*the plains of Moab*," lying on the borders of the Jordan River. The prophet Micah relates to what took place prior to Israel's transgression. "*O my people, remember now what Balak king of Moab consulted, and what Balaam the son of Beor answered him from Shittim unto Gilgal; that ye may know the righteousness of the LORD*" (Mic. 6:5). Even in the book of Revelation we have a reference to this sad event. "*But I have a few things against thee, because thou hast there them that hold the doctrine of Balaam, who taught Balac to cast a stumblingblock before the children of Israel, to eat things sacrificed unto idols, and to commit fornication*" (Rev. 2:14).

> "*And the people began to commit whoredom with the daughters of Moab. And they called the people unto the sacrifices of their gods: and the people did eat, and*

bowed down to their gods. And Israel joined himself unto Baalpeor: and the anger of the LORD was kindled against Israel" (Num. 25:1–3).

The verb *"called,"* is in the feminine and implies that the invitation was given by these daughters of Moab. They probably made themselves very attractive to the men of Israel, thus luring them into their snare. As a result, some of Israel were soon seen engaging in the worship of Moab's gods, which would embrace licentious activity with these immoral, foreign women. It seems that the offering unto idols always included fornication as part of the idolatrous worship.

The LORD had formerly warned of such occasions in the giving of the law forty years previously, stating:

> *"Take heed to thyself, lest thou make a covenant with the inhabitants of the land whither thou goest, lest it be for a snare in the midst of thee: But ye shall destroy their altars, break their images, and cut down their groves: For thou shalt worship no other god: for the LORD, whose name is Jealous, is a jealous God: Lest thou make a covenant with the inhabitants of the land, and they go a whoring after their gods, and do sacrifice unto their gods, and one call thee, and thou eat of his sacrifice; And thou take of their daughters unto thy sons, and their daughters go a whoring after their gods, and make thy sons go a whoring after their gods"* (Ex. 34:12–16).

Israel wantonly disregarded the Law and plunged into the cesspool of polluted and prostituted worship. The psalmist laments: *"They joined themselves also unto Baal-peor, and ate the sacrifices of the dead. Thus they provoked Him to anger with their inventions: and the plague brake in upon them. Then stood up Phinehas, and executed judgment: and so the plague was stayed"* (Ps. 106:28–30). They ate the sacrifices of the dead. Not only was the idol itself dead, but the hero who it represented had also been long dead. We see a similar thing in the Church of

Rome, whose worshippers bow down to the images of canonized saints, who have been dead for ages.

Israel joining himself unto Baal-peor was certainly an unequal yoke which involved the abandonment of modesty. Matthew Henry has aptly put it: "Those that have broken the fences of modesty will never be held by the bonds of piety." So many of the people, including the princes, were guilty, that the sin became a national affront against the Almighty, thus, God was rightfully fiercely angry with the whole nation of Israel.

OFFENDERS HANGED

"And the LORD said unto Moses, Take all the heads of the people, and hang them up before the LORD against the sun, that the fierce anger of the LORD may be turned away from Israel" (Num. 25:4).

The question arises, who are the heads? Are they the chief actors in the transgression, or are they the leaders and princes of the people? Or does it mean to take the rulers of the people as assistants in executing judgment on the transgressors. In other words, take the heads of the people (the rulers) and let them hang them, the transgressors. Or does the text imply to take the rulers (who were the heads of the people) and hang them for allowing such atrocities in Israel? We submit other versions of this difficult text to you. "Take the princes of the people, sit in judgment, and slay him who shall be worthy of death" (Chaldean Version). "Take all the chiefs of the people with thee; and let them slay those men who have worn the badges of Baal-Peor; and hang them up before the Lord until sunsetting" (Geddes Translation).

However, there are a great number of interpreters whose current runs the other way. Those leaders and princes (subordinate officers, who were rulers of tens or hundreds) that went out of the camp with others, to commit this terrible sin of fornication and idolatry, were to be dealt with in a special way. They were to be stoned to death, and then hanged upon a tree, in broad daylight, until the setting of the sun. Thus, the ringleaders in sin were made examples of justice. We are convinced that this is the right interpretation. We have a similar action in 1 Timothy 5:20, where an elder has been convicted of sinning. *"Them (any overseer) that sin, rebuke before all."* Their place of responsibility calls for public rebuke. This does not apply to the rank and file of God's people. Thus, their judgment is more severe.

These leaders in the transgression were to be hanged "before the Lord," or, "*for* the Lord," as an offering to His just displeasure. The Greek would read, "Make a public example of them, for the Lord against the sun." Hanging a living person, or crucifixion, was never practiced in Israel. However, hanging subsequent to stoning was considered a mark of divine anathema. It was a sign of being accursed of God. *"His body shall not remain all night upon the tree, but thou shalt in any wise bury him that day; (for he that is hanged is accursed of God;) that thy land be not defiled, which the LORD thy God giveth thee for an inheritance"* (Deut. 21:23). Let us be clear on this, "the person was not accursed because he was hanged, but he was hanged because he was accursed" (Jerome).

Thus, Israel beheld numbers of corpses, hanging in broad daylight, as a public example. It was exceedingly sad to behold. So much so, that the godly had gathered together before the door of the tabernacle to weep. The day before, they were at the verge of entering into their promised land. It was in view, just over the Jordan. But having almost finished their course, the sensual men were snared by foreign women, and the lust of their flesh had brought them miserably down to the dust. What a lesson for us! Paul, in referring to this incident, writes: *"Neither let us commit fornication, as some of them committed, and fell in one day three and twenty thousand. ... Wherefore let him that thinketh he standeth take heed lest he fall"* (1 Cor. 10:8, 12).

"Slay every one his men" (Num. 25:5). The judges were to examine and ascertain the heads who were guilty, who were under

their jurisdiction, and then have them put to death. Thus, we see that the judicial system suggested by Jethro was continued all the time that they journeyed in the wilderness.

Poor Israel! Their sin commenced with idleness. They had years of toil now behind them and they were relaxed. The end of the wilderness journey was now about over. Nothing but good awaited them. They had won the victory! Ah yes, such circumstances were fertile ground for temptation and consequent departure.

Let us be careful brethren, we who through all the years have sought to live a sanctified life for God, lest we too fall in like manner. The world, with all its ungodly allurements, surrounds us, tempting us to succumb. Carnal pleasure was thrown in Israel's way, and instead of resisting, they miserably failed. They had not the stamina and fortitude of Joseph, who victoriously resisted Potiphar's wife (Gen. 39). If only the Moabites had come out in war against Israel, all would have been different. But the devil with his wiles devised a successful means of bringing Israel down – they approached them as friends, and invited them to join their idolatrous activities and feasts. One thing led to another, as is always the case in departure. Israel began conversing with the daughters of Moab, and this led to whoredom, but alas, that illicit pleasure led to idolatry, which invoked the wrath of God.

TODAY'S UNEQUAL YOKE

The prayer of our Lord for us did not involve us being taken out of the world, but rather that we be kept from the wicked one. How delighted the devil must have been to see the men of Israel forfeiting their separation, their protection from God, and their strength in God, all for a moment of licentious pleasure.

It has been said, "a *kick* from the world is far less dangerous, than a *kiss* from the world." When the world is antagonistic to a Christian, usually that Christian will become stronger in his faithfulness to God. However, when the world caters to a Christian, and appears to be sweet and friendly, then the danger of one losing his testimony becomes far greater. "Come, join us!" is the cry of the world today. "Let us be friends. Join our associations, our clubs, and get involved with us in community activities. After all, we want what is right, and you are valuable to us to help make this a better world. Come out of your shell, and enjoy life. We have pleasures for you. The sports arena is great. Be like us, and cheer for your team. Get involved in our worldly projects and cease being anti-social. Enjoy the movies, the bowling alley, the pool room, the golf course, after all, what is wrong with an occasional social drink? Join the P.T.A.. Your help is needed. Go to the voting booth. You have a responsibility to try your utmost to get the "right" man into office. Enroll your children in the Boy Scouts and the Girl Scouts, it is good clean activity for them. We love you Christians, you have such qualities and a great potential for enlarging your coasts. Oh yes, we also have wonderful religious musicals that you should attend, and don't forget, when a noted speaker comes to our "church," be sure to join us. And by the way, we have some wonderful stock brokers that will gladly help you to invest your savings into stocks that will give you tremendous dividends. By purchasing them you will be yoked with, and automatically become a partner of the company, to your financial advantage. Some "deadbeats" say that investing in stocks is gambling. Don't listen to them, you deserve to be rich and increased with goods"

Ah, my friend, doesn't all this sound most plausible and convincing? But wait! What does God say about it? *"Love not the world, neither the things that are in the world. If any man love the world, the love of the Father is not in him. For all that is in the world, the lust of the flesh, and the lust of the eyes, and the pride of life, is not of the Father, but is of the world. And the world passeth away, and the lust thereof: but he that doeth the will of God abideth for ever"* (1 Jn. 2:15–17). James, through the Spirit, is even more blunt. *"Pure religion and undefiled before God and the Father is this, To visit the fatherless and widows in their affliction, and to keep himself unspotted from the world"* (Jas. 1:27). *"Ye adulterers and adulteresses, know ye not that the friendship of the world is enmity with God? whosoever therefore will be a friend of the world is the enemy of God"* (Jas. 4:4). Paul takes a firm stand against the world. *"But God forbid that I should glory, save in the cross of our Lord Jesus Christ, by whom the world is crucified unto me, and I unto the world"* (Gal. 6:14).

Now I have no problem with these inspired statements, and I trust that you do not either. Any intelligent Christian knows that the word *"world"* in all of these passages does not refer to the planet Earth, nor does it mean the people on that planet. No, no! The word *"world"* in these quotations refers to the *"adornment"* of this world. That is, the system that corrupt man has devised to keep fallen humanity happy and prosperous without God. That is the *"world"* referred to here. God's people are termed *"saints,"* which basically means, *"holy and separated."* We are a unique identity down here, separated from the world in all its false ways. As Peter writes, we are *"strangers and pilgrims,"* and as such, we are to abstain from fleshly lusts which war against the soul (1 Pet. 2:11). Let us be ever watchful! Let us keep up our guard!

SOLOMONS' WARNING

Solomon warned his son; *"Keep my words, and lay up my commandments with thee. Keep my commandments and live; and my law as the apple of thine eye."* He then warns about *"the strange woman"* that flattereth with her words, enticing a young man into her house. In the street, she boldly catches him and kisses him, and with an impudent face persuades him to take his fill of love with her. Then Solomon adds, *"With her much fair speech she caused him to yield, with the flattering of her lips she forced him. He goeth after her straightway, as an ox goeth to the slaughter, or as a fool to the correction of the stocks."* This woman is a picture of this world in relation to a Christian. The final warning is; *"Let not thine heart decline to her ways, go not astray in her paths. For she hath cast down many wounded: yea, many strong men have been slain by her"* (Prov. 7). This woman pictures the world.

PHINEHAS

"And, behold, one of the children of Israel came and brought unto his brethren a Midianitish woman in the sight of Moses, and in the sight of all the congregation of the children of Israel, who were weeping before the door of the tabernacle of the congregation. And when Phinehas, the son of Eleazar, the son of Aaron the priest, saw it, he rose up from among the congregation, and took a javelin in his hand; And he went after the man of Israel into the tent, and thrust both of them through, the man of Israel, and the woman through her belly. So the plague was stayed from the children of Israel. And those that died in the plague were twenty and four thousand" (Num. 25:6–9).

Thus, a priestly man springs into action! There is no hesitation. Phinehas is not so much concerned at this time about holding a censer in his hand to offer incense to Jehovah. Instead, he has a javelin in his hand to execute judgment for sin. The sin was flagrant, open, and a bold act against the Most High. Some were weeping at the door of the tabernacle because of conditions. This was all well and good, for there is nothing wrong with mourning over sin, but there are times when sin must be immediately, and righteously dealt with, and this is seen in Phinehas. His name means "mouth of brass." Brass in the Scripture is usually associated with judgment, and here was a man living up to his name. As the psalmst remarked, he *"executed judgment"* (Ps. 106:30).

It is interesting to note that farther down the line of Israel's history, we find another priest with the same name, but instead of him executing judgment for God, it was God that executed judgment on him. Phinehas, the son of Eli, openly laid with the women that gathered at the door of the tabernacle of the congregation. Consequently, he was slain by the Lord in battle (1 Sam. 4:11). So, the first Phinehas *executed* judgment *for* God, while the second Phinehas *experienced* judgment *from* God.

PUTTING AWAY

When problems arise in the assembly, calling for "putting away," what do we do? Do we sit back and say, "Oh my, we had better pray about this"? Do we reason what the repercussions might be? Do we worry what may be the reaction of the sinning one's relatives. Do we fear man, or do we fear God? When dealing with serious sin, there should be no coldness, legality, fleshly anger, or unwise zeal. Ah no, that is not the way to deal with sin. Brethren are not to put away a person in order to merely get even with him. You would hardly term that righteous judgment. Nor does the assembly excommunicate the wicked person to permanently get rid of him. Oh no, for one reason for excommunication is to put the sinning one in a position where God will bring him down to the place of repentance, that restoration to God and to the assembly might become a reality.

The meeting for putting away is a special meeting. I have sat in such meetings, and there have been tears. That is the spirit we covet for such meetings, is it not? Tender love for the offender, yet dealing righteously, unwaveringly, and immediately, regarding the sin.

Sin is righteously dealt with in order to maintain the purity of the assembly; to furnish a warning to all the saints; to vindicate the name of God, and as already stated, for the restoration of the offender.

The sins calling for *immediate* excommunication are listed in 1 Corinthians 5:11, and Matthew 18:15–17, that sin being rebellion against the oversight. I do not believe that *"reject"* in Titus 3:10, refers to putting away. The late William Warke said that any sin calling for the death penalty in the Old Testament, calls for excommunication in the New Testament. In most cases that might be true.

Calvin makes a profitable remark on the action of Phinehas:

> "If any private person should in his preposterous zeal take upon himself to punish a similar crime, in vain will he boast of being an imitator of Phinehas, unless he shall be thoroughly assured of the command of God. In order that our zeal may be approved of God, it must be tempered by spiritual prudence, and directed by His authority; in a word, the Holy Spirit must go before, and dictate what is right."

We add that any such action against the sinning one is not an individual matter, but that of the whole assembly of God. That is what the Holy Spirit has dictated.

Moses records that 24,000 died from the plague, and Paul records in 1 Corinthians 10:8, that 23,000 died. Thus skeptics cry out that the Word of God contradicts itself. What careless readers! Notice Paul's report. *"Neither let us commit fornication, as some of them committed, and fell **in one day** three and twenty thousand"* (2 Cor. 10:8). That is how many died before the day ended at sundown. The rest died after sunset, which was considered the next day. Moses gives the total number of those who died.

When the judgment was righteously executed, and the plague was stayed, then the LORD spoke unto Moses.

> *"Phinehas, the son of Eleazar, the son of Aaron the priest, hath turned My wrath away from the children of Israel, while he was zealous for My sake among them, that I consumed not the children of Israel in My jealousy. Wherefore say, Behold, I give unto him My covenant of peace: And he shall have it, and his seed after him, even the covenant of an everlasting priesthood; because he was zealous for his God, and made an atonement for the children of Israel"* (Num. 25:11–13).

A reward was given to Phinehas for his heroic act. The LORD gave him His covenant of peace, meaning a promise of abundant prosperity, comfort, and happiness. Due to his earnest regard to the honor of Jehovah's majesty, coupled with his love of the truth, and his concern for the well-being and security of his brethren, God was now going to honor him with a long succession of high priesthood. In this, his posterity would be included in this high office, instead of possibly being transferred later to some other branch of Aaron's descendants. In this respect, Phinehas was a type of Christ, Who through His defeat of sin, death, and hell, rose triumphantly to become our Great High Priest, forever after the order of Melchisedek.

"And the LORD spake unto Moses, saying, 'Vex the Midianites, and smite them." This infliction of vengeance would be the last public act of Moses. Notice chapter 31:2. *"Avenge the children of Israel of the Midianites: afterward shalt thou be gathered unto thy people"* (Num. 31:2). It would seem that the Midianites had taken the lead in the conspiracy suggested by Balaam, thus, the judgment was denounced against them, rather than against the Moabites. The Midianites had probably retained Balaam in their company, for it was among them that he was slain (31:8). Brethren, the world is wily, and beguiling. Satan is the god of this world. *"Put on the whole armour of God, that ye may be able to stand against the wiles of the devil"* (Eph. 6:11). *"The serpent beguiled Eve through his subtilty"* (2 Cor. 11:3). Brethren, let us be careful, vigilant, and strong. Don't allow the world to get a grip on our hearts, and drag us down, until we become useless for God.

35

THE NEW CENSUS THE DAUGHTERS OF ZELOPHEHAD

NUMBERS 26

The following census is in comparison to the census taken 38 years prior, and listed in Numbers 1.

	Chapter 26	Chapter 1	
Reuben	43,730	46,500	(2770 *decrease*).
Simeon	22,200	59,300	(37,100 *decrease*).
Gad	40,500	45,650	(5,150 *decrease*).
Judah	76,500	74,600	(1,900 increase).
Issachar	64,300	54,400	(9,900 increase).
Zebulon	60,500	57,400	(3,100 increase).
Manasseh	52,700	32,200	(20,500 increase).
Ephraim	32,500	40,500	(8,000 *decrease*).
Benjamin	45,600	35,400	(10,200 increase).
Dan	64,400	62,700	(1,700 increase).
Asher	53,400	41,500	(11,900 increase).

| Naphtali | 45,400 | 53,400 | (8,000 *decrease*). |
| Total | 601,730 | 603,550 | (1,820 *decrease*). |

Of seven tribes, there was an increase of 59,200.

Of five tribes there was a *decrease* of 61,020

For a moment, let me take you back to the beginning. What strength, what power, and what faith was seen in that throng, as they marched out of Egypt. *"He brought them forth also with silver and gold: and there was not one feeble person among their tribes"* (Ps. 105:37). *"And the children of Israel journeyed from Rameses to Succoth, about six hundred thousand on foot that were men, beside children"* (Ex. 12:37). What a glorious sight that must have been! A redeemed and rejoicing people marching in rank out of slavery, with their eyes fixed forward on the land of their inheritance.

However, the divine record saddens. *"But with whom was He grieved forty years? Was it not with them that had sinned, whose carcases fell in the wilderness?"* (Heb. 3:17). Alas, they sinned, they fell, and never entered into the Land of Promise. Their unbelief brought them down to the desert dust. How solemn was the verdict of Jehovah at Kadesh:

> *"Your carcases shall fall in this wilderness; and all that were numbered of you, according to your whole number, from twenty years old and upward, which have murmured against Me, doubtless ye shall not come into the land, concerning which I sware to make you dwell therein, save Caleb the son of Jephunneh, and Joshua the son of Nun. But your little ones, which ye said should be a prey, them will I bring in, and they shall know the land which ye have despised. But as for you, your carcases, they shall fall in this wilderness. And your children shall wander in the wilderness forty years, and bear your whoredoms, until your carcases be wasted in the wilderness"* (Num. 14:29–33).

Now, the *"little ones"* have grown into men. Almost forty years has come and gone. The trail of Israel's journeys could have been traced by the graves in the desert sand. The former generation had all fallen, their carcasses rotting in the graves strewn along the way. Only Joshua, Caleb, and the Levites, remained of the former generation. So now we have a nation of men, of which none are over sixty years of age. They are going to cross Jordan in a short time and possess the land under the leadership of Joshua. Aaron and Miriam have been laid to rest with their fathers, and Moses is soon to go the way of all the earth. There is a bit of sadness to this whole thing, yet there is much to thank God for. A new generation, ready, and eager to fight the foe! Many lessons had been learned, many scenes had been viewed, and a few conflicts had been fought. They are ready for war, 601,730 men!

SIMEON'S DECREASE

Out of all the tribes, Simeon had decreased in number more than any other tribe. In fact, this tribe had decreased more that all the others put together. Almost forty years previously they were the largest tribe, and now they had been reduced to the smallest of all the tribes. One wonders if the words of Jacob's dying words would not have a bearing on their decrease. *"Simeon and Levi are brethren; instruments of cruelty are in their habitations.... Cursed be their anger, for it was fierce; and their wrath, for it was cruel: I will divide them in Jacob, and scatter them in Israel"* (Gen. 49:5,7). This prophecy was fulfilled, for when they first entered Canaan they had only a small portion; a few towns and villages in the worst part of Judah's lot.

COLDNESS AND CRUELTY

You will remember how Simeon acted treacherously and barbarously when destroying the Shechemites. They held the sword, not as a weapon of defense, but as a weapon of violence, to do others wrong. Their deed was shameful, which grieved the heart of their father, Jacob, greatly. Hundreds of years later, we find Simeon's descendents still out of order. While

Moses and others are mourning at the door of the tabernacle, the plague already commencing, here marches a man into the camp with a Midianitish woman. His impudent wickedness is publicly declared. He was a prince of a chief house among the Simeonites. It seemed that this man prided himself in that in which he should have been ashamed. There was defiance in the man. Little did he care about the testimony of God, and intergrity was the least of his concern. However, Phinehas immediately took care of the problem, and slew this wretched man and his Midianitish lover.

Can you see the general characteristic of this tribe? Their father manifested coldness, and cruelty. His posterity manifested fleshly lust and a total disregard for the Law of God. No wonder that they suffered the greatest loss of all the tribes in thirty-eight years. Now then, bring this to our day. What is one way in which an assembly can be reduced? Namely this. A legal spirit, a cold and perhaps even cruel attitude in maintaining "the truth," coupled with a carnal satisfying of the flesh in various forms. People that are hard on others, but easy on themselves are to be watched, and avoided. Such people if placed into the position of leadership of an assembly, will in time, bring it down.

HOW TO RUIN AN ASSEMBLY

Now please do not think that this is the only reason assemblies become numerically smaller. There can be far more reasons than the ones enumerated. If there is a lack of gospel outreach, a lack of gospel zeal among the saints, there is the danger of the assembly becoming smaller, for when the older saints are called home, there is no one to fill the ranks. Again, if saints lose their first love, they are in danger of experiencing what the Ephesian assembly experienced, namely, the removal of the lampstand. Ephesus was a thriving community, and the assembly in that city held a straight line, labored for His sake, and manifested endurance. However, they had left their *first love,* consequently, there is no assembly there today, and even the city lies desolate, merely a malaria-infested swamp.

Bringing the world into God's assembly may also be a contributing factor to its ruin. Going through Christian-like motions on Lord's Day, then flirting with the world the rest of the week, will surely affect the testimony in a negative way. The church at Pergamos held the doctrine of Balaam. Where is that testimony today?

Self-centeredness can adversely affect an assembly. As Paul lamented, *"For all seek their own, not the things which are Jesus Christ's"* (Phil. 2:21). The church of the Laodiceans was characterized by this, and where was Christ in relation to them? Outside!

PHILADELPHIA

On the other hand, let me say that quality is far more important than quantity. The church at Philadelphia was numerically weak, yet pleasing to the Lord. They had kept His word, and had not denied His name, consequently, the Lord had opened a door for them for the spreading of the gospel. There are assemblies, that for years, have been few in number, yet are godly. It is a joy to be with them, and refreshing to the soul. On the other hand, there are some large assemblies, with much activity, but there is not the same "family atmosphere" as in some of our smaller assemblies. However, one does like to see growth, and we often wonder why in the general census of all the assemblies in our land, we seem to be shrinking, instead of swelling. Could it be worldly prosperity, lack of true love to Christ, a lack of gospel zeal, self-centeredness, worldliness, legality, or even perhaps hidden sin? You be the judge.

MANASSAH"S GROWTH

Of all the tribes, Manassah experienced the most growth, an increase of 20,500 men from twenty years of age and upward. Strange to say, before crossing the Jordan, half of that tribe manifested a half-hearted, and self-indulgent spirit (Num. 32). The father of this tribe, unlike the fathers of the other tribes, was born in Egypt, and named Manassah by his father Joseph, who declared: *"For God, hath made me forget all my toil, and all my father's house"* (Gen. 41:51). Thus, we see prosperity and fruitfulness connected with the first mention of the name, Manassah. However, at the end of the wilderness journey, after forty years of testing, we see failure to follow through and claim all the promises of God. This condition can be traced to the professing Church. At its commencement, there was a tremendous outburst of blessing and fruitfulness. But as time wore on, we observe in its history, a faltering and a failure to grasp and enjoy the spiritual blessing that were allotted to it. Just as one half of that tribe failed to enter in and secure their blessing, so today in Christendom, we find five foolish virgins with lamps, but with no oil in their vessels, and five wise virgins with their lamps, and oil in their vessels. Their lamps would speak of their profession, and the oil would typify the Holy Spirit (Matt. 25:1–12). Those of the tribe of Manassah who entered into the land would typify earnest believers, who by God's grace, have secured, and are enjoying the heavenly blessings that they possess in a risen Christ.

FIVE HONORABLE WOMEN

Connected with the tribe of Manasseh, we find five honorable women – the daughters of Zelophehad. They have a serious problem and were very much concerned about it. There was no provision in the Law for them. An inheritance for women was unheard of. Their father had died in the wilderness, leaving no sons. Since he had no sons, there would be no inheritors to claim the inheritance. These ladies had full respect for their parents, and were not ashamed to mention their father. Yes, he had died, but not because of a rebellious nature or a crowning sin. He had gone the way of all the earth as all men do eventually.

It took courage for these five sisters to approach, as it were, the supreme court of Israel. They had no advocate to plead for them. They were plain and honest, loyal and honorable! What a beautiful group of sisters! I will tell you my brethren, women of their character are most valuable in an assembly. We can use all the ladies of this character that we can get! I can just picture these devout ladies standing before Moses, Eleazar the high priest, the princes, and all the congregation, unblushingly presenting their case. These women manifested great faith in that they spoke of entering the land as if already in it! They had full confidence in the word of the Lord, and confidence in Jehovah to completely fulfill His word. They felt that they were entitled to an inheritance. One writer says that they were concerned about their sons. However, I do not read of them having husbands at this point in their life, and thus being virtuous women, they would naturally have no sons when approaching Israel's supreme court. They were virgins, clean in their testimony and life! Consequently, what they said publicly carried tremendous weight, simply because of what they were privately.

Later, when contemplating marriage, these ladies were instructed to marry only into the family of the tribe of their father, so that their inheritance would not move to another tribe (Num. 36:6–7). It was said of them, *"Let them marry to whom they think best."* One can readily see that their way of thinking was in absolute correspondence with the mind of God. They had no thought whatsoever of marrying outside of their tribe. If you are a young sister or a young brother contemplating marriage, let me advise you. Never marry one from another tribe. You may say, "Of what tribe am I?" You are in the tribe of *Christians gathered together unto the name of our Lord Jesus Christ.* For your benefit, let me name a few other tribes. The *denominations* tribe. The *world* tribe. The *unconverted* tribe. Be careful whom you choose. It is unlawful to marry an unconverted person. It is most unwise to marry a denominational "saint." It is wrong to marry a clean-living, moral, and upright worldling. *"Can two walk together, except they be agreed?"* (Amos 3:3). The answer is, NO! Let us maintain the path of separation, touching not the unclean thing, and then and only then, will the Lord Almighty play the part of a loving and caring Father to us (2 Cor. 6:14–18).

Allow me to add one more thought. It will be noticed that the daughters of Zelophehad were required not to just marry within their own tribe, but within their own *family* of that tribe. That stipulation greatly narrowed the prospects for marriage. The application is this. If an assermbly is likened to a tribe, then within that assembly you have various families. Not all in God's assembly are of the same character. There is the family of the carnal, and there is the family of the spiritual. You dear ones contemplating marriage, be careful with whom you associate in your assembly. If you are a young man looking for a wife, and you want to please the Lord in your own life, then do, above all things, seek out a godly lady in the assembly. There is the question of cosmetics or character; shapeliness or saintliness; silly attire or sober adornment. Be careful, for the person that you marry will become one flesh with yourself, and she will either drag you down or lift you up spiritually.

Young ladies, what are you looking for in a husband? Muscles? Popularity? Flamboyancy? Good looks? A joker? Or, are you interested in a man that can lead God's people into the presence of the Lord when he prays? Are you looking forward to being united in one flesh to a man that is keenly interested in the Scriptures, and delights to speak of the Lord Jesus Christ? A man that is devoted to the assembly, contributes to its functions, and has a genuine love for the saints, is the kind of a man that a spiritual lady will invariably seek. Remember, the family into which you marry will set the pattern of your Christian life in years to come. Be careful!

36

JOSHUA'S INAUGURATION WAR ON THE MIDIANITES

NUMBERS 27, 31

"And the LORD said unto Moses, Get thee up into this mount Abarim, and see the land which I have given unto the children of Israel. And when thou hast seen it, thou also shalt be gathered unto thy people, as Aaron thy brother was gathered. For ye rebelled against My commandment in the desert of Zin, in the strife of the congregation, to sanctify Me at the water before their eyes: that is the water of Meribah in Kadesh in the wilderness of Zin" (Num. 27:12–14).

THE DEATH OF MOSES

Moses is called upon by the LORD to die. He was to be gathered unto his people. He would soon be in the same realm as Abraham, Isaac, and Jacob. He would soon join the ranks of former godly saints. Now it would seem to me that such an event would be something to look forward to. I will grant you, that death is not what any person would term a pleasant thing.

It still seems to lurk as an enemy, an enemy not yet destroyed (1 Cor. 15:26). On the other hand, we look at it as a porter, ushering us into another world, the world of spirits in an unclothed state. When our time comes, we shall go to meet those whom we loved, that have gone on before. Most blessed of all, we shall enter the Father's house to see our blessed Lord, face to face. No mortal can fully comprehend what that will be like, but certainly we can say like Paul, it will be far better. Perhaps Aaron set an example for Moses how to die. Moses would have remembered with what ease his brother had died. Aaron allowed his younger brother to strip him of his priestly garments, then put them on his son Eleazar. Then, with dignity, and composure, quietly lay down and allowed Jehovah to strip him of his earthly tabernacle, only to wing his way to Sheol below, to await the day of the Lord's entry, after Calvary, which would make it a virtual paradise. *"Precious in the sight of the LORD is the death of His saints"* (Ps. 116:15).

Before dying, Moses blessed the children of Israel (Deut. 33:1). Naming the tribes one by one, he blessed them in this order: Reuben, Judah, Levi, Benjamin, Joseph, Ephraim, Manasseh, Zebulun, Issachar, Gad, Dan, Naphtali, and Asher. You will notice that Simeon is not mentioned. "The lot of Simeon was an appendage to that of Judah, that tribe is included in the blessing of Judah. Some copies of the LXX join Simeon with Reuben: 'Let Reuben live and not die; and let Simeon be many in number.'" [89]

Up to the very moment of his death, Moses had God's people upon his heart. He had led them out of bondage, forsaking the riches of Egypt, and had suffered their impudence for forty years in the wilderness. He had been unappreciated, railed on, abused, falsely charged, threatened with death, yet he dearly loved them! What an example of the grace of God! What meekness, what lowliness, and what godly love radiated from this man of God. His thoughts ran parallel to the Lord's, when it was said of Jehovah, *"yea, He loved the people"* (Deut. 33:3). Let

---

89 Matthew Henry. Commentary on the Whole Bible, Vol. 1. World Bible Publishers. P. 875

me ask you, in spite of the way some of God's people have treated you, do you still love them?

Another thing to notice is that this mighty man of God expressed deep concern for the future of God's people. In view of his departure, he speaks to the LORD.

> "Let the LORD, the God of the spirits of all flesh, set a man over the congregation, which may go out before them, and which may go in before them, and which may lead them out, and which may bring them in; that the congregation of the LORD be not as sheep which have no shepherd" (Num. 27:1517).

This mighty man is not bemoaning his death. He certainly is not manifesting self-pity. What a tremendous man! In love to the Lord's people, one thing occupied his mind, and that was the future welfare of God's people, that they might have a man to shepherd them. He addresses the LORD as, *"the LORD, the God of all flesh."* He acknowledges that God is the original Creator of all men's spirits, and that He is the Bestower of the various spiritual gifts which are termed "spirits" in 1 Corinthians 14:12. God alone knew who would be fitted for the leadership of His people, and Moses thus appeals to God in this way. The desire was for a man of great activity, a man able to go in before the people, and then lead them out, just as a shepherd does with his flock.

Let me ask, do you pray, like Moses, that God will raise up men in His assemblies that will be shepherd-like in their activities for the benefit of God's people? Men that are not on a high pedestal, but men that dwell among God's people, and are conversant with them, men that can lead them out to green pastures for their health's sake. True shepherds know the state of their flock, simply because they visit them in their homes. They are men that can *feed*, for that is what the word *shepherd* implies. At the assembly Bible reading, the true shepherd opens up the Word of God and feeds the sheep with the finest of the wheat, so that they return home more intelligent in divine things than when they came. When a sheep breaks a leg, the shepherd mends the bone. When sickness invades the flock, the shepherd has the right medicine for a cure. He protects his flock from wolves, or any other creature that would do his flock harm. He is a very busy man. Are there men of this character in your assembly, and if not, why not? I am ashamed to admit that some assemblies have no true shepherds. The poor sheep are starving spiritually, and some are becoming infected with spiritual disease as the result of the lack of food and care.

JOSHUA

Joshua had proven himself to be a fearless soldier, a faithful spy, and a fruitful minister unto Moses. There was nothing but good to say about him. He was the man of God's choice. It was not a matter of Moses choosing Joshua. Oh no! It was a matter of God choosing the man for the position. Not only this, but God instructs Moses regarding the process in placing Joshua into the office of leadership. It was to be a public positioning. Moses was to lay his hand upon Joshua, set him before Eleazar, and all the congregation, and give him charge in sight of the congregation. In so doing, Moses was visibly transferring the office of leader of Israel, from himself to his successor. Accompanying this was Moses' charge to Joshua: *"Be strong and of a good courage: for thou must go with this people unto the land which the LORD hath sworn unto their fathers to give them; and thou shalt cause them to inherit it. And the LORD, He it is that doth go before thee; He will be with thee, He will not fail thee, neither forsake thee: fear not, neither be dismayed"* (Deut. 31:7–8). It was only *some* of Moses' honor that was to be transferred to Joshua. The spiritual gifts conferred upon Moses had rendered him honorable in the sight of the people, and a portion of this was to be given to Joshua so that he might be held in high esteem by the congregation. In laying his hands on Joshua before the congregation, Moses was as much as declaring: "This is your new leader, and I am now dedicating him to this noble work."

During his leadership, Moses spoke to God face to face, but not Joshua. He was dependent on the high priest for the revelations of God. Men who lead God's assemblies, and men who fight the battles of the Lord in the gospel, are very dependent on our Great High Priest for direction in leading the flock and fighting the enemy. Paul was in constant contact with His risen Lord as to his movements. How men can plan evangelistic meetings years in advance, and have the time set when they will end their series, long before they even commence, is beyond me. Such movements are a flagrant denial of the intimate leading of the Holy Spirit, and the guidance of our Great High Priest. Consider the apostle Paul, an exemplary model for all evangelists. Passing through the region of Galatia, they were *"forbidden of the Holy Ghost to preach the word in Asia. After they were come to Mysia, they assayed to go into Bithynia: but the Spirit suffered them not"* (Acts 16:6–7). What is this? Why the answer is simple! It is a scriptural declaration of how sensitive those godly men were to the total guidance of God. It wasn't if they wanted to go or not. Ah no, it was a matter of, does God want me to go or not? I am afraid that in our modern day of intellectualism and organizing, we have lost the sense of the guidance of God. This appalling failure was not to be seen in Joshua. How wonderful it would be if it was to cease among us!

WAR WITH MIDIAN

I am sure by now, that you suspect that the writings of Moses are not all in chronological order – and you are correct. We have partially read about God's notice to Moses regarding his death. However, Israel's conflict with the Midianites took place before that, though not mentioned until later in chapter 31.

> *"And the LORD spake unto Moses, saying, Avenge the children of Israel of the Midianites: afterward shalt thou be gathered unto thy people. And Moses spake unto the people, saying, Arm some of yourselves unto the war, and let them go against the Midianites, and avenge the LORD of Midian. Of every tribe a*

thousand, throughout all the tribes of Israel, shall ye send to the war" (Num. 31:1–4).

If you were to consider this war and not know the circumstances, you would cry out that it was an atrocity! Israel, having won the war, returned back with captives who were women with their little children, and also women that were virgins. How the soldiers determined who were virgins, we are not told, but having divided the captives into two groups, the soldiers methodically killed every mother and their little male children without mercy. The virgins were spared a horrible death. Can you picture this? I believe that mothers would be pleading with the soldiers to spare them, and if not, to at least not kill their little sons and their babies. But no, every one of them was mercilessly slain in cold blood, with the sword. There must have been hideous screams as the swords began to pierce their bodies. What horror it must have been to see soldiers taking little children and plunging a cold, steel sword, into their little bodies, thus hurling them into eternity. Writers estimate that there were perhaps 50,000 women to deal with. As one writer puts it; "The very soul sickens to think upon the cruel details of their slaughter." Why such brutality? Let us proceed with the answer.

THE REASON FOR WAR

First of all, let us consider the reason for this conflict. The Midianites were a semi-nomad people, descended from Abraham and Keturah. Those who were dealt with by Israel occupied a portion of land that lay east and southeast of Moab, on the eastern coast of the Dead Sea. Some of the other Midianites settled south of Canaan, among whom Jethro lived. These people retained the worship of the true God. However, the ones we are presently considering are those who settled east of Canaan, and had fallen into idolatry. They were neighbors to, and in confederacy with, the Moabites. Their land was not designated to be given to Israel, nor would Israel have meddled with them if they had not made themselves detestable to Israel by sending their sensuous women among them to lure them to idolatry and whoredom. They were very wicked people, and God was going to judge them, using Israel as His weapon of destruction. Since the men of Israel had been judged for their fornication, and died, so also the women, who were just as guilty of fornication, must die. That was the verdict of God. It must be carried out.

It was a war of vengeance. You will notice that the Lord said: *"Avenge the children of Israel of the Midianites."* But we also read that Moses said: *"Let them go against the Midianites, and avenge the LORD of Midian."* In other words, the LORD emphasized His tender concern regarding the welfare of His people, yet Israel, on the other hand, was to manifest a supreme concern for the glory of Jehovah. A dishonor had been done to God and an injury inflicted on His people. The interests of God and Israel were identical.

The Moabites were at this time spared in consideration of Lot, and because the measure of their iniquities was not yet full (Deut. 2:9). Seeing that this war resulted because of the express command of God against idolaters who had seduced the Israelites to practice their abominations, it was a religious war, and fully justified. The destruction inflicted upon the Midianites appears to have been only partial, being limited to those who were in the neighborhood of the Hebrew camp and who had been accomplices in the evil plot of Baal-peor.

PHINEHAS SENT

> *"And Moses sent them to the war, a thousand of every tribe, them and Phinehas the son of Eleazar the priest, to the war, with the holy instruments, and the trumpets to blow in his hand. And they warred against the Midianites, as the LORD commanded Moses; and they slew all the males"* (Num. 31:6–7).

Since Eleazar was the high priest, why was his son Phinehas sent, and not he? The answer is simple. You will remember when we discussed the red heifer in dealing with Numbers 19, a law of purification was passed for those who had come in contact with a dead body. They were to be sprinkled with the water of separation on the third day, and then again on the seventh day, in order to become ceremonially undefiled, so that they could enter the camp of Israel. If Eleazar had gone to war with the 12,000 men, upon returning, he would have not been able to function as Israel's high priest for at least seven days. Such a thing would never do! Thank God, we have a Great High Priest, Who can never be defiled, and Who will never cease to function.

TWO TRUMPETS

Accompanying Phinehas were the holy instruments and in his hand the two trumpets to blow. Scripture does not relate to us what the holy instruments were. They certainly were not the Urim and Thummin, which were worn only by the high priest. Perhaps the Ark may have been included in the expression, "the holy instruments," but where Scripture is silent, it would only be conjecture to name what we feel was taken by Phinehas into the battle. One thing we do know, the presence of the LORD was with them. The army could have been much larger, but God designed it so that they were in total dependence upon Him for a victory. They would never be able to exclaim that their might wrought a wonderful victory. Ah no, there was no room for bragging, for the battle was God's. Can we not claim the same when engaged in warfare against all the powers of darkness, and preaching the gospel? When souls are saved, do we give ourselves the credit? I should certainly hope not! No! The godly warrior meekly gives God all the credit for the victory, and rightly so! God help the man that says, "I saw so many saved here and so many saved there." What imbecility to have a mind geared like that! The truth of the matter is, that a man can preach fervently, scripturally, and forcefully, but if the Spirit of God is not accompanying the message to the unsaved, he will be like sounding brass or a tinkling symbol (1 Cor. 13:1).

The blowing of the trumpets would certainly urge the soldiers on, giving them fresh courage at every step that the LORD was with them in the battle. How wonderful it is to know that while laboring in the gospel, we have One at our right hand encouraging us on, as we fight the foe. Consider a man away from all the fellowship of like-minded saints, walking from door to door, seeking to find souls to come and hear the gospel in some little building that he has rented. Perhaps insulted by some, smiled on by others, and welcomed by a few, he works daily in the battle. His meals are purchased in some eating-place, and he dwells alone in a little rented room, with his wife and family many miles distant. Why doesn't he fall? Why doesn't he throw up his hands in despair, and say, "What's the use?" I will tell you why my friend. It is because he realizes that the Lord is at his side, and he is fighting the Lord's battles. The fact that he is fulfilling the great commission: *"Go ye into all the world, and preach the gospel to every creature"* (Mark 16:15), brings joy to his soul.

We are not told who was the human commander of Israel's army. It may have been Joshua, for one can see no reason, with the position he was then occupying, why he should be staying with the stuff at home. In the invasion of the enemy, their cities and homes were destroyed by fire. The Israelites plundered all the enemy's cattle, flocks, and goods. Nothing was spared, the devastation was total.

MEETING THE VICTORS

Coming forth out of the camp to meet and congratulate the victors were Moses, Eleazar, and all the princes of the congregation. Since the soldiers had become polluted by slaying victims, and touching dead bodies, they would have to undergo the week-long process of purification before being allowed to enter the camp. Thus, the congratulating party meet them outside the camp. However, as soon as Moses saw the captives, and realized that the army had failed in carrying out the whole word of God, he was wroth with the officers of the host, being the captains over thousands, and captains over hundreds. Even though victorious, the army had failed, and it was the army's leaders that were to blame. Bring this to today's circumstances. When an assembly fails, or when an assembly drifts from the truth, who is to blame? Why the elders of course! It is they who shall give an account of the condition of the flock when they stand before the Judgment Seat of Christ. Theirs is the responsibility to maintain the divine pattern laid out for the church of God, of which they rule.

MOSES' RIGHTEOUS ANGER

Moses, the meek man, was filled with holy indignation because the Lord's honor was at stake. The sparing of the females, instead of putting them to death, occasioned his righteous anger. These non-virgin women in all probability were the very women that were immorally active in the iniquity of Peor. If spared, there would be the grave danger that they would spread their snares again, defile the men of Israel and bring them down in disgrace to the dust. Not only that, there was the danger that their little sons, upon growing up, would vent themselves against Israel. They too, must be destroyed. Only the virgins, who were female children and ladies, were to be spared and incorporated into the nation of Israel. Israel's receiving of them was a mercy. These girls would be distributed throughout the households of the children of Israel, and rapidly absorbed into their way of life, having no natural parents to influence them. Consequently, their prospects of a brighter and better future were far greater than if they had been allowed to remain in the ruined villages of the Midianites. Perhaps many of them came to trust under the wings of Jehovah as a result of this, and if so, we shall meet them in the sweet bye and bye, on that heavenly shore.

I look upon the slaying of the little male children as a mercy, and for this reason. These little ones did not know their right hand from their left, thus, when slain, their souls would find their place in the realm of comfort, where Moses would soon be, to await the resurrection of the just. It is horrible to think of the millions of abortions of unborn infants in our land. Nevertheless, there is a silver lining to this dark cloud, and it is that these little ones are Christ's, and they will be in heaven with us for eternity. God had little Midianite children destined for the glory, consequently, they were slain as babes. *"O the depth of the riches both of the wisdom and knowledge of God! How unsearchable are His judgments, and His ways past finding out!"* (Rom. 11:33).

In the war, the army of Israel took 32,000 female prisoners, 61,000 asses, 72,000 beeves (beef cattle, or an animal of the ox family), 675,000 sheep and small cattle; besides the large number of males who fell in battle, and the women and children who were slain. Then, the officers said unto Moses; *"Thy servants have taken the sum of the men of war which are under our charge, and there lacketh not one man of us"* (Num. 31:49). Utterly amazing! The warriors entering an "extreme danger" zone had Divine life insurance! Not one man lost his life!

DIVIDING THE SPOIL

Following the return and ceremonial cleansing of the army, the Law of the Division of the Spoil comes into being.

> *"And the LORD spake unto Moses, saying, Take the sum of the prey that was taken, both of man and of beast, thou, and Eleazar the priest, and the chief fathers of the congregation: And divide the prey into two parts; between them that took the war upon them, who went out to battle, and between all the congregation"* (Num. 31:25–27).

The spoil taken in battle was to be divided between the soldiers, and those who remained in the camp. The amount to be divided was to be in two equal parts, half to the 12,000 soldiers, and half among the rest of the Israelites, because all were concerned in a common cause. Later in Israel's history, David enacted a similar law. *"For who will hearken unto you in this matter? but as his part is that goeth down to the battle, so shall his part be that tarrieth by the stuff: they shall part alike"* (1 Sam. 30:24).

To prevent partiality, the distribution was given over to the heads of the tribes in concert with the high priest. All was holy, and done aboveboard. I have no doubt that when those 12,000 men were out in the thick of the battle, that the folks at home would be engaged in earnest prayer on their behalf. I believe that every man in the camp would have eagerly gone into the battle, but they were not chosen of the LORD, thus, they remained at home. Why should not all have their portion in the spoil?

REALEASING AN EVANGELIST

Bring this to your day, fellow believer. Not every man has been chosen by the Spirit, to leave the assembly and his family, in order to engage in the battles of God in the great harvest field. While you abide by the stuff, safe and secure, do you spend time in earnest prayer for the soldiers of the Cross? How many assemblies have you heard of holding a couple of weeks of prayer meetings for the purpose of praying for all the evangelists out in the harvest field? Would it be too much to expect an assembly to assemble a list of all the preachers known to them, obtain a report of their present activity, and then gather for a couple of weeks to pray for them? Would this be wrong? You know the answer, but you don't see it being done, do you? Are we all in the battle together? We should be! In the day of recompense and reward, we shall part (divide) alike. That is, those who went to the battle, and those who remained at home, supporting the work with their substance and their supplications, shall have their reward.

THEIR OFFERING

Another feature of the division was that they were to levy a tribute unto the LORD. From the soldiers were to be deducted a five hundreth part of every kind of spoil. This was to be an offering unto God in acknowledgment of Him as the rightful Owner of all, and the cause of all their success. It was to be presented as a heave offering to the priests.

In like manner, the children of Israel also were to offer of their spoil. However, there was a difference. They were to offer a fiftieth from each article of the spoil. However, instead of offering to the priests, their portion offered was given to the Levites. There were far more Levites than priests, thus, they received more. What was offered would be used of the Levites for the service of God in the tabernacle of the LORD. Matthew Henry provides a very salient thought on this subject, stating:

> "Whatever we have, God must have his dues out of it. And here (as before) the soldiers are favored above the rest of the congregation, for out of the people's share, God required one in fifty, but out of the soldier's share, only one in 500, because the people got theirs easily, without any peril or fatigue. The less opportunity we have of honoring God with our personal services, the more it is expected we should honor him with our substance."

Even though in this dispensation of grace there has been no levy as a tribute unto the LORD, yet there are exhortations for us to give of our substance. *"Honour the LORD with thy substance, and with the firstfruits of all thine increase"* (Prov. 3:9). Does God honor such exercise? Read the next verse! *"So shall thy barns be filled with plenty, and thy presses shall burst out with new wine"* (Prov. 3:10). Paul relates to this, writing; *"But this I say, He which soweth sparingly shall reap also sparingly; and he which soweth bountifully shall reap also bountifully"* (2 Cor. 9:6). The question arises, how much should I give to the Lord of my substance? Here is the answer; *"Every man according as he purposeth in his heart, so let him give; not grudgingly, or of necessity: for God loveth a cheerful giver"* (2 Cor. 9:7). Whether you give 10% or 50% of your income to the Lord, is strictly your business, it is between you and the Lord. **The true value of any person's sacrifice is not necessarily determined by how much is given, but rather, how much is left for one's self after giving.** Let me illustrate it like this. A millionaire may give $1,000, and have only $999,000 left, while a poor person with only $20 to her name, may give $20, leaving her nothing. Needless to say, the woman left with nothing would be offering the greater sacrifice.

When saints are gathered together for the Lord's Supper and the basket is passed, who puts their money into the basket? Is giving to the Lord limited only to husbands, maidens, and bachelors? Are wives excluded? Not at all! Notice the wording in 1 Corinthians 16:2. *"Upon the first day of the week let **every one** of you lay by him in store, as God hath prospered him, that there be no gatherings when I come"* (2 Cor. 16:2). Notice, **"*every one,*"** not merely every husband. The term is generic, indicating males and females. Wives have the responsibility, and the privilege, to give as well as widows, maidens, and men. The word *"every one of you,"* confirms this. What my wife gives is *her* exercise, not mine, and what I give is *my* exercise, not hers. We are individual priests, ministering to the Lord. I do not partake of the bread and cup for her, neither does she partake of the bread and cup for me. Let us be intelligent in the matter of giving. The tribute was levied, and the people gave accordingly.

As this chapter draws to a close, we find the officers of the army saying to Moses: *"We have therefore brought an oblation for the LORD, what every man hath gotten, of jewels of gold, chains, and bracelets, rings, earrings, and tablets, to make an atonement for our souls before the LORD"* (Num. 31:50). The officers brought their oblation to express their gratitude to God for His marvelous protection for all of their fighting men, for the spoil they had received, and for an atonement (or an amend) for their error in sparing those who should have been slain in the battle. Moses accepted their offering, and laid it up in the tabernacle as a *"memorial for the children of Israel before the LORD."* It was placed there as a monument of God's goodness to them. This would give them confidence to trust the LORD in future battles, being ever-reminded of His favors bestowed upon them in their battle with the Midianites.

Their giving of these precious spoils would enrich the tabernacle. As the soldiers of the Cross engage in the battles of God today, one view is to see souls saved, but also, there should be the desire that upon seeing souls saved, that they be incorporated into the testimony, thus enriching it. Consequently, the evangelist must be prepared to teach his converts the right ways of God, so that they will respond to his teachings and be baptized, and gathered outside the camp, unto His name.

MIDIAN – THE FLESH

Before closing this chapter, I want to draw an analogy, and liken Midian to the flesh that so plagues the Christian. Midian's attack, prior to the war, was subtle. It was unprovoked, crafty, and very successful, bringing thousands of Israel's men down to infamy in the dust. Because of their misbehavior, the plague slew 24,000 foolish men. Can you picture such devastation in the camp of Israel? Corpses lying everywhere, women weeping, and men solemnly digging graves everywhere. Oh the horror of it! Oh the sadness of it! Those men had journeyed through the wilderness all those years, awaiting the day when they would enter into the good land, that large land, that land flowing with milk and honey. But now, all their prospects are lost, all over a moment's licentious pleasure. The folly of it all is immeasurable!

Brethren, there are dangers lurking all around us that are just as subtle, crafty, and dangerous. How the flesh within us would seek to take control. Its approaches can be very subtle at times, and sometimes saints are caught unawares. *"Now the works of the flesh are manifest, which are these; Adultery, fornication, uncleanness, lasciviousness, idolatry, witchcraft, hatred, variance, emulations, wrath, strife, seditions, heresies, envyings, murders, drunkenness, revellings, and such like"* (Gal. 5:19–21). What a morbid, God-given list! The solemn thing is, that we are capable of such things. When God saved us, He never eradicated the flesh. When Paul considers the flesh within, he cries out, *"O wretched man that I am!"* (Rom. 7:24). Peter warns us; *"Dearly beloved, I beseech you as strangers and pilgrims, abstain from fleshly lusts, which war against the soul"* (2 Pet. 2:11).

Considering these solemn verities, what can be done to defeat this subtle enemy? The answer is found in the Holy Scriptures.

"But put ye on the Lord Jesus Christ, and make not provision for the flesh, to fulfil the lusts thereof" (Rom. 13:14). The Christian's clothing is different from that of the unsaved. He is to be clothed with the graces of Christ. This will protect him from the temptations and assaults of the flesh. It will help him to divert his attention from the yearnings of his corrupt nature, which provide a means for the gratification of the flesh.

"Having therefore these promises, dearly beloved, let us cleanse ourselves from all filthiness of the flesh and spirit, perfecting holiness in the fear of God" (2 Cor. 7:1). One way to cleanse one's self is to keep looking upward. *"And every man that hath this hope in him purifieth himself, even as he is pure"* (1 Jn. 3:3). We find another means of cleansing in Psalm 119:11. "Thy word have I hid in mine heart, that I might not sin against Thee."

This I say then, walk in the Spirit, and ye shall not fulfil the lust of the flesh" (Gal. 5:16). It has been said; "The best way to keep tares out of a bushel is to fill it with wheat." Rightly so. You will notice the text does not say; *"Walk in the Spirit, and ye shall not feel the lust of the flesh."* No, no, it never says that. No matter how godly we walk, as long as we are in the body, we will *feel* the lust of the flesh. However, if we walk in the Spirit, that is, constantly under His control and guidance, we will be preserved from fulfilling the lust of the flesh.

"Balaam also the son of Beor they slew with the sword" (Num. 31:8). It would seem that this soothsayer was not slain in the battle, but fell by way of judicial execution. Rebelling against the convictions of his own conscience, he went down slain to the pit with the uncircumcised. It would seem that this corrupt man, on his dismissal from Balak, set out for his home in Mesopotamia. But somehow, along the way, he remained among the Midianites without traveling farther. His purpose was to provoke them into action by using their women to snare Israel, and then to watch

the effects of his wicked counsel. Thus, in God's sight, he became an object of merited vengeance. Approached by Israeli solders, Balaam received the just reward of his wicked deeds. His desire was to die the death of the righteous, but instead, he died the death of the uncircumcised, and perished in his sins.

Brethren, we have a subtle foe that incites the flesh in us, but take courage in these words: *"I would have you wise unto that which is good, and simple concerning evil. And the God of peace shall bruise Satan under your feet shortly. The grace of our Lord Jesus Christ be with you. Amen"* (Rom. 16:20).

37

REUBEN AND GAD – COMING SHORT

NUMBERS 32

> *"Now the children of Reuben and the children of Gad had a very great multitude of cattle: and when they saw the land of Jazer, and the land of Gilead, that, behold, the place was a place for cattle; The children of Gad and the children of Reuben came and spake unto Moses, and to Eleazar the priest, and unto the princes of the congregation, saying, Ataroth, and Dibon, and Jazer, and Nimrah, and Heshbon, and Elealeh, and Shebam, and Nebo, and Beon, Even the country which the LORD smote before the congregation of Israel, is a land for cattle, and thy servants have cattle: Wherefore, said they, if we have found grace in thy sight, let this land be given unto thy servants for a possession, and bring us not over Jordan"* (Num. 32:1–5).

Before entering the request of the tribes of Reuben and Gad, let me bring before you just what entering the Land of Canaan implies. Taking possession of the Promised Land is a picture of a child of God taking possession of all the privileges and blessings that have come to him by way of the Cross. It is the thought of progress in the things of God, coupled with sacrifice resulting from obedience to the Lord. We are not our own, therefore, we are to *"glorify God in our body, and in our spirit, which are God's"*

(1 Cor. 6:20). We rejoice like Paul, and say; *"Blessed be the God and Father of our Lord Jesus Christ, Who hath blessed us with all spiritual blessings in heavenly places in Christ"* (Eph. 1:3). Our Great High Priest, our citizenship, our treasures, our affections, our blessed hope, and our inheritance, are all in heaven. Have we laid hold upon those truths? Are we living in the enjoyment of them? Are we witnessing it to a gloomy world? If so, you are living in the spiritual Canaan of God!

Now then, let us come back to earth, and go to the land of Gilead. Ah, what a picturesque place! The whole of this region is now called the Belka. The Bedouins say of it, "Thou canst not find a country like the Belka." It was superior to any part of the country west of the Jordan, possessing a fine climate, and exuberant fertility, even east of the Jordan. It was famous for its rich and extensive pastures, vibrant with luxuriant vegetation.

REUBEN AND GAD

In the camp of Israel, Reuben and Gad were pre-eminently pastoral. These two tribes were under the same standard, thus affording frequent opportunities of conversing. Thus, they united in proclaiming a request that the Belka, so well suited to the habits of a pastoral people, might be assigned to them. They were not interested in crossing Jordan and having God's allotted portion given to them. No, no, it was not a matter of what *God* wanted, it was a matter of what *they* wanted. It appears that two things common in the world induced these tribes to make this choice, namely, *"the lust of the eyes* and the *pride of life"* (1 Jn. 2:16). Such a choice was not of the Father, but of the world.

They thought more of their cattle than their children's "religious" welfare. They knew that the Ark would be going over Jordan with the congregation of Israel, and that God would be setting up His dwelling place on the other side of the river. However, that made no difference with these people. It wasn't a matter of honoring God, and entering into His blessings that concerned them. Their greatest concern was self, and present comfort. They were influenced by their secular interest and advantage to possess an area that was short of the promised Canaan. They were rich and increased with goods, and had need of nothing.

SELF-CENTERED SAINTS

The question arises, just whom do these tribes represent today? Well, they represent a certain class of people that have experienced salvation, but proceed no further in the things of God. In reality, they are selfish, and self-centered. They have used Christ as a fire escape from hell, but have little thought of acknowledging Him as total Lord over every phase of their life. They never seem to go on to perfection. They have never realized that the purposes of God were to be a great rule of life for them. Ah no, they seem to presume that a man is in himself the best judge of his own interests. (This is humanism). Their conception of heaven is vague, and they prove it by their conduct. Their material possessions occupy their mind, and heaven becomes a far off place. They are willing to confess that they are Christians, and saved by His blood, but they are not willing to totally forsake the world for His cause. Their living is less strict because of society or business. They are more interested in seeking their own, not the things that are Jesus Christ's (Phil. 2:21). Their life is moral and commendable as far as society is concerned, but the truth of separation from the world seemingly does not appeal to them. They are half-hearted, lukewarm, self-indulgent, and carnal. They are not interested in linking themselves with a scriptural testimony, let alone gathering on a Lord's Day morning to break bread with fellow believers. Oh no, that is not in their agenda. To them, there is more freedom and enjoyment than the spiritual Canaan, which to them appeared more limited, and uninteresting. These are the Reubenites, and the Gadites of our modern day, people that have advanced just far enough to feel free from judgment. They can sing:

> "I lived for myself, for myself alone.
> For myself, and none beside.
> Just as if Jesus had never lived.

And as if He had never died."

Let us remember brethren, all that we possess, essentially comes from the Father of lights. All that we have, we owe to Him. We should then be quite willing, not to live unto ourselves, but unto Him Who died for us and rose again (2 Cor. 5:15).

Little did these tribes realize the potential danger in which they were placing themselves. The Holy Land was separated from all other lands by geographical features, but the territory that Reuben and Gad desired, was totally exposed to a great number of hostile heathen in every direction but the west. Christians that dwell in the land of "coming short," are in greater danger of falling when under attack, than the Christian dwelling in the spiritual Canaan.

It is interesting to also notice, that when the Assyrian captivity took place, this area was overcome and carried away first (2 Kgs. 15:29).

Questioned by Moses, these tribes agreed to leave their little ones, their wives, their flocks, and all their cattle in the cities of Gilead, while every one of their men armed for war went with Israel into Canaan to battle.

ISRAEL'S ENCAMPMENTS

Moses then records all the encampments of Israel during their forty-year sojourn in the wilderness. The children of Israel had pitched their tents no less than 41 times, and the tabernacle had been taken down and set up. Their guidance was solely through the cloudy pillar, which directed their way. In spite of the promises of God to them, and His rich provision and attentive care, they had murmured constantly along the desert pathway. Even before the 38 years of wandering, God stated that they had murmured ten times. They had doubted:

(1) God's ability to preserve at the Red Sea (Ex. 14:11).

(2) **God's goodness** at Marah (Ex. 15:24).

(3) **God's provision** in the Wilderness of Sin (Ex. 16:2).

(4) **God's instructions**, they kept the Manna overnight (Ex. 16:20).

(5) **God's commandments**, they hunted for Manna on the Sabbath (Ex. 16:27).

(6) **God's presence** at Rephidim (Ex. 17:3).

(7) **God's existence**, they made a golden calf at Sinai (Ex. 32:1).

(8) **God's guidance** at Taberah (Num. 11:1).

(9) **God's ability to satisfy**, they lusted after Egypt's food (Num. 11:4).

(10) **God's omnipotence** at Paran (Num. 14:2).

After recording the various encampments of the children of Israel, the LORD instructed Moses to address the nation concerning their attitude to the inhabitants of Canaan.[90] They were told to drive them out and destroy everything pertaining to idolatry. Then they were informed about the dividing of the land among the tribes, and giving to the Levites their inheritance. Their inheritance was cities and their suburbs that were designated for their cattle.

THE DEATH PENALITY

Cities of refuge were to be appointed once they conquered the land, providing shelter for the manslayer that would kill any person unawares. They were warned to take no satisfaction for the life of a murderer which was guilty of death. He was to

---

90 From Numbers 33:50, to Numbers 36:13.

be "surely put to death." Failure to do so would defile the land. They were informed that the land could not be cleansed of the blood shed therein, but by the blood of him that shed it. Thus, the death penalty was firmly established. In fact in Numbers 35, the murderer and the death penalty are mentioned five times! Compare verses 16, 17, 18, 21, and 31.

The first indication of a death penalty is found in Genesis 9:6, during Noah's day. *"Whoso sheddeth man's blood, by man shall his blood be shed: for in the image of God made He man."* We find the same requirement in Moses' day. *"He that smiteth a man, so that he die, shall be surely put to death"* (Ex. 21:12). *"He that killeth a man shall surely be put to death"* (Lev. 24:17). In our modern and sophisticated day, men have reasoned this law practically out of existence, consequently, many nations are defiled with blood. The death penalty has proven to be a strong deterrent against murder. It cannot be denied that governments who strictly hold to the death penalty have a lower crime rate than governments that allow the murderer to live. One thing for certain, if a murderer is put to death, he will never be able to go out and murder again. This is often the case when a cold-blooded murderer is given a parole. However, that is not the main reason for enacting the death penalty. The main reason is that God must be satisfied for the death of a murderer. It is required by Him, because in His image made He man.

> "The man accused of the crime of murder; of this crime he is guilty or he is not: if he be guilty of murder he should die; if not, let him be punished according to the demerit of his crime. Taking away the life of another is the highest offense that can be committed against the individual, and against society; and the highest punishment that a man can suffer for such a crime is the loss of his own life. As punishment should be ever proportioned to crimes, so the *highest punishment* due to the *highest crime* should not be inflicted for a *minor offense*. The law of God and the eternal dictates of reason say, that if a man kill another,

the loss of his own life is at once the highest penalty he can pay, and an equivalent for his offense as far as civil society is concerned."[91]

"Willful murderers must be put to death. This is the sin which is here designed to be restrained by the terror of punishment. (1) God will punish murderers: *At the hand of every man's brother will I require the life of man,* that is, 'I will avenge the blood of the murdered upon the murderer.' (Compare 2 Chron. 24:22). When God requires the life of a man at the hand of him that took it away unjustly, the murderer cannot render that, and therefore must render his own in lieu of it, which is the only way left of making restitution. Note, The righteous God will certainly make inquisition for blood, though men cannot or do not. One time or other, in this world or in the next, he will both discover concealed murders, which are hidden from man's eye, and punish those which are too great for man's hand. The magistrate must punish murderers: *Whoso sheddeth man's blood,* whether upon a sudden provocation or having premeditated it (for rash anger is heart-murder as well as malice prepense), (Matt. 5:21–22), *by man shall his blood be shed,* that is, by the magistrate, or whoever is appointed or allowed to be the avenger of blood. There are those who are ministers of God for this purpose, to be a protection to the innocent, by being a terror to the malicious and evildoers, and they must not *bear the sword in vain,* (Rom. 13:4). Before the flood, as it would seem by the story of Cain, God took the punishment of murder into his own hands; but now he committed this judgment to men, to masters of families at first, and afterwards to the heads of countries, who ought to be faithful to

---

91 Clark. Macintosh Computer Mac OS X Software.

the trust reposed in them. Note, willful murder ought always to be punished with death. It is a sin which the Lord would not pardon in a prince (2 Kgs. 24:3–4), and which therefore a prince should not pardon in a subject. To this law there is a reason annexed: *For in the image of God made He man* at first. Man is a creature dear to his Creator, and therefore ought to be so to us. God put honour upon him. Let not us then put contempt upon him. Such remains of God's image are still even upon fallen man as that he who unjustly kills a man defaces the image of God and does dishonour to him. God allowed men to kill their beasts, yet he forbade them to kill their slaves; for these are of a much more noble and excellent nature, not only God's creatures, but His image (Jas. 3:9). All men have something of the image of God upon them; but magistrates have, besides, the image of His power, and the saints the image of His holiness, and therefore those who shed the blood of princes or saints incur a double guilt." [92]

The USA was founded by God-fearing men. Those men carried out the death penalty. However, this nation is now filled with self-esteeming, obnoxious, and godless liberals, who think that they know more than God. In many North American states, they have succeeded in abolishing the death penalty. Consequently, millions of dollars, supplied by taxpayers, is diverted to the building of fancy prisons, in hope of rehabilitating murderers that should have been put to death. The cost of housing these murderers is phenomenal, and you, the taxpayer, are footing the enormous bill. To sum the whole affair up, all that can be said is – this country is defiled by blood!

Let me relate a tragedy that took place in our city lately.

---

92   Matthew Henry. Macintosh Computer MacSword OS X software.

An individual spent time in prison for murder, and then, after serving his time, was released into society. He married a young woman, and three days later entered into her sister's house and brutally shot his wife to death. He also shot and killed her sister, and the sister's little twin sons, and her little daughter. He also shot her nine-year-old son, but he survived. Five innocent people were needlessly ushered into eternity. Consider this. If God's law regarding murder, *"the murderer shall surely be put to death"* (Num. 35:17), had been carried out the first time, five innocent people would still be alive today. But no, our court system seems to know more than God, allowing murderers to prowl the streets, after serving time, to murder more people. Again I repeat, our land is defiled with blood!

DEUTERONOMY – INSIDE THE LAND

The first four books of the Bible present to us the history of Israel *outside* of the land. The following eight books give us Israel's history *inside* the land. It is good to see this, for then we can hold the Book of Deuteronomy in its right perspective. Since this statement may seem strange to you, allow me to show you why I believe this to be the case. The answer is found in the way each book commences. The Hebrew word *"ye"* is employed as the first word in Exodus, Leviticus, and Numbers, and is translated, *"and,"* or *"now."* Consequently, Exodus is connected to Genesis by its first word *"ye,"* translated *"now."* Moving on to Leviticus, you find the same first word of that book, *"ye,"* translated, *"and."* So that links Leviticus to the chain of Genesis and Exodus. That is simple to understand, isn't it? Now, look at the first word in the book of Numbers. What is it? Why it is the same little word *"ye,"* translated, *"and."* So by this we see that Genesis, Exodus, Leviticus, and Numbers are all chained together.

Now, step into Deuteronomy and what do you find? Do you find the first word to be *"ye"* like the four previous books? Not at all! Instead, you read these words: ***"These** be the words which Moses spake unto all Israel on this side Jordan in the wilderness."* So you can readily see that the chain is broken, and we are entering a different section altogether. Take the time to look at the first word in the next eight books following Deuteronomy, and you will discover them all "chained" together by the same first word "ye." Sometimes that little word is translated *"and,"* and other times *"now,"* or *"then,"* but they are all the same word, *"ye."* Consequently Joshua is hooked to Deuteronomy; Judges is linked with Joshua; Ruth is welded to Judges; 1 Samuel is joined to Ruth; 2 Samuel is glued to 1 Samuel; 1 Kings is welded to 2 Samuel; 2 Kings is married to 1 Kings; and there the link stops! As said before, we find four books concerning Israel *outside* the land, followed by eight books relative to Israel *inside* the land.

Consequently, the book of Deuteronomy deals with God's people and their behavior in the land of Canaan. Considering this, one major theme runs through Deuteronomy, and that is obedience! God expects it, God demands it, and God deserves it – unwavering obedience! This book is like a sword against the Devil. As you will remember, this is the very book with which the Lord confronted the Devil in the wilderness. Time and again our Lord refuted that wicked one with these words: *"It is written."* All the writings that our Lord referred to were found in Deuteronomy.

Critics claim that this book was written under the reign of Hezekiah, or Manasseh, or Josiah, and some go so far as to say that it was composed after the Babylonian captivity. However, a reading of the gospels shows that the Lord Jesus claims Moses to be the author. At least 54 verses from this book are quoted in the New Testament. The writing is over 3,500 years old, yet relevant to our day, proving that it is divinely inspired.

Deuteronomy opens and immediately gives us the place and date of Moses' final address to the nation on which he had mediated during their forty-year sojourn through a waste-howling wilderness. He is about to leave them, and they, under the leadership of Joshua, will be crossing the Jordan and claiming their inheritance. It is a most searching and sobering occasion. In the Hebrew Bible, this book is given its proper title, *"elleh hadd ba-*

rim," meaning, *"these are the words."* This correct title describes more accurately the content of Deuteronomy. This book must be understood in the context of Israel's past history, and in the assessment of their future history.

The book of Exodus records the redemption of Israel from Egyptian bondage. God became their king, yet they were a nation without a land, and without a constitution. Arriving at Sinai, a constitution for the nation was formed, and the covenant was sealed between the LORD and Israel. On that occasion, Moses was the mediator. Forty years later, a new generation stands near Jordan, ready to pass over. There is compassion and love in the heart of Moses for them. The LORD has informed him that he cannot go in, but being a man of God, we do not detect a bitter spirit whatsoever. Instead, he seeks to instruct and warn the nation relative to the warfare that lay before them. His desire is for them to succeed, thus he addresses the nation, and those parting words of their great leader is what has been recorded in Deuteronomy.

The book is portioned into five distinct addresses by Moses. (1) 1:6 – 4:43. (2) 4:44 – 26:19. (3) 27:1 – 29:1. (4) 29:2 – 30:20. (5) 31:1 – 34:12. Following the introduction, Moses reminds the nation of Horeb, Kadesh-barnea, Mount Seir, Moab and Ammon, and their conquest of Heshbon and Bashan; the allocation of the land east of Jordan; and God's refusal to allow him to enter the land. Chapter four begins with a call for obedience to the Law, showing that it was the foundation of the nation and that they were to take heed to themselves. This was followed by a notice on the cities of refuge.

The second section begins in 4:44, with an announcement of the basic commandments, that they *"may learn them, keep them, and do them."* He mentions God writing these commandments on tables of stone and delivering them unto him. Then, they are exhorted to love the LORD their God, and given instructions concerning the promised land. He mentions their stubbornness, the Ark, God's requirement of them, and then, blessings and cursings.

As chapter 12 opens, we find Moses announcing regulations relating to the sanctuary; the dangers of idolatry; laws concerning various religious practices, the year of release, the sanctification of firstlings, the observance of major feasts, the appointment of officers and judges, various laws relating to transgressions of the covenant, laws concerning the Levites, followed by warnings concerning false prophets. Chapter 19 begins with instructions concerning the cities of refuge, the conduct of war, laws relating to murder, and family affairs. They are told to remember Amalek, and to bring their baskets of first fruits unto the LORD.

Commencing at chapter 27, we come to Moses' third address to the nation. He opens with an exhortation to keep all the commandments, the building of an altar of stones, the uttering of curses upon the disobedient, and the uttering of blessings upon the obedient.

Moses' fourth address begins at 29:2. He reminds the people what God did unto Pharaoh; how they were sustained through their wilderness journey; and an appeal for covenant faithfulness, setting before them life and good, and death and evil.

THE SONG OF MOSES

Finally, his fifth appeal to the nation begins at chapter 31, encouraging them with the fact that the LORD their God will go over before them, and will destroy those nations before them, that they might possess the land. He speaks to Joshua in the sight of all Israel, exhorting him to be strong and of a good courage, assuring Him that the LORD would be with him and would not forsake him. Moses then wrote a song that same day and taught it to the children of Israel. The song is recorded in chapter 32. Let me pull some statements from that song for our benefit.

"He is the Rock, His work is perfect: for all His ways

> *are judgment: a God of truth and without iniquity, just and right is He"* (v. 4).

The Lord is described as a Rock, emphasizing His stability and permanence. This title comes up in verses 15, 18, 30, and 31, and reveals God as the One who formed them and saved them; and the One Who was superior to their enemies. Credit is also given to His character, as the One who is righteous in judgment, without iniquity, just and right. Thus, He is also seen as the Judge of His people. Rabbi Moses ben Maimon, writes that the word *tsur*, which is ordinarily translated *rock*, signifies "*origin, fountain*, and *first cause*." Thus, the text could read, *"He is the first principle, His work is perfect."* Since He is the *cause* of all things, He therefore must be infinitely perfect; and consequently, all His works must be *perfect* in their respective kinds. This verse also declares that God had been true to His covenant, and that even though severe trials had befallen them because of their perverse conduct, yet He remained true to His word. He was now about to fulfill His promise given to the fathers, and to them. Jordan lay before them, and on the other side Canaan!

What a contrast to mere mortal man. The best of man's works are imperfect, but not so with our God. All His works and actions are unblameable, wise, totally righteous, and perfect. He is a God of truth Who cannot be accused of unfaithfulness in any realm.

> *"When the most High divided to the nations their inheritance, when He separated the sons of Adam, He set the bounds of the people according to the number of the children of Israel"* (v. 8).

"When He separated" means that He divided them in their languages and habitations according to their families. He set the bounds, that is, He disposed of the several lands and limits of the people so as to reserve a sufficient place for the great numbers of the people of Israel. Therefore, He so guided the hearts of several people, that the posterity of Canaan, which was accursed of God and devoted to ruin, should be seated in that country which God intended for the children of Israel. Consequently, when the iniquities of those nations were ripe they would be rooted out, and the Israelites would come in their stead. His people: It is no wonder God had so great a regard for this people, for He chose them out of all mankind to be His peculiar portion." [93]

After Noah's flood, in the days of Peleg, the earth was divided among the sons of men, and each family having their own lot where they were to settle, would eventually grow up into a nation. Even back then, God had Israel in His thoughts for designing this good land as Israel's future inheritance. The posterity of Canaan was chosen to be planted there in the meantime, to keep possession until the time would come for Israel to possess it as their inheritance. According to Genesis 9:25, those families were under the curse of Noah, by which they were condemned to servitude and ruin. Thus, Israel was just and honorable in executing judgment upon the inhabitants of Canaan. The fulness of the time had now arrived when Israel should take possession, and as long as they would be obedient to the LORD, the Canaanites would be easily, and effectually, rooted out. Consequently, God set the bounds of that people with a view to the designed number of the children of Israel.

Moses continues to relate how their Rock triumphantly led them out of Egyptian bondage, and brought them into the land of Canaan. Yet in their prosperity, they would kick against Him and make to themselves strange gods, thus provoking Him to anger. The song continues with the threatening of God against the nation. The threatening is heavy:

> "I will heap mischiefs upon them; I will spend Mine arrows upon them. They shall be burnt with hunger, and devoured with burning heat, and with bitter destruction: I will also send the teeth of beasts upon them, with the poison of serpents of the dust. The sword without, and terror within, shall destroy both

---

[93] John Wesley. Mac Sword for Macintosh OS 10h

the young man and the virgin, the suckling also with the man of gray hairs. I said, I would scatter them into corners, I would make the remembrance of them to cease from among men" (Deut. 32: 23–26).

They are reminded of their future in the land. God looked upon them as a sluggish, inconsiderate people, who constantly refused to trust their God. The prophetic notes of Moses' song continue. He would consider them deserving of utter ruin and to be wiped off the face of the earth. Their vine would be like the vine of Sodom. They would be planted as a choice vine, but would become degenerated and be like Sodom. Their principles and practices would be detestable. Their fruits would become loathsome to Him, for they would be bitter.

However, as the song draws to a close, there is a silver lining to the dark cloud. The song ends with these bright words: *"Rejoice, O ye nations, with His people: for He will avenge the blood of His servants, and will render vengeance to His adversaries, and will be merciful unto His land, and to His people"* (Deut. 32:43).

MOSES' FINAL APPEAL

He then makes His final appeal, saying unto them, *"Set your hearts unto all the words which I testify among you this day, which ye shall command your children to observe to do, all the words of this law. For it is not a vain thing for you; because it is your life: and through this thing ye shall prolong your days in the land, whither ye go over Jordan to possess it"* (Deut. 32:46–47).

Times have not changed regarding these two verses. How important the heart is, for out of it are the issues of life. We are enjoined to *"keep it with all diligence"* (Prov. 4:23). The seat of their mind was to be solidly established upon the word of God. Thus, we see the vital importance of daily reading and meditating upon the Word of God. Our failure today, our drift into worldliness, and our lack of discernment and godly judgment can all be traced back to the fact that we have neglected the consistent study of the Book. The subtle thing is, that the drift is so gradual, that we do not seem to notice it.

Not only this, they were commanded to teach their children the Word of God. I heard a two-year old girl quote the whole twenty-third Psalm and the first six verses of Isaiah 53. The three-year old sister did the same. Parents, are you instilling into your children the Holy Scriptures? Their memory is far more retentive than yours. Timothy learned the alphabet from the Holy Writings, because he had a godly mother and grandmother who cared. Do you discuss the Scriptures with your children? When you are called upon by God to punish them with the rod, do you explain to them from the Bible why you are going to spank them? When the late Albert Joyce was going to spank his little boy, he made him kneel at the bed alongside his father, who told the Lord all about what he was going to do, in the presence of his little son. Have you ever tried that? Do you have a daily Bible reading at one of the family meals, with each member reading a couple of verses out loud, until the chapter is completed? Or do you set them in front of a TV to teach them the evil principles of the world? The responsibility of parents is tremendous.

Just before the death of Moses, he blesses the people. How touching this must have been. I would not be surprised to know that there were many tears shed. What a noble man. What a prince among men. He was Israel's mediator, shepherd, leader and true friend, and now his days were about to terminate, and in his last moments, all his energy was spent addressing God's people, to warn, and to encourage them. He writes for them a song, and then blesses them. What a tremendous man!

When all was accomplished, he bid them goodbye. Alone, he walks away from the congregation he so loved. He walked the valley alone with his God. The land of Moab received his precious remains over against Beth-peor. He had spoken to God face to face for over 40 years, and God became his Undertaker in the day of his death. To this day, the location of his grave remains known only to God. God honored him before his brethren at the end of life's journey, and God buried him with all the dignity of a king.

38

JOSHUA AND RAHAB

JOSHUA 1–2

"Now after the death of Moses the servant of the LORD it came to pass, that the LORD spake unto Joshua the son of Nun, Moses' minister, saying, Moses My servant is dead; now therefore arise, go over this Jordan, thou, and all this people, unto the land which I do give to them, even to the children of Israel. Every place that the sole of your foot shall tread upon, that have I given unto you, as I said unto Moses" (Josh. 1:1–3).

Before considering the crossing of Jordan, and the nation setting its foot in the land of promise, I believe it would be well to consider the man chosen to lead this multitude of people into their inheritance. What an important occasion this would be for Israel. Forty years later, a whole generation of people had passed away since leaving Egypt. Only those under twenty years of age when leaving the land of bondage were spared. Consequently, the oldest people would have been sixty years old, except Caleb, Joshua, and the Levites, who were spared from dying in the wilderness because of their faithfulness.

JOSHUA – HIS RECORD

The first exposure of Joshua was in Exodus 17, where he led Israel's forces against Amalek, and was victorious in the battle.

JOSHUA – THE SOLDIER. In Exodus 24:13, we behold him as a minister to Moses, climbing Mount Sinai with him. Moses had confidence in this trustworthy man. ***JOSHUA – THE SERVANT.*** In Numbers 13, we see him with eleven others, entering Canaan on a secret mission, and then bringing back the report to the nation. Only two of the twelve gave a good report, Caleb being one, and Joshua the other. The other ten were plagued with unbelief, causing Israel to wander for 38 more years in the wilderness. ***JOSHUA – THE SPY.*** In Numbers 32:12, tribute is given by Moses to this mighty man as one who had wholly followed the LORD. ***JOSHUA – THE SINGULAR OF HEART.*** In Deuteronomy 34:9, we read that Joshua was full of the Spirit of wisdom. Thomas Newberry puts a capital *"S"* on the word *"spirit,"* and we believe this to be accurate. This would give Joshua the authority needed when he spoke to the people. His words would be wise and weighty, simply because they would be uttered in the power of the Spirit. This was Paul's deep concern when he entered Corinth. *"My speech and my preaching was not with enticing words of man's wisdom, but in demonstration of the Spirit and of power: That your faith should not stand in the wisdom of men, but in the power of God"* (1 Cor. 2:4–5). Solomon said; *"Through wisdom is an house builded; and by understanding it is established"* (Prov. 24:3). Israel was about to enter the land, to make it their permanent home. Wisdom was needed, and God, through the Spirit, supplied their leader with that very quality. ***JOSHUA – THE SPIRITUAL.***

With these credentials, is it any wonder that the LORD put into Moses' heart to choose this man? Let us apply this to men coming up in the assemblies. When the older men pass away, who will carry on? Is it not the responsibility of elders to observe the younger generation coming up, and for them to encourage worthy young men to assume responsibility? Let us compare the four qualities of Joshua and apply them to young men coming up in the ranks of the assembly.

First: Is the young man a successful *soldier*? If Amalek is a picture of the flesh, has that particular young man been successful in subduing the flesh? Is he walking in the Spirit, not fulfilling the lusts of the flesh? (Gal. 5:16). Is he temperate in all things? Is he meek and lowly?

Second: Is the prospective overseer-to-be a man that has been a servant to older men? In other words, has he been willing to take godly advice? Has he a mind to wait on his older brethren? When they seek to instruct him, does he gladly receive their instruction? Or does he have "new" ideas on how to accomplish things? Beware of men with "better" ways. Is he an "old path" brother? Good if he is! Joshua played the part of a servant until promoted to a higher rank. It is refreshing to see young men occupying the place of *servants* in the assembly.

Third: Can it be said of a young man aspiring for leadership in God's assembly, that through searching out, (by spying out) the Word of God, he has the ability to witness to God's people what he has found?

Fourth: Is he a man of a single heart? Does he give a good report, having wholly followed the Lord? Is his ministry scriptural, or is it a lot of "fluff"? Is his word as "good as gold"? I remember on one occasion listening to a young man who was very self confident. He said, "I am going to speak on stress." He read a little verse, but never referred to it in his "lecture." One would think that he was a psychology student by the way that he rambled on and on. No Scripture was explained, and as far as I was concerned, the whole "bushel of words," was nothing more than a lot of palaver (prolonged and idle talk). When he finished, I was distressed, and stressed!

If young men with a Joshua-like character are lacking in any assembly, that assembly is doomed to one of two things – becoming a part of Christendom, or extinction! May the Lord stir us who are older, to pray more fervently for young men who are not interested in sports, entertainment, or worldly foolishness, but are rather men of the Book. We need men who spend much time in prayer, and much time searching their Bibles. It is our only hope of survival.

Fifth: Is the person under consideration for leadership *spiritual?* The spiritual men that I have known in days gone by had faces like lions when it came to defending the truth, but they had hearts like lambs when it came to caring for God's people. Gathering young people together for *a sing* is easy. However, to gather them together for *a supplication meeting,* (getting together just to pray) is more difficult. To educe them *to a "shepherding meeting,"* that is, visiting the sick and shut-in elderly saints, is even more difficult. Let us be serious and honest about this. We hear announcements about young people's sings. How often have you heard an announcement for the young and old to get together to pray? Meetings for a "sing" are announced at some conferences. These are usually held after the last conference meeting on Saturday. Mostly young folks attend. I wonder if the announcement were changed that a "supplication meeting" would be held, instead of a "sing meeting," how many would attend? Since when have you heard of a young brother, or a young married couple, taking a day or an evening, to visit some elderly saints?

PRACTICAL MINISTRY

I remember many years ago a group of young Christians went to a poor elderly sister's humble abode. What did they go for? Well, let me gladly tell you. They hung new curtains and drapes. They painted the walls, and even hung wallpaper in her little living room. They placed a beautiful oval rug on the bare living room floor, and scrubbed and waxed her linoleum in the kitchen. They brought lots of groceries and filled her fridge, and scrubbed the place from "stem to stern." What do you think of that kind of ministry? Well, that really doesn't matter what you think, does it? What matters is, what did the Lord think of it? That answer is in the Bible. *"For God is not unrighteous to forget your work and labour of love, which ye have shewed toward His name, in that ye have ministered to the saints, and do minister"* (Heb. 6:10). That precious time could have been spent on pleasure of various sorts. But no, they were wise young ones, in love with the Lord, and in love with the Lord's saints. What a day of reaping for them that will be, for God is not unrighteous to forget.

JOSHUA – HIS CHARGE

What a word of encouragement given to Joshua by the LORD. *"There shall not any man be able to stand before thee all the days of thy life: as I was with Moses, so I will be with thee: I will not fail thee, nor forsake thee. Be strong and of a good courage: for unto this people shalt thou divide for an inheritance the land, which I sware unto their fathers to give them"* (Josh. 1:5–6). It reminds me of our exhortation; *"If God be for us, who can be against us? ... Nay, in all these things we are more than conquerors through Him that loved us"* (Rom. 8:31, 37).

However, for Joshua, there was a price to pay for the good of this promise. *"Only be thou strong and very courageous, that thou mayest observe to do according to all the law, which Moses My servant commanded thee: turn not from it to the right hand or to the left, that thou mayest prosper whithersoever thou goest"* (Josh. 1:7). This is interesting, for the same principle holds good today. Don't blindly expect the Lord to prosper your way if you are willfully disobedient to His Word. Such thinking is foolishness, to say the least! Joshua was to be courageous to observe the law. The word *"observe"* means *"to look narrowly,"* also, *"to guard and protect."* Did you ever consider that it takes courage to guard and protect the truths of God? Not only this, but to also *DO* them, to carry them out in our lives. That attitude could involve much reproach, not only from the world, but sadly, also from worldly-minded Christians.

He was not to turn to the right hand when accomplishing the will of God. Since the *right hand* denotes power, we consider that to mean that he should not go beyond what the Word of God stated. Such an attitude supports legalism. On the other hand, he should not turn to the left hand. The left hand speaks of weakness. Thus, it was not allowable for Israel's leader to come short of fulfilling the divine precepts. To do so would indicate looseness. It is interesting that among us we have both types of brethren. Some would find fault if a brother had a bit of red in his tie, or a little feather in his hat, or even perhaps a very faint stripe in his shirt. Such critics have turned to the right hand. They are legalists. On the other hand, we have the other extreme. There are brethren that would tear down a proper dress code for an assembly gathering. No dress shirt, no tie, blue jeans if one felt like it, or no coat, just a shirt, or perhaps a sweater. What is the problem? Why they have turned to the left hand, and are slack.

JOSHUA – AND THE BOOK

Joshua was to be a very careful man, not an extremist. How often legal men have driven saints away with their bullishness, which they excuse for "standing for the truth." We have also seen loose men, who hold divine truths very slackly, bring the character of the assembly down to the level of a denomination in Christendom. One can readily see the need for divine wisdom when leading an assembly of God. Turn neither to the right hand, nor to the left.

Joshua was the first man recorded who was called upon to regulate his conduct by the words of a Book. It was to be a lamp to his feet and a light unto his path. With such a lamp and light, he could not possibly miss the way. It is interesting to observe the following exhortation.

> *"This book of the law shall not depart out of thy mouth; but thou shalt meditate therein day and night, that thou mayest observe to do according to all that is written therein: for then thou shalt make thy way prosperous, and then thou shalt have good success. Have not I commanded thee? Be strong and of a good courage; be not afraid, neither be thou dismayed: for the LORD thy God is with thee whithersoever thou goest"* (Josh. 1:8–9).

What does it mean that the book of the law should not depart out of Joshua's mouth? Perhaps the answer could be found in the following verse. *"For out of the abundance of the heart the mouth speaketh"* (Matt. 12:34). *"As a man thinketh in his heart, so is he"* (Prov. 23:7). The mouth reveals what is in the heart. Through meditation on the law, Joshua's heart was to be filled with the Scriptures, and if that would be so, then naturally, his mouth would speak what filled his heart.

One might say, "You mean to tell me that this mighty man, commanding a host of warriors, and going into a full scale battle, is to stop and take time to read the law and meditate upon it on a daily basis? Where would he ever find the time to do such a thing?" My first answer is, yes, if he expected to be successful in his endeavour as a soldier. Second, no, he wouldn't be able to *find* the time, he must *take* the time. It was vital, it was absolutely necessary, if he were to be prosperous and have good success.

Now let me say this. It is not enough to admire the Bible and to fill one's head with the root meaning of Hebrew and Greek words, and their tenses and so on. That is all well and good, but that is not the paramount thing in one's association with the Bible. No, no! There is something more vital than being an expert in Hebrew and Greek, and a dissector of words and phrases. The prime thing is to *obey* what one reads! That is the all-important thing! *"Do!"* Do what? *"DO according to ALL that is written therein."* Not 10%. Not 50%. Not even 99%. No, God says 100%! Are you prepared to implicitly obey ALL the Word of God, no matter how much it may cost you? If not, then forget about God marching with you to spiritual success. Saul was reminded by Samuel, that to obey was better than sacrifice, and to hearken than the fat of rams (1 Sam. 15:22). That same principle remains today.

It is worthy to note that six times Joshua was exhorted to be strong. Twice by Moses (Deut. 31:7, 23); thrice by the Lord (Josh. 1:6–9); and once by Israel (Josh. 1:18). This strength was totally dependent upon his obedience to the Word of God.

ELDERS ENCOURAGING YOUNGER MEN

It is most comforting when the Lord speaks to us words of assurance, encouraging us to be strong. It gives one confidence in his spiritual endeavor. Then again, it is nice to see an older leader of men, exhorting and encouraging younger men that show promise and gift. There is a class of older men, who when a godly young man shows gift in the assembly and seeks to be of a little help, they feel threatened, and actually try to hinder the younger man. This attitude and activity is a very serious thing. We who are older should rejoice when we perceive in a young brother a godly spirit and a God-given ability to give a little word from time to time. Some older brethren who have never applied themselves to the study of the Word, and are ignorant men, feel threatened when a young man can give a good and an acceptable word. Shame on such older men. No, we need to encourage these young, godly men, all that we can, for after all, they will be the ones carrying on the testimony after we are called home. When an older preacher sees an evangelistic gift in a young man, in fellowship with the elders of that man's assembly, he ought to encourage him. If that man eventually enters full-time service in evangelistic work, that older preacher should take him under his wing, introducing him to the saints elsewhere, and having him help him in various gospel series. Leaving my secular work in 1963 to launch out into the great harvest field, there were four older men that took me under their wing. I pay tribute to them; William Warke, George Graham, Oswald MacLeod, and Archie Stewart. We slept in rented rooms, ate in dinky restaurants, and tramped the streets with invitations to come and hear the gospel in a rented building, or a tent. I was glad to play the part of "second fiddle." I did what they said, and took their advice with thankfulness. They taught me much, and what to expect in that type of labor. They took turns taking me with them. They were great men, and I owe much to their private ministry to me, and their skill in the Lord's work.

Some young men today do not want to play the "second fiddle" part. They have their own ideas, and are not about to take advice from an older man. Furthermore, they are more interested in going from conference to conference, and assembly to assembly, where everything is laid at their feet and all expenses are paid. Taking the gospel to new places holds no attraction for them. Renting a room in a boarding house and renting a building in which to preach is out of the question. The lime-light holds a greater attraction than the candlelight. I feel sorry for them, for they are missing one of the most rewarding experiences a man could have, by taking the gospel to the regions beyond. Then too, the Judgment Seat of Christ lies before us all, and I wonder what their loss will be by not fulfilling the great commission of Mark 16:15.

JOSHUA ENCOURAGED

It is most blessed to see the congregation encouraging Joshua to be strong. How wonderful! What tremendous assurance he must have gotten from this three-fold exhortation to be strong. If a young man is worthy, by all means, the whole assembly should be behind him. It is true, there are some young men that need to be restrained. But on the other hand, there are young men that need to be encouraged by all.

If you are a young man and exercised about the Lord's work in the harvest field, and have the confidence of all your brethren, and a mature evangelist wants you to come with him, by all means go! Be willing to be his minister. Be willing to listen to his advice, and be willing to suffer a little hardship for the Lord, and for the gospel's sake. Don't worry about support. You will not have to run to conferences to be supported. Ah no, just do the Lord's bidding, and even though you may be out of sight for months at a time, let me assure you that you will not be out of mind, for *"the eyes of the LORD are in every place, beholding the evil and the good"* (Prov. 15:3). He will meet not only all of your need, but many of your wants beside.

When comparing verses 6, 7, and 9, you will see that verse 7 says, *"very courageous,"* while verses 6 and 9 just say, *"courageous."* The thought is, that it would take Joshua more courage to observe to do all the law, than to divide the land and fight the battles. The fact that Joshua was encouraged to be strong and of good courage, may be an indication that he felt himself weak for this tremendous task of leading a nation of over 2,500,000 people in the Promised Land. Thus the exhortation, *"be strong."* He may have been affrighted at the very thought of it, thus the assured word, *"be of good courage."* He was told to not be dismayed. The force of that word is *"to be terrified and break down."* Perhaps he feared that he would not be able to finish this great work being laid to his hand.

JOSHUA – GOD'S CHOICE

It is so good to see a powerful man void of self-confidence. Joshua was no boaster, nor was he proud of any former achievements. I believe that this noble man felt in himself his total inadequacy to fill this great commission being placed upon him. Did Moses have Joshua in mind for the task? I wonder. In fact, Moses really didn't know whom the Lord would pick for the position of leadership, for in Numbers 27:15–21 we read:

> "And Moses spake unto the LORD, saying, Let the LORD, the God of the spirits of all flesh, set a man over the congregation, which may go out before them, and which may go in before them, and which may lead them out, and which may bring them in; that the congregation of the LORD be not as sheep which have no shepherd. And the LORD said unto Moses, Take thee Joshua the son of Nun, a man in whom is the spirit, and lay thine hand upon him; And set him before Eleazar the priest, and before all the congregation; and give him a charge in their sight. And thou shalt put some of thine honour upon him, that all the congregation of the children of Israel may be obedient. And he shall stand before Eleazar the priest, who shall ask counsel for him after the judgment of Urim before the LORD: at his word shall they go out, and at his word they shall come in, both he, and all the children of Israel with him, even all the congregation. And Moses

did as the LORD commanded him: and he took Joshua, and set him before Eleazar the priest, and before all the congregation: And he laid his hands upon him, and gave him a charge, as the LORD commanded by the hand of Moses."

Thus, Moses had the divine assurance from the LORD Himself, that Joshua was the man of God's choice. Joshua had well proven himself before the call of God to the work of Israel's commander in chief. Time has not changed this concept when it comes to men being called to a responsible position. How are elders to know when God has called another man to join them in the work of overseeing an assembly? They can only know by having observed the man's past achievements for God. Has he manifested a shepherd care for the saints? Has he manifested an aptness to teach? If he has children, are they under control. Are the qualifications listed in 1 Timothy 3, seen in him? Does he have a desire to take on the responsibility of overseership? These are the vitals overseers must consider before accepting a man into their governing body.

It is the same when releasing a man from the assembly's responsibilities, to enter into the harvest field to preach the gospel. I would find it very difficult to commend a man who couldn't hold a job; or a man that was not respected in his place of employment; or a man that loved to preach for attention's sake; or a man that had little desire to pioneer with the gospel; or even a man that had never won a soul to Christ. A sensible oversight would hardly allow a man with these faults to enter the great harvest field as a full-time worker.

The work Joshua was being called to was no easy task. The inhabitants of Canaan were well versed in warfare. They had gained their position by soldiery, and would be well prepared to fight for every foot of territory by the most effective methods of warfare. Israel was comparatively an infant nation, and the nations that they were going to fight were hardened and mature. Little wonder that Joshua felt his own impotence, facing such a formidable foe. However, bringing God into the situation changed everything! Joshua was given the assurance that the foe would literally melt away before them, since the Almighty would be going before them to conquer the foe.

Is the battle of God dangerous today? Is the evangelist warring against a dangerous and powerful foe? Yes he is! I am not advocating that a preacher wantonly position himself in a place of danger. Not at all! We are called upon to use common sense. On the other hand, there are times when a pioneer of the gospel finds himself in a place of extreme danger due to unforeseen circumstances. Notice, I said a *pioneer* of the gospel, not a gentleman preacher, who only preaches in established churches, and is well taken care of by the saints. The pioneer moves out in faith to regions where he is not known. And what does he find? Sometimes he finds enemies and opposition. The opposition can be subtle, or it can become physically violent. In such situations, what is the pioneers resource? What is his strength? What is his protection? Why, it is the Lord, of course! Many men of such caliber can exclaim like David: *"In my distress I cried unto the LORD, and He heard me"* (Ps. 120:1). God's voice rang in Joshua's heart; *"The LORD thy God is with thee whithersoever thou goest"* (Josh. 1:9).

RAHAB'S FAITH

While encamped in Shittim (approximately 8 or 10 miles from the Jordan River) Joshua sent out two spies to view the land, even Jericho. How they crossed the Jordan we are not told. Their spying mission was a success. It also proved a blessing to a Gentile named Rahab, for by faith she received the spies, and hid them from the enemy, thus, as James writes, she *was "justified by works"* (Jas. 2:25).

If the spies had never been sent, she wouldn't have had the opportunity to manifest her faith. Whether she was saved before, or upon their coming, is not the issue. What a wondrous confession from the lips of this woman to the messengers. *"I know that the LORD hath given you the land ... for the LORD your God, He is God in heaven above, and in earth beneath"* (Josh. 2:9, 11).

JOSHUA AND RAHAB

The terror of Israel had fallen upon the inhabitants of the land, and they were faint. They recognized that God was with Israel. Their hearts did melt, neither did there remain any courage in any man. Can you see how God was working? This woman recognized the power of Israel's God, and that God was in them of a truth. Thus, with her self-confidence gone, and a melted heart, she trusted in the living God of Israel. Her reputation certainly wasn't the best, but God had mercy on this dear woman and saved her. Not only this, she was a vital instrument in the hand of God to save her family. How amazing is the grace of God!

Her conversion runs parallel to what we have today in the salvation of a soul. While in their sins, having heard of the penalty for sin, the wrath of God, and their ultimate doom, the sinner's heart melts within, as terror grips his soul. This is termed, "conviction of sin." Apart from this process, there can be no salvation. That is why it is imperative that preachers warn sinners of their sins, and coming hell fire.

> "When first, o'erwhelmed with sin and shame,
> To Jesus Cross I trembling came,
> Burdened with guilt, and full of fear,
> Yet drawn by love to venture near,
> Pardon I found, and peace with God,
> In Jesus' rich atoning blood." [94]

Rahab was a woman like the Gentiles in Ephesus; *"Ye were without Christ, being aliens from the commonwealth of Israel, and strangers from the covenants of promise, having no hope, and without God in the world"* (Eph. 2:12). She was perhaps worse than the Samaritan woman in John 4, of whom it was said; *"Thou hast had five husbands; and he whom thou now hast is not thy husband"* (John 4:18). She would relate to some of the Corinthians, who were classified as fornicators, idolaters, and adulterers, before they were saved. What grace! What mercy! So rich, abounding, and free!

---

94 James G. Deck. The Believer's Hymn Book, P. 274. John Ritchie Ltd.

This woman was low, but the God of Israel reached down with His mighty hand, and delivered her from the pit of depravity and sin, and placed her feet firmly on redemption ground. The Samaritan woman at Jacob's well, the Corinthians, and the Ephesians, all experienced the same. Most reading this book were not perhaps as immoral as the folks just mentioned. However, like they, we were strangers from the covenants of promise, without Christ, without God, and having no hope in this world. It is wonderful that God in His matchless grace went over the Jewish wall, and with His mighty and loving hand, plucked us as brands fit only for the burning.

> "Grace it was, yea, grace abounding,
> Brought Thee down to save the lost;
> Ye above, His thone surrounding,
> Praise Him, praise Him all His host:
> Saints! Adore Him!
> Ye are they who owe Him most." [95]

She was not saved through the preaching of the spies, for we never read of them witnessing to her. Ah no, it was the other way around, she witnessed to them! It is wonderful to see the providence of God working in her case. For years she had been "listening to the news." Those "news reports" included Israel's movements and God working on their behalf. It was through this that she put her faith in the God of Israel, and her faith was proven by her works in receiving the spies and witnessing to them.

Just think that this stranger to grace and to God was brought into the kingly family and genealogically linked to Christ! Amazing! Her name is spelled "Rachab," in Matthew 1:5. We too, even though most of us Gentiles, have been incorporated into the royal family, and our blessed Lord, Who is King of kings, is not ashamed to call us brethren (Heb. 2:11).

---

[95] Thomas Kelly. <u>The Believer's Hymn Book,</u> P. 200. John Ritchie Ltd.

JOSHUA'S REPORT

Upon returning to Joshua, the spies gave a good report, assuring their commander with these words. *"Truly the LORD hath delivered into our hands all the land; for even all the inhabitants of the country do faint because of us"* (Josh. 2:24). I wonder how well Joshua slept that night? It was early in the morning when he rose. The silver trumpets would sound, and over two and one half million people would break camp, and begin their last march outside the land. The Jordan River lay about ten miles to the east. It was that time of the year when Jordan was swollen by the spring floods. Normally, ninety feet wide and four to six feet deep, this sharply descending river at Israel's crossing time was a raging torrent of water one mile wide. Nobody but a fool would venture into such a torrent of turbulent, rushing water. But wait! If God directs a man to do something contrary to all nature and he obeys, what is he? He is certainly not a fool. Oh no! He is a man of faith. Israel's faith is radiant at this time. There is no murmuring, no weeping of unbelief. Ah no, that generation had passed away, and on the banks of Jordan stands a new generation that is willing to trust God, and eager to vanquish the foe. This army of men would be fulfilling the will of God in performing massacres. The question arises in the hearts of many – is it right to deliberately murder helpless, innocent men, women, and their children? Under certain conditions, certainly! If God commanded it so, how could it be wrong? Let me explain the situation, and why God called upon Israel to inflict such cruel punishment upon the inhabitants of Canaan.

When God spoke to Abraham regarding Israel's time to enter the land, He said that it would not take place until the iniquity of the Amorites was full (Gen. 15:16). That time had now arrived, and the Amorites were to be brought down because of their iniquity. The nations in Canaan had abandoned all decency, and had sunk into the most loathsome immorality. Not only this, they were saturated in spiritualism. Their worship of idols had brought them into familiar contact with the demon world. The land was full of enchanters, sorcerers, wizards, and necromancers. Israel was solemnly warned against these occult practices.

> *"When thou art come into the land which the LORD thy God giveth thee, thou shalt not learn to do after the abominations of those nations. There shall not be found among you any one that maketh his son or his daughter to pass through the fire, or that useth divination, or an observer of times, or an enchanter, or a witch, or a charmer, or a consulter with familiar spirits, or a wizard, or a necromancer. For all that do these things are an abomination unto the LORD: and because of these abominations the LORD thy God doth drive them out from before thee. Thou shalt be perfect with the LORD thy God. For these nations, which thou shalt possess, hearkened unto observers of times, and unto diviners: but as for thee, the LORD thy God hath not suffered thee so to do"* (Deut. 18:9–14).

Israel, in driving out and destroying these corrupt nations, were only the weapons in the hand of God, in His holy war against the demon world. This conflict was really against principalities and powers, against all the host of demons in the heavenly places. When Paul preached the gospel, we have the same connection. Notice what he says. *"We wrestle not against flesh and blood, but against principalities, against powers, against the rulers of the darkness of this world, against spiritual wickedness in high places"* (Eph. 6:12). It is very interesting to note that just prior to this statement, he exhorts the Ephesian believers in the same manner as Moses exhorted Joshua. *"My brethren, be strong in the Lord, and in the power of his might. Put on the whole armour of God, that ye may be able to stand against the wiles of the devil"* (Eph. 6:10–11).

Seven years of war lay ahead for Israel, and then the promised rest would be theirs to enjoy, in full fellowship with their God. There is a distinct analogy between the Book of Joshua, and the Epistle to the Ephesians. It is good to remember Paul's words when he spoke of Israel's wilderness experiences. *"Now all these things happened unto them for ensamples: and they are writ-*

ten for our admonition, upon whom the ends of the world are come" (1 Cor. 10:11). In other words, the experiences of Israel in Old Testament times, gives us a set of applicable rules, or behavior designs, for New Testament times. This immediately leads us to Hebrews, chapters three and four, where we find the first generation of Israel failing to enter into God's rest, and the Hebrews of Paul's day exhorted to enter into the present rest that God had provided. He exhorts them to labor to enter into that rest, referring to those not yet saved. For those who were saved, he assures them with these words; *"For we which have believed do enter into rest"* (Heb. 4:3).

THE LAND TODAY

Israel, in possessing the land, faced a battle. Now *the land* today speaks to us of all our spiritual blessings in the heavenlies. However, they are not ours to enjoy until we have claimed them by a living faith. They lie before us, but we must avail ourselves, through warfare, to claim them for ourselves, thus, like Joshua, we need to be strong and very courageous.

What are these spiritual blessings? They are all things that have been provided for us in Christ, to experience and enjoy. We have *salvation*, and will never perish! We have been justified as *righteous* before God, and will never be condemned! We have *redemption*, thus rescued from the powers of darkness! We have been placed before God as His *sons,* and *indwelt* with the Holy Spirit. We have Christ as our Shepherd, Advocate, High Priest, and Bridegroom. We have an inheritance incorruptible, undefiled, and reserved in heaven for us. We have the Holy Scriptures which are a lamp to our feet and a light to our path. Christ is unto us wisdom, so that our intelligence can surpass the normal. We possess divine love and a sound mind. The list could go on and on, but I believe that you can see what a blessed people we are.

Now comes the big question. As a believer, have you entered into these blessings? Are you rejoicing in them? Are they regulating your conduct as a possessor of the land? Are you living in the power of them? Or, to use the language of the Old Testament, have you failed to enter into the Land of Promise? Have you not yet occupied the cities that you have never built? Have you not yet eaten of the olive-yards, and the vineyards that you have never planted? Are you not dwelling in the houses you never built? Have you come short of dwelling in that good land that is wet with the dew of heaven, and bringing forth lush fruits from its rich soil? It is all yours my Christian friend, if only you will go in and possess it! Your full enjoyment of your spiritual blessings is determined by your obedience to God and denial of yourself. That is one of the reasons why the Scriptures have been given to us, that we may know how to possess the good land, and thus enjoy our spiritual blessings.

Neither the religious rites of Rome, nor the Law will never bring a soul into the good land. Good works fail to bring us over Jordan, and reformation still leaves us outside of the good land. Ah, but our blessed Lord has provided a way to cross the turbulent Jordan, and to place our feet into Canaan. Through His blood, every spiritual blessing has been secured for us, if only we go in and possess it! He has hushed the roar of the river, and held it back, allowing us to enter in to the promises of God on dry land. If you have never claimed the land, if you are not enjoying its blessings, I urge you to confess your sin, lay down your self-will, and commit yourself entirely to Him saying, "Not my will, but Thine be done." Having done this, you will begin, my dear Christian, to enjoy your spiritual blessings. Do not be like the tribes of Reuben, Gad, and half the tribe of Manasseh, who had much cattle, and were quite satisfied to dwell outside of the land, in Gilead. They represent brethren who are willing to fight the foe with their brethren, but they are not willing to abandon the strong allurements of the world, and to settle down, separating themselves from the world, to a hidden life of spiritual joy in Christ.

Let me ask you again, have you entered in? Have you taken possession of the land? Are you enjoying your spiritual blessings in Christ. Do they occupy your mind? Do you meditate day and night upon them? Are you living in the joy of them, or do you belong to the tribe of Reuben and Gad, being quite content to know that you are saved and will never be in hell, but still groveling in the muck and mire of this poor world's vain pleasures? Are you a Demas, who started out well, laboring with Paul, but of whom it was said, *"Demas hath forsaken me, having loved this present world, and is departed unto Thessalonica"* (2 Tim. 4:10). Where do you stand today my beloved, in the land of Canaan, or in the land of Gilead? Do the activities of this world fascinate you, or is your joy dependent on spiritual things? What occupies your mind, sports or Scriptures, the world's festivities, or God's spiritual feasts?

> *"But God forbid that I should glory, save in the cross of our Lord Jesus Christ, by whom the world is crucified unto me, and I unto the world"* (Gal. 6:14).

Let us beware of falling short of occupying the spiritual blessings that God has set before us. The world, the flesh, and the devil, constantly seek to rob us of our enjoyment of them.

39

CROSSING JORDAN

JOSHUA 3 – 4

After the spies returned, *"Joshua rose early in the morning; and they removed from Shittim, and came to Jordan, he and all the children of Israel, and lodged there before they passed over"* (Josh. 3:1).

This would afford the congregation quite a sight I am sure! The roaring of the water, and the turbulence seen as the waters swiftly passed by their encampment, on to the Dead Sea, would produce awe in their hearts. They were to cross to the other side. How? They lodged there for three days before receiving their instructions for the following day, thus giving them time to consider before acting.

It is instructing to note that the Scripture plainly states that they lodged *"three days"* before receiving instruction from the officers. The number "three" in Scripture often speaks of *"death, burial, and resurrection."* Our Lord spoke of it that way when mentioning Jonah as a figure of Himself (Matt. 12:40). That is exactly what these people were going to experience in a spiritual sense. Even so we ourselves must be dead with Christ, buried with Christ, and raised to walk in newness of life, [96] ere we can enter into the land to enjoy the spiritual blessings in the heavenlies.

---

96 Romans 6:3–4.

THE ARK OF THE COVENANT

One cannot help but notice the first thing mentioned prior to their crossing was that Ark of the covenant of the LORD their God. Fifty nine references had been made of the Ark in all the writings of Moses, but when we come to Joshua chapters 3 and 4, we find it mentioned 22 times! Of all the vessels of the tabernacle, the Ark was the most perfect expression of Jehovah.

The first thing that they were informed of was that when they saw the Ark being borne by the Levites they were to immediately remove from their place and go after it. Notice first the title given to the Ark on this momentous occasion. It was termed, *"the Ark of the covenant."* This pictures Christ as the Mediator of the new covenant. When it is called, *"the Ark of the testimony,"* that indicates its character in the wilderness. It is never termed this after crossing Jordan. Another description given was, *"the Ark of Jehovah."* This points to the fact is that it is solely in Christ in Whom all the rights of Jehovah are maintained. As Israel followed the solemn procession toward Jordan, God insisted that there be a space between the Ark and the people of about two thousand cubits. That way, those in the rear of the procession would be able to see the Ark being borne, as well as those in the front row. However, the spiritual lesson is that our Mediator was a separated Person in His lifetime. True, He sat and ate with sinners, yet there was something vastly different in His glorious Person. He was harmless, undefiled, and separate from sinners. He did not act like them. He did not talk like them. He did not think like them. There was a distance.

The next injunction was, *"come not near unto it."* If you know the Lord in a personal way, you will admit that there is an intimacy. It is not a mere human intimacy, but rather a divine and reverential intimacy. Let us all be careful to give Him due reverence. In addressing a judge we say, "your honor." In addressing a king we say, "your majesty." A soldier addresses his superiors as "sir." Luke addressed Theophilis, a political dignitary as, "most excellent." I am appalled at some youngsters addressing a much older person by their first name, instead of showing respect and calling them by their last name with Mr. preceding it. Here is an example. Johnny is 10, and Mr. Robert Smith is 50. So here comes little Johnny, and upon seeing Mr. Smith, he hollers out, "hi Bob," instead of saying, "hello Mr. Smith." What does this little boy lack? Two things; teaching and reverence. When I hear Christians addressing the Lord as just "Jesus," or using the pronoun "you," I surmise two things. Either they are ignorant, or they want to prove something. They want to show everybody that they do not respect the teachings of older, godly brethren. They have an "axe to grind," and a point to prove. People with such a spirit, have never entered into the spiritual land of Canaan.

The Ark was to show them the way they must go, a way that they had not passed before (Josh. 3:4). It was to be an entirely new experience for them. It would be a new experience also for the Ark. The Scriptures reveal to us about the Saviour's Cross, that He had never passed that way before? Is it any wonder, when He contemplated Calvary, and the abandoning of His God, that His soul became exceeding heavy, even unto death? See Him prostrate in the garden. Notice His sweat, and what doctor Luke reports. *"And being in an agony He prayed more earnestly: and His sweat was as it were great drops of blood falling down to the ground"* (Luke 22:44).

Some have thought that the meaning of the words is, that the sweat was so profuse that every drop *was as large as a drop of blood*, not that the *sweat* was *blood* itself. However, this does not appear likely. Cases have been reported in which persons in a weakened state of body, or through extreme distress of soul, have had their sweat tinged with blood. Some medical men have testified that there are cases in which, through *mental pressure*, the pores may be so dilated that the blood may issue from them, so that there is a bloody sweat. The medical term for this is *"hematidrosis."* This we believe to be the Saviour's case. He had *"not passed this way heretofore."*

INFLATED CHRISTIANS

During this encounter at Jordan, the LORD spoke to Joshua three times (Josh. 3:7; 4:4; 4:15). Each commenced with a divine command, followed by Joshua speaking to the people, expecting them to obey. God was going to magnify Joshua in the sight of all Israel on that day so that they might know that the LORD was with him, as He was with Moses. A godly man never has to magnify himself. He never promotes himself, nor seeks to look big in the eyes of the people. Have you ever observed inflated Christians? They are sickening, especially if they have a gift. They insist on being number one. They push themselves. They order their lives, through political correctness, to be popular. Away with such hypocrisy! May God give us all grace to be just what we are! No, my dear friends, the godly man will hide and shun popularity as a plague. There is a divine principle that runs through the Word of God, and it is this: *"Whosoever exalteth himself shall be abased; and he that humbleth himself shall be exalted"* (Luke 14:11). If God is pleased to exalt a humble man, let that man thank God, and continue to walk the path of humility before all. Self-exaltation is a principle in the world, but a plague to God's people. Bragging and self-praise are the characteristics of the inflated man. God says, *"Let another man praise thee, and not thine own mouth; a stranger, and not thine own lips"* (Prov. 27:2). This will undoubtedly take place if God magnifies that person.

JOSHUA – HIS ADDRESS

After hearing the voice of God, Joshua addresses the congregation with these assuring words. *"Hereby ye shall know that the living God is among you, and that He will without fail drive out from before you the Canaanites, and the Hittites, and the Hivites, and the Perizzites, and the Girgashites, and the Amorites, and the Jebusites. Behold, the Ark of the covenant of the Lord of all the earth passeth over before you into Jordan"* (Josh. 3:10 –11).

The statement of Joshua is interesting. First of all, he addresses God as "the living God." That particular expression is found 30 times in the Scriptures, this being its second occurrence. The first one is found in Deuteronomy 5:26. Israel was about to invade a land full of dead gods, idols of gold, silver, stone, and wood. Israel's God was far different, He was living! For God, Joshua uses the word *"El."* This signifies *"strong,"* or *"first."* Mr. Newberry informs us that "His attributes are connected generally with the singular name for God, El." Thus, He is portrayed as "the Mighty One, the First Great Cause of all." What a fitting way to present God to the people on this occasion. Joshua is wise in his selection of descriptive titles. Notice also that when he speaks of "the Ark of the covenant of the Lord," that the word is "Lord," not "LORD." The KJV translators, when speaking of Jehovah, put the word *"LORD"* in capital letters, but when the word is *"Adon,"* they wrote it in upper and lower case – *"Lord."* The word Lord (*"Adon"*) is singular, and means *"Sovereign Lord, Master,"* or *"Possessor,"* the root coming from *"to rule, govern,"* or *"to judge."* Israel was to take the land, and their God was to be the *Master* of all operations and the One behind Israel's success in becoming *possessors* of that land.

THE FIRST STEP

Standing at the bank of the river, bearing the Ark of the covenant the priests take their first step into the muddy and rushing waters. Immediately at Adam, upstream about twenty miles, the waters were miraculously blocked by an unseen force. A huge lake must have formed, and the remaining waters rushed downstream with the dry bed of Jordan being revealed. Finally, after an undisclosed time, the waters rushed by the priests, leaving them standing on dry ground! This is absolutely impossible, isn't it? However, with God all things are possible! What a tremendous token to the nation on that occasion of the prevailing power of God on their behalf. I would have liked to have seen their faces as they suddenly were looking at dry ground where a rushing river had just been.

> *"And the priests that bare the Ark of the covenant of the LORD stood firm on dry ground in the midst*

of Jordan, and all the Israelites passed over on dry ground, until all the people were passed clean over Jordan" (Josh. 3:17).

STANDING FIRM

The priests bearing the Ark stood firm in the midst. What a picture of our blessed Lord, crucified in the midst of two thieves, standing, as it were, firm, until all the redeemed from every age passed over to the other side. He never wavered, He never faltered, nor did He fail! Not until the tremendous debt of every single sin of every redeemed soul was entirely paid for, did he shout, *"It is finished,"* meaning, *"paid in full."* The death of Christ, entering the cold waters of death, has paid the price, allowing us entrance into the promised land, that is, the spiritual blessings already discussed. Blessed be His holy Name!

BACK TO ADAM

The fact that the waters were backed up to the city of Adam, presents another spiritual truth. The man named Adam was the first of the human race, and the one that introduced sin into that race. When Christ entered into the judgment waters of God to put away sin, how many sins, and whose sins, were righteously dealt with? Let the Scripture answer. *"He is the propitiation for our sins: and not for ours only, but also for the sins of the whole world"* (1 Jn. 2:2). *"Whom God hath set forth to be a propitiation through faith in His blood, to declare His righteousness for the remission of sins that are past, through the forbearance of God"* (Rom. 3:25). *"The sins that are past"* means, all sins committed *before* Calvary, all the way back to Adam. Thus we see the all-inclusive results of Calvary.

TWELVE STONES SET UP AT GILGAL

With all the people on the Canaan side of Jordan, Joshua is told by the LORD to take twelve stones out of the midst of Jordan where the priests feet stood firm, and to carry them to the place where they were to lodge that night. One man from each tribe was selected for this unusual task. Thus, carrying the stones on their shoulders, when they came to their lodging place, being Gilgal, they were set up as a memorial unto the children of Israel for ever.

OUR CHILDREN

Having established the stones in Gilgal, Joshua spoke to the children of Israel saying: *"When your children shall ask their fathers in time to come, saying, What mean these stones? Then ye shall let your children know, saying, Israel came over this Jordan on dry land. For the LORD your God dried up the waters of Jordan from before you, until ye were passed over, as the LORD your God did to the Red sea, which He dried up from before us, until we were gone over: That all the people of the earth might know the hand of the LORD, that it is mighty: that ye might fear the LORD your God for ever"* (Josh. 4:21–24).

God is interested in children, and so should we be. As the years rolled by, children would be born unto them. Having reached maturity, they would be asking questions, and their parents would be responsible to give them sensible answers. Seeing the stones would spark the curiosity of the children, and at the same time prompt the parents to tell them just why those stones were there. Gilgal was to be the religious center of the nation for years, and as parents came to worship, naturally, they would bring their children, and that is when they would see the stones.

MEMORIALS

Let us come to our day. Do we have memorials? Most certainly we do! The bread and the wine at the Lord's Supper are memorials, they are symbols, and they are tokens of our Lord's body given, and His blood shed. Do we bring our children to view the supper being carried out? Some parents seem to think that little ones disturb the sacred gathering, thus, they keep them at home. Disturb the gathering? Let me tell you of a mother who had twelve children who never disturbed any assembly gathering. When they were babies, she would waken them hours before the Supper, so that when entering the hall, she gave them a bottle, wrapped them in a blanket, and laid them on the floor beside her chair. No problem! They slept through the meeting. When a little older, if they squirmed, if they made a noise, they were taken out and spanked. This woman was consistent, firm, yet loving, and thus, her children never missed a single meeting, nor did they cause any noticeable disturbance. Today, all of those children profess to be saved except two. This woman honored the Lord, and in return the Lord has honored her.

God would have us to instruct our children in the things of God. Do we bring them to the assembly meetings and force them to behave, thus instilling into them reverence? We certainly cannot make them Christians, but we can raise them in such a way that when they do get saved, there won't be much of a change in their lifestyle. The raised stones were to be memorials.

SUBMERGED STONES

Joshua was also commanded to take twelve stones from the dry land, and set them up in the midst of Jordan, in the place where the feet of the priests which bare the Ark of the covenant stood. There they were to be buried out of sight when the waters returned. Notice, when speaking of this, the next thing we read are these informative words: *"For the priests which bare the Ark stood in the midst of Jordan, until everything was finished"* (Josh. 4:10). One cannot but help to think of our Lord's victorious cry on the Cross, *"It is finished!"*

Considering the *standing* stones, and the *submerged* stones, there is a lesson in them for us. Just as the stones were placed in the midst of Jordan, in the place where the feet of the priests which bare the Ark (Christ) stood, so we (the stones) have died with Him. This is exactly what Paul is expounding in Romans 6:3. *"Know ye not, that so many of us as were baptized into Jesus Christ were baptized into His death?"* (Rom. 6:3). Before explaining this verse, let me ask you, when were you baptized *into* Christ? If you answer and say, it was when you were immersed in water, then you are admitting that you never were a member of His body, flesh, and bones until you submitted to the ordinance of water baptism. But that would be false doctrine, would it not? No, that will never do. You became a member of the body of Christ the moment you were saved. At that moment, the Holy Spirit baptized you into the body of Christ, and that is the truth of this verse under consideration. Water is not in the picture whatsoever!

So the stones represent the fact that *"I am crucified with Christ"* (Gal. 2:20). *"For the love of Christ constraineth us; because we thus judge, that if one died for all, then were all dead"* (2 Cor. 5:14). Many commentators state that the words, *"then were all dead,"* refers to the fact that His death proved all men to be dead in their sins. However, the correct interpretation seems to be, as Dean Alford comments: "This death is the result of His death in the believer." Romans 6:8 states *"… we be dead with Christ."* Christ dying is exactly the same as if all believers had died. They had died to sin and self. It is not the thought of being dead *in* one's sins, but rather being dead *to* sin as a master. This is the teaching of Romans 6:11. *"Likewise reckon ye also yourselves to be dead indeed unto sin, but alive unto God through Jesus Christ our Lord"* (Rom. 6:11).

Before passing on to Gilgal, let me make a few more remarks regarding the import of these stones relative to the believer today. Romans 6 is a very challenging chapter, and opens with a question: *"What shall we say then? Shall we continue in sin, that grace may abound?"* In other words, if it is true that the greater my sin, the greater God's grace in dealing with it, then why not sin more to enhance the grace of God? Paul rebukes this false notion, and goes on to show that the believer is dead to sin, and has been linked to a new Master, even to Christ. We have died to sin's reign, power, and rule over us. *"For by one Spirit are we all baptized into one body, whether we be Jews or Gentiles, whether we be bond or free; and have been all made to drink into one Spirit"* (1 Cor. 12:13). We are joined with Him, and are participants in what has happened to Him.

CHRIST DIED UNTO SIN

When He died *unto* sin, so did we. Notice, Paul does not state here that He died *for* sin (which is true), but that *"He died unto sin"* (Rom. 6:10). That is, Christ has no more to do with sin as requiring atonement. He has died in His relationship to it. His life is now lived in a new sphere. We too share this broken relationship with sin. We now live in a new sphere. A new quality of life has been imparted to us. We now walk in newness of life. We have no more to do with the sinful nature. The death of Christ broke the power of indwelling sin in the believer's life. Thus, Peter tells us; *"Forasmuch then as Christ hath suffered for us in the flesh, arm yourselves likewise with the same mind: for he that hath suffered in the flesh hath ceased from sin; That he no longer should live the rest of his time in the flesh to the lusts of men, but to the will of God"* (1 Pet. 4:2). Christ suffering for us in the flesh means His death. Consequently, we are told to arm ourselves with the same mind. In other words, we are to reckon ourselves dead. We are to put to death the body of sin by self-denial and mortification. We have died with Him (2 Tim. 2:11); We are dead with Christ (Col. 2:20). We are crucified with Christ (Gal. 2:20). These are what the stones buried in the depths of Jordan symbolize.

STANDING STONES

The stones taken out of Jordan, and erected in Gilgal symbolize what the believer is essentially. He is on resurrection ground. The judgment of God for sin, now lies behind him. He has been grafted into the likeness of Christ's death, consequently, he now walks in the likeness of His resurrection. Notice, the walk is not identical, but *in the likeness* of His resurrection. The thought is, that just as Christ entered into a different sphere upon being raised, so we too, enter into a different sphere (Rom. 6:5). He also states, *"Now if we be dead with Christ, we believe that we shall also live with Him"* (Rom. 6:8). The word, *"we shall,"* is something subsequent to our death. Thus, it means *now*. However, the full and final sense is yet coming. Paul enlarges on this in Ephesians 2:5–6. *"Even when we were dead in sins, hath quickened us together with Christ, (by grace ye are saved;) And hath raised us up together, and made us sit together in heavenly places in Christ Jesus."* Our walk is in Canaan, taking possession of, and enjoying all the spiritual blessings that we have in the heavenlies in Christ. We have died with Christ, consequently, we are dead unto sin (the submerged stones), and we are alive unto God through Jesus Christ our Lord (the standing stones). That is the truth of Romans 6:11.

THE OLD MAN

In all of these truths, we have the *"old man,"* entering the picture. The question arises, who is he, and what is he? You will notice that the text does not say *"the old nature,"* but rather *"the old man."* Let us not confuse the two, as so many have done. In fact, the term *"old nature"* does not occur even once in the Bible. However, we do have an old nature called *"the flesh."* That nature has never been eradicated from us. It dwells within, constantly waiting to overcome us. Only through the power of the indwelling Holy Spirit can we keep it subdued. When you have an evil thought, that is the flesh. Anything you may foolishly do that is contrary to the teachings of Scripture, is a manifestation of the flesh in action. It would seek to dethrone the supremacy of the Lord in your heart. It would have you bring dishonor to His holy name if it could. Before salvation, we were in the flesh. After conversion, that standing changed and we were baptized into Christ. However, the flesh still remaineds in us. We are not in the flesh, but the flesh is still in us. It is listed with two other enemies, thus, we speak of them as the flesh, the world, and the devil. Peter speaks of *"fleshly lusts, which war against the soul"* (1 Pet. 2:11).

"The old man" is mentioned three times in the New Testament, and we are going to explain them to you in simple terms. The truths connected with them are very challenging regarding our Christian behavior. First of all, let me say that the term *"the flesh,"* or *"the old nature,"* is in relationship to my **state**, or, how I

behave myself. On the other hand, the term, *"the old man,"* is in relationship to, not my state, but rather to my ***standing***, or, my position before God on the basis of redemption.

> *"Knowing this, that our old man is crucified with Him, that the body of sin might be destroyed, that henceforth we should not serve sin"* (Rom. 6:6).
>
> *"That ye put off concerning the former conversation the old man, which is corrupt according to the deceitful lusts; And be renewed in the spirit of your mind; And that ye put on the new man, which after God is created in righteousness and true holiness"* (Eph. 4:22–24).
>
> *"Lie not one to another, seeing that ye have put off the old man with his deeds; And have put on the new man, which is renewed in knowledge after the image of Him that created him"* (Col. 3:9–10).

The term *"old man,"* indicates something worn out, and fit only for the scrap pile. It is what I was in Adam. In that position or state, we served sin as a master over us. We were under its dominion and power. "The body of sin" is termed that way, for our physical body was the vehicle in which sin had taken possession, enabling us to sin. We sinned using our body to do so. Our body was ruled by sin's tremendous power. We were powerless to deliver ourselves from that awful state.

A man can commit suicide through many means, but he cannot crucify himself to inflict death. Yes, he could lay himself on a cross and nail his feet to that tree, and one hand, but he cannot nail the remaining free hand, nor could he lift the tree upright to stand. It is utterly impossible for a man to crucify himself! However, our *"old man,"* in other words, *our old standing before God*, has been put to death, never to raise its ugly head again. It has been put to death, certainly not by our own efforts, but by the work of Another, even God! Our *"old man"* was crucified with Christ! Essentially, when Christ died on the Cross, my old standing in Adam died. It was miraculously removed!

But you may counter my remarks and say, "Well then, how come in the Ephesian and the Colosssian passages we are told to put off the old man, yet you say that God has crucified him? How can one put off something that does not exist? That is a good question. However, it can be explained like this. We are to put off the *characteristics* of the life of the old man. In other words, don't live as if you were still that old man. You are not being told to get rid of him, or crucify him, for he is already gone! Just don't live as if he were still alive!

How challenging this is to all of us who profess to be Christians! We were slaves to sin, and now we are the bondslaves of our Lord Jesus Christ. My brother, my sister, do you fully realize what this involves? You have a body that you do not own. You have a will that has been divinely placed under the will of Another. You are not allowed to serve sin, but as Christ's slave, you are expected to bear fruit unto holiness. You are to move away from the sins of the works of the flesh, and become devoted to God at His service. Your members are no longer instruments of unrighteousness unto sin. You must not allow sin to have dominion over you. Do not let it reign in your mortal body, that you should obey it in the lusts thereof. The fruit of the flesh is death. Looking back to pre-conversion days, we remember the fruits of our flesh, and are ashamed.

We have *"put on the new man,"* which has been created in righteousness and true holiness. What is this? Why, it is your new nature my friend! The moment you were saved, you became a new creation, you obtained a *"new man."* You received the indwelling of the Holy Spirit of God, Who immediately instilled in your soul a fervent desire, not to live unto yourself, but unto Him Who died for you and rose again. You changed. Let me add to that. You dramatically changed! Your outlook on life changed. Your desires changed. Consequently, your friends changed. Your old hell-bound companions began to shun you, and you bid them farewell. You obtained true friends, those who were of like mind, and were true Christians.

Have you been challenged by these remarks about the standing and the submerged stones? I trust so! Remember, all that you are, all that you own, essentially belongs to the One Who died for you. Consequently, you owe your all to Him. May God help you to live out the truth of the two kinds of stones.

40

GILGAL

JOSHUA 5

CIRCUMCISION

The wilderness now lies behind us. The wanderings are over, and Israel is in the land that has yet to be possessed through seven years of warfare. However, before representing the God of Israel in any conflict, there was a requirement needed, and that was, the men must be circumcised. It seems that the last time this rite was carried out would have been at Sinai, before eating the Passover. None were circumcised after that, during their 38 years of wandering in the wilderness, and the question arises; why? There is a definite reason. Due to their unbelief in not entering the land, there was a temporary suspension of the covenant. Because of their unbelief, they were rejected of the Lord, and were doomed to perish in the wilderness.

Even before their turning back at Kadesh (Num. 13), it would seem that there was a disruption in their relationship with their God through making a golden calf to worship. Moses breaking the two tables of stone seemed an appropriate consequence to the breaking of the covenant. Their children had to bear the iniquity of their fathers from that time on to the crossing of Jordan, as one by one, the former generation passed away in the wilderness (Num. 14:33). It would seem that the suspension of circumcision was included in the punishment of their sins. God forbade them to place upon their children the sign and the seal of the covenant made with their father Abraham, a covenant that they had broken through their idolatry and unbelief.

However, the suspension was only temporary, and the time had now come when it was to be restored. They had now entered into the land which God sware to Abraham, Isaac, and Jacob, to give unto them. Thus, the first thing was to give back to the people the holy sign of the covenant, which was circumcision. Every man that had not been circumcised was to undergo this rite. Through this we see the covenant was renewed unto them. It is reckoned that those who did not need to be circumcised were more than fifty thousand. Thus, there were enough men to defend the camp if an attack were to be made upon it.

One may wonder why an attack was not made upon them the moment they crossed Jordan. It would seem that the words of Rahab to the spies provides the answer. *"I know that the LORD hath given you the land, and that your terror is fallen upon us, and that all the inhabitants of the land faint because of you ... our hearts did melt, neither did there remain any courage in any man, because of you: for the LORD your God, He is God in heaven above, and in the earth beneath"* (Josh. 2:9–11).

Even prior to Rahab's witness, Jehovah had told Israel what the condition of the enemy in the land would be.

> *"This day will I begin to put the dread of thee and the fear of thee upon the nations that are under the whole heaven, who shall hear report of thee, and shall tremble, and be in anguish because of thee"* (Deut. 2:25).
>
> *"There shall no man be able to stand before you: for the LORD your God shall lay the fear of you and the dread of you upon all the land that ye shall tread upon, as He hath said unto you"* (Deut. 11:25).
>
> *"And all people of the earth shall see that thou art called by the name of the LORD; and they shall be afraid of thee"* (Deut. 28:10).

TREMBLING JERICHO

The city of Jericho, as fortified and strong as it was, had been brought down mentally by Jehovah. The whole city was terror stricken and trembling. Not one person had any strength. With hearts melted, they were as weak as water spilt upon the ground. If you could have walked the streets of Jericho just prior to Israel's invasion, you would have been struck with the silence and look of dread on the faces of the people. Instead of dancing, they were trembling. Instead of laughing, they were languishing. Instead of courage, there was cowardice. The city was straightly shut up. The massive wall doors were securely bolted. There they sat, a city full of immoral, wicked, godless people, and their time of visitation had come.

Ah my friend, are we not living in a virtual Jericho? Apart from God's redeemed, this world produces nothing but a stench to the nostrils of God. Thousands of years ago *"The LORD looked down from heaven upon the children of men, to see if there were any that did understand, and seek God"* (Ps. 14:2). What did He find? How sobering are His words! *"They are all gone aside, they are all together become filthy: there is none that doeth good, no, not one"* (Ps. 14:3). The word "filthy" means, *"turned to corruption."* Let me give you a picture of this age with all its intellectualism, achievements, programs, and honors. Place a number of dead rats into a garbage pail, and secure the lid. Let the pail stand in the hot and humid weather of the tropics for one month. Then (be prepared) lift the lid, bend over and smell. Will the odour delight you? Hardly! In fact, it might make you vomit. If Christ was ready to vomit over the condition of the Laodicean Church, how much more nauseous must this world be to Him!

The day of God's reckoning with this sinful world has not yet occured. However, God *"hath appointed a day, in the which He will judge the world in righteousness by that Man whom He hath ordained; whereof He hath given assurance unto all men, in that He hath raised Him from the dead"* (Acts 17:31). The Lord Jesus gives us the characteristics of that dreadful day. *"And there shall be signs in the sun, and in the moon, and in the stars; and upon the earth distress of nations, with perplexity; the sea and the waves roaring; Men's hearts failing them for fear, and for looking after those things which are coming on the earth: for the powers of heaven shall be shaken. And then shall they see the Son of man coming in a cloud with power and great glory"* (Luke 21:25–27).

SEVEN DAYS – SEVEN YEARS

For *seven days*, Israel marched around the walls of Jericho, before they fell. For *seven years*, the Lord will bring unprecedented plagues on this earth, until all kingdoms are toppled, and Christ comes as King of kings, and Lord of lords.[97] God will speak to the kings of the earth in His wrath, and vex them in His sore displeasure. Then He will set His King, the Lord Jesus, upon His holy hill of Zion. Christ will break the earthly kingdoms with a rod of iron, and dash them in pieces like a potter's vessel (Ps. 2:5–9). Thank God, the saints of this dispensation will be delivered from that wrath to come (1 Thess. 1:10). He will deliver us from the hour of temptation (trial) (Rev. 3:10). He will snatch us away at the last trump, and while this poor world will be suffering great tribulation, we shall be with Him, with glorified bodies, in the Father's house above. Praise God!

THE REPROACH OF EGYPT

It was first **standing** stones, then **submerged** stones, and then **sharp** stones, which were stones of flint used to circumcise the males. After the rite of circumcision was completed *"the LORD said unto Joshua, This day have I rolled away the reproach of Egypt from off you. Wherefore the name of the place is called Gilgal unto this day"* (Josh. 5:9).

Israel had come out of Egypt, and were thought of as part of Egypt (Num. 22:5). To Israel, this was a great reproach. However, by their circumcision they were distinguished from the

---

[97] The most enlightening reading of this coming event can be found in the Book of the Revelation, chapters 6 to 19.

Egyptians, and manifested to be another people. With many in the wilderness, there was no distinction between the men and the Egyptians, for they were not circumcised. At Gilgal, that reproach was rolled away. It also may be said that the shame of their idolatry, and lustfulness stemming from Egypt, was rolled away.

Keil presents another thought. "The taunts industriously cast by that people upon Israel as *nationally* rejected by God by the cessation of circumcision and the renewal of that rite was a practical announcement of the restoration of the covenant."

To enhance this thought, allow me to give you the convictions of another writer, written over 100 years ago.

> "How could the suspension of circumcision be called the reproach of Egypt? The words imply that, owing to the want of the sacrament, they had lain exposed to a reproach from the Egyptians, which was now rolled away. The brevity of the statement, and our ignorance of what the Egyptians were saying of the Israelites at the time, make the words difficult to understand. What seems most likely is, that when the Egyptians heard how God had all but repudiated them in the wilderness, and had withdrawn from them the sign of His covenant, they malignantly crowed over them, and denounced them as a worthless race, who had first rejected their lawful rulers in Egypt under pretext of religion, and, having shown their hypocrisy, were now scorned and cast off by the very God whom they had professed themselves so eager to serve. We may be sure that the Egyptians would not be slow to seize any pretext for denouncing the Israelites, and would be sure to make their jibes as sharp and as bitter as they could. But now the tables are turned on the Egyptians. The restoration

of circumcision stamps this people once more as the people of God. The stupendous miracle just wrought in the dividing of the Jordan indicates the kind of protection which their God and King is sure to extend to them. The name of Gilgal will be a perpetual testimony that the reproach of Egypt is rolled away." [98]

SPIRITUAL CIRCUMCISION

Coming to the New Testament, we find circumcision used in a spiritual sense. On some occasions *"the circumcision,"* means the Jews as a people, while the expression, *"the uncircumcision,"* means the Gentiles as a people. But the word is used other ways, and this is what we wish to deal with for a few moments

The first occurrence of this word being used in a spiritual sense is found in Romans 2:28–29.

> "For he is not a Jew, which is one outwardly; neither is that circumcision, which is outward in the flesh: But he is a Jew, which is one inwardly; and circumcision is that of the heart, in the spirit, and not in the letter; whose praise is not of men, but of God."

Notice, we have circumcision of the heart. That is different, isn't it? What does it mean? Simply this, it is the putting away of all impurity from the heart. Paul, no doubt, had in mind the passage in Deuteronomy 30:6: *"And the LORD thy God will circumcise thine heart, and the heart of thy seed, to love the LORD thy God with all thine heart, and with all thy soul, that thou mayest live."* The words of Jeremiah 4:4, may also bear upon this. *"Circumcise yourselves to the LORD, and take away the foreskins of your heart, ye men of Judah and inhabitants of Jerusalem: lest my fury come forth like fire, and burn that none can quench it, because of the evil of your doings."*

---

[98] William Garden Blaikie. <u>The Book of Joshua</u>, P. 120. Klock & Klock Christian Publishers.

This circumcision is not an outward mark in the flesh of the body, but is in the spirit. This simply means that the spirit of man is under the influence of the Holy Spirit. It is *"not in the letter,"* that is, it is not literal, but rather spiritual. The true Jew (whether Jew or Gentile), may be ill-spoken of by men, but that means very little, for he shall have praise of God, and that is all that really matters.

The circumcision of the heart meant separation from the heathen world, and consecration to God. It involved the renunciation and forsaking of all sin; or the cutting off of everything that was offensive to God. This was heart-work.

STRANGE TEACHING

Before proceeding any further, let me warn you about a strange teaching concerning circumcision. Allow me to quote a well-respected, and godly writer on this subject.

> "He is not a Christian that is one outwardly, nor is that **baptism** which is outward in the flesh; but he is a Christian that is one inwardly, and **baptism** is that of the heart, in the spirit, and not in the letter, whose praise is not of men but of God" (Matt. Henry).

Now just where does Matthew Henry find *"baptism"* in the word *"circumcision?"* They are two completely different words. *"Circumcise"* means *"to cut off,"* while *"baptize"* means *"to immerse."* Perhaps a little exposition on this subject might help. Please bear with me.

One reason some groups within Christendom baptize babies instead of believers is because they believe that baptism in the New Testament is what circumcision was in the Old Testament. They reason that if those born into Jewish households could be circumcised in anticipation of the Jewish faith in which they would be raised, then those born in Christian households can be baptized in anticipation of the Christian faith in which they will be raised. Thus, they claim that the pattern is the same. Consequently, they state that baptism replaces circumcision. Nothing could be further from the truth! Let me explain why it is erroneous to teach that baptism replaced circumcision.

"The covenant of circumcision" (Acts 7:8), was confined to the descendants of Abraham, Isaac, and Jacob, and those converted to Judaism (Gen. 17:12–13; Exodus 12:48). However, baptism is for all nations (Matt. 28:19–20). There is no similarity between the two.

Circumcision was confined to males, but baptism is for both male and female. Also, if baptism replaced circumcision, then those Jews who were already circumcised according to the law could not be baptized. But it is readily seen that this was not the case, for at the commencement of the Church they were all circumcised Jews, yet they all submitted to the rite of baptism. Thus, if baptism was a replacement of circumcision, how could they both be in effect at the same time, among the Jews?

FAITH BEFORE BAPTISM

Please also notice, that in every New Testament command of baptism, the requirement of faith precedes it. Consequently, infants are excluded, for they are incapable of exercising faith. There are no recordings in Scripture of infant baptism. When you read of households being baptized (Lydia's household; the Philippian Jailor's household; and the household of Stephanus, Acts 16:15; 30–33; 1 Corinthians 1:16), no mention is made of infants. In fact, the story of the jailor indicates that it was to all in his house that the Word of the Lord was spoken, implying that the whole household was old enough to understand the preaching of the gospel. Infants do not have the mental capacity to understand.

HOUSEHOLD BAPTISM?

Many years ago, the late Fred Watson, while riding on a train, became engaged in conversation with another man who believed in "household baptism." The conversation turned to Lydia (Acts 16) and what the Scripture said about her. *"She was baptized and her household."* Smiling, the opposing brother said to Mr. Watson, "See there it is, all her little infants were baptized!" Mr. Watson countered with this remark, "Oh no, her daughter was a college graduate, and her two sons were grown business men." Quite surprised at Mr. Watson's rapid reply, the other man said, "And just where do you find that in the Bible?" Mr. Watson was a very alert man, and with no hesitation he replied, "The very same place where you find that her children were infants." The man was speechless.

When the church met in Jerusalem to discuss whether circumcision should still be required of believers upon becoming Christians, it is very interesting to see that not once in that entire conference did anyone say one thing about baptism standing in the place of circumcision as a sign of the new covenant, and thus valid for children as well as adults, as circumcision was. If any time would have been appropriate for such a discussion to show that circumcision was being replaced by baptism, and was no longer necessary, it was then. But baptism was not even discussed.

THE CHURCH IS NOT A REPLAY OF ISRAEL

The whole reason for this confusion lies in the fact that there has been an assumption that there is a similarity between the people of God in the Old Testament and the people of God today. They assume that the way God gathered His covenant people Israel, and the way that He is gathering His New Testament saints is so similar that baptism and circumcision can be administered in the same way. Thus they conjecture, that if circumcision placed Old Testament saints under a covenant, then baptism, in like manner, places New Testament saints under a covenant. However, it is not baptism that places us under a covenant. The New Covenant has been ratified by the precious blood of Christ, and made good to us by faith in His Person as Lord and Saviour. Our children are not born under a covenant. They are born sinners in need of the new birth when reaching the age of responsibility.

But no, the infant baptism group won't have it the scriptural way, but strongly assert that the children of Christian believers belong to the visible Church by reason of their birth and consequently, should receive the sign and seal of the covenant just as the eight-day-old infants of Israel did in the Old Testament. No my friend, the Church is not a *replay* of Israel, it is an *advance* on Israel. A separate identity altogether! Baptism is *not* circumcision, neither is it for infants!

THE CIRCUMCISION OF CHRIST

The next occurrence of the word *"circumcision"* is found in Colossians 2:11.

> *"In Whom also ye are circumcised with the circumcision made without hands, in putting off the body of the sins of the flesh by the circumcision of Christ."*

"With the circumcision made without hands." That circumcision was carried out in the heart by the renunciation of all sin. The Jewish teachers insisted on the necessity of a literal circumcision in order to obtain salvation as we see from Acts 15:1. *"And certain men which came down from Judaea taught the brethren, and said, Except ye be circumcised after the manner of Moses, ye cannot be saved."* Thus, the subject of circumcision is often introduced into the writings of Paul, and he constantly shows that, by believing in Christ, all was secured which was required in order to obtain salvation. The word *"circumcision"* means, *"to cut off,"* thus, spiritual circumcision denoted that all sin was to be cut off or renounced, and that he who was spiritually circumcised was to be devoted to God and to a

holy life. Paul declares that this was obtained by the gospel. What Christians had obtained was related *to the heart*; it was not a mere ordinance pertaining *to the flesh*. In other words, the abandonment of sin through spiritual union with Christ was the only circumcision that was required. It was a "cutting off" spiritually of the former way of life.

Having established what spiritual circumcision involves, one might ask the question, "What does the circumcision of Christ mean?" Regarding this, there are two thoughts that somewhat differ, and I will present them to you and let you decide for yourself which is the most accurate.

We cut off, or lay aside all that is connected with the old nature by that spiritual circumcision which Christ works in our heart. Joshua, after the wilderness journey, circumcised the Israelites in Canaan the second time. So. Jesus, the Antitype, is the Author of the true circumcision, which is therefore called *"the circumcision of Christ."* (Rom. 2:29). As Joshua was *"Moses' minister,"* so Jesus is *"minister of the circumcision for the truth of God"* unto the Gentiles" (Rom. 15:8).

"By the circumcision of Christ." Alfred Barnes states, "Not by the fact that Christ was circumcised, but that we have that kind of circumcision which Christ established – to wit, *the renouncing of sin*. The idea of the apostle here seems to be, that since we have thus been enabled by Christ to renounce sin, and to devote ourselves to God, we should not be induced, by any plausible arguments, to return to an ordinance pertaining to the flesh, as if that were needful for salvation.

The other thought is that the circumcision of Christ is His being cut off in the midst of His years.

> *"He was taken from prison and from judgment: and who shall declare His generation? for He was **cut off** out of the land of the living: for the transgression of my people was He stricken"* (Isa. 53:8).

*"And after threescore and two weeks shall Messiah be **cut off**, but not for Himself"* (Dan. 9:26).

Thus, through His death, we have been saved and indwelt with the Spirit. Thus, we are enabled to perform spiritual circumcision on ourselves, namely the cutting off of a former way of life.

So, Israel ate the *manna*, they ate *roast lamb*, and they ate the *old corn of the land*. In like manner, we feast on the holy humanity of Christ, the living Manna. We enjoy the sacrifice of Christ, the Lamb of God, our Passover sacrificed for us. Finally, we enjoy the resurrected Christ, of which the old corn of the land typifies. We are in the land brethren. We have been raised with Christ, and seated with Christ in the heavenlies, and as such, we have been blessed with all spiritual blessings in the heavenlies.

We have been saved by grace, apart from any works of our own. That was a miracle! However, we learn the Scriptures, and we grasp and enjoy the spiritual blessings that are ours, all by works. It is no miracle to have a profound knowledge of divine things my brethren. Ah no! Salvation may come by grace, but a knowledge of the Scriptures comes only by work.

THE SAINT'S THREE SPHERES

Just as there were three spheres for the children of Israel, so there are three spheres for us as His people today. (1) Israel was in Egypt (the world). So we too, even though not of the world, are still in the world. The assembly at Corinth would correspond to this. (2) Israel was in the wilderness. We also are in a wilderness, and as such, we are pilgrims and strangers. This corresponds to Peter's Epistles. (3) Finally, Israel occupied the promised land. In like manner, we too have been positioned to enjoy all the spiritual blessings in the heavenlies given to us in Christ. This truth is wondrously presented in the Epistle to the Ephesians.

Israel's journey forty years prior to entering the land commenced with the Passover. The nation's end of the journey concluded as it began – with the Passover. Having already expounded some truths relative to the Passover in chapter 4, we will be brief in dealing with the subject here.

> *"And the children of Israel encamped in Gilgal, and kept the Passover on the fourteenth day of the month at even in the plains of Jericho. And they did eat of the old corn of the land on the morrow after the Passover, unleavened cakes, and parched corn in the selfsame day. And the manna ceased on the morrow after they had eaten of the old corn of the land; neither had the children of Israel manna any more; but they did eat of the fruit of the land of Canaan that year"* (Josh. 5:10–12).

There are three major things worth noticing in the above portion. Namely this:

THE MANNA. This speaks of Christ's *humanity*. This affects my practical walk.

THE PASSOVER. This is a picture of Christ's *death*. This affects my devotion to Him.

THE OLD CORN OF THE LAND. This affords a shadow of the *resurrection* of our Lord. This affects my hope.

Thus, we have our practical walk, our positional relationship, and our prevailing hope. The circumcising of all the uncircumcised males in the camp would have been a time of great rejoicing. The visible token of every man being one of God's children was now manifested in all the males. They could now fully consider themselves heirs to the covenant made with their fathers. This alone would help them to rest with firmer trust on the promise that God gave saying; *"I will bless them that bless thee, and curse him that curseth thee"* (Gen. 12:3). Not only this, being circumcised would allow them to partake of the Passover, for as we all know, no uncircumcised person was allowed to eat thereof (Ex. 12:28).

ISRAEL'S THIRD RECORDED PASSOVER

This was the third recorded occasion when Israel kept the Passover. The first occasion was in Egypt, the night before their departure. The second occasion was the first month of the second year after they were come out of the land of Egypt, when they reached Sinai. All through their wilderness wanderings they were denied the Passover. Now, after 38 years, the privilege is theirs once again. What joy this must have brought to their souls. The Passover itself could never be repeated. That was history. However, the feast of the Passover could be kept yearly as a commemoration of that fact.

In keeping the feast of the Passover, Israel would have their mind automatically turned back to their great day of redemption in Egypt. They would be reminded that the blood of the lamb was the very basis of their redemption. Also brought to mind would be Sinai, the giving of the Law, and the majesty and glory of God revealed midst *"the thunderings, and the lightenings, and the noise of the trumpet, and the mountain smoking"* (Ex. 20:18). It is good to have our mind turned back to the former mercies of God on our behalf, for meditating on those most blessed truths has a tendency to strengthen us for trials yet to come.

It is most blessed to see the activity of all of Israel just prior to entering the battles of the Lord. I don't read of military training. There is no mention of a "boot camp." There seems to be no emphasis on physical fitness. Nothing of the sort! What is occupying this nation and its army prior to the battle? The answer is, they were giving the LORD the very first place. They were making sure that they had a proper relationship with their God. Thus, instead of pursuing a battle, they participated in the Passover.

STARTING YOUR DAY

Let me ask you, when you start a fresh day, a day in which you are going out to battle a cruel world, do you give the Lord the first place? Or do you rise at the last minute, and hastily devour your breakfast, then rush out the door to press against the cold, godless blast of a Christless world? Ah my friend, that is the formula for weakness. That is the blueprint on how to fail as an effective witness for Himself. No, my dear soul, such hurried behavior will never do. What you want to do is to get your priorities right, and give the Lord first place. Give Him a little time to speak to you through His Word, and give yourself a little time to speak to Him through prayer. That is the secret of being able to face a cruel world successfully, as a faithful witness of the Lord Jesus Christ.

> "Oh for just a quiet moment.
> Sweetly all alone with Thee.
> Drawing from Thy rich resources.
> That I might successful be." [99]

Just two miles from the River Jordan, and six miles from Jericho, they sat in fellowship with Jehovah, and ate the Passover. Forty years had come and gone. Over two million of them had died in the wilderness, the memories of the past would remind them of the mercies, grace, and unfailing provision of their God as they wandered in a waste-howling wilderness. The past was over, and new days lay ahead. They were about to claim their inheritance and witness the almighty power of God for them. They were about to face seven nations well trained in warfare, but this did not frighten them, nor did the fact weaken them. How wonderful to see the complete faith that this new generation was placing in their God. There was no wavering, no doubting, no sidestepping, no faltering, and no complaining. Ah no, they were enjoying roast lamb, in fellowship with each other, and in fellowship with their God.

> *"And they did eat the old corn of the land"* (Josh. 5:11).

Naturally, the question arises, where did they obtain the *"old corn?"* It would seem that as a result of Israel's invasion, the inhabitants of the land fled elsewhere for refuge from the

---

[99] R. E. S.

coming judgment to be inflicted by Israel. Whether the people took refuge in Jericho we are not told, but at that particular season of the year, their barns would have been full from the previous harvest. Thus, the army of Israel simply helped themselves, bringing back to the camp enough provision for the people to make cakes of unleavened bread, in order to keep the feast of unleavened bread that immediately followed the Passover.

In Leviticus 23:9–11, we read these words. *"And the LORD spake unto Moses, saying, speak unto the children of Israel, and say unto them, when ye be come into the land which I give unto you, and shall reap the harvest thereof, then ye shall bring a sheaf of the firstfruits of your harvest unto the priest: And he shall wave the sheaf before the LORD, to be accepted for you: on the morrow after the sabbath the priest shall wave it."* That is, on the *fifteenth* day; for then the feast of unleavened bread began. However, they were not allowed to eat bread, nor parched corn, nor green ears, till the *first-fruits* of the harvest had been *waved* at the tabernacle, as seen in Leviticus 23. Therefore, it would seem that the Israelites had offered a sheaf of the *barley-harvest*, the only grain that was then ripe, before they ate of the unleavened cakes and parched corn. Thus, the new corn, was reaped by them from the abandoned fields, and waved before the Lord, and the old corn stored in barns from the previous year's harvest was used in the making of unleavened bread for the feast following the Passover.

On the ***fourteenth*** of Nisan they sacrificed the paschal lamb; then on the ***fifteenth***, the same day after sunset, they prepared themselves for eating it. On the morrow, the ***sixteenth***, after having offered to God the *homer*, they began eating the corn of the country; and on the ***seventeenth***, the manna ceased to fall from heaven. What supports this thought is that the *homer* or *sheaf* was offered on the sixteenth of Nisan, in broad daylight, although near the evening. Consider the fact that the manna did not fall until night, or very early in the morning; so that it could not be stated to have ceased falling the same day that the Israelites began to eat of the produce of the country.

HONORING THE LORD

It is refreshing to see that the moment the fruits of this good land came to their hands, they had an opportunity to honor God with them, and employ them in His service according to His appointment. They were very careful to give the LORD His portion first. It reminds me of Solomon's advice. *"Honour the LORD with thy substance, and with the firstfruits of all thine increase: So shall thy barns be filled with plenty, and thy presses shall burst out with new wine"* (Prov. 3:9–10).

There is a tendency in some people to waste their money. Help them with your substance, and they will spend it on frivolous things, or perhaps even gamble it away. Such people are fools. They simply cannot manage money. They have no sense of values.

TREASURES ON EARTH – OR IN HEAVEN?

On the other hand, we have people that are greedy, and hoard all that they can. They will live frugal lives in order to stash their substance safely in a bank or vault. The Scripture warns: *"If riches increase, set not your heart upon them"* (Ps. 62:10), but they heed not God's advice. They scrimp, and hoard, and stash away as much silver and gold as they can. They seem to fall in love with money. However, lurking in the corner is a danger. Solomon describes it. *"Wilt thou set thine eyes upon that which is not? for riches certainly make themselves wings; they fly away as an eagle toward heaven"* (Prov. 23:5).

Now do not misunderstand me. I am not referring to being wise and setting a little aside for a rainy day. Doing that is wisdom and common sense. I believe the Bible sanctions that. *"In the day of prosperity be joyful, but in the day of adversity consider: God also hath set the one over against the other, to the end that man should find nothing after him"* (Eccl. 7:14). What I am seeking to impress upon you is the folly of laying up treasures upon earth *"where moth and rust doth corrupt, and where thieves break through and steal"* (Matt. 6:19). That's the point. That's what we want to consider.

When a person loses money in the stock market, I do not feel sorry for him at all. In the first place, why did he invest his money in stocks, thus making himself a partner in an ungodly business? Why did he become unequally yoked together with unbelievers? The answer is simple. He wanted more money than he presently possessed! He was willing to be a sophisticated gambler! He was covetous for more! You can't deny it! The facts proclaim it! You may counter my blunt remarks and say, "He was using his money wisely." Nonsense! Let me tell you how a wise man uses his money. Listen to this! *"But lay up for yourselves treasures in heaven, where neither moth nor rust doth corrupt, and where thieves do not break through nor steal"* (Matt. 6:20). Now, that is wisdom par-excellence! That is godly advice from the Teacher of all teachers, even the Lord Himself! Are you like the Laodiceans, rich and increased with goods and in need of nothing? Well then, if that is the case, the Lord has some pertinent advice for you. *"I counsel thee to buy of me gold tried in the fire, that thou mayest be rich; and white raiment, that thou mayest be clothed, and that the shame of thy nakedness do not appear; and anoint thine eyes with eyesalve, that thou mayest see"* (Rev. 3:18).

Are you seeking the Lord's face relative to your riches? Are you wondering where to send some of your substance? Then pray, and keep your eyes and ears open for evident avenues in which to funnel your substance. Perhaps there are some believers struggling to erect a new hall in which to meet. Would you be willing to help them? Or, is the interest you are receiving from your bank more important to you? Are you aware of believers in need of food or clothing? Are you concerned about the spread of the gospel into new places, and the cost to the men pioneering with the good news? Do these realities ever enter your mind? Or do you mutter to yourself, "That may all be true, but after all, I must think of my future. Things may fail and I need something to fall back on."

Ah yes, if you give to the Lord He just might abandon you in the future and let you starve to death, out on the street with no shelter. Is that what you are saying? "Oh no, not at all!" you might hurriedly reply. Well now, that is what you are implying. You are acting as if God were dead and totally unaware of you, and that He has no concern for your welfare whatsoever.

LENDING TO GOD

At this particular time I am staying with a lovely Christian couple along the banks of the Ohio River. Every morning after breakfast, a chapter from the book of Proverbs is read that corresponds to the monthly date. This morning, being March 19, the nineteenth chapter was read and commented on. One of the verses read like this: *"He that hath pity upon the poor lendeth unto the LORD; and that which he hath given will He pay him again"* (Prov. 19:17).

Imagine, God taking the place of a debtor, and you lending to Him! The word *"lent"* signifies *"lent upon interest."* Consequently, a tremendously rich recompence shall be made for it: He will repay the lender in temporal, and in spiritual blessings here, and with eternal blessings in the glory. So, it is very evident, that prayerful, and careful giving to those less fortunate than ourselves, is the surest and safest way of thriving. The New Testament counterpart to this truth is found in Matthew 25:40. *"And the King shall answer and say unto them, Verily I say unto you, inasmuch as ye have done it unto one of the least of these My brethren, ye have done it unto Me."*

Anybody would be a fool to say that lending to the Lord would be an unwise investment. You may lend to the bank, or be foolish enough to invest in stocks, thus lending to some corporation. But remember this, banks can fail, and corporations can go bankrupt, leaving you with nothing but a written guarantee that has failed. Now then, do you believe that the Lord can fail? Do you believe that He can go bankrupt? Answer me! Do you? Well, you sputter and meekly acknowledge that He can never fail. If so, then why not place your investment with Him? Why not let Him be, as it were, your Debtor? Since He never can fail, or go bankrupt, would not this be the wisest investment in all the universe? Certainly so! The Lord is open for business, if I may so put it that way, so why not place your investment with Him, and have pity upon the poor? You have nothing to lose, and everything to gain.

PROVISIONS THE ORDINARY WAY

After the Passover, they were to keep *the feast of unleavened bread,* which they could not do when they had nothing but manna to live on. Perhaps this was one reason why the Passover was suspended in the wilderness. However, the army found old corn enough in the barns of the Canaanites to supply them plentifully for that occasion.

> *"And the manna ceased on the morrow after they had eaten of the old corn of the land; neither had the children of Israel manna anymore"* (Josh. 5:12).

God miraculously supplied Israel with the manna as long as they needed it. While they were in the wilderness they were dependent on this provision; nor could such a multitude, in a waste-howling wilderness, be supported without such a miracle. Now they have entered into the promised land, and have found the old corn of the land. They were also brought in just at the commencement of the barley harvest; hence, as there is an ample provision made in the *ordinary* way of Providence, there is no longer any need of a *miraculous* supply. Therefore the manna, which was their provision for forty years, ceased. You will notice that the manna ceased as soon as they ate the *old corn of the land.* This fact goes to prove that the manna did not come by chance or common providence, as snow or rain does, but by the special process of divine wisdom and grace; for, as it came just when they needed it, so it continued as long as they had occasion for it and no longer.

As stated, the manna was not an ordinary production of nature, but an extraordinary and special gift of God to supply their necessity. It ceased because God would not be extravagant of his favors, by working miracles where ordinary means were sufficient. There is a saying in the world that may bear a little truth: "God helps those who help themselves." Now that is not always true, for there have been saints brought into situations beyond their control and they cannot help themselves. Then miraculously, God steps in and brings help. On the other hand, there are people who may be in need, yet they are healthy enough to go out and seek employment, but they are too lazy to work to purchase food for their mouth. Instead, they sit at home and pray to God to send food in some miraculous way. Now this is folly! I can fully understand and appreciate a person crying out to God in his desperation and weakness for help, and God intervening and rescuing that person from his dilemma. But I cannot sympathize with a slothful person, too lazy to better himself, crying to God to meet his wants. No, no! That does not go down with me!

Solomon *"went by the field of the slothful, and by the vineyard of the man void of understanding; And, lo, it was all grown over with thorns, and nettles had covered the face thereof, and the stone wall thereof was broken down. Then I saw, and considered it well: I looked upon it, and received instruction. Yet a little sleep, a little slumber, a little folding of the hands to sleep: So shall thy poverty come as one that travelleth; and thy want as an armed man."* Rightly so, he deserved to go hungry and live in rags (Prov. 24:30–34).

"HOMELESS – WILL WORK FOR FOOD"

There was a character at our corner supermarket who parked himself in the parking lot with a big sign stating, "Homeless, will work for food." Silly people were tossing him money right and left. One day, the owner of the store approached him and offered him a job in his supermarket. Now just what do you think that poor homeless character replied? Did he leap up and rejoice at the offer of a job? Why no! Why work, when one can get more money begging? Naturally, he flatly refused the store owner's generous offer. The owner was an Italian man that had worked hard all his life to establish a reputable business, and he was looking at a tramp that was too lazy to put his hand to his mouth to feed himself. I am not prepared to print the Italian's fiery response, but the tramp was ordered off the premises immediately, and rightly so.

DILIGENCE REQUIRED

We as the children of God are exhorted to be *"not slothful in business"* (Rom. 12:11). You cannot occupy the seat of the slothful and carelessly say, "The Lord will provide." That is spiritual ignorance. The word rendered *slothful* refers to those who are slow, idle, destitute of promptness of mind and activity. That type of person is described by our Lord in Matthew 25:26.

The word, "business," is rendered "diligence" in Romans 12:8, and carries the thought of *"haste intensity,"* or, *"ardour of mind;"* and hence it also denotes *"industry,"* and, *labour*. The whole thought is that we should be diligently occupied in our proper employment. We are exhorted to be faithful and industrious in the discharge of all our appropriate duties. God's people are to be industrious, hard-working, and honest people. Time is valuable, and we are to redeem it, not fritter it away with indolence.

When our Lord called certain ones to be his apostles, he chose industrious men. When he chose Simon and Andrew, they were busy casting a net into the sea. When He called James and John, they were employed in mending their nets. You find the same principle in the Old Testament with Elijah. When he called Elisha to the work, the man was busy plowing with twelve yoke of oxen. Even the Lord in His youth was employed in carpentry. *"Is not this the carpenter, the Son of Mary?"* (Mark 6:3). In His ministry, He never was indolent. He was a tireless Worker. *"My Father worketh hitherto, and I work"* (John 5:17). If any man was aware of lazy people, it was Solomon. He observes the beggar.

What has made the man a begger? Well, he has made himself a beggar, simply because when he could work, he refused. So, Solomon writes, *"The sluggard will not plow by reason of the cold; therefore shall he beg in harvest, and have nothing"* (Prov. 20:4). Paul states, *"For even when we were with you, this we commanded you, that if any would not work, neither should he eat"* (2 Thess. 3:10). That is a divine principle.

An *idle* man and a *Christian* are names which are not compatible. They do not blend together. The Lord has given every Christian enough to do to that will occupy *all* of his time; and those who spend their life loafing in ease, and in doing nothing, should doubt whether the root of the matter is really in them or not. The Lord has assigned us much to accomplish and He will hold us answerable for the faithful performance of it. Paul did not mince his words with the Thessalonian saints: *"For even when we were with you, this we commanded you, that if any* **would not work,** *neither should he eat. For we hear that there are some which walk among you disorderly***, working not at all***, but are busybodies. Now them that are such we command and exhort by our Lord Jesus Christ, that with quietness they* **work,** *and eat* **their own** *bread"* (Not someone else's bread) (2 Thess. 3:10–12).

Our prosperous and promiscuous nation promotes immorality and laziness through its welfare system. Hard working people are paying taxes to support people that, through lame excuses, will not work. Single women can live a life of ease, simply by having children, and receiving government funds to support them. To increase their "income" they simply have more babies. The whole affair is gross. It is true that the welfare system has helped legitimate people, but the general picture is that it has produced, and encouraged a lazy, and immoral class of people, to continue in their wayward ways. Married couples have been known to obtain a divorce, yet remain living together, so that they might be supported from the welfare program, since it caters to women with children who have no husband.

THE "ENTITLEMENT" GROUP

Many have degenerated so much as to join a group of people that believe in *entitlement*. In other words, they feel that they are entitled to receive government handouts, though they won't labor to provide their own income. They feel that everybody owes them a free living. Their thinking is warped. No true Christian would ever pursue such a path, or develop such a way of thinking. The whole concept is foreign to the teachings of Holy Scripture. Such wicked behavior is contrary to Christianity altogether. The godly Christian recognizes one thing concerning *entitlement*, and that is, the only thing he ever was entitled to was to be consigned to hell fire for eternity.

When Israel finally settled in the land, they worked to make provision for themselves. They plowed their fields, they harvested their crops, and they stored their surplus in view of the coming winter months. One cannot help but mention the virtuous woman of Proverbs 31. *"She riseth while it is yet night, and giveth meat to her household, and a portion to her maidens."* Is she looking for a handout? Not at all! She is virtuous! Do you know what that means? It means a woman that has an excellent character, one who is strong in faith, and worthy of praise. King Lemuel continues his appraisal, saying; *"She looketh well to the ways of her household, and eateth not the bread of idleness."* Young and healthy sisters, how do you spend your time?

SHARING WITH OTHERS

Now then, there is a little verse following the exhortation to be diligent in business, and it is this: *"Distributing to the necessity of saints; given to hospitality"* (Rom. 12:13). In other words, to share with others. The word *"necessity"* can also be translated, *"destitution." "Hospitality"* means to *"entertain."* Now in order to help others, you need substance. That substance is gained by work. So you work to provide for your family, and you lay aside a little for a "rainy day." But something happens. A calamity befalls a couple in your assembly. So what do you do? Do you sit back and say, "We are praying for you." What good is that? Tell me, just what does that accomplish? Does it put clothes on their back, and food on their table? Not at all! If you have any means, what is your responsibility? It is simply this, you are to distribute to their necessity. There are no ifs and ands about it! It is in black and white that you are to share your substance with them. But if you are a lazy person, always looking for a free handout, you will have no ability to help others.

What about hospitality? How can a slothful man entertain others with a table laden with good food? How can he provide a comfortable room for the stranger? He can't! He has nothing! He has never considered others, other than to beg from them, so there he sits, with no ability to fulfill the exhortation of Romans 12:13.

May the Lord give us to see that we are to labor diligently, and handle our substance prudently. We are not to hoard our money, yet on the other hand we are not to waste our money, and are called upon to be aware of the needs of others less fortunate than ourselves. May we also be aware of the fact that if we are to prosper, we *must* honor the Lord with our substance, giving to Him what we have purposed in our hearts.

REQUIREMENTS FOR SUCCESSFUL POSSESSION

Looking at Israel in the land in a spiritual way, we have another picture before us. They were to obey the Lord in every phase of their life, and thus, God being with them, they would finally possess all that had been given to them though His covenant with their fathers. However, God had requirements.

FEARING THE LORD

"And now, Israel, what doth the LORD thy God require of thee, but to fear the LORD thy God, to walk in all His ways, and to love Him, and to serve the LORD thy God with all thy heart and with all thy soul, to

keep the commandments of the LORD, and His statutes, which I command thee this day for thy good?" (Deut. 10:12–13).

Just as Israel was given the land, in like manner, the Lord has given to us all spiritual blessings in the heavenlies. Just as God laid before Israel requirements in order to possess the land, so we too, have requirements given us by the Lord, to enable us to fully enjoy our spiritual blessings. The requirements are the same for us, as they were for Israel.

First of all, we are to *fear the Lord.* You might inquire, "What does that mean? What does that involve?" In preparing an answer, let me give you first what the Scripture says. *"The fear of the LORD is to hate evil: pride, and arrogancy ... The fear of the LORD is the beginning of wisdom: and the knowledge of the holy is understanding ... In the fear of the LORD is strong confidence: and his children shall have a place of refuge"* (Prov. 8:13; 9:10; 14:26). These are some of the things that the fear of the Lord produces in the lives of individuals. They hate anything of an evil nature. They hate pride and arrogancy, for they are meek and lowly. They manifest an unusual wisdom, especially relative to divine things, and in their normal behavior, place strong confidence in the Lord. He makes provision for his children, through his wise dealings in life. These are the qualities of a person that fears God.

The fear of God was resident in the midwives of Egypt, when the children of Israel were being persecuted (Ex. 1:17). It was manifested in Nehemiah's brother Hanani, and Hananiah the ruler of the palace. They feard God above many (Neh. 7:2). Job was a man that feard God and fled from evil (Job 1:1). Even though not saved at the time, Cornelius was a devout man and one that feared God with all his house (Acts 10:2). These people had a reverential fear of God. They would be deathly afraid to do anything contrary to His will. They held total respect and highest esteem toward the Almighty. This is the fear of the Lord, and to expect to enjoy your spiritual blessings, this is also required of you.

WALKING IN HIS WAYS

The next thing we see is, *"to walk in all His ways."* This is, if I may say, a "byproduct" of the fear of God. *"Thus saith the LORD, Stand ye in the ways, and see, and ask for the old paths, where is the good way, and walk therein, and ye shall find rest for your souls"* (Jer. 6:16). In our modern day and age, we liken *"the old paths"* to the teachings received from former brethren regarding our Christian walk. Do we consider and obey the old teachings? Or, have we foolishly gone modern? Are we devising better methods to accomplish the Lord's work? Ah brethren, let us consider the former days, when our conferences were totally guided by the Holy Spirit, not by the selective programs of men. Let us consider the old preachers, how, without any political correctness, they thundered out the blunt truths of sin, hell, and the judgment to come. Remember the former ministry, when the saints were searched to the very core, and often brought to tears as a result of the faithful ministry searching them relative to their wayward condition.

Today, in many circles, the cry is the same as in Isaiah's day; *"Prophesy not unto us right things, speak unto us smooth things, prophesy deceits"* (Isa. 30:10). Ah yes, let us be nice. Let us be smooth. Let us not ruffle any feathers. Let us never preach anything that might make people not like us. You mean to tell me that a brother could walk into a holy meeting dressed like a tramp, and nothing be said? Is it right to overlook a sister dressed like a harlot venturing into the gathering, and nothing be said? Away with such cowardice! Preach the word! Tell it as it is! Tell it with convictions, but oil it with genuine love. If preachers want to fully enjoy God's spiritual blessings in Christ, they must be faithful in telling forth the Word of God, and if saints expect the same, they must bow to the teachings of faithful, and God-fearing men.

The word *"walk,"* simply means our way of life, or, our way of living. We should walk *"in the steps of that faith of our father Abraham"* (Rom. 4:12). *"We also should walk in newness of life"* (Rom. 6:4). We *"walk not after the flesh, but after the Spirit"* (Rom. 8:1). *"Let us walk honestly, as in the day; not in rioting and drunkenness, not in chambering and wantonness, not in strife and envying"* (Rom. 13:13). *"For we walk by faith, not by sight"* (2 Cor. 5:7). We are to *"walk worthy of the vocation wherewith ye are called"* (Eph. 4:1). We are to *"walk not as other Gentiles walk, in the vanity of their mind"* (Eph. 4:17). We should *"walk in love, as Christ also hath loved us"* (Eph. 5:2). Let us *"walk as children of light"* (Eph. 5:8). *"See then that ye walk circumspectly, not as fools, but as wise"* (Eph. 5:15). *"As ye have therefore received Christ Jesus the Lord, so walk ye in Him"* (Col. 2:6). *"Walk in wisdom toward them that are without, redeeming the time"* (Col. 4:5). We should *"walk worthy of God, Who hath called you unto His kingdom and glory"* (1 Thess. 2:12). Let *us "walk honestly toward them that are without"* (1 Thess. 4:12). *"He that saith he abideth in Him ought himself also so to walk, even as He walked"* (1 Jn. 2:6). There is the supreme example and standard for our behavior. Walking as our Lord walked, brings joy to the godly, and perhaps reproach from the carnal. John exclaimed; *"I have no greater joy than to hear that my children walk in truth"* (3 Jn. 1:4).

LOVING THE LORD

The third requisite in order to enjoy our spiritual blessings is *"to love Him."* The church at Ephesus was scripturally correct (Rev. 2:1–7). They were a very strict assembly, and very active laboring for the Lord. However, there was a fly in the ointment! They had abandoned their first love! Oh how sad! What a depressing condition to be in! Yes, people can be very knowledgeable in the Scriptures, and be holding the truth tenaciously, yet not enjoying their spiritual blessings! Why? Simply because their love to Christ has diminished, and what used to be a bright light from a fervent fire within, had lessened to just a faint glow of dying embers. I have met them. They are so legal! They have lost (if they ever had it), the ability to tenderly restore a wayward saint. Instead, they have the knack of hammering the erring one into the ground with their 40-pound spiritual sledgehammer. They cannot see themselves. There is no self soul-searching on their part, but they are famous with finding fault with others. They are like floating icebergs, chilling every village on the way, as do the icebergs floating down the Straits of Belle Isle.

Such behavior will never do brethren. If the love of Christ is not burning in the believer, he certainly cannot manifest the lowliness and meekness of his blessed Lord. It is impossible! Such people cannot be enjoying their spiritual blessings.

WHOLEHEARTEDNESS IN SERVING HIM

The fourth requirement is, *"to serve the LORD thy God with all thy heart and with all thy soul."* Wholeheartedness in serving the Lord! God wants our heart, our whole heart. Are you enthused in whatever you endeavor to do for the Lord, or are you half-hearted? A saint all "wrapped up" and enthusiastic in his labors for God is just evidencing the fact that he is enjoying his spiritual blessings. Did not Solomon exhort us saying, *"Whatsoever thy hand findeth to do, do it with thy might"*? (Eccl. 9:10). Paul said, *"I laboured more abundantly than they all: yet not I, but the grace of God which was with me"* (1 Cor. 15:10). *"Fervent in spirit; serving the Lord,"* is a tremendous quality. Paul said; *"So, as much as in me is, I am ready to preach the gospel to you that are at Rome also"* (Rom. 1:15). There you have it in a nutshell! Paul put everything he had into his preaching, and he was always ready. What a noble servant of Christ.

GOSPEL PREACHING

Preaching the gospel is not standing before an audience and reading a bunch of typed out notes in a monotone voice, and waving your hand on certain points. Neither is it a stage for dramatics to mesmerize silly people with one's antics. Neither is it a stage to impress people with yourself. The gospel is a solemn declaration from God to man, through the clay lips of a fervent, soul-convicted individual interested in one's conviction of sin and conversion to God. He is scriptural and wholehearted in his presentation. He is desperately earnest, deliberate, plain, searching, scriptural, and full of love in his declaration.

The preaching of the gospel is not a lecture! Neither is it a seminar! Nor is it a little "come-to-Jesus-talk." It is a solemn and divine announcement from the throne of God to the heart of man. It is a forceful revelation of divine truth about eternity, and man's desperate need of salvation.

May God bless such men who, in their preaching, fill this criteria! It is very evident, that men of that caliber are men who are enjoying their spiritual blessings in Christ.

KEEPING HIS COMMANDMENTS

The last, and fifth necessity to enjoy one's spiritual blessings is; *"To keep the commandments of the LORD, and His statutes."* Tell me, if one knowingly transgresses the commands of our Lord, how can that person expect to enjoy the spiritual blessings God has for him? The answer is, he can't!

May the Lord help us all to be aware of what He expects of us. He has a storehouse of rich blessings for us to enjoy. All He asks of us is to fear Him; to walk in all His ways; to love Him; to be wholehearted for Him in service; and to keep His commandments. You are able, for if saved, the enabling Spirit dwells within you. Are you willing? I trust so, for if you possess the spiritual Canaan, and are enjoying the good of that land, you will be the most content and happy Christian in the world. May the Lord bless you thus, and prosper you, until we all reach that blissful heavenly shore. AMEN!